EASTERN AND WESTERN PERSPECTIVES ON SURROGACY

EASTERN AND WESTERN PERSPECTIVES ON SURROGACY

Edited by
Jens M. Scherpe
Claire Fenton-Glynn
Terry Kaan

intersentia
Cambridge – Antwerp – Chicago

Intersentia Ltd
Sheraton House | Castle Park
Cambridge | CB3 0AX | United Kingdom
Tel.: +44 1223 370 170 | Fax: +44 1223 370 169
Email: mail@intersentia.co.uk
www.intersentia.com | www.intersentia.co.uk

Distribution for the UK and Ireland:
NBN International
Airport Business Centre, 10 Thornbury Road
Plymouth, PL6 7PP
United Kingdom
Tel.: +44 1752 202 301 | Fax: +44 1752 202 331
Email: orders@nbninternational.com

Distribution for Europe and all other countries:
Intersentia Publishing nv
Groenstraat 31
2640 Mortsel
Belgium
Tel.: +32 3 680 15 50 | Fax: +32 3 658 71 21
Email: mail@intersentia.be

Distribution for the USA and Canada:
Independent Publishers Group
Order Department
814 North Franklin Street
Chicago, IL 60610
USA
Tel.: +1 800 888 4741 (toll free) | Fax: +1 312 337 5985
Email: orders@ipgbook.com

Image on cover: Radachynskyi Serhii - Shutterstock

ISBN 978-1-78068-652-3
D/2019/7849/4
NUR 822

British Library Cataloguing in Publication Data. A catalogue record for this book is available from the British Library.

PREFACE AND ACKNOWLEDGEMENTS

This book is the culmination of a research project spanning more than three years and events on two continents. It has involved 29 contributors from 19 jurisdictions, coming from the fields of law, medicine and philosophy. A project of this magnitude could not have been undertaken without the generous support of the WYNG Foundation of Hong Kong. It was through their funding that we were able to bring together experts from Europe, Asia, Africa, America and the Middle East at a conference held under the auspices of the Centre for Medical Ethics and Law (CMEL) of the University of Hong Kong and Cambridge Family Law on 9 and 10 September 2016, which served as a foundation for this volume. We wish to thank the Foundation for giving us this opportunity and hope that this book furthers their mission to acquire, exchange, disseminate and apply knowledge to achieve a more advanced and a more caring society. We also wish to particularly thank Au Yun Ling, for her exceptional administrative support in organising the Hong Kong conference, and St John's College and its Master, Rev. Dr Eric Chong, for providing accommodation for some of our speakers (and authors of this volume).

The Hong Kong conference was followed by a conference on 'Law and Practice of Surrogacy', held at Cambridge on 25 and 26 June 2018 and organised jointly by Cambridge Family Law and the Academy of European Law (ERA), with a focus on European developments. We would particularly like to thank Dr Angelika Fuchs, the Head of Section for Private Law at ERA, as well as Tabea Lüth from ERA for the very fruitful and efficient cooperation on this event.

The (probably) final event to which this project is tied, and where the book will be officially launched, will be the 'International Surrogacy Forum' in Cambridge on 27 and 28 June 2019, organised jointly by Cambridge Family Law, the International Academy of Family Lawyers and the American Bar Association (ABA) Section of Family Law. We would like to thank, in particular, Anne-Marie Hutchinson OBE, QC (Hon) for taking the initiative on this event and being so supportive throughout the process.

Thanks are also due to Matt Jordan, who provided research and editing assistance for this book as well as support at and for the Cambridge Conferences; Elizabeth Aitken for making sure that our accounts were in order; Shirley Bidgood for her assistance with the booking system; and Daniel Bates for setting up and maintaining the websites.

As always, the collaboration with Intersentia Publishing was wonderful (at least from the editors' side!), and we would like to thank Rebecca Moffat and Ann-Christin Maak-Scherpe for their exceptional support and patience in ensuring that this book was published.

Finally: Surrogacy is ultimately about family, and our thanks go to ours for the unwavering support they have given us over the course of this project. To Ann-Christin, Helma and Lilo, who had to put up with absences, long working nights, telephone conferences when we should have been playing UNO together (but in your father's defence, it was past bedtime!) and foul moods when things did not go as planned. To Luke, who was uncomplaining when birthdays were missed because of conferences. And to Eva, who was born as the project reached its completion, and over whose sleeping head proofs were finalised.

The Editors
Cambridge/Hong Kong, 20 February 2019

CONTENTS

LIST OF CONTRIBUTORS

Paul Beaumont
University of Aberdeen, Scotland, United Kingdom

Naomi Cahn
George Washington University, United States of America

June Carbone
University of Minnesota, United States of America

Daisy Cheung
University of Hong Kong, Hong Kong SAR

Anatol Dutta
Ludwig Maximillians University, Germany

Esther Farnós Amorós
Pompeu Fabra University, Barcelona, Spain

Claire Fenton-Glynn
University of Cambridge, England, United Kingdom

Hrefna Friðriksdóttir
University of Iceland, Iceland

Shinichiro Hayakawa
University of Tokyo, Japan

Sir Mark Hedley
England and Wales High Court (retired)

Chih-Hsing Ho
Academia Sinica, Taiwan

Soraj Hongladarom
Chulalongkorn University, Thailand

Terry Kaan
University of Hong Kong, Hong Kong SAR

Mary Keyes
Griffith University, Australia

Olga A. Khazova
The Moscow School of Social and Economic Sciences, Russia; National Research University 'Higher School of Economics', Russia

Ock-Joo Kim
Seoul National University, South Korea

Frank Klinkhammer
Federal Court of Justice, Germany

Prabha Kotiswaran
King's College London, England, United Kingdom

Byung-Hwa Lee
Dongduk Women's University, South Korea

John Pascoe
Family Court of Australia, Australia

Walter Pintens
Catholic University of Leuven, Belgium; Saarland University, Germany

Jens M. Scherpe
University of Cambridge, England, United Kingdom; University of Hong Kong, Hong Kong SAR; University of Aalborg, Denmark

Rhona Schuz
Sha'arei Mishpat Academic Center, Israel

Lei Shi
Southwest University of Political Science and Law, People's Republic of China

Julia Sloth-Nielsen
University of the Western Cape, South Africa; University of Leiden, the Netherlands

Rute Teixeira Pedro
University of Porto, Portugal

Katarina Trimmings
University of Aberdeen, Scotland, United Kingdom

Debra Wilson
University of Canterbury, New Zealand; New Zealand Law Foundation Rethinking Surrogacy Laws Project

Eleni Zervogianni
Aristotle University of Thessaloniki, Greece

EASTERN AND WESTERN PERSPECTIVES ON SURROGACY

An Introduction

Jens M. Scherpe and Claire Fenton-Glynn

The issues arising out of surrogacy are global ones. Whether one approves of surrogacy or not (or indeed just some forms of it), it is a simple fact that there is a global surrogacy market, and people are making use of it. Jurisdictions therefore cannot avoid taking a position on surrogacy, and the aim of this volume is to canvas and analyse how jurisdictions worldwide have reacted to the 'phenomenon' of surrogacy in general and international surrogacy arrangements in particular, and then to draw some comparative conclusions.[1]

For this it is necessary to look at both 'Eastern' and 'Western' jurisdictions (being aware of how difficult, imprecise and even inappropriate such categorisations can be). Much of the legal research undertaken so far is focused on what can broadly be called 'Western' jurisdictions. Some of these jurisdictions are what can be called 'receiving jurisdictions' with regard to surrogacy, meaning that couples from these jurisdictions often turn to international surrogacy as a result of the very restrictive legal rules on surrogacy in their home jurisdictions. By contrast, several of the 'Eastern' jurisdictions are, or at least have been until fairly recently, destinations for what rather deprecatorily is called 'surrogacy tourism'. This may be because of the permissive legal rules, or indeed the absence of legal rules, but may also be driven by differences in wealth and income, meaning that commercial surrogacy could be offered at lower rates than in 'Western' jurisdictions, some of which also have very permissive rules

1 It should also be noted that the issues arising with regard to the regulation of surrogacy are part of a wider debate concerning the definition of parenthood, and the ways in which the law can recognise and protect relationships between adults and children arising in increasingly diverse family forms. On this point see, for example, J. Sosson, G. Willems and G. Motte (eds), *Adults and Children in Postmodern Societies*, Intersentia, Cambridge 2019 and J.M. Scherpe, 'Breaking the Existing Paradigms of Parent-Child Relationships', in G. Douglas, M. Murch and V. Stephens (eds), *International and National Perspectives on Child and Family Law: Essays in Honour of Nigel Lowe*, Intersentia, Cambridge 2018, pp. 343–59.

on surrogacy. In addition, the cultural differences regarding the concept and importance of 'family' can also justify drawing a distinction between 'East' and 'West', and so the book was divided in this way.

One of the main aims of the book and research project is to look at how the global surrogacy market has had an impact on the law in different jurisdictions and different societies – and in particular, how legislatures have reacted to the social and political pressures resulting from the realities of surrogacy in a globalised world. Have restrictions been relaxed and/or even some form of surrogacy legalised in 'receiving' jurisdictions, given that there is an obvious demand which is only met elsewhere, with all the legal and other difficulties this brings with it? And in other, more permissive jurisdictions, has the 'tourism' practice led to changes in the law that restricted surrogacy? Unsurprisingly, the answer to both questions, as can be seen in several of the chapters of this book, is affirmative, so we are seeing a clear impact of the global realities on national surrogacy laws; this also allows looking at the actual efficacy of national legislation (or absence of legislation) in what, for better or worse, is a 'global marketplace'. As will be explained below, the book therefore also attempts to map emerging patterns in national legislations.

But the chapters of this book of course go further, exploring and explaining the historical, cultural and religious influences on the current approaches to surrogacy in the jurisdictions canvassed for this book and research project. The chapters also engage with the national and international fundamental legal, social and ethical debates surrounding surrogacy, and in particular the human rights of the surrogate, the commissioning parents and the child. Key issues include the potential commodification of children and of gestation (and thus women's bodies), the possible exploitation of women acting as surrogates, but also the autonomy rights of the women concerned. This volume will not seek to provide a definitive answer as to what constitutes exploitation or commodification, as this has been explored (though not conclusively) at length elsewhere,[2] but instead explores how these concepts are defined and understood in different jurisdictions. In doing so, it will also look to the consequences of decisions made by national legislatures on the basis of these concerns. Restriction or even prohibition of surrogacy may protect against perceived

2 See, for example, S. Wilkinson, 'The Exploitation Argument against Commercial Surrogacy' (2003) 17(2) *Bioethics* 169; S. Wilkinson, 'Exploitation in International Paid Surrogacy Arrangements' (2016) 33(2) *Journal of Applied Philosophy* 125; M. Brazier, 'Can you Buy Children?' (1999) 11(4) *Child and Family Law Quarterly* 345; R.A. Epstein, 'Surrogacy: The Case for Full Contractual Enforcement' (1995) 81 *Virginia Law Review* 2305; H. McLachlan and K. Swales, 'Commercial Surrogate Motherhood and the Alleged Commodification of Children: A defense of legally enforceable contracts' (2009) 72 *Law and Contemporary Problems* 91; R.A. Posner, 'The Ethics and Economics of Enforcing Contracts of Surrogate Motherhood' (1989) 5 *Journal of Contemporary Health Law and Policy* 21; A. Van Niekerk and L. Van Zyl, 'The Ethics of Surrogacy: Women's Reproductive Labour' (1995) 21 *Journal of Medical Ethics* 345.

exploitation in some situations, but in others they may unduly restrict the autonomy of the persons concerned – and entice people to seek international surrogacies instead, thus merely 'exporting' the very issues the restrictive approach sought to tackle. How do, how should, laws react to this and safeguard the interests of the parties involved, while striking a balance with the autonomy rights of others who may not want this protection? Can national legislation deal with the issues arising out of 'surrogacy tourism'?

The issues arising out of surrogacy are complex and concern many areas of law. In particular, core family law and status questions arise concerning the allocation of the legal position as a parent, and what this position should be based on: gestation and giving birth; being married to the surrogate; genetic contribution; intention; or social parenthood. That is, the regulation of surrogacy demands that we consider no less a question of what 'being a parent' really means.[3]

What is also apparent from the many debates in many jurisdictions is the struggle to balance the best interests of the child with the desires and actions of commissioning parents. In particular, prohibitive, or even regulated schemes, have struggled with ways to prevent commissioning parents from undertaking a surrogacy abroad, and returning with the child. The crux of this debate in particular is that domestic authorities inevitably are faced with a *fait accompli*, i.e. a child born as a result of a surrogacy arrangement, and they are then forced to deal with this reality. Any attempts to argue that 'it would be better if this child had not been born' are self-defeating, and 'punishing' the innocent child for the way it was conceived and brought into this world is unacceptable.[4] But, of course, this is problematic as it may, and undoubtedly does, encourage circumventing the law to 'reap the reward' in the form of the child.

Further central issues concern the surrogacy arrangement/contract as such. Should such arrangements be capable of being regarded as binding contracts, and if so with what consequences? Again, fundamental issues with regard to potential exploitation, commodification and autonomy arise and must be answered. The same is true for considerations as to who should be eligible

---

3 See A. Bainham, 'Arguments About Parentage' (2008) 67(2) *Cambridge Law Journal* 322; M. Johnson, 'A Biomedical Perspective on Parenthood' in A. Bainham et al., *What is a parent?* Hart Publishing, Oxford 1999; J. Carbone and N. Cahn, 'Which ties bind? Redefining the parent-child relationship in an age of genetic certainty' (2003) 11 *William & Mary Bill of Rights Journal* 1011; R. Probert, 'Families, Assisted Reproduction and the Law' [2004] *Child and Family Law Quarterly* 273.

4 I.G. Cohen, 'Regulating Reproduction: The Problem with Best Interests' (2012) 96 *Minnesota Law Review* 423; I.G. Cohen, 'Beyond Best Interests' (2012) 96 *Minnesota Law Review* 1187; K.M. Mutcherson, 'In Defense of Future Children: A Response to Cohen's Beyond Best Interests' (2012) 96 *Minnesota Law Review Headnotes* 46.

as surrogates and commissioning parents, once one accepts that surrogacy is happening and ought to be regulated, as many jurisdictions have done.

The fact that the problems arising seem insurmountable, and that any position taken inevitably can be criticised for its imperfection and inability to deal with all surrogacy situations, does not mean that debates on these issues are futile – on the contrary, it makes them even more necessary. It probably is inevitable that any regulation, be it national or international, will only be partially able to achieve its policy aims. In many ways, the best one can hope for is that while not all, at least *more* people are protected by the legal rules. Still, this certainly is an aim worth working for, and it is hoped that this book and research project can make a contribution to the debates and legal reform.

For this, specific jurisdictions were chosen and categorised for this book and research project. The 'Western perspectives' begin with chapters on the 'Prohibitive Approach', namely reports on France, Germany and Spain. These jurisdictions have in common that they prohibit surrogacy as a matter of principle, but when confronted with a child born as a result of an international surrogacy arrangement, will recognise the commissioning parents as legal parents of the child mainly because that was in the best interest of the child concerned (in the case of France only after decisions of the European Court of Human Rights, on which there is a specific chapter later in this volume).

That is also true for those jurisdictions which have been categorised as having a 'Tolerant Approach', namely England and Wales and the jurisdictions of Australia. These jurisdictions are named 'tolerant' as they do not regulate surrogacy itself, but the effects of surrogacy – namely the transfer of parenthood from the surrogate to the commissioning parents through surrogacy specific mechanisms. In these jurisdictions, somewhat reluctantly, altruistic surrogacy is permissible, but the lack of available surrogates has led to many couples seeking surrogacies abroad, just like those in 'prohibitive' jurisdictions.

The next group of jurisdictions is the one where jurisdictions have an express and clear 'Regulatory Approach', i.e. a specific legal framework to regulate the use of surrogacy, as an attempt to accept the realities of surrogacy (and indeed international surrogacy) and deal with the issues arising from this. The jurisdictions in this group are Greece, Israel, South Africa, New Zealand, Portugal and Iceland (although in the latter jurisdiction the proposed regulatory framework so far has not become law). What differentiates this approach from the 'tolerant approach' is the regulation of surrogacy *before* the conception of the child, with permission needing to be sought before this can go ahead, rather than trying to deal with the consequences of surrogacy on an *ex post facto* basis (i.e. when the child is already in existence).

The final group has been termed the 'Free Market Approach' and comprises several jurisdictions of the United States of America and Russia. The term was chosen because in these jurisdictions the contractual obligations arising from surrogacy arrangements, in principle, are binding and thus enforceable, making these jurisdictions destinations for 'surrogacy tourism' as well.

These chapters on the national jurisdictions, written by academics in the field of law, philosophy and medicine, are complemented by 'Judicial Perspectives' to explain what the various approaches mean in practice. These perspectives serve to enlighten readers as to the quandaries faced by judges – in their own words – when dealing with competing interests arising in surrogacy (and in particular, international surrogacy).

In addition, given the impact that the decisions of the European Court of Human Rights have had (and will continue to have) on the European jurisdictions, a chapter focuses exclusively on these decisions. In particular, this chapter draws out the implications for families born through surrogacy in establishing legal ties in the receiving jurisdictions and how a human rights analysis can support – or indeed hinder – this aim.

The book then turns to the 'Eastern' perspectives, where the rapidly changing legal landscape, even in the period between when this research project was started and concluded, made categorisation even more difficult. Again, the analysis begins with jurisdictions which have a 'Prohibitive Approach' such as the People's Republic of China, Taiwan and Singapore, followed by the (more or less) 'Tolerant Approach' seen in Hong Kong. After this, two jurisdictions, Japan and South Korea, are looked at together as neither of them so far has enacted laws on surrogacy and the practice is governed by medical/ethical guidelines of the medical profession. This part concludes with India and Thailand, which both used to be popular destinations for 'surrogacy tourism' but recently have enacted legislation to close down that particular practice – but without prohibiting surrogacy altogether. These jurisdictions are particularly important as they show ways in which destination jurisdictions, as well as receiving jurisdictions are reacting to the rise in global surrogacy, and in particular, concerns regarding the exploitation of women.

The final chapter of this book then is a *comparative analysis* with some tentative comparative conclusions, drawing on the experiences of the jurisdictions canvassed in this volume. While it cannot possibly provide answers to the myriad of issues facing surrogacy – both national and international – it hopes to provide a starting point for analysis, and a framework through which to view the various legislative options.

QUESTIONNAIRE

Jens M. Scherpe and Claire Fenton-Glynn

1. GENERAL LEGAL FRAMEWORK

1. Are there specific legal rules dealing with surrogacy in your jurisdiction (especially: is there a specific statute or merely an administrative/court practice)?
   - Please provide information including the general constitutional/legal framework where appropriate.
   - If there are no specific legal rules, is surrogacy nevertheless regulated through other mechanisms (e.g. medical boards/professional bodies)?
2. Is there a specialised authority set up to oversee surrogacy in your jurisdiction?

   If so, please provide information concerning the role, and powers, of this authority.
3. What is the reasoning behind the law/rules on surrogacy (or lack thereof) in your jurisdiction?

   Please describe the historic development leading up to the current law, and any significant legislative or judicial debates.

   Please note if there is any distinction drawn between traditional and gestational surrogacy.
4. Please give *statistical information* (where available), concerning:
   - (estimated) number of surrogate births in your jurisdiction;
   - (estimated) number of surrogacy arrangements undertaken by citizens in another jurisdiction;
   - number of clinics in which surrogacy can take place;
   - any other relevant/interesting statistical information.

2. SURROGACY ARRANGEMENTS IN GENERAL

1. Are surrogacy contracts legal in your jurisdiction? Are they binding/enforceable?

If so, please provide information concerning the terms that can, and cannot, be included.

2. Can a surrogate be remunerated for her participation in the surrogacy arrangement?

   In particular:

   - Are there guidelines concerning appropriate levels of payments? If so, who are they provided by?
   - Are there any limits on payments?
   - How are payments to the surrogate monitored?

   Please provide any statistical information concerning payments made to surrogates in your jurisdiction.

3. LEGAL PARENTHOOD AT THE TIME OF BIRTH

1. Who are the legal parents of a child born through surrogacy at the time of birth?

   How does this relate to the way in which your jurisdiction views parenthood in general, and motherhood in particular?

2. Will there be any indication on the birth certificate, or other document, that the child was born as a result of a surrogacy arrangement?
3. Is information concerning the surrogate – as the person who gave birth – preserved by the relevant authorities if she is not the legal mother of the child?

   If so, please provide information concerning, inter alia:

   - What information is collected?
   - Can the child access this information?
   - What are the conditions for being able to access this information?

4. ELIGIBILITY FOR SURROGACY

4.1. ELIGIBILITY CRITERIA FOR WOMEN ACTING AS A SURROGATE

1. If surrogacy is permitted in your jurisdiction, are there any eligibility criteria for women acting as surrogates?

   For example, are there criteria related to: age; number of surrogate births; marital status; nationality or residency; financial status; any other factor?

   What are the justifications for these criteria?

2. Has there been any research in your jurisdiction on the characteristics of women acting as surrogates, or their reasons for doing so?

   Please provide information (where available) concerning: age; marital status; socio-economic status; ethnicity and any other factor.

4.2. ELIGIBILITY CRITERIA FOR COMMISSIONING PARENTS

3. If surrogacy is permitted in your jurisdiction, are there any eligibility criteria for commissioning parents?

   In particular, are there criteria related to: age; medical condition/infertility; marital status; sexual orientation; nationality or residency; relationship with the surrogate; any other factor?

   What are the justifications for these criteria?

4. Are there any rules in your jurisdiction concerning the gametes used in the surrogacy arrangement?

   In particular:

   - Is sperm, egg and/or embryo donation permitted in your jurisdiction in general and for surrogacy in particular?
   - If so, is it anonymous?
   - If so, is there any way for a child to later access information concerning their genetic origins?
   - Can payments be made for the donation of gametes/embryos by commissioning parents?
   - Whose gametes can be used in the surrogacy?
   - Is there a requirement that there be a genetic relationship between the commissioning parents and the child?

5. TRANSFERRING PARENTHOOD

5.1. LEGAL PROCESS

1. If the commissioning parents are not the legal parents at birth, how can they acquire parenthood?

   Is there a specific mechanism for transfer of parenthood for surrogate births, or are general mechanisms such as adoption used?

2. Who is responsible for overseeing the transfer of parenthood? Is this a judicial or administrative procedure?

   Please describe the conditions that must be met before (transferred) parenthood can be recognised. In particular, please provide details concerning the consent of the surrogate, and any conditions on this, for example: time limit; provision of information; legal advice; any other factor.

3. In the event of a dispute concerning the surrogacy arrangement, how would this be adjudicated upon, and by whom?

   Please provide any available information concerning the frequency of disputes following surrogacy, and the outcomes of such disputes.

4. If legal parenthood can be transferred, is information concerning the surrogate – as the person who gave birth – preserved by the relevant authorities if she is not the legal mother of the child?

   If so, please provide information concerning, inter alia:

   - What information is collected?
   - Can the child access this information?
   - What are the conditions for being able to access this information?

5.2. RIGHTS OF CHILDREN

5. In your jurisdiction, to what extent are the child's rights/interests relevant to a determination of whether to permit a transfer of parenthood?

   How are these rights and interests articulated? What are the relevant factors considered?

6. AGENCIES AND CRIMINALISATION

1. What is the role of mediators/agencies/middlemen in your jurisdiction?

   Are there rules and regulations concerning their involvement?

   Please comment on any rules concerning: introducing surrogates and commissioning parents; providing advice and information; advertising their services; payments; any other factor.

2. What are the penalties for a breach of laws concerning surrogacy?

   In particular:

   - Are the penalties different for: commissioning parents; surrogates; mediators/agencies/middlemen?
   - Do they apply extra-territorially?
   - To your knowledge, have these penalties ever been imposed?

7. INTERNATIONAL SURROGACY ARRANGEMENTS

1. Does your jurisdiction have specific rules/laws/regulations concerning surrogacy arrangements that take place in other jurisdictions?

   Is foreign surrogacy regulated separately from domestic surrogacy? If so, are there any differences between the applicable rules?
2. Which jurisdiction's law applies to assigning parenthood arising from surrogacy – for example, the law of the commissioning parents; the law of the place of birth; the law of the surrogate?

   What happens if there is a conflict between assignment of parenthood in different jurisdictions?
3. Is parenthood arising out of a surrogacy arrangement in another jurisdiction recognised in your jurisdiction?

   If so, what are the requirements or pre-conditions for such recognition?

   Please provide details of any relevant decisions in this area.
4. Will a child born under an international surrogacy arrangement require special authorisation to return to your jurisdiction?

   If so, please provide details of the applicable rules, and any relevant decisions in this area.
5. Will a child born to an international surrogacy arrangement automatically acquire your jurisdiction's nationality (and if so, at what point in time)? If not, how can it be acquired later?

8. CONCLUSION

Please evaluate the status quo and the development that led up to it.

Is the law regarded as workable?

What do practitioners/academics/the courts/the competent authorities think about the current state of the law?

Are there suggestions for reform?

PART I

WESTERN PERSPECTIVES

THE PROHIBITIVE APPROACH

SURROGACY IN FRANCE

Walter PINTENS

1. GENERAL LEGAL FRAMEWORK

Surrogacy is forbidden in France without any distinction between altruistic or commercial surrogacy, between traditional or gestational surrogacy or between domestic and international surrogacy. When in the 1980s surrogacy became more popular, the legality of agencies and associations dealing with surrogacy was disputed.[1] In 1988 the Conseil d'État, the highest administrative court of France, confirmed a decision to deny legal registration of those bodies.[2]

---

1 M. MEILHAC-PERRI, 'National Regulation and Cross-Border-Surrogacy in France' in A. BONOMI and G.P. ROMANO (eds), *Yearbook of Private International Law Vol. XVI – 2014–15*, Otto Schmidt, Cologne 2015, pp. 275–88.

2 Conseil d'État 22 January 1988, no. 80936.

In the same year the French Supreme Court, the Cour de cassation, ruled that those associations were null and void because their object was illegal and that they had to be dissolved.[3] In 1991 the Cour de cassation, sitting in plenary assembly, ruled in a domestic case that surrogacy agreements, even in non-commercial cases, violated public policy and were void because the human body, and the status of a person, could not be seen as commodities. They are both inviolable and inalienable.[4] Changes in the civil status of a person may derive from events, the operation of law, judgments or administrative decisions but not from private arrangements.[5] Furthermore, surrogacy was seen as an instrument to circumvent the adoption procedure.[6] This case law was integrated in the Bioethics Act of 30 July 1994 and later codified in Art. 16-7 of the Civil Code. This article states that any surrogacy agreement is null and void. Such nullity is a matter of public policy (Art. 16-9 of the Civil Code). Since surrogacy agreements are illegal and contrary to public policy, they are not binding and not enforceable.

Today, the reasons behind this public policy principle still lie in the inalienability of the human body and the civil status of a person as argued by the Cour de cassation. The prohibition is also justified by ethical concerns. It seeks to avoid the situation that the child is treated as merchandise between infertile couples and surrogates. The prohibition aims also to protect the interest of the child which is seen as psychologically at risk in such transactions. The prohibition is also meant to prevent the exploitation of surrogates, as they are mostly from a lower economic status than the commissioning parents. This approach was until recently supported by a majority of the French population. But a recent poll of December 2017 shows that society is changing. 64 per cent of the population is in favour of surrogacy, but only 18 per cent in all cases. 46 per cent only accept surrogacy for medical reasons.[7]

2. SURROGACY ARRANGEMENTS IN GENERAL

As stated above, surrogacy contracts are null and void in France as a matter of public policy. They are illegal, and can be subject to criminal sanctions (see below Section 6). This is the case for both commercial and altruistic arrangements.

---

3 Cass. 13 December 1989, JCP 1990 II 21526, note A. Sériaux.

4 Cass. (Ass. plén.) 31 May 1991, D. 1991, note D. Thouvenin, JCP 1991 II, 21752, note J. Bernard. In the same sense: Cass. 29 June 1994, JCP 1995 II, 22362, note J. Rubbelin-Devichi; Cass. 9 December 2003, D. 2004, 1998, note E. Poisson-Drocourt.

5 L. Perreau-Saussine and N. Sauvage, 'France', in P. Beaumont and K. Trimmings (eds), *International Surrogacy Arrangements. Legal Regulation at the International Level*, Hart Publishing, Oxford 2013, p. 121.

6 Above n. 4.

7 IFOP, *Les Français et les questions liées à la bioéthique*, Paris 2017, p. 13.

3. LEGAL PARENTHOOD AT THE TIME OF BIRTH

The prohibition of surrogacy does not preclude that in practice surrogacy agreements are concluded. But since they have no legal effect, they cannot alter the rules on affiliation, nor transfer parenthood from the birth parents to the commissioning parents, even when there is no disagreement between the parties.[8]

It is not the commissioning mother but the person who gives birth – i.e. the surrogate – who is the legal mother, even in cases of gestational surrogacy where an egg of the commissioning mother is used. This is in accordance with general law on affiliation, which considers the woman who gave birth to the child as the legal parent. Only she can be registered on the birth certificate as the mother of the child. In accordance with the *mater semper certa est* principle, genetics are not taken into consideration.[9] In all cases of artificial procreation, ties of affiliation cannot be established between the donor of the egg and the child (Art. 311-19 of the Civil Code).

If the surrogate is married, her husband is presumed to be the legal father of the child (Art. 312 of the Civil Code). Therefore, surrogacy agreements exclude the parental rights of the husband of the surrogate. Even if the gametes of the commissioning father are used, parenthood cannot be established between the donor of the sperm and the child (Art. 311-19 para. 1 of the Civil Code).

There will be no indication on the birth certificate or other document that the child was born as a result of a surrogacy arrangement.

4. ELIGIBILITY FOR SURROGACY

As surrogacy is not permitted in France, there are no criteria laid down for the eligibility of either surrogates or commissioning parents to enter into surrogacy arrangements.

5. TRANSFERRING PARENTHOOD

In principle, a transfer of parenthood in domestic cases is excluded. Exceptionally, some techniques are used to establish affiliation between the commissioning parents and the child:

1. The birth certificate is falsified. It does not mention the name of the surrogate but the name of the commissioning mother.[10] This procedure

---

8 M. Meilhac-Perri, above n. 1, p. 277.

9 M. Meilhac-Perri, above n. 1, p. 277.

10 I. Gutton, *GPA en France: législation, jurisprudence, sanctions et débat*, <https://babygest.com/gestation-pour-autrui-en-france/#devenir-mere-porteuse-en-France> accessed 04.09.2018.

is risky because such a substitution is a criminal offence (see below Section 6);

2. The surrogate mother makes use of the possibility of anonymous birth (*accouchement sous X*). In this case the mother will not appear on the birth certificate. The commissioning father recognises the child, and his wife – the commissioning mother – adopts the child as a second parent. This possibility is only available to married commissioning couples, because the adoption of the child of one's unmarried partner is still forbidden. Also here there is a risk: if it comes into the open that a child has been relinquished by a surrogate, then the adoption will be refused or declared void.

6. AGENCIES AND CRIMINALISATION

As discussed above, agencies and associations dealing with surrogacy are prohibited. The French courts have confirmed that it is legal to deny legal registration of surrogacy agencies, as their object – the bringing about of surrogacy arrangements – is prohibited under French law. Moreover, acting as a middleman in a surrogacy arrangement is penalised with imprisonment of up to one year and a fine of €15,000 (Art. 227-12 para. 3 of the Penal Code). In commercial cases on a regular basis (rather than just a one off) the penalty is up to two years' imprisonment and a fine of €30,000 (Art. 227-12 para. 3 of the Penal Code).

The prohibition of surrogacy has consequences also for others involved in the process, as it is penalised as an attempt on affiliation (*atteinte à la filiation*).[11]

Recourse to surrogacy by convincing a mother to abandon her child is a criminal offence, punishable by up to six months' imprisonment and a fine of €7,500 (Art. 227-12 of the Penal Code). Wilful substitution and simulation leading to the modification of the civil status of a child are also criminalised, with the penalty of up to three years' imprisonment and a fine of €45,000 (Art. 227-13 para. 1 of the Penal Code). Medically assisted procreation using techniques other than those permitted under the Public Health Code – which surrogacy is not – is penalised by up to five years' imprisonment and a fine of €75,000 (Art. 511-24 of the Penal Code). Having said this, in practice prosecution is seldom, extenuating circumstances apply and the penalty is reduced to a fine or a suspended sentence.

---

11 See M.X. Catto, 'La gestation pour autrui: d'un problème d'ordre public au conflits d'intérêts?' (2013) 3 *La Revue des droits de l'homme. Revue du Centre de recherches et d'études sur les droits fondamentaux* 45 <https://journals.openedition.org/revdh/201?lang=en> accessed 04.09.2018; L. Perrau-Saussine and N. Sauvage, above n. 5, p. 121.

If the acts are performed by a French citizen in a foreign state, they can only be prosecuted in France if these acts are also illegal in that foreign state. Concluding a surrogacy agreement in California where surrogacy is legal, for example, can therefore not be prosecuted in France.[12]

7. INTERNATIONAL SURROGACY ARRANGEMENTS

The strict rules against domestic surrogacy cannot prevent French citizens having recourse to surrogacy abroad. Informal statistics indicate that every year 200 children are born abroad with French citizens as commissioning parents.[13] Some of those parents have had great difficulties returning to France with their children and registering them in the civil status records, as will be explained through the following cases.

7.1. THE STRICT POSITION OF THE COUR DE CASSATION

In 2011 the Cour de cassation, sitting in plenary assembly, had to rule on three cases concerning international surrogacy arrangements.[14] This chapter will mainly focus on two of these cases – *Mennesson* and *Labassée* – because they are at the root of the case law of the ECtHR.

In both cases the applicants were husband and wife, and due to the infertility of the wife, had recourse to surrogacy in the United States, respectively in California and Minnesota. The embryos were produced with the gametes of the husbands. As a result, the Mennesson twins, Valentina and Fiorella, and Juliette Labassée were born. Californian and Minnesota judgments ruled that Mr and Mrs Mennesson were the twins' parents and that Mr and Mrs Labassée were Juliette's parents. The judgments specified that the applicants should be recorded in the birth certificate as the father and mother. Upon their return to France, the French authorities, suspecting that the cases involved surrogacy arrangements, refused to enter the particulars of the birth certificates into the French register of births, marriages and deaths. In the *Mennesson* case, the birth certificates were nevertheless entered in the register on the instructions of the public prosecutor, who subsequently brought proceedings

---

12 Articles 113-2 and 113-6 of the Penal Code; TGI Créteil 30 September 2004, D. 2005, 476.

13 L. Perreau-Saussine, above n. 5, p. 119.

14 Cass. 6 April 2011 (nos 09-17.130, 09-66.486 and 10-19.053); X. Labbe, 'La gestation pour autrui devant la Cour de cassation' [2011] *Recueil Dalloz* 1064; L. Perreau-Saussine and N. Sauvage, above n. 5, p. 124; W. Pintens, How the European Court of Human Rights changed the life of surrogacy children, in Ars docendi et scribendi. Essays in honour of Johan Scott, Pretoria 2018, p. 118.

against the couple in order to have these entries annulled. In the *Labassée* case, the couple did not challenge the refusal to register the birth, but sought to have the legal relationship recognised on the basis of de facto enjoyment of status (*possession d'état*). They obtained an *acte de notoriété*, a document issued by a judge attesting the status of son or daughter, that is, the existence of a de facto parent-child relationship, but the public prosecutor refused the registration.

In judgments of 6 April 2011 the Cour de cassation, in line with a judgment of 1994,[15] ruled that under the current law, it was against the principle of inalienability of the status of persons, a fundamental principle of French law, to give effect, in respect of parenthood, to a surrogacy agreement, which, while it may be legal abroad, is null and void on public policy grounds under Arts 16-7 and 16-9 of the Civil Code. Therefore, the foreign decision could not be recognised and the request for transcription in the French register of birth was dismissed. The parents invoked a violation of Art. 8 of the ECHR, but the court found that there had been no infringement of the right to respect for private and family life since the refusal or the annulment of the entries in the register had not deprived the children of the maternal and paternal legal relationship recognised by the laws of California and Minnesota and had not prevented them from living in France with their commissioning parents. Indeed, although the French consulate refused to issue passports for the children, they could enter France with American passports on which the commissioning parents were named as their legal parents.

The fact that the court applied a general ban, including in these cases where at least one of the commissioning parents was the biological parent of the child, is questionable. The court could at least have recognised this part of the birth certificate.[16]

In 2013, the court had to deal again with surrogacy in two cases of children born in India which would lead to a new ECtHR judgment in the case *Foulon and Bouvet*.[17] Didier Foulon recognised his child Emilie in Paris before she was born a few days later in Bombay. Philippe Bouvet also recognised his children Adrien and Romain some days before their birth. In both cases, the Court of Appeal stated that the infringement of the prohibition of surrogacy had to be considered as fraud, but nevertheless decided that the birth certificates had to be registered. Justifications were the best interests of the children and the conformity of those certificates with Art. 47 of the Civil Code.

---

15 Above n. 2.

16 C. Bidaud-Garon, 'A Chronicle of French Family Law' in B. Atkin (ed.), *The International Survey of Family Law*, Family Law, Bristol 2014, p. 143.

17 Cass. 13 September 2013 (no. 12-30.1398 and 12-18.315), D. 2013, 2377, note M. Fabre-Magnan. See C. Bidaud-Garon, above n. 16, p. 143; W. Pintens, above n. 14, p. 119.

This article prescribes that faith must be given to the civil-status certificate of a French citizen, drawn up in a foreign country in the forms used in the said country, unless the certificate is illegal or forged or the facts declared therein do not correspond to reality. The birth certificates were in conformity with Art. 47 of the Civil Code since the parents listed therein were the biological parents. The attorney general appealed.

The Cour de cassation did not take into account the criticisms of its 2011 judgment, and in fact took an even more radical approach, basing the new decision on fraud. It found that when the birth results from an overall process based on a surrogacy agreement which is legal abroad but illegal in France on public policy grounds, parenthood established abroad cannot be registered in France. *Fraus omnia corrumpit.* The recognition by the biological father in France was annulled. Deviating from the 2011 decision, the court added that in the presence of fraud neither the interest of the child as guaranteed by Art. 3 of the UNCRC nor the respect for private and family life as guaranteed by Art. 8 of the ECHR could be invoked. The result of this decision was devastating. The child became a *res nulla* without affiliation and nationality, without parental authority and inheritance rights. A new kind of pariah was created. Legal scholars criticised this case law and argued that although the child was born from a prohibited surrogacy agreement, the parenthood of the father was not fraudulent since he was the biological father.[18]

In 2014 a new judgment confirmed the fraud approach but the court did not repeat its questionable formula that the rights of the child could not be invoked.[19]

From the rulings of the Cour de cassation, it can be concluded that a foreign surrogacy agreement is null and void as a violation of public policy, as it is in contradiction with the principle of the inalienability of personal status, which is still an essential principle of French law. Therefore, the foreign birth certificate of a child born under such a surrogacy agreement is a fraud and cannot be transcribed on the French civil-status register. This rule applies also when the father and the mother, as stated on the birth certificate, are the biological father and the woman who gave birth to the child. The surrogacy agreement contaminates the whole procedure and excludes the application of Art. 47 of the Civil Code. As long as the court bases its decision on fraud, parenthood established abroad cannot have any effect in France and the salvation of the children had to come from the ECtHR.[20]

---

18 H. Fulchiron and C. Bidaud-Garon, '"L'enfant de la fraude ...". Réflexions sur le statut des enfants nés avec l'assistance d'une mère porteuse: note sous Civ. 1re, 19 mars 2014' (2014) 15 *Recueil Dalloz* 905–11.

19 Cass. 19 March 2014, no. 13-50.005.

20 C. Bidaud-Garon, above n. 16, p. 144; W. Pintens, above n. 14, p. 120.

7.2. THE POSITION OF THE ECtHR

7.2.1. Mennesson *and* Labassée

The parents in *Mennesson* and *Labassée* applied to the ECtHR and invoked a violation of the right to respect for private and family life guaranteed by Art. 8 of the ECHR.[21] The applicants argued that, to the detriment of the children's best interests, they were unable to obtain recognition in France of a parent-child relationship that had been legally established abroad. The applicants in the *Mennesson* case further invoked a violation of Art. 14 of the ECHR on the prohibition of discrimination taken in conjunction with Art. 8 of the ECHR. They argued that their inability to obtain recognition placed the children in a discriminatory legal situation compared with other children when it came to exercising their right to respect for their family life.

In the *Mennesson* case the court found that Art. 8 of the ECHR was applicable in both its 'family life' aspect and its 'private life' aspect.

The court examined whether the interference by the State was in accordance with the conditions of Art. 8(2) of the ECHR. Firstly, the interference has to be in accordance with the law.[22] The court noted that the interference with the applicants' right to respect for their private and family life resulting from the French authorities' refusal to recognise the legal parent-child relationship was in accordance with the law as prescribed by Art. 8 of the ECHR. Secondly, the interference has to be necessary in a democratic society in the interests of certain protected values.[23] The interference by the State had pursued the protection of health and the protection of the rights and freedoms of others, both listed as legitimate aims in Art. 8 of the ECHR. The court observed that the State wanted to discourage French citizens from having recourse abroad to a reproductive technique that was prohibited under French law with the

21 ECtHR 26 June 2014 (*Mennesson v France*) no. 65192/11; ECtHR 26 June 2014 (*Labassée v France*), no. 65941/11. See K. Duden, 'International Surrogate Motherhood – Shifting the Focus to the Child – Judgments of the European Court of Human Rights of 26 June 2014 and of the German Bundesgerichtshof of 10 December 2014' (2015) 23 *Zeitschrift für Europäisches Privatrecht*, pp. 637–60; F. Chenede, 'Les arrêts Mennesson et Labassée ou l'instrumentalisation des droits de l'homme' (2014) 31 *Recueil Dalloz* 1797–1805; N. Hervieu, 'La Cour européenne des droits de l'homme, stratège juridictionnel face aux enjeux brûlants de société. Gestation pour autrui, transsexualisme et mariage des couples de meme sexe (Art. 8 et 12 CEDH)' (2014) 5 *Revue des droits de l'homme. Revue du Centre de recherches et d'études sur les droits fondamentaux*, <https://journals.openedition.org/revdh/870> accessed 04.09.2018; H. Fulchiron and C. Bidaud-Garon, 'Reconnaissance ou reconstruction? À propos de la filiation des enfants nés par GPA, au lendemain des arrêts Labassée, Mennesson et Campanelli-Paradiso de la Cour européenne des droits de l'homme' (2015) 104 *Rev. crit. DIP* 1; W. Pintens, above n. 14, p. 121.

22 *Mennesson v France*, above n. 21, para. 50.

23 *Mennesson v France*, above n. 21, para. 76.

aim, as the authorities saw it, of protecting the children and the surrogate. As to whether the interference was necessary in a democratic society, the court stressed that a wide margin of appreciation had to be left to states in making decisions relating to surrogacy, in view of the difficult ethical issues involved and the lack of a European consensus on these matters.[24] Nevertheless, that margin of appreciation had to be reduced when it came to parenthood.[25] The court examined whether a fair balance had been struck between the interests of the State and those of the individuals directly concerned, with regard to the fundamental principle according to which, whenever the situation of children is an issue, their best interests are paramount.[26]

But the court distinguished between the right of the commissioning parents, and the right of the children themselves, to respect for their private and family life.[27]

The court observed that the commissioning parents' family life was inevitably affected by the refusal to recognise the parent-child relationship between Mr and Mrs Mennesson and the twins, but that they had not been prevented from the enjoyment in France of their right to respect for their family life. They had been able to settle in France shortly after the birth of the children, and they lived there together in circumstances which were comparable to those of other families. There was no risk that they would be separated by the French authorities.[28] The court concluded that a fair balance had been struck between the applicants' interests and those of the State, in so far as their right to respect for their family life was concerned.[29]

With regard to the children's right to respect for their private life, the court noted that they were in a state of legal uncertainty: the French authorities, although aware that the twins had been identified in another country as the children of the applicants, had nevertheless denied them that status under French law. The court considered that this contradiction undermined the children's identity within French society.[30] Moreover, although their biological father was French, they faced worrying uncertainty as to the possibility of obtaining French nationality, a situation that was liable to have negative repercussions for the definition of their personal identity.[31] The court further observed that the children did not have any intestate inheritance rights but could only inherit from their parents as legatees, which meant that their

---

24 *Mennesson v France*, above n. 21, paras 78–79.
25 *Mennesson v France*, above n. 21, para. 80.
26 *Mennesson v France*, above n. 21, para. 81.
27 *Mennesson v France*, above n. 21, para. 86.
28 *Mennesson v France*, above n. 21, para. 92.
29 *Mennesson v France*, above n. 21, para. 94.
30 *Mennesson v France*, above n. 21, para. 96.
31 *Mennesson v France*, above n. 21, para. 97.

inheritance rights would be less favourable. The court regarded this as depriving them of a further component of their identity in relation to their parenthood.[32] The children's right to respect for their private life and especially the establishment of the essence of their identity, including parenthood, was therefore significantly affected. There was therefore a serious issue as to the compatibility of the situation with the children's best interests, which must guide any decision in their regard.[33] This analysis takes a special dimension where one of the parents is also the child's biological parent. The court found that, given the importance of biological parenthood as a component of each individual's identity, it is not in the best interests of the child to deprive him or her of a legal tie when the biological reality of that tie is established and the child and the parent claim its full recognition. In preventing the recognition and establishment of the children's legal relationship with their biological father, the French state has overstepped the permissible margin of appreciation.[34] Therefore, the court held that the children's right to respect for their private life had been infringed, in violation of Art. 8 of the ECHR.[35]

In view of the violation of Art. 8 concerning the children, the court did not find it necessary to examine the applicants' complaint under Art. 14 of the ECHR.

The court came to the same conclusion in the *Labassée* case.

7.2.2. Foulon and Bouvet

In the *Foulon and Bouvet* case the French government applied to strike out the applications on the basis of Art. 37(1) of the ECHR given that, due to the 2015 judgments of the Cour de cassation (discussed below), the position of surrogate children had improved. But the court decided that important questions remained and that the procedure concerning the execution of the judgments in *Mennesson* and *Labassée* were still pending before the Committee of Ministers of the Council of Europe.[36]

The court observed the similarity of the case with both of the *Mennesson* and *Labassée* cases. The argument of the French government that after the 2015 judgments of the Cour de cassation affiliation could be established by recognition or possession of status had still a hypothetical character. Therefore, the court came to the same ruling as in *Mennesson* and *Labassée*.

32 *Mennesson v France*, above n. 21, para. 98.
33 *Mennesson v France*, above n. 21, para. 99.
34 *Mennesson v France*, above n. 21, para. 100.
35 *Mennesson v France*, above n. 21, para. 101.
36 ECtHR 21 July 2016 (*Foulon and Bouvet v France*), no. 9063/14 and 10410/14.

7.2.3. *Conclusions*

From the *Mennesson* and *Labassée* cases can be concluded that the prohibition of surrogacy itself does not violate the ECHR. The Contracting States have a large margin of appreciation in this area. Also, the refusal on the ground of surrogacy to transcribe a birth certificate drawn up abroad is compatible with the right to respect for private and family life. But the refusal to transcribe the filiation of the children as mentioned on the foreign certificate, with respect to the biological father, constitutes a disproportionate prejudice to the children's private life. Each person should have the right to see his identity as a human being established and this should include his filiation.

It is important that the court affirmed its earlier case law and confirmed that family life is not restricted to traditional families but that also de facto families enjoy the rights of Art. 8 of the ECHR. The court extend the de facto family to the relationship between the commissioning biological parents and the children.

7.3. SURROGACY AFTER *MENNESSON* AND *LABASSÉE*

How did France react to the case law of the European Court? After *Mennesson* and *Labassée* a distinction has to be made between cases where the commissioning father has a biological tie with the child and cases where there is no tie at all.

7.3.1. *Biological Tie*

7.3.1.1. Parenthood

The French legislature did not react to the *Mennesson* and *Labassée* judgments but awaited a new decision by the Cour de cassation. In 2015, the court had to rule on two surrogacy cases which took place in Russia.[37] In each of them, the French biological father recognised the child in France before the birth. The birth certificate drawn up in Russia mentioned the biological father as being the legal father and the woman who gave birth as being the mother. The fathers then asked for the transcription of the Russian birth certificate on the French birth

---

37 Cass. (Ass. plén.) 3 July 2015, nos 14-21.323 and 15-50.002. See C. Legrand and C. Escuillie, 'Statut juridique de l'enfant issu d'une GPA à l'étranger: Une avancée jurisprudentielle en demi-teinte. Droit au respect de la vie privée et familiale (art. 8 CEDH)' [2016] *La Revue des droits de l'homme. Revue du Centre de recherches et d'études sur les droits fondamentaux* <https://journals.openedition.org/revdh/1772> accessed 04.09.2018; H. Fulchiron and C. Bidaud-Garon, 'Gestation pour autrui international: Changement de cap à la Cour de cassation' (2015) 31 *Recueil Dalloz* 1819–27; W. Pintens, above n. 14, p. 124.

register. But the Public Prosecutor opposed the transcription, suspecting the use of a surrogate. In one of the cases, the court of appeal refused the transcription. In the other case, the court ordered the transcription, but the attorney general appealed.

The Cour de cassation had to decide, in light of the European case law, if the refusal to transcribe the birth certificate, duly drawn up in a foreign country, of a child who has at least one French biological parent, could be justified by the sole fact that the birth was the result of surrogacy.

The court did not explicitly refer to the European case law. This is normal given that the traditional style of the court is not to mention any case law or legal doctrine. Only in one of the cases did the court refer to Art. 8 of the ECHR. But in both cases the court stated that the birth certificates declared the man who had acknowledged being the father to the child as the father, and the woman who had given birth as the mother. The rules of Art. 47 of the Civil Code were not violated since the birth certificate was not forged and reflected the reality. Therefore, the theory of fraud could not hinder the transcription of the birth certificate. The decision which dismissed the request for transcription on the sole basis that the birth resulted from a process involving surrogacy was quashed and reversed. The appeal against the second decision, which ordered the transcription notwithstanding the existence of a surrogacy agreement, was dismissed.

In a press release of 3 July 2015 which was also published in English,[38] the court explicitly stated that the cases referred to the court did not deal with the issue of the transcription of filiation established abroad with respect to non-biological commissioning parents and that the court therefore had not ruled on this matter.

7.3.1.2. Nationality

Before the *Mennesson* and *Labassée* judgments, surrogacy babies were denied French nationality because of the suspicion of surrogacy. Even if the commissioning father was the biological father, the French consulates refused to recognise the parenthood. They argued that the recognition of parenthood between the commissioning father and the child would be contrary to French public policy. Under French law, only a child who has at least one French parent is French (Art. 18 of the Civil Code). This means that such a child could not enter France except when a passport indicating family ties with the parents was issued, which was problematic.

The Conseil d'État took a more liberal standpoint than the Cour de cassation. In an Indian surrogacy case where the children could not obtain

38 <https://www.courdecassation.fr/IMG/Press_release_surrogate_motherhood.pdf> accessed 04.09.2018.

Indian nationality since the mother had relinquished the child, and the *ius soli* principle was not applicable, the Conseil accepted that the Indian birth certificate was in conformity with Art. 47 of the Civil Code. The birth certificate stated that the commissioning father was the biological father (which was confirmed by a DNA test) and the biological mother legally ended her parental rights in accordance with Indian law. The Conseil relied on Art. 3 of the UNCRC and gave primary consideration to the best interests of the child.[39] The Conseil did not decide on the nullity of the surrogacy contract, but stated that the French administration, even if the contract was void, had to allow the child of a French citizen to enter France considering the best interests of the child. Therefore, a laissez-passer had to be issued.

In 2013, a circular letter from the Minister of Justice took this a step further, and stated that a nationality certificate cannot be refused when the parenthood of a French national is established in a foreign civil-status certificate, in accordance with Art. 47, even if there is a presumption that the parent made use of a surrogacy agreement.[40] However, a DNA test is required to confirm this parenthood. An appeal against this possibility to grant French nationality was rejected by the Conseil d'État.[41]

After *Mennesson* and *Labassée* there is no other solution than to grant French nationality when biological parenthood is established.

7.3.2. No Biological Tie

The present state of law and practice do not offer a solution for the recognition of the birth certificate of children who have no genetic tie with either of the commissioning parents. In light of the judgments of 2015, the solution has to lie in the application of Art. 47 of the Civil Code. But if the commissioning parents mentioned on the birth certificate as legal parents are not the biological parents, recognition is impossible because the facts declared therein do not correspond to reality.

The *Paradiso and Campanelli* case before the ECtHR does not offer a solution.[42] In this case Italy refused to register the Russian birth certificate

---

39 Conseil d'État 4 May 2011, no. 348778. See L. Perreau-Saussine and N. Sauvage, above n. 5, p. 122.

40 Circulaire de la Garde des Sceaux du 25 janvier 2013 relative à la délivrance des certificat de nationalité française – Convention de mère porteuse <http://www.textes.justice.gouv.fr/art_pix/JUSC1301528C.pdf> accessed 04.09.2018.

41 X. Domino, 'La circulaire "Taubira" sur les certificats de nationalité française validée: concl. sur CE 12 déc. 2014.' (2015) 6 *Recueil Dalloz* 352–357; H. Fulchiron and C. Bidaud-Garon, 'La circulaire "Taubira" sur les certificats de nationalité française validée' (2015) 6 *Recueil Dalloz* 357–62.

42 ECtHR 27 January 2015 (*Paradiso and Campanelli v Italy*), no. 25358/12. See P. Beaumont and K. Trimmings, 'Recent jurisprudence of the European Court of Human Rights in

indicating the commissioning parents as the legal parents. Neither of them had a biological link with the child, and thus the birth certificate contained false information and violated public policy.[43] The ECtHR dismissed the complaint concerning the registration of the birth certificate because domestic remedies were not exhausted.[44] But the applicants complained also that the child was removed from the parents, and placed into foster care. The Second Chamber of the court found that family life did exist between the commissioning parents and the child, even if it was of short duration. The Italian authorities had not properly considered the balance between public policy and the best interests of the child.[45] But given that the child had undoubtedly developed emotional ties with the foster family with whom he was placed at the beginning of 2013, this finding of a violation could not therefore be understood as obliging the State to return the child to the commissioning parents.[46]

The conclusion was that de facto family life could exist between the commissioning non-biological parents and the child. The court noted that the child received a new identity only more than two years after his birth, and underlined that it is necessary to ensure that a child is not disadvantaged on account of the fact that he or she was born to a surrogate, especially in terms of citizenship or identity, which are of crucial importance.[47]

But on appeal, the Grand Chamber came to another conclusion.[48] Having regard to the absence of any biological tie between the child and the commissioning parents, the short duration of the relationship with the child and the uncertainty of the ties from a legal perspective, and in spite of the existence of a parental project and the quality of the emotional bonds, the court considered that the conditions which would enable it to conclude that there existed a de facto family life had not been met.[49] The court did not underestimate the impact which the immediate and irreversible separation from the child must

---

the area of cross-border surrogacy: Is there still need for global regulation?' in *Centre for Private International Law, University of Aberdeen Working Paper 2015/2*, p. 6; C. Kohler and W. Pintens, 'Entwicklungen im europäischen Personen- und Familienrecht 2010–2011' (2015) 58 *FamRZ* 1433–40; W. Pintens, above n. 14, p. 126; M. WellsGreco and H. Dawson, 'Inter-Country Surrogacy and Public Policy: Lessons from the European Court of Human Rights' in A. Bonomi and G.P. Romano (eds), *Yearbook of Private International Law Vol. XVI 2014/15*, Otto Schmidt, Cologne 2016, pp. 315–41; M. Winkler, 'Senza identità: il caso Paradiso e Campanelli' (2015) 1 *GenIUS* 243.

43 The commissioning father claimed that unknown gametes instead of his own were erroneously used.

44 *Paradiso and Campanelli v Italy*, above n. 42, para. 4.

45 *Paradiso and Campanelli v Italy*, above n. 42, paras 86 and 87.

46 *Paradiso and Campanelli v Italy*, above n. 42, para. 88.

47 *Paradiso and Campanelli v Italy*, above n. 42, para. 85.

48 ECtHR (Grand Chamber) 24 January 2017 (*Paradiso and Campanelly v Italy*), no. 25358/12, FamRZ 2017, 444, note K. Duden.

49 *Paradiso and Campanelli v Italy* (Grand Chamber), above n. 48, para. 157.

have had on the applicants' private life. It found that while the Convention does not recognise a right to become a parent, the court cannot ignore the emotional hardship suffered by those whose desire to become parents has not been or cannot be fulfilled. However, the public interests at stake weigh heavily in the balance, while comparatively less weight is to be attached to the applicants' interest in their personal development by continuing their relationship with the child. Agreeing to let the child stay with the applicants, possibly with a view to becoming his adoptive parents, would have been tantamount to legalising the situation created by them in breach of important rules of Italian law. The court accepted that the Italian courts, having assessed that the child would not suffer grave or irreparable harm from the separation, struck a fair balance between the different interests at stake, while remaining within the wide margin of appreciation available to them in the present case.[50] Therefore, there had been no violation of Art. 8 of the ECHR.

But it is clear that under certain circumstances family life may exist: for example, in case of a longer duration of the relationship between the child and the commissioning parents. In such cases, the identity of the child is not complete without the establishment of parenthood in relation to both commissioning parents. It is not clarified if this implies that the foreign birth certificate mentioning the commissioning parents has to be recognised. The ECtHR will have to answer the question whether the Contracting States have a margin of appreciation in establishing parenthood and if adoption could satisfy as a solution.

At present French law does not provide a solution for the establishment of parenthood of the non-biological parents, but the Conseil d'État took a first step.[51] A French commissioning mother asked for a laissez-passer to enter France with a child born in Armenia. The Armenian birth certificate indicated her as the mother of the child having parental authority. The French embassy refused to issue the document because the French citizen could not be regarded as the mother of the child given the indications of surrogacy. Although a laissez-passer is only delivered after verification of the nationality of the child (which was contested), the Conseil d'État in a final appeal, ordered the Minister of Foreign Affairs to issue the document. The Conseil d'État did not decide on nationality and parenthood because the competence lay with the civil courts, but argued that the best interests of the child as guaranteed by Art. 3 of the UNCRC had to prevail in all decisions concerning children. A void (from the perspective of French law) surrogacy agreement cannot justify an exception regarding this obligation.

---

50 *Paradiso and Campanelli v Italy* (Grand Chamber), above n. 48, para. 215.

51 Conseil d'État 3 August 2016, no. 401924.

In a recent judgment the Cour de cassation took a step further and allowed the adoption of the child by the wife of the biological father under the condition that all requirements for the adoption are fulfilled and that the adoption is in the best interests of the child.[52]

Even in the *Mennesson* and *Bouvet* cases there is a positive development. The Cour de cassation, sitting as a *Cour de réexamen*, decided on the basis of the Act of 18 November 2016 permitting a judicial review after a judgment of the ECtHR that the Cour de cassation, sitting in a plenary assembly, has to review those cases.[53] But in the *Mennesson* case the plenary assembly of the Cour de cassation did not take a final decision but made use of the new Protocol no. 16 to the ECHR and asked the ECtHR for an advisory opinion.[54] The following questions were submitted: (1) Does a Member State exceed its margin of appreciation under Art. 8 of the ECHR by refusing to transcribe on the civil-status registers the birth certificate of a child born abroad from a surrogate mother, when this certificate refers to the intended mother as the legal mother, while the transcription regarding the father has been accepted when he was the biological father of the child? Is it necessary to distinguish between whether or not the child is conceived with the gametes of the intended mother? (2) If the answer to one of the two questions is positive, does the possibility for the intended mother to adopt her husband's biological child, which constitutes a mean of establishing parentage open to her, comply with the requirements of Art. 8 of the ECHR?

8. CONCLUSION

Although the ban on surrogacy was introduced in order to protect children, it works against children. It is not in their interest to be left without an identity or with only a partial identity. The European Court of Human Rights can take credit for changing the life of those children. The new approach by the Cour de cassation, following the Strasbourg case law, is an important step forward but offers no solution for commissioning parents who have no biological link with the child. Several proposals were made by the Senate and the Conseil d'État but they were not taken into account.[55] After the disaster with 'le marriage pour tous' which was implemented but divided France, it was decided to exclude surrogacy from a larger reform of family law. It seems that an international approach is favoured. The Hague Conference on Private International Law has taken an

---

52 Cass. 5 July 2017, no. 16-16.455.

53 Cour de réexamen 16 February 2018, nos 001 and 002.

54 Cass. (Ass. plén.) 5 October 2018, no. 10-19053.

55 Rapport d'information, Sénat 2007–08, no. 421; Conseil d'État, La révision des lois de bioéthique, 2011.

initiative but progress is slow, and there is no certainty that an international instrument will see the light of day.

But an international approach does not solve all the problems. It raises the question for how long a ban on domestic surrogacy can be upheld. It is not reasonable that in an international case everything is possible, but in a national case nothing is permitted. Further, the legislator should not only keep in mind that the best interests of the child should be a primary consideration (Art. 3(2) of the UNCRC), but that the State has to take all appropriate measures to ensure that a child is protected against punishment on the basis of the activities of his or her parents (Art. 2(2) of the UNCRC).

SURROGACY IN GERMANY

Anatol Dutta

1. GENERAL LEGAL FRAMEWORK

Germany – to start with the result of this report – was correctly placed by the editors of this volume in the group of legal systems which follow a prohibitive approach towards surrogacy. Most of the questions posed in the questionnaire for the national reports have to be answered in the negative: No, there are no specific legal rules dealing with surrogacy, apart from criminal law provisions which ban surrogacy (see below Section 2.1.). No, there is no authority set up to oversee surrogacy in Germany, except the public prosecutor which will start criminal proceedings if he or she finds out that there has been a case of surrogacy in Germany. And no, there is, as far as I can see, no relevant statistical data on the number of surrogate births in Germany or the number of surrogacy arrangements undertaken by German citizens in another jurisdiction. Interestingly, the official annual criminal statistics of the Federal

Ministry of the Interior, which counts with German efficiency all criminal offences committed on German soil, do not specifically mention, at least not in the last years, any violations of the provisions banning surrogacy. It appears that criminalising surrogacy has restrained the medical profession from implementing surrogacy arrangements in Germany. Doctors, of course, face losing their medical licence if found violating the provisions against surrogacy, and surrogacy without medical assistance is rather difficult. The surrogacy hostile attitude of German law can mainly be explained by the fact that the pertinent provisions date back to the beginning of the 1990s and reflect the ethical, scientific and political debates of the 1980s.

2. SURROGACY ARRANGEMENTS IN GENERAL

2.1. THE ILLEGALITY OF SURROGACY IN GERMANY

Therefore, the starting point of a report on the German law of surrogacy[1] has to be criminal law. German criminal law tackles surrogacy not directly but rather indirectly from two different angles, outside general criminal law, by special legislation.

First and foremost, most reproduction techniques required for a successful surrogacy are forbidden by the provisions of the *Embryonenschutzgesetz* ('ESchG'), the German Act for the protection of gametes. In its §1 under the headline 'misuse of reproduction techniques' ('*Mißbräuchliche Anwendung von Fortpflanzungstechniken*') the Act sanctions egg donations in general (§1(1) no. 1 of the ESchG) and the transfer of human embryos to a surrogate, which is defined in the Act as a woman who intends to leave her child permanently to a third person (§1(1) no. 7 of the ESchG). The Act also bans any artificial insemination of a surrogate (§1(1) no. 7 of the ESchG) and the artificial insemination of an egg or removal of a human embryo in order to transfer the egg or embryo to a third woman (see §1(1) no. 2, 6 of the ESchG). Furthermore, already the impregnation of an egg is punishable by the *Embryonenschutzgesetz* (§1(2) of the ESchG), if not done with the aim to induce a pregnancy of the woman from whom the egg originates. The criminal sanctions provided in the *Embryonenschutzgesetz* range from a monetary penalty to imprisonment for up to three years. However, the Act is clearly directed against the medical profession: The commissioning parents and the surrogate cannot be prosecuted (see §1(3) of the ESchG, cf. §11(2) of the ESchG).

---

1 See on German law also the report by S. Gössl, 'Germany' in P. Beaumont and K. Trimmings (eds), *International surrogacy arrangements: Legal regulation at the international level*, Hart Publishing, Oxford 2013, p. 130.

Following the principle of 'nulla poena sine lege scripta', the principle that there is to be no penalty without written law, there are rare situations where surrogacy is not explicitly forbidden by the *Embryonenschutzgesetz*.[2] For example, the natural insemination of the surrogate is not covered by the Act. The same applies for the artificial self-insemination of the surrogate which is forbidden but at least not punishable (§11(2) of the ESchG). Finally, the Act does also allow the use of so called left-over eggs. Eggs, which have been inseminated for the donor but which cannot be used anymore for the donor, can be transferred to another woman as long as this woman will carry the child as her own child.

German criminal law, however, does not only focus on the reproduction technique as such, but also tries to control – and this is the second toehold for criminalising surrogacy – the market for surrogacy. This is mainly implemented by the *Adoptionsvermittlungsgesetz* ('AdVermiG'), the Act on agencies in the area of adoption. The Act does not only regulate the adoption agencies and their activities, however: it also bans without exception in §§13c and 13d of the AdVermiG agencies offering surrogacy services (as defined in §§13a and 13b of the AdVermiG), as well as advertisement of such services. The arrangement of surrogacy services is even a criminal offence punishable with fine or imprisonment up to one year (§14b of the AdVermiG). The *Adoptionsvermittungsgesetz* does not distinguish between commercial and non-commercial activities. Both are sanctioned alike.

2.2. CONTRACTUAL ENFORCEABILITY

There is also a rather small scope for contractual arrangements between surrogate and commissioning parents. Although private autonomy is one of the cornerstones of German private law, a contract between commissioning parents and a surrogate will in most cases be unenforceable. Legal transactions which violate a statutory prohibition are void according to German law (see §134 of the BGB). Hence, contracts, which oblige the parties to do acts which are forbidden by the criminal provisions on surrogacy in Germany (above Section 2.1.), will not be effective.[3] This does not require that the acts are punishable. As already mentioned, especially the *Embryonenschutzgesetz* does not punish the surrogate and the commissioning parents. This, however, does not mean that those acts are legal. They are illegal but not punishable. Yet in any case, the surrogate cannot oblige herself in the contract to consent

2 See M. Coester, 'Ersatzmutterschaft in Europa' in H.-P. Mansel et al. (eds), *Festschrift für Erik Jayme*, vol. II, Sellier European Law Publishers, Munich 2004, pp. 1243 and 1245.

3 See, for example, AG Hamm 22 February 2011, no. XVI 192/08; OLG München 13 May 2016, *FamRZ (Zeitschrift für das gesamte Familienrecht)* 2017, 72, 74, 75.

to the later adoption of the child (see as to adoption below Section 5.4.). This consent is a personal act which cannot be the object of a contractual arrangement. Otherwise, the cooling-off period in §1747(2)1 of the BGB could be circumvented[4] which provides that the mother can only consent to the adoption eight weeks after birth. However, contractual agreements on surrogacy arrangements as far as they are not illegal (above Section 2.1.) are valid and, in particular, do not as such violate good morals (see §138(1) of the BGB).[5]

Whether the commissioning parents can reclaim a remuneration already paid to the surrogate or whether the surrogate can claim damages for the maintenance of the child if the commissioning parents do not take the child – these are all open questions. Against the right to reclaim the surrogate fees militates a special provision in the German law of restitution: §817 of the BGB which provides in its second sentence that a reclaim of unjustified performance is excluded if the performance and the receiving of performance was illegal or immoral.[6] However, this provision has been interpreted rather narrowly by the German courts in the past,[7] and the same could be true in cases of immoral agreements on surrogacy.[8] There might, however, be a basis for damages by the surrogate. At least the German Federal Court of Justice has held that in case of sperm donation the partner of the mother who consented to the assisted insemination of the mother, but later did not recognise his fatherhood, is obliged to pay maintenance based on an implicit contract.[9] The same should apply for commissioning parents who do not care for the child.[10]

3. LEGAL PARENTHOOD AT THE TIME OF BIRTH

The surrogacy hostile attitude is also reflected by German family law when it comes to the question of legal parenthood concerning a child born through

---

4 Cf. D. Coester-Waltjen, *Die künstliche Befruchtung beim Menschen – Zulässigkeit und zivilrechtliche Folgen – Gutachten B für den 56. Deutschen Juristentag*, C.H. Beck, Munich 1986, pp. 92 et seq.

5 See for details D. Coester-Waltjen, above n. 4, pp. 79 et seq.; M. Coester, above n. 2, p. 1251; E. Deutsch and A. Spickhoff, *Medizinrecht*, 7th ed., Springer, Berlin and Heidelberg 2014, p. 718: violation of good morals and invalidity of the arrangement only if remuneration exceeds the reimbursement of the surrogate's expenses; for a general violation of good morals according to §138(1) of the BGB, however, e.g. OLG Hamm 2 December 1986, *FamRZ* 1986, 159, and A. Diel, *Leihmutterschaft und Reproduktionstourismus*, Wolfgang Metzner, Frankfurt a. M. 2014, pp. 85 et seq.

6 Applying this provision in case of surrogacy E. Deutsch and A. Spickhoff, above n. 5, p. 718; A. Diel, above n. 5, pp. 86 et seq.

7 See for details M. Schwab, in *Münchener Kommentar zum Bürgerlichen Gesetzbuch*, vol. V, C.H. Beck, Munich 2013, §817 of the BGB paras 20 et seq.

8 D. Coester-Waltjen, above n. 4, p. 92.

9 See BGH 3 May 1995, *FamRZ* 1995, 861; BGH 23 September 2015, *FamRZ* 2015, 2134.

10 Cf. D. Coester-Waltjen, above n. 4, pp. 93 et seq.

surrogacy. Criminal law (above Section 2.1.) is, of course, only one side of the coin. It can sanction surrogacy but it cannot avoid surrogacy altogether. There have to be provisions on parenthood even if the child was born through surrogacy, be it because the commissioning parents, the surrogate and the medical staff did not stick to the rules (which will be rarely the case) or be it because the criminal sanction did not apply: As already seen, there can be cases where surrogacy is not forbidden. Furthermore, in principle, German criminal law applies only within German territory, as §§3 et seq. of the *Strafgesetzbuch* ('StGB'), the German Criminal Code provide. Hence, violations of the provisions on surrogacy committed outside Germany are generally not prosecuted; based on a special provision on the international scope of German criminal law as to abetment (§9(2) of the StGB) only acts assisting the implementation of an illegal surrogacy abroad committed on German soil could be punishable.[11]

German family law treats surrogacy as a 'normal' birth assuming that the surrogate (and her partner) aim to have the child for their own family and that the commissioning parents play, if at all, only a role as donors of gametes.[12] This ignorance of the law towards the social background of surrogacy, of course, causes considerable inconsistencies.[13]

Since 1998, an explicit provision in the *Bürgerliche Gesetzbuch* ('BGB'), the Civil Code, the famous §1591 of the BGB, explicitly provides that the mother of a child is the woman who has given birth to the child. Hence, in cases of surrogacy, it is only the surrogate who is the legal mother of the child; the commissioning mother has no position at all. Biological motherhood legally prevails over genetic, intentional or social motherhood. The provision in §1591 of the BGB was introduced by the German legislator on purpose. Violations of the provisions in the *Embroyenschutzgesetz* should not only be sanctioned by criminal law but by family law also.[14] There should be no scission of legal

---

11 See BGH 8 October 2015, *FamRZ* 2016, 714, 715; OLG München 13 May 2016, *FamRZ* 2017, 72, 74, 75; for details see D. Magnus, 'Kinderwunschbehandlungen im Ausland: Strafbarkeit beteiligter deutscher Ärzte nach internationalem Strafrecht (§9 StGB)' [2015] *NStZ (Neue Zeitschrift für Strafrecht)* 57; and A. Diel, above n. 5, pp. 131 et seq.

12 K. Duden, *Leihmutterschaft im Internationalen Privat- und Verfahrensrecht*, Mohr Siebeck, Tübingen 2015, p. 22.

13 T. Helms, *Rechtliche, biologische und soziale Elternschaft – Herausforderungen durch neue Familienformen, Gutachten F zum 71. Deutschen Juristentag*, C.H. Beck, Munich 2016, p. 52, speaks of 'Inkonsistenzen im Abstammungsrecht' with regard to surrogacy.

14 See Gesetzentwurf der Bundesregierung zur Reform des Kindschaftsrechts of 13 June 1996, BT-Drucks. 13/4899, pp. 82 et seq.: 'Eine Klarstellung der Mutterschaft im Zivilrecht erscheint dennoch im Hinblick auf die Fälle geboten, in denen eine Eispende entweder im Ausland oder verbotenerweise im Inland vorgenommen wird. Denn hierbei handelt es sich um eine reine Konfliktregelung, die [...] nicht dahin mißverstanden werden kann, daß das Zivilrecht eine öffentlich-rechtlich verbotene Methode der künstlichen Befruchtung billigt oder gar praktikabel macht'.

motherhood among different women but a clear-cut rule.[15] Additionally, §1591 of the BGB should exercise a deterrent effect towards surrogacy by legally refusing commissioning parents and the surrogate the result they aim to accomplish: that is legal parenthood for the commissioning parents.[16] Prevention by the means of family law is, of course, a problematic approach: Family law should balance private interests and should not primarily be a tool of behavioural control.[17]

The recognition of legal motherhood solely lying with the surrogate has, of course, considerable consequences for the attribution of legal fatherhood, which is derived in German law mainly from the motherhood of the child: According to German family law the legal father of the child is, at least in the first instance, the man who is married to the mother (§1592 no. 1 of the BGB). If the surrogate is married, consequently, her husband is legally the father of the child born through surrogacy.[18] The market reacts to this legal rule. German commissioning parents apparently often use the Ukrainian surrogacy market, and it is reported that the Ukrainian surrogacy agencies – knowing about German family law – only offer unmarried surrogates to German couples.[19] If the mother is not married, according to German law the father of the child is the man who has – with consent of the mother – recognised his fatherhood by formal declaration (§1592 no. 2, §§1594 et seq. of the BGB). Hence, in cases of surrogacy the commissioning father can, with consent of the surrogate as the legal mother of the child, obtain legal fatherhood.[20] The relevant declaration can already be made before the birth (§1594 Abs. 4 of the BGB), although – at least according to the prevailing opinion – not before the conception of the child.[21] A formal recognition of fatherhood by the commissioning father with

---

15 Gesetzentwurf der Bundesregierung zur Reform des Kindschaftsrechts of 13 June 1996, BT-Drucks. 13/4899, pp. 51 et seq.

16 Gesetzentwurf der Bundesregierung zur Reform des Kindschaftsrechts of 13 June 1996, BT-Drucks. 13/4899, p. 82: 'Diese klare Regelung dient auch der Verhinderung von Leihmutterschaften'.

17 Cf. recently T. Helms, above n. 13, p. 53: 'Darüber hinaus erscheint es fragwürdig, abstammungsrechtliche Regeln für ein Kind so zuzuschneiden, dass die rechtliche Elternschaft von vornherein einer Person zugesprochen wird, die als soziale Mutter ausscheidet. [...] Auch für die Zuordnung zur Mutter sollte eigentlich der Grundsatz gelten, dass abstammungsrechtliche Regeln unabhängig davon zu konzipieren sind, ob Art und Umstände der Zeugung des Kindes (gesellschaftlich oder rechtlich) missbilligt werden'.

18 See VG Berlin 5 September 2012, *FamRZ* 2013, 738, 739; VG Köln 20 February 2013, *NJW (Neue Juristische Wochenschrift)* 2013, 2617, 2618.

19 A. Bernard, *Kinder machen – Neue Reproduktionstechnologien und die Ordnung der Familie*, S. Fischer, Frankfurt a. M. 2014, pp. 364 et seq.

20 See e.g. AG Nürnberg 14 December 2009, *FamRZ* 2010, 1579; OLG Düsseldorf 26 April 2013, *FamRZ* 2013, 1495, 1497; BGH 10 December 2014, *FamRZ* 2015, 240, 241.

21 See e.g. R. Hepting and A. Dutta, *Familie und Personenstand*, 2nd ed., Verlag für Standesamtswesen, Frankfurt a. M and Berlin, 2015, para. V-57.

consent of the surrogate is even possible if the sperm cell was not donated by the commissioning father; genetic fatherhood is not a prerequisite of legal fatherhood by virtue of formal recognition.[22] The only substantive condition is that legal fatherhood has not been attributed to a different man (§1594(2) of the BGB), for example, by virtue of the surrogate's marriage or a valid prior recognition of fatherhood by another man.

In relation to the registration of the child's birth, once a child is born, the civil status registrar is required by the *Personenstandsgesetz* ('PStG'), the German Civil Status Act, to certify in the birth register, the child's name, place, day, hour and minute of birth, and the child's legal gender. It must also state the legal parents' names (see §21(1) no. 3 of the PStG), that is at least the name of the surrogate as the legal mother, but potentially also the name of her husband as the legal father. The fact that the child was born through surrogacy is not mentioned. In particular, the commissioning parents are not registered unless the commissioning father is the legal father of the child, for example, based on a valid recognition of fatherhood.

4. ELIGIBILITY FOR SURROGACY

As surrogacy is prohibited, there are no provisions setting out eligibility criteria for either surrogates or commissioning parents.

5. TRANSFERRING PARENTHOOD

Against the background of this hostile attitude German law takes against surrogacy, it is of no surprise that the transfer of legal parenthood to the commissioning parents is also not an easy task under German law. German law does not provide for any special transfer rules for surrogacy. On the contrary, the transfer of parenthood might even be more difficult in case of surrogacy than in other situations (see, especially as to adoption, below Section 5.4.).

5.1. CHALLENGING THE LEGAL FATHERHOOD OF THE SURROGATE'S PARTNER

The difficulties already start when a legal fatherhood of the surrogate's partner shall be challenged, especially if the surrogate was married. One option under

---

[22] R. Hepting and A. Dutta, above n. 21, paras V-20 et seq.; cf. BGH 10 December 2014, *FamRZ* 2015, 240, 241.

German family law to obtain legal fatherhood – besides marriage to the mother or formal recognition of fatherhood (see above Section 3) – is a legal fatherhood established by a court decision (§1592 no. 3 of the BGB). The biological father of a child, among other persons, can apply to the court to establish his legal fatherhood based on his biological fatherhood. Such proceedings, however, require that the child currently has no legal father (§1600d(1) of the BGB). If legal fatherhood is already attributed to a different man, first, this legal fatherhood has to be challenged, which can also only happen by a court decision on the application of certain persons within a certain period of time (see §§1600 et seq. of the BGB). In case of surrogacy, the commissioning father can, in effect, only establish legal fatherhood by a court decision if he donated the sperm cell – and even in that case there are considerable legal hurdles:

- If there is already a legal father of the child (by virtue of marriage or recognition) this fatherhood can only be challenged by the commissioning father as the genetic father if there is no factual family relationship between the legal father and the child (§1600(1) no. 2 and (2) of the BGB). Legal fatherhood which coincides with social fatherhood is rather highly protected against attacks by the genetic father under German law. Of course, in cases of surrogacy the legal father – for example, the husband of the surrogate – will normally not entertain a factual family relationship with the child. This would, according to §1600(3)1 of the BGB, require the father to bear or to have borne factual responsibility for the child. However, there is a presumption that such a factual family relationship exists if the legal father is married to the mother (cf. §1600(3)2 of the BGB).
- Furthermore, in case of surrogacy a rather delicate interpretation issue arises. The German Civil Code only allows the genetic father to challenge another man's legal fatherhood if the genetic father affirms that he has '*beigewohnt*' the mother during the period of conception (§1600(1) no. 2 of the BGB). The verb '*beiwohnen*' is rather weird; most Germans will not understand this term, although it is the traditional word for having sexual intercourse. Hence, the commissioning father has to affirm that he had sexual intercourse with the surrogate in order to challenge the legal fatherhood, for example, of the husband of the surrogate. Actually, the German Federal Court of Justice has taken a rather liberal view towards the concept of '*beiwohnen*'. The Court of Justice held that except in case of an anonymous sperm donation the self-insemination with sperm acquired privately with the consent of the sperm donor can be qualified as '*beiwohnen*'.[23] I assume that the Court of Justice would take the same view once it comes to surrogacy

[23] BGH 15 May 2013, *FamRZ* 2013, 1209, 1210.

and the use of sperm cells of the commissioning father,[24] at least if the parties concerned know each other.

If the commissioning father successfully challenges the fatherhood of the partner of the surrogate, the court at the same time establishes the legal fatherhood of the biological father.[25]

5.2. CHALLENGING THE LEGAL MOTHERHOOD OF THE SURROGATE?

As seen in the previous section, the legal fatherhood of the man who was married to the mother, or who has recognised fatherhood, but who is not the genetic father of the child, can be challenged under German law. However, a corresponding revision mechanism is missing for legal motherhood.[26] There is no possibility to replace the legal motherhood of the biological mother in favour of a legal motherhood of the genetic or social mother.[27] Of course, there are procedural provisions on establishing legal parenthood by court (see §169 no. 1 of the FamFG). Also the *Personenstandsgesetz* provides that the birth registry can be amended (§§47, 48 of the PStG). Those provisions, however, only allow a clarification of the legal motherhood based on §1591 of the BGB (for example, if it later turns out that another woman has given birth to the child). Yet they do not allow a challenge to the legal motherhood of the actual biological mother.

5.3. RECOGNISING GENETIC MOTHERHOOD WITHOUT AFFECTING LEGAL MOTHERHOOD

Furthermore, it is not even possible under German law to apply for a declaratory judgment solely on the genetic motherhood of the commissioning mother,

---

24 At least with a similar result A. DIEL, above n. 5, pp. 91 et seq.; C. MAYER, 'Ordre public und Anerkennung der rechtlichen Elternschaft in internationalen Leihmutterschaftsfällen' (2014) 78 *RabelsZ (Rabels Zeitschrift für ausländisches und internationales Privatrecht)* 551, 566; N. WITZLEB, '„Vater werden ist nicht schwer"? – Begründung der inländischen Vaterschaft für Kinder aus ausländischer Leihmutterschaft' in N. WITZLEB et al. (eds), *Festschrift für Dieter Martiny zum 70. Geburtstag*, Mohr Siebeck, Tübingen 2014, pp. 203, 212 et seq.; cf. T. HELMS, 'Leihmutterschaft – ein rechtsvergleichender Überblick' [2013] *StAZ (Standesamt)* 114, 115 with note 9; for a different view K. DUDEN, above n. 12, p. 26.

25 See §182(1) of the *Gesetz über das Verfahren in Familiensachen und in den Angelegenheiten der freiwilligen Gerichtsbarkeit* ('FamFG'), the Act on Family Proceedings and Matters of Non-Contentious Jurisdiction.

26 M. COESTER, above n. 2, p. 1247; N. WITZLEB, above n. 24, p. 209.

27 OLG Stuttgart 7 February 2012, *FamRZ* 2012, 1740, 1741; VG Berlin 5 September 2012, *FamRZ* 2013, 738, 739; BGH 10 December 2014, *FamRZ* 2015, 240, 241 et seq.

if she has donated the egg, in order to recognise her genetic relation to the child without affecting the legal motherhood of the surrogate. In particular, the commissioning mother cannot avail herself of mechanisms which allow to recognise the genetic parenthood of a person under German law. The German legislator has so far not introduced a general mechanism to recognise genetic parenthood without status effects.[28] Also, remedies by general procedural law are only available to a limited extent.[29] Furthermore, the German Civil Code grants the right to claim the consent of the child or the legal father for a genetic testing solely to the legal mother – not the commissioning mother (§1598a of the BGB).

There is another rather problematic provision in German law which grants rights to merely genetic parents who are not legal parents. But this provision does not help the commissioning mother either. Based on decisions of the European Court of Human Rights,[30] the German legislator introduced recently a provision which gives the biological father some information and access rights regarding the child if another man is the legal father of the child (§1586a of the BGB). This provision, however, only applies to genetic fathers, not mothers – which is regarded as a discrimination by some authors.[31] It is only the commissioning father who, as far as he is the genetic but not the legal father, could invoke those rights.

5.4. ADOPTION BY THE COMMISSIONING PARENTS

Of course, the classic transfer mechanism for parenthood – adoption – is also available under German law. The commissioning parents could adopt – at least if married – the child born by the surrogate as a common child (see §1741(2)2 of the BGB). Where the commissioning parents are registered partners, only a so-called 'successive adoption' would be an option (see §9 Abs. 7 of the *Lebenspartnerschaftsgesetz* ('LPartG'), the German Act on registered partnerships[32]). If the commissioning father is already the father of the child (because of a recognition of fatherhood with consent by the surrogate, see above Section 3), a stepchild adoption by the commissioning mother or (in case

---

28 As proposed e.g. by D. Coester-Waltjen, 'Künstliche Fortpflanzung und Zivilrecht' [1992] *FamRZ* 369, 373.

29 See as to a general *Feststellungsklage*, an action for a declaratory judgment, based on §256 of the *Zivilprozessordnung*, the German Civil Procedure Code, for further details e.g. A. Diel, above n. 5, p. 89.

30 ECHR 21 December 2010, no. 20578/07 (*Anayo/Germany*) *FamRZ* 2011, 269; ECHR 15 September 2011, no. 17080/07 (*Schneider/Germany*) *FamRZ* 2011, 1715.

31 For example, by M. Löhnig, 'Die leibliche, nicht rechtliche Mutter' [2015] *FamRZ* 806.

32 This option was introduced on the basis of the decision of the German Constitutional Court in BVerfG 19 February 2013, *FamRZ* 2013, 521.

of a same-sex couple) the second commissioning father would be possible, however, only if the commissioning parents are married or live in a registered partnership (see §1741(2)3 of the BGB, §9(7)1 of the LPartG).

However, the adoption requires the consent by the legal parents (see §1757 of the BGB), hence, at least by the surrogate as the legal mother, but potentially also by a legal father (for example, the surrogate's husband), and consent by the child (or his or her legal representative respectively, see §1746 of the BGB). In most surrogacy cases those consent requirements will easily be met. The true hurdle will be another requirement for adoption under German law: An adoption decree will only be granted by the court (see §1752 of the BGB) if it is established that the adoption will be conducive to the best interests of the child (§1741(1)1 of the BGB). This will be the case if the commissioning parents are in the meantime also the social parents, because the surrogate does not wish to assert her legal parenthood.[33] Of course, checking the best interests of the child in surrogacy cases is potentially inconsistent with the general notion of German law that genetic parenthood has normally not to be socially tested;[34] this applies at least if the commissioning parents are the genetic parents of the child. However, there might be an extra hurdle in cases of surrogacy. §1741(1)2 of the BGB provides that a person who has participated in illegal or immoral child arrangement or has mandated or rewarded a third person to do so shall only be allowed to adopt the child if adoption is necessary to protect the best interests of the child – a provision against child trafficking. Hence, the standard of testing the best interests of the child is considerably raised (it is not sufficient that the adoption is *conducive* to the best interests of the child; it rather has to be *necessary to protect* the best interests of the child). It was argued by some courts that this provision should also apply in cases of illegal surrogacy[35] – a view which is criticised in legal literature.[36]

---

33 See for details M. Coester, above n. 2, pp. 1249 et seq.; N. Dethloff, 'Leihmütter, Wunscheltern und ihre Kinder' [2014] *JZ (Juristenzeitung)* 922, 931; cf. BGH 10 December 2014, *FamRZ* 2015, 240, 244. See, however, also the reservations made by H.-U. Maurer, in *Münchener Kommentar zum Bürgerlichen Gesetzbuch*, 7th ed., vol. IX, C.H. Beck, Munich 2017, §1741 of the BGB para. 130.

34 T. Helms, above n. 13, p. 53: 'Das für die Adoption zentrale Erfordernis der Kindeswohldienlichkeit [...] ergibt bei der Adoption durch die eigenen genetischen Eltern keinen Sinn. Genetische Elternschaft muss im Allgemeinen keine soziale Bewährungsprobe überstehen, um rechtliche Anerkennung zu erfahren'.

35 See e.g. AG Düsseldorf 19 November 2010, no. 96 XVI 21/09; AG Hamm 22 February 2011, no. XVI 192/08; LG Düsseldorf 15 March 2012, no. 25 T 758/10; against an application of §1741(1)2 of the BGB, however, LG Frankfurt a. M. 3 August 2012, *NJW* 2012, 3111 et seq.

36 See e.g. recently A. Botthof and A. Diel, 'Voraussetzungen für die (Stiefkind-)Adoption eines Kindes nach Inanspruchnahme einer Leihmutter' [2013] *StAZ* 211; N. Dethloff, above n. 33, pp. 930 et seq.; M. Löhnig and I. Plettenberg, 'Künstliche Fortpflanzung im deutschen Recht' in A. Dutta and D. Schwab et al. (eds), Künstliche Fortpflanzung und europäisches Familienrecht, Gieseking, Bielefeld 2015, pp. 10, 20 et seq.

5.5. SECRET SURROGACY

The only option in merely internal cases is a factual transfer of parentage to the commissioning parents by secret surrogacy. If surrogate and commissioning parents agree and the surrogate leaves the child with the commissioning parents and they register the child as their own child, factually legal parenthood will be established. If the gametes of the commissioning parents have been used it will be practically impossible to challenge legal parentage later on – the more so as nobody will have an interest in challenging the legal parenthood of the commissioning parents.

6. AGENCIES AND CRIMINALISATION

As discussed in Section 2.1. above, criminal sanctions apply to medical professionals involved in surrogacy procedures, as well as agencies offering surrogacy services.

7. INTERNATIONAL SURROGACY ARRANGEMENTS

There is, of course, another option to attribute legal parentage to the commissioning parents which leaves the boundaries of German law: using international surrogacy arrangements and establishing legal parenthood to the commissioning parents by the means of foreign law. That international surrogacy arrangements are a viable solution for commissioning parents was shown by a seminal decision of the German Federal Court of Justice.[37] This report refrains from presenting that decision as one of the judges rendering the decision will address cross-border issues of surrogacy from a German perspective in his contribution to this volume.[38]

8. CONCLUSION

Surrogacy has been made unattractive by German legislation, not only by criminal law but also by family law, at least in merely internal cases. The reasons behind this anti-surrogacy attitude are the classic concerns towards a

37 BGH 10 December 2014, *FamRZ* 2015, 240; see also BGH 20 April 2016, *FamRZ* 2016, 1251.

38 See the chapter in this volume authored by F. Klinkhammer; on the relevant case law of the European Court of Human Rights; see also the contribution by W. Pintens.

commercialisation of motherhood with all its potential risks for the surrogate and the child.[39]

There is currently a political discussion in Germany on reforming the law of parenthood fundamentally. For example, the German *Juristentag*, the biannual meeting of the German Lawyers Association has discussed the topic on its 2016 meeting. Tobias Helms who was the reporter for the *Juristentag* considers in his extensive opinion also a slight liberalisation of the German provisions on surrogacy.[40] One should not, however, overlook that surrogacy will not be at the focus of those discussions. There are much more important issues to be discussed currently in German law, for example, concerning sperm donation and same-sex parentage – in those area German law has lost contact to the international developments. If at all, pressure will come from abroad if more and more commissioning parents avail themselves of foreign law.

---

39 Gesetzentwurf der Bundesregierung zur Änderung des Adoptionsvermittlungsgesetzes of 9 March 1989, BT-Drucks. 11/4154, pp. 6 et seq.

40 T. Helms, above n. 13, pp. 51 et seq.; see also R. Müller-Terpitz, '„ESchG 2.0" – Plädoyer für eine partielle Reform des Embryonenschutzgesetzes' [2016] *ZRP* (*Zeitschrift für Rechtspolitik*) 51, 54.

SURROGATE MOTHERHOOD UNDER GERMAN NATIONAL AND INTERNATIONAL PRIVATE LAW

A Judicial Perspective*

Frank KLINKHAMMER

The German legislature first addressed surrogate motherhood at the end of the 1980s. It rejected it then and has continued to do so, a position clearly expressed in the laws surrounding the recognition of parenthood. The German government seeks to maintain this dismissive position in the future as well.

---

* The majority of this contribution was previously published in [2016] *International Family Law* 131; the section on the Swiss decision was added for publication in this volume.

Regardless of this dismissal, there is a need for reproduction by way of surrogacy. For heterosexual (married) couples it is needed to bridge the problem of female infertility, and for male homosexual couples it is needed to fulfil their desire to have children. As surrogacy is forbidden in Germany, these couples turn to other more liberal countries where it is permitted, and where there are agencies that assist couples in finding women who agree to give birth to a child for a fee. However, when the couples then desire to return to Germany with the child and start a family, this leads to a variety of legal problems. It is in this context that the Federal Court of Justice issued its landmark decision on 10 December 2014.[1] In the decision, the Federal Court of Justice developed standards for the recognition of foreign judgments, including the legality of parenthood derived through foreign surrogacy, and how this relates to German public policy. Other significant questions, however, remain unanswered.

1. GERMAN MEDICAL LAW, ADOPTION LAW AND LAW CONCERNING PARENTAGE

In Germany surrogate motherhood is expressly prohibited by statute. The physician who performs artificial insemination on a surrogate mother or who transfers an embryo to her is criminally liable, as is an agent who procures a woman for this purpose. If a surrogacy nevertheless takes place, however, the surrogate mother is the sole legal mother of the child.

2. MEDICAL LAW AND ADOPTION LAW

Criminal law provisions seek to discourage surrogate motherhood in a variety of ways. Pursuant to s. 1(1) no. 7 of the Act on the Protection of Embryos (*Embryonenschutzgesetz*; 'ESchG'), a person is liable if they artificially inseminate, or transfer an embryo to, a woman who is planning to give her child to a third party after birth (surrogate mother). Pursuant to s. 1(3) no. 2 of the Act on the Protection of Embryos, however, neither the surrogate mother nor the person who plans to raise the child is subject to criminal liability. However, under s. 13c of the Adoption Placement Act (*Adoptionsvermittlunsgesetz*; 'AdVermiG'), the procurement of women for the purposes of surrogacy is prohibited. Further, under s. 14b(1) and (2) of the Adoption Placement Act, a person who procures a surrogate mother or receives or is promised

---

1 XII ZB 463/13, FamRZ 2015, p. 240, with comment by Helms.

remuneration for the procurement of a surrogate mother is committing a criminal offence, however s. 14b(3) makes clear that neither the surrogate mother nor the intended parents is subject to criminal liability in this respect.

3. FILIATION

In principle, German law only permits joint parentage by filiation by the father and mother. Joint parentage for two women or two men by filiation is not provided for. Only in exceptional cases where one person has changed their legal gender can joint parentage be established by filiation for same-sex couples.

Paternity, in accordance with s. 1592 of the German Civil Code (*Bürgerliches Gesetzbuch*; 'BGB'), is based upon the man being married to the mother at the time of the birth (s. 1592 no. 1 of the German Civil Code), acknowledgement (no. 2), or the judicial establishment of paternity (no. 3), whereby only the last alternative requires the proof of genetic filiation. Pursuant to s. 1591 of the German Civil Code the mother is the woman who gave birth to the child. This excludes a different woman from claiming legal motherhood even if the child is genetically related to her. Joint parentage by two men is not provided for in German law, just as recognition of the parenthood of a female life partner; or the same is true for cohabitants/partners of one of the parents (mother or father) is not. As such, in every instance, the surrogate mother, as the woman who gave birth to the child, always holds definite parental status under German law, according to s. 1591 of the German Civil Code. As German law does not provide a mechanism to challenge legal motherhood, the genetic mother of a child born through surrogacy can only acquire parental status through adoption of the child.

Thus, the only possibility for the intended parents of a child born through surrogacy to become parents jointly in Germany is adoption (compare the decision of the Federal Constitutional Court)[2]. While a married couple who seek to become parents can adopt a child jointly as a couple, adoption by same-sex partners under the current legal system can only take place if the child is a stepchild, or as a 'successive adoption' (adoption of one partner, after the other partner adopted the child before; s. 9(7) of the Act on Registered Life Partnerships (*Gesetz über die Eingetragene Lebenspartnerschaft*; 'LPartG')).

Therefore a child born of a surrogate mother born abroad can only become the legal child of the intended parents if the foreign legal system provides for this.

---

2 FamRZ 2013, p. 521.

4. RECOGNITION OF FOREIGN JUDGMENTS ON PARENTAGE OF THE INTENDED PARENTS

If a judicial decision on the parental status of a child born through surrogacy has been made in a foreign country, it must be given priority under private international law. If the foreign judgment is to be recognised in Germany, it will have full effect. German courts will not examine whether, from the German perspective, foreign law would have been applicable and especially will not examine whether the foreign law was properly applied (prohibition on review as to substance).

The primary goal of the law on the recognition of foreign judgments is the preservation of harmony of international decision-making and, particularly, as to questions concerning civil status – the avoidance of 'limping' legal relationships. Section 109(1) no. 4 of the Act on Proceedings in Family Matters and in Matters of Non-contentious Jurisdiction (*Gesetz über das Verfahren in Familiensachen und in den Angelegenheiten der freiwilligen Gerichtsbarkeit*; 'FamFG') thus, is to be interpreted narrowly in the interests of harmony, so that a failure to recognise a judgment based upon a violation of the public policy remains limited to exceptional cases.

5. JUDGMENTS THAT MAY BE RECOGNISED

The recognition of family law judgments is governed by ss. 108 and 109 of the FamFG. A 'judgment' within the meaning of s. 108 FamFG is not made when the kinship relationship has only been certified or entered into a registry. In cases of mere certification or registry entry, a judicial examination did not occur to ensure that the registration also complied with the law. Judicial decisions – according to German law – may have a constitutive effect establishing a right, or may have only a declaratory effect stating a right. However, in this respect, whether the decision establishes a right or only has the effect of stating a right has no decisive significance, according to consistent past decisions of the Federal Court of Justice. This is because even when a decision only sets forth the existing legal situation recognition is available pursuant to s. 108 of the FamFG. Contrary to mere registration or certification of the kinship relationship, such a judgment is based on an examination of the substance by the court, which in addition to the validity of the surrogacy agreement also deals with the legal status of the child as a result of the agreements.

The case decided by the Federal Court of Justice concerned a Californian surrogacy agreement based on s. 7960(f)(2) of the California Family Code. Even a court decision which is merely declaratory is therefore subject to procedural law recognition. It has the commensurate full legal effect and, as long as no impediments to recognition exist, is binding in Germany.

6. IMPEDIMENT TO RECOGNITION BASED UPON LACK OF INTERNATIONAL JURISDICTION BY THE FOREIGN COURT

Jurisdiction for recognition within the meaning of s. 109(1) no. 1 of the FamFG must be assessed in accordance with German law, which is to be applied as a mirror to the jurisdiction of the foreign court ('Mirror Principle'). In accordance with this principle, the foreign court has international jurisdiction if there would also be a foundation for international jurisdiction upon corresponding application of German provisions. International jurisdiction is assessed in accordance with s. 100 of the FamFG, and in the case under consideration is connected to the citizenship of the child, mother, or father (s. 100(i) of the FamFG) or his or her usual place of residence (s. 100(ii) of the FamFG). Accordingly, the foreign court always has international jurisdiction based upon the habitual place of residence of the surrogate mother.

7. IMPEDIMENTS TO RECOGNITION BASED UPON VIOLATION AGAINST PUBLIC POLICY

Under s. 109(1) no 4(iv) of the FamFG, the recognition of a foreign judgment is excluded if this would lead to a result that is obviously incompatible with fundamental principles of German law, especially if recognition is incompatible with the basic rights enshrined in the German Basic Law, the German Constitution (violation of public policy). As to the question of recognition of a foreign judgment, it is not national public policy that the German courts must consider in the application of foreign law, but rather the more generous law of recognition under international public policy. Following this approach, a foreign judgment is not incompatible even if the German judge – if he had adjudicated the proceeding – would have reached a different decision on the basis of compulsory German law (prohibition of review on the merits). Rather, of greater relevance is whether the result of the application of foreign law in the case at issue is so fundamentally contrary to essential ideas of German regulations and concepts of justice that it appears untenable from a German legal perspective.

Prior to the decision of the Federal Court of Justice, there was dispute about whether a foreign (court) judgment that formed or established parentage for the intended parents based upon a surrogacy agreement is incompatible with German public policy. The Federal Court of Justice emphasised that in the case of surrogate motherhood a foreign judgment that allocates legal parentage to the intended or surrogate parents does not in itself present a violation of German public policy if one intended parent – and not the surrogate mother – is genetically related to the child.

The Federal Court of Justice based its decision to a large extent on the rights of the child born of the surrogacy and on the welfare of the child. The finding of the court based on foreign law – that there is a legal parent-child relationship between the child and the intended parents – does not contravene significant principles of German law to such an extent that the recognition of such a judgment would appear untenable. Likewise, the basic rights or human rights of the surrogate mother and the child would not in principle prohibit recognition. Rather, the welfare of the child militates strongly in favour rather than against recognition.

The prohibitive position of the Adoption Placement Act and the Act on the Protection of Embryos are more fundamental; their aim simply is to prevent surrogacy arrangements in Germany. In addition, the criminal law provisions discussed above remain limited to surrogate motherhood conducted domestically (s. 7 of the Criminal Code (*Strafgesetzbuch*; 'StGB')). The Federal Court of Justice weighed the general preventive considerations against the fact that regardless of the intended prohibition, a surrogacy had taken place in a foreign country in a permitted manner, and now the child as a legal entity must be taken into consideration. Although the German regulation in s. 1591 of the Civil Code is designed to be compulsory, and is aimed at the prevention of surrogate motherhood in foreign countries beyond the area of applicability of criminal law provisions, it does not automatically follow that it must be attributed to public policy.

The Federal Court of Justice above all referred to the right of the child to be able to establish a parent-child relationship as recognised by the European Court of Human Rights under Art. 8(1) of the ECHR.[3] The fact that the intended father, as the genetic father, would have legal status, is insufficient as the child would still only have one parent instead of two, in contravention of Art. 6(2) first sentence of the Basic Law. Legal classification as parent and child also cannot be dispensed with just because the child, even without this, could remain in the care of the intended parents. This is because the welfare of the child also includes the reliable legal classification of the parents as the persons who assume ongoing responsibility for his welfare and needs.

In contrast to surrogate motherhood conducted in a prohibited manner within Germany, as to which the law specifies two full legal parents, the limping kinship relationship to the surrogate mother, which is not effective in her home country, does not fulfil the requirements arising from Art. 2(1) in conjunction with Art. 6(2) of the Basic Law and from Art. 8(1) of the European Convention on Human Rights. If the welfare of the child is the focal point of consideration, it must be recognised that the child had no influence over its creation and, thus, cannot be held responsible for the consequences of it. Following on from this,

3 ECtHR judgment of 26 June 2014 – Application no. 65192/11 [*Mennesson*] no. 96.

the assessment of the welfare of the child is not limited to the aspect of the psychosocial relationship between the child and the surrogate mother. Rather, within the framework of a comprehensive assessment, it cannot be ignored that the intended parents accept the role of parent (unlike the surrogate mother).

The human dignity of the surrogate mother is not violated merely as a result of the occurrence of a surrogate birth. This also applies to the child who, without the surrogacy, would not have been born. In this way, if the effectiveness of the surrogacy agreement and the legal parentage of the intended parents was established by a competent foreign court in a proceeding in compliance with the requirements of the rule of law, the judgment, in the absence of contrary indications, offers a guarantee of a voluntary decision by the surrogate mother including as to voluntarily giving up the child to the intended parents.

Whether a different assessment would be appropriate if neither intended parent was genetically related to the child or if the surrogate mother was also the genetic mother, did not fall to be decided because in the case at issue one of the partners was the genetic father of the child and there was no genetic connection between the surrogate mother and the child at issue.

The argument often asserted that the welfare of the child can be better ensured through adoption is not contravened by this. It is true that adoption would enable the individual examination of the welfare of the child, but in cases of stepchild adoption it would regularly lead to the same result as the immediate recognition of the intended parents. The result takes a clear position against the assumption that there is a violation of public policy. Further, in comparison to parentage recognised upon birth by operation of descent, adoption contains additional dangers for the child. This is because after the birth of the child the intended parents still have a choice as to whether they will accept the child as their own or whether – for example because of a disability of the child – they change their mind about wanting the child. If the intended parents separate or regret their decision, the intended parent not genetically related would be able to avoid legal parentage. In the case of rejection by the intended parents, the child would remain in the country of its birth without parents, from where he would not be able to assert his relationship to the surrogate mother applicable under German law. On the other hand, the intended parents would be relieved of their responsibility although they were the initiators of the medically assisted conception and the child exists because of them. The situation is distinguishable in this way from adoption because without the surrogacy agreement the child would not have been conceived and born. In contrast to adoptive parents, in the case of surrogate motherhood the intended parents will undoubtedly play a vital role as responsible persons in the child's later search for identity as to its origins, which however would not be reflected by corresponding legal parental responsibility.

In summary it can be stated that the Federal Court of Justice gave precedence to the welfare of the child over the general preventive goals of the German prohibition on surrogate motherhood. If at least one parent is genetically related to the child and it is ensured that both the surrogacy and the giving up of the child to the intended parents were undertaken voluntarily, the parentage of the intended parents will be recognised. Because parentage of same-sex persons is possible through adoption, ultimately it is not surprising that the Federal Court of Justice did not view the fact that the intended parents were of the same sex as an impediment to the recognition of parentage by filiation.

8. IN CONTRAST TO THE GERMAN DECISION: DECISION OF THE SWISS FEDERAL COURT OF JUSTICE OF 21 MAY 2015

The decision of the Swiss Federal Court of Justice of 21 May 2015[4] is diametrically opposed to the decision of the German Federal Court. As with Germany, the Swiss legal system takes a prohibitive approach to surrogacy. But in a similar factual scenario to one described above, the Swiss Federal Court of Justice came to a very different conclusion. The case involved a male same-sex couple – both Swiss citizens – who had entered into a Registered Partnership, and undertaken a surrogacy agreement in California. After the birth of the child, a Californian Superior Court had made an order that recognised the commissioning couple as the legal parents.

While the Swiss Federal Court of Justice accepted the parenthood of the commissioning parent who was genetically related to the child, it refused to recognise the Californian judgment in relation to the non-genetically related commissioning parent. In contrast to the German decision, the Swiss Federal Court of Justice mainly based its decision on the need to deter Swiss citizens from going abroad to circumvent the national prohibition on surrogacy. Thus, when considering the best interests of the child, the court focused on promoting children's welfare generally by preventing child trafficking and protecting children from being treated as commodities rather than on the individual welfare of the child in question. One argument of the Swiss Federal Court of Justice in particular may appear somewhat odd, namely that accepting the deliberate violation of the law by the commissioning parents would deprive the child of the right of the child to feel as a victim (at 6.7) It is not clear what exactly the child gains by such a 'right'.

In comparison to the German law there are two particular provisions in Swiss law which may have had an impact on the decision: the prohibition of surrogacy in Swiss law is part of the constitution (Art. 119(2) lit d of the Swiss constitution (*Bundesverfassung*, 'BV')) and adoption by same-sex couples

[4] 5A 748/2014 BGE (Bundesgerichtsentscheidungen) 141 III, p. 312.

currently is not permitted under Swiss law. It may be that these divergences contributed to the difference in outcomes between the German and Swiss decisions.

9. CONFLICT OF LAWS APPLICABILITY OF FOREIGN LAW

The decision of the German Federal Court of Justice, despite the fact that the standards of the public policies concerning the law as to recognition and conflict of laws are not completely identical, indicates that an assessment based upon Art. 6 of the Introductory Act to the Civil Code would have led to the same result. However, it is not guaranteed that the application of substantive law would lead to parentage of the intended parents, as this would only be the case if the German conflict of laws (international private law) rules led to the application of the foreign law.

In Art. 19(1) of the Introductory Act to the Civil Code German law provides for three alternatives as to the descent of a child. In accordance therewith, the descent of the child is governed by the law of the State in which the child has his habitual residence (first sentence). In relation to each parent the descent can also be determined by the law of the country of this parent's nationality (second sentence). If the mother is married, the descent can also be determined by the law that governs the general effects of the marriage at the time of the birth of the child (third sentence).

Following from this, allocation of the child to the German intended parents is only considered when the child has his habitual residence in the country of birth. The habitual residence of a person is the location where he primarily stays, where his home is. Small children are so dependent on their caregivers and custodians that their habitual residence generally is tied to them. Accordingly, the habitual residence of infants and small children generally depends upon where the actual caregivers (usually the parents) have their habitual residence. Thus, a newborn infant who was born during a short stay in a country that was time-limited from the outset does not have his habitual residence in the place of birth. During the primarily factual consideration, however, legal aspects may play a role, especially if the legal framework can be implemented reliably and, then, the residence of the child can be determined from the factual perspective as well.

If, for example, the child's entry into Germany is barred, habitual residence in a foreign country must be initially assumed. The question then arises whether the status in accordance with the principle of acquisition of acquired rights extends beyond the change in residence, on which until now there has not been a decision by the highest court.

If, on the other hand, there is no impediment to entry into Germany, this suggests that habitual residence of the child is not in the country of birth. He merely had a short stay there and habitual residence is first established in Germany. In such cases, legal parenthood of both intended parents can only be established by adoption. A different result would be reached if German national law concerning descent was unconstitutional, which however is highly unlikely.

10. CONCLUSION

Whether a legal parent-child relationship arises with the intended parents after a surrogacy undertaken in a foreign country initially depends upon whether a court decision that is capable of recognition has been issued in the country of birth. If there are no special issues, in accordance with the decision of the Federal Court of Justice, in such a case when one of the intended parents is a genetic parent there generally is no violation of public policy.

In the absence of a court decision in the country of birth, the issue will be determined based upon the applicability of the foreign law. The conflict of laws assessment relies on the habitual residence of the child and leads to the result that in cases of unimpeded entry with the child into Germany, German law is applicable and an adoption is required. If on the other hand entry is refused, foreign law will be applicable, and there is a strong argument that public policy considerations cannot stand in the way of the application of foreign law.

SURROGACY IN SPAIN

Esther Farnós Amorós*

* This chapter, last revised in January 2019, forms part of a research project on reproductive freedom and building family relationships ('Libertad reproductiva y formación de relaciones familiares', DER2014-55573-R) funded by the Spanish Ministry of Economy, Industry and Competitiveness, and directed by Prof. Josep Ferrer-Riba (Pompeu Fabra University, Barcelona).

Spanish case law cited in this chapter is taken from *Aranzadi*, a private database accessible from the main law libraries. It can also be accessed from *Cendoj*, a free-access database owned by the Spanish General Council of the Judiciary (*Consejo General del Poder Judicial*): <http://www.poderjudicial.es/search/index.jsp> accessed 11.10.2018. The *Aranzadi* database references include AC (Court of First Instance and Appellate Court decisions), AS or JUR (regional High Courts of Justice decisions) and RJ (General Board of Registers and Notaries and Supreme Court decisions) followed by the year in which the decision was published and its identification number.

1. GENERAL LEGAL FRAMEWORK

The first assisted reproductive technologies ('ART') regulation in Spain was Act 35/1988 of 22 November (BOE no. 282, 24 November 1988).[1] This was followed some years later by Act 14/2006 of 26 May on assisted human reproductive technologies (BOE no. 126, 27 May 2006),[2] which persisted in denying surrogacy arrangements any legal effects.[3] Article 10.1 declared commercial or altruistic gestational surrogacy arrangements 'fully null and void', and thus these arrangements have typically been considered to be contracts with unlawful purpose (Arts 1271 and 1275 of the Spanish Civil Code).[4] The main consequence of the nullity is that any child's legal mother is the woman who gave birth to it (Art. 10.2 of Act 14/2006), in accordance with the Roman law principle *mater semper certa est*.

Spain has become one of the top 'fertility tourism' destinations for couples and single women from other European countries.[5] Factors such as permission to use third-party gametes; 'compensation' policies fostering gamete surplus; donor anonymity; non-exclusion of unmarried and lesbian couples; and – in the private sector – lower costs and shorter waiting lists compared to other Member States which also have liberal ART regulations all go some way to explaining this phenomenon. However, Spanish citizens themselves need to leave Spain and visit other legal systems when matters of surrogacy are concerned. Popular destinations so far have been – in this order – the United States (US), Ukraine, India, Mexico and Thailand.[6] Although providing official data on a reality which takes place outside the control of the law is extremely difficult,[7] there is some evidence which leads to the conclusion that cross-border surrogacy is an ever-increasing phenomenon in Spain, often encouraged by private agencies

---

1 BOE is the abbreviation for *Boletín Oficial del Estado*, the Spanish official bulletin.

2 *Ley 14/2006, de 26 de mayo, sobre técnicas de reproducción humana asistida*, Act 14/2006 from now on.

3 On the background to this rule, see the Report on Spain (pp. 351–67) by M. Roca i Escoda, in L. Brunet, J. Carruthers, K. Davaki, D. King, C. Marzo and J. Maccandless, *A comparative study on the regime of surrogacy in EU Member States*, Directorate General for Internal Policies – European Union, 2013, pp. 351–53: <http://www.europarl.europa.eu/RegData/etudes/STUD/2013/474403/IPOL-JURI_ET(2013)474403_EN.pdf> accessed 04.09.2018.

4 *Código civil*, from now on CC. An English version of the Spanish Civil Code is accessible from the website of the Spanish Ministry of Justice: <http://www.mjusticia.gob.es/cs/Satellite/es/1288774502225/TextoPublicaciones.html> accessed 04.09.2018.

5 F. Shenfield, J. De Mouzon, G. Pennings, A.P. Ferraretti, A. Nyboe Andersen, G. De Wert and V. Goossens, 'Cross border reproductive care in six European countries' (2010) 25(6) *HR (Human Reproduction)* 1361, 1366–67. Instead of 'fertility tourism', these authors favour the more neutral expression 'cross-border reproductive care'.

6 P. Álvarez, 'El 80% de los hijos por gestación subrogada proceden de EE UU y Ucrania', *El País*, 18.12.2017: <https://politica.elpais.com/politica/2017/12/13/actualidad/1513185337_622133.html> accessed 04.09.2018.

7 On this point see also the report cited in n. 3, pp. 366–67.

and intermediaries.[8] It is estimated that around 1,000 children with Spanish commissioning parents were allegedly gestated in this way and born in the US in 2003.[9] According to data from the Spanish Consulate in Los Angeles, the birth rate among Spanish nationals resident in this consular territory in 2008 was 50.01 per 1,000 residents, which is five times higher than that among Spanish nationals residing in Spain that same year (9.8 per 1,000). This rate can only be explained because the Consulate has allowed for the registration of sons and daughters of non-residing couples of different sex.[10] In 2011 it was estimated that around 500 Spanish couples, of whom 85 per cent were of different sex, travel to the US every year to access surrogacy.[11] In 2016 the advocacy group *Son Nuestros Hijos* ('SNH') put the number of Spanish couples resorting to surrogates in the US annually at around 800.[12] More recent data provided by the Spanish government, based on registries at Spanish consulates and embassies, point out that around 975 children gestated in this way were born between 2010 and 2016.[13] However, the same source reports that the number of births after a surrogacy process carried out abroad may be higher, since these data do not reflect the surrogacy cases processed as if they were adoptions by the Spanish embassies.

---

8 While the number of foreign agencies – mainly Ukrainian – offering their services to Spanish citizens is increasing, Spanish agencies are also flourishing. The following are only a few examples: <http://subrogalia.com/>, <http://www.vientredealquiler.com/>, <http://www.alfinpadres.com/?gclid=COjugOvEnNECFVTnGwodfZ4B3g>, <http://www.agar-asociacion.org/reproduccion-asistida/> accessed 04.09.2018.
The first agency mentioned is involved, at least, in two criminal proceedings (decrees of the Barcelona Court of Appeal, 4th Section, of 17.05.2017, JUR 2017/267636; and 5th Section, of 28.12.2017, JUR 2017/77133) for breach of contract, fraud, deceit and false advertising resulting from not providing several Spanish male gay couples, who hired a surrogate in Mexico, with the embryos created with sperm of one of the commissioning parents and anonymous eggs. According to the contracts signed by the couples, the mentioned embryos must be sent to Mexico but this was finally not possible because the ART centre ran by the agency did not have the mandatory authorisations to do so. The agency has also been fined by the Catalan government for advertising a non-licensed activity in Spain: see R. Quelart, 'Un juez obliga a devolver casi todo el dinero cobrado para dos procesos de maternidad subrogada', *La Vanguardia*, 08.11.2017: <http://www.lavanguardia.com/sucesos/20171108/432716467628/sentencia-caso-subrogalia.html> accessed 04.09.2018.

9 A. Durán Ayago, and P. Blanco-Morales Limones, 'Los vientres de alquiler (La cara y la cruz)' (2014) 881 *AJA (Actualidad Jurídica Aranzadi)* 1, 2.

10 See the figures in the document cited in n. 3, pp. 354–55. Please note that the information provided in the mentioned document is not very accurately explained.

11 R. Ruiz and G. Abril, 'Hijos muy buscados', *El País*, 29.05.2011: <http://elpais.com/diario/2011/05/29/eps/1306650415_850215.html> accessed 04.09.2018.

12 SNH, which means literally 'They are our children', is a highly active Spanish society of mainly same-sex families which has launched an initiative in order to register in Spain the parentage of children gestated abroad through surrogacy: <http://www.sonnuestroshijos.com/> accessed 04.09.2018. Source: J.A. Cañas, 'Spanish police arrest three over illegal womb-for-rent arrangement', *El País*, 29.11.2016: <http://elpais.com/elpais/2016/11/29/inenglish/1480426054_414168.html> accessed 04.09.2018.

13 It is estimated that 553 of these children were born in the US, 231 in Ukraine, 97 in India, 51 in Mexico, 27 in Thailand, four in Canada, four in the United Kingdom (UK), four in Greece and four in Russia: see P. Álvarez, above n. 6.

As the above information shows, the Spanish authorities have already had to deal with surrogacy in a cross-border context (see Section 7). The lack of any specific surrogacy prohibition, together with the absence of criminal and/or administrative sanctions (see Section 6) has led to surrogacies undertaken abroad being recognised by judicial and administrative bodies. Although the Spanish parliament remains silent on the issue, this quasi-tolerant approach offers another example of the existing tendency among legal systems that do not allow surrogacy to legalise it when it is carried out abroad. In doing so, the public authorities have frequently invoked the principle of the child's best interests.

2. SURROGACY ARRANGEMENTS IN GENERAL

As is clear from Art. 10.1 of Act 14/2006, Spanish law unambiguously denies the enforceability of surrogacy arrangements, irrespective of whether they are entered into on an altruistic or commercial basis. Therefore, the parties to such contracts cannot request the fulfilment of the usual reciprocal obligations (e.g. the surrogate's obligation to waive maternity and give the baby away and the commissioning parents' obligation to pay the surrogate's expenses and – where the surrogacy is commercial – financial compensation).[14]

3. LEGAL PARENTAGE AT THE TIME OF THE BIRTH

According to Art. 10.2 of Act 14/2006 the legal mother is the woman who gives birth to the child. If she is married, her husband will be considered the legal father because the marital paternity presumption will apply (Art. 116 of the CC).[15] If the child is born out of wedlock, her legal father will be the man who acknowledges paternity in the birth certificate, a will, a public deed or a statement before a Civil Registry official (Art. 120, paras 1–3 of the CC).[16]

---

14 P. Orejudo Prieto de los Mozos, 'Spain', in K. Trimmings and P. Beaumont (eds), *International Surrogacy Arrangements. Legal Regulation at the International Level*, Hart Publishing, Oxford and Portland 2013, p. 348.

15 Similarly in Catalonia, Art. 235-5.1 of the Catalan Civil Code (from now on CCCat). Book 2 of the Catalan Civil Code dealing with personal and family law was approved by Act 25/2010 of 29 July (BOE no. 203, 21.08.2011), which came into force on 01.01.2011. An English version of Act 25/2010 is available on the Catalan Parliament website: <http://www.parlament.cat/web/documentacio/altres-versions/lleis-versions/index.html> accessed 04.09.2016.

16 This rule was amended by Act 19/2015 of 13 July (BOE no. 167, 14.07.2015), which reforms the Civil Registry. For this acknowledgement to be valid it must be subject to the requirements

Acknowledgement is the most common way of establishing paternity since unlike paternity claims it occurs at extrajudicial level and DNA tests do not therefore need to be carried out. However, as extrajudicial means for establishing parentage, both the acknowledgement of paternity and the marital paternity presumption can be disrupted by a paternity claim which proves that the man acknowledging the child's paternity, or the mother's husband, is not the biological father. This is so because where the biological father is concerned, Art. 10.3 of Act 14/2006 provides that paternity claims to be brought according to the 'general rules' (see below Section 5).[17] In addition to this option, the biological father can acknowledge paternity according to the procedure described by Art. 120, paras 1–3 of the CC as long as paternity has not been established in favour of another man. However, if the commissioning father who provided the sperm accessed surrogacy with a woman (the commissioning mother), she cannot legally be considered the mother because the '*mater semper certa est*' Roman law principle will prevail, at least at the beginning (see below Section 5). Therefore, it is not relevant whether the commissioning mother gave her eggs in order for the child to be conceived or not.

4. ELIGIBILITY FOR SURROGACY

As a logical consequence of applying the '*mater semper certa est*' principle as described in Sections 1 and 3, Spain regulates neither the legal requirements for the surrogate and commissioning parents nor the rights and duties of the persons involved – such as the woman's right to terminate her pregnancy, contact rights between parents and children, and the right to know one's biological origins.

5. TRANSFERRING PARENTAGE

As mentioned in Section 3 with regard to the man providing the sperm for the child's conception (i.e. the biological father), Art. 10.3 of Act 14/2006 allows the commissioning biological father to bring a paternity claim according to the 'general rules', in order to establish his paternity. However, as mentioned above, initially there is nothing to prevent either the paternity presumption from being applied to the surrogate's husband, or a man who is not married to the surrogate

stated in Arts 123 and 124 of the CC. Along similar lines, Arts 235-9.1.a) and 235-12 of the CCCat.

17 'Queda a salvo la posible acción de reclamación de la paternidad respecto del padre biológico, *conforme a las reglas generales*.'

from acknowledging paternity. In those cases, bringing the paternity claim allowed in Art. 10.3 of Act 14/2006 will allow paternity previously established through extrajudicial means to be disrupted.

According to Art. 7.1 of Act 14/2006, which states that parentage of children conceived through ART will be subject to 'civil rules', any possible paternity claim by the biological father (Art. 10.3) will be subject to the rules in the Spanish Civil Code or whichever regional civil code is applicable on the basis of the child's *vecindad civil* (Art. 9.4 of the CC in connection with Arts 9.1 and 14). *Vecindad civil*, a sort of civil status for the purposes of applying general or territorial laws, is usually passed on from parents to children via *ius sanguinis*; it may also be acquired by the free decision of the person after two years of continuous residence in the region, or if an individual has been domiciled in a territory for an unbroken 10-year period, provided the person does not file a contrary declaration during this period (Art. 14.5 of the CC).[18] The lack of a homogeneous 'Spanish family law', which explains the legal diversity surrounding the establishing of parentage, is a consequence of territorial diversity and a highly relevant feature of Spanish private law. Spain never completed the process of unifying its private law. Therefore, what is called *derecho común* (Spanish general law), whose basic private law text is the Spanish Civil Code, coexists with *derechos autonómicos* (territorial laws), also called *derechos forales* in some regions. The 1978 Spanish Constitution acknowledged this diversity by awarding regions which still had *derechos forales o especiales* the power to preserve, modify and develop their own private law (Art. 149.1 no. 8).[19] Catalonia has developed an almost complete system of family law – including extensive regulation of parentage – the only exceptions being the requirements for marrying, for separating or divorcing, and for requesting annulment of marriage, which are governed by Spanish general law. The Catalan parliament brought traditional family law up to date by means of several specific regulations passed in the last decade of the twentieth century, which were merged into the 1998 Family Code (except for Act 10/1998 concerning non-marital relationships, which remained outside the Code). This Code was replaced by Book 2 of the Catalan Civil Code dealing with personal and family law.[20]

---

18 See J. Ferrer-Riba, 'Marital Agreements and Private Autonomy in Spain', in J. Scherpe (ed.), *Marital Agreements and Private Autonomy in Comparative Perspective*, Hart Publishing, Oxford and Portland 2012, p. 352.

19 *Constitución española de 1978*, SC from now on. An English version of the SC as published in the BOE is available here: <https://www.boe.es/legislacion/documentos/ConstitucionINGLES.pdf> accessed 04.09.2018.

20 Cited at n. 15. For more information on the topic some years before Book 2 entered into force, see E. Arroyo I. Amayuelas, 'The Plurality of Civil Codes in Spain. Spanish Decodification *versus* Catalan Codification', in A. Zaccaria (ed.), *Verona Lectures on European Private Law*, 1, Aracne, Roma 2006, pp. 18–21. More recently, see J. Ferrer-Riba, above n. 18, pp. 351–52. On the existence of an almost complete 'Catalan family law', see also A. Lamarca Marquès,

As can be seen from the previous paragraph, the parentage of children who are not subject to any regional civil code is established through a judicial procedure following Art. 131 of the CC and ff., which includes DNA testing.[21] Article 131 allows not only the commissioning biological father to bring a paternity claim, but also any other person with legal standing.[22]

Once the surrogate has agreed to the adoption according to the procedure described below in this same paragraph and paternity has been established in favour of the commissioning father through extrajudicial (see Section 3) or judicial means (see above), it has been suggested that the commissioning mother can adopt the child.[23] As described in Section 7.1, so far this modus operandi has only been reported with reference to Spanish citizens accessing surrogacy abroad, probably because cases of domestic surrogacy remain hidden.[24] When surrogacy is practised inside Spanish borders, it could seem at first glance that subsequent adoption by the commissioning mother – or the other commissioning father, in cases involving male gay couples – would be unlikely to gain judicial approval, since its origins lie in a null and void surrogacy contract (Art. 10.1 of Act 14/2006). However, 'stepparent adoption', allowed in Art. 176.2.II.2 of the CC, can be a valid mechanism for circumventing this nullity. Stepparent adoption, which has to follow a judicial procedure like any other adoption in Spain (Art. 176.1 of the CC), needs no prior proposal, so there is no requirement for an official certificate of suitability. As it is a sort of 'private adoption', which needs to be confirmed by the judiciary, it is only possible in exceptional circumstances – such as when parentage had never been established for one parent; this parent died; was deprived of parental rights or was under a deprivation cause, *or should he or she assent to the adoption* (Art. 235-32.1.a) of the CCCat. Therefore, if the surrogate agrees to the adoption six weeks or more after the birth (Art. 177.2.IV of the CC),[25] the public authorities will not control her waiving of rights unless

'The changing concept of "family" and challenges for family law in Spain and Catalonia', in J. Scherpe (ed.), *European Family Law*, vol. 2, Elgar, Cheltenham and Northampton 2016, p. 291.

21 In Catalonia this procedure, with some special features, is regulated in Arts 235-20 to 235-22 of the CCCat.

22 Article 131.I of the CC refers to any person with a 'legitimate interest' if parentage was demonstrated by the possession of 'parental status' ('Cualquier persona con *interés legítimo* tiene acción para que se declare la filiación manifestada por la constante *posesión de estado*'). When this 'parental status' is lacking, Art. 132 of the CC confers legal standing on the 'father', the 'mother' and 'children'. The children's heirs also have legal standing. The Catalan Civil Code disregards the 'parental status' category and merely confers legal standing on the 'father', the 'mother' and 'children'. The children can act by themselves or through their legal representatives. The claim can be transmitted to the children's offspring and heirs (Arts 235-21 and 235-22 of the CCCat).

23 P. Orejudo Prieto de los Mozos, above n. 14, p. 349.

24 With remarkable exceptions, such as the one which gave room to the case cited in n. 28.

25 Similarly, see Arts 235-38.1 and 235-41.2 of the CCCat regarding Catalonia.

the child is in need. Since any child in this situation would already have a legal father (i.e. the commissioning father), there seems to be nothing to prevent the other commissioning parent from adopting the child. In any case, since domestic surrogacy remains hidden because of Art. 10 Act of 14/2006, and there is no need to state the form of conception to the public authorities (Art. 7.2 of Act 14/2006), there is no evidence about how many domestic surrogacy arrangements are being legalised in this way in Spain every year.

6. AGENCIES AND CRIMINALISATION

The absence of any specific prohibition of surrogacy in Art. 10 of Act 14/2006 or the Criminal Code means that Spanish law also lacks administrative sanctions against individuals involved in this practice. At first glance, there are no express references to any surrogacy related actions in the list of offences in Art. 26 of Act 14/2006, which establishes three kinds of offences relating to ART: minor, serious and very serious. Serious and very serious infringements are certain behaviours such as the lack of informed consent to ART or practice of ART in non-licensed centres, which are explicitly included in the list, while minor infringements are any non-fulfilments of duties or transgressions of a prohibition established in the Act but not explicitly considered either serious or very serious infringements. Surrogacy could be considered a very serious infringement, since Art. 26.2.c).2 considers 'practising any technique which is not included in the Act's annex or accepted as a testing technique according to article 2' as such. The penalty for practicing surrogacy in Spain could therefore be a fine of between €10,001 and €1,000,000, as well as the closing down of the centre where the practice was carried out (Art. 27.1 of Act 14/2006). However, as these fines are aimed at ART centres and their staff (Art. 25 of Act 14/2006), there is no rule that directly punishes the commissioning parents, the surrogate or third persons such as mediators, agencies, middlemen, advertisers or lawyers.

As stated in Section 1, the Spanish Criminal Code does not specifically address surrogacy either, but it does deal with cases where one woman pretends to have given birth to a child (*suposición de parto*), as well as with cases of misrepresentation of parentage (*alteración de la paternidad*) resulting from baby trafficking (Arts 220 to 222). In practice these provisions are applied when family members try to hide teenage pregnancies by assuming legal parentage themselves, as well as in cases of 'baby trading' and the switching of babies at birth. Although Art. 221.2 also provides for both the person who receives the child and the intermediary if the delivery takes place abroad to be penalised, Art. 23 of Act 6/1985 of 1 July on the judicial branch (BOE no. 157, 2 July 1985) bases criminal prosecution by the Spanish jurisdiction on territoriality. This consideration and the principles of minimum intervention of criminal law and proportionality explain why the articles of the Criminal Code mentioned above have not so far been applied to international surrogacy cases.[26] Although to date Spanish case law databases contain no domestic cases of surrogacy where the former provisions have been applied,[27] the growing demand for surrogacy could explain the fact that a recent domestic case is probably subject to prosecution under the Criminal Code.[28]

7. INTERNATIONAL SURROGACY ARRANGEMENTS

As mentioned in Section 1, one of the main consequences of the lack of surrogacy regulation in Spain is that Spanish citizens access surrogacy in other legal systems where it is explicitly permitted or simply tolerated. In this context, ever since the first case arose in 2009 (see Section 7.1.) the Spanish authorities have dealt with applications from Spanish commissioning parents aimed at establishing their parentage and being granted social security benefits (paternity and maternity leave) regarding a child or children gestated abroad by a surrogate. As described below, these cases have been resolved not through legislative norms but through case law and administrative solutions, leading to great legal uncertainty.

7.1. TRANSFERRING PARENTAGE

7.1.1. The Case which Opened Pandora's Box

A case reported in 2009 opened Pandora's box where the effects of foreign surrogacy in Spain were concerned and triggered the Spanish administrative authorities' current surrogacy friendly approach.[29] Until then, when a man

---

[26] On this complex issue at general level, see G. Cohen, 'Circumvention Tourism' (2012) 97 *CLR (Cornell Law Review)* 1309, 1373.

[27] On the same conclusion in 2013, see L. Brunet, J. Carruthers, K. Davaki, D. King, C. Marzo and J. Maccandless, above n. 3, p. 108.

[28] According to the alleged facts of the case, which took place in the southern region of Andalusia, a male gay couple established contact with a woman who was then inseminated in a private ART centre and 'rented' her womb to them for €10,000. After the birth the woman gave the baby girl to the couple and told social workers that her daughter had died during birth. On the basis of the suspicions of the social services and the contradictions between the woman's version and the hospital's, both the woman and the couple were arrested and the child was taken into care. For more information on the case, see J.A. Cañas, above n. 12.

[29] P. Orejudo Prieto de los Mozos, above n. 14, pp. 349 and ff. For more information about the story of the case, see M. Requejo, 'Spanish homosexual couple and surrogate pregnancy', Blog *Conflict of Laws.net. News and Views in Private International Law* (29.11.2008): <http://conflictoflaws.net/2008/spanish-homosexual-couple-and-surrogate-pregnancy/> accessed 04.09.2018. See also the document cited in n. 3, pp. 126–30.

and woman of childbearing age asked for their child's birth from a surrogacy arrangement to be entered in the Spanish Civil Registry, parentage registration was granted.[30] But when the commissioning parents were two men, an increasingly common phenomenon since same-sex marriage was approved in Spain by Act 13/2005 of 1 July (BOE no. 157, 2 July 2005),[31] the fact that the baby had clearly been born to a surrogate implied that parentage registration was denied.[32] This is exactly what happened in the case detailed below, which opened the debate about what the effects of surrogacy practised abroad by Spanish citizens should be in Spain.

After several failed attempts at international adoption, a Spanish male gay couple who were married in Valencia in 2005 decided to pursue surrogacy in San Diego (California), and twins were born there to a surrogate on 24 October 2008. The Spanish consulate registrar in Los Angeles refused to register their parentage and once back in Spain the spouses lodged an application for review before the General Board of Registers and Notaries ('DGRN'), an administrative body in charge of Civil Registers attached to the Spanish Ministry of Justice.[33] On 18 February 2009 the DGRN upheld the appeal (RJ 2009/1735),[34] stating that the request to register parentage declared on birth certificates issued by a foreign administrative authority in San Diego in Spain raised only questions of recognition, and concluding that the legality test regarding the foreign authority's international jurisdiction, due process and compatibility with Spanish *ordre public* was satisfied. Where *ordre public* was concerned, the DGRN argued that since Spanish law already allowed double paternity resulting from adoption, as well as double maternity resulting either from adoption or ART, refusing the registration would constitute discrimination. In the end, according to the DGRN, such a denial would also jeopardise the best interests of the children, who were already in Spain living with the commissioning couple.

Since civil status and registration decisions are subject to judicial review, the Spanish public prosecutor appealed against the decision on the grounds of Art. 10 of Act 14/2006. On 15 September 2010 a Court of First Instance in

---

30 See the data provided in relation to nn. 9 and 10. On the same opinion, see C. Marín Pedreño and J.A. Marfil, 'Surrogacy in Spain: reality v legality' June [2014] *IFL* (*International Family Law*) 100, 101. See also V. Gutiérrez Calvo, 'Spain seeks solution for surrogate babies stuck in legal limbo', *El País*, 05.07.2014: <http://elpais.com/elpais/2014/07/04/inenglish/1404469559_678105.html> accessed 04.09.2018.

31 See the data provided by A. Lamarca Marquès, above n. 20, pp. 294–95. See also, by the same author, 'Same-sex marriage in Spain: the decision of the Constitutional Court' March [2013] *IFL* 76.

32 In relation to this issue, connected to discriminatory arguments, see below n. 39.

33 *Dirección General de los Registros y del Notariado*, from now on DGRN.

34 M. Requejo, 'Spanish homosexual couple and surrogate pregnancy (II)', Blog cited in n. 29 (14.03.2009): <http://conflictoflaws.net/2009/spanish-homosexual-couple-and-surrogate-pregnancy-ii/> accessed 04.09.2018.

Valencia (AC 2010/1707) declared the registration of parentage null and void on the basis that Spanish law *prohibits* gestational surrogacy (§3).[35] The court was especially severe with regard to the discrimination argument that had been successful before the DGRN, arguing that the registration of the children's parentage had been denied not because the claimants were men but because the children had been born as a result of a null and void arrangement, and the same consequence would therefore apply to both different and same-sex couples as well as single men and women. The court also disregarded the argument in favour of registration based on the children's best interests because the Spanish legal system has enough means and instruments (among them, the paternity claim allowed by Art. 10.3 of Act 14/2006 in respect of the biological father and subsequent adoption or fostering by the other commissioning parent) to register the twins as both spouses' legal children (§5.11).

On 23 November 2011 the 10th Section of the Valencia Appellate Court upheld the Court of First Instance's decision (AC 2011/1561). The most serious obstacle encountered by the Appellate Court was that registration of legal parentage was contrary to Spanish law and therefore failed to comply with the test of legality (§1) and violated Spanish *ordre public* (§2). Secondly, the court stated that the foreign certificate recorded in the proceedings was not a 'judicial' decision.[36] This requirement is especially important when the link between the appellants and the foreign country is not substantial, as happened in this case. At this point, the court warned about the commissioning parents' fraudulent use of Spanish rules on legal parentage (§3). Relying on the Court of First Instance's thesis, the Appellate Court rejected the discrimination argument put forward by the commissioning parents (§4). Finally, the court reiterated the argument made by the Court of First Instance according to which Spanish law already allows a relationship resulting from a surrogacy arrangement to be registered through valid mechanisms, such as a paternity claim by the biological father (Art. 10.3 of Act 14/2006) and subsequent adoption by the other commissioning parent.

The commissioning parents appealed against this decision and on 6 February 2014 the Civil Chamber of the Supreme Court (RJ 2014/833) upheld the Appellate Court decision in a five to four ruling.[37] Although

---

35 M. Requejo, 'Spanish homosexual couple and surrogate pregnancy (III)', Blog cited in n. 29 (20.09.2010): <http://conflictoflaws.net/2010/surrogate-motherhood-and-spanish-homosexual-couple-iii/> accessed 04.09.2018.

36 On this point, see the *Guidelines for recognition of parentage established abroad by means of surrogacy* in this subsection and the references to the DGRN's Order of 05.10.2010 there.

37 See also P. de Lora, 'Are you my mother? The Spanish Supreme Court and Surrogacy Tourism', Blog *Bill of Health – Harvard Law Petrie-Flom Center* (16.02.2014): <http://blogs.harvard.edu/billofhealth/2014/02/16/are-you-my-mother-the-spanish-supreme-court-and-surrogacy-tourism/> accessed 04.09.2018.

the high court used a better method in international private law terms,[38] it ultimately fell back on the substantial arguments invoked by the lower courts. These arguments are, briefly, that surrogacy is contrary to Spanish *ordre public*; since surrogacy is forbidden to everybody there is no discrimination with regard to lesbian couples who could access ART in Spain with double maternity effects (§4.2),[39] and the principle of the child's best interests. I will now turn to the arguments related to the *ordre public* exception and the child's best interests, since the court placed special emphasis on them both.

7.1.2. Is Recognition of Parentage Contrary to Spanish Ordre Public?

The Spanish Supreme Court considered it relevant that the parentage status which the parties tried to transfer to the Spanish Civil Registry was the direct and main consequence of a surrogacy arrangement, a practice contrary to Spanish *ordre public* (§11). This is undoubtedly one of the most controversial points of the court's decision, since it is difficult to maintain today that Art. 10 of Act 14/2006 is contrary to Spanish *ordre public*. The provision has no prohibitive content per se, merely declaring that surrogacy contracts are 'null and void' and only establishing the civil consequences of nullity. Furthermore, as emphasised in Section 6, the Spanish Criminal Code does not directly address surrogacy at all. The possibility of establishing paternity in favour of the biological father, expressly stated by the law (Art. 10.3), and thus reconstituting the family also prompts the conclusion that surrogacy is no longer contrary to Spanish *ordre public*. Ultimately, the quasi-tolerant approach to international surrogacy arrangements endorsed by administrative and judicial bodies reflects the fact that surrogacy is widely accepted by the Spanish public if practised abroad.

From a methodological point of view, the most debatable aspect of the Supreme Court decision is the test carried out, since the court refused to check whether Spanish *ordre public* was violated in the case in question.[40] It concluded instead that any surrogacy arrangement is contrary to the dignity of the surrogate and the child involved because it commodifies gestation and

---

38 See especially the next subsection.

39 Although I agree with this line of reasoning it is necessary to point out that this argument was not raised until 2009, on the occasion of the male gay couple case analysed here. Spanish different sex couples had already entered into surrogacy arrangements before 2009 but these cases remained 'legal secrets', 'invisible' or 'taboo'. On the same opinion, P. Orejudo Prieto de los Mozos, above n. 14, p. 350. This author discusses factual (rather than legal) discrimination. On this discussion, see also the references cited in n. 30 and the document cited in n. 3, pp. 125 and 354–55.

40 This modus operandi was severely criticised by the dissenting opinion, according to which 'breach of international *ordre public* can only be examined on a case-by-case basis'. See also C. Marín Pedreño and J.A. Marfil, 'Surrogacy in Spain: reality v legality' June [2014] *IFL* 100, 102.

parentage, treating women and children as objects, allowing intermediaries to make money out of them, exploiting the situation of young women in need and creating a kind of privileged citizenship restricted to people with extensive financial resources (§3.6).

7.1.3. Is Recognition of Parentage Contrary to the Principle of the Child's Best Interests?

Although the Supreme Court was aware that non-recognition of children's parentage can damage their legal status (§§5.8 and 5.11), it accepted that appealing to the general principle of the child's best interests does not enable judges to arrive at any solution which would have the effect of turning the children into objects of commercial trafficking (§§5.6 and 5.8). This argument is in conflict with the dissenting opinion, according to which the *ordre public* principle cannot be invoked if the child's best interests are not effectively damaged in a particular case (§2.3).

The leading case analysed here is highly unusual, since the commissioning parents brought neither the Californian surrogacy contract to the proceedings nor the Californian pre-birth judgment which transferred parentage to them and contained the surrogate's waiver of maternity.[41] They provided only the US birth certificates, which stated their paternity. Therefore, since it was not clear who the children's biological father was (§1.7), the Supreme Court urged the civil prosecutor to press the commissioning parents to begin judicial claims to establish the children's parentage (namely, a paternity claim on the part of the biological father, ex Art. 10.3 of Act 14/2006, followed by the adoption process described in Section 5). Unlike the method of recognition of foreign decisions, this is a long burdensome process during which various upheavals can occur, such as divorce or the death of one or both commissioning parents. This circumstance, together with the fact that on 26 June 2014 the ECtHR (Fifth Section) ruled on two similar cases, *Mennesson* and *Labassée v France* (application nos 65192/11 and 65941/11) and found against France in both,[42] probably explains why the commissioning parents raised the nullity

---

41 On this critical point, see a preliminary analysis of the case in E. Farnós Amorós, 'Surrogacy arrangements in a global world: the case of Spain' March [2013] *IFL*, 68, 70–71.

42 An analysis of the French cases can be found in the chapter written by Prof. W. Pintens in this book, pp. 17 and ff. Both cases are accessible through the ECtHR database (HUDOC), although the *Labassee* case is not available in English (accessed 31.12.2016). Apart from *Mennesson* and *Labassee*, which have inspired other similar French cases which have also accessed the ECtHR (*Foulon and Bouvet v France*, application nos 9063/14 and 10410/14, Fifth Section, 21.07.2016; and *Laborie v France*, application no. 44024/13, Fifth Section, 19.01.2017), see *Paradiso and Campanelli v Italy* (application no. 25358/12), decided by the ECtHR (Second Section) on 27.01.2015. It is important to note that the latter is a more complex and very unusual case, in which it was proven that the child had no genetic link with

of the February 2014 decision before the Supreme Court itself.[43] However, on 2 February 2015 the Court's Civil Chamber confirmed the previous ruling (JUR 2015/45930). Consciously differentiating between the Spanish and French cases, the court attached special relevance to the fact that France does not allow the commissioning parents to establish parentage in any way at all, unlike Spain, where parentage can be established in favour of the biological father and the other commissioning parent can then resort to adoption.

The option that the Supreme Court offered the commissioning parents can be considered 'second best', since it only allows the children's parentage to be established at some time after the birth. During the time between the birth and the resolution of judicial claims aimed at transferring parentage (paternity claim plus adoption process), the children have no established parentage. However, as hypothesised in Sections 3 and 5 in relation to domestic surrogacy, this critique could be softened if one of the commissioning parents acknowledged the children's paternity once in Spain, in accordance with the extrajudicial proceeding mentioned above. Once the surrogate has agreed to the adoption, the other commissioning parent could adopt the children through a stepparent adoption process.

In the specific case analysed here, and maybe due to ideological issues, the appellants did not only oppose bypassing the regular parentage circuit via paternity claim and subsequent adoption but also failed to take the Californian judicial decision stating their parentage to the proceedings in order for it to be recognised in Spain.[44] The Supreme Court's decision is likely to be scrutinised

either of the commissioning parents, who had been found guilty of circumventing legislation on international adoption, among other offences, in Italy. As the ECtHR press release stresses, in this case the court focused on the removal of the child and his placement under guardianship, *and not on the issue of surrogacy*: 'Questions and Answers on the Paradiso and Campanelli v. Italy judgment (27 January 2015)', 1: <http://www.echr.coe.int/Documents/Press_Q_A_Paradiso_and_Campanelli_ENG.pdf> accessed 04.09.2018.
In spite of this, the ECtHR's reference to *ordre public*, assuming that it 'could not, however, be considered as giving *carte blanche* for any measure, since the State had an obligation to take the child's best interests into account irrespective of the nature of the parental link, genetic or otherwise,' is worthy of note (§80). The ruling, which considered the Italian authorities to have violated the applicants' right to respect for their private and family life and ordered Italy to pay the applicants €20,000 in respect of non-pecuniary damages, was referred to the Grand Chamber by the Italian government. On 24.01.2017 the Grand Chamber reversed the ruling. The court held by 11 votes to six that there had been no violation of Art. 8 of the Convention. Despite admitting 'the impact which the immediate and irreversible separation from the child must have had on the applicants' private life', the court concluded that 'Agreeing to let the child stay with the applicants, possibly with a view to becoming his adoptive parents, would have been tantamount to legalising the situation created by them in breach of important rules of Italian law' (§215).

43 It has been said that the ECtHR rulings could help dozens of couples in Spain: see V. Gutiérrez Calvo, above n. 30.

44 The commissioning parents only brought the US birth certificates to the proceedings. This was probably an entirely conscious decision. The fact that they were a male gay couple could

by the Constitutional Court, and a subsequent appeal before the ECtHR cannot be ruled out either.

7.1.4. *Guidelines for Recognition of Parentage Established Abroad by Means of Surrogacy*

On 5 October 2010, while the leading case described above was still before the courts, the DGRN issued an Order on the registration in Spain of parentage of children gestated abroad through surrogacy (BOE no. 243, 7 October 2010).[45] This could have been an *administrative* response (it is important to stress that it was not a *legal* response) to the ever-increasing number of Spanish couples and single persons going abroad in order to access surrogacy[46] and returning with one or more children whose gestational mother had legally waived maternity in the country where the surrogacy was practised. As well as requiring one of the claimants to be Spanish, the Order demands a judicial decision establishing the child's legal parentage from a competent court in the country where the child was born. This prerequisite is apparently imposed to ascertain that international child trafficking is not involved, that the principle of the child's best interests is respected, especially in relation to the right to know one's biological origins, and that the capacity of surrogate women and the freedom and revocability of their consent are guaranteed. However, there is another explanation that the DGRN fails to mention, which has to do with the fact that following a Supreme Court decision on 21 September 1999 (RJ 1999/6944), Spanish law has rejected the possibility of anonymous births. Thus, under Spanish law there must always be a mother, who according to Art. 10.2 of Act 14/2006 is the woman who gives birth, and it is impossible to register a birth if the medical certificate does not mention her.[47] By requiring a *judicial* decision which establishes the child's legal parentage from a competent court in the country where the child was born, the Order makes it clear that foreign birth certificates or declarations of birth are not valid documents for registering the birth and subsequent parentage. This explains why the Order could not apply to the case described above. Although the surrogacy in the case occurred in a legal system such as the Californian one, which bases transfer of parentage resulting from surrogacy on a pre-birth *judgment*, the commissioning

---

explain why they wanted to hide the identity of the children's biological father in order to be treated equally by the law.

45 See M. Requejo, 'Another twist in surrogacy motherhood saga', Blog cited in n. 29 (08.10.2010): <http://conflictoflaws.net/2010/another-twist-in-surrogacy-motherhood-saga/> accessed 04.09.2018. See also R.F. Storrow, '"The Phantom Children of the Republic": International Surrogacy and the New Illegitimacy' (2012) 20(3) *Journal of Gender, Social Policy and the Law* 561, 601–02.

46 See the estimated data provided in Section 1.

47 On this additional explanation, see P. Orejudo Prieto de los Mozos, above n. 14, p. 351.

parents did not include this document in the proceedings.[48] Requiring a *judicial* decision also explains why the Order cannot be applicable when surrogacy has taken place in a legal system where parentage is not transferred through this means. This applies in Ukraine, for example, which for reasons of cost has become one of the most popular destinations among Spanish citizens wishing to access surrogacy. Since same-sex marriage is not legal there, Ukrainian law only allows surrogacy for different-sex spouses and the resulting child is registered by a written request from the commissioning parents. In such cases the latter can be named as the parents on the birth certificate if the surrogate gives written permission in the pre-pregnancy notarial contract.[49] Since the document establishing parentage is not judicial but notarial, once the commissioning parents are back in Spain, it is not possible to obtain recognition of the foreign decision establishing parentage. Therefore, when the biological father's paternity has been established (see Sections 3 and 5) and the Ukrainian surrogate has agreed to the adoption in the terms of Art. 177.2.2.IV of the CC (see Section 5), the child can be adopted by the commissioning mother.

The next step is obtaining recognition of the foreign judgment in Spain. Since the recognition of foreign judgments establishing legal parentage based on surrogacy arrangements is treated as a non-contentious judicial proceeding (*jurisdicción voluntaria*), it is generally unnecessary for Spanish courts to intervene via *exequatur*, and recognition is automatic.[50] The DGRN lays down several conditions in these circumstances, namely recording the judgment in a document that fulfils all the requirements for a foreign public document to be considered equivalent to a national one; that the foreign court bases its jurisdiction on criteria equivalent to those prescribed by Spanish law; that procedural safeguards have been met;[51] that the child's best interests and the surrogate's rights are respected, with special attention to the fact that the latter's consent has been freely obtained without error, violence or fraud, and that she has sufficient natural capacity; that the ruling is final, and that the surrogate's

48 See above n. 44.

49 In Ukraine, where the law allows commercial surrogacy, the contract includes provision for many other aspects, such as the surrogate's obligations during the pregnancy or the total amount to be paid by the commissioning parents. Sources: <http://vittoriavita.com/surrogacy-law-in-ukraine/> and <http://en.surrogacy-ukraine.com/> accessed 04.09.2018.

50 On this point, see P. Orejudo Prieto de los Mozos, above n. 14, p. 352, with special attention to further references made by this author in n. 21 of her chapter. Cases where *exequatur* is necessary are subject to Arts 52–55 of Act 29/2015 of 30 July on international judicial cooperation (BOE no. 182, 30.07.2015).

51 Since *ordre public* is not expressly mentioned, P. Orejudo Prieto de los Mozos (above n. 14, p. 353) sees it as clear evidence of the DGRN's surrogacy friendly approach. According to this author, fulfilment of this requirement can mostly be taken for granted, since if the authorities in charge of the civil status register are competent to recognise the foreign judgment, it is because the judgment was issued in a non-contentious proceeding, i.e. because there was no claimant or defendant but only interested parties.

consent to the agreement is irrevocable. Reference to the child's best interests and those of the surrogate seems to seek a sort of *ordre public* test.[52]

The DGRN's approach is in stark contrast with that taken by the Supreme Court vis-a-vis the case described above, where there was no foreign judicial decision to be recognised. This would explain why, despite the harsh 2014 and 2015 Supreme Court rulings, the DGRN doctrine is still applied in Spain, allowing both the parentage of children gestated abroad through surrogacy to be registered and the commissioning parents to have access to related social security benefits such as paternity and maternity leave.

7.2. PATERNITY AND MATERNITY LEAVE: THE PREVALENCE OF ATTENUATED *ORDRE PUBLIC*

The DGRN's doctrine has not only been applied to establish parentage in favour of the commissioning parents, but also to grant them social security benefits such as paternity and maternity leave. The doctrine has frequently been invoked by different regional high court of justice ('HCJ') labour chambers to grant maternity or paternity leave when parentage had been declared abroad in favour of the commissioning parent or parents by means of a judicial decision, thus contradicting a previous decision by an administrative body and leading to a sort of attenuated *ordre public*.[53] In contrast, other regional court decisions have produced opposite outcomes.[54] The latter approach is based on two CJEU decisions, both of 18 March 2014, about whether the respective Member States should guarantee maternity leave to two female employees, one British and one Irish, who had become mothers by means of surrogacy.[55]

---

52 P. Orejudo Prieto de los Mozos, above n. 14, p. 353.

53 The first reported case involving a request of this type was a Madrid High Court of Justice (HCJ from now on) decision of 30.11.2009 (AS 2010/277), which granted paternity leave to the commissioning father, a single man who had accessed surrogacy in Idaho. In the same vein, see the Asturias HCJ decision of 20.09.2012 (AS 2012/2485), granting the request of a commissioning mother in a different-sex marriage and thus placing surrogacy cases on a level with adoption or fostering (§§4–5), and the Madrid HCJ decision of 18.10.2012 (AS 2012/2503), granting the request of a commissioning father in a same-sex marriage on a similar basis (§§5–7). See also subsequent decisions by the HCJ of Catalonia, 23.11.2012 (AS 2013/845); Madrid, 13.03.2013 (JUR 2013/291496) and 23.12.2014 (AS 2015/406); Catalonia, 09.03.2015 (AS 2015/954); the Canary Islands, 27.03.2015 (JUR 2015/214175); Castile-La Mancha, 27.05.2015 (AS 2015/1332); Catalonia, 01.07.2015 (AS 2015/1826); Madrid, 17.07.2015 (JUR 2015/202928); Catalonia, 15.09.2015 (AS 2015/2019), and Madrid, 12.02.2016 (JUR 2016/79841) which took the same line of reasoning.

54 See the decisions by the HCJ of the Basque Country, 13.05.2014 (AS 2014/1228); Madrid, 07.07.2014 (JUR 2014/244222); Andalusia, 04.02.2015 (AS 2015/720), and Madrid, 05.10.2015 (JUR 2015/253456).

55 See case C-167/12, *C.D. v S.T.* (ECLI:EU:C:2014:169), and case C-363/12, *Z. v A Government Department and The Board of Management of a Community School* (ECLI:EU:C:2014:159).

In the preliminary rulings the court stated that failing to grant the employees the maternity leave they had requested did not constitute discriminatory treatment on grounds of sex or disability, as stated by EU Directives.[56]

Although this latter approach has only been taken in a minority of HCJ decisions,[57] the question of paternity or maternity leave resulting from international surrogacy arrangements has caused great legal uncertainty. The Spanish Supreme Court Labour Chamber therefore published in 2016 three leading decisions, unifying the doctrine on the issue and granting this social benefit in cases of access to surrogacy abroad.[58] The first of these was a ruling on 19 October 2016 (JUR 2016/247184) concerning two Spanish men who had accessed surrogacy in California and whose genetic connection with the resulting child remained unclear. Once in Spain, the commissioning father who was registered for social security applied for paternity leave, but the administrative body in charge of social security benefits, the *Instituto Nacional de la Seguridad Social* ('INSS'), rejected his application. He appealed against the INSS's decision before the Labour Court, which duly reversed it. Both the Catalonia HCJ[59] and the Supreme Court confirmed the Labour Court ruling. According to the Supreme Court, surrogacy recognised by means of a judicial decision in the country of birth, i.e. when both birth and parentage have been registered at the consulate, can be safeguarded by paternity and maternity leave since these benefits also apply to adoption and fostering. Although the court admitted that the cases resolved by the CJEU differed from that in question, especially because in those cases the genetic connection with the children was proven, it seems to have assumed that the CJEU guidelines were minimum guidelines which were open to improvement by Member States.

The second decision on the topic was issued on 25 October 2016 (JUR 2016/273617) and is more straightforward. The claimant was a Spanish commissioning father who had accessed surrogacy in India, where twin girls were born in September 2013. The girls were conceived with the surrogate's eggs and claimant's sperm and were registered at the Spanish consulate in

56 It should be noted that while the claimant in the English case had had the child's parentage established by means of a Parental Order since surrogacy is legal in the UK if it is not for commercial gain, in the Irish case the woman was the child's legal guardian and was only considered the legal mother under Californian law. In spite of the CJEU's declarations, the British government approved granting leave and benefits to commissioning parents similar to those provided for adoptive parents: see s. 122 and sch. 7 of the Children and Families Act 2014.

57 According to nn. 53 and 54 above, four out of a total of 17 decisions.

58 The Spanish Ministry of Employment and Social Security website now includes surrogacy among the situations which create a right to this benefit: <http://www.seg-social.es/Internet_1/Trabajadores/PrestacionesPension10935/Maternidad/RegimenGeneral/Situacionesprotegid28301/index.htm> accessed 04.09.2018.

59 Decision of 09.03.2015, cited above n. 53.

New Delhi as daughters of both of them. In October 2013 the surrogate waived her rights and responsibilities regarding the girls in a notarised document and they were thus free to go to Spain with their father. Once they were in Spain the INSS denied the commissioning father paternity leave. He appealed to the Labour court, which confirmed the decision. However, the Catalonia HCJ reversed the INSS decision[60] and the Spanish Supreme Court confirmed the ruling. In doing so, the court took into account the Spanish Public Prosecutor's approach which, perhaps surprisingly, argued in favour of protecting the family relationship which already existed. Although the INSS invoked a case in which the Basque Country HCJ had denied maternity leave to a Spanish woman who had accessed surrogacy in California,[61] the Supreme Court considered that the approach was not correct. The court first invoked *Mennesson* and *Labassée v France* and *Paradiso and Campanelli v Italy*, paying particular attention to the importance the ECtHR attached to the need to protect family relationships that already existed in the home country[62] regardless of whether a parentage link between the children and the commissioning parents had been established. Second, the court was aware that although EU law provides no solution to this problem, offering minimum guidelines to Member States does not exclude allowing maternity leave either.[63] In the end the court did confirm the concession of the social security benefit, on the basis of an analogy with the concession of maternity leave in cases of *adoption* or *fostering*, but also stressed that the commissioning father was also the biological father in the case in question. The basic arguments raised by the court in reaching this outcome were the children's best interests principle, their right to establish family ties with their parents from their first weeks of life, and their right not to be discriminated against on grounds of parentage (§9).

The last reported decision on the topic shares many features with the previous decision and was issued on 16 November 2016 (JUR 2016/270902).[64] This decision originated in an application for maternity leave made by a commissioning mother who had accessed surrogacy in California with her male partner and whose application was also rejected by the INSS. The commissioning mother appealed against the decision in the Labour Court and then in the Madrid HCJ, which confirmed the administrative decision.[65] On the basis of the CJEU doctrine mentioned above, the INSS and the courts involved considered

---

60 Decision of 15.09.2015, cited above n. 53.

61 Decision of 13.05.2014, cited above n. 54.

62 Cases cited above n. 42.

63 The court particularly invoked the CJEU cases cited above n. 55.

64 At the time of revising this chapter (January 2019), the Spanish Supreme Court Labour Chamber had issued other decisions granting this social benefit in cases of cross-border surrogacy: e.g. the decisions of 30.11.2016 (RJ 2016/6516 and RJ 2016/6514), 30.11.2017 (RJ 2017/5969), 14.12.2017 (RJ 2017/6015) and 22.03.2018 (RJ 2018/1414).

65 Decision of 07.07.2014, cited above n. 54.

that Spanish law only recognised maternity leave in cases of *birth*, *fostering* and *adoption*. However, the Supreme Court reversed this line of reasoning and granted maternity leave on the basis of a conciliatory interpretation of the CJEU doctrine. The decision was also grounded in the child's best interests principle and the duty of the public authorities to ensure full protection for children, as recognised in Art. 39.2 of the 1978 Spanish Constitution, since, above and beyond health issues and the right to rest, maternity leave also aims to protect family and childhood. On the basis of the ECtHR *Mennesson* and *Labassée v France* cases,[66] the Supreme Court invoked Art. 8 of the European Convention on Human Rights to safeguard the protection of children gestated through surrogacy, whose 'de facto' family relationships are paramount. According to the court, a contrary approach would result in discriminatory treatment on grounds of parentage (§9).

The Supreme Court decisions made on 25 October and 16 November 2016 contain some interesting dissenting opinions, which were mainly based on the mistaken reference to the child's best interests principle and having resorted to the analogy method. With regard to principle of the child's best interests, the dissenting judges do not consider this approach to be applicable in Spain, where – contrary to France or Italy – the parentage of children gestated through surrogacy abroad can somehow be legally reconstituted. The dissenting judges also criticise the analogy method used by the majority of the court, invoking the absence of a legal gap which would justify access to this method, as well as the lack of equivalence between adoption or fostering and surrogacy. According to these judges, not including surrogacy among the causes which can legally justify conceding paternity and maternity leave is not an unconscious act on the part of the Spanish legislature, but a consistent response to Art. 10 of Act 14/2006 as currently drafted. Ultimately, these dissenting opinions are based on the existence of a *fraus legis* to Art. 10 of Act 14/2006 on the part of the commissioning parents, which caused harm to a third party, namely the INSS. Following this argument, the dissenting judges maintain that surrogacy is a null and void act (Art. 10 of Act 14/2006) from which no effects can be inferred unless the question is specifically dealt with in the Spanish Parliament.

7.3. AUTHORISATION TO RETURN TO THE COMMISSIONING PARENTS' JURISDICTION WITH THE CHILD AND ACQUISITION OF NATIONALITY

Problems resulting from international surrogacy arrangements can arise when the commissioning parents try to return to Spain with the child or children, or

[66] Cited above n. 42.

once they are all in situ. One such situation affects children born to surrogates in countries where surrogacy is either banned or unregulated. Since surrogacy arrangements which consider both members of the commissioning couple to be the legal parents have no legal effects in these countries and they do not recognise 'birthright citizenship', the children are stateless, caught between two legal systems and with uncertain parentage, waiting for a court decision that requires an exception to the law in their best interests by means of diplomatic solutions or international adoption.[67]

A second situation occurs fairly frequently when an individual or couple accesses surrogacy in a legal system which permits it. Since according to Art. 17.1.a) of the CC the main criteria for acquiring Spanish nationality is having a Spanish father or mother at birth (*ius sanguinis*), children gestated through surrogacy abroad can be considered Spanish and can thus have Spanish passports if one of the commissioning parents can prove he or she is the father or the mother, as derives from the Spanish acquisition of parentage conflict rule (Art. 9.4 of the CC). In such circumstances, paternity is based on the existence of a genetic link (Art. 131 of the CC and ff.) and maternity on the fact of the birth (Act. 10.2 of Act 14/2006). Spanish consulates only issue Spanish passports to children gestated through surrogacy abroad if one of these two requirements is proven.[68] This is not required in relation to children gestated through surrogacy

---

[67] In this regard, see a case concerning a Spanish male gay couple who accessed surrogacy in the Mexican state of Tabasco, reported by V. Calderón, 'Gay couple stuck in Mexican legal limbo after birth of surrogate twins', *El País*, 12.02.2015: <http://elpais.com/elpais/2015/02/12/inenglish/1423748151_686685.html> accessed 04.09.2018.
The Mexican state of Tabasco has typically been one of the first destinations of Spanish citizens wishing to access surrogacy. Unlike other common destinations such as India, Ukraine or the US, Tabasco offers Spanish citizens unquestionable language advantages. However, on 13 January 2016 (a few days after the birth of the twins in the news item reported above) Tabasco's official bulletin published Decree 265, which added a new chapter on surrogacy to the 1997 Tabasco Civil Code. Apart from limiting access to surrogacy to different-sex couples, married or not, and then only if there is some medical reason why the commissioning mother is unable to bear a child, the new regulation requires the parties to the arrangements to be Mexican citizens. This regulation aims to provide a response to the previous regulation, which tolerated – and thus promoted – commercial surrogacy.
A similar case involving a Spanish different-sex couple occurred when India reformed its previous regulation on surrogacy to require a letter from the Spanish consul or ambassador in India confirming that the adoption process was legal in Spain. See P. Pareja, 'Couple faces legal battle to take babies out of India', *El País*, 27.08.2013: <http://elpais.com/elpais/2013/08/27/inenglish/1377620485_555486.html> accessed 04.09.2018.

[68] See V. Calderón, above n. 67, where the children – twins gestated in the Mexican state of Tabasco – were able to obtain Spanish passports because sperm from one of the commissioning parents had been used in the fertilisation process, thus making the twins Spanish nationals. This fact could not be proved in the case which lead to the Madrid HCJ (Administrative Chamber) decision of 13.03.2017 (JUR 2017/79536). Therefore, the HCJ confirmed the decision by the Spanish consulate in Moscow denying the safe-conduct requested by the Spanish commissioning parents, who formed a different-sex marriage which had accessed surrogacy in Russia.

in American states where surrogacy is legal, such as California, since children born in the US are automatically US citizens, so the commissioning parents can take the children back to Spain on their US passports. Once in Spain, commissioning parents can register their parentage with the national authorities according to the proceedings described in Section 7.1.4.

8. CONCLUSION

More than eight years after the DGRN issued the Order allowing recognition of parentage of children gestated by means of international surrogacy under certain circumstances, Art. 10 of Act 14/2006 remains intact. Although the Order is the product not of a parliamentary process but of an administrative body answerable to the Ministry of Justice, the fact that it is currently applied by Spanish courts and administrative bodies to establish the parentage of children gestated by means of international surrogacy and to grant paternity or maternity leave means that there is an urgent need for the Spanish legislature to consider a legal reform providing a well-grounded response to what already seems to be a real social demand.[69] Any solution requires not only approaching the topic from an *ex post* or pragmatic point of view, which only seeks a solution from an international private law approach when the child already exists. It also demands an ex ante approach which questions from a democratic point of view which takes into account the symbolic value of domestic laws[70] whether surrogacy in Spain really requires a response at domestic level.[71] Apart from raising discrimination issues among individuals who can afford to access surrogacy abroad and those who cannot, legislative silence, together with the quasi-tolerant approach endorsed by administrative and judicial bodies, will only promote legal uncertainty for Spanish citizens who wish to access surrogacy and for children gestated in this way.

---

69 Quoting Fenton-Glynn and Scherpe's analysis of the law governing surrogacy in the UK, 'there is a limit to what can be achieved without parliamentary reform': see the authors' analysis in 'Is the law governing surrogacy keeping pace with social change? Submission by Claire Fenton-Glynn and Jens M. Scherpe on behalf of Cambridge Family Law', p. 11: <https://www.family.law.cam.ac.uk/sites/www.law.cam.ac.uk/files/images/www.family.law.cam.ac.uk/documents/cambridge_family_law_submission.pdf> accessed 04.09.2018.

70 See B. Van Beers, 'Is Europe 'Giving in to Baby Markets?' Reproductive Tourism in Europe and the Gradual Erosion of Existing Legal Limits to Reproductive Markets' (2014) 23(1) *MLR* (*Medical Law Review*) 103.

71 'In providing an ex post facto examination of surrogacy arrangements, the courts are being asked to undertake a retrospective investigation of an agreement that has taken place outside their jurisdiction, with no real opportunity to examine its contents'. With this approach we are also 'exporting our ethical issues, and the problems associated with surrogacy, elsewhere': see C. Fenton-Glynn and J. Scherpe, above n. 69, p. 8.

As already observed in this chapter, there are now enough arguments for it to be possible to state that surrogacy is not contrary to Spanish *ordre public*. Unlike other legal systems referred to here, mainly the French one, the lack of a real prohibitive approach in Spain is evidenced by the declaration in Act 14/2006 (Art. 10.1) that all surrogacy arrangements are null and void as well as the fact that surrogacy is not specifically addressed in the Spanish Criminal Code. The law's express statement as to the possibility of establishing paternity in favour of the biological father (Art. 10.3) and therefore of reconstituting the family also leads to the conclusion that surrogacy is not contrary to Spanish *ordre public*. Indeed it is difficult to maintain that something which can be legalised according to valid Spanish legal mechanisms is opposed to Spanish *ordre public*. An additional argument for regulating surrogacy in Spain is the fact that the establishment of maternity by birth (Art. 10.2) is no longer the only mean for establishing maternity in Spain, especially since the admission of double maternity resulting from access to ART by Art. 7.3 of Act 14/2006.[72]

In this context, the possible reform of Art. 10 not only has awakened great interest at academic level but it is also on the political debate.[73] So far *Ciudadanos*, a political party affiliated with the Alliance of Liberals and Democrats for Europe Party, has submitted a bill on the 'right' to surrogacy, while the party currently in the government ('PSOE') is openly contrary to it.[74] The Bill, which advocates for regulating altruistic surrogacy at a domestic level, foresees a 'reasonable payment' to the surrogate, aimed at the reimbursement of actual expenses and loss of profit attached to gestation (Art. 5). Taking into account the demands of certain social groups, it also excludes any consanguinity relationship between the commissioning parent(s) and the surrogate (Art. 4.3). Beyond the loud calls for the current situation to be changed, the voices raised against regulating surrogacy in Spain are also strong and will have to be heard during any eventual legislative process.[75] There seems

---

72 This provision was introduced by a subsequent legal reform to Act 14/2006 by Act 3/2007 of 15 March regulating the rectification of register entries relating to a person's gender (BOE no. 71, 23.05.2007).

73 C. López, 'España prepara una ley de vientres de alquiler', *La Vanguardia*, 14.12.2016: <http://www.lavanguardia.com/vida/20161214/412602666192/espana-prepara-ley-vientres-alquiler.html> accessed 04.09.2018.

74 The Bill is available, only in Spanish, at the official bulletin of the Congress of the Deputies no. 145-1, 08.09.2017: <http://www.congreso.es/public_oficiales/L12/CONG/BOCG/B/BOCG-12-B-145-1.PDF> accessed 04.09.2018.

75 One of the most significant movements against surrogacy regulation, led by some feminists, has produced the slogan *No somos vasijas*, which literally means 'We are not receptacles'. A brief version of their manifesto, published in 2015, is available in English: <http://nosomosvasijas.eu/?page_id=733> accessed 04.09.2018.
In May 2017 the Spanish Bioethics Committee published a report, only available in Spanish, which condemns the practice even at international level: <http://assets.comitedebioetica.es/

to be widespread acceptance of women who cannot bear a child for medical reasons having access to surrogacy, especially when the surrogate is someone within the family or from the commissioning parents' immediate circle. However, beyond the most common objections to regulating surrogacy there is probably some degree of prejudice about which family models we are ready to accept as a society, as well as the 'slippery slope' argument which considers that accepting surrogacy will open the door to commodification of women and children and exploitative practices in general.

Regulating surrogacy does not imply accepting a free market in this field. Surrogacy will never be successfully regulated in Spain if ART centres, intermediaries and agencies are not subject to government monitoring. Furthermore, in line with the 'reasonable payment' for gamete and embryo donation in Spain, which – in principle – at least is aimed strictly at covering 'physical discomfort and moving and working expenses',[76] domestic surrogacy arrangements negotiated on a commercial basis should be prohibited. Finally, measures limiting access to surrogacy in function of certain links with the home country or only allowing transfer of parentage to individuals domiciled there[77] should be taken into account when regulating in order to avoid exploitation risks promoted by so-called 'fertility tourism'.[78]

---

files/documentacion/es/informe_comite_bioetica_aspectos_eticos_juridicos_maternidad_subrogada.pdf> accessed 04.09.2018.

76 Article 5.3 of Act 14/2006.

77 This is the line already taken by other European legal systems such as the UK (ss. 54(4)(b) and 59 of the Human Fertilisation and Embryology Act 2008, in relation to the Surrogacy Act 1985). This seems also to be the approach followed in Mexico after the experience in the 'procreative paradise' of Tabasco (see above n. 67).

78 See above n. 5.

THE TOLERANT APPROACH

SURROGACY IN AUSTRALIA

Mary KEYES

1. GENERAL LEGAL FRAMEWORK

Surrogacy is specifically regulated in Australia. Australia is a federation in which most matters of family law are regulated nationally, but some issues including surrogacy and assisted reproductive technology are principally regulated by the states and territories. All six states[1] and the Australian Capital Territory ('ACT')[2] have legislation dealing with surrogacy.[3] The laws in these seven jurisdictions

---

1 New South Wales ('NSW'), Queensland ('Qld'), South Australia ('SA'), Tasmania ('Tas'), Victoria ('Vic') and Western Australia ('WA').

2 The legal systems of the Australian Capital Territory ('ACT') and the Northern Territory ('NT') operate in a way which, for the purposes of this chapter, is similar to the six states.

3 The relevant statutes are the Parentage Act 2004 (ACT); the Surrogacy Act 2010 (NSW); the Surrogacy Act 2010 (Qld); the Family Relationships Act 1975 (SA); the Surrogacy Act 2012 (Tas); the Assisted Reproductive Treatment Act 2008 (Vic); the Status of Children Act 1974 (Vic); and the Surrogacy Act 2008 (WA). As of October 2018, the South Australian Law Reform Institute's inquiry into the South Australian surrogacy legislation was still in progress.

are broadly similar in three respects. First, commissioning parents[4] in altruistic[5] arrangements can apply, post-birth, for a 'parentage order', transferring parental status from the surrogate parents to the commissioning parents. Second, the surrogate mother[6] can enforce the commissioning parents' promise to reimburse her reasonable expenses associated with the arrangement. Third, commercial surrogacy is prohibited.

Federal family law does not specifically regulate surrogacy, but is relevant because commissioning parents sometimes apply under federal family legislation for orders that they have parental responsibility for children born in surrogacy arrangements,[7] declarations of parental status,[8] or leave to adopt.[9] Federal immigration and citizenship law is also relevant to international surrogacy arrangements.

There is currently no legislation in the Northern Territory regulating surrogacy. Australian medical practitioners, including those in the Northern Territory, must adhere to the National Health and Medical Research Council's *Ethical Guidelines on the Use of Assisted Reproductive Technology in Clinical Practice and Research.*[10]

There is no specialised authority which oversees surrogacy nationally. Statutory authorities in Victoria and Western Australia have a role in regulating some surrogacy arrangements. In Victoria, registered assisted reproductive treatment providers can only carry out surrogacy arrangements that were approved before conception by the Patient Review Panel of the Victorian Assisted Reproductive Treatment Authority ('VARTA').[11] This is only permitted

---

4 In this chapter, I refer to the commissioning parents in the plural because there are usually two parents. Unless otherwise stipulated, the plural includes the singular commissioning parent; in most jurisdictions, single commissioning parents can apply for parentage orders. See below nn. 85–86.
The term 'commissioning' parents is used for consistency with the other chapters. This term is only used in the legislation of two Australian jurisdictions; others use the terms 'intended', 'arranged', and 'substitute' parents.

5 An 'altruistic arrangement' is one in which the commissioning parents promise to pay the surrogate no more than reimbursement of reasonable expenses: see below at nn. 50–52.

6 For consistency with the other chapters, the term 'surrogate mother' is used in this chapter. In Australia, the term 'birth mother' is used in the legislation in most jurisdictions.

7 Such an order is referred to as a 'parenting order': Family Law Act 1975 (Cth) Pt VII, Div 2.

8 Referred to as a 'declaration of parentage': Family Law Act 1975 (Cth) s. 69VA.

9 State and territory courts determine applications to adopt; the Family Court only grants leave to adopt: Family Law Act 1975 (Cth) s. 60G.

10 National Health and Medical Research Council, *Ethical Guidelines on the Use of Assisted Reproductive Technology in Clinical Practice and Research* (2017) <https://www.nhmrc.gov.au/about-us/publications/ethical-guidelines-use-assisted-reproductive-technology> accessed 22.01.2019 ('NHMRC, *Ethical Guidelines*').

11 Assisted Reproductive Treatment Act 2008 (Vic) s. 39. The criteria that must be satisfied before an arrangement can be approved are set out in s. 40. In NSW, a registered assisted reproductive technology provider cannot provide services in a surrogacy arrangement unless

in altruistic surrogacy cases. If the arrangement was commissioned with the assistance of a registered assisted reproductive treatment provider, a Victorian court can only make a parentage order if the Patient Review Panel approved the arrangement.[12]

In WA, a parentage order can only be made if the Western Australian Reproductive Treatment Council ('RTC') approved the arrangement before conception.[13] This is only possible in altruistic arrangements.

In the other jurisdictions, there is no authority which oversees surrogacy arrangements.[14] Compliance with legislative requirements is only considered if commissioning parents apply for a parentage order, in which cases the courts are responsible for policing the requirements. If commissioning parents do not apply for a parentage order, the requirements are not monitored.

The main effect of the surrogacy legislation is to enable the transfer of parentage to commissioning parents in altruistic arrangements. Altruistic agreements are generally unenforceable;[15] in most jurisdictions, aspects of such arrangements, including advertising and brokering, are criminalised.[16]

The legislation enabling transfer of parentage was intended to achieve a balance between minimising harm and protecting liberty.[17] It aims to minimise uncertainty for children and commissioning parents; to prevent discrimination against children born in surrogacy arrangements, and their families;[18] and to respect reproductive autonomy by minimising state intervention in family life.[19] The surrogate mother's right not to relinquish the child is protected by

they have been provided with an 'assessment report' by an independent counsellor: Assisted Reproductive Technology Act 2007 (NSW) s. 15A.

12 Status of Children Act 1974 (Vic) s. 22(1)(b).

13 Surrogacy Act 2008 (WA) s. 16(1). The relevant criteria are set out in s. 17.

14 The possibility of establishing an authority to monitor the requirements was discussed by parliamentary committees in NSW, Queensland and Tasmania prior to enactment of the surrogacy legislation in those states. The Queensland and Tasmanian committees recommended establishing authorities to approve surrogacy arrangements, but the legislation in these states does not do so: Investigation into Altruistic Surrogacy Committee, *Report*, Queensland Parliament, Brisbane, 2008, pp. 60–61; Parliament of Tasmania, Legislative Council Government Administration Committee 'A', *Inquiry into Surrogacy Bill 2011 and Surrogacy (Consequential Amendments) Bill 2011 Report*, Hobart, 2011, p. 26. This option was dismissed by the NSW Legislative Council Standing Committee on Law and Justice on the basis that 'the regulation of surrogacy should be left largely in the hands of [medical and para-medical] practitioners in the field': *Legislation on Altruistic Surrogacy in NSW*, Sydney 2009, p. 100.

15 The only exception is that the commissioning parents' promise to reimburse the surrogate mother's reasonable costs is enforceable. See below nn. 50–52.

16 See below Section 6.

17 Investigation into Altruistic Surrogacy Committee, above n. 14, p. 29.

18 Surrogacy Act 2010 (Qld) s. 6(2)(b); Surrogacy Act 2012 (Tas) s. 3(2)(b).

19 Standing Committee of Attorneys-General, Australian Health Ministers' Conference, Community and Disability Services Ministers' Conference Joint Working Group, *A Proposal for a National Model to Harmonise Regulation of Surrogacy*

making altruistic agreements unenforceable;[20] by only allowing applications for parentage orders to be made post-birth;[21] and by maintaining the rule that the birth mother is the legal parent.[22] The criminalisation of advertising and brokering is intended to avoid commercialisation of surrogacy.[23]

The prohibition of commercial surrogacy[24] reflects concerns that commercial surrogacy commodifies children and exploits poor women,[25] and creates risks for children in terms of their rights to know their parents and their genetic heritage.[26]

Prior to the current legislation, four jurisdictions had enacted legislation prohibiting surrogacy.[27] The ACT was the first jurisdiction to permit transfer of parental status to the commissioning parents, in 2000.[28] The ACT legislation was modelled on the United Kingdom's Human Fertilisation and Embryology Act 1990. From 2006, the Standing Committee of Attorneys-General attempted to develop uniform national legislation based on the ACT model.[29] While unsuccessful, this attempt influenced the development of legislation in the states.

Surrogacy is contentious in Australia.[30] The legislation has been described as ambivalent and cautious because

> '... many legislators have reservations about the practice. In consequence, the laws they have made combine an unwillingness to give effect to surrogacy arrangements with a recognition that these arrangements will continue to be made. The resulting laws ...

(January 2009), pp. 2, 5 (Joint Working Group); Investigation into Altruistic Surrogacy Committee, above n. 14, pp. 26–27, 29; Surrogacy Act 2010 (Qld) s. 6(2)(d), Surrogacy Act 2012 (Tas) s. 3(2)(d).

20 E.g. Surrogacy Act 2010 (NSW) s. 6(1); Surrogacy Act 2012 (Tas) s. 10(1).

21 E.g. Parentage Act 2004 (ACT) s. 25(3); Surrogacy Act 2008 (WA) s. 20(2).

22 Joint Working Group, above n. 19, pp. 2–3; Investigation into Altruistic Surrogacy Committee, above n. 14, pp. 55–56; Victorian Law Reform Commission, *Assisted Reproductive Treatment and Adoption: Final Report*, Victorian Law Reform Commission, Melbourne 2007, p. 188. In Australia, a person who undergoes a procedure as a result of which that person becomes pregnant is conclusively presumed to be the parent of the child: e.g. Parentage Act 2004 (ACT) s. 11(1) and (2); Family Relationships Act 1975 (SA) s. 10C(1). See further below Section 3.

23 Investigation into Altruistic Surrogacy Committee, above n. 14, p. 37.

24 See below Section 6. Similarly, the NHMRC *Ethical Guidelines* state that 'it would be ethically unacceptable for clinics to facilitate commercial surrogacy': above n. 10, p. 57.

25 Joint Working Group, above n. 19, pp. 2, 5.

26 Ibid, p. 20.

27 Some jurisdictions prohibited all forms of surrogacy: Family Relationships Act 1975 (SA); Surrogate Parenthood Act 1988 (Qld); Surrogacy Contracts Act 1993 (Tas). In Victoria, only commercial surrogacy was prohibited, but the legislation gave no legal effect to altruistic arrangements: Infertility Treatment Act 1995 (Vic) Pt 6.

28 Artificial Conception (Amendment) Act 2000 (ACT).

29 Standing-Committee of Attorneys-General, Communiqué (28 March 2008) p. 7 <www.nswbar.asn.au/circulars/scag.pdf> accessed 05.09.2018.

30 For example, one member of the Tasmanian Legislative Council's Government Administration Committee, 'A', dissented from that committee's Report on its Inquiry into Surrogacy because she was 'fundamentally opposed' to the Surrogacy Bill: above n. 14, p. 77.

acknowledge that answers must be given to the question of the parentage of a child born following such an agreement.'[31]

One view is that regulation should be minimal and largely left to the medical profession;[32] the alternative view is that regulation is required to address concerns that arise uniquely in surrogacy arrangements.[33] The legislation reflects a combination of these views.

There has been limited research in Australia on what motivates these views, and whether there are significant differences between the views held by different groups and communities in Australian society. Some organisations are especially vocal participants in the public discussions and debates about surrogacy; particularly, some support groups for commissioning parents which are in favour of surrogacy, and some religious groups which oppose it.[34]

There is no significant distinction in Australia between traditional and gestational surrogacy.[35]

There are no comprehensive statistics available about surrogacy in Australia. Information is published in the Australian New Zealand Assisted Reproduction Database ('ANZARD'),[36] and by VARTA and the RTC. ANZARD publishes data supplied by Australian and New Zealand clinics; information for Australia is not separately reported.[37] Australian and New Zealand clinics reported 36 liveborn babies in surrogacy cycles in 2014,[38] 36 in 2013,[39] and 19 in 2012.[40]

---

31 J. Seymour and S. Magri, *A.R.T., Surrogacy and Legal Parentage: A Comparative Legislative Review*, Victorian Law Reform Commission, Melbourne 2004, p. 50. See similarly NSW Legislative Council Standing Committee on Law and Justice, above n. 14, p. 49.

32 This was the majority position adopted by the NSW Legislative Council Standing Committee on Law and Justice, above n. 14, pp. 6, 67.

33 The minority of the NSW Legislative Council Standing Committee on Law and Justice preferred this view: above n. 14, p. 67.

34 A range of individuals and government, academic and community organisations engage in public debates and make submissions to reviews and inquiries about surrogacy, including providers of fertility services, individual academics and academic research centres, action and support groups and networks (such as the Australian Adoptee Rights Action Group and Families through Surrogacy) and community and religious organisations (such as the Australian Catholic Bishops Conference and the Australian Christian Lobby).

35 In the ACT, a court cannot grant a parentage order if either surrogate parent is a genetic parent; in Victoria, a surrogacy arrangement cannot be approved if the surrogate is the genetic mother: see below n. 99.

36 This database is available at <https://npesu.unsw.edu.au/data-collection/australian-new-zealand-assisted-reproduction-database-anzard> accessed 06.09.2018.

37 In 2016, 92 per cent of all treatment cycles (not just in surrogacy arrangements) were from Australian clinics: K. Harris et al., *Assisted Reproductive Technology in Australia and New Zealand 2014*, National Perinatal Epidemiology and Statistics Unit, UNSW, Sydney 2016, p. 4.

38 Ibid.

39 A. Macaldowie et al., *Assisted Reproductive Technology in Australia and New Zealand 2013*, National Perinatal Epidemiology and Statistics Unit, UNSW Sydney, 2015, p. 4.

40 A. Macaldowie et al., *Assisted Reproductive Technology in Australia and New Zealand 2012*, National Perinatal Epidemiology and Statistics Unit, UNSW, Sydney, 2014, p. 4.

VARTA and the RTC also publish information about altruistic arrangements which are subject to their regulation. In Victoria, in the six years to June 2015, 36 babies were born in regulated surrogacy arrangements.[41] In WA, between 2010 and 2015, five births were reported to the RTC.[42] In 2015–16, the RTC 'received fewer than five' surrogacy applications.[43]

There is no comprehensive data about the number of surrogacy arrangements undertaken by Australians in other countries, but it is clear that many more children are born in international than in domestic arrangements. The Department of Immigration and Border Protection, which deals with applications for citizenship for children of Australians and for visas to bring children into Australia, estimates that 'it deals with approximately 250 offshore surrogacy cases each year'.[44]

Approximately 10 Australian clinics offer surrogacy services. In some altruistic arrangements, the parties engage the services of clinics in other Australian jurisdictions,[45] or overseas.[46]

2. SURROGACY ARRANGEMENTS IN GENERAL

The commissioning parents' agreement to reimburse the surrogate mother for her reasonable expenses incurred in the surrogacy arrangement is enforceable.[47]

41 In 2014–15, 11 babies were born; in 2013–14, six babies were born; in 2012–13, seven babies were born; in 2011–12, 10 babies were born; and one baby was born in each of 2010–11 and 2009–10: VARTA, *Annual Report 2016*, Melbourne 2016, p. 34; VARTA, *Annual Report 2015*, Melbourne 2015, p. 32; VARTA, *Annual Report 2014*, Melbourne 2014, p. 25; VARTA, *Annual Report 2013*, Melbourne 2013, p. 26; VARTA, *Annual Report 2012*, Melbourne 2012, p. 24; VARTA, *Annual Report 2011*, Melbourne 2011, p. 18.

42 Western Australian RTC, *Annual Report, 1 July 2014 to 30 June 2015*, WA RTC, Perth 2015, p. 13.

43 Western Australian RTC, *Annual Report 2015–2016*, WA RTC, Perth 2016, p. 13.

44 Frances Finney, Department of Immigration and Border Protection, *Committee Hansard*, Canberra, 02.03.2016, p. 2, cited in House of Representatives Standing Committee on Social Policy and Legal Affairs, *Inquiry into the Regulatory and Legislative Aspects of Surrogacy*, Canberra 2016, p. 22.

45 See e.g. *Interstate Substitute Parentage Order Registration: Child AB* [2015] VCC 988.

46 See e.g. *BB v DD; Re AA and the Surrogacy Act 2010 (NSW)* [2015] NSWSC 1095.

47 Surrogacy Act 2008 (WA) s. 7(3). In NSW, this is so only if the agreement was made pre-conception: Surrogacy Act 2010 (NSW) s. 6(2). In Queensland, South Australia and Tasmania, this is so only if she relinquishes the child and consents to the making of the parentage order: Surrogacy Act 2010 (Qld) s. 15(2), Family Relationships Act 1975 (SA) s. 10N(2). Surrogacy Act 2010 (Tas) s. 10(2)(c). In the ACT and Victoria, the legislation is silent as to the surrogate's entitlement to enforce the agreement, but it is consistent with the legislation in those jurisdictions that she should be entitled to do so: see M. Keyes, 'Cross-border Surrogacy Agreements' (2012) 26 *Australian Journal of Family Law* (*AJFL*) 28, 38–39. The legislation is also silent as to whether the commissioning parents are obliged to reimburse the surrogate mother if they refuse to or are unable to take the child; it is suggested that they would be bound to do so.

Otherwise, surrogacy contracts are unenforceable.[48] Terms purporting to restrict a woman's right to manage her pregnancy,[49] or obliging the surrogate mother to relinquish the child, are unenforceable.

A surrogate mother can be remunerated, but only by reimbursing her for 'reasonable' costs incurred in relation to the arrangement. The laws in the seven jurisdictions differ in terms of the detail in the costs that are specifically referred to as recoverable. The Victorian legislation is the least specific, stating that the surrogate mother can be reimbursed for costs 'actually incurred … as a direct consequence of entering into the surrogacy arrangement'.[50] The statutes in the other jurisdictions list expenses that can be reimbursed, including costs associated with the pregnancy,[51] and the birth and care of the child.[52] In most jurisdictions, costs of counselling, legal advice and applications for parentage orders are recoverable; as well as of health, disability and life insurance; and a limited amount of lost earnings.

Payments to the surrogate mother are weakly monitored. The Victorian and West Australian laws do not explicitly require VARTA or the RTC to scrutinise proposed payments in determining whether to approve arrangements. It therefore falls to the courts to monitor payments in determining whether to make parentage orders. In the published decisions, payment to surrogate mothers is rarely mentioned.[53]

3. LEGAL PARENTHOOD AT THE TIME OF BIRTH

The surrogacy legislation is premised on the assumption that the surrogate mother and her spouse or partner are the legal parents of the child; it enables the commissioning parents to apply for a parentage order, post-birth,

---

48 Parentage Act 2004 (ACT) s. 31; Surrogacy Act 2010 (NSW) s. 6(1); Surrogacy Act 2010 (Qld) s. 15(1); Family Relationships Act 1975 (SA) s. 10G; Surrogacy Act 2012 (Tas) s. 10(1); Assisted Reproductive Treatment Act 2008 (Vic) s. 44(3); Surrogacy Act 2008 (WA) s. 7(1). In all jurisdictions, the courts can dispense with the surrogate mother's consent in exceptional cases; it has therefore been suggested that this means surrogacy arrangements are enforceable: Legislative Council of Western Australia Standing Committee on Legislation in Relation to the Surrogacy Bill 2007, *Report 12*, Perth 2008, p. 57.

49 Surrogacy Act 2010 (Qld) s. 16(2); Family Relationships Act 1975 (SA) s. 10HAB(1); Surrogacy Act 2012 (Tas) s. 11(2).

50 Assisted Reproductive Treatment Act 2008 (Vic) s. 44(2); Status of Children Act 1974 (Vic) s. 22(1)(d).

51 The legislation refers only to costs associated with the pregnancy generally; it is not specific as to whether, for example, costs of medical emergencies, or costs of medical conditions resulting from and continuing after the pregnancy can be recovered.

52 Parentage Act 2004 (ACT) s. 40; Surrogacy Act 2010 (NSW) s. 7; Surrogacy Act 2010 (Qld) s. 11; Family Relationships Act 1975 (SA) s. 10HA(2a)(i); Surrogacy Act 2012 (Tas) s. 9(2) and (3); Surrogacy Act 2008 (WA) s. 22.

53 But see *Application MJC and CSC; re EMC* [2012] NSWSC 1626.

which transfers the legal status of parents from the surrogate parents to the commissioning parents. The assumption that the surrogate parents are the child's legal parents is always true under Australian law if the child was conceived following a fertilisation procedure.[54] In that case, the surrogate mother and her spouse or partner are the parents of the child, irrespective of whether either of them is a genetic parent.[55] Genetic parents who are not the birth parents are not the legal parents.[56] Although these rules were designed with in vitro fertilisation in mind, they were intentionally retained in the context of surrogacy in order to protect the surrogate mother by preventing forced relinquishment.[57] If the child was not conceived following a fertilisation procedure, and a court has not already made a determination,[58] it is a question of fact as to whether a person is legally a parent. In determining that, a number of rebuttable presumptions may be relevant, including that a child born to a woman during the course of a relationship is the child of that woman and her spouse or partner,[59] that someone who is registered as a parent is a parent,[60] and that a man who has acknowledged paternity is a parent.[61]

Parental status is relevant in international arrangements, because children can only be brought into Australia if they are citizens,[62] or have been granted a visa.[63] This depends on whether one of the commissioning parents is determined to be a parent for the purposes of citizenship or immigration law. The Full Court of the Federal Court of Australia held that the word 'parent' in the Australian Citizenship Act should be given its ordinary meaning, and

54 Traditional surrogacy is rare in Australia, but see *Lowe & Barry* [2011] FamCA 625.

55 E.g. Parentage Act 2004 (ACT) s. 11(1), (2); Status of Children Act 1996 (NSW) s. 14(1), (1A), (4); Status of Children Act 1978 (Qld) s. 17; Status of Children Act 1974 (Vic) s. 10C. As explained further below, parental status for the purposes of citizenship and immigration law is determined separately.

56 E.g. Parentage Act 2004 (ACT) s. 11(3), (4); Status of Children Act 1996 (NSW) s. 14(2)–(4); Status of Children Act 1978 (Qld) s. 17(2)(b).

57 NSW Legislative Council Standing Committee on Law and Justice, above n. 14, p. 119; Investigation into Altruistic Surrogacy Committee, above n. 14, pp. 55–56.

58 If a court has made a determination as to parentage, this conclusively establishes parentage: e.g. Parentage Act 2004 (ACT) s. 10.

59 E.g. Family Law Act 1975 (Cth) ss. 69P, 69Q; Parentage Act 2004 (ACT) ss. 7, 8; Status of Children Act 1974 (Vic) s. 5.

60 E.g. Family Law Act 1975 (Cth) s. 69R; Parentage Act 2004 (ACT) s. 9; Status of Children Act 1978 (Qld) ss. 25, 28.

61 E.g. Family Law Act 1975 (Cth) s. 69T; Status of Children Act 1978 (Qld) s. 27.

62 A person born outside Australia is eligible to become an Australian citizen if 'a parent of the person was an Australian citizen at the time of the birth': Australian Citizenship Act 2007 (Cth) s. 16(2)(a).

63 A child visa may be granted to a 'dependent child' of an Australian citizen or permanent resident: Migration Regulations 1994 (Cth) Sch. 2, cl. 101.21. There is no published case in Australia of a child born in an international surrogacy arrangement being stateless. The liberal definition of 'parent' in the Australian citizenship legislation means it is not likely to arise in practice.

that determining whether someone is a parent may depend on 'social, legal and biological' factors.[64] This differs from the rules of parental status outlined above, particularly if a child was conceived using reproductive treatment, and therefore a commissioning parent may be determined to be a parent for the purposes of citizenship law, but not otherwise.

The determination of parental status for the purposes of citizenship and immigration is done administratively by delegates of the Minister for Immigration,[65] by reference to the Department of Immigration's *Citizenship Policy*,[66] which identifies factors that may be taken into account, including any biological connection between the child and a commissioning parent. The policy lists the following factors as relevant to determining parentage for children born in surrogacy arrangements:

- whether the commissioning parent consented to being named as a parent on the birth certificate;
- whether the commissioning parent was involved in providing care and support to the surrogate mother during pregnancy;
- social acknowledgment by the commissioning parent that the child is part of the commissioning parent's family;
- the existence of a 'formal surrogacy agreement' entered into before conception and 'lawful transfer of parentage' in the country where the child was born; and
- evidence that the commissioning parents treated the child as 'their own'.[67]

The difference between these factors and the determination of parental status under the general rules usually will create a conflict between the child's status for the purposes of citizenship and immigration law, and for the purposes of the law of parentage: commissioning parents are likely to be treated as parents for the purposes of citizenship and immigration law, and not likely to be parents under the Australian law of parentage. It is very unlikely that children of Australian commissioning parents would be stateless and there has been no consideration of how that possibility would be addressed in the Australian law or commentary.

The legal parents of the child at the time of birth are obliged to register the birth,[68] and the original birth certificate should list them as the child's parents. Commissioning parents should only apply for registration if they are legally a parent. The original birth certificate will not indicate that the child was born

64 *H v Minister for Immigration and Citizenship* (2010) 188 FCR 393; [2010] FCAFC 119 at [129].

65 An appeal can be taken to the Administrative Appeals Tribunal: see e.g. *Brinkman & Minister for Immigration and Border Protection (Citizenship)* [2016] AATA 716.

66 Department of Home Affairs, Citizenship Policy, 01.06.2016 <https://www.homeaffairs.gov.au/Citizenship/Documents/acis-june-2016.pdf> accessed 06.09.2018.

67 Ibid, p. 215.

68 Surrogacy Act 2010 (Qld) s. 18; Surrogacy Act 2012 (Tas) s. 31.

as a result of a surrogacy arrangement. In several published cases in which commissioning parents have applied for parentage orders, commissioning fathers had wrongly applied for registration as a parent, and had been registered as a parent on the birth certificate.[69] In *BB v DD*, Robb J noted that only the legal parents could apply for registration, and required rectification of the birth registration before considering the application for parentage orders.[70]

The circumstances of the child's birth are not referred to in either the original or the amended birth certificate.

The surrogate mother is usually the legal mother of the child at the time of birth, and should be registered as the mother of the child at birth.

There has been very little consideration of the issue of choice of law for determining parental status in international surrogacy cases.[71] Australian courts assume that Australian law applies even where the child was conceived and born outside Australia, although they sometimes refer to the law of the place where the child is born without explaining why.[72] As a consequence, in the cases in which the issue of parental status is considered, the surrogate mother is held to be the legal parent, and the commissioning parents are not.

4. ELIGIBILITY FOR SURROGACY

4.1. ELIGIBILITY CRITERIA FOR WOMEN ACTING AS A SURROGATE

There are no 'eligibility' criteria as such, but various requirements must be satisfied before the Victorian or Western Australian authorities approve altruistic arrangements before conception, and before courts can grant a parentage order. The requirements are not identical in any two jurisdictions. No jurisdiction requires that the surrogate mother is married or is an Australian resident, domiciliary or citizen. The financial status of the surrogate mother is not a relevant consideration in any jurisdiction. The only requirements are in relation to age and 'suitability'.

Most jurisdictions impose minimum age requirements for surrogate mothers.[73] In one, the minimum age is 18,[74] and in the remaining five it is 25.[75]

---

69 *S v B; O v D* [2014] NSWSC 1533; *BB v DD* [2015] NSWSC 1095.

70 *BB v DD* [2015] NSWSC 1095, para. 103.

71 M. Keyes and R. Chisholm, 'Commercial Surrogacy – Some Troubling Family Law Issues' (2013) 27 Australian *Journal of Family Law* 105, 119–20.

72 Ibid, 120.

73 There is no minimum age requirement for surrogate mothers in the ACT.

74 Family Relationships Act 1975 (SA) s. 10HA(2a)(b).

75 Surrogacy Act 2010 (NSW) s. 27; Surrogacy Act 2010 (Qld) s. 22(2)(f); Surrogacy Act 2012 (Tas) s. 16(2)(c); Assisted Reproductive Treatment Act 2008 (Vic) s. 40(1)(b), Status

In South Australia and Western Australia, the surrogate mother must have been assessed as being suitable as a surrogate.[76] In three jurisdictions, the surrogate mother must have already given birth to a live child.[77] There is no other explicit requirement of suitability of the surrogate mother; in most jurisdictions, the surrogate mother must have undergone counselling.[78]

There is a lack of research in Australia about surrogacy generally. There have been some studies of commissioning parents,[79] but none of surrogate mothers, including as to their characteristics and motivations. In most published cases concerning intra-Australian surrogacy arrangements, surrogate mothers are related to the commissioning parents.

4.2. ELIGIBILITY CRITERIA FOR COMMISSIONING PARENTS

There are no 'eligibility' criteria as such that apply to commissioning parents. There are requirements that must be satisfied before the Victorian and Western Australian authorities approve altruistic surrogacy arrangements, and before the courts make parentage orders. These requirements differ between jurisdictions and are as follows:

- Age: In most jurisdictions, the legislation stipulates minimum ages of the commissioning parents, which range between 18,[80] 21,[81] and 25.[82]
- Medical or social need: In most jurisdictions, there must be a justification for the surrogacy arrangement;[83] in some, only medical reasons suffice.[84]

---

of Children Act 1974 (Vic) s. 23(2)(a); Surrogacy Act 2008 (WA) s. 17(a)(i). In NSW, the minimum age is 25 but this is not a mandatory requirement; the surrogate must be at least 18: Surrogacy Act 2010 (NSW) s. 27(3).

76 Family Relationships Act 1975 (SA) s. 10HA(2a)(f); Surrogacy Act 2008 (WA) s. 17(c)(ii).

77 Surrogacy Act 2012 (Tas) s. 16(2)(d); Assisted Reproductive Treatment Act 2008 (Vic) s. 40(1)(ac); Surrogacy Act 2008 (WA) s. 17(a)(ii).

78 Assisted Reproductive Technology Act 2008 (NSW) s. 35(2); Surrogacy Act 2008 (WA) ss. 17(c)(ii), 21(2)(b). This is not a strict requirement in some jurisdictions: Parentage Act 2004 (ACT) s. 26(3)(e).

79 E.g. D.W. Riggs, 'Narratives of Choice Amongst White Australians who Undertake Surrogacy Arrangements in India' (2016) 37 *Journal of Medical Humanities* 313.

80 Parentage Act 2004 (ACT) s. 26(3)(a); Surrogacy Act 2010 (NSW) s. 28; Family Relationships Act 1975 (SA) s. 10HA(2a)(b). While the minimum age is 18 in NSW, the court must be satisfied of the maturity of a commissioning parent who is under 25: Surrogacy Act 2010 (NSW) s. 29.

81 Surrogacy Act 2012 (Tas) s. 16(2)(b).

82 Surrogacy Act 2010 (Qld) s. 22(2)(g); Surrogacy Act 2008 (WA) s. 19(1)(a). The Victorian legislation does not stipulate a minimum age for commissioning parents.

83 Surrogacy Act 2010 (NSW) s. 30; Surrogacy Act 2010 (Qld) s. 22(2)(d); Surrogacy Act 2012 (Tas) s. 16(2)(h). There is no requirement to show a reason for the arrangement in the ACT.

84 Family Relationships Act 1975 (SA) s. 10HA(2a)(e); Surrogacy Act 2008 (WA) s. 19(2) a social need is sufficient, except where the commissioning parent is a woman or both commissioning parents are women, in which case, only a medical reason will suffice).

- Marital status: The commissioning parents' relationship status is relevant in two jurisdictions. In SA, they must be married or in a de facto heterosexual relationship of at least three years' duration, and a single person cannot apply for parentage orders.[85] In WA they must be married or in a de facto heterosexual relationship, and a single male cannot apply for parentage orders.[86]
- Residence: In all jurisdictions, the commissioning parents must be resident[87] or domiciled[88] in the jurisdiction.
- Suitability: In most jurisdictions, the suitability of the commissioning parents is not an explicit requirement.[89] Robb J noted that their suitability and capacity evidently fall to be considered in relation to whether making a parentage order is in the child's best interests.[90] Victoria is the only jurisdiction which requires criminal records and child protection order checks for all parties, in cases in which VARTA's approval is required.[91] In Western Australia, commissioning parents must have been assessed as being 'psychologically suitable to be involved in the surrogacy arrangement' prior to conception;[92] in the ACT, the court must consider whether the surrogate and commissioning parents received 'assessment from an independent counselling service'.[93]

The donation of gametes and embryos is regulated by the National Health and Medical Research Council's *Ethical Guidelines*,[94] as well as by legislation in some jurisdictions.[95] Gamete and embryo donation is permitted, including in surrogacy cases, but anonymous donation is not, because children are entitled to access information about their genetic parents.[96] It is not permitted to pay for gametes[97] or embryos.

In Victoria, this is a requirement in cases in which VARTA is required to approve surrogacy arrangements (Assisted Reproductive Treatment Act 2008 (Vic) s. 40(1)(a)), but not otherwise.

85 Family Relationships Act 1975 (SA) s. 10HA(2a)(d).

86 Surrogacy Act 2008 (WA) s. 19(2).

87 Parentage Act 2004 (ACT) s. 24(e); Surrogacy Act 2010 (NSW) s. 32; Surrogacy Act 2010 (Qld) s. 22(2)(g)(ii); Surrogacy Act 2012 (Tas) s. 16(2)(j)(ii); Status of Children Act 1974 (Vic) s. 20(1)(b); Surrogacy Act 2008 (WA) s. 19(1)(a).

88 Family Relationships Act 1975 (SA) s. 10HA(2a)(c).

89 South Australia is the only jurisdiction which explicitly requires the court to consider whether the commissioning parents are 'fit and proper persons to assume the role of parents of the child': Family Relationships Act 1975 (SA) s. 10HB(10).

90 *BB v DD* [2015] NSWSC 1095, para. 42.

91 Assisted Reproductive Treatment Act 2008 (Vic) s. 42.

92 Surrogacy Act 2008 (WA) s. 17(c)(ii).

93 Parentage Act 2004 (ACT) s. 26(3)(e).

94 NHMRC *Ethical Guidelines*, above n. 10.

95 Artificial Reproductive Technology Act 2007 (NSW); Assisted Reproductive Treatment Act 2008 (Vic); Human Reproductive Technology Act 1991 (WA).

96 NHMRC *Ethical Guidelines*, above n. 10, paras 6.1, 6.11, 7.1, 7.2.

97 Ibid, para. 6.5.

In two jurisdictions, at least one commissioning parent must be genetically related to the child.[98] In the ACT, neither surrogate parent can be a genetic parent and in Victoria, the surrogate mother cannot be genetically related to the child.[99]

5. TRANSFERRING PARENTHOOD

5.1. LEGAL PROCESS

The commissioning parents are usually not the legal parents of the child at birth.[100] In altruistic arrangements they may apply, post-birth, for 'parentage orders', which transfer the legal status of parent to the commissioning parents. Commissioning parents may also apply to adopt the child,[101] although this is rarely done.

State and ACT courts determine whether legal parenthood should be transferred. The legislation in each jurisdiction stipulates requirements which must be met before the court can make a parentage order.[102] These include the eligibility criteria already described;[103] in Victoria and WA, the arrangement must also have been approved prior to conception. An application for parentage orders must be made within six months of the birth.[104] In all jurisdictions, the surrogate mother's consent is required,[105] and the parties, including the surrogate mother, must have received counselling.[106] In most jurisdictions, the

98 Parentage Act 2004 (ACT) s. 24(d); Family Relationships Act 1975 (SA) s. 10HA(2a)(h)(ii).

99 Parentage Act 2004 (ACT) s. 24(b); Assisted Reproductive Treatment Act 2008 (Vic) s. 40(1)(ab).

100 Above nn. 54–56.

101 E.g. *Blake & Another* [2013] FCWA 1.

102 Many of the requirements are not strictly mandatory in some jurisdictions; the legislation gives the court the discretion to relax some requirements: Surrogacy Act 2010 (NSW) ss. 30, 31(2), 32–36; Surrogacy Act 2010 (Qld) s. 23; Surrogacy Act 2012 (Tas) s. 16(3).

103 Above Sections 4.1. and 4.2.

104 Parentage Act 2004 (ACT) s. 25(3); Surrogacy Act 2010 (NSW) s. 16; Surrogacy Act 2010 (Qld) s. 21(1); Family Relationships Act 1975 (SA) s. 10HB(5); Surrogacy Act 2012 (Tas) s. 15(1); Status of Children Act 1974 (Vic) s. 20(2); Surrogacy Act 2008 (WA) s. 20(3).

105 Parentage Act 2004 (ACT) s. 26(1)(b); Surrogacy Act 2010 (NSW) s. 31(2); Surrogacy Act 2010 (Qld) s. 22(2)(e)(iii); Family Relationships Act 1975 (SA) s. 10HB(7); Status of Children Act 1974 (Vic) s. 22(1)(e); Surrogacy Act 2012 (Tas) s. 22(2)(c)(iv); Surrogacy Act 2008 (WA) s. 21(2)(d).

106 Parentage Act 2004 (ACT) s. 26(3)(e); Surrogacy Act 2010 (NSW) s. 35; Surrogacy Act 2010 (Qld) s. 22(2)(e)(ii); Family Relationships Act 1975 (SA) s. 10HA(2a)(g), (3); Surrogacy Act 2012 (Tas) s. 16(2)(f); Assisted Reproductive Treatment Act 2008 (Vic) s. 40(1)(c); Status of Children Act 1974 (Vic) s. 23(2)(b); Surrogacy Act 2008 (WA) s. 21(2)(b).

parties must have received legal advice.[107] In four jurisdictions, the surrogacy agreement must be in writing.[108]

The family courts deal with disputes concerning the surrogacy arrangement. There are two published cases of disputes between the commissioning and surrogate parents,[109] as well as media reports of disputes.[110] In one case, the court granted parenting orders in favour of the surrogate parents,[111] and in the other, in favour of the commissioning parents.[112] In each case, parenting orders were made in favour of the parents with whom the child was living.

Following the grant of a parentage order, the order will be noted in the entry relating to the birth of the child in the Register of Births, Deaths and Marriages,[113] and the child's birth must be re-registered, removing reference to the surrogate parents and replacing it with details of the commissioning parents. The new birth certificate will not refer to the surrogate parents or to the change of parentage.[114] Information concerning the surrogate mother is preserved in court records and in the internal entry relating to the child's birth in the Register of Births, Deaths and Marriages. In most jurisdictions, the legislation explicitly recognises the child's entitlement to access information both in court records[115] and the entry in the Register.[116]

---

107 Surrogacy Act 2010 (NSW) s. 36; Surrogacy Act 2010 (Qld) s. 22(2)(e)(i); Family Relationships Act 1975 (SA) s. 10HA(6); Surrogacy Act 2012 (Tas) s. 16(2)(a)(i); Assisted Reproductive Treatment Act 2008 (Vic) s. 40(1)(c); Surrogacy Act 2008 (WA) s. 21(2)(c).

108 Surrogacy Act 2010 (NSW) s. 34(1); Surrogacy Act 2010 (Qld) s. 22(2)(d); Family Relationships Act 1975 (SA) s. 10HA(6); Surrogacy Act 2008 (WA) s. 17(b).

109 *Re Evelyn (No. 2)* (1998) 23 Fam LR 73; *Farnell & Chanbua* [2016] FCWA 17.

110 T. Barliss, 'When altruistic surrogacy goes wrong' 10.08.2014, *Sydney Morning Herald*, <http://www.smh.com.au/national/when-altruistic-surrogacy-goes-wrong-20140807-101bo5.html> accessed 06.09.2018; M. Morris, 'Surrogacy laws: legal tug of war highlights flaws of current system', 19.04.2016, *ABC News*, <http://www.abc.net.au/news/2016-04-18/surrogacy-battle-laws-north-queensland-alexa/7334712> accessed 06.09.2018.

111 *Re Evelyn (No. 2)* (1998) 23 Fam LR 73.

112 *Farnell & Chanbua* [2016] FCWA 17.

113 The court must generally notify the Registrar of Births, Deaths and Marriages of the parentage order, and the Registrar must re-register the child's birth: e.g. Births, Deaths and Marriages Registration Act 1997 (ACT) Pt 2, Div. 2.4; Births, Deaths and Marriages Registration Act 1995 (NSW) Pt 4A; Surrogacy Act 2012 (Tas) ss. 33–34.

114 E.g. Births, Deaths and Marriages Registration Act 1995 (NSW) s. 25D(2); Births, Deaths and Marriages Registration Act 1996 (SA) s. 22A(3)(b); Surrogacy Act 2008 (WA) s. 39(1).

115 E.g. Surrogacy Act 2012 (Tas) s. 46(3)(a); Status of Children Act 1974 (Vic) s. 34(2)(a).

116 E.g. Births, Deaths and Marriages Registration Act 1996 (SA) s. 22A(4); Surrogacy Act 2008 (WA) s. 38(1)(a). Under the legislation in NSW, Queensland and SA, the child must be 18 to access the information, but there is no such limitation in the legislation in the other states. The legislation in the ACT makes no specific provision for the child's entitlement to access information in court records or the entry in the Register.

5.2. RIGHTS OF CHILDREN

Although the legislation is intended to protect the child's interests, there is little explicit reference to the child's rights or interests in the legislation. The putative child's best interests are not explicitly identified as a factor that must be considered by VARTA or the RTC in determining whether to approve a surrogacy arrangement. In all jurisdictions, the legislation states that the court should consider the child's best interests in determining whether to make a parentage order.[117] The WA legislation presumes it to be 'in the best interests of the child for the [commissioning] parents to be the parents of the child'.[118] The legislation in the other six jurisdictions does not elaborate as to what factors are relevant to determining a child's best interests, and there is little consideration of this in the case law.

In *BB v DD*, Robb J noted that the legislation provides 'little guidance as to how the court should determine whether or not the making of a parentage order is in the best interests of the child.'[119] His Honour observed that:

> 'Whether the making of a parentage order is in the best interests of the child is likely to be determined by the consideration that there is no reasonably viable alternative [to granting the parentage order] that could be in the interests of the child at all. ... unless there is some reasonably strong evidence to the contrary, by the time the Court comes to consider the issue of what is in the best interests of the child, circumstances will generally create a *fait accompli*.'[120]

6. AGENCIES AND CRIMINALISATION

The surrogacy legislation creates a number of offences. In each jurisdiction, several offences apply to people who are involved in surrogacy arrangements, other than the commissioning parents and surrogate mother.[121] Six jurisdictions prohibit advertising; in five, this includes advertising in relation to altruistic

---

117 Parentage Act 2004 (ACT) s. 26(1)(a); Surrogacy Act 2010 (NSW) s. 22; Surrogacy Act 2010 (Qld) s. 22(2)(a); Family Relationships Act 1975 (SA) s. 10HB(6); Surrogacy Act 2012 (Tas) s. 16(2)(k); Status of Children Act 1974 (Vic) s. 22(1)(a); Surrogacy Act 2008 (WA) s. 21(2 (g).

118 Surrogacy Act 2008 (WA) s. 13(2).

119 *BB v DD* [2015] NSWSC 1095, para. 41.

120 Ibid, para. 44.

121 In five jurisdictions, it is a criminal offence to enter into a commercial surrogacy agreement: Parentage Act 2004 (ACT) s. 41; Surrogacy Act 2010 (NSW) s. 8; Surrogacy Act 2010 (Qld) s. 56; Surrogacy Act 2012 (Tas) s. 40; Surrogacy Act 2008 (WA) s. 8. In Victoria, the relevant offence is the receipt by the surrogate mother of a 'material benefit or advantage': Assisted Reproductive Treatment Act 2008 (Vic) s. 44(1).

arrangements.[122] In some jurisdictions, brokering or procuring[123] arrangements is an offence; in some, the provision of services in commercial arrangements is prohibited.[124]

The penalties differ between jurisdictions but in all jurisdictions the maximum penalties are substantial. In most jurisdictions, the offences are punishable by imprisonment,[125] ranging from six months to five years.[126] Most offences are also punishable by fines; the maxima of which are substantial.[127] In most jurisdictions, the maximum penalties are the same for commissioning parents, surrogates and agents. However, in Western Australia, the maximum penalty for providing services to facilitate commercial surrogacy is five years,[128] and in the ACT, the advertising offences attract lesser penalties than all other offences.[129]

In three jurisdictions, the offences are explicitly given an extraterritorial effect, applying to ordinary residents, or domiciliaries, in relation to their activities outside the jurisdiction.[130]

There have been few reported prosecutions of the offences. Under the previous Queensland legislation,[131] at least six people were prosecuted for their

---

122 Parentage Act 2004 (ACT) s. 43; Surrogacy Act 2010 (NSW) s. 10; Surrogacy Act 2010 (Qld) s. 55; Surrogacy Act 2012 (Tas) s. 41(2)(c); Assisted Reproductive Treatment Act 2008 (Vic) s. 45; In NSW, the publishing offences do not apply to altruistic cases if a fee was not paid for publishing the information: Surrogacy Act 2010 (NSW) s. 10(2). There are no advertising offences in South Australia. The advertising offences in WA only apply to commercial arrangements: Surrogacy Act 2008 (WA) s. 10.

123 Parentage Act 2004 (ACT) s. 42; Family Relationships Act 1975 (SA) s. 10H; Surrogacy Act 2012 (Tas) s. 41; Surrogacy Act 2008 (WA) s. 9.

124 Parentage Act 2004 (ACT) s. 44; Surrogacy Act 2010 (Qld) s. 58; Surrogacy Act 2008 (WA) s. 11.

125 In Tasmania, the only penalties are fines, the maximum of which is 100 penalty units ($15,900 in June 2018).

126 In the ACT, the maximum penalty for most offences is one year's imprisonment or 100 penalty units ($15,000 in June 2018). In NSW, the maximum penalty is 1,000 penalty units ($110,000 in June 2018) or two years' imprisonment: Surrogacy Act 2010 (NSW) s. 8. In Queensland, the maximum penalty for all offences is 100 penalty units ($12,615 in June 2018) or three years' imprisonment: Surrogacy Act 2010 (Qld) ss. 55–58.

127 See above nn. 125–126. In SA, the only penalty is one year's imprisonment: Family Relationships Act 1975 (SA) s. 10H.

128 In WA, the penalties are the most diverse, ranging from a fine of $6,000 for advertising, to imprisonment for five years for providing services to facilitate commercial surrogacy: Surrogacy Act 2008 (WA) ss. 10, 11(1).

129 Whereas all other offences are punishable by one year's imprisonment or 100 penalty units ($15,000), the advertising offences are punishable by 50 penalty units ($7,500) or, in the case of advertising for commercial arrangements, six months' imprisonment: Parentage Act 2004 (ACT) s. 43(1).

130 Parentage Act 2004 (ACT) s. 45(1); Surrogacy Act 2010 (NSW) s. 11(2); Surrogacy Act 2010 (Qld) s. 54(b).

131 Surrogate Parenthood Act 1988 (Qld).

involvement in surrogacy arrangements.[132] In two more recent cases,[133] Watt J noted that the commissioning parents' act of entering into a commercial surrogacy agreement in Thailand was illegal under Queensland legislation, and referred the matter to the Queensland Director of Public Prosecutions; but no prosecution was pursued. There is a widespread perception among commissioning parents that the offences are unlikely to be prosecuted, based on the well-known lack of recent prosecutions, and this appears to influence the decisions of some commissioning parents to enter into commercial surrogacy agreements abroad.

7. INTERNATIONAL SURROGACY ARRANGEMENTS

The only explicit treatment of international arrangements in the surrogacy legislation is in the provisions in the ACT, Queensland and NSW legislation giving the offences an extraterritorial effect.[134] Parentage orders can only be granted in altruistic arrangements, which excludes most international cases that come before the Australian courts. In some jurisdictions, parentage orders could not be made in international altruistic arrangements, because of the requirement in those jurisdictions that medical procedures were carried out within the jurisdiction.[135] There are other requirements which would be difficult to satisfy in international altruistic arrangements.[136] There are no published decisions in which parentage orders were granted in an international arrangement.

In cases involving international arrangements, the courts invariably apply Australian domestic law to determine parental status, usually without reference to choice of law.[137]

Parenthood arising out of a surrogacy arrangement in another jurisdiction has been recognised in several recent cases.[138] In *Re Halvard*,[139] the Family

132 Two women were charged in 1991, and another two in 1992. In 1993, a doctor and a woman were charged: G. Emmerson, *Surrogacy: Born for Another*, Research Bulletin No. 8/93, Queensland Parliamentary Library, Publications and Resources Section, Brisbane 1996, pp. 38–39. See also Investigation into Altruistic Surrogacy Committee, above n. 14, p. 9 (referring to five reported prosecutions).

133 *Dudley & Chedi* [2011] FamCA 502; *Findlay & Punyawong* [2011] FamCA 503.

134 Above n. 129.

135 Parentage Act 2004 (ACT) s. 24(a); Family Relationships Act 1975 (SA) s. 10HA(2a)(h)(i); Status of Children Act 1974 (Vic) s. 20(1)(a).

136 Some counselling and legal advice requirements require that the person providing the service is a member of an Australian association, or an Australian practitioner: e.g. Surrogacy Act 2010 (NSW) s. 36(1); Surrogacy Act 2010 (Qld) s. 19.

137 Cf. *Farnell & Chanbua* [2016] FCWA 17, para. 368. For criticism, see M. Keyes and R. Chisholm, above n. 71, 119–20.

138 In *Re Mark* [2003] FamCA 822, the commissioning parents did not seek to have the Californian court order, which determined that one of the commissioning fathers was the legal father, recognised but the point was argued. Brown J held that the foreign order did not come within the terms of the Australian legislation enabling recognition of foreign orders: para. 33.

139 *Re Halvard* [2016] FamCA 1051.

Court registered orders[140] of a Tennessee court that the commissioning parents, who lived in the United States but intended to visit Australia in the future, were the child's legal parents. Forrest J noted that the arrangement was altruistic, and observed that 'an overseas child order that came into existence as a consequence of a commercial surrogacy agreement might have difficulty attracting a favourable exercise of the discretion to register it in this Court for public policy reasons'.[141] However, he has since registered orders in two other cases in which the surrogacy arrangement was commercial.[142]

As described above, a child born in an international surrogacy arrangement will only be permitted to enter Australia if they have been granted a visa or Australian citizenship, in both cases, on the basis of the child's relationship to a commissioning parent.[143]

Children born in international surrogacy arrangements can acquire Australian nationality if they are found to be the child of an Australian citizen or permanent resident.[144]

8. CONCLUSION

The current laws regulating altruistic surrogacy are relatively new and their effectiveness is difficult to measure because, in most jurisdictions, the courts' decisions are not published. The laws impose minimal requirements, many of which are not mandatory. In most jurisdictions, the requirements are only considered post-birth, and only if the commissioning parents apply for parentage orders. As the application is made post-birth, the courts' ability to ensure compliance with requirements is compromised. Notwithstanding these issues, it is sometimes asserted that the regulation of altruistic arrangements is unacceptably prescriptive, onerous and expensive.[145]

It is frequently asserted that the diversity in the surrogacy legislation of the seven different jurisdictions is problematic;[146] there have been many calls to develop uniform legislation. In May 2016, the House of Representatives Standing Committee on Social Policy and Legal Affairs recommended the

140 Under Family Law Act 1975 (Cth) ss. 70G, 70H.

141 *Re Halvard* [2016] FamCA 1051, para. 35.

142 *Sigley & Sigley* [2018] FamCA 3; *Re: Grosvenor* [2017] FamCA 366.

143 See above nn. 62–67.

144 Ibid.

145 J. Millbank, 'The New Surrogacy Parentage Laws in Australia' (2011) 35 *Melbourne University LR* 165.

146 This is commonly identified as a justification for commissioning parents seeking overseas arrangements: House of Representatives Standing Committee on Social Policy and Legal Affairs, above n. 44, pp. 30–31.

development of a model national law facilitating altruistic surrogacy in Australia, to ensure greater protection for children as well as the adult parties.[147] To date, there has been no reaction to that recommendation.

Although there is a widespread perception that the surrogacy offences are not prosecuted, there is also a perception that the prohibition of advertising is an impediment to the success of altruistic surrogacy. This led to reform of the South Australian legislation in 2015 in which the advertising offences were repealed. The legislation now provides for the preparation of a State Framework for Altruistic Surrogacy, and the establishment of a Surrogate Register of women who are willing to act as surrogate mothers.[148] These have not yet been implemented, and in 2018 they are being reviewed.

Australian commissioning parents are far more likely to engage in international commercial than in domestic altruistic arrangements. A number of serious concerns arise in relation to international commercial arrangements. The first is the inconsistency between the laws relating to parental status, and the determination of parental status for the purposes of federal immigration and citizenship laws. The second is the lack of interest in scrutinising international commercial arrangements by government departments and authorities,[149] and in prosecuting breaches of the criminal laws. At least some commissioning parents are therefore undeterred by the prohibition of commercial surrogacy. The third is the lack of effective controls in international commercial arrangements, in terms of protecting surrogate mothers, commissioning parents, and children, and controls on the suitability of the commissioning parents. In two known cases, Australian commissioning fathers entered into international arrangements to acquire children for the purpose of sexual exploitation,[150] and in one known case, a commissioning father had prior convictions for multiple counts of child sexual assaults.[151]

Surrogacy remains highly contentious, including among legal practitioners, academics, legislators and judges. Many agree that the existing law is imperfect, but there is a lack of agreement as to how it should be remedied, and a lack of political will to introduce reforms. Few suggestions for legal reform have come to fruition. In 2013, the Family Law Council recommended that the Family Court should have 'a discretionary power to transfer parentage from

---

147 Ibid p. 7.

148 Family Relationships Act 1975 (SA) Div 1A.

149 House of Representatives Standing Committee on Social Policy and Legal Affairs, above n. 44, p. 32.

150 *DPP (Commonwealth) v McIntosh* [2016] VCC 622; N. Ralston, 'Couple offered son to paedophiles', *Sydney Morning Herald* (01.07.2013) <http://www.smh.com.au/national/couple-offered-son-to-paedophiles-20130630-2p5eg.html> accessed 06.09.2018.

151 *Farnell & Chanbua* [2016] FCWA 17.

the surrogate mother to the [commissioning] parents where certain "safeguard" criteria have been met',[152] which the Council anticipated should be possible in international commercial arrangements. This recommendation has not been implemented.

There have been repeated calls for the de-criminalisation of commercial surrogacy, which, it has been argued, would resolve problems with altruistic surrogacy and prevent Australians from engaging in international commercial arrangements.[153] The House of Representatives Standing Committee on Social Policy and Legal Affairs recommended that commercial surrogacy remain illegal because 'even if a regulated system of commercial surrogacy could be implemented, the risk of exploitation of both surrogates and children remains significant.'[154] Given the diversity of views on surrogacy in Australia, it seems unlikely that significant reforms will be achieved in the short term.

152 Family Law Council, *Report on Parentage and the Family Law Act*, Commonwealth of Australia, Canberra 2014, p. 100.

153 A. Stuhmcke, 'The Criminal Act of Commercial Surrogacy in Australia: A Call for Review' (2011) 18 *Journal of Law and Medicine* 601; J. Millbank, 'Rethinking "Commercial" Surrogacy in Australia' (2015) 12 *Bioethical Inquiry* 477.

154 House of Representatives Standing Committee on Social Policy and Legal Affairs, above n. 44, p. 6.

A VIEW FROM THE BENCH IN AUSTRALIA

John Pascoe*

1. INTRODUCTION

I would like to provide a view from the Bench. Interestingly, that view may be different depending upon which Bench you are sitting both from an International perspective and from an Australian perspective given that Australia, like America, is a federation and state laws may, and indeed do, often differ from federal laws.

The focus of this conference, different perspectives of surrogacy, is, in my mind, its great strength. It encourages of us all to see the same problem through different lenses, to see the issue of surrogacy from the perspective of different cultures and traditions, different professions and different goals. The issue may be approached completely differently if one is a scientist interested in human reproductive technology as opposed to an advocate for children's rights.

However, at the centre of the conference is the bringing into existence of a child – an issue that goes to the heart of our humanity – it literally defines who we are – and must therefore be an issue for humanity as a collective as a whole.

---

* Any views expressed in this contribution are the author's personal views and are expressed in an academic rather than a judicial capacity. His Honour would like to thank his legal associates, Benedict Porter and Lisa Churcher, for their assistance in preparing this contribution.

It will be no surprise that, from my perspective, what is critical is the best interests of the child, regardless of the manner in which that child was brought into existence. This *is* the focal point of any decision made by me as a judge notwithstanding a myriad of other matters to be considered.

Australia is a signatory to the (almost) universally accepted Convention on the Rights of the Child ('the CRC').[1] The child's inalienable and inviolate human rights are therefore part of the fabric of Australian law and central to how a judge in my court considers issues relating to children, especially in relation to international commercial surrogacy. In other words, there is an inescapable truth and an inescapable logic that makes the best interests of the child central to the decision-making process rather than issues of contracting rights, adult desires, or technological advances.

The reality from the Bench is that the welfare of the child is at issue, and that must be the primary focus.

As mentioned, quite apart from the child's best interests, there are many other matters to be taken into account. I would like to discuss three of them. Firstly, the Australian legal framework; second, the international framework via Private International Law; and third, what constitutes the best interests of the child and the compromises a judge might have to make.

2. COMMERCIAL SURROGACY

I want to begin by looking at commercial surrogacy. It is banned in most countries, and most states in Australia, some of which apply extraterritorial laws to its citizens to prevent them engaging in the practice either locally or overseas. Sadly, the prohibition is often ignored, especially with regards to international commercial surrogacy.

The rapid retreat by countries that once permitted commercial surrogacy has been well noted and may be regarded as driven by concern about the potential abuse commercial surrogacy poses to their citizens, especially poor women, and to the children who are the subject of such arrangements. Relatively few countries now permit commercial surrogacy and fewer still allow commercial surrogacy services to be provided to foreigners. However, where there is demand and a profit to be made, a market almost inevitably will open up.

Agents, middlemen, clinics and facilitators advertise surrogacy services, usually illicitly, to wealthier foreign commissioning parents, and recruit local women, who are usually poor, uneducated, and desperate to earn some money. Obviously a commercial enterprise, the surrogacy industry bears all the usual hallmarks, including financial lures, cost cutting, competitive pricing, and

---

1 United Nations General Assembly resolution 44/25 of 20 November 1989.

techniques (which may be morally reprehensible but which) guarantee certain results. Moreover, the foreign location, lax laws, and/or poor law enforcement assists the industry by providing commissioning parents a back-out option if they decide not to go through with the arrangement – what can be seen as a crude 'returns policy'. If they are unhappy with the arrangement or indeed the resulting child, they can back-out and abandon the pregnant surrogate mother or child, retreating to the safety of their home jurisdiction without any adverse legal consequences. Such a scenario occurred in the now infamous 'Baby Gammy' scandal. The acceptance that international commercial surrogacy is an industry has led many to aptly describe it as a multi-million dollar 'booming business'.[2]

At no point are the rights of the child of concern. The child's rights are at best apparently 'suspended', whilst the child is regarded purely as a commercial, tradeable and disposable commodity.

The view from the Bench is spent looking at litigants and facts; either the mundane and the ordinary or the few but notable far fringes – the degenerate and the depraved. Depressingly, the fringe example is presently set by a 49-year-old Australian paedophile (recently gaoled for 22 years) for sexually assaulting his specifically commissioned-for-abuse twin daughters when they were just 27 days old.[3] The view from the Bench is that this is deplorable, just unacceptable, the prevention of which is worth 1,000 happy 'complete' families.

3. THE AUSTRALIAN SITUATION

Australia is a Federation; it has six states and two territories, each with its own body of laws and a federal government with powers stipulated in the Australian Constitution. The federal government is empowered to legislate with regards to 'marriage'[4] and 'divorce and matrimonial causes; and in relation thereto, parental rights, and the custody and guardianship of infants.'[5] Thus, 'human creation' is not a matter for the federal government but rather for the states. I do note however that, with regard to the international aspect of Australians entering into surrogacy arrangements abroad, the federal government does have power to act as it has the jurisdiction to legislate 'for the peace, order, and good government of the Commonwealth with respect to … external affairs.'[6]

2 S. Mohapatra, 'Stateless Babies and Adoption Scams: A Bioethical Analysis of International Commercial Surrogacy' (2012) 30 *Berkeley Journal of International Law* 412, 413.

3 N. Bucci, 'Man pleads guilty to sexually abusing his twin surrogate babies' (21.04.2016) *Sydney Morning Herald*. <http://www.smh.com.au/national/man-pleads-guilty-to-sexually-abusing-his-twin-surrogate-babies-20160421-goc83m.html> accessed 06.09.2018.

4 Commonwealth of Australia Constitution Act s. 51(xxi).

5 Commonwealth of Australia Constitution Act s. 51(xxii).

6 Commonwealth of Australia Constitution Act s. 51(xxix).

This power enables treaty implementation, such as the CRC, and may be used to regulate Australian citizens' behaviour abroad.

I have previously discussed the powers of the states and will not specifically enumerate the many disparate and divergent pieces of relevant legislation, other than to say that in some states commercial surrogacy is criminal, in others it's simply illegal, in some states there are laws with extraterritorial application, and in one territory the word 'surrogacy' is not mentioned at all. The descriptions of the inconsistencies of surrogacy legislation across the states and territories as 'a patchwork of regulatory stitching'[7] and 'chaotic'[8] seem apt. The inconsistencies have created a labyrinthine obstacle course for desperate parents to run. This is a type of 'regime shopping' and is anathema to courts everywhere.

Many commissioning parents seem undeterred by the criminal sanctions or legal consequences that may result from their actions. In fact they may be encouraged to act by lawyers, intermediaries and medical clinics (all of whom collect a fee). These parties are emboldened by an absence of prosecution from state and territory law enforcement agencies against those who very publicly break the law. Indeed, on the front page of a local newspaper recently, a couple appealed for money for international commercial surrogacy via 'crowd-funding'. Whilst gaoling a commissioning parent for actualising the dream of becoming a parent, thus leaving a newborn without a carer may not seem appropriate to some, the current public policy position against commercial surrogacy needs to be respected and to be enforced. Otherwise, simply repeal the law. To do nothing, as is presently the case, is to bring the Rule of Law into disrepute. Judges are left to deal with the consequences of the failure to enforce clear statutory prohibitions.

The only consistency in Australia is with regard to altruistic surrogacy, an arrangement that does not permit the exchange of money other than for 'reasonable expenses'. Importantly, altruistic surrogacy arrangements cannot compel the surrogate to abort the child, (or not abort the child), nor to give the child up should the surrogate mother change her mind after she gives birth.[9]

4. COMMONWEALTH LEGISLATION

In Australia, Family Law matters are dealt with by the Federal Circuit Court of Australia and the Family Court of Australia. Nearly 90 per cent of Family Law

7 E.A. Schneller, 'The Right of Donor Inseminated Children to Know their Genetic Origins in Australia' (2005) 19 *Australian Journal of Family Law* 222, 228, quoting H. Szoke, 'Australia – A Federated Structure of Statutory Regulation of ART' in J. Gunning and H. Szoke (eds), *The Regulation of Assisted Reproductive Technology*, Ashgate, Burlington 2003, p. 75.

8 E.A. Schneller, above n. 7, p. 244.

9 M. Keyes, 'Cross-Border Surrogacy Agreements' (2012) *Australian Journal of Family Law* 28, 39.

matters are dealt with in the, 'district court level', Federal Circuit Court. The Family Law Act 1975 ('the FLA') acknowledges children who were born from assisted reproductive technology procedures and surrogacy respectively so as to allow the FLA to be applied to them.[10] Otherwise, federal legislation does not engage on the surrogacy question at all. This silence in the FLA does not provide guidance to a judge when presented with a child, the subject of a surrogacy arrangement, which is illegal under state law. Moreover, the FLA's silence has allowed a party to approach the family courts seeking orders relating to the parentage and parenting for the child. The courts' lack of relevant jurisdiction in relation to parentage orders of a surrogate child can leave the child vulnerable and without clear acknowledgement of the circumstances of birth.

The family courts *may* make a parentage order if a state or an overseas court has made such a declaration so that the court's jurisdiction may be applied to the child and parents.[11] Furthermore, the court may make a declaration of parentage in circumstances where maternity or paternity is in issue in proceedings before the Court. A declaration is made on the balance of probabilities and is regarded as conclusive across Australia.[12] The refusal of a judge to make a parentage declaration is not a conclusive denial of parentage, simply that insufficient evidence was supplied or that the evidence relied upon was not accepted.

5. FAMILY COURTS' HANDLING OF INTERNATIONAL COMMERCIAL SURROGACY ARRANGEMENTS

To date, there have been only two cases where a family court has made parentage orders in circumstances where the commissioning couple had engaged in an international commercial surrogacy arrangement. I note that these cases were relatively 'early on' in the use of commercial surrogacy. The Full Court of the Family Court of Australia has now conclusively rejected the approach taken in these earlier cases, finding that FLA leaves it to the states and territories to regulate the status of children born under surrogacy arrangements, and that will be recognised for the purposes of the FLA. It is not open to the Court to fill any lacuna created when state legislation does not apply to the particular circumstances of the case.[13] The middle-ground that seeks only to protect the best interests of the child – the paramount consideration to family courts is that the commissioning parents may seek parenting orders from the court.

---

10 Family Law Act 1975 (Cth) ss. 60H and 60HB respectively.
11 Family Law Act 1975 (Cth) ss. 69P–69U.
12 Family Law Act 1975 (Cth) ss. 69V–69ZD.
13 *Bernieres and Anor & Dhopal and Anor* (2017) 57 Fam LR 149.

'Parentage' orders are to be distinguished from 'parenting' orders. A parentage order is a declaration as to who is the legal parent of the child. Such an order may be used to apply to the state or territory authority responsible for birth certificates for reissuance.[14] This is a problem which I will address later. Parenting orders are, however, altogether different. The family courts have the power to regulate who and how a person may care for the child, including how much time a certain person may spend with the child and under what circumstances. Importantly, the carer is not necessarily the legal parent. A commissioning parent in receipt of parenting orders is in effect a legally appointed carer, responsible for the safety of the child but not necessarily the child's legal parent with all the rights and duties that accompany such a position. For the applicant commissioning parent this may be an unsatisfactory situation. More importantly, the child lacks the formal protection of a legal parent.

I leave this point noting, as Professor Mary Keyes mentioned, that the courts' encounter with these sorts of applications in relation to international surrogacy is relatively seldom – however we suspect (to the point of surety) that there are more cases, more children, in Australia whose parents have illicitly created them and brought them to Australia and who now hide them in fear of prosecution. As aforementioned, this prosecution is, ironically, unlikely to be enforced. These children will remain hidden – their rights ignored and supressed – until needs push the issue into the light which may be too late in the circumstances to save the child from their unnecessary fate.

6. PRIVATE INTERNATIONAL LAW

As mentioned above, a judge may be presented with the judgment of a foreign court which states that the commissioning parents are the legal parents of the child. The judge must decide whether he or she can recognise that foreign judgment or indeed give it weight in his or her parentage decision, which, as stated earlier, is made on the balance of probabilities.

In the family law courts, regulations provide for the recognition of overseas child orders from prescribed jurisdictions, which is limited to New Zealand, Papua New Guinea, Switzerland and most states of the United States of America.[15] Where a decision does not fall within the limited scope of the regulations, the answer is that there is no mechanism to allow a judge to recognise a foreign parentage order. It can be given some weight (if it were not

[14] See Parentage Act 2004 (ACT) s. 24(c); Surrogacy Act 2010 (NSW) s. 31(1); Surrogacy Act 2010 (Qld) s. 20; Family Relationships Act 1975 (SA) s. 10HB(2)(a); Surrogacy Act 2012 (Tas) ss. 14 and 15; Status of Children Act 1974 (Vic) s. 20(1)(a); Surrogacy Act 2008 (WA) s. 12.

[15] Family Law Regulations 1984 (Cth) reg. 23 and Sched. 1A.

contrary to public policy) but it is not conclusive and it will be outweighed by considerations as to the best interests of the child.

Further, of the approximate 200 countries in the world, Australia only prescribes 32 foreign superior courts for registration and enforcement of their judgments.[16] Indeed, these arrangements largely apply to civil in personam matters. Enforcement of a parentage order would be very new ground and no judge has so far been prepared to entertain such a novel argument, preferring the more orthodox but discretionary path – namely, the balance of probabilities and best interests of the child.

Under state laws, parentage orders can be issued by a judge of that state, however public policy explicitly precludes a judge from recognising or giving weight to orders made in a foreign jurisdiction if the child was conceived via a commercial surrogacy arrangement. The result is that, in the absence of any parenting order from a relevant court, the child's parentage is simply a matter of conjecture. A person may appear to be the legal parent, even act as one, but if challenged by a police officer, or if the child wanted to go to a public hospital, or be enrolled in a school, serious legal parentage questions may arise which can adversely affect the child.

Private International Law may provide some solutions which do not leave a child at the mercy of discretion. A convention similar to the Hague Convention on Intercountry Adoption[17] may provide a mechanism for recognition of the orders made by a court in the jurisdiction where the child was born. This mechanism might provide a layer of protection for the rights of the child who – however he or she was conceived or born – is now before the court.

The possible benefits of a Hague-like convention do not, in my view, remove the need to address the very serious human rights abuses that are well documented in commercial surrogacy. However such a mechanism may save a judge being caught between *pro*-active state and territory policies based on the prevention of citizens engaging in commercial surrogacy on one hand, and on the other, the *re*-active federal family law policy that looks to the best interests of the child. Justice Hedley of the High Court of England and Wales concisely summarised this dilemma:

> 'What the Court is required to do is balance two competing and potentially irreconcilably conflicting concepts. Parliament is clearly entitled to legislate against commercial surrogacy and is clearly entitled to expect that the courts should implement that policy consideration in its decisions. Yet it is also recognised that as the full rigour of that policy consideration will bear on one wholly unequipped to comprehend it let

[16] Foreign Judgments Regulations 1992 (Cth) Sched. 1. See also: Foreign Judgments Act 1991 (Cth).

[17] Convention of 29 May 1993 on Protection of Children and Co-operation in Respect of Intercountry Adoption.

> alone deal with its consequences (that is, the child concerned). That rigour must be mitigated by the application of a consideration of that child's welfare. That approach is both humane and intellectually coherent. The difficulty is that it is almost impossible to imagine a set of circumstances in which by the time the case comes to court, the welfare of any child (particularly a foreign child) would not be gravely compromised by a refusal to make an order. If public policy is truly to be upheld, it would need to be enforced at a much earlier stage than the final hearing. The point of admission to this country is in some ways the final opportunity in reality to prevent the effective implementation of a commercial surrogacy agreement.'[18]

This last statement is endorsed by Justice Ryan, of the Family Court of Australia, echoing submissions made by the Australian Human Rights Commission:

> 'The Court is faced with having children in front of it and needs to make orders that are in the best interests of those children, and at that stage it's probably too late to inquire into the legality of the arrangements that had been made. The court really needs to take the children as it finds them.'[19]

Interestingly, we are in the early stages of considering a Private International Law approach through the work of the Experts Group on Surrogacy and Parentage under the auspices of the Permanent Bureau for Private International Law at the Hague. This group, of which I am a member, is discussing the possibility and feasibility of a coordinated international approach that provides legally binding standards, a system of supervision that protects the rights of the child as set out in the CRC, establishes appropriate modes of communication between states, and ensures cooperation between the surrogate and the commissioning countries.

Clearly there would need to be safeguards as to identity and the preservation of documentation. All of the information relating to the circumstances of the child's birth, including accurate and complete information as to the genetic history of donor material, the birth mother's identity (subject to her rights of privacy), her ethnicity and the country in which the child was born must be preserved and be available to the child upon reaching adulthood, with specific and purposeful disregard of the wishes or convenience of the commissioning parents or donors who may wish to suppress the information. Such a provision meets the child's right to know. Any convention would most certainly be subject to the provisions of the CRC.

Private International Law will not, however, solve the problems of commercial surrogacy, especially the exploitation of vulnerable women and children, nor the commodification of human life. It may provide some relief

---

18 *X and Y (Foreign Surrogacy)* [2008] EWHC 3030, para. 24 per Hedley J.

19 *Ellison and Karnchanit* [2012] FamCA 602, para. 87 per Ryan J.

to the judge in addressing the best interests of the child, now in existence, and some limited legal protection for the child. The court is thus shielded from a discussion about the morality of particular conduct and matters of public policy; which are the prerogative of Parliament.

7. THE CHILD'S RIGHT TO KNOW

A significant issue, on which I wish to conclude, leads me back to my opening statement; that the discussion of surrogacy may involve many issues (indeed, that is part of the problem), but the core consideration must be the child and his or her inalienable human rights.

In the case of surrogacy, as with adoption, the child's right to know, including his or her genetics is often overlooked. Today, we know much more about the adverse effects loss of a sense of identity can cause. To say the least, it is devastating psychologically and may have life-threatening consequences. With medical advances, knowledge of genetic history can be the key to life-saving treatment. It is also critical to answering the question: 'who am I?' Further, with advances in reproductive technology, traditional methods of recognising parentage are now simply no longer adequate.

The limitation of a two-person birth certificate denies the distinction between biological and legal parentage. Indeed the term biological has changed meaning too – it can mean the gestational mother, which used to be conclusive, or the person who provided the gametes. Further, legal parentage can change with a court order, with the birth certificate changing each time without reference to the existence of a previous (different) certificate.

The phenomena of 'thruples', a legal three-person union, and 'rainbow families', lesbian, gay, bisexual, transgender or intersex persons who have a child further indicates the expanding number of people with whom the child may have a relationship. A denial of recognition of what 'is' may cause great distress and anguish in later life.

The CRC – a universal document – states that the child has the right to know his or her parents, which includes nationality and genetic heritage, as well as all the people who actually raised the child. Therefore it is a positive duty incumbent upon the custodial parent to ensure that such knowledge is acquired, retained, and imparted to the child. Wilful blindness or indifference to these obligations is no excuse to the suppression of a child's human rights.

8. CONCLUSION

A parent is charged with a responsibility to act in the child's best interests and so must not be allowed to choose to ignore or suppress a child's rights. Of course, tact and timing is important. However, it is the child's right that is critical, not the parent's convenience or feelings of jealousy that there may be another, or indeed others, to whom the child may refer as a parent.

The saying 'what they don't know, can't hurt them' is a fallacy when applied to identity. It very much hurts, and it lasts a lifetime. The duty is on the custodial parent to have all the details surrounding the identity of the donor material used to create the child and it is their duty to pass that information on to their child. They are merely custodians of the information – it truly belongs to the child.

Domestic and international legal frameworks should be in harmony. However, with technological advances, the law (at least in Australia) has been slow to react in order to provide protection to vulnerable parties and guidance to assist judges, despite the provisions in the CRC.

What is left is a disharmony. The judge is left to be the ultimate arbiter of confused, questionable, haphazard, and perhaps reckless actions in what should be a well-guided and well-regulated process. The judge is left with a feeling of dissatisfaction both in relation to the ambiguity which he or she faces in adequately protecting the best interests of the child and the insufficiency of the remedies available.

The judge can only pick up the shattered pieces after the event and do what is possible – however limited. The judge is not immune to the sea of pain and desperation – past, present and future – that exists in most commercial surrogacy cases. This is indeed a heavy burden, and, in my view, not one a judge should carry.

Ultimately, in Australia at least, a judge sitting in family law jurisdiction can only interpret the law to try and protect the best interests of the child. It is only Parliament that can act to remove the ambiguity and the potential for human rights abuse we regularly see.

SURROGACY IN ENGLAND AND WALES

Claire Fenton-Glynn

1. GENERAL LEGAL FRAMEWORK

1.1. THE LEGAL FRAMEWORK FOR SURROGACY

Surrogacy in England and Wales is regulated by two key pieces of legislation: the Surrogacy Arrangements Act 1985, and the Human Fertilisation and Embryology Act 2008 ('HFEA 2008'). Having said this, there has been a large body of jurisprudence built up by the courts in this area which has substantially affected the way in which this legislation is applied. In examining the English law, it is important to note that it does not regulate when, how, or by whom a surrogacy arrangement can be entered into.[1] Rather, it regulates the effects of the surrogacy – how legal parenthood can be transferred after birth.

While England has been lauded as a jurisdiction that is very permissive towards surrogacy, in truth, the legislative framework for recognising parenthood through a surrogacy arrangement is highly restrictive. Although it does provide a specific mechanism for transferring parental status from the surrogate to commissioning parents – unlike in so many countries where adoption laws have been co-opted to this purpose – the circumstances in which this can be granted are narrow.

The opposition of the British government to surrogacy can be traced back to the Report of the Warnock Committee, which was set up in 1982 to inquire into the technologies of IVF and embryology. The Committee argued that surrogacy constituted an attack on the value of the marital relationship, as it introduced a third party into the process of procreation, which they believed should be confined to the 'loving partnership between two people.'[2] They suggested that it was inconsistent with human dignity for a woman's womb to be used for financial profit, and treated 'as an incubator for someone else's child'[3] and that given the risks relating to pregnancy, no woman should be asked to undertake it for another person in order to earn money.[4] Furthermore, the Committee felt that the relationship between mother and child was distorted by surrogacy and argued that it was degrading for a child to be treated as a commodity and 'bought for money'. The Committee concluded that the danger of exploitation was so great that it outweighed any benefits that could be perceived in permitting surrogacy. It stated: 'That people should treat others as a means to their own ends, however desirable the consequences, must always be liable to moral objection. Such treatment of one person by another becomes positively exploitative when financial interests are involved.'[5]

Shortly after the Warnock Report was published, the case of Kim Cotton hit the headlines. Cotton – a British national – had been hired by a Swedish couple, in a deal brokered by a US agency, to give birth to a surrogate child. She was paid £6,500 for the surrogacy and a further £20,000 to sell her story to the tabloid press, and the ensuing 'babies for cash' scandal led to the government taking swift legislative action. Thus the Surrogacy Arrangements Act 1985 – which has been described by one commentator as 'morally panicked'[6] – was introduced. The Act followed the recommendations of the Warnock Committee,

---

1 Except to say that the agreement cannot be enforced under law (see Section 2).

2 *Report of the Committee of Inquiry into Human Fertilisation and Embryology*, HMSO, London 1984, (reprinted 1988) Cm 9314 ('Warnock Report'), 8.10.

3 Ibid.

4 Ibid, 8.12.

5 Ibid, 8.17.

6 M. Freeman, 'Does Surrogacy Have a Future After Brazier?' (1999) 7 *Medical Law Journal* 1, 12.

and prohibited surrogacy being undertaken on a commercial basis, while also providing that any surrogacy arrangement would not be enforceable by law.

It was not until five years later that the government came to regulate the effects of surrogacy arrangements, when it introduced a mechanism for the transfer of parenthood in the Human Fertilisation and Embryology Act 1990 ('HFEA 1990'). Section 30 of this Act set out conditions that the commissioning parents must meet before they can be recognised as the legal parents of the surrogate child, through what is known as a Parental Order, which are now contained in s. 54 of the HFEA 2008. Such a Parental Order transfers parenthood from the surrogate to the commissioning parents, and will be discussed in more detail below.

We can thus see that there is a clear legal framework for the regulation of surrogacy in England and Wales, setting out rules to be followed if the parties wish to have their parenthood recognised. What is less certain, however, is the extent to which these rules can be enforced, or whether the legislation is simply an empty shell that sets out clear principles, but is of little benefit in practice.

1.2. THE PREVALENCE OF SURROGACY IN ENGLAND AND WALES

We do not have accurate statistics concerning the number of surrogacy arrangements taking place within England, or by British commissioning parents in other countries. In the latter case, there is no requirement that a Parental Order be obtained once the child enters this jurisdiction, and as such, it is unclear how many children are living in England and Wales with people who are not legally recognised as their parents in this jurisdiction. It has been frequently stated by commissioning parents when coming before the courts that they were not aware of the need for a Parental Order and thought that their recognition as parents in the foreign jurisdiction would automatically be given effect in England.[7] As a result, we often have children in England and Wales with an uncertain legal status, being cared for by people who are not recognised as their legal parents.

Even where we do have 'official' statistics – in the form of the number of Parental Orders being made by the courts each year – they are internally inconsistent and thus demonstrably unreliable, with government departments unable to agree between themselves as to the exact number being made. The Ministry of Justice indicated that in 2013, 162 children were the subject of Parental Orders, with 240 in 2014.[8] However, the General Register Office

7 See *Re X (Time Limit)* [2014] EWHC 3135 (Fam).

8 Surrogacy UK, 'Surrogacy in the UK: Myth busting and reform' (2015), <https://www.familylaw.co.uk/system/froala_assets/documents/27/Surrogacy_in_the_UK_report.pdf> accessed 06.09.2018, 14.

reports 185 in 2013 and 258 in 2014. While it may be argued that some of the confusion arises from international surrogacy arrangements, even with children born within the United Kingdom (UK), the Ministry of Justice records 102 in 2013 and 163 in 2014, as opposed to the Registrar's 116 and 151.[9]

In consequence, we cannot be certain of the exact number of surrogate births in England and Wales, nor can we know how many British couples travel to other jurisdictions to achieve their desire of becoming parents. What we can see, however, is that there are a growing number of children being registered following surrogacy arrangements, potentially indicating a growth in the practice, both within and outside the jurisdiction.

2. SURROGACY ARRANGEMENTS IN GENERAL

2.1. THE ENFORCEABILITY OF SURROGACY ARRANGEMENTS

Section 1A of the Surrogacy Arrangements Act 1985 (inserted by the Human Fertilisation and Embryology Act 1990) states: 'No surrogacy arrangement is enforceable by or against any of the persons making it.' As such, although it is not illegal to enter into such a contract, it is not enforceable in a court of law. This lack of enforcement has multiple consequences. First, as will be discussed below, this means that the surrogate can refuse to hand over the child to the commissioning parents as she is the legal mother. Second, the commissioning parents cannot enforce requirements on the surrogate mother concerning questions of pre-natal testing, abortion, dietary choices or any other pre-birth choices. But it also means that the commissioning parents can walk away at any time if their requirements are not met, or choose not to take the child when it is born. This means that there must be a great degree of trust between the parties, to be confident that both will fulfil their side of the bargain. If not, the surrogate mother may be left with a child she never wanted, or the commissioning parents left thousands of dollars out of pocket, with nothing to show for it.

Despite the lack of ability to enforce an agreement, there appears to be an assumption that one will be in place. This can be seen domestically, where hospitals have requested a copy of the agreement when parties arrive for pre-birth checks[10] – but also in international surrogacy cases, where the Home Office requires commissioning parents applying for a passport for a child born through surrogacy to produce 'a surrogacy agreement on official headed paper'.[11]

---

9 These figures were provided by the Registrar's Office to Dr Marilyn Crawshaw, University of York.

10 *JP v LP* [2014] EWHC 595.

11 'Surrogacy Overseas', Foreign and Commonwealth Office, <https://www.gov.uk/government/uploads/system/uploads/attachment_data/file/477720/new_1.pdf> accessed 06.09.2018.

This is made more complicated in the UK by the fact that the Surrogacy Arrangements Act 1985 prohibits individuals from entering into negotiations for a surrogacy arrangement on a commercial basis. Although this provision was primarily intended to prohibit commercial surrogacy agencies and profit-making middlemen, it also applies to legal professionals, as was made clear in the case of *JP v LP*.[12] In this case, the surrogate mother and commissioning parents had attended a pre-birth consultation at the hospital, and on becoming aware that this was a surrogate birth, the hospital asked the parties to enter into, and provide the hospital with a copy of, a surrogacy agreement. The parties thus asked a firm of solicitors to draw up an agreement on their behalf, and the solicitors naturally charged for their time. When the case came before the High Court, the judge pointed out that by drafting this agreement, the solicitors could have been committing an offence under the Act.

We therefore have the odd situation in which parties are being asked to enter into agreements that are not enforceable, and the individuals who draft these agreements must either donate their time free of charge, or breach the criminal law.

2.2. REMUNERATION FOR SURROGACY

One reason for not permitting a surrogacy contract to be enforced was the strong opposition of the Warnock Committee to women being forced by legal sanctions to part with 'their' child – a position that reflects the English position on parenthood (discussed below). A second reason lies in the reluctance of English law to allow child bearing – and child rearing – to enter the commercial sphere, and to come within the scope of contract law. According to this view, surrogacy should be a labour of love, an altruistic offering from one woman to another, rather than a commercial agreement that can be litigated and enforced. This ties in with the issue of payments to surrogate mothers, and the extent to which they can be remunerated for entering into an agreement.

In 1998, the government set up a Committee to consider the issue of commercialisation of surrogacy, and whether surrogate mothers should be permitted to receive payments. The Brazier Committee, as it was known, articulated three principal concerns that arose in relation to payments beyond recompense for genuine expenses incurred, namely: the danger that women will not be giving free and fully formed consent to act as a surrogate; that payments risk commodifying the child to be born as a result of the surrogacy; and that payments contravene social norms in England that, like body parts, intimate services cannot be bought and sold.[13]

---

12 *JP v LP* [2014] EWHC 595.

13 'Surrogacy: Review for Health Ministers of Current Arrangements for Payments and Regulation – Report of the Review Team' (HMSO, London 1998) Cm 4068 ('Brazier Report'), i.

This position is reflected in s. 54(8) of the Human Fertilisation and Embryology Act 2008, which states that in order to be able to make a Parental Order:

> 'The court must be satisfied that no money or other benefit (other than for expenses reasonably incurred) has been given or received by either of the applicants for or in consideration of—
>
> (a) the making of the order,
> (b) any agreement required by subsection (6),
> (c) the handing over of the child to the applicants, or
> (d) the making of arrangements with a view to the making of the order,
>
> unless authorised by the court.'

Having said this, it must be noted that this provision is largely ignored, or at least widely circumvented. Brazier and her colleagues observed that, despite both a formal restriction of payment to expenses only and declarations inimical to commercialisation: 'it is clear that in many cases a component of the amount paid to the surrogate mother is a direct payment for services rendered rather than the reimbursement of actual expenses.'[14]

In deciding whether to authorise payments beyond reasonable expenses, and thus confirm a Parental Order, the courts must consider the child's best interests. While originally this was viewed as being a primary consideration, in 2010 this was elevated to 'the paramount consideration', leaving courts with little choice but to make the Parental Order. In the case of *Re X and Y (Foreign Surrogacy)*, Mr Justice Hedley articulated the difficulty faced by the court in coming to this decision:

> 'I feel bound to observe that I find this process of authorisation most uncomfortable. What the court is required to do is to balance two competing and potentially irreconcilably conflicting concepts. Parliament is clearly entitled to legislate against commercial surrogacy and is clearly entitled to expect that the courts should implement that policy consideration in its decisions. Yet it is also recognised that as the full rigour of that policy consideration will bear on one wholly unequipped to comprehend it let alone deal with its consequences (i.e. the child concerned) that rigour must be mitigated by the application of a consideration of that child's welfare. That approach is both humane and intellectually coherent. The difficulty is that it is almost impossible to imagine a set of circumstances in which by the time the case comes to court, the welfare of any child (particularly a foreign child) would not be gravely compromised (at the very least) by a refusal to make an order.'[15]

As a result, we have seen that courts have routinely authorised payments in excess of reasonable expenses, as to do otherwise would be contrary to the welfare

---

14 Ibid, 43.
15 *Re X and Y (Foreign Surrogacy)* [2008] EWHC 3030 (Fam), [2009] 1 FLR 733, para. 24.

of the child. Despite payments ranging from US$23,000[16] and US$53,000[17] in California, around £3,000 in India,[18] and £8,812 in Russia,[19] no application for a Parental Order has been refused on the grounds of payments contrary to s. 54(8).[20]

Despite this, the courts have been active in trying to define parameters for when payments will be acceptable. In *Re X and Y (Foreign Surrogacy)*, Mr Justice Hedley listed three factors that the court should consider when deciding whether to authorise payments:

1. Was the sum paid disproportionate to reasonable expenses?
2. Were the applicants acting in good faith and without 'moral taint' in their dealings with the surrogate mother?
3. Were the applicants party to any attempt to defraud the authorities?

When determining whether expenses have been 'disproportionate to reasonable expenses', the court will not look to an objective standard based on the level of profit-making or commercial activity, but will instead take a subjective view of what is permitted in the country in which the surrogacy takes place. In *Re C (Parental Order)*,[21] concerning a Russian surrogate birth, the payment was found to be proportionate, notwithstanding the fact that it was an amount equivalent to one to two years' average local wage, on the grounds that it was 'less than the amount reported to be paid to surrogate mothers in St Petersburg, and does not appear unusually high in the context of what is paid in other areas in Russia'.[22]

The same approach has been taken to payments made to surrogacy agencies or middlemen working on a commercial basis. In *Re PM*, despite the commissioning couple paying US$21,000 to the surrogacy agency in California, Mrs Justice Theis noted that 'the level of profit is unlikely, in circumstances such as here where it is in compliance with the legal framework in the country that it is entered into be a reason for refusing to make an order, save in the most exceptional case.'[23]

What we can see is that there is a tacit acceptance on the part of the courts that payments are an ordinary, and inescapable, part of surrogacy arrangements,

---

16 *Re S (Parental Order)* [2009] EWHC 2977 (Fam), [2010] 1 FLR 1156.
17 *J v G* [2013] EWHC 1432 (Fam), [2014] 1 FLR 297.
18 *Re X and Y (Parental Order: Retrospective Authorisation of Payments)* [2012] EWHC 3147 (Fam), [2012] 1 FLR 1347; *Re A and B (Surrogacy: Domicile)* [2013] EWHC 426 (Fam), [2014] 1 FLR 169.
19 *Re C (Parental Order)* [2013] EWHC 2413 (Fam), [2014] 1 FLR 654.
20 There have been refusals for other reasons, for example, lack of domicile within the UK (see *Re G (Surrogacy: Foreign Domicile)* [2007] EWHC 2814 (Fam), [2008] 1 FLR 1047, discussed below).
21 *Re C (Parental Order)* [2013] EWHC 2413 (Fam), [2014] 1 FLR 654.
22 Ibid, at p. 658.
23 *Re PM* [2013] EWHC 2328 (Fam), [2014] 1 FLR 725.

especially with the increase in international surrogacy and medical tourism. As Mrs Justice Theis has said: 'The reality is there is a legal commercial framework which is driven by supply and demand.'[24] As the English experience has shown, an *ex post facto* consideration of the payments, at the time when the only question is who should be recognised as the child's parents, cannot stop that reality.

3. LEGAL PARENTHOOD AT THE TIME OF BIRTH

Under s. 33(1) of the HFEA 2008, '[t]he woman who is carrying or has carried a child as a result of the placing in her of an embryo or of sperm and eggs, and no other woman, is to be treated as the mother of the child'. This applies whether the woman was in the UK or elsewhere at the time of the placing in her of the embryo, or the sperm and eggs. This provision simply reaffirms the application of the general law of motherhood to cases involving assisted reproduction – the woman who gives birth is always the mother.

Fatherhood, on the other hand, is slightly more complicated. If the surrogate mother is married at the time when the sperm or embryo is placed in her, her husband will be the legal father of the child, unless he has not consented to her treatment.[25] This will be the case even if the sperm of the commissioning father has been used in the surrogacy arrangement. If she is not married, then the source of the sperm becomes more important. If the sperm of the commissioning father is being used, he may be treated as the father of the child – as the genetic father at common law. This will be the case if no other man is treated as a father by virtue of the HFEA (e.g. the surrogate's husband or unmarried partner). If donated sperm is used, the sperm donor is explicitly excluded from legal parenthood.[26] Instead, the surrogate mother will be the only legal parent.

There will be no indication on the birth certificate that the child has been born as a result of a surrogacy arrangement, except after the transfer of parenthood, which will be discussed below.

4. ELIGIBILITY FOR SURROGACY

4.1. ELIGIBILITY CRITERIA FOR SURROGATES AND COMMISSIONING PARENTS

In line with the lack of regulation surrounding the legality and enforceability of surrogacy agreements (as opposed to regulating the transfer of parenthood

24 Ibid.
25 HFEA 2008 s. 35.
26 HFEA 2008 s. 41.

post-birth) there are no criteria that restrict the eligibility of women to act as surrogates. Where artificial reproductive techniques have been used within this jurisdiction, however, the legislation places certain restrictions on receiving this type of treatment.

Section 13(5) of the HFEA 1990 (as amended by HFEA 2008) requires that:

> 'A woman shall not be provided with treatment services unless account has been taken of the welfare of any child who may be born as a result of the treatment (including the need of that child for supportive parenting), and of any other child who may be affected by the birth.'

Guidance issued by the Human Fertilisation and Embryology Authority suggests that relevant factors are those that are likely to cause a risk of significant harm or neglect to the child who may be born, or to any existing child of the family, including, inter alia: previous convictions relating to harming children; child protection measures taken regarding existing children; family violence; or conditions that are likely to lead to an inability to care for the child, including mental or physical conditions, drug or alcohol abuse.[27] The guidance also emphasises that it should not only be the commissioning parents who are evaluated according to these criteria, but the surrogate (and her partner, if she has one) as well.[28]

The regulation surrounding commissioning parents is similar to that relating to surrogates. There are no eligibility criteria for the surrogacy arrangement to take place, beyond those imposed in receiving artificial reproductive treatment under the HFEA 1990. However, in order to have their parenthood recognised under English law, commissioning parents must apply for a Parental Order, which transfers parentage from the surrogate (the legal mother) to the commissioning parents.

The full criteria for a Parental Order are discussed in Section 5, but there are two criteria that relate specifically to the commissioning parents, and thus are of relevance to this section also: that the commissioning parents must be married, civil partners, or living together in an 'enduring family relationship' (s. 54(2)); and that they must be domiciled within the UK, Channel Islands, or Isle of Man (s. 54(4)(b)).

Previously, the criteria under s. 54(1) required that an application for a Parental Order be made by 'two people', and as such, single persons who commissioned surrogacy arrangements were not able to gain legal recognition of their parenthood through this mechanism. However, in the case of *Re Z (A Child) (No. 2)*, decided in 2016,[29] the government conceded that this

---

27 'Code of Practice' (Edition 8.0), the Human Fertilisation and Embryology Authority, London, October 2017, 8.10.

28 Ibid, 8.4.

29 *Re Z (A Child) (No. 2)* [2016] EWHC 1191 (Fam).

restriction was discriminatory, in violation of Art. 14 in conjunction with Art. 8 of the European Convention on Human Rights ('ECHR') in so far as it prevents the father from obtaining a Parental Order on the sole ground of his status as a single person, as opposed to being part of a couple. The court issued a declaration of incompatibility under s. 4 of the Human Rights Act 1998. This change has now been incorporated into legislation with the Human Fertilisation and Embryology Act 2008 (Remedial) Order 2018.

With regard to the criteria relating to the domicile of commissioning parents, we have seen that it has been interpreted in a very expansive manner. In the case of *Re A (Foreign Surrogacy: South Africa)*,[30] although the couple had been living abroad for the last nine years, and had no plans to return to the UK for the next 10 to 15 years, they were deemed to have been domiciled for the purposes of s. 54(4)(b) of the HFEA 2008. Having said this, there have been some cases where the court simply has not been able to stretch the facts to fit within the statutory criteria. In *Re G (Surrogacy: Foreign Domicile)*,[31] a Turkish couple came to England to enter into a surrogacy arrangement, as such procedures are not permitted in Turkey. When they applied for a Parental Order, the court found that this could not be granted, as the requirement for domicile was expressed in mandatory terms, and could not be departed from. Nevertheless, the court found another mechanism to transfer legal parenthood to the commissioning parents, using s. 84 of the Adoption and Children Act 2002 to enable the intended parents to return to Turkey with the child with a view to initiating adoption proceedings.

4.2. THE DONATION AND USE OF GAMETES IN SURROGACY

There is no restriction on whose gametes can be used in the surrogacy. In particular, there are no rules on whether the surrogacy can be traditional or gestational. However, in order for a Parental Order to be granted, there must be a genetic relationship between the commissioning parent(s) and the child (s. 54(1)(b) of the HFEA 2008).

Sperm and egg donation, as well as embryo donation, are permitted in England and Wales. Payment of donors is prohibited, although a sperm donor may receive compensation of up to £35 per clinic visit, and an egg donor may receive compensation of up to £750 per cycle of donation, to cover financial losses in connection with the donation.[32] Donors can also make a claim for additional expenses to cover travel, accommodation and childcare.[33]

---

30 *Re A (Foreign Surrogacy: South Africa)* [2015] EWHC 1756 (Fam).

31 *Re G (Surrogacy: Foreign Domicile)* [2008] 1 FLR 1047.

32 'Code of Practice' (Edition 8.0), the Human Fertilisation and Embryology Authority, London, October 2017, 13A.

33 Ibid.

Donor-conceived children who were conceived on or after 1 April 2005 are able to receive non-identifying information on the donor once they reach 16, and identifying information (including last-known address) at 18.[34]

5. TRANSFERRING PARENTHOOD

5.1. THE LEGAL PROCESS

The primary way in which surrogacy is regulated in England and Wales is through the criteria for the transfer of parenthood. As stated above, the surrogate will always be recognised as the child's parent at birth, and in order to gain legal recognition of their parenthood, commissioning parents must apply to the courts for a Parental Order under s. 54 of the HFEA 2008.

The key requirements of s. 54 are as follows:

- There must be two commissioning parents (s. 54(1))[35]
- there must be a genetic relationship between the commissioning parents and the child (s. 54(1))
- the commissioning parents must be either married, civil partners, or in an enduring family relationship (s. 54(2))
- the application must be made within six months of the child's birth (s. 54(3))
- the child must already be living with the commissioning parents (s. 54(4)(a))
- the commissioning parents must be domiciled in the UK (s. 54(4)(b))
- the commissioning parents must both be over 18 (s. 54(5))
- both the surrogate mother, and any other man or woman recognised as a legal parent, must have freely, unconditionally, and with full understanding, consented to the making of the order (s. 54(6)) – unless such parent cannot be found or is incapable of giving consent (s. 54(7))
- the consent of the surrogate mother must be given more than six weeks after birth (s. 54(7))
- unless authorised by the court, no money other than 'expenses reasonably incurred' can be given in relation to making the surrogacy arrangement, handing over the child, or consenting to the order (s. 54(8)).

The new s. 54A, inserted by the Human Fertilisation and Embryology Act 2008 (Remedial) Order 2018, which covers Parental Orders for single applicants, contains equivalent provisions.

---

34 HFEA, <https://www.hfea.gov.uk/donation/donors/rules-around-releasing-donor-information/> accessed 06.09.2018.

35 Though on this point see above Section 4.

In theory, the court must be satisfied that all these conditions have been met before it can make a Parental Order. However, in practice, we have seen that the courts have been willing to liberally interpret these criteria, as the overriding consideration must be the best interests of the child, whose welfare would be harmed if the order is not made.

This was discussed in Section 2 in relation to commercial surrogacy, and payments in excess of reasonable expenses under s. 54(8). In addition, Section 4 highlighted the expansive definition of 'domicile' under s. 54(4)(b).

Another area in which the court has been active in judicially reinterpreting the statutory criteria is in relation to s. 54(3), which requires that an application for a Parental Order be made within six months of the child's birth. Initially, the courts interpreted this very strictly, with Mr Justice Hedley in *Re X and Y (Foreign Surrogacy)* describing the time limit as 'non-extendable'.[36] However, in the case of *Re X (A Child) (Surrogacy: Time Limit)*,[37] the President of the Family Division, Sir James Munby, held that the courts had the power to grant a Parental Order after the six-month time limit. Moreover, they had a duty to exercise this power in the interests of the child's welfare.

He held that:

> 'Given the subject matter, given the consequences for the commissioning parents, never mind those for the child, to construe section 54(3) as barring forever an application made just one day late is not, in my judgment, sensible. It is the very antithesis of sensible; it is almost nonsensical.'[38]

He emphasised that a Parental Order goes not just to the legal status of the child, but to their very identity as a human being, and that the impact of the decision to grant or refuse an order will extend decades into the future. As such, he granted an application for a Parental Order made over two years after the child's birth – thus well outside the six-month limit. Subsequent cases have followed this precedent, including a case where a Parental Order was made in relation to a child aged 13.[39]

We can see from the discussion in Sections 4 and 5 that the courts have been generous in their interpretation of the statutory requirements for surrogacy. But we must also accept that they have had little choice in the matter. Where they are presented with a child who is living with the commissioning parents, who will be his or her parents for all intents and purposes, there is little, if any, scope for the courts to refuse an order. The imperative to make the child's best interests the paramount consideration prevents them from doing anything but making

---

36 *Re X and Y (Foreign Surrogacy)* [2008] EWHC 3030 (Fam), [2009] 1 FLR 733.

37 *Re X (A Child) (Surrogacy: Time Limit)* [2014] EWHC 3135 (Fam).

38 Ibid, para. 55.

39 *A v C* [2016] EWFC 4.

an order that reflects their current status. It is for this reason that England and Wales is described as taking a 'tolerant' approach to surrogacy. While it sets out strict requirements for the transfer of parenthood, in reality, many of them can be circumvented or expansively interpreted to achieve the desired aim.

5.2. ADJUDICATING DISPUTES BETWEEN COMMISSIONING PARENTS AND SURROGATES

In order for the court to make a Parental Order, both the surrogate mother, and any other legal parent, must have consented to the order 'freely, unconditionally, and with full understanding' (s. 54(6)). This consent cannot be dispensed with, even if it were in the best interests of the child.

However, there is an exception where the parent cannot be found or is incapable of giving consent (s. 54(7)), and this has been used quite liberally. One example of this can be seen in the case of *Re D and L (Minors) (Surrogacy)*.[40] This case involved a surrogacy arrangement that had taken place in India, but where the consent given by the surrogate mother was invalid, as it had been given within six weeks of the child's birth. The commissioning parents, after having returned to England with the surrogate children, sought to obtain additional consent after this time period, but were unable to do so. The inquiry agent they hired was unable to locate the surrogate, as the address that they had been given by the surrogacy clinic was the residence of the agent, rather than the mother, and the clinic itself, when asked for its assistance, replied with a single piece of paper printed with an 'obscene gesture'. As a result, the court admitted that all the documents and evidence provided by the clinic had to be treated with caution. Nevertheless, Mr Justice Baker was willing to make the Parental Order under s. 54, and dispense with the mother's consent under s. 54(7), on the grounds that the she could not be found. Importantly, when considering how to apply the exception to parental consent, Mr Justice Baker suggested that although the consent of the surrogate given before the expiry of the six-week period was not valid for the purposes of s. 54(7), he was entitled to take into account evidence that the consent *had* been given at this earlier time. This is a curious conclusion, as it is difficult to see how the earlier consent of the surrogate has any bearing on whether or not the court should rule that the mother cannot be found. It may, however, be relevant as to whether or not it is in the best interests of the child for the Parental Order to be made, as it may indicate that the surrogate no longer believes, or intends, that she has legal ties to the child.

The result of this case, and others like it, is to allow foreign agencies the possibility of circumventing rules concerning consent by ensuring that the

---

40 *Re D and L (Minors) (Surrogacy)* [2012] EWHC 2631 (Fam).

surrogates cannot be located after the birth of the child. This is achieved by maintaining strict separation between the commissioning parents and surrogate, and giving false names and addresses on official forms. This was seen in the case of *Re D (A Child)*,[41] where the court was trying to locate a surrogate in Georgia, to establish whether she had been married or not at the time of birth. When an international detective arrived at the address given by the surrogacy agency, three women living there claimed to answer to the name given on the documents, yet none of them admitted to bearing the child. As a result, the court was forced to cease its enquiries.

Having said this, these cases in all likelihood reflect a problem with the surrogate's consent as a matter of procedure, rather than there being a substantive issue of the surrogate wanting to keep the child.[42] Where the surrogate does want to retain her parenthood of the child, and does not consent to the making of a Parental Order, then it is not possible to dispense with her consent. Instead, ordinary private law rules apply in relation to parenthood, and the custody of the child.

This was seen in the case of *Re P (Surrogacy: Residence)*,[43] which was a domestic UK case that involved rather unusual facts. The surrogate in this case already had three children, and wanted more, but was inhibited by the fact that her husband had had a vasectomy. Following an incident in which the mother falsely laid claim to an abandoned child, her husband tried unsuccessfully to have the vasectomy reversed, and when this was not successful, the couple sought fertility treatment by donor insemination, but were considered unsuitable. The woman then registered with a surrogacy agency, and was soon matched with a commissioning couple. She became pregnant, but although the pregnancy progressed smoothly, she informed the biological father and his wife that she had miscarried, and raised the child as her own. A few years later, she re-registered with the agency, and once again was matched with a commissioning couple. Again she falsely claimed that she had had a miscarriage, but the agency discovered the truth, and upon the child's birth, the biological father issued proceedings to gain custody of the child, with a view to adoption. The court found that the case should be viewed simply as a dispute between two biological parents and their respective spouses, and as such, the question before the court was in which home the child was more likely to mature into a happy and balanced adult, and achieve their fullest potential as a human being. Mr Justice Coleridge stressed that the mother's deceptive conduct in relation to the surrogacy was only relevant to the issue of whether she was suitable for the parental role – she should not be penalised for breaking the agreement, as such

---

41 *Re D (A Child)* [2014] EWHC 2121 (Fam).

42 Although it should be noted that such procedures are important to ensure that the surrogate mother has a chance to consent or object should she wish.

43 *Re P (Surrogacy: Residence)* [2008] 1 FLR 177.

agreements are not enforceable under English law, and a legal mother (as the birth mother will always be) has every right to decide to keep the child should she so wish. However, the court ultimately ruled in favour of the child living with the commissioning parents, as they would provide the most beneficial environment for the child.

In this way, while surrogacy agreements are unenforceable, and a Parental Order cannot be made without the surrogate's consent, the courts have been willing to use other mechanisms to transfer the care of the child from the surrogate to the commissioning parents, even if it cannot transfer legal parenthood, if this is in his or her best interests.

5.3. THE PRESERVATION OF INFORMATION ON ORIGINS

As the surrogate will be the legal mother at birth, she will be listed on the child's birth certificate. If and when a Parental Order is granted, the child's birth will be re-registered, and a fresh entry will be made on a special register held at the General Register Office, showing the commissioning parents as the child's legal parents. This new entry will supersede the original entry, which will be annotated to reflect this. Once the child reaches 18, he or she will be able to access the original birth certificate, and thus will be able to find out the name of the surrogate.

5.4. THE IMPACT OF THE RIGHTS OF CHILDREN

As has been seen in the discussion above, the rights of children are the cornerstone of the regulation of surrogacy in England and Wales. When deciding to make a Parental Order, courts are required to give paramount consideration to the welfare of the child.[44] As Mr Justice Hedley said in *Re L (Commercial Surrogacy)*:

> 'The effect of that must be to weight the balance between public policy considerations and welfare ... decisively in favour of welfare. It must follow that it will only be in the clearest case of the abuse of public policy that the court will be able to withhold an order if otherwise welfare considerations supports its making.'[45]

While it was only in 2010 that this requirement was put into legislative form, it has been a feature of judicial decision-making since the very first cases of

---

[44] Human Fertilisation and Embryology (Parental Orders) (Consequential, Transitional and Saving Provision) Order 2010.

[45] *Re L (Commercial Surrogacy)* [2010] EWHC 3146 (Fam), [2011] 1 FLR 1423, 1425.

surrogacy in this country. In 1985, when deciding the case of *Re C (A Minor) (Wardship: Surrogacy)*, the judge stated:

> 'Plainly, the methods used to produce a child as this baby has been, and the commercial aspects of it, raise difficult and delicate problems of ethics, morality and social desirability ... In my judgment they are not relevant. The baby is here. All that matters is what is best for her now that she is here and not how she arrived.'[46]

The priority given to the child's best interests by the courts has been buttressed by references to the UN Convention on the Rights of the Child (UNCRC), and the European Convention on Human Rights. In the case of *A v P (Surrogacy: Parental Order: Death of Applicant)*[47] the court was asked to grant a Parental Order to the surviving spouse of a couple who had commissioned a surrogate to bear their child. Her husband had died after the child had been born, but before the couple had been granted a Parental Order. Section 54(4)(a) requires not only that there be two applicants at the time of the application, but also at the time at which the order is made, leaving the commissioning mother on tenuous legal ground.[48] In deciding whether to grant the Parental Order, Mrs Justice Theis emphasised that the requirements under s. 54 must be interpreted in a manner consistent with the child's best interests. She relied on Art. 8 of the UNCRC, and the obligation on the State to protect the child's right to identity. She also highlighted the implications of the Parental Order on the child's right to respect for private and family life under Art. 8 of the ECHR, and the fact that the effect of not making an order would mean that the factual relationship between the child and both his parents would not be recognised by law. Mrs Justice Theis held that the court must consider itself bound to take a purposive construction of s. 54(4) to ensure the child's identity, and to preserve the link between the child and both his parents.

As such, we have seen the child's best interests dominate decision-making in this area of law, with courts interpreting the law as widely as possible to ensure that a Parental Order is made to reflect the reality of the child's lived experiences.

6. AGENCIES AND CRIMINALISATION

Section 2 of the Surrogacy Arrangements Act 1985 provides that 'no person shall on a commercial basis do any of the following acts in the UK: (a) initiate any negotiations with a view to the making of a surrogacy arrangement; (aa) take

---

[46] *Re C (A Minor) (Wardship: Surrogacy)* [1985] FLR 846, 847–48.

[47] *A v P (Surrogacy: Parental Order: Death of Applicant)* [2011] EWHC 1738.

[48] She was also not herself genetically connected to the child, as is required under s. 54(1).

part in any negotiations with a view to the making of a surrogacy arrangement; (b) offer or agree to negotiate the making of a surrogacy arrangement, or (c) compile any information with a view to its use in making, or negotiating the making of, surrogacy arrangements'; and no person shall in the UK knowingly cause another to do any of those acts on a commercial basis. The Act excludes surrogate mothers and commissioning parents from the ambit of this provision, although surrogates may be caught in the prohibition of advertisement (s. 3), which applies to any person who indicates that they are, or may be, willing to enter into a surrogacy arrangement, or to negotiate or facilitate such an arrangement. An offence under either of these sections is liable to a fine not exceeding £5,000, but an offence under s. 2 carries with it also the possibility of imprisonment not exceeding three months.

This is a very comprehensive provision, and has caused difficulties for commissioning parents and surrogate mothers in seeking professional assistance when undertaking surrogacy arrangements. This was highlighted in the case of *Re G (Surrogacy: Foreign Domicile)*,[49] where the couple in question had brought about a surrogacy arrangement with the assistance of the organisation COTS (Childlessness Overcome Through Surrogacy). As discussed above, the court held that a Parental Order could not be granted, as the commissioning parents were Turkish, and not domiciled in the UK as is required by the legislation. Mr Justice MacFarlane emphasised that the agency's lack of knowledge of 'one of the basic requirements needed to obtain a Parental Order is a matter of some real concern'. However, he acknowledged that it was the legislation itself that gave such agencies no alternative. He stated:

> 'The court's understanding is that surrogacy agencies such as COTS are not covered by any statutory or regulatory umbrella and are, therefore, not required to perform to any recognised standard of competence. I am sufficiently concerned by the information uncovered in these two cases to question whether some form of inspection or authorisation should be required in order to improve the quality of advice that is given to individuals who seek to achieve the birth of a child through surrogacy. Given the importance of the issues involved when the life of a child is created in this manner, it is questionable whether the role of facilitating surrogacy arrangements should be left to groups of well-meaning amateurs.'[50]

Subsequently, the Human Fertilisation and Embryology Act 2008 amended these provisions, allowing non-profit agencies to receive 'reasonable payment' for work relating to initiating negotiations with a view to making a surrogacy arrangement – for example, making introductions. Nevertheless, this stopped short of providing a system of regulatory oversight, as was proposed by

---

49 *Re G (Surrogacy: Foreign Domicile)* [2008] 1 FLR 1047.

50 Ibid, para. 29.

the Brazier Report in 1998, and there is still no mechanism for registering, inspecting or controlling their activities.

7. INTERNATIONAL SURROGACY ARRANGEMENTS

International surrogacy arrangements that take place outside the UK are treated in exactly the same way as those that take place within the jurisdiction. When determining parenthood, English law always applies, no matter where in the world the child was conceived or born. As such, even where the foreign birth certificate names the commissioning parents as the child's parents, English law will still consider the surrogate (and her husband if she has one) as the legal parents of the child until a Parental Order is made.

This has caused significant difficulties, for example in the case of *Re X and Y (Foreign Surrogacy)*, discussed above. In this case, a British couple had travelled to Ukraine to enter into a surrogacy arrangement. When the Ukrainian surrogate gave birth to twins, they went to the British embassy to seek passports for the children to return to the UK. The British embassy informed the couple that under English law, the surrogate and her husband were the children's legal parents, and therefore the children had no connection to the UK, and could not obtain British passports. They recommended seeking assistance from the Ukrainian authorities. However, the Ukrainian authorities informed the commissioning parents that, according to Ukrainian law, they were the legal parents listed on the birth certificate, and therefore the children could not obtain Ukrainian passports either. As a result, the children were left stateless, and were only able to leave Ukraine when the British authorities allowed them to enter outside the Immigration Rules.

When determining whether a child born through surrogacy can enter the UK, the applicable rules will depend on the marital status of the surrogate, and to whom the child has a biological connection. Where the surrogate mother is unmarried, and the commissioning father has a genetic connection to the child, as long as he is identified on the birth certificate, he will be able to pass on his British citizenship to his child, who will then be able to enter the country freely. On the other hand, where the surrogate is married, or where the commissioning father has no genetic connection with the child (but the commissioning mother does), he will not be considered the father, as the fatherhood of the surrogate's husband is not rebuttable in cases of artificial reproduction.[51] In order to return to the UK, the surrogate mother and her husband will have to give up their parental responsibility for the child, and the commissioning parents will have to apply for entry clearance to bring the child to the UK outside the Immigration

[51] British Nationality Act 1981 s. 50(9).

Rules. Entry outside the rules is at the discretion of the Secretary of State, and will only be granted on the condition that a Parental Order is applied for within six months of birth, and where evidence suggests that such an order is likely to be granted.[52] Where there is no genetic connection between the child and either of the commissioning parents, then this route cannot be utilised, as a Parental Order requires a genetic connection (s. 54(1)). As such, the case would be treated as an intercountry adoption, and those legal rules applied.

When the child returns to the UK, if he or she has not already obtained British citizenship at birth, the child will be granted citizenship upon the making of a Parental Order.

8. CONCLUSION

There is widespread consensus amongst practitioners, academics, and even the judiciary, that the current law surrounding surrogacy in England and Wales is deeply unsatisfactory. While there is a clear legislative framework under the Surrogacy Arrangements Act 1985 and the HFEA 2008, the system of *ex post facto* scrutiny of surrogacy arrangements has proved unworkable in practice. As Mr Justice Hedley has pointed out, the courts are required to balance two potentially competing interests: the statutory requirements for transferring parenthood, and the best interests of the child. However, by the time the case comes before the court, the child will already have been living with the commissioning parents for some time, and the child's welfare would be gravely compromised if the court does not make the order to reflect this lived reality. As such, judges are being forced to be creative with their interpretation of the statutory requirements to ensure that the rights of the child are adequately protected.

This is made even more difficult in light of the global surrogacy market. In the case of *Re D (A Child)*, Mr Justice Moylan opened his judgment with this strong statement:

> 'This case provides a clear example of the difficulties created as a result of surrogacy arrangements being subject to varying degrees of domestic regulation, from significant regulation to none at all, and also because of the existence of significant differences in the effect of such domestic regulation. There is, in my view, a compelling need for a uniform system of regulation to be created by an international instrument in order to make available an appropriate structure in respect of what can only be described as the surrogacy market.'[53]

---

52 The UK Border Agency, 'Inter-Country Surrogacy and the Immigration Rules', <https://www.gov.uk/government/uploads/system/uploads/attachment_data/file/261435/Intercountry-surrogacy-leaflet.pdf>, accessed 06.09.2018.

53 *Re D (A Child)* [2014] EWHC 2121, para. 1.

Absent the prospect of international regulation anytime in the near future, however, we must make do with domestic reform. In 2018, the Law Commission of England and Wales announced that it would review the laws surrounding surrogacy. It is hoped that this will be the beginning of a re-evaluation of the way that we regulate surrogacy in this jurisdiction, and a move towards a system that not only provides strong principles, but is able to be enforced in practice.

THE LEGAL IMPLICATIONS OF INTERNATIONAL SURROGACY AGREEMENTS

A View from the Bench in England and Wales

Sir Mark HEDLEY

Any rational consideration of surrogacy is bound to be inadequate. The desire to parent has a deep emotional, not to say emotive, component and lawyers and legislators ignore that at their peril. Rationality, however, remains necessary, for the closing words of the Book of Judges in the Hebrew Scriptures – 'In those days Israel had no King and every man did what was right in his own eyes'[1] – describe not utopia but anarchy. What is required is a judicious blend of rationality and human empathy.

This becomes the more so where the subject matter of our consideration is both complex and morally controversial as well as emotive. It means that every judgment is value-laden and not only may those values be controversial, there will be more than one value system in play at any one time. So we will have to take into account the values of the society in which we are engaged as well as the values of the particular parties involved. Moreover, we have to recognise that in any value-laden discretionary decision, account must also be taken of the values of the individual trial judge. I suspect that, even amongst the small group of judges in England and Wales who do this work, there will be a wide range of personal values. Were you to read any judgment of mine, you may or may not be able to detect my own value system but it will nevertheless have played a part in any discretionary decision. It will be clear then that these different value systems may not all pull in the same direction. It should not therefore surprise us if we encounter difficulties in this area of law.

The usual (but not the only) expression of surrogacy is the fertilisation of a donated egg, using the sperm of a commissioning parent, which is then

1 Judges 21:25 (KJV).

implanted in the surrogate who gives birth in due course. The requirement in English law is provided as follows:

> '... (a) the child has been carried by a woman who is not one of the applicants as a result of the placing in her of an embryo or sperm and eggs or her artificial insemination,
>
> (b) the gametes of at least one of the applicants were used to bring about the creation of the embryo ...'[2]

Anecdotally it appears that commissioning couples have usually already explored other routes to parenthood with no success though for some, especially same-sex male couples, this may well be the first and only route as an alternative to adoption. Surrogacy has a 'natural' component to it which adoption generally lacks and which many would-be parents regard as important.

There is no common view on surrogacy in our world. Some societies ban it altogether whereas others not only allow it but allow its exploitation for commercial gain. There is no common view in the West where Germany, Italy and France simply do not allow it whilst other countries take other views. It is likely to be controversial within countries, across religions and probably in any social context. Thus legislation relating to surrogacy, even where it exists, is likely to be specific to that jurisdiction.

The first formal legislation in England and Wales came in 1985[3] and has since been supplemented by the Human Fertilisation and Embryology Act 2008 ('HFEA 2008') which in itself replaced a similarly named Act of 1990. It represents a compromise. It permits and regulates surrogacy but only on an altruistic basis in that it prohibits payments beyond 'reasonable expenses'.[4] Whilst it permits surrogacy agreements, it treats them as unenforceable. It provides that the surrogate mother is to be treated as the mother for all purposes and the surrogate's husband (but only a husband) is treated as the father for all purposes unless he did not know of or consent to the surrogacy.[5] The combined effect of legislation and judicial decision is that these provisions have extra-territorial effect.[6] What the Act does provide by s. 54 is the right for commissioning parents to apply for a Parental Order which has much the same effect as an adoption order in that it confers legal parenthood exclusively on the applicants and requires in effect that the child be treated as though born of those applicants. A Parental Order is as difficult to set aside as

---

2 Human Fertilisation and Embryology Act 2008 s. 54(1).

3 The Surrogacy Arrangements Act 1985.

4 HFEA 2008 s. 54(8).

5 Ibid ss. 33 and 35.

6 Sections 33(3) and 35(1) of the HFEA 2008 and *Re X & Y (Foreign Surrogacy)* [2008] EWHC 3030 (Fam).

an adoption order for both are recognised as according status and not merely being arrangements for the care and upbringing of the child.[7]

Surrogacy is used in England and Wales but tends usually to be confined to private arrangements between those already known to each other, or linked through specialist groups or publications no doubt because of its altruistic requirement. There was then a move amongst interested couples in the United Kingdom (UK) to explore surrogacy abroad where it was not only legal and regulated but where payment was allowed and thus it was easier to find a surrogate who was a stranger. Our subsequent judicial experience, in ways that I shall describe, demonstrated that the whole process was very much more difficult and complicated than any involved in it had expected to find. Moreover, we found that many applicants, despite their going to properly recognised agencies, were receiving advice that was seriously inadequate and sometimes plain wrong. As was observed in one of the cases, 'the path to parenthood has been less a journey along a primrose path and more a trek through a thorn forest.'[8]

These cases first came before the courts of England and Wales in 2008. The then President of the Family Division, Sir Mark Potter, in an effort to provide some uniformity of approach, directed that initially all these cases should be listed before me. Accordingly it became my responsibility to furnish a system under legislation drafted by those who may not actually have foreseen in 1990 the concept of overseas commercial surrogacy arrangements. One of the strange features is that, so far as I know, not a single one of these cases has come before an appellate court. The development of this area of the law in England and Wales has been undertaken by trial judges on a case-by-case basis with the support of the President.

Since that is the way it has happened, it is probably best to look at three of the earlier cases (inevitably decisions of mine) in order to understand the issues and difficulties that arose. These cases provide some stark examples of conflict of laws points not least because of the absence of any semblance of international agreement over surrogacy.

The first case, *Re X and Y (Foreign Surrogacy)*,[9] involved a professional couple who turned to surrogacy as a last resort in their quest to become parents. They received poor advice from those from whom they were entitled to expect better and went to the Ukraine where commercial surrogacy was legal and enforceable. The provision of regulated health care in Ukraine was good in respect of surrogacy and the couple complied scrupulously (as did the surrogate and her husband) with all the requirements of Ukrainian law and in due course the couple received twins of whom the male member of the couple was the biological father. It was at this point that unanticipated difficulties first emerged.

---

7 *G v G* (Parental Order: Revocation) [2012] EWHC 1979 (Fam).
8 *Re X & Y (Foreign Surrogacy)* [2008] EWHC 3030 (Fam), para. 2.
9 Ibid.

Under Ukrainian law the surrogates lost all parental rights and duties when the children were handed to the commissioning couple who then acquired all such rights and duties. Accordingly under Ukrainian law the children were the children of the commissioning couple and took their nationality. The position in English law was quite different. English law would not recognise the Ukrainian position because it had been achieved by means (i.e. payment other than for 'reasonable expenses') which in England and Wales would have been unlawful. In English law the surrogate and her husband (for they were married) were the parents of the children 'for all purposes'. Accordingly the children had no right of entry to the UK. They were in international terms both legal orphans and stateless – not a great way to start your life.

In the end the couple got limited permission to enter 'outside the Rules' for the purposes of allowing them to apply for a Parental Order which they did, in the event successfully. There were, however, two further difficulties in their way: the question of the payment made to the surrogate and the basis on which an order would be made since, upon compliance with the statutory conditions, a court 'may' (not 'must') make an order.[10] It was accepted both that the court had power retrospectively to authorise the payments and that the court had to consider the 'welfare' of the children. Those matters tended to pull in different directions and the real issue was the weight to be given to the welfare of the child. The court expressed it thus:

> '[24] I feel bound to observe that I find this process of authorisation most uncomfortable. What the court is required to do is to balance two competing and potentially irreconcilably conflicting concepts. Parliament is clearly entitled to legislate against commercial surrogacy and is clearly entitled to expect that the court should implement that policy consideration in its decisions. Yet it is also recognised that as the full rigour of that policy consideration will bear on one wholly unequipped to comprehend it let alone deal with its consequences (i.e. the child concerned) that rigour must be mitigated by the application of a consideration of that child's welfare. That approach is both humane and intellectually coherent. The difficulty is that it is almost impossible to imagine a set of circumstances in which by the time the case comes to the court, the welfare of any child (particularly a foreign child) would not be gravely compromised (at the very least) by a refusal to make an order. … If public policy is truly to be upheld, it would need to be enforced at a much earlier stage than the final hearing of [an] application. In relation to adoption this has been substantially addressed by rules surrounding the bringing of the child into the country and by the provisions of the Adoption with a Foreign Element Regulations 2005. The point of admission to this country is in some ways the final opportunity in reality to prevent the effective implementation of a commercial surrogacy agreement. It is, of course,

10 HFEA 2008 s. 54(1).

not for the court to suggest how (or even whether) action should be taken, I merely feel constrained to point out the problem.'[11]

In a second case, *Re S (Parental Order)*,[12] involving a surrogacy agreement in California, similar problems arose. In the United States (US) jurisdictions there is provision for pre-birth orders which in those jurisdictions settle the question of parenthood (and thus also of nationality) before birth. However, they raise in England and Wales all the same issues as in the previous case. On this occasion the court offered a test as to what would be considered when the question of retrospective authorisation of payments arose. Three principles were suggested in an attempt to address the potential conflict between public policy and welfare:

> '(1) To ensure that commercial surrogacy agreements are not used to circumvent childcare laws in this country, so as to result in the approval of arrangements in favour of people who would not have been approved as parents under any set of existing arrangements in this country.
> (2) The court should be astute not to be involved in anything that looks like the simple payment for effectively buying children overseas. That has been ruled out in this country and the court should not be party to any arrangements which effectively allow that.
> (3) The court should be astute to ensure that sums of money which might look modest in themselves are not in fact of such a substance that they overbear the will of the surrogate.'[13]

Parliament did have the opportunity to reconsider this legislation when debating HFEA 2008. In the end only two changes were made. The first widened the scope of potential applicants by including unmarried and same-sex couples; the second adopted the approach suggested by the court in the first case above by importing the concept of welfare in adoption, giving welfare a 'lifelong' perspective. In fact they went further by making the child's welfare the court's paramount consideration.[14]

That brings us to the third case: *Re L (Commercial Surrogacy)*.[15] This too involved a state in the US. All the same problems were raised. However, in this case, welfare now had to be regarded as the 'paramount' consideration. That led to this expression of view:

> 'The effect of that [legislative change] must be to weight the balance between public policy considerations and welfare (as considered in *Re X and Y* (*supra*)) decisively in

---

11 *Re X & Y (Foreign Surrogacy)* [2008] EWHC 3030 (Fam) para. 24.
12 *Re S (Parental Order)* [2009] EWHC 2977 (Fam).
13 Ibid at para. 7.
14 Human Fertilisation and Embryology (Parental Orders) (Consequential, Transitional and Savings Provision) Order 2010.
15 *Re L (Commercial Surrogacy)* [2010] EWHC 3146 (Fam).

> favour of welfare. It must follow that it will only be in the clearest case of the abuse of public policy that the court will be able to withhold an order if otherwise welfare considerations support its making. It underlines the court's earlier observation that, if it is desired to control commercial surrogacy arrangements, those controls need to operate before the court process is initiated, i.e. at the border or even before.'[16]

The effect was to emasculate any attempt to honour the public policy provisions that underpinned the English concept of legal surrogacy. Bluntly, the effect was that if you were sufficiently determined and sufficiently wealthy you could simply circumvent the domestic restrictions on surrogacy by relying on the welfare needs of the child. It also meant that welfare played a double role in the decision making: in the discretionary act of the authorisation of payment and also in the decision as to whether to grant an order upon fulfilment of the statutory conditions which was, of course, its proper role.

I have concentrated on these three cases since I had to decide them – a wonderful stimulus to careful thought! There have been of course many others. Some have raised questions already considered but others have dealt with issues foreseen but not then requiring decision. For example, the statute[17] imposes a time limit of six months after birth for the making of an application and appears to confer no power to extend that limit. Given the sort of difficulties being discussed above, that was eventually going to have to be confronted. It is a very serious matter not to be able to apply for a Parental Order as will be apparent from our discussion so far. It took a titanic feat of reasoning by the current President Sir James Munby[18] to conclude that Parliament could not really have meant that and to find that the court had power to extend. In at least one other case[19] the judge had to have recourse to the concepts of human rights so as to construe a provision so that it was compliant with Convention Rights; indeed he went so far as to issue a Declaration of Incompatibility, which the government duly accepted.[20]

If you have formed the impression that this sort of complex (and of course necessarily expensive) reasoning is not the ideal approach to an issue which engages with some of our deepest human feelings, I am not going to disagree with you. Surely it need not be that complicated. The difficulty, however, arises out of there being no internationally agreed approach to surrogacy and thus the inevitable conflicts of private international law generated by a combination of the right of individual states to legislate as they think best on a morally

---

16 Ibid at para. 10.

17 HFEA 2008 s. 54(3).

18 *Re X (a child) (Surrogacy: Time Limit)* [2014] EWHC 3135 (Fam).

19 *A v P (Surrogacy: Parental Order: Death of Applicant)* [2011] EWHC 1738 (Fam).

20 Convention on the Rights of the Child (United Nations General Assembly resolution 44/25 of 20 November 1989).

controversial and complex issue and passionate human feelings which can find readier expression in an age of comparatively easy international travel.

We have perhaps encountered again what every practitioner in personal law will have discovered one way or the other: we know what we can do so much better than we know what we ought to do. In other words our technical skills have outstripped our ethical skills in modern society. Medically surrogacy is now a fairly straightforward and safe process but the conception of the child that is not the child of both parents, and the means by which that is achieved, remain ethically controversial across the world.

Some states have dealt with this by simply outlawing surrogacy but that does not solve the problem of dealing with children so born overseas but returning to the commissioning couple's country of origin. The judges in Germany have wrestled with this issue and have concluded that the best interests of the child must take precedence, and have recognised legal parenthood. Others have acknowledged the fact of surrogacy and have responded by allowing but regulating it. That is the approach of a number of American states and of the Ukraine, for example. Many, like the UK, have sought a third way. Such variations will inevitably spawn the sort of issues that I have been trying to describe.

Another issue arises from the variety of countries involved which can pose a further problem for the domestic judge. Perhaps I may illustrate by comparing and contrasting California and India simply because I have dealt with cases from both. I do not think that the UK is alone in insisting on an altruistic regime in which the only money that may change hands is in relation to 'reasonable expenses'. That inevitably means considering the authorisation of sums when the child has been born in a foreign surrogacy. I have tried to demonstrate the principles that the courts of England and Wales have adopted over that.

However, one cannot simply do it by arithmetic. My impression is that a lawful surrogate birth in California will involve an outlay of about US$200,000 when all procedures legal and medical are taken into account. Of that the surrogate mother seems to receive a 'compensation' payment (over and above expenses) of some US$25,000; that is not probably far off 75 per cent of the average American annual wage. In India the sums are much smaller and the 'compensation' payment seems more like the equivalent of US$1,500–US$2,000. However, that represents considerably more than the annual salary of a clerk in India. Thus much smaller sums have a much greater potential to overbear the free choice of the surrogate. Now India seems well regulated (even though that is done privately by the medical profession) and, in my experience, insists that one of the commissioning couple have Indian ethnicity. Since those cases India has now banned overseas commercial surrogacy agreements. What happens, as surely it must, when surrogacy is explored in Third World countries? It seems to me that this judicial gatekeeper role will become very much more difficult.

That may be even more so in an area that already threatens difficulty: parental consent. At present the consent of the surrogate (and where relevant her husband) are usually well evidenced at or before birth. However, English law (following our adoption law) requires consent not earlier than six weeks after the birth.[21] Even in a legally sophisticated regime this can produce difficulties; in other circumstances it may be very difficult to produce adequate evidence. In accordance with the English principle of non-enforceability of a surrogacy agreement, the court has no power to dispense with consent save in two circumstances: first, where the mother cannot be found; and secondly where she lacks the mental capacity to consent.[22] Otherwise the applicants must prove the required consent on the balance of probability. This issue has recently been addressed in England and Wales[23] and, whilst consent was dispensed with on the grounds that the surrogate could not be found, it was made clear that this would only be after full enquiry with all its attendant anxiety and expense. If this decision does nothing else, it reminds potential commissioning parents that this may be a long, uncertain and expensive exercise. It also appears that not only are potential parents still not necessarily receiving good advice from those whom they are entitled to rely on, but also not doing sufficient research of their own so that they are forewarned and thus forearmed.

I hope that this description of experience from the Bench of England and Wales resonates in other jurisdictions. I would be surprised were it not to do so. It raises two fundamental issues for the judiciary: first, the essential law is a matter of political judgment to be made by the domestic legislature; and secondly, legal rationality will have to take account of the profound feelings engendered by the desire to become a parent. In the absence of international agreement about surrogacy (and that seems at present most unlikely) each legislature will reflect its own culture, religion and judgment of prevailing social mores in what is enacted. That may, of course, result in either outlawing domestic surrogacy or rendering it at least manageable (insofar as any aspect of private family law is truly manageable) in the domestic context. It will, however, give rise in the field of international surrogacy to all the issues that we have been considering and no doubt human ingenuity will unearth a few more. What we are considering now will haunt our courts (albeit in different forms) for some time to come. All this has to be dealt with in a context in which rationality is not the only intellectual driver. Experienced family practitioners are, of course, familiar with this but the desire to parent does evoke particularly powerful feelings. Indeed it often goes beyond desire so as to create an expectation of

21 HFEA 2008 ss. 54(6) and (7).

22 HFEA 2008 s. 54(7), and ss. 1–3 of the Mental Capacity Act 2005.

23 *Re D & L (Surrogacy)* [2012] EWHC 2631 (Fam) and *Re WT (Foreign Surrogacy)* [2014] EWHC 1303 (Fam).

a right to parent, something which surely no legal or political system is in truth in a position actually to deliver.

International surrogacy has confronted judges and practitioners with new problems. Developing medical science allied to relatively cheap international travel suggests, however, that the problems of international surrogacy are only a prelude to other issues yet to arise, or perhaps yet to be thought of, with which the courts will be faced. Our attempts to deal with surrogacy may additionally provide us with the expertise for dealing with the as yet unknown.

THE REGULATORY APPROACH

SURROGACY IN GREECE

Eleni ZERVOGIANNI

1. GENERAL LEGAL FRAMEWORK

The right to reproduce is guaranteed in Art. 5 para. 1 of the Greek Constitution, as an expression of the right to free development of one's personality. It covers not only natural but also medically assisted reproduction,[1] both homologous and heterologous,[2] and is further concretised though special legal provisions.

In 2002 a comprehensive law for medically assisted reproduction was enacted,[3] that introduced a special chapter in the Greek Civil Code setting the conditions for medically assisted reproduction,[4] while it also amended

[1] See the Explanatory Memorandum of Law 3089/2002, Point I 4 (p. 1), available at: <www.hellenicparliament.gr/UserFiles/2f026f42-950c-4efc-b950-340c4fb76a24/i-human-eisig.pdf> accessed 07.09.2018 and the Explanatory Memorandum of Law 3305/2005, p. 1, available at: <www.hellenicparliament.gr/UserFiles/2f026f42-950c-4efc-b950-340c4fb76a24/e-medipar-eis.pdf> accessed 07.09.2018.

[2] See AP. GEORGIADES, *Family Law*, 2nd ed., Sakkoulas, Athens/Thessaloniki 2017, §24 no. 3 (in Greek) and explicitly so I. SPYRIDAKIS, *Family Law*, Ant. N. Sakkoulas, Athens/Komotini 2006, p. 402 (in Greek); Cf. Law 3305/2005 Art. 1 para. 1.

[3] Law 3089/2002, *Official Gazette*, issue A, no. 327/23.12.2002.

[4] Articles 1455–1460 of the Greek Civil Code (hereinafter: 'GrCC').

accordingly the rules on maternal and paternal descent.[5] The regulatory framework on medically assisted reproduction was complemented three years later by a subsequent law on specific issues of the application of medically assisted reproduction methods, the donation of genetic material and its cryopreservation as well as on the establishment and operation of medical centres on assisted reproduction.[6] The same law provided also for the foundation of the National Authority of Assisted Reproduction, which is an independent authority, the main responsibilities of which lie on the oversight of the implementation of the legal framework on medically assisted reproduction, the issue of regulations on special issues, as well as the submission of proposals for the amendment of the current provisions.[7] In January 2017 the National Authority of Assisted Reproduction issued a Code of Ethics of medically assisted reproduction[8] that includes a set of detailed binding rules on the applicable procedures.

The abovementioned legal framework includes explicit rules on surrogacy. Namely, gestational, but not traditional, surrogacy is permitted in Greece under specific conditions set by the law.[9] Although the issue has been undoubtedly contentious, the legislator's decision to opt for the permissibility of surrogacy has been driven by pragmatic considerations: As mentioned in the Explanatory Memorandum of the law,[10] a prohibition of surrogacy could never be enforced entirely. On this assumption, the regulation of surrogacy, rather than its prohibition, was thought to serve the best interests of the children that would be born using this method of assisted reproduction. Notwithstanding remote reactions from the Church, the relevant bill passed from the parliament with large majority.

Judging from the experience of the application of the legal framework on surrogacy in the 15 years since it entered into force, it can be ascertained that it has been indeed successful and well accepted by Greek society, without substantial objections of moral, religious, political or other character.[11]

Statistical data on surrogacy agreements confirm the aforementioned conclusion. Namely, as will be discussed below,[12] a condition of surrogacy is that a court has granted its authorisation. Two recent studies delved into the relevant court decisions. The first one is based on 256 decisions of the years 2003–16 of the courts of Athens and of Piraeus, as well as of other courts, the rulings

---

5 Article 2 of Law 3089/2002 amended Arts 1464, 1465, 1471, 1475, 1478 and 1479 of the GrCC.

6 Law 3305/2005, *Official Gazette*, issue A, no. 17/27.01.2005.

7 See Arts 19 and 20 of Law 3305/2005.

8 Decision 73 of 24.1.2017, *Official Gazette*, issue B, no. 293/7.02.2017.

9 See in more detail below Sections 2 and 4.

10 See the Explanatory Memorandum of Law 3089/2002, Point I 4 (p. 1).

11 See on this point the empirical research of K. Panagos, *Surrogacy. Greek Legal Regime and Criminological Extensions*, Sakkoulas, Athens/Thessaloniki 2011, p. 133 ff. (in Greek), performed on 120 students of Aristotle University of Thessaloniki.

12 See Section 2.

of which have been made available in electronic data bases,[13] while the second one considered 71 decisions of the Court of Athens of the years 2005–09 and 19 decisions of the Court of Piraeus of the years 2007–12.[14] Both studies focus on qualitative data referring to characteristics (nationality, marital status, age, medical reason for surrogacy) of both the intended parent(s) and the surrogate, rather than quantitative data.[15] They therefore do not provide information on the total number of children that have been actually born by surrogate mothers in the whole of Greece. However, on the basis of court rulings that authorise surrogacy (as it is required by law in all cases of surrogacy) it can be estimated that hundreds of children have been born by surrogate mothers. Given that surrogacy arrangements are unproblematic, or even widespread, in Greece there do not seem to exist many cases of surrogacy arrangements undertaken in other jurisdictions.[16]

2. SURROGACY ARRANGEMENTS IN GENERAL

Surrogacy arrangements are in principle legal in Greece. Such agreements must be concluded in writing between the intended parents and the surrogate. If the surrogate is married or is in a registered partnership, the consent of the spouse or of the registered partner is also needed.[17] The agreement must be then submitted to the court before the embryo transfer takes place, so that judicial authorisation for the surrogacy can be granted.[18] The court is bound to authorise surrogacy if all conditions set forth in the law are met.[19] This decision is crucial for the establishment of the parental descent of the child.[20]

---

13 See P. Ravdas, 'Surrogate Motherhood in Greece: statistical data derived from Court Decisions' (2017) 3(2) *BIOETHICA*, available online at: <http://www.bioethics.gr/images/pdf/JOURNAL/BIOETHICA_Vol_3_Issue_2_FINAL.pdf> accessed 07.09.2018, pp. 40 ff.

14 See the reference to the research of Kokkinaki, in D. Papadopoulou-Klamari, '*Post-Mortem* Artificial Insemination and Surrogacy in Practice' in *Assisted Reproduction in Europe: Social, Ethical and Legal Issues*, Sakkoulas, Athens/Thessaloniki 2015, pp. 117 ff. at 121 ff. (in Greek).

15 See in more detail below Section 4.

16 In published court decisions only one, very problematic, such case is documented. See on this issue below Section 7.

17 See Art. 1458 sent. 1 of the GrCC. For the application of this provision by analogy in case of a registered partnership see Art. 12 of Law 4356/2015 (*Official Gazette*, issue A, no. 181/24.12.2015).

18 See Art. 1458. According to Arts 740 para. 1 sent. 2 and 799 para. 1 of the Greek Code of Civil Procedure (hereinafter 'GrCCP'), as amended, this case falls within the competence of the multi-membered Court of First Instance of the place of the habitual residence of the surrogate or of the intended mother.

19 The procedure is non-adversarial and therefore according to Art. 744 of the GrCCP, the court has the power of ex officio investigation. For the conditions under which surrogacy is permitted in Greece see below Sections 2 and 4.

20 See below Section 3.

The surrogacy agreement is considered to be a special type of contract of mandate:[21] which is binding, gratuitous[22] and of a personal nature.[23] It is therefore possible for all parties to withdraw from the contract any time before the embryo transfer, even if the court authorisation has been already granted.[24] In the lack of special provisions, the general provisions of contract law apply to surrogacy arrangements as well. The surrogate must observe the general standards for a healthy pregnancy (such as abstinence from smoking or drinking alcohol). If she does not comply and this affects the health of the child, she may be held liable both in contract and in tort, vis-à-vis the intended parties and the child born.[25] Terms of the contract that lead to the undue restriction of the surrogate's freedom are considered immoral and therefore void.[26] Such terms may refer, for example, to the surrogate's deprivation of her right to proceed to a legal abortion,[27] to the surrogate being subject to the constant control from the intended parents, or even to extreme precautions she must take during pregnancy.[28]

On the other hand, commercial surrogacy arrangements, where the surrogate is promised remuneration, are unlawful, and as such will not be authorised by the court.[29] This even constitutes a criminal offence.[30] This rather controversial provision was included in the law at the last moment, during its discussion in the parliament.[31] However, a few clarifications need to be made on this point: The reimbursement of all costs related to achieving pregnancy, to the pregnancy itself and post-partum period are not considered as remuneration. In addition the surrogate may be granted compensation for her lost profits due to the

---

21 This contract is regulated in Arts 713 ff of the Greek Civil Code.

22 See Art. 1458 sent. 1 of the GrCC and in more detail below, Section 2 *in fine*.

23 See Ap. Georgiades, above n. 2, §25 no. 19.

24 See Art. 1458 sent. 1 of the GrCC in combination with Art. 1456 para. 2 sent. 1 of the GrCC.

25 See P. Agallopoulou, 'Surrogacy' (2004) *Digesta* 1 ff. at 9–10 (in Greek); Ap. Georgiades, above n. 2, §25 no. 20.

26 See Arts 178 and 179 of the GrCC. On this issue see also P. Agallopoulou, above n. 25, at 9; P. Agallopoulou, 'Surrogacy' in M. Kanellopoulou-Boti and F. Panagopoulou-Koutnatzi (eds), *Medical Liability and Bioethics. Contemporary Approaches and Future Perspectives*, Paschalidis, Athens 2014, pp. 173 ff. at 177 (in Greek); Ap. Georgiades, above n. 2, §25 no. 20.

27 See above n. 26 and also K. Rokas, 'Greece' (Ch. 9), in K. Trimmings and P. Beaumont (eds), *International Surrogacy Agreements*, Hart Publishing, Oxford 2013, pp. 143 ff. at 147; Cf. however Th. Papachristou, *Artificial Reproduction in the Civil Code*, Sakkoulas, Athens/Thessaloniki 2003, p. 55 (in Greek). On the conditions of legal abortion see Art. 304 of the Greek Penal Code.

28 See Ap. Georgiades, above n. 2, §25 no. 20.

29 See Art. 1458 sent. 1 of the GrCC. See also Art. 13 para. 4 sent. 1 of Law 3305/2005.

30 See Art. 26 para. 8 of Law 3305/2005 and in more detail below Section 6.

31 For a critique of the provision see esp. A. Hatzis, 'The Law in the Books and the Law in the Practice' (2012) *Efimerida Dioikitikou Dikaiou* 250 ff., 258 (in Greek). See also on this issue K. Panagos, above n. 11, pp. 96 ff.

pregnancy.[32] If the surrogate is unemployed, this compensation is assessed on the basis of the (hypothetical) salary she would get, if she were employed in a position which corresponded with her qualifications. However, in any case, this compensation may not exceed €10,000.[33] In practice, it is often a family member (usually the sister or the mother) of the intended mother who acts as a surrogate.[34] In the remaining cases, it is doubtful if parties actually comply with the prohibition of remuneration.[35] According to research performed on the basis of court decisions that approved surrogacy arrangements, in more than half of the cases the surrogate is a foreign national, residing in Greece, coming mostly from countries of Eastern Europe.[36] Journalistic sources mention that the remuneration of surrogates in practice is between €20,000 and €40,000.[37]

3. LEGAL PARENTHOOD AT THE TIME OF BIRTH

Provided that surrogacy has been authorised by the court, the legal mother of the child already at the time of birth is the intended mother.[38] This is stated on the birth certificate of the child, without any reference to the surrogate[39] and it holds even if the genetic material used is not of the intended mother but of a third person.[40] In the rare, but actual, cases where a single man has commissioned a surrogacy,[41] it should be accepted that the child has no legal mother, but only a legal father, whose kinship with the child is directly derived from the court decision authorising surrogacy.[42]

---

32 See Art. 13 para. 4 of Law 3305/2005.

33 See Art. 4 of the Decision 36/2008 of the National Authority of Assisted Reproduction, *Official Gazette*, issue B, no. 670/16.04.2008.

34 See in more detail below Section 4.1.

35 See esp. P. Ravdas, 'Surrogacy: The Legislator's Expectations under the Challenge of Statistical Data' in Th. Papachristou and E. Kounougeri-Manoledaki (eds), *Family Law in the 21st Century*, Sakkoulas, Athens/Thessaloniki 2012, p. 99 (in Greek); K. Rokas, above n. 27, p. 148; Cf. A. Hatzis, above n. 31, p. 257 ff.

36 See P. Ravdas, above n. 13, p. 52, as well as the research of Kokkinaki, referred to by D. Papadopoulou-Klamari, above n. 14, p. 123.

37 See the article 'Greek Industry with surrogates', in the daily newspaper *Kathimerini* of 13.04.2014 available at: <http://www.kathimerini.gr/762582/article/epikairothta/ellada/ellhnikh-viomhxania-me-paren8etes-mhteres> (in Greek) accessed 07.09.2018.

38 See Art. 1464 para. 1 of the GrCC.

39 See Art. 20 para. 1 of Law 344/1976 on Civil Registry Certificates, as amended.

40 On this issue see below Section 4.3.

41 See on this controversial issue below Section 4.2.

42 See D. Papadopoulou-Klamari, *Kinship. Establishment, Registration, Protection*, Ant. N. Sakkoulas, Athens/Komotini 2010, p. 108 (in Greek); G. Lekkas, 'Medically Assisted Reproduction and Kinship in Greek Law. Introduction of "Social-Emotional Kinship" or Reproduction without Kinship?' in Th. Papachristou and E. Kounougeri-Manoledaki (eds), *Family Law in the 21st Century*, Sakkoulas, Athens/Thessaloniki 2012, p. 63 (in Greek);

Once legal motherhood is determined, paternal descent is established on the basis of the provisions on kinship applicable in case of artificial reproduction. Thus, if the legal mother of the child is married or in a registered partnership, it is presumed that her spouse or registered partner is the legal father of the child.[43] This presumption cannot be contested, even if the genetic material used were donated, provided that the presumed father had given his consent to its use.[44] If the intended parents were neither married nor had concluded a registered partnership, paternal descent is established by acknowledgement. Namely, the consent of the legal mother's partner to medically assisted reproduction holds as an acknowledgement of the child as his own and the consent of the legal mother to medically assisted reproduction holds as a consent to this acknowledgment.[45] This acknowledgement is also unchallengeable.[46] If the legal mother is single the child has no legal father.

In general, the Greek legislative framework of medically assisted reproduction grants priority to the so-called social-emotional bond between the intended parents and the child, that prevails over biology.[47] Nevertheless, maternal descent may be contested if it is proved that the ovum that has been actually fertilised has been of the surrogate.[48] The surrogate can then bring a claim challenging the legal motherhood of the child within six months of birth.[49] If the claim succeeds, the surrogate becomes the legal mother of the child.[50] This brings about changes as to the paternal descent of the child as well. Thus if the surrogate is married or in a registered partnership, the spouse or registered partner is presumed to be the father of the child,[51] unless he contests fatherhood.[52]

With the exception of the rare cases where legal motherhood is successfully contested, the surrogate has no legal relation to the child she gave birth to and

---

Ap. Georgiades, above n. 2, §28 no. 6. *Contra*: Expert Opinion 261/2010 of the Legal Council of the State (*Nomiko Symboulio tou Kratous*), available at: <www.nsk.gov.gr/webnsk/gnwmodothsh.jsp?gnid=112719> accessed 07.09.2018, according to which in this case the surrogate should be registered in the birth certificate as the legal mother of the child.

43 See Art. 1465 of the GrCC for married couples and Art. 9 of Law 4356/2015 for couples that have concluded a registered partnership.

44 See Art. 1471 para. 2 Nr. 2 of the GrCC and Art. 9 sent. 3 of Law 4356/2015.

45 See Art. 1475 para. 2 of the GrCC.

46 See Art. 1477 para. 2 of the GrCC.

47 For the notion of 'social-emotional' kinship see already I. Deliyannis, 'Establishment and Challenge of Kinship according to Greek Law' (1992) *Elliniki Dikaiosyni* 1 ff. (in Greek). For the use of this notion in the framework of (heterologous) artificial reproduction see the Explanatory Memorandum of Law 3089/2002, Point II 1 (p. 4) and also in detail E. Kounougeri-Manoledaki, *Family Law*, 7th ed., vol. II, Sakkoulas, Athens/Thessaloniki, 2018, p. 85 (in Greek); G. Lekkas, above n. 42, pp. 57 ff.

48 See Art. 1464 para. 2 of the GrCC.

49 See Art. 1464 para. 2 of the GrCC.

50 See Art. 1464 para. 3 of the GrCC.

51 See Art. 1465 para. 1 of the GrCC and Art. 9 of Law 4356/2015 on registered partnerships.

52 See Art. 1467 of the GrCC and Art. 9 sent. 3 of Law 4356/2015 that stipulates, among others, that Art. 1467 of the GrCC applies by analogy in cases of registered partnership.

therefore also has no rights. If she does not willingly hand over the child to his/her legal parents, the latter may compel her to do so on the basis of the provisions of the Code of Civil Procedure on judicial execution.[53] Along the same lines, the surrogate has no right to contact the child.[54] Relevant agreements between the intended parents and the surrogate granting her such a right are not enforceable, since the legal parents have the sole competence to make decisions on the upbringing of their child.[55]

Similarly, although the law does not explicitly provide for the anonymity of the surrogate,[56] there is no rule granting the child the possibility to access the relevant information. No indication of surrogacy may be found in any official document, other than the court decision that granted authorisation to it. Court decisions are kept in the court's archives, but given the protection of personal data, in principle third parties may have access to them once they have been anonymised.[57] In the cases in question this protection is even more enhanced, since the procedure may take place behind closed doors.[58]

4. ELIGIBILITY FOR SURROGACY

4.1. ELIGIBILITY CRITERIA FOR WOMEN ACTING AS A SURROGATE

The sole criterion for the eligibility of the woman acting as a surrogate is that she must be in the physical and psychological condition that allows her to bear a child. This has to be proved by means of a medical expert opinion.[59] Although the law already since 2005 set a maximum age for the intended mother,[60]

---

53 See Art. 946 para. 1 of the GrCCP. So E. Kounougeri-Manoledaki, 'The Bill on Medically Assisted Human Reproduction and the Response to the Reactions against it' (2002) *Chronika Idiotikou Dikaiou* 676 ff., 676 (in Greek); P. Agallopoulou, 'The Grant of Judicial Authorisation for Surrogacy' (2003) 2 *Kritiki Epitheorisi Nomikis Theorias kai Praxis* 235 ff., 241 (in Greek); Ap. Georgiades, above n. 2, §25 no. 29; cf. however K. Pantelidou, 'Issues of the New Institution of "Surrogate" Motherhood' (2004) *Harmenopoulos* 977 ff., 986 (in Greek) and K. Panagos, above n. 11, p. 67.

54 See also K. Rokas, above n. 27, p. 151.

55 See Art. 1510 ff. of the GrCC on the right of parental care. On the contents of this right see in detail P. Agallopoulou in Ap. Georgiades and M. Stathopoulos (eds), *Commentary of the Civil Code*, vol. VIII, 2nd ed., P.N. Sakkoulas – Dikaio kai Oikonomia, Athens 2003, Art. 1510 no. 80 ff. (in Greek).

56 Only the anonymity of the donors of genetic material is granted. See below Section 4.3.

57 See on this point the Expert Opinion 2/2006 of the Hellenic Data Protection Authority, available at: <http://www.dpa.gr/portal/page?_pageid=33,120923&_dad=portal&> accessed 07.09.2018.

58 See Art. 799 para. 2 of the GrCCP.

59 See Art. 13 para. 2 of Law 3305/2005.

60 See below Section 4.2.

until recently no such restriction applied as to the surrogate. This gap has been filled by the relevant provision of the Code of Ethics of 2017, according to which the surrogate should be between 25 and 45 years of age.[61] The Code further stipulates that a woman is eligible as a surrogate provided that she has already had at least one child of her own and has not undergone more than two caesarean sections.[62] It is furthermore in principle immaterial if the surrogate is married or in a registered partnership or not. In the latter case though, her spouse or registered partner has to consent to the surrogacy arrangement.[63]

The original version of the law stipulated that both the surrogate and the intended parents should be domiciled in Greece.[64] The rationale for this rule was to avoid reproductive tourism. However, the conformity of this rule to EU law was questioned early on,[65] and it was rather ineffective in practice, since domicile was considered proved rather easily. A residence in Greece for a few months, sometimes evidenced by a leasehold agreement, was often sufficient.[66] In July 2014 the relevant provision was amended, so that it is now enough that either the surrogate or the intended mother has a domicile or a temporary residence in Greece.[67] This new provision should be embraced, since it acknowledges the reality that reproductive tourism is unavoidable,[68] as long as the legal framework of medically assisted reproduction, and surrogacy in particular, is in most other countries more restrictive than in Greece.[69]

According to the research performed on the basis of 256 court decisions that granted authorisation to surrogacy in the years 2003–16,[70] the mean age

61 See Art. 9 para. 1 of the Code of Ethics of Medically Assisted Reproduction.

62 Ibid.

63 See Art. 1458 of the GrCC, in case of registered partnership in combination with Art. 12 of Law 4356/2015.

64 See the original version of Art. 8 of Law 3089/2002 and also P. Agallopoulou and A. Koutsouradis (eds), *Medically Assisted Human Reproduction. The Law 3089/2002. Preparatory Works – Discussions in the Parliament*, Sakkoulas, Athens/Thessaloniki 2004, p. 238.

65 See A. Koutsouradis, 'Issues on Surrogacy, especially after the Law 3305/2005' (2006) *Nomiko Vima* 337 ff. at 343 ff. (in Greek).

66 See esp. P. Ravdas, above n. 35, p. 98; K. Rokas, above n. 27, p. 157.

67 Article 8 N 3089/2002 has been amended by Art. 17 of Law 4272/2014, *Official Gazette*, Issue A, no. 145/11.07.2014.

68 An indication of the existence of reproductive tourism in Greece is the fact that many medical centres of assisted reproduction have internet sites in English, French or German. Nevertheless, reproductive tourism in Greece seems to pertain mainly to ova donation. As regards surrogacy, in more than 80 per cent of the cases the intended mother is Greek. See P. Ravdas, above n. 13, p. 48.

69 See E. Zervogianni, 'Künstliche Fortpflanzung in Griechenland' in A. Dutta, D. Schwab, P. Gottwald, D. Henrich and M. Löhnig (eds), *Künstliche Fortpflanzung und Europäisches Familienrecht*, Gieseking Verlag, Bielefeld 2015, pp. 205 ff. at 217–18. Cf. A. Grammaticaki-Alexiou, 'Fertility Tourism, European Law and Conflict of Laws Issues' in *Essays in Honour of Professor Ioannis Voulgaris*, vol. I, Ant. N. Sakkoulas, Athens/Komotini 2011, pp. 87 ff. at 95.

70 See P. Ravdas, above n. 13, p. 52.

of women acting as surrogates was almost 35 years old. Almost half of them were married and more than half already had children of their own. In addition, about two-thirds of them were foreign nationals, coming mostly from countries of Eastern Europe. It is worth noting that the Greek surrogates were on average older and more likely to be married as compared to the surrogates of foreign nationality. As regards their relations to the intended parents, in around a quarter of cases the surrogate has been a relative of the intended mother (usually sister or mother), with the rest being either 'close friends' of the intended mother, in more than half of the cases, or previously employed by her (usually as household help or nurse). These results are also confirmed by the second relevant research.[71]

4.2. ELIGIBILITY CRITERIA FOR COMMISSIONING PARENTS

An important principle of the Greek regulation on medically assisted reproduction in general is that natural reproduction, if possible, is granted priority over medically assisted reproduction.[72] On this basis, surrogacy is an option only for persons who cannot have a child in the natural way, due to a medical condition, such as for example, uterine anomalies of the intended mother or her suffering from a serious condition or disease which could be transmitted to the foetus, such as HIV.[73]

In addition, following the general provisions on medically assisted reproduction, the age limit for such procedures is set by the age until which reproduction in the natural way would be possible. For women, including mothers commissioning a surrogate, this limit is set at 50 years.[74] This provision is meant to ensure the parents' capability to take good care of the child and is therefore thought to serve best the interests of the child that will be born, which according to the law is always to be taken into account.[75] For the same reasons, intended parents are subject to medical screening prior to the authorisation of surrogacy.[76]

The nationality of the commissioning parents, and after July 2014 also their domicile, is in principle irrelevant.[77]

---

71 See research by Kokkinaki, mentioned by D. Papadopoulou-Klamari, above n. 14, p. 123.

72 See esp. Art. 1455 para. 1 sent. 1 of the GrCC.

73 See Art. 1458 sent. 2 of the GrCC. On this issue see also Ap. Georgiades, above n. 2, §25 no. 23.

74 See Art. 4 para. 1 of Law 3305/2005.

75 See Art. 1 para. 2 of Law 3305/2005 and also in detail A. Koutsouradis, above n. 67, esp. pp. 355 ff.; Th. Trokanas, 'The Application of Methods of Assisted Reproduction and the Best Interests of the Child Born' in Th. Papachristou and E. Kounougeri-Manoledaki (eds), *Family Law in the 21st Century*, Sakkoulas, Athens/Thessaloniki 2012, pp. 135 ff. (in Greek).

76 See Art. 13 para. 3 of Law 3305/2005.

77 See above Section 4.1.

Moreover, it is immaterial if the commissioning parents are married or have concluded a registered partnership or not, as long as they are a heterosexual couple. The sexual orientation of the commissioning mother is not per se a criterion for her eligibility as a commissioning parent. However, although same-sex couples have been legally recognised in Greece,[78] they cannot be granted parental rights as a couple, meaning that Greek law does not accept the possibility of same-sex parents.[79] In the law it is also explicitly stipulated that single women may also commission a surrogate.

A question that still remains open is whether single men, who face a health condition due to which they cannot have a child in a natural way,[80] may commission a surrogate. No explicit regulation of this issue can be found in the law.[81] In two such cases the courts approved the surrogacy arrangement on the grounds of non-discrimination on the basis of sex.[82] This approach finds also strong support in the legal literature.[83] In one of these cases, however, the

---

78 See Law 4356/2015, *Official Gazette*, Issue A, no. 181/24.12.2015, on registered partnership, which according to Art. 1 of the said law is an option for all adult persons, irrespective of their sex.

79 It is worth noting though that according to Art. 8 para. 1 of Law 4538/2018 on foster care and adoption (*Official Gazette*, issue A, no. 85/16.05.2018) same-sex couples can act as foster parents.

80 This is a general condition which shall be fulfilled in all cases of medically assisted reproduction. See Art. 1455 para. 1 of the GrCC.

81 In the Explanatory Memorandum of Law 3089/2002, Point II 1 (p. 3) though, there is a relevant reference of the possibility of widowers to proceed to assisted reproduction through surrogacy, with the ova of their late wives, provided that the conditions for post-mortem reproduction set by law are fulfilled. On these conditions see Art. 1457 of the GrCC and in more detail in English see P. Agallopoulou, 'Assistant Reproductive Technology: Forcing a Rethink of Parenthood in Greek Law' in B. Feuillet-Liger, K. Orfali and T. Callus (eds), *Reproductive Technology and Changing Perceptions of Parenthood around the World*, Bruylant, Brussels 2014, p. 116 ff. at 133–34.

82 See Decisions 2827/2008 of the Single-member Court of First Instance of Athens, *Chronika Idiotikou Dikaiou* 2009, 816 and 13707/2009 of the Single-member Court of First Instance of Thessaloniki, *Chronika Idiotikou Dikaiou* 2011, 267.

83 See I. Spyridakis, *The New Regulation of Artificial Reproduction and Kinship*, Ant. N. Sakkoulas, Athens/Komotini 2003, p. 29 (in Greek); I. Spyridakis, above n. 2, p. 414; Th. Papachristou, 'Comment to the Decision 2827/2008 of the Single-member Court of First Instance of Athens' (2009) *Chronika Idiotikou Dikaiou* 818 (in Greek); N. Koumoutzis in Ap. Georgiades and M. Stathopoulos (eds), *Commentary of the Civil Code*, vol. VII, 2nd ed., P.N. Sakkoulas – Dikaio kai Oikonomia, Athens 2007, Arts 1457–1458 no. 77; N. Koumoutzis, 'The Artificial Reproduction of the Single Man' (2011) *Chronika Idiotikou Dikaiou* 316 ff. (in Greek); N. Koumoutzis, 'The Artificial Reproduction of Single Persons and the European Convention on Human Rights' in *Assisted Reproduction and Alternative Forms of Family*, Sakkoulas, Athens/Thessaloniki 2014, pp. 25 ff., esp. p. 37 (in Greek); E. Kounougeri-Manoledaki, above n. 47, pp. 55–56; E. Kounougeri-Manoledaki, 'Medically Assisted Reproduction: Redefining the Notion of Family' in *Medically Assisted Human Reproduction. 10 Years Application of Law 3089/2002*, Sakkoulas, Athens/Thessaloniki 2013, pp. 35 ff. at 47–48 (in Greek); Th. Trokanas, *Human Reproduction. Private Autonomy and its Limits*, Sakkoulas, Athens/Thessaloniki 2011, p. 222; V. Peraki, in Ap. Georgiades (ed.),

States Attorney brought an appeal,[84] leading to the Court of Appeal quashing the decision of the Court of First Instance that had granted authorisation for the surrogacy. The Court of Appeal argued that the goal of the regulation of surrogacy is to redress medical problems that lead to the impossibility of pregnancy and not to override nature.[85] Thus, according to the Court of Appeal, since a man has neither ova not a uterus, the reason he is unable to achieve a pregnancy cannot be considered to be a medical problem.

The aforementioned argument is not terribly convincing, since a single woman, who may according to the law commission a surrogate if she is unable to bear a child herself, overrides nature to the extent that in such a procedure she is necessarily provided with the element she is missing due to her biology, namely with the sperm of a man.[86]

4.3. THE GAMETES USED IN THE SURROGACY ARRANGEMENT

The gametes used in the surrogacy arrangement do not need be of the commissioning parents.[87] Sperm, ova and embryo donation are a legal option, if the genetic material of the intended parents cannot be used due to medical

---

Brief Commentary of the Civil Code, vol. II, P.N. Sakkoulas - Dikaio kai Oikonomia, Athens 2013, Art. 1458 no. 21; P. Agallopoulou, 'Surrogacy' in M. Kanellopoulou-Boti and F. Panagopoulou-Koutnatzi (eds), above n. 26, p. 180; cf. Explanatory Memorandum of Law 3089/2002, Point II 1 (p. 3); cf. also. I. Androulidaki-Dimitriadi, 'The Contract for Medically Assisted Reproduction' in *Essays in Honour of Apostolos S. Georgiades*, vol. I, Ant. N. Sakkoulas, Athens/Komotini, pp. 27 ff. at 31 (in Greek). *Contra*: D. Papadopoulou-Klamari, above n. 42, pp. 220 ff., esp. at 224; K. Pantelidou, 'Non-Discrimination and Medically Assisted Human Reproduction' in *Essays in Honour of Penelope Agallopoulou*, vol. II, Ant. N. Sakkoulas, Athens/Komotini 2011, pp. 1095 ff., esp. at pp. 1099–100 (in Greek); P. Nikolopoulos, 'Comment on the Decision 3357/2010 of the Athens Court of Appeals' (2012) *Nomiko Vima* 1440 (in Greek); A. Koutsouradis, 'Entwicklungen des griechischen Familien- und Erbrechts 2013–2014' (2014) *Zeitschrift für das gesamte Familienrecht* 1509 ff., 1509.

84 See Art. 761 of the GrCCP according to which in non-adversarial proceedings the competent State Attorney of the Court of First Instance may appeal the decisions of the court.

85 See Decision 3357/2010 of the Athens Court of Appeals, *Nomiko Vima* 2012, 1437. The same argumentation has been then used by the Court of First Instance of Thessaloniki in Decision 8641/2017, published in *Efarmoges Astikou Dikaoiu* 2017, 925, that rejected the application of a single man for the authorisation of surrogacy.

86 See esp. N. Koumoutzis, 'The Artificial Reproduction of Single Persons (...)', above n. 3, pp. 35–36.

87 See E. Kounougeri-Manoledaki, above n. 47, p. 52; Th. Papachristou, *Family Law*, P.N. Sakkoulas - Dikaio kai Oikonomia, Athens 2014, p. 218; N. Koumoutzis in Ap. Georgiades and M. Stathopoulos, above n. 83, Arts 1457–1458 no. 38–40; D. Papadopoulou-Klamari, above n. 42, pp. 96 and 207; Th. Trokanas, above n. 83, p. 375; Ap. Georgiades, above n. 2, §25 no. 18; cf. P. Agallopoulou, above n. 83, p. 176. This opinion is also followed by case law. See below n. 91 for the relevant statistics. *Contra*: A. Koutsouradis, above n. 65, at 350, according to whom surrogacy with donated ova

reasons. It is therefore possible that the intended parents have no genetic relation with the child born by the surrogate.[88] In practice this is not the usual case.[89] Given that only gestational surrogacy is permitted in Greece, the only restriction as to the genetic material used in case of surrogacy is that the ovum that shall be fertilised should not be of the surrogate herself.[90]

The donation of sperm, ova and embryos is regulated comprehensively in the law. No consideration shall be paid for their use,[91] but donors may receive a refund of their costs, such as the expenses for the necessary medical tests and for their travel, as well as a compensation for their lost profits, due to their absence from work, and their physical exertion.[92] According to the decision of the National Authority of Assisted Reproduction the total amount should not exceed €300 in case of sperm donation and €2,000, not including the medical expenses, in cases of ova donation.[93] As to the donation of embryos it is worth noting that only embryos that have been left over from efforts of medically assisted reproduction of other persons may be donated,[94] provided that the latter have granted their consent.[95]

If donated genetic material is used, the anonymity of the donor is preserved.[96] Upon deciding this issue, the legislator apparently concluded

---

is not permitted. See further A. Koutsouradis, 'Zum Aktuellen Stand des griechischen Abstammungsrechts' in A. Spickhoff, D. Schwab, D. Henrich and P. Gottwald (eds), *Streit um die Abstammung. Ein europäischer Vergleich*, Gieseking Verlag, Bielefeld 2007, pp. 205 ff., at p. 245 fn. 113; A. Kotzampasi, 'The Right to Reproduction: Between the Freedom of Natural Reproduction and the Legally Provided Right of Artificial Reproduction' in A. Kotzampasi, *Views and Ideas on Issues of Interpretation of Civil Law*, City Publish, Thessaloniki 2006, pp. 245 ff. at pp. 265–66 (in Greek).

88 This has been actually the case in the two instances where courts granted their authorisation to surrogacy by single men. See above Section 4.2.

89 According to the research of P. Rabdas, above n. 13, p. 51, donated ova were used in around 10 per cent of cases of surrogacy, whereas donated sperm was used in less than two per cent of the cases.

90 See Art. 1458 sent. 1 of the GrCC.

91 See Art. 8 para. 1 of Law 3305/2005. See also Art. 9 para. 1 of the Code of Ethics of Medically Assisted Reproduction.

92 See Art. 8 paras 1 and 5 of Law 3305/2005. The 'donation' of genetic material with consideration is a criminal offence, according to Art. 26 para. 2 of Law 3305/200.

93 See Arts 1 and 3 of the Decision 36/2008 of the National Authority of Assisted Reproduction, above n. 33, as amended by Decision 54/2014 of the same Authority, *Official Gazette*, issue B, no. 2683/09.10.2014, that provides that: In case of sperm donation, the refund for the donor's travel expenses should not exceed the amount of €200 and his compensation for lost profits should not exceed the amount of €100. In case of ova donation, the donor is entitled to travel expenses up to €600 and compensation for corporal strain up to €1,000, while the sum of travel costs and compensation for corporal strain should not exceed €1,200. The donor may also receive compensation for lost profits up to the amount of €800.

94 See Art. 8 para. 3 of Law 3305/2005. The non-observance of this rule constitutes a criminal offence. See Art. 26 para. 4 of Law 3305/2005.

95 See Art. 1459 of the GrCC.

96 See Art. 1460 para. 1 sent. 1 of the GrCC. The revelation of the identity of the donor constitutes a criminal offence according to Art. 26 para. 11 of Law 3305/2005.

that the privacy of the donor and the protection of the so-called 'social family' outweighs the child's right to gain knowledge over his/her genetic origins. The child may only have access to an archive with medical information about the donor, if this is deemed necessary because of health reasons.[97] Nevertheless, even then, the identity of the donor is not revealed. In extreme cases of medical necessity (e.g. when the child is in need of organ donation) it is supported that the child shall be granted access to the archive of the National Authority of Assisted Reproduction that also includes information on the identity of the donor.[98] Under no circumstances though can the donor be informed about the identity of the child and his legal parents.[99]

At the time when the law on medically assisted reproduction entered into force, the prevailing opinion in the literature had been in favour of the anonymity rule. Since then though, there are more and more voices in support of the child's right to know his/her genetic origins, with convincing arguments.[100]

5. TRANSFERRING OF PARENTHOOD IN THE ABSENCE OF A COURT'S AUTHORISATION OF SURROGACY

Before the enactment of the special regulation of surrogacy, commissioning parents could become legal parents of the child only through adoption. This possibility had been accepted by case law as well.[101] Since 2002, adoption

[97] See Art. 1460 para. 1 sent. 2 of the GrCC.

[98] See Ap. Georgiades, above n. 2, §25 no. 41. About the archive of the National Authority of Assisted Reproduction see Art. 20 para. 2 of Law 3305/2005.

[99] See Art. 1460 para. 2 of the GrCC.

[100] See Ch. Stampelou's opinion in P. Agallopoulou and A. Koutsouradis (eds), above n. 64, p. 59 (in Greek); Ch. Stampelou in Ap. Georgiades and M. Stathopoulos, above n. 83, Art. 1460 no. 6 ff.; Ch. Stampelou, 'The Anonymity of the Donor of Genetic Material' in *Current Tendencies in Family Law*, Nomiki Vivliothiki, Athens 2013, pp. 16 ff., esp. p. 31 (in Greek); P. Agallopoulou, 'Medically Assisted Human Reproduction and Anonymity of the Third Donor of Genetic Material' in *Essays in Honour of Michael P. Stathopoulos*, vol. I, Ant. N. Sakkoulas, Athens/Komotini 2010, pp. 1 ff., at p. 19 (in Greek); cf. A. Kotzampasi, 'The Anonymity of the Donor in Artificial Reproduction as a Legal and Moral Question' (2000) *Harmenopoulos* 710 ff. at 716 (in Greek); G. Lekkas, above n. 42, pp. 65–66; E. Zervogianni, above n. 69, at pp. 227–28. *Contra* (in favour of anonymity); K. Fountedaki, 'The Information of the Child that has been Born by Heterologous Artificial Reproduction about his Descent' in *Artificial Reproduction and Genetic Technology: The Moral-Legal Dimension*, Publications of the Association of Jurist of North Greece, vol. 48, Thessaloniki 2003, p. 129 ff., esp. p. 138 (in Greek); E. Kounougeri-Manoledaki, above n. 47, pp. 83–84; Th. Papachristou, above n. 89, p. 222; cf. also T. Vidalis, *Life without a Face*, Ant. N. Sakkoulas, Athens/Komotini 2003, pp. 153 ff., esp. at p. 159 (in Greek).

[101] See Decision 31/5803/176/1999 of the Multi-member Court of First Instance of Heraklion, *Nomiko Vima* 2000, 495, commented by F. Skorini-Paparrigopoulou and by Th. Papachristou (in Greek). See also P. Agallopoulou, 'Surrogacy (on the Occasion of

may play a role if the parties proceeded to surrogacy without the court's authorisation, as in this case the surrogate will be irrevocably the legal mother of the child at the time of birth, irrespective of the gametes used.[102] The legitimacy of adoption could be challenged on the grounds that it would constitute an evasion of the law.[103] The rather prevailing opinion in the literature though accepts adoption as a legitimate option, given that it would undoubtedly serve the best interests of the child.[104]

On this basis, the general provisions on adoption would apply,[105] taking also into account that in Greece adoptive parents may seek an adoptive child independently and not necessarily through an adoption agency. A court decision is always required for adoption, as is the consent of the parents of the child, i.e. the consent of the surrogate, who is the legal mother of the child, and of her partner, if he is the legal father.[106] However, adoption of a child by more than one person is only possible if these are spouses.[107] The provisions on adoption also set minimum and maximum age limits for the adoptive parents,[108] but courts often deviate from them, on the basis that it is in the best interests of the child to be adopted by the applicant, even if the latter is older than stipulated in the law.[109] Finally, in case of adoption the law grants the child the right to be fully informed about his/her adoption as soon as he/she reaches majority. Thus the child could come to know the identity of the surrogate and possibly also of her spouse or partner.[110]

Decision 31/5803/176/1999 Multi-member Court of First Instance of Heraklion)' (2000) 1 *Kritiki Epitheorisi Nomikis Theorias kai Praxis* 227 ff. (in Greek); Th. Trokanas, above n. 83, pp. 366 ff.

102 See Art. 1463 sent. 1 of the GrCC. If such an authorisation has been granted, the intended parents become directly the legal parents of the child. See above Section 3.

103 See Th. Papachristou, above n. 27, pp. 75–76; cf. F. Skorini-Paparrigopoulou, above n. 101, p. 498; K. Pantelidou, above n. 53, at 984. Cf. K. Panagos, above n. 11, p. 69.

104 See Decision 122/2008 of the Single-member Court of First Instance of Heraklion, Legal Database Intrasoft-Nomos; F. Skorini-Paparrigopoulou in Ap. Georgiades and M. Stathopoulos (eds), above n. 83, Arts 1463–1464 no. 50; E. Pournaras, in Ap. Georgiades (ed.), *Brief Commentary of the Civil Code*, above n. 83, Arts 1463–1464 no. 9; I. Spyridakis, above n. 2, p. 431 n. 2; E. Kounougeri-Manoledaki, above n. 47, pp. 94 ff.; E. Kounougeri-Manoledaki, *Artificial Reproduction and Family Law*, 2nd ed., Sakkoulas, Athens/Thessaloniki 2005, pp. 110–11 (in Greek); Georgiades, above n. 2, §28 no. 3; cf. P. Agallopoulou, above n. 25, at 12.

105 See Art. 1542 ff. of the GrCC.

106 See Art. 1550 of the GrCC.

107 See Art. 1545 of the GrCC. It is disputed whether (heterosexual) registered partners may proceed to adoption as a couple. See A. Georgiades, above n. 2 §36 nr. 13 and 41.

108 See Art. 1543 of the GrCC.

109 See, among many other, Decision 25358/2007 of the Multi-member Court of First Instance of Thessaloniki, *Harmenopoulos* 2008, 65.

110 See Art. 1559 of the GrCC.

6. AGENCIES AND CRIMINALISATION

The non-observance of almost any legal provision on medically assisted reproduction is criminally sanctioned.[111] As to surrogacy in particular, it is stipulated that whoever participates in a surrogacy procedure that does not comply with all conditions set by the law shall be imprisoned for at least two years and pay a fine of at least €1,500. This includes, among others, the surrogate herself, the commissioning parents as well as the doctor that performs the procedure. These penalties refer to breaches of the relevant Greek legislation and thus they do not apply extra-territorially.

The same sanctions apply also to whomever

> '(...) publicly or though the circulation of relevant documents, illustrations or by representation announces, promotes or advertises, even in a concealed way, the possibility to have a child borne by a third woman or provides as a professional activity against any consideration his services as a middle-man or offers in the same way his services or the services of a third person to this end.'[112]

Thus the Greek legal order does not reserve any (legitimate) role for middlemen in surrogacy.

In spite of this rather excessive criminalisation of all breaches of the rules on medically assisted reproduction, in practice it seems these penalties are not often imposed, as no relevant judgment could be retrieved in electronic databases.

7. INTERNATIONAL SURROGACY ARRANGEMENTS

The Greek provisions on surrogacy, referring both to the conditions under which surrogacy is permissible and its consequences as to the establishment of the child's parental descent, apply irrespective of the nationality of the surrogate or of the commissioning parents in all procedures that take place in Greece provided that either the surrogate or the intended mother have a domicile or temporary residence in the country.[113] Given that gestational surrogacy is broadly available in Greece, international surrogacy arrangements, meaning arrangements concluded abroad, appear rather seldom in practice. Thus it

---

111 See Art. 26 of Law 3305/2005, covering almost all possible instances of breach of the relevant rules.

112 See Art. 26 sent. 2 of Law 3305/2005.

113 In this sense it has been supported that Art. 8 of Law 3089/2002 is a somehow concealed conflict of law rule. See T. Korka, 'Developments in the Field of Family Law – The Institution of Surrogacy' in Ch. Tsouka (ed.), *International Family Law*, Nomiki Vivliothiki, Athens 2016, pp. 89 ff., at p. 111, n. 110 (in Greek). See also K. Rokas, above n. 27, pp. 156 ff., who ascertains that this approach has been followed consistently by case law, but expresses his reservations to it.

comes as no surprise that there exist no special rules as to such arrangements that take place in other jurisdictions, while the legal literature has not dealt in depth with this issue.

In addition, given the permissibility of surrogacy in Greece, the recognition of parenthood arising out of a surrogacy arrangement in another jurisdiction does not seem problematic in principle. This is no longer the case if there arise issues as to the compatibility of such recognition with the Greek *ordre public*. Case law has dealt with this issue in an extreme case,[114] where a woman, after the death of her son, commissioned two surrogates in Russia who, using the sperm of the deceased and their own ova, gave birth to four children in total. The intended mother (or grandmother) then adopted the children in Russia and filed a request before the Greek courts for the recognition of the relevant Russian court decision. The court denied the request on the grounds that the Russian judgment contravened the Greek *ordre public*. This has been due to many concurring reasons: First, the deceased had never granted his consent to post-mortem artificial reproduction. Secondly, even if he had consented, it would be up to his partner and not up to his mother to proceed to the use of his genetic material. Thirdly, the ova that were fertilised were the ones of the surrogates (traditional surrogacy). Fourthly the intended mother (or grandmother) had exceeded all age limits that are set by the law both for surrogacy and for adoption. Lastly, the commissioning of two surrogates at the same time also gives rise to questions.

In cases where the deviations from Greek law are neither so blatant nor act cumulatively it does not seem probable that the assignment of parenthood to the intended parents would be considered to be against the *ordre public*.[115] This assignment would actually serve the best interests of the child that form an integral part of the *ordre public*.[116] In the (rather unlikely) case that this were

---

114 See Decision 7013/2013 of the Single-member Court of First Instance of Thessaloniki, *Efarmoges Astikou Dikaiou* 2013, 337, commented by K. Pantelidou.

115 According to the established case law of the Greek Supreme Court (Areopag) the *ordre public* comprises all fundamental rules and principles of highest importance that prevail in Greece at a specific point in time and reflect social, financial, political, religious, moral and other views. See, among others, plenary Decisions 4/2012, *Efarmoges Astikou Dikaiou* 2012, 578; 11/2009, Legal Database Intrasoft-Nomos; 17/2008 *Elliniki Dikaiosyni* 2008, 977; 6/1990, *Elliniki Dikaiosyni* 1, 990, 552.

116 The pursuit of the best interests of the child is a fundamental principle of Greek Family Law (see esp. Art. 1511 para. 1, 1542 and 1648 of the GrCC). See on this issue S. Koukouli-Spiliotopoulou in Ap. Georgiades and M. Stathopoulos (eds), above n. 55, Introduction to Arts 1505–1541, no. 204 ff.; E. Kounougeri-Manoledaki, above n. 47, vol. I, p. 13. See also the UN Convention on the Rights of the Child (esp. Art. 3 para. 1), that has been ratified by Law 2101/1992, *Official Gazette*, issue A, no. 192/2.12.1992. On the close connection between the best interests of the child and the *ordre public* see also, among many others, the decisions of the Court of Appeals of Thessaloniki, Legal Database Intrasoft-Nomos and 2438/2009 of the Multi-member Court of First Instance of Thessaloniki, *Efarmoges Astikou Dikaiou* 2010, 311.

not accepted, legal parenthood could be established between the child and the intended parents through adoption. This result seems to be also supported by the recent judgments of the European Court of Human Rights in the cases of *Mennesson v France* and *Labassée v France*.[117]

Finally, as to the nationality of the child born to an international surrogacy arrangement, there arise no particularities. The Code of Greek Nationality would apply, according to which if one of the (legal) parents is a Greek national, the child also acquires the Greek nationality already at birth.[118]

8. CONCLUSION

Overall, the legal framework of surrogacy in Greece is regarded as liberal and innovative. It has also been proven workable in practice. In particular the legislator's decision to determine the child's descent ex ante, by coupling it to the court's authorisation of surrogacy before the embryo transfer is seen as particularly successful. Thanks to this clear-cut solution, Greek courts have not been confronted with complex ethical problems that may arise in cases where the surrogate does not give up the child, or the commissioning parents no longer wish to have the child, (for example, because of an illness or disability).[119]

Currently there are no suggestions for reform of the regulation of surrogacy. In the last years though the voices in favour of commercial surrogacy become louder. In fact practice has shown that the provisions on altruistic surrogacy are rather unenforceable and there is little doubt that the interest of the surrogate would be better protected if she were paid on the basis of a valid contract, controlled by a judge, rather than under the table.[120]

A more general issue of medically assisted reproduction which according to a great part of the legal literature should be revisited is the anonymity of donors of genetic material.[121] The legislator's balancing of the donor's privacy and of the protection of the 'social family' against the child's right to know his/her genetic origins is put to question. A provision similar to the one of adoption, according to which once the child reaches majority has the right to be informed on his/her

---

117 See Decisions of 26.06.2014 (on applications 65192/11 and 65941/11) nos 96 ff. and 75 ff. respectively.

118 The same holds for children born in Greece by a parent who was also born in Greece and has been domiciled in the country permanently ever since. See Arts 1 and 2 of Law 3284/2004.

119 See on this point also K. Rokas, above n. 27, p. 148.

120 See esp. T. Vidalis, 'Surrogacy "Tourism"' in (2016) *Assisted Reproduction in Europe. Social, Ethical and Legal Issues*, available at: <https://ejournals.lib.auth.gr/culres/article/download/4956/4921> accessed 07.09.2018 and A. Hatzis, 'From Soft to Hard Paternalism and back: The Regulation of Surrogate Motherhood in Greece' (2009) *Portuguese Economic Journal* 205 ff.

121 See above n. 100.

biological parents[122] would seem preferable in case of assisted reproduction as well. In any case, this should not bring about changes as to legal parenthood.[123]

A question which is not yet settled is the possibility of single men who cannot have a child in the natural way to commission a surrogate.[124] Finally, the debate concerning the possibility of same-sex couples of accessing medically assisted reproduction techniques in order to have a child has hardly opened. This issue is parallel to the question as to whether same-sex partners should be granted the right to adopt a child, which has been likewise not sufficiently discussed. This discussion constitutes logically the next step, after the relatively recent legal recognition of same-sex couples.[125]

122 See Art. 1559 of the GrCC.

123 Of this opinion P. Agallopoulou, above n. 100; E. Zervogianni, above n. 100. Cf. also Ch. Stampelou, above n. 100; G. Lekkas, above n. 42, pp. 65–66.

124 See above Section 4.2.

125 See above n. 78.

SURROGACY IN ISRAEL

Rhona SCHUZ

1. GENERAL LEGAL FRAMEWORK

1.1. LEGAL RULES RELATING TO SURROGACY

Israel was the first country in the world to regulate surrogacy by legislation. The Surrogate Motherhood Agreements (Approval of Agreement and Status of Newborn Law) 1996 (hereinafter 'the Surrogacy Law') legalised gestational surrogacy agreements which fulfilled the conditions set out in the Surrogacy Law and received approval from a Statutory Committee (hereinafter 'the Approvals Committee'), set up under that Law.[1] The Surrogacy Law specifically allows for payments to be made to the surrogate mother to compensate her for her time and suffering and thus surrogacy in Israel is commercial. Whilst the scheme is widely considered successful, over the years it became clear that some aspects needed improving. As will be explained below, a recent amendment law[2] made some improvements, but did not address all of the problems. The Surrogacy Law relates only to cases where the implantation of the embryo takes place in Israel. In recent years, for reasons which will be set out below, a growing number of Israelis have entered into agreements with foreign surrogates. Since Israeli law does not forbid this practice, it is not illegal. In the absence of legislative regulation, the procedure for determining the status of the children born as a result of such arrangements is governed by administrative guidelines, as modified by judicial decisions, which will be explained below.

1.2. THE APPROVALS COMMITTEE

Surrogacy arrangements have to be authorised by the Approvals Committee, set up under the Surrogacy Law.[3] The Committee is appointed by the Minister of Health and includes two doctors with expertise in gynaecology and obstetrics;

1 For detailed analysis of this Law, see R. Schuz 'Surrogacy in Israel: An Analysis of the Law in Practice' in R. Cook and S.D. Sclater (eds), *Surrogate Motherhood: International Perspectives*, Hart Publishing, Oxford 2003, pp. 35–54. See also S. Shakargy, 'Israel' in K. Trimmings and P. Beaumont, *International Surrogacy Arrangements*, Hart Publishing, Oxford 2013.

2 The Surrogate Motherhood Agreements (Approval of Agreement and Status of Newborn Law) (Amendment No. 2) Law 2018.

3 The Surrogate Motherhood Agreements (Approval of Agreement and Status of Newborn Law) 1996 s. 1.

one doctor with expertise in internal medicine; a clinical psychologist; a social worker; a lawyer; and a religious cleric (according to the religion of the parties).[4]

The Surrogacy Law[5] provides that applications to the Committee have to include a draft surrogacy agreement, a medical opinion confirming that the commissioning mother is unable to carry a pregnancy or that pregnancy would involve a significant risk to health; opinions from doctors and psychologists as to the suitability of each of the parties to participate in the process; confirmation from a psychologist or social worker that the commissioning parents received appropriate professional advice, including in relation to other possibilities of parenthood. The Committee is required to hear all the parties and is entitled to request additional information.

Surrogacy agreements may be authorised where the Committee is satisfied, on the basis of all the facts arising from the documents and the hearing that: (a) all the parties are entering into the agreement voluntarily and understand its significance and its consequences; (b) there is no risk to the health of the surrogate or the welfare of the child to be born; (c) that the surrogacy agreement doesn't contain conditions which harm or prejudice the rights of the child to be born or those of one of the parties.[6]

The Committee has formulated requirements over and above those contained in the Surrogacy Law, which have been published in Guidelines to Applicants. Whilst not strictly binding, the Committee is allowed to give weight to these requirements in exercising its discretion.[7]

1.3. BACKGROUND TO THE SURROGACY LAW

1.3.1. Legal Background

The Surrogacy Law was born as a result of challenges by childless couples to the Public Health (In Vitro Fertilization) Regulations 1987 ('IVF Regulations'), which provided inter alia that fertilised eggs could only be implanted into the womb of the woman who was intended to be their mother. After the Nachmani couple[8] petitioned the High Court of Justice ('HCJ') in 1991, claiming that

---

4 Ibid. s. 2. Under s. 3 of the Amendment Law (above n. 2), one member of the Committee must be a State employee and the term for serving on the Committee is four years, with a possibility of an additional four-year extension.

5 Ibid. s. 4.

6 Ibid. s. 5.

7 HCJ 625/10 *Plonit and Ploni v The Approvals Committee* (26.07.11).

8 In relation to the compromise reached in this case and the later dispute between the couple, see R. Schuz, 'The Right to Parenthood: Surrogacy and Frozen Embryos' in A. Bainham (ed.), *The International Survey of Family Law*, Kluwer Law International, The Hague 1996, pp. 237–56.

these regulations were ultra vires, a committee headed by Justice Aloni was set up to consider the question of surrogate motherhood in Israel. Its report, published in 1994,[9] recommended a regulatory approach to surrogacy, under which agreements should be allowed, provided that they would be approved by a statutory committee, and the child would be treated as that of the intended parents.

A year later, a group of childless couples petitioned the HCJ for judicial review of the IVF Regulations on the basis that they breached the fundamental right to parenthood and discriminated against couples who were unable to reproduce naturally.[10] The Minister of Health accepted that the question of surrogacy should be dealt with in primary legislation and asked the court to allow the Regulations to remain in force for six months to allow for the enactment of such legislation. This gave the necessary impetus for the enactment of the Surrogacy Law, which adopted most of the recommendations of the Aloni Committee.

1.3.2. Sociological, Religious and Cultural Background

There are a number of explanations for the fact that Israel, in contrast to most other Western countries (barring some states in the United States) expressly sanctions commercial surrogacy. Firstly, the prevailing view is that principles of autonomy and privacy require minimum State interference in human reproduction[11] and there has been express judicial recognition of the right to become a parent.[12] Secondly, allowing only altruistic surrogacy was not a realistic option since a close family relationship between the surrogate and one of the commissioning parents raises doubts about the status of the child in Jewish law, as will be seen below. The third reason is the centrality of procreation in Israeli society[13] and the corresponding policy of encouraging childbirth.[14]

---

9 Report of the Public Committee on In Vitro Fertilization 1994 ('The Aloni Report').

10 HCJ 94/5087 *Zabaro and others v Minister of Health* (17.07.95).

11 Aloni Report at para. 1A5; 'Report of the Public Committee for Examining Legislative Regulation of Fertility and Childbirth in Israel' (May 2012) ('Mor-Yosef Committee') available at <www.health.gov.il/PublicationsFiles/BAP2012.pdf> accessed 07.09.2018 (in Hebrew) at p. 9.

12 R. Schuz, 'The Developing Right to Parenthood in Israeli Law' in B. Atkin (ed.) *The International Survey of Family Law*, Jordan Publishing Limited, Bristol 2013, pp. 197–225.

13 See generally: R. Landau, 'Religiosity, Nationalism and Human Reproduction: The Case of Israel' (2003) 23 *International Journal of Sociology & Social Policy* 12, 64, 68; E. Waldman, 'Cultural Priorities Revealed: The Development and Regulation of Assisted Reproduction in the United States and Israel' (2006) 16 *Health Matrix: Journal of Law-Medicine* 65.

14 The birth rate is currently 3.1, whilst most other OECD countries the rate is less than two, <https://www.oecd.org/els/family/SF_2_1_Fertility_rates.pdf> accessed 07.09.2018. Israel enjoys the highest rate of infertility therapy per capita coverage worldwide (C. Shalev and S. Goldin, 'The Uses and Misuses of In Vitro Fertilization in Israel' (2006) 12 *Nashim: A Journal of Jewish Women's Studies* 151–76) and is the only country in the world to finance unlimited numbers of treatments from public funds (Ministry of Health, Handbook on IVF,

Various explanations have been advanced for these pro-natalist attitudes, including religious,[15] political,[16] historical[17] and security reasons.[18]

1.4. STATISTICS

The number of applications to the Approvals Committee has risen steadily over the years, with 119 in 2014.[19] Out of the 1,042 applications submitted between 1996 and the end of 2014, there were only 408 births,[20] even though 98 per cent of the applications were approved.[21] Surrogacy can be carried out in any clinic which gives IVF treatment and in 2013 there were 25 such clinics in Israel.[22] In a random research sample of 210 surrogate births, a third involved caesarean section, even though the vast majority of the surrogates had given birth vaginally previously.[23]

The only method of ascertaining the number of foreign surrogacy arrangements undertaken by Israeli citizens is from the number of petitions to court to recognise parenthood following foreign surrogacy. In 2014, there were 232 such petitions.[24] The most popular countries for such surrogacy in 2014

<http://www.health.gov.il/PublicationsFiles/IVF-handbook.pdf> accessed 07.09.2018 (in Hebrew)); approximately four per cent of births in Israel result from IVF <http://www.health.gov.il/PublicationsFiles/IVF1986_2013.pdf> accessed 07.09.2018; <www.health.gov.il> accessed 07.09.2018 (in Hebrew).

15 The first religious commandment in the Bible is to 'be fruitful and multiply' (Genesis 1:28), and the importance of reproduction is a recurring theme in the Old Testament and later Jewish sources. E.g. Rachel's plea 'Give me children, or else I die' (Genesis 30:1) (quoted frequently in the cases concerning the right to parenthood of infertile couples). Reproduction is also important in Muslim tradition, see 'Mor-Yosef Report', above n. 11, p. 4.

16 Zionist ideology and demographic reality require a high rate of childbirth among the Jewish population in order to ensure that there remains a Jewish majority in the Jewish State, E. Waldman, above n. 13, pp. 73–74.

17 The need to replenish the Jewish people after the massacre of six million Jews in the Holocaust, E. Waldman above n. 13, at p. 72.

18 The need to replenish those who fell in the many wars and terrorist attacks and to provide soldiers who will continue to defend Israel from those who seek its destruction, R. Landau, above n. 13.

19 <http://www.health.gov.il/PublicationsFiles/SurrogacyApproved.pdf> accessed 07.09.2018.

20 Ibid.

21 <http://www.health.gov.il/Subjects/fertility/Surrogacy/Pages/default.aspx> (in Hebrew) accessed 07.09.2018. In a random research sample, 61 per cent of the agreements did not end in a birth, N. Lipkin and E. Samama, 'From a Heroic Act to a Shelf Product – the Crawling Normalization of Surrogacy in Israel', (2013) 15 *Mishpat Umimshal* 464 (in Hebrew).

22 Ministry of Health IVF Handbook, above n. 14.

23 E. Samama, 'A Womb to Rent, The Surrogate Motherhood Agreements Law: Vision, Policy and Reality' (Doctoral Thesis, Ben Gurion University, 2014) (in Hebrew) at p. 136.

24 R. Zafran and D. Hacker, 'Research Report: International Surrogacy in Israel, submitted to the Mission of Research for Law and Justice – the Ministry of Justice of the French Republic' (2016) (on file with author). This figure should be contrasted with the 65 births of children born as a result of surrogacy in Israel in that year, above n. 17.

were Georgia (86), US (29), India (15), Thailand (66), Nepal (29). However, since then the latter three countries have closed their doors to foreign commissioning parents.[25]

2. SURROGACY ARRANGEMENTS IN GENERAL

2.1. STATUS AND TERMS OF SURROGACY AGREEMENTS

As stated above, contracts to perform surrogacy in Israel are legal so long as they are approved by the Approvals Committee. They are binding in the sense that the surrogate may not renege on the agreement and refuse to hand over the child, unless a court is convinced that there has been a change of circumstances which justifies her change of mind and this will not harm the welfare of the child.[26]

The Committee will not approve a surrogacy agreement unless the surrogate and commissioning parents have received independent and separate legal advice in relation to the terms of the agreement and their implications.

The Committee publishes detailed guidelines about the terms to be included in the agreement.[27] In relation to some issues, the guidelines mandate the terms to be included. In relation to other issues, they simply state that a provision relating thereto should be included. For example, the parties must state the remedies for breach of the agreement, but no guidance is given in relation to the content of these remedies. Most of the provisions relate to financial matters (discussed below) and medical matters.

The agreement must state that all medical procedures will be carried out with the informed written consent of the surrogate[28] and that she is entitled to obtain a second opinion from a doctor of her choice. In particular, it should be made clear that the surrogate is entitled to terminate the pregnancy in accordance with the law.[29] However, where this is done for non-medical reasons, the remedies provided for in the contract will apply.[30]

The parties are to make provision for the period of time over which the attempts to secure a pregnancy will continue (not more than 18 months) and

---

25 R. Zafran and D. Hacker, ibid.

26 Section 13 of the Surrogacy Law.

27 <http://www.health.gov.il/DocLib/pon_tofes13.pdf> accessed 07.09.2018 (in Hebrew).

28 This reflects s. 18 of the Surrogacy Law, which provides that nothing in that Law or the surrogacy agreement derogates from the need for informed consent for every medical procedure or from the surrogate's right to any medical treatment, including termination of pregnancy in accordance with the law.

29 This has happened in at least one case (lecture by Legal Advisor to Minister of Health on 22.01.17).

30 This may mean that the surrogate will have to return payment which she has received, N. Lipkin and E. Samama, above n. 21, p. 462.

the number of attempts at implanting embryos (no more than six).[31] In addition, the parties should make provision for the maximum number of embryos to be implanted[32] and for reduction in the case of multiple pregnancy.

The agreement should include provision in relation to the abstinence of the surrogate from dangerous behaviour, such as smoking,[33] or from other conduct forbidden by the doctor responsible. In addition, the surrogate should agree not to have sexual intercourse from the date of her last period until 21 days after the implantation and not to have unprotected intercourse throughout the entire period of the treatment.

2.2. REMUNERATION OF THE SURROGATE

Whilst the payments have to be approved, in practice the Approvals Committee does not interfere with the sums agreed which are determined by market forces, other than in relation to the items set out below. Currently, the average cost of the process is around US$66,000, of which US$40,000 is the basic sum paid to the surrogate, to compensate her for her time, suffering and impaired earning capacity and the remainder covers expenses and other extras provided for in the agreement (discussed below).[34]

The Committee's guidelines provide various items of expenditure for which the commissioning parents must be responsible, in addition to the basic sum paid to the surrogate for carrying the embryo. These items include independent legal advice, life insurance,[35] psychological counselling[36] and direct and indirect expenses incurred due to hospitalisation resulting from the pregnancy. In addition, the agreement must provide for additional payment for extra tests or procedures, such as amniocentesis and caesarean section. Similarly, an additional payment must be made for multiple pregnancies. Where it is necessary to use a foreign donated egg and the embryo implantation is to take place abroad, the commissioning parents have to cover all the expenses involved and take out full health insurance for the surrogate.

---

31 This maximum is now enacted in the Draft Amendment Law, above n. 2.

32 The parties are referred to Ministry of Health guidelines which recommend implanting two embryos for the first three attempts, unless there are special circumstances, and not exceeding four embryos.

33 Also sometimes the eating of certain foods is forbidden, N. Lipkin and E. Samama, above n. 21, p. 460.

34 <http://www.poriyut-guide.com/2011/09/06/surrogacy/?gclid=CODtsbf6_dECFeUV0wodEr8FwQ#A7> accessed 07.09.2018 (in Hebrew).

35 But it is not possible to acquire insurance cover for loss of fertility or other medical problems which can be caused by the process, N. Lipkin and E. Samama, above n. 21, p. 463.

36 But many surrogates don't make use of this and sometimes the money is then paid to them, ibid, p. 461.

The commissioning parents must deposit in a trustee account in the name of a lawyer or accountant, agreed by the parties, sufficient funds to cover all potential payments to the surrogate. Confirmation by the trustee of this deposit is a condition for the granting of the approval by the Committee. The trustee releases the sums to the surrogate in accordance with the agreement.

Concern has been expressed that the usual structure of payments means that in cases where the treatment fails or the surrogate miscarries, she is poorly remunerated.[37] This is likely to exacerbate the stress and anguish caused by the failure of the treatments.

3. LEGAL PARENTHOOD AT THE TIME OF BIRTH

3.1. LEGAL PARENTHOOD

Section 10(b) of the Surrogacy Law provides that a social worker, appointed by the chief social worker, will be the child's legal guardian from the time of his birth until a parenthood order is granted to the commissioning parents. There is no express legislative provision in Israeli law providing who are the parents of a child, but it is generally assumed that the legal parents are the child's biological father and gestational mother.[38] Thus, the Surrogacy Law is an exception to this basic rule.

3.2. REGISTRATION

The name of the surrogate mother, together with her identity number, nationality and religion are recorded in the register of parenthood orders.[39]

3.3. ACCESS TO INFORMATION

The child upon reaching 18 is entitled to look at the details in the register, subject to the approval of the Chief Social Worker.[40] The Registrar of Marriages also has access to the register.[41]

---

37 N. Lipkin and E. Samama, above n. 21, p. 462.

38 R. Schuz and A. Blecher-Prigat, 'Child and Family Law in Israel: Dynamism and Schizophrenia' in E. Sutherland (ed.), *The Future of Child and Family Law: International Predictions*, Cambridge University Press, Cambridge 2012, p. 191.

39 Surrogacy Agreement (Approval of the Agreement and Status of the Child)(Registration) Regulations 1998.

40 Ibid. Section 16 of the Law provides that the provisions in relation to access to the register of adoption orders shall also apply to the register of parenthood orders.

41 Ibid.

4. ELIGIBILITY FOR SURROGACY

4.1. ELIGIBILITY CRITERIA FOR SURROGATES

Under the Surrogacy Law, the surrogate must fulfil the following criteria: (a) be over 18; (b) be a resident of Israel; (c) not be married, but the Committee may allow married surrogates where it is satisfied that the commissioning parents could not with reasonable effort locate an unmarried surrogate; (d) not be a relative of either of the commissioning parents; (e) be the same religion as the commissioning mother (unless none of the parties are Jewish and the cleric on the Committee agrees).

The last three criteria reflect controversies in Jewish law relating to the status of a child born as a result of a surrogacy arrangement. Firstly, it is not clear whether the child is treated as the offspring of the genetic mother or the gestational mother and so the requirement that both the mothers are Jewish avoids any doubts as to whether the child is Jewish (which is determined by the religion of the mother). Secondly, it is not entirely clear that a child born to a married Jewish surrogate is not treated like a child born from an adulterous or incestuous relationship, who is called a *mamzer* (usually translated inaccurately as a bastard), and subject to serious marriage restrictions. The majority view is that a child born as a result of IVF cannot be a *mamzer* because there was no forbidden sexual contact, but a minority opinion takes the view that the status derives from the presence of a forbidden man's gametes in the married woman's womb. Accordingly, to avoid any doubt, the Surrogacy Law requires that the surrogate usually be unmarried and not related to the commissioning parents.

In addition to the criteria contained in the Surrogacy Law, the Approvals Committee added a number of criteria. Three of these, with small variations, have now been enacted in the Surrogacy Amendment Law:[42] that the surrogate (a) is aged 22 to 38; (b) must have already given birth not as a surrogate mother and the child must not have been placed out of home by a court order; (c) must not have given birth more than four times; (d) must not have been a surrogate more than twice previously.

4.2. CHARACTERISTICS OF SURROGATES

It will be noted that the combination of these criteria means that surrogates are divorced, widowed or single mothers. Indeed, research on a sample of 275 surrogacy applications submitted between 1996 and 2002 revealed

[42] Above n. 2. The requirement that the surrogate should not have a criminal record was not enacted.

that 75 per cent of the surrogates were divorced and 22 per cent were single mothers.[43] Additional data from the research sample relating to the characteristics of the surrogate mother include the following: average age was 31;[44] 30 per cent were born abroad[45] (of whom 20 per cent in the former Soviet Union);[46] only seven per cent had post-high school education; 25 per cent did not work and 33 per cent worked in menial jobs;[47] 49 per cent were of average intelligence and 21 per cent of low intelligence.[48] 80 per cent of the surrogates in this sample stated that their motives for participating in the process were financial.[49] However, there is some evidence of a change in the profile of surrogates in recent years, with an increase in the number of surrogates who have had higher education and whose motives are altruistic.[50]

4.3. ELIGIBILITY CRITERIA FOR COMMISSIONING PARENTS

Under the Surrogacy Law, the commissioning parents must fulfil the following criteria: (a) be a heterosexual married couple; (b) be Israeli residents; (c) the commissioning mother must have medical problems preventing her from bearing a child (or making it medically risky for her to do so); and (d) the sperm must be that of her husband. Petitions claiming that the first condition is unconstitutional because it discriminates on the basis of marital status, gender and sexual tendency have been submitted to the HCJ.

The first challenge was by a single woman, who wished to have her eggs, which had been fertilised by donor sperm, implanted into the womb of a surrogate mother. The HCJ, whilst accepting that the statutory requirements discriminated against single women, rejected her petition on the basis that a decision to extend the use of surrogacy had to be made by the legislature, in the light of the novel, delicate and complex nature of surrogacy.[51] Indeed, the

---

43 N. Lipkin and E. Samama, above n. 21, p. 457.

44 Ibid.

45 Ibid. (among the general population, 7.9 per cent were born abroad).

46 Ibid.

47 Ibid.

48 Ibid.

49 E. Samama, above n. 23, p. 231, but some of these (32 per cent) stated a combined financial and altruistic motive.

50 Legal Adviser to the Health Ministry at a conference on 26.01.17; lecture by a surrogate who is a clinical psychologist in a conference on 19.6.2018.

51 HCJ 2458/01 *New Family v Approvals Committee for Surrogate Motherhood Agreements, Ministry of Health*, 57(1) PD 419; for detailed discussion of this case, see R. Schuz, 'Surrogacy And PA In The Israeli Supreme Court and The Reports Of The Committee On Children's Rights' in A. Bainham (ed.), *The International Survey of Family Law 2004 Edition*, Family Law, Bristol 2004, p. 247.

Surrogacy Amendment Law,[52] now allows single women who are unable to bear children to enter into a surrogacy arrangement, provided that they use their own egg.

More recently, a similar challenge was brought by a homosexual couple and is awaiting a decision by the HCJ.[53] The position of the State, submitted to the HCJ by the Attorney-General,[54] is that there it is legitimate to distinguish between men and women because there is a material difference between women who cannot bear a child because of medical problems and men, who were not intended by nature to bear children. Moreover, in deciding whether surrogacy arrangements should be available other than in extreme medical cases, it is necessary to take into account the need to protect the interests of surrogates and the interests of those women who need surrogacy because of medical problems. This view mirrors that of the Mor-Yosef Committee,[55] which unanimously recommended that the current commercial scheme should not be extended to men, out of concern that the huge rise in demand would lead to unsuitable women being surrogates[56] and increased undesirable commercialisation.[57]

In addition to the statutory eligibility criteria for commissioning parents, a further two were added by the Committee (a) that the commissioning mother is no older than 53; and (b) that the couple does not have more than two joint children already. Challenges were brought against both of these criteria. In the first,[58] the refusal was based on the age of the parties, who were aged 58 (man) and 53 (woman) at that date of submission of the application, four years previously.[59] The Family Court held that the considerable weight which had been given to the age of the parties in this case was appropriate, balanced and

52 Above n. 2.

53 HCJ 781/15 *Arad-Pinkas v The Approvals Committee and the Knesset*. In a decision, dated 03.08.17, the HCJ decided to suspend the hearing of the case to allow for exhaustion of the legislative process of amending the law, even though at no stage during the legislative process did the Amendment Law allow men without a female partner to be commissioning parents. However, a few of the judges did make comments suggesting a tendency to support the petitioners' claim that the Law is an unconstitutional violation of the right to equality. However, the HCJ did hold that a condition requiring use of the gametes of one of the commissioning parents was legitimate and that this requirement ensured a distinction between surrogacy and creation of children for adoption.

54 On 07.07.16, <http://www.justice.gov.il/Pubilcations/News/Pages/State'sResponseRegardingSurrogacyJuly16.aspx> accessed 07.09.2018.

55 Mor-Yosef Committee, above n. 11, pp. 56–59.

56 The difficulty in finding suitable surrogates is evidenced by the fact that this now takes around a year, at least double the time previously, N. Lipkin and E. Samama, above n. 21, p. 458.

57 The solution of the majority was to set up a parallel altruistic scheme for men, allowing some relatives to serve as surrogates. The solution of the minority was to revoke the current scheme and allow only altruistic surrogacy for all, above n. 11, p. 55.

58 FamC 26140/07 *Plonit and Ploni v State Attorney's Department – Central District* (15.02.2010).

59 At that time, the guidelines required the Committee to take into account the parties' age where this is above that of natural fertility, i.e. 48 to 50.

in accordance with the objective of the Surrogacy Law. The Amendment Law has now introduced a requirement that at least one of the commissioning parents is not yet 54, but gives the court discretion to dispense with it in special circumstances.

The second challenge was to an *in limine* refusal by the Committee of an application by a couple with three children and was upheld on the basis that the Surrogacy Law did not limit the number of children of applicants. Accordingly, there was no basis for *in limine* rejection of the application, but the fact that the applicants already had three joint children was a relevant factor in exercising the discretion whether to give approval. The Amendment Law has now introduced such a limitation.[60] The Surrogacy Amendment Law has also added the requirement that the intended parents have not been convicted of an offence which, in the light of its severity or circumstances, constitutes a risk to the welfare of the child and criminal proceedings are not pending against them in relation to such an offence.[61]

4.4. DONOR GAMETES

As stated above, donor eggs, but not donor sperm, may be used for surrogacy arrangements.[62] Where the egg is donated in Israel, the requirements of the Egg Donation Law 2010 must be satisfied. This Act requires that the donor be aged 21–35; unmarried; not related to the donee and of the same religion as the donee.[63] The Act severs any connection between the donor and the child for civil law purposes, but expressly does not impact on the status under religious law in matters of marriage and divorce or on the powers of the religious courts. The Law sets up a confidential Registry of children born as a result of egg donations. The Register will inform adult applicants whether they were born as a result of egg donation and, if so, whether there is any genetic relationship between them and a potential marriage partner. Whilst generous payment is made to donors,[64]

60 Providing that couples must not have more than two joint children and single women must not have more than two genetic children, above n. 2. Interestingly, the Law allows the Minister of Health, with the approval of the Committee for Employment, Welfare and Health, to increase this provision to three children, but not before 1 August 2023.

61 Above n. 2.

62 In a research sample, around a quarter of the cases involved egg donation, N. Lipkin and E. Samama, above n. 21, p. 478.

63 A committee may make exceptions to some of these requirements, s. 22 of the Egg Donation Law.

64 The original payment of 10,000 NIS (US$2,500) was almost doubled to 19,000 NIS in 2013, in the hope that this would attract more donations, <http://www.mako.co.il/news-israel/health/Article-7fecdf5544f1241004.htm> accessed 07.09.2018 (in Hebrew).

in practice relatively few eggs are donated in Israel[65] and most women in need of a donations use foreign eggs.

The importation of eggs from abroad is regulated by secondary legislation, which allows implantation in recognised IVF units in Israel of eggs donated abroad, where the medical staff are satisfied that a series of requirements, relating to the donor and the procedure for egg donation, are satisfied.[66] In practice, in order to ensure compliance, egg harvesting is carried out abroad under the supervision of Israeli doctors.[67] Foreign eggs are donated anonymously and the donee does not obtain any information about the donor.

5. TRANSFERRING PARENTHOOD

5.1. LEGAL PROCESS

Section 10 of the Surrogacy Law provides for the formal handing over of the baby to the commissioning parents in the presence of a social worker as soon as possible after the birth. While, as noted above, the social worker is the legal guardian of the child, the commissioning parents have physical custody.

The commissioning parents must apply for a parenthood order within seven days of the child's birth and the court must make this order unless it is satisfied that this course of action would not be consistent with the welfare of the child.[68] The consequence of the parenthood order is that the commissioning parents are the legal parents and sole guardians of the child for all intents and purposes.[69] There are no known cases where parenthood orders have not been granted, but there has been criticism of the delays caused by the need for a social report, which can result in practical difficulties due to the fact that in the meantime any act which requires parental consent, such as medical treatment, has to be approved by the social worker.

---

65 During the four years 2013–16 inclusive, 133 women donated eggs (communication from Ministry of Health).

66 Public Health (IVF) Regulations 1987 s. 2A (added in 2001).

67 <https://www.health.gov.il/Subjects/fertility/ovum_donation/Pages/default.aspx> accessed 07.09.2018 (in Hebrew). There is anecdotal evidence that this practice means that eggs of the same donor are used by a number of women, resulting in a proliferation of genetic siblings.

68 Under the original law, a parenthood order could not be granted without a social report. Under the Surrogacy Amendment Law, above n. 2, there is no need for a social report unless a social worker informs the court that there is a risk to the welfare of the child or the court requests a report.

69 Section 12 of the Surrogacy Law.

5.2. DISPUTES

Section 13 of the Surrogacy Law provides that the surrogate may not renege on her undertaking to hand over the child, unless a court is satisfied that there has been a change in the circumstances which justify her change of mind and this will not harm the child's welfare.

In practice, there have not been any cases where the surrogate has asked to keep the child.

Any disputes concerning alleged breach of the terms of a surrogacy arrangement would be adjudicated by a court. No such cases have been reported. However, an NGO report about surrogacy[70] mentions a case where a commissioning mother sued the Approvals Committee for lack of care in authorising the surrogate, claiming that she had suffered psychological harm. The parties came to a settlement under which the mother received some compensation.

5.3. INFORMATION ABOUT THE SURROGATE

A special register, set up under the Surrogacy Law, records details of the parentage order, the surrogate mother, the commissioning parents and the child. These details include the name, identity number, religion and nationality of the birth parent. The child may access these details on reaching the age of 18, subject to the agreement of the Chief Social Worker.[71]

5.4. CHILD'S RIGHTS

As stated above, the stringent screening of the parties is intended inter alia to protect the child's right to be born healthy and his future welfare. In addition, his right to privacy is protected by the fact that the Register of children born under surrogacy arrangements is confidential[72] and by the prohibition of publishing identifying information about the child.[73] Similarly, his right to know his parents is protected by the fact that he may receive information about the surrogate mother upon reaching 18. However, in the case of an egg donation, he will not be able to obtain any identifying information about his genetic mother.

---

70 N. Lipkin and E. Samama 'Surrogacy in Israel – Status Report 2010 and Proposals for Legislative Amendment' (2011), p. 47, <http://isha.org.il/wp-content/uploads/2014/08/surrogacy_Eng001.pdf> accessed 15.10.2018.

71 In any event, in contrast to adoption, the commissioning parents are in possession of identifying information about the surrogate and can pass this onto the child.

72 It may only be accessed by the Registrar of Marriages and the Chief Social Worker.

73 Surrogacy Law s. 19.

6. AGENCIES AND CRIMINALISATION

6.1. AGENCIES

There are a number of agencies in Israel who mediate between commissioning parents and surrogates. Most of the agencies specialise in either local surrogacy or surrogacy abroad, but some of them deal with both types of surrogacy. There is no regulation of the activities of these agencies. In the case of surrogacy in Israel,[74] the contract with the agency must be submitted to the Approvals Committee, but to the best of the author's knowledge, that Committee does not actually interfere in any way with it.[75]

In relation to international surrogacy, there was a law reform proposal to license agencies and to require Israelis making surrogacy arrangements abroad to use the services of one of these recognised agencies.[76] The agencies would have been responsible for ensuring the suitability of the commissioning parents and that the clinic used abroad fulfilled criteria fixed by the law.[77] Following the change of the Minister of Health after the parliamentary elections of 2014, this proposal was dropped and it is understood that there is no intention at the moment to proceed with it.

6.2. PENALTIES

It is a criminal offence to implant fertilised eggs into a surrogate mother other than in accordance with the provisions of the Surrogacy Law.[78] In addition, offering or accepting payment in relation to the carrying out of a surrogacy arrangement, other than that authorised by the Approvals Committee is a criminal offence.[79] Furthermore, it is forbidden to publish, without permission of a court, anything said in a session of the Approvals Committee or documents submitted to it or any information which would enable identification of the surrogate, the commissioning parents or the child.[80] In relation to all the offences, the maximum punishment is imprisonment of one year.

---

74 In Samama's sample, an agency was involved in more than 60 per cent of the cases, but more agencies have opened up since then, N. Lipkin and E. Samama, above n. 21, p. 458.

75 The agency fee is around US$7,500, ibid.

76 Surrogate Motherhood Agreements (Amendment No. 2) Draft Law – 2014.

77 There was criticism of this proposal, inter alia, on the basis that the agencies were profit-making bodies, unlike those licensed to deal with inter-country adoption, and that there would therefore be a conflict of interests.

78 Surrogacy Law s. 19.

79 Ibid.

80 Ibid. In the case of FamC 4580/98 *Plonit v A-G*, the Family Court rejected an application to allow screening of a film about the first surrogate birth in Israel in a way which would allow

7. INTERNATIONAL SURROGACY ARRANGEMENTS

7.1. THE PHENOMENON

During the last few years, more and more Israeli couples have turned to foreign surrogacy.[81] About half of these couples are homosexuals who, as seen above, are unable to use the Israeli surrogacy scheme. Others are heterosexual married couples, who do not meet the eligibility criteria of the Surrogacy Law or the guidelines of the Approvals Committee; cannot find a surrogate in Israel or see foreign surrogacy as a method of saving the long-winded bureaucracy involved in the Israeli scheme and sometimes also money.[82]

7.2. THE LAW

In contrast to domestic surrogacy arrangements, there is no regulation of international surrogacy arrangements. Accordingly, it is permissible for an Israeli citizen to enter into a contract with a surrogate abroad, provided that the implantation of fertilised eggs takes place abroad.

The status of the child born as a result of a foreign surrogacy arrangement is determined by the usual laws of parentage. Thus, where the sperm used is that of the commissioning father, he will be a legal parent for all purposes. This means that the child is entitled to Israeli citizenship and to be registered as the child of his father in the Population Registry. However, there is no Law providing for the procedure to be followed in such cases.

7.3. THE ADMINISTRATIVE GUIDELINES

In the light of the lack of express regulation, the Ministries involved formulated guidelines,[83] which reflect the view of State officials as to the general principles of determining parenthood and their concern to prevent illegal trafficking in children. The guidelines have not been published, but are mentioned in court decisions, which, as will be seen below, have required some modification of them.

Under the guidelines, the intended parents have to produce documents evidencing the surrogacy agreement, its legality under the foreign law and the

---

identification of the parties, in order to protect the child's right to privacy. The film was screened with the faces of the parties blurred.

81 For statistics, see above Section 1.4.

82 R. Zafran and D. Hacker, above n. 24.

83 Ibid.

birth mother's consent to the child's removal to Israel, which has to be given at the Israeli consulate in the country of birth. In addition, the intended father of the child has to bring proof that he is the biological father of the child before the child can be allowed to enter the country. This involves obtaining a court order allowing paternity testing. Then, a DNA sample (usually saliva) is taken from the child in the foreign country and sent to Israel via diplomatic post to check that it matches the DNA sample of the intended father, taken before he left Israel. Once paternity is proven, the child is given Israeli citizenship; the biological father is registered as his parent and can bring the child to Israel. However, according to the guidelines, the father's partner (whether this is his wife or a homosexual partner) does not have any status in relation to the child, until he or she adopts him.[84] One of the problems with the procedure is that of time. The parent (or at least one of them) and the newborn child have to stay in the foreign country for a few weeks until paternity is proven.[85] Even once the child comes into Israel, it can take more than a year for the adoption process to be completed.

7.4. JUDICIAL INTERVENTION

The legal challenges against the guidelines can be divided into three categories. The first relates to the situation where the commissioning mother is the genetic mother of the child. Courts have held in a number of cases that the genetic mother is to be treated as the mother of the child, without the need for an adoption or parenthood order.[86]

The second category of case relates to the question of the need to prove biological paternity. In the case of *Mamat-Magad*,[87] a homosexual couple entered into a surrogacy arrangement with a surrogate in the US and donor eggs were fertilised with the sperm of one of them. The couple obtained an order from the court in Pennsylvania declaring them to be the parents of the child to be born and a birth certificate was issued in their names. Their petition to the HCJ to allow them to register the child on the basis of the court order and birth certificate was denied on the basis that the status of the child in Israel can only be recognised upon proof of biological connection. The court took the view that the best method of proving biological connection was via DNA testing, but left

84 This condition was later modified to allow for the granting of a judicial parenthood order, instead of an adoption order (see below n. 91). Whilst this order is constitutive (*A-G v Plonit* (24.05.2018)), the court has discretion to make it retroactive to the date of birth, ibid. and FamC 16-11-49653 *Z.A. v Ministry of Welfare* (12.03.2018), FamA 17-03-28901.

85 Apart from cases where the child is entitled to citizenship in the country where he is born (as in the US), in which case he can enter Israeli with a passport of that country.

86 See e.g. FamC 10509-10-11 *YP and NP v A-Gl*, (05.03.2012); FamC 21170-07-12 *Plonit v A-G*, (03.02.2013).

87 HCJ 566/11 *Mamat-Magad v The Interior Minister* (28.01.2014).

open the possibility that other methods of proof could suffice. The petitioners then brought medical evidence[88] that the chance that the first petitioner was not the father of the child was less than one per cent. This evidence was accepted by the Family Court, since paternity could be proved on the balance of probabilities,[89] but this decision was overturned on appeal by the District Court, in the light of flaws in the expert evidence.[90]

The third category of case relates to the status of the partner of the biological parent. In the case of *Tabak-Aviram*, the homosexual couple proved by a DNA test that one of them was the biological father of the child, born to a US surrogate, and then sought to register the other partner as a father in the population register, on the basis of the US birth certificate.[91] The State refused to allow registration without the non-biological father obtaining an adoption order or a judicial parenthood order.[92] The majority of the High Court of Justice upheld the petition, relying on case law requiring registration of couples who got married abroad on production of a foreign marriage certificate, without any investigation as to whether the marriage is recognised under Israeli law.[93] However, the judges strongly advised the parties to apply for a parenthood order, because otherwise the non-biological father would not in fact be the legal parent of the child.

7.5. PROBLEM SITUATIONS

A number of problem situations have arisen over the past few years. The first involves the policy of the foreign country. The best example of this is the decision in 2015 of the authorities in Nepal to freeze all surrogacy arrangements. Only after great diplomatic efforts was consent obtained to allow the babies conceived before this date to leave.[94]

Secondly, in a few cases, there was found to be no genetic tie between the child and the commissioning parents. In one of these cases, the foreign country did not allow the twins to leave and put them up for adoption locally.[95]

88 Testimony of the doctor in charge of the clinic where the procedures were carried out.

89 FamC 14-05-32901 *Ploni v A-G* (07.08.2016).

90 FamA 41530-10-16 *State of Israel v M.M.* (03.04.2018).

91 HCJ 6569/11 *Tabak-Aviram v The Interior Minister* (28.01.2014).

92 In the course of the proceedings, the A-G announced (on 11.05.2013) that they would no longer require adoption orders and that a judicial parenthood order in favour of the non-biological parent would suffice.

93 E.g. in HCJ 3045/05 *Ben-Ari v Population Registry PD* 61(3) 537, the HCJ ordered registration of the marriage of a homosexual couple on the basis of the Canadian marriage certificate, even though it is clear that such a marriage is not recognised according to the personal law of the parties, which is the applicable law in Israel.

94 R. Zafran and D. Hacker, above n. 24.

95 Ibid.

In another case, the Israeli courts allowed the commissioning parents to bring the children to Israel so that they could institute legal proceedings to determine the future of the children, but they had to deposit large sums to guarantee that they would take the child out of the country if required to do so.[96]

Finally, a sad case illustrates the limits of the recognition of foreign surrogacy.[97] A seriously disabled woman suffering from muscular dystrophy, who was desperate to have a child, arranged for an egg from a South African donor[98] to be fertilised with the sperm of a friend of hers and implanted into her niece in India. After the child was born in Israel, the woman applied for a parenthood order. The Israeli courts rejected her claim that foreign law should be applied, since the child was born in Israel, and denied her request as she did not have a genetic or physiological connection with the child, nor was she the partner of a legal parent. The fact that she had engineered, paid for and accompanied the whole process could not make up for the fact that she did not meet any of the criteria for being recognised as a legal parent. So, the child was placed with adoptive parents.

8. CONCLUSION

On the whole, the current domestic surrogacy scheme works well and there is evidence that Israeli surrogates who succeed in giving birth consider the experience very rewarding, personally as well as financially.[99] Nonetheless, as seen above, some areas of concern have been identified,[100] including the impact of repeated failed attempts to secure a pregnancy on the physical and mental health of surrogates; contractual restrictions on the behaviour of the surrogate and the sudden termination of the intimate relationship between the (often emotionally vulnerable) surrogate and the commissioning parents.[101] These problems could be significantly alleviated by closer regulation of the content of surrogacy agreements and by more social work involvement. In addition, there is a need for more research to assess the long-term effects on the surrogate and her children.

---

96 RFamA 7414/11. Later the couple adopted the child after the surrogate came to Israel and gave her consent (communication from couple's lawyer).

97 RFamA 1118/14 *Plonit v The Ministry of Welfare* (01.04.2015).

98 Previous attempts to implant her own eggs into a foreign surrogate had failed.

99 E. Teman, *Birthing a Mother: The Surrogate Body and the Pregnant Self*, University of California Press, 2010, p. 305. However, this may be dependent on the extent to which she feels appreciated by the commissioning parents, N. Lipkin and E. Samama, above n. 21, p. 479.

100 N. Lipkin and E. Samama, ibid, pp. 480–85.

101 E. Samama, above n. 23, p. 57, found that 66.8 per cent of the surrogates expected to have continued contact after the birth, as opposed to 19 per cent of the commissioning parents.

It is unclear what would the repercussions be of an HCJ ruling that the Surrogacy Law is unconstitutional because it discriminates against men without a female partner. Given the current political constellation, the passing of a law extending the scheme to men seems highly improbable. Even if this became politically feasible, it is difficult to see how the scheme in its present form would be able to cope with the substantially increased demand. In particular, it would be necessary to find means to ensure that the current level of screening of the parties is maintained and that women in need of surrogacy arrangements are not left without a solution. In addition, it would be necessary to consider the impact on the public interest of surrogacy arrangements becoming much more common, especially the risks of increasing commercialisation, as a result of the competition among commissioning parents for the limited number of suitable surrogates.

In any event, both men and women will continue to turn to surrogates abroad. There is little doubt that there is a need to regulate international surrogacy, but how this can be done is far from clear. Unilateral regulation of the type proposed by the Ministry of Health in 2014[102] is likely to be of limited effectiveness, given the difficulty in supervising clinics abroad. It was at Israel's request that the Hague Conference on Private International Law initiated its project in relation to international surrogacy,[103] but whether it will be possible to draft a Convention which will be acceptable to sufficient countries remains to be seen.

---

102 See 2014 Draft Amendment Law, above n. 76.

103 'Private International Law Issues Regarding the Status of Children, including issues arising from international surrogacy arrangements', <https://assets.hcch.net/docs/f5991e3e-0f8b-430c-b030-ca93c8ef1c0a.pdf> accessed 07.09.2018.

SURROGACY IN SOUTH AFRICA

Julia SLOTH-NIELSEN

1. GENERAL LEGAL FRAMEWORK

Steps to regulate surrogacy in South Africa predate the advent of democracy. In 1987, in a much publicised case, Karen Ferreira Jorge gave birth to triplets, born of the gametes of her daughter (she was the gestational mother and the biological grandmother). At the time there was no legal regulation for this unprecedented state of events, leading to a project committee of the South African Law Commission (now the South African Law Reform Commission (hereafter 'SALRC') being appointed to investigate the issue. Although this Committee had completed its work in the 1990s,[1] there was no further legislative action (notwithstanding a post-1994 Ad Hoc Parliamentary Committee being convened to conduct public hearings on surrogacy) to

[1] Draft Bill on Surrogate Motherhood, proposed by SALRC, GN 512 GG 16479, 14 June 1995.

finalise new laws. Ultimately surrogacy was added as a final chapter to the Children's Act 38 of 2005, which came fully into force in April 2010. The project committee which had deliberated upon the development of the omnibus Children's Act had not considered surrogacy during its lifespan, so the impetus to add surrogacy to the Children's Act came from within the SALRC. The initial work of the SALRC has survived, and many of the current provisions can be traced to the original report. The location of regulations on surrogacy within the overarching tenets of the Children's Act has, however, shaped the current interpretation of the provisions, as will be shown below. By way of a preliminary point, the Act allows only altruistic surrogacy: commercial surrogacy is barred.

South Africa stands out for its progressive constitution, with two particular clauses worthy of discussion. First, s. 28 provides a mini charter of children's rights, including the injunction that the best interests of the child are of paramount concern in all matters affecting the child. As a justiciable constitutional right, the best interests provision has provided an important standard which has at times been overriding. Second, South Africa's equality clause (s. 9) prohibits discrimination on a wide range of bases, including gender, marital status and sexual orientation. All have proved to be relevant in the context of surrogacy, which is equally available to hetero and same-sex couples.

Apart from the Children's Act, of added relevance are the Regulations Relating to the Artificial Fertilisation of Persons[2] promulgated by the Minister of Health under the Health Act 2003.[3]

There are no available statistics to indicate how many surrogacy agreements are concluded annually in the country. Since the Children's Act requires confirmation of surrogacy agreement prior to fertilisation of the surrogate by a High Court, of which there are more than 12 in the country, it could be possible to establish a quantum, but that would require perusal of the documents at each court. Since fertility clinics are mainly in private hands, data from that source is not available either.

However, both the requirement of a written agreement, which would necessarily be prepared by an attorney,[4] and the requirement of a High Court application which is costly, means that generally surrogacy will be the preserve of the middle and upper classes, and figures are estimated to be fairly low (in the tens or hundreds rather than thousands).

---

2 R 175 of Government Gazette no. 1165 of 20.09.2016, read together with R 175 of Government Gazette no. 35099 of 12.03.2012.

3 Act 61 of 2003. Section 296(2) of the Children's Act provides that the fertilisation of any person in consequence of the confirmation of a surrogate agreement must be effected in terms of these regulations.

4 See the stringent requirements for papers laid down in the first reported surrogacy matter, *Ex Parte WH and others* 2011 (6) SA 514.

2. SURROGACY ARRANGEMENTS IN GENERAL

With the coming into force of Chapter 20 of the Children's Act, surrogacy agreements acquired legal validity, provided that the various requirements established by the Act are met. First, the agreement must be in writing, and signed by all the parties.[5] Of primary importance is that only non-commercial surrogacy (altruistic) is permitted, as will be further detailed below.

The contractual agreement must be entered into in South Africa, and at least one of the commissioning parents, or where the commissioning parent is a single person, that person, must be domiciled in South Africa.[6] So, too, the surrogate and her husband or partner, if any, must be domiciled in South Africa at the time of entering into the agreement.[7] The intention of the legislator was clearly to prevent South Africa from becoming an international surrogacy destination.

Further, where a commissioning parent is married or is involved in a permanent relationship, a court may not confirm an agreement unless that husband, wife or partner gives consent to the agreement and becomes party to it. Similarly, the husband or partner of the surrogate must consent and become party to the agreement.[8]

Before proceeding to detail the requirements of s. 294, s. 295 provides what the Constitutional Court of South Africa has termed the 'threshold requirement'. This entails that the commissioning parent or parents must not be able to give birth to a child and that such condition must be permanent and irreversible. A person is 'conception infertile' if they are unable to contribute a gamete[9] for the purposes of conception through artificial fertilisation. A person is 'pregnancy infertile' if they are permanently and irreversibly unable to carry a pregnancy to term. In other words, both situations would meet the requirements of s. 295(a) of the Children's Act.

Section 294 contains the now famous genetic link requirement: no surrogacy agreement is valid unless the child whose conception is contemplated in the

---

5 Section 292(1)(a).

6 There have been concerns expressed that South Africa may have been or be a destination for international surrogacy as in an early case, the commissioning fathers were respectively a Danish and Dutch citizen; however they alleged they were domiciled in South Africa. See *Ex Parte WH and others* 2011 (6) SA 514 (GNP) and J. Heaton, 'The pitfalls of international surrogacy: A South African family law perspective' (2015) 74 *THRHR* 24.

7 Section 292(1)(c) and (d). The domicile requirement pertaining to the surrogate may be waived by a High Court on reasonable cause shown, e.g. if the intended surrogate is a relative living abroad.

8 Section 293(1) and (2). If the husband or partner of the surrogate who is not genetically related to the child to be born unreasonably withholds consent, his consent may be dispensed with by a court.

9 Section 1 of the Children's Act 38 of 2005 defines a gamete as 'either of the two generative cells essential for human reproduction.'

agreement is to be effected with the gametes of both of the commissioning parents, or, if that is not possible due to biological, medical or other valid reasons, the gametes of at least one of them. This requirement was the subject of protracted litigation, finally ending in the Constitutional Court in *AB and others v Minister of Social Development and Others (Centre for Child Law intervening as Amicus Curiae)* in 2016.[10] Upon being advised that, because she was unable to provide gametes as a single person, she was ineligible for surrogacy, the applicant mounted a constitutional challenge to the validity of s. 294, arguing that the genetic link requirement violated her rights to equal treatment, to reproductive autonomy and to dignity (amongst others). Pitted against this was the question whether the child's best interests and right to know his or her genetic origins outweighed the applicant's claims to the constitutional violations alleged.[11]

In the High Court, *AB* was successful, insofar as the judge ruled the 'genetic link' requirement to be unconstitutional, striking down the impugned section, and referring the matter to the Constitutional Court for confirmation (as required by the Constitution). A critical factor which prompted the High Court to declare s. 294 provisionally unconstitutional was the differentiation in law between the use of surrogacy and the use of IVF procedures, as spelt out in the regulations to the Health Act (referred to above). The IVF regime does not require that the parent or parents of a child to be conceived through IVF donate their gametes. In the view of the High Court, this amounted to differential treatment, even though it was conceded that the two procedures – IVF and surrogacy – were fundamentally different.

The Constitutional Court reversed the decision of the High Court. The Constitutional Court regarded it as significant that the impugned provision falls under the overarching principles of the Children's Act, such as the principle that the best interests of the child must be applied in all decisions taken under the Act. Turning to the question of discrimination, the Constitutional Court

---

10 *AB and others v Minister of Social Development and Others (Centre for Child Law intervening as Amicus Curiae)* CCT 155/15, discussed in S. Florescu and J. Sloth-Nielsen, 'Visions on Surrogacy: From North to South: the approach of the Netherlands and South Africa to the issue of surrogacy and the child's right to know his origin' [2017] *International Survey of Family Law*, 239–58.

11 The Minister of Social Development, as the custodian of the Children's Act, opposed the application on several grounds, namely that:
(a) It was not only *AB*'s rights that were at issue, but also those of the child to be created by the surrogate mother and donor(s). The prospective child had the right to know its genetic origins.
(b) The adoption process in South Africa catered for *AB*'s need to have a child.
(c) To allow a single infertile person to create a child with no genetic link to her would result in the creation of a 'designer' child. This would not be in the public interest.
(d) Section 294 assists to prevent commercial surrogacy from taking root.

majority[12] affirmed that mere differentiation does not necessarily amount to 'irrational' discrimination; moreover, IVF and surrogacy were regulated under completely different statutes, with different objectives.

According to the court, '[t]he requirement of donor gamete(s) within the context of surrogacy indeed serves a rational purpose – the public good chosen by the lawgiver – of creating a bond between the child and the commissioning parents or parent. The creation of a bond is designed to protect the best interests of the child-to-be born so that the child has a genetic link with its parent(s). Therefore, a rational connection exists.'[13] Second, it is rational because it safeguards the child's genetic origin, in the best interests of the child, in the view of the court.[14] And third, an IVF parent using a double donation gametes would have gestational links to the child to be born.

Having established the rationality of the provision, the next issue to consider was whether it discriminated unfairly against the applicant on the grounds of her infertility? It did not, according to the court. 'The parent still has available options afforded by the law: a single parent has the choice to enter into a permanent relationship with a fertile parent, thereby qualifying the parent for surrogacy. It is therefore the exercise of this personal choice that disqualifies her, not her infertility or the impugned section.'[15] Having found no discrimination, the court did not need to deal with the question as to whether the discrimination was unfair.

This majority decision has not been welcomed in all quarters, as the reasoning of the majority was not entirely convincing. Moreover, the suggestion that the infertile applicant find a fertile partner for the purposes of conception with non-donor gametes does not seem judicious, and smacks of a different form of baby shopping. The finding of the Constitutional Court has, however, lead to a South African Law Reform Commission investigation into the rights of children to know their biological origins[16] more generally and an Issue paper was released on the topic in 2017.[17]

---

12 The majority/minority split was 7-4. The minority also wrote a lengthy judgment (which is reproduced first, with the majority following).

13 *AB and others v Minister of Social Development and Others (Centre for Child Law intervening as Amicus Curiae)* CCT 155/15 para. 287, above n. 10.

14 Ibid. para. 288. The court compares the disqualification of persons unable to donate a gamete to those with defective vision (blindness) or uncontrolled epilepsy and uncontrolled diabetes mellitus, who are disqualified from obtaining a driver's license.

15 Ibid. para. 302.

16 Section 41 of the Children's Act provides that a child born as a result of artificial fertilisation or surrogacy or the guardian of such child is entitled to have access to any medical information concerning that child's genetic parents and to any other information concerning the child's genetic parent but not before the child reaches the age of 18 years. Subsection 41(2) provides however, that information disclosed as set out here may not reveal the identity of the person whose gamete was or gametes were used for the artificial insemination of the identity of the surrogate mother.

17 'The Right to Know One's Own Biological Origins' *South African Law Reform Commission Issue paper 32, Project 40*, 20.05.2017. The Issue paper expresses the concern that the

Section 295 sets out the requirements for a court to confirm a surrogacy agreement, which are elaborated[18] more closely under Section 4 below, as they pertain mainly to the eligibility requirements of for the commissioning parents and for the surrogate. Section 295 requires that the agreement contain details of the consents, genetic origin of the children, when artificial fertilisation will take place, termination of the agreement and the effect of termination of the agreement.[19] Furthermore, the agreement must spell out adequate provisions for the care, contact, upbringing and general welfare of the child that is to be born in a stable home environment, including the child's position in the event of the death of the commissioning parents or one of them, or their divorce or separation before the birth of the child.[20]

The bare requirements of the Children's Act in respect of the contents of a surrogacy agreement have been supplemented by judicial guidance on the contents of surrogacy agreements. Notably, in *Ex parte WH*,[21] a case in which an agency had facilitated the contact between the commissioning parents and the prospective surrogate, the court wanted considerable additional details to be filed on the role of that agency, such as all agreements concluded between the commissioning parents, the agency and the surrogate, and details of any sums paid by the commissioning parents to the agency. Full details of payments made by the agency to the surrogate were also required to be produced. The court adversely commented on the provision for payment of 'lump sum' or general amounts under the various categories (health insurance, life insurance, surrogate's various expenditure (maternity clothes, transport)) as these could disguise the payment of compensation.[22] The court must be appraised of any previous applications for confirmation of a surrogacy agreement, in which jurisdiction they were brought and whether they were successful or not. Proof must be given of police clearance having been obtained, of a report from a clinical psychologist for both the surrogate and a separate one for the commissioning parents confirming their suitability, and a medical report in respect of the surrogate must be attached. In that jurisdiction (Gauteng North, i.e. the Pretoria region), the rules laid down adding requirements to be included in confirmation applications have been supplemented by a Practice Manual for the guidance of legal practitioners. These will be referred to in this chapter where appropriate.

---

provision of s. 41 of the Children's Act may, especially in the light of the reasoning in *AB*, be unconstitutional.

18 Section 296 provides emphatically that no artificial fertilisation of the surrogate may take place before confirmation of the agreement by a court, or after the lapse of 18 months after confirmation by a court.

19 *Ex parte WH and others* 2011 (6) SA 514 (GNP), para. 39.

20 Section 295(d).

21 Above n. 20.

22 *Ex parte WH*, above n.19, para. 29.

The Act does not provide for regulations to be promulgated in relation to surrogacy. Amendments that have been prepared for the Department of Social Development, but which as yet have not been introduced to Parliament, will seek to add a provision empowering the Minister to produce regulations, and with a view to implementing the requirements added by the court in *Ex parte WH*, which will probably feature in these Regulations.[23]

The Children's Act creates a number of offences related to surrogacy. These are contained in s. 303. First, no person may fertilise a woman in the execution of a surrogate motherhood agreement until the artificial fertilisation has been authorised by a court in accordance with the Act. Second, no person may in any way or with a view to compensation make it known that any person is or might be willing to enter into a surrogate motherhood agreement.

3. LEGAL PARENTHOOD AT THE TIME OF BIRTH

The effect of a legally valid surrogacy agreement is that the child once born is to all intents and for all purposes the child of the commissioning parent(s) from birth, according to s. 297(1).[24] Sections 297(b) and (c) provide that the surrogate mother must hand over the child as soon as reasonably possible after the birth, and neither she nor her partner (if any) or relatives will enjoy any legal status in respect of the child. Unless specified in the agreement, she will also have no right to have contact with the child. In turn, the surrogate-born child will have no maintenance or inheritance claim against the surrogate mother or her partner or relatives. She may not terminate the agreement once artificial fertilisation has taken place,[25] subject to her inalienable right to opt for a termination of pregnancy (see s. 300).

However, a different position prevails if she is genetically related to the child (through ovum donation): in this case, she has 60 days after the birth of the child to terminate the agreement. In this instance, the court must confirm her withdrawal from the contract, and she then incurs no liability to the commissioning parents save for the reimbursement of any expenses that they have covered.[26] The effect, according to s. 299, is that where the agreement is terminated after the child is born, parental rights vest then in the surrogate, her partner or husband,

---

23 A draft Children's Act Amendment Bill, which includes these proposed provisions, was issued for public comment during September 2018.

24 In respect of legally *invalid* surrogacy agreement, the consequences would be that the child is for all purposes the child of the surrogate (and her partner, if any) even if there is no genetic link to either of them, Conversely, the commissioning parents would have not status as legal parents (even in one of them is genetically related to the child): s. 297(2).

25 Section 297(1)(e).

26 Section 298.

or if she does not have one, the commissioning father.[27] Where the agreement is terminated before the child is born, parental rights vest in the surrogate, her husband or partner if any, or if none, the commissioning father as from the time of birth.[28] The surrogate mother, her husband or partner, or where applicable the commissioning father, are obliged to accept the responsibilities of parenthood. Subject to the instance that the surrogate has no husband or partner, triggering the allocation of parental rights to the commissioning father, the commissioning parents in all other instances have no rights towards the surrogate-born child.[29]

A child born of a surrogacy arrangement which does not comply with the requirements of the Act is deemed for all purposes the child of the surrogate and not the commissioning parent(s).[30]

No artificial fertilisation of the surrogate may take place before the confirmation of the agreement by a court, or after the lapse of 18 months from the date of confirmation.[31] In *Ex parte M and others*[32] the court was confronted with just such a fait accompli as this section tried to prevent. The application for confirmation was made when the surrogate was already 33 weeks pregnant.[33] The fertilisation had taken place on the basis of a verbal agreement between the parties, who had used the father's sperm. The questions facing the court were twofold: was the court competent to confirm the agreement notwithstanding non-compliance with s. 296? And what is to be required in cases like the present, i.e. on what basis could the court exercise its discretion to confirm an agreement for which prior authorisation was not obtained? For the record, the pregnancy resulted from the use of a donor egg and sperm from the commissioning father.

The court held that the Act does not clearly state what powers such court may have to confirm *ex post facto* an agreement, and what the status of such agreement (valid or invalid) might be. However, at common law, this would be an unlawful agreement, and therefore unenforceable. Courts would normally be slow to interpret a statute in such a way as to condone illegality. But, the court noted, a surrogacy contract is a contract of a special kind, raising issues such as the best interests of the child to be born, the right to dignity, and the

27 Section 299(a).

28 Section 299(b).

29 Section 299(d). The agreement may also be terminated by the surrogate exercising her right to undergo a termination of pregnancy, which is guaranteed under the sexual and reproductive autonomy clause of the Constitution and provided for in the Choice on Termination of Pregnancy Act 1996. She is required to inform the commissioning parents of her decision and to consult with them prior to the termination.

30 Section 297(2).

31 Section 296.

32 2014 (3) SA 415 (GP).

33 Pre-confirmation conception is actually an offence in terms of s. 301.

surrogate's right to security in and control over her body. Hence, the judge interpreted her mandate to include a discretionary power to condone the late submission of the agreement, for the most part inspired by the best interests of the child whose birth was imminent. It is widely thought, though, that the judgment involved considerable stretching of legal principle to arrive at the desired result.

4. ELIGIBILITY FOR SURROGACY

4.1. ELIGIBILITY CRITERIA FOR WOMEN ACTING AS A SURROGATE

Section 295 spells out the eligibility criteria for women desiring to act as a surrogate. These are: that she is competent to enter into the agreement; that she is in all respects suitable to act as a surrogate mother; that she understands and accepts the legal consequences of entering into an agreement in terms of this Act; that she is not using surrogacy as a source of income and that she is entering into the contract for altruistic reasons; that she has a documented history of at least one pregnancy and viable delivery; and that she has a living child of her own. *Ex Parte WH* confirmed that a court will require a proper psycho-social report relating to the surrogate to be attached to the papers.

A recent case did illustrate the willingness of the court to probe the suitability of would-be surrogates with some diligence. In *Ex Parte K*,[34] the court raised as a matter of concern (inter alia) that the prospective surrogate was only 20 years old, that she had met her husband (the fourth applicant) when she was only 13 years old, had had her first child at 16, whereupon she dropped out of school prematurely. She had another child two years later. The court was concerned that, as regards her psycho-social status, she did not appear to have made good decisions in her best interests as a teenager, and that there was nothing in the papers to indicate that she had gained the maturity to understand the implications of her decisions.[35] For this, and other reasons discussed below, the court did not find her suitable to serve as a surrogate mother.[36]

Although there is no explicit age (upper or lower), one website of a local clinic involved in surrogacy requires the surrogate to be no older than 42 years of age.

---

34 Case no. 14341/17, Gauteng Local Division, Johannesburg.

35 This was relevant to the assessment of whether she understood the implication of handing over the child upon birth.

36 Paragraphs 21 and 22 of the judgment.

4.2. ELIGIBILITY CRITERIA FOR COMMISSIONING PARENTS

As mentioned, according to s. 295, the commissioning parents must be unable to give birth to a child, and that condition must be permanent and irreversible. They must be competent to enter into the agreement, be in all respects suitable to accept the parenthood of the child that is to be conceived; and understand and accept the legal consequences of the agreement to be confirmed. Case law has confirmed that medical supporting evidence of the pregnancy or conception infertility of the would-be commissioning parents must be provided (unless the commissioning parent is single or a same-sex (male) couple).

The issue of age(s) of the commissioning parents has not surfaced *eo nomine*, although there were informal concerns raised by child rights advocates at the time of the *AB* decision that the principal applicant was already in her late fifties by the time of the application for a declaration of constitutional invalidity which, if successful, would have paved the way for her to enter into a surrogate motherhood agreement.

4.3. ROLE OF THE CHILD'S BEST INTERESTS IN ASSESSING ELIGIBILITY

A potentially controversial judgment was recently handed down by the High Court in Pretoria.[37] Two men seeking confirmation of a surrogacy agreement were unsuccessful. It came to the attention of the judge before whom the matter served that the second applicant, HN, did not want his sexual orientation made public and that he and partner CJD do not live together.[38] The court noted that his need to be discreet about his sexual orientation was occasioned by his career as a medical specialist, as rumours about his sexual orientation had in the past impacted negatively on his practice. However, the court raised this as a flag with potential consequences for the child's best interests:

> 'The questions that need to be considered by the Court is how the fact that the parties do not live together, and how the fact that HN does not want his sexual orientation to be made public will impact on the best interest of the child. It is of no importance at all that CJD and HN are homosexual, the fact however is that the specific situation may impact on the interest of the child to be born.'[39]

37 *Ex Parte CJD and others (Centre for Child Law intervening as amicus curiae)* (2018 (3) SA 197 (GP), North Gauteng High Court).

38 The third and fourth applicants are the potential surrogate and her partner.

39 Paragraph 4 of the (as yet unreported) judgment.

The fact that the parties wanted to be discreet about their private life, according to the court, did not extend to being discreet about their role(s) as parents of a child born of a surrogacy agreement. The court provided examples of such possible impact: an excited toddler running to his father in a public place shouting 'Daddy Daddy' – would the father then pretend not to be a parent? What will they tell kindergarten and teachers about who the parents are? Who would attend parent days at school?

Citing the requirement that the court must have as uppermost the best interests of the child or children to be born from the surrogacy agreement,[40] the court opined that however wide the Act is in permitting persons involved in different (permanent) family type relationships to qualify for confirmation of a surrogacy agreement, the court will still have to determine whether the way that the permanent relationship is structured will be supportive of raising a family.[41] The court found it difficult to conceptualise of a family unit when it is clear from the start that the commissioning parents would not be living together and sharing a household.[42] By way of analogy, the court cited those instances where the legislation permits joint adoption,[43] noting that there must be a joint household with shared rights and responsibilities, according to the intention of the legislature. In this application, the applicants did not explain how they will operate as a family unit, whilst not sharing a household. Stressing that the judgment did not preclude an application by one partner as prospective commissioning parent, or a joint application if the second applicant were to be more open about his sexual orientation and status in the relationship, in future, the best interests of the child (to be born) resulted in the court refusing to confirm the application.

5. TRANSFERRING PARENTHOOD

5.1. LEGAL PROCESS

Due to the a priori *legislative* determination of the allocation of legal parental status once a surrogacy agreement has been confirmed by a High Court (as discussed in Section 3 above), there is no post-birth transfer of parenthood, as is the case in other jurisdictions.

---

40 *Ex parte WH* 2011 (6) SA 514 at 517 para. 4: 'Children occupy a special place in the cultural, social and legal arrangement so most societies. That this is so is understandable in recognition of both the vulnerability of children and the almost instinctive need to advance their well-being and ensure their protection, as well as the compelling human and social imperative to pursue and further their best interests ….'

41 Paragraph 18 of the unreported judgment.

42 Paragraph 21.

43 Section 231(1) of the Children's Act.

5.2. RIGHTS OF CHILDREN

Section 41 of the Children's Act makes provision for a child born as a result of surrogacy, or the guardian of that child, to have access to any medical information or other information concerning the child's genetic parent(s) after the child reaches the age of 18 years. This is consistent with the object of s. 294 to ensure that the child becomes aware of its genetic origin. This is so even if the provision does not allow access to information regarding the identity of the surrogate mother in terms of s. 41(2) (*AB* para. 254).

6. AGENCIES AND CRIMINALISATION

The involvement of agencies surfaced in the first reported case after the coming into operation of the Children's Act, *Ex parte WH*, where the court was at pains to emphasise that the involvement of agencies raised the real risk of 'wombs for hire' and unauthorised payments passing between commissioning parents and agency, or agency and surrogate. The court then stressed that only payments authorised by the Act are permitted. Section 301 lists these as follows: claims directly related to the artificial fertilisation and pregnancy and birth of the child; expenses related to the confirmation of the surrogacy agreement itself; loss of earnings suffered by the surrogate in consequence of the surrogacy agreement; insurance for the surrogate mother to cover for death or disability; and bona fide professional medical or legal services.

The court required, further, when an agency was involved in the surrogacy arrangement, for the following additional documents to be submitted with the papers: the business of the agency; whether any form of payment is being paid to or by the agency for any aspect of the surrogacy; what exactly the agencies involvement was regarding: (i) the introduction of the surrogate mother; (ii) how the information regarding the surrogate mother was obtained by the agency; (iii) whether the surrogate mother received any compensation at all from the agency or from the commissioning parents.[44]

In a recent matter, *Ex parte HPP*,[45] the court noticed that a particular person was to act as a so-called surrogacy coordinator providing 'surrogacy facilitation services'. This raised the question as to whether s. 301 of the Children's Act was being contravened by the submission of a contract (between the parties and the surrogacy coordinator), and whether the court could confirm a surrogacy agreement if it found that the agreement between the parties and the coordinator was unlawful, but all other requirements were met.

---

44 Paragraph 66.

45 Unreported case no. 45037/16.

Upon inquiry as to what this service entailed, and whether it was to be paid for, the court established that it included: guiding and advising the surrogate; a referral to a clinical psychologist; assisting with any mediation with the surrogate, if applicable, during the gestational period; if required, to manage any dispute resolution; in general, to oversee the entire surrogacy 'journey'. An amount of R5,000 was to be invoiced for this service, which the applicants were happy to pay. It was explicit that no fee would be earned for introducing the surrogate to the intended parents.

The court, having noted the interests of the surrogacy facilitator, advised her of its intention to declare the agreement between herself and the applicants unlawful, so that she could file an affidavit. She responded that she had been offered full-time employment by a fertility clinic as a surrogacy coordinator, which she accepted.

She explained that she herself had acted as a surrogate six times in the past 11 years, and was uniquely placed to provide support services to surrogates; she added that her services included offering round-the-clock emotional support, running a surrogacy support group, and monitoring the surrogate throughout the process. This includes reminders to the surrogate to take her medication, explaining complicated doctors' reports to the surrogate, and preparing the surrogate emotionally for medical procedures.

On evaluation of this supplementary evidence, the court was not convinced that her services do not encroach on legal, medical and psychological terrains. Moreover, the court emphasised, that, like it or not, commercial surrogacy was prohibited in South Africa, and that s. 301 reinforces that only prescribed payments are permitted, on pain of criminal sanction. Payments of introductory fees to facilitate the link between commissioning parents and a potential surrogate are specifically prohibited (and the surrogacy coordinator categorically stated that she did not levy a fee for services other than those authorised by the Act or to persons other than authorised by the Act), and any affidavit founding an application for confirmation must state this fact.[46]

The applicant's lawyer argued that the facilitator's fee fell within the ambit of s. 301 exceptions, on the basis that they were expenses 'related to the artificial fertilisation and pregnancy' or those 'related to the birth of the child'. The court dismissed this, stating that invaluable though her services might be, they are not authorised by the Act and therefore the agreements between her and the commissioning parents were declared unlawful and unenforceable. The primary concern of the court was the possibility of commercial surrogacy being furthered through the back door, particularly that fees will be charged de facto for recruiting surrogates and introducing them to commissioning parents.

---

46 In *WH*, the surrogates were introduced to the commissioning parents by an egg donation agency, free of charge.

As to the impact of an illegal collateral agreement upon the surrogate motherhood agreement, the court held that there was no danger that the rights of the unborn child would be affected, as the fertilisation process had not yet commenced. The rights of the commissioning parents would be impinged only to a limited extent as they could still enter into another surrogacy agreement which was not affected by a tainted collateral agreement. The court had a discretion according to applicable contract law to establish whether the unlawful contract had tainted the lawful contract to the extent that the lawful contract cannot be endorsed. The surrounding circumstances in this case having been briefly perused, including the fact that the applicants were unaware of the possible illegality of a facilitation agreement, the court confirmed the surrogate motherhood agreement sans the collateral illegal agreement.

In *Ex parte K*,[47] the court expressed grave concern about the purportedly altruistic nature of the surrogate's willingness to act as such. She came seemingly from poor socio-economic circumstances, and had no other income. The municipal rates bill for the property where she lived with extended family members was deeply in arrears. The surrogate and her husband had not provided a full statement of assets and liabilities to the court. She was to receive a flat fee of R4,000 (US$340) per month to start with, escalating to R6,000 (US$500) per month once a pregnancy was confirmed (for her to hire a domestic worker to assist with the extra burden of the pregnancy and her own two small children). Noting that the court in *WH* had specifically discouraged the payment of generic amounts, the court said it was not convinced that these amounts (of R4,000 and R6,000) were justified, as insufficient information had been placed before the court to warrant that the prospective surrogate mother was not using surrogacy as a form of income. The contract was not confirmed.

The court also commented adversely on some other aspects of third-party involvement in this surrogacy arrangement. The court noted that the surrogate and commissioning parents were introduced to one another by a clinic which operates an internal surrogacy programme. They also offer other services; the assessment report reflects that the psychologist had an office based at the same premises as the clinic; the same psychologist compiled the reports for both the surrogate and the commissioning parents; it also appeared that the same medical doctor who would undertake the artificial fertilisation was also responsible for compiling the reproductive medical reports. His address also was the same as that of the clinic. No information was provided to the court as to whether these complementary services were paid for by any of the parties or not. Further, if they were paid for, this might hamper the objectivity of the professional assessment. Given that it was found that it was unlikely that the potential surrogate in this case had the necessary maturity to realise the implications of her decision, the

[47] Above, n. 34.

court said 'this points for the need for medico-legal experts involved in the surrogacy process to be impartial in perception and in fact, given the assistance they offer to the Court in this regard. They owe their allegiance to the Court and not to the parties to the SMA.'[48]

In the premise, the court was not satisfied about the non-disclosure of the relationship between the medico-legal professionals and the clinic, such that the risk of a commercial surrogacy could be eliminated.

7. INTERNATIONAL SURROGACY ARRANGEMENTS

The terrain of international surrogacy relative to South Africa is at once simple and complicated. As pointed out, the starting point is that unless authorised by a court in the case of an intended surrogate, the parties must be domiciled in South Africa. Domicile is a legal concept, and is not equatable to habitual residence. It can be established quite quickly, provided that the requisite intention to establish a domicile is in place. The *WH* case, as mentioned, involved a Dutch and a Danish national, who did aver that their domicile was South Africa, though this has been disputed in academic circles, who have raised the spectre of international surrogacy tourism.[49] A surrogacy agreement concluded by foreign nationals who are not domiciled in South Africa would be invalid and unenforceable, regardless of whether the surrogacy is altruistic or commercial. The commissioning parents would acquire no rights in respect of the surrogate-born child, and would also likely be ineligible for adoption, given the requirements of s. 25 of the Children's Act which foresees such applications as being treated as inter-country adoptions, which must be dealt with in accordance with the Hague Convention on Intercountry Adoption (1993), which South Africa has ratified. Satisfying Hague Convention requirements include the principle of subsidiarity, meaning that no suitable domestic adoption possibilities exist.[50]

The position of a South African engaging in surrogacy abroad is murky. The law does not prohibit South Africans from engaging in surrogacy abroad. There would be little reason for them to do so, since altruistic surrogacy is legal, unless they lacked or did not want to donate their own gametes, or preferred medical services offered elsewhere.[51] Their legal parentage status could be uncertain, and if commercial surrogacy was at stake, the public policy exception of common law might result in South African courts declining to recognise the legal tie between the commissioning parents and the child. Recently, an enquiry regarding

48 At para. 27. SMA is the abbreviation for surrogate motherhood agreement.
49 J. Heaton, above n. 6, p. 32.
50 For this reason, the Children's Act established a Register of Adoptable Children and Prospective Adoptive Parents, to enable domestic matching to occur: s. 232.
51 J. Heaton, above n. 6, p. 40.

parentage was received by a child rights advocacy clinic regarding twins born to a South African mother arising from a surrogacy agreement concluded and fulfilled abroad. Upon her return to South Africa, she died, and an uncle, based in South Africa, was exploring the possibility of formalising his parentage status in respect of the two children. The matter is yet to be resolved.[52]

The *HPP* case discussed above records that the surrogacy coordinator advertised her services on a website and offered services to national and international clients. This included providing for intended parents living out of state, and personal consultation with the surrogate via home visits. This position is potentially illegal in view of the prohibition on payments being received for surrogacy services in s. 301, subject to the exceptions provided for therein. Recently, an anecdotal report surfaced of commissioning parents based in the United Kingdom who have two children born of a South African surrogate. Since there are additional concerns relating to the legality of the alleged court approval, the matter is being investigated.[53]

8. CONCLUSION

There is an evident need to foster better oversight over surrogacy as a whole in South Africa. As matters stand at present, the reliance has been exclusively placed on the judiciary to exercise oversight and ensure that the intention of the legislature, especially to prevent commercial surrogacy, is upheld. The cases discussed in this chapter show that, as far as can be ascertained, many judges are performing an excellent job in delving into the details of surrogate motherhood agreements coming before them for confirmation. However, too little information exists about the overall picture: how many surrogacy agreements are being concluded in the country as a whole? What is the overall profile of surrogate mothers? How are the actual payments to surrogate mothers and others (lawyers, clinics) being monitored?

It is therefore proposed that two solutions would improve the surrogacy situation in South Africa: first, the enactment of regulations to the principal law contained in the Children's Act, to spell out in more detail the criteria that the courts are developing related to (for instance) eligibility of surrogates and commissioning parents, authorised payments and the benchmark amounts,[54] and the role of intermediaries and third parties.

---

52 K. Ozah, presentation at the Miller du Toit Cloete/University of the Western Cape 21st conference on child and family law, Cape Town 02.03.2018 (copy on file with the author).

53 Personal communication wth a lawyer representing the South African mother in court proceedings being pursued in the United Kingdom for the return of the children on 25 September 2018.

54 As has been done in the Regulations to the Children's Act prescribing payments for intercountry adoption.

Second, there appears to be a need for a central authority to collate information and monitor developments. Such agency would have to be established under one or another legal regime, in order for it to have the necessary powers and functions (e.g. to require reporting by fertility clinics and other role players, to investigate cases of potential malpractice and so forth).

South Africa's history of surrogacy is not a recent one: even prior to the enactment of legislation in 2010, clinics had been performing surrogacy services for some 30 years.[55] However, with the advent of the Children's Act, surrogacy is much more in the public domain,[56] and subject to judicial scrutiny.

55 Presentation by an obstetrician at a conference on surrogacy in October 2015, Stellenbosch University Faculty of Law. He acknowledged having birthed more than 3,000 surrogate-born babies over the course of his career.

56 Although the Children's Act does prescribe that the identities of the commissioning parent, the surrogate, and the surrogate-born child may not be made public: s. 302.

SURROGACY IN NEW ZEALAND

Debra WILSON

1. GENERAL LEGAL FRAMEWORK

Surrogacy is regulated in New Zealand under the Human Assisted Reproductive Technology Act 2004 (the 'HART Act'). The specific provisions are found in ss. 14 and 15. Section 14 states that a surrogacy arrangement 'is not of itself illegal, but is not enforceable by or against any person'. The section continues that it will be an offence to give or receive valuable consideration for the participation or arranging for the participation of a person in the arrangement, although exceptions are made for payments directly to medical and legal professionals for specified services. Section 15 prohibits advertising in relation to commercial surrogacy. Altruistic surrogacy is not specifically mentioned, and therefore appears to be permitted by default. Should a dispute arise, the language of s. 14 gives judges little guidance as to Parliament's intention, except that the arrangement is unenforceable.

This is not, however, the extent of the regulation of surrogacy in New Zealand. The HART Act also requires that the Minister of Health set up two national-level committees: an advisory committee and an ethics committee. It then categorises reproductive procedures as either 'established procedures', 'prohibited actions' or 'regulated activities'. Established procedures (which must be declared as such by the Governor-General and are currently found in the Schedule to the Human Assisted Reproductive Technology Order 2005) are those which can be carried out by fertility clinics without any external approval. Prohibited actions (which are listed in Sched. 1 of the HART Act) are those which can never be carried out. Under s. 8, carrying out a prohibited action is an offence punishable by a term of imprisonment not exceeding five years, or a fine not exceeding NZ$200,000, or both. All other procedures are classified by default as regulated activities. Surrogacy falls into this last category. Under s. 16 it is an offence for a fertility clinic to carry out a regulated activity 'without the prior approval in writing of the ethics committee.'

The advisory committee established under the HART Act is known as the Advisory Committee on Assisted Reproductive Technology ('ACART'). The ethics committee is known as the Ethics Committee on Assisted Reproductive Technology ('ECART').

Under the HART Act, both ACART and ECART are to be guided by the following principles:[1]

'(a) the health and well-being of children born as a result of the performance of an assisted reproductive procedure or an established procedure should be an important consideration in all decisions about that procedure:
(b) the human health, safety, and dignity of present and future generations should be preserved and promoted:
(c) while all persons are affected by assisted reproductive procedures and established procedures, women, more than men, are directly and significantly affected by their application, and the health and well-being of women must be protected in the use of these procedures:
(d) no assisted reproductive procedure should be performed on an individual and no human reproductive research should be conducted on an individual unless the individual has made an informed choice and given informed consent:
(e) donor offspring should be made aware of their genetic origins and be able to access information about those origins:
(f) the needs, values, and beliefs of Māori should be considered and treated with respect:
(g) the different ethical, spiritual, and cultural perspectives in society should be considered and treated with respect.'

1 Section 4 of the Human Assisted Reproductive Technology Act 2004.

ACART consists of 8–12 members, at least half of which must be lay members. Members are appointed for a term of three years, and can be reappointed (but cannot serve more than six consecutive years). The membership must contain experts in assisted reproductive research, human reproductive research, ethics, Māori customary values, and law. In addition, there must be members able to articulate issues from the perspectives of Māori, consumers, persons with disabilities and children.

Under its terms of reference, ACART has two key functions. First, it provides advice to the Minister of Health on aspects of, or issues arising out of, assisted reproductive procedures. Second, it issues Guidelines and Advice to ECART. 'Guidelines' are general rules which ECART must follow in determining whether to approve applications for assisted reproductive procedures. They can only be issued after consultation with both the public and the Minister of Health. 'Advice' is a response to a specific question arising from an application for approval of a regulated activity.

ECART also consists of 8–12 members, at least half of which must be lay members (including the Chairperson). Members are appointed for terms of three years, and can be reappointed (but cannot serve more than six consecutive years). The membership must contain experts in assisted reproductive procedures, human reproductive research, ethics and law. In addition, there must be members able to articulate issues from the perspectives of consumers and persons with disabilities.

ECART's primary function is to consider and determine applications for regulated activities. If ACART has issued relevant Guidelines, ECART can consider an application and decide whether to approve (with or without conditions or recommendations); defer; or decline the application. Decisions are to be made by consensus where possible (or at minimum by a two-thirds majority). If no Guidelines have been issued, ECART must refer the application to ACART for Advice.

Before discussing how ECART will determine applications, it is worthwhile discussing the process through which the application is made. The ECART website,[2] which contains the application form, specifies that the application is to be completed and submitted by a fertility clinic on behalf of the potential commissioning parents. It will be remembered that under s. 16, the fertility clinic will commit an offence if it carries out the surrogacy related assisted reproductive procedures without ECART approval, and so its involvement in relation to the application process is understandable. It should be noted that under s. 14(4)(ii) the fertility clinic's steps in preparation for the application will be considered 'counselling' and therefore a permitted expense payable by the

---

2 Ethics Committee on Assisted Reproductive Technology, New Zealand, *Application Form, Surrogacy Arrangements Involving Providers of Fertility Services* <https://ecart.health.govt.nz/publications-and-resources/application-forms> accessed 21.01.2019.

commissioning parents regardless of the success or otherwise of the application. If the commissioning parents and the surrogate do not intend to use a fertility clinic (known as a 'private' surrogacy arrangement) ECART approval is not required.

There are currently four fertility clinics in New Zealand that are licensed to carry out fertility treatments. These are: Fertility Associates (18 offices in five cities), Repromed (Auckland), Fertility Plus (Auckland) and Genea Oxford Fertility (Christchurch). All but Genea Oxford currently deal with surrogacy applications. These clinics employ specialist fertility counsellors who meet with the commissioning parents and surrogate in separate and joint sessions. They will also meet with any existing children (of either party) who are old enough to understand the effects of the surrogacy arrangement. The counsellors cannot introduce parties to each other but only meet with parties who have a pre-existing relationship.

The application requires that the parties have had independent medical and legal advice, and individual and joint counselling sessions. Reports on these sessions by the relevant professionals must be attached to the application. In addition, the application may include additional medical reports, or letters from the commissioning parents, surrogate, or any other relevant person.

Decisions on applications are made at bi-monthly meetings. They are made 'on the papers' and applications are anonymous. In making their decision, ECART must follow any Guidelines issued by ACART. The initial ACART Guidelines on surrogacy were the 'Guidelines on Surrogacy Arrangements involving Providers of Fertility Services' published in 2007. These were replaced in 2013 by the 'Guidelines on Surrogacy involving Assisted Reproductive Procedures ('ACART Guidelines')'.[3] The current guidelines read:

> '2. When considering an application for surrogacy involving an assisted reproductive procedure:
> (a) ECART must determine that:
> (i) where there is one intending parent, he or she will be a genetic parent of any resulting child, or
> (ii) where there are two intending parents, at least one will be a genetic parent of any resulting child; and
> (iii) there has been discussion, understanding, and declared intentions between the parties about the day-to-day care, guardianship, and adoption of any resulting child, and any ongoing contact; and
> (iv) each party has received independent medical advice; and

3 Advisory Committee on Assisted Reproductive Technology, New Zealand, *Guidelines on Surrogacy involving Assisted Reproductive Procedures* <https://acart.health.govt.nz/publications-and-resources/guidelines-and-advice-issued-ecart/guidelines-surrogacy-arrangements> accessed 21.01.2019.

- (v) each party has received independent legal advice; and
- (vi) each party has received counselling in accord with the current Fertility Services Standard;

(b) ECART must be satisfied that:

- (i) the proposed surrogacy is the best or only opportunity for an intending parent, or at least one intending parent in a couple, to be the genetic parent of a child because, for example, an intending parent is:
  - unable to gestate a pregnancy; or
  - unable to conceive a child for medical reasons; or
  - unlikely to survive a pregnancy or birth; or
  - likely to have her physical or psychological health and wellbeing significantly affected by a pregnancy or birth; or
  - likely to conceive a child who is unlikely to survive the pregnancy or birth or whose health would be significantly affected by the pregnancy or birth; and
- (ii) the surrogacy is not for reasons of personal or social convenience; and
- (iii) the risks associated with a surrogacy for the adult parties and any resulting child are justified in the proposal. These risks are:
  - risks to the health and wellbeing of the intending surrogate, including
    - risks associated with pregnancy, childbirth and relinquishment of a resulting child to the intending parent(s);
    - the risk that the intending parent(s) may change their mind about parenting a resulting child;
  - risks to the health and wellbeing of the intending parent(s), including that the surrogate may change her mind about relinquishing a resulting child; and
  - risks to the health and wellbeing of a resulting child, including becoming the subject of a dispute if the relationship between the surrogate and intending parents breaks down.

(c) In addition to the risks identified in (b)(iii) above, ECART must take into account the following relevant factors:

- (i) whether the intending surrogate has completed her family;
- (ii) whether the relationship between the intending parent(s) and the intending surrogate safeguards the wellbeing of all parties and especially any resulting child;
- (iii) whether legal reports indicate that the parties clearly understand the legal issues associated with surrogacies;
- (iv) whether counselling has:
  - included implications counselling for all parties
  - included joint counselling for all parties
  - been culturally appropriate
  - provided for whānau/extended family involvement
  - provided for the inclusion of any children of the parties;

(v) whether counselling will be accessible to all parties before and after pregnancy is achieved; and
(vi) whether the residency of the parties safeguards the wellbeing of all parties and especially any resulting child.'

There are two significant changes from the 2007 Guidelines. First, is the insertion of guideline 2(a)(i), which now enables an application to be made by only one intended parent. Second, is the removal of the 2007 requirement that the 'intending mother has: a medical condition that prevents pregnancy or makes pregnancy potentially damaging to her and/or any resulting child; or a medical diagnosis of unexplained infertility that has not responded to other treatments.' This is replaced by the requirements in guideline 2(b) which uses the more gender-neutral language of 'intending parent' and 'genetic parent'. These changes were the result of public consultation following a 2011 complaint to the Human Rights Commission, which alleged that the provisions discriminated on the basis of sex and sexual orientation through the requirement that there be an 'intending mother', and that the requirements linked to pregnancy effectively prevented single men or a homosexual couple applying.

It is worth noting that guideline 2(a) requires ECART to be satisfied that one intended parent will be a genetic parent of the child. In September 2017 ACART began the public consultation process which is a prerequisite for altering four of its Guidelines.[4] In a document entitled 'Proposed donation guidelines'[5] it sought submissions on whether the requirement of a 'biological link' ought to remain, in order to provide advice to the Minister of Health. This process was ongoing at the time of writing.

There is little evidence available as to the reasoning behind the surrogacy provisions. It is probably a safe assumption that the surrogacy provisions were introduced in response to the *Baby M* case in the United States and the *Baby Cotton* case and the enactment of the Surrogacy Arrangements Act 1985 in the United Kingdom. The HART Act was initially introduced into Parliament as a Private Members' Bill in 1996. The debates in Parliament became dominated in 1997 by the topical issue of human reproductive cloning, with surrogacy receiving only a brief mention. In 1998 a government Bill, the Assisted Human

4 Advisory Committee on Assisted Reproductive Technology, New Zealand, *Guidelines on Embryo Donation for Reproductive Purposes, (2008), Guidelines on the Creation and Use, For Reproductive Purposes, of an Embryo created from Donated Eggs in conjunction with Donated Sperm (2010), Guidelines on Donation on Eggs or Sperm Between Certain Family Members (2013), Guidelines on Surrogacy Arrangements involving Assisted Reproductive Procedures (2013)* <https://acart.health.govt.nz/publications-and-resources/guidelines-and-advice-issued-ecart> accessed 21.01.2019.

5 Advisory Committee on Assisted Reproductive Technology, New Zealand, *Proposed Donation Guidelines: For Family Gamete Donation, Embryo Donation, Use Of Donated Eggs With Donated Sperm And Surrogacy: Consultation Document (2017)* <https://acart.health.govt.nz/consultations/past-consultations> accessed 21.01.2019.

Reproduction Bill, was also introduced into Parliament. It contained no reference to surrogacy. Both Bills were finally considered by the Health Committee in 2003, which recommended that the Private Members' Bill proceed. The final debate again contained little reference to surrogacy. At the time the Bill was being debated there had been only one, uncontroversial, case on surrogacy in New Zealand[6] with a second case, similarly uncontroversial,[7] being heard late in the legislative process.

Identifying statistics in relation to the practice or prevalence of surrogacy in New Zealand is difficult. In relation to domestic surrogacy, the ECART reports of meetings[8] provide an accurate record of the number of applications made. From the period of its establishment in September 2005 through to the end of 2017, ECART has heard 253 applications, at a rate of 16–29 applications per year. Of these, 157 were approved outright, 41 were approved with conditions, 10 were approved with recommendations, 7 were declined and 38 were deferred. ECART does report outcomes of assisted reproductive procedures, but this information can be delayed in being published. Reports to the end of 2014 suggest a total of 47 live births recorded by fertility clinics. There is no information on private domestic surrogacy arrangements (those not involving fertility clinics). There is also no data available in relation to international surrogacy arrangements.

There have been 31 reported applications for adoption or guardianship in relation to surrogacy, of which 14 were domestic cases and 17 were international (although three of these were familial arrangements where one of the parties lived in Australia). Applications have occurred at an average of one–two per year from 2007–10, four–five per year from 2012–15, but only one per year in 2016–17 (although from discussions with lawyers, many more cases have occurred, but remain unreported).

2. THE LEGALITY OF SURROGACY CONTRACTS

According to s. 14(1) of the HART Act, 'a surrogacy arrangement is not of itself illegal, but is not enforceable by or against any person.'

According to s. 14(3) of the HART Act:

> 'Every person commits an offence who gives or receives, or agrees to give or receive, valuable consideration for his or her participation, or for any other person's participation, or for arranging any other person's participation, in a surrogacy arrangement.'

---

6 *Re Adoption of G* ADOPT 6-92 03.02.1993, Judge Neal.

7 *Re H* [2003] NZFLR 529.

8 Advisory Committee on Assisted Reproductive Technology, New Zealand, *Minutes* <https://ecart.health.govt.nz/meetings> accessed 21.01.2019.

A breach of this section is punishable by imprisonment for a term not exceeding one year, or a fine not exceeding NZ$100,000, or both.

Section 14(4) provides an exhaustive list of exceptions to subs. (3):

> 'Subsection (3) does not apply to a payment:
>
> (a) to the provider concerned for any reasonable and necessary expenses incurred for any of the following purposes:
> (i) collecting, storing, transporting, or using a human embryo or human gamete:
> (ii) counselling 1 or more parties in relation to the surrogacy agreement:
> (iii) insemination or *in vitro* fertilisation:
> (iv) ovulation or pregnancy tests; or
>
> (b) to a legal adviser for independent legal advice to the woman who is, or who might become, pregnant under the surrogacy arrangement.'

The inclusion of a prohibition on commercial surrogacy in s. 14(3) is similar to that occurring in both countries in response to those cases, although it should be noted that the UK approach in s. 2(2) of the Surrogacy Arrangements Act 1985 of exempting the commissioning parents and surrogate from liability has not been adopted in New Zealand. The s. 14(4) exception for payment to professionals reflects (unadopted) recommendations in the UK Warnock report to ensure that the surrogate would not be deterred from receiving appropriate professional advice.

The language in s. 14(1) is the interesting part of the section: A surrogacy arrangement is not of itself illegal, but is not enforceable by or against any person. There appear to be several policy considerations underpinning this language. The first part reads that the arrangement 'is not of itself illegal'. This wording aims to prevent the child being born under a taint of criminality due to the nature of his or her conception, gestation and birth. The second part reads 'but is not enforceable by or against any person'. This addresses the *Baby M* situation, where the commissioning parents sought a court order for custody of the child when the surrogate changed her mind shortly after the birth and refused to hand over the child. The wording of the section reflects the position that, similar to adoption, the surrogate ought to be able to change her mind and retain custody of the child. While both policy considerations are logical, the juxtaposition of both in the one subsection makes it difficult to understand whether the intention of Parliament is to encourage altruistic but not commercial surrogacy, discourage all forms of surrogacy, or simply remain neutral. Possibly for this reason, only three reported Family Court applications for adoption following surrogacy refer to s. 14[9] even though a further 11 cases have a clear commercial element to them.

[9] *Re BWS* [2011] NZFLR 621; *Re SCR* [2012] NZFC 5466; and *Re Kennedy* [2014] NZFLR 367.

Section 25(1) of the Adoption Act 1955 ('Adoption Act') is also relevant, as adoption is the only mechanism available under New Zealand law by which to transfer legal parentage to the commissioning parents:

> 'Except with the consent of the court, it shall not be lawful for any person to give or receive or agree to give or receive any payment or reward in consideration of the adoption or proposed adoption of a child or in consideration of the making of arrangements for an adoption or proposed adoption.'

The penalty for breach of this section is imprisonment for a term not exceeding three months, a fine not exceeding NZ$15,000, or both.

When an application is made to ECART, the report from the legal adviser must include verification that the parties have been provided with a copy of s. 14 of the HART Act with the offences sections highlighted, and that they have been advised about the Adoption Act provision.

Of the 31 reported applications for adoption of a child born as the result of a surrogacy arrangement, 14 specifically refer to payments being made to the surrogate (although two of these are before the HART Act was enacted). In all of these cases the judge either did not discuss the issue of payment or determined that since the payments related to the surrogacy and not to the adoption, s. 25 of the Adoption Act was not relevant. Only three cases refer to s. 14 of the HART Act. In *Re BWS*[10] Judge Walker commented only that the payment to the surrogate in that case 'does not sit well with New Zealand's efforts to "prohibit certain commercial transactions relating to human reproduction"' (referring to one of the purposes of the HART Act as found in s. 3). In *Re SCR*[11] it was considered relevant that the payments were made by the commissioning father's father, who lived in the United States and was therefore not subject to the s. 14 prohibition. Finally, in *Re Kennedy*,[12] the judge classified the payments of NZ$20,000 payment for pain and inconvenience and NZ$5,000 for general expenses as amounting to a 'paid' surrogacy arrangement as opposed to a 'commercial' surrogacy arrangement. In none of these cases, therefore, did the judge find a breach of s. 14, or that the payment in any way affected the outcome sought. A further nine applications related to international arrangements which were likely to have been commercial, but the judges did not consider whether ss. 14 of the HART Act or 25 of the Adoption Act had been breached.

The cases discussing commercial surrogacy often include commentary that the Family Court judges consider themselves caught between two competing

10 *Re BWS* [2011] NZFLR 621.
11 *Re SCR* [2012] NZFC 5466.
12 *Re Kennedy* [2014] NZFLR 367.

policy objectives when deciding the cases: the prohibition on commercial surrogacy, and the principle of acting in the best interests of the child. In these cases the judges consistently conclude that their role is to determine the application in front of them and not to enforce the wider policy considerations in relation to commercial surrogacy.

3. LEGAL PARENTHOOD AT THE TIME OF BIRTH

Under s. 5 of the Status of Children Act 1969, the general rule is that:

> 'a child born to a woman during her marriage, or within 10 months after the marriage has been dissolved by death or otherwise, shall, in the absence of evidence to the contrary, be presumed to be the child of its mother and her husband, or former husband, as the case may be.'

The New Zealand law therefore reflects the Latin maxims *mater certa semper est* ('the mother is always certain') and *pater est quem nuptiae demonstrant* ('the father is determined by the marriage').

In 2004 specific provisions in relation to parentage following assisted reproduction were inserted into the Status of Children Act. These provisions refer to assisted reproduction generally and do not consider the specific situation of surrogacy. They state that the woman who becomes pregnant is the mother, even if the ovum has been donated. If the woman has a partner who did not provide the sperm or ovum, but consented to the woman undergoing the procedure, then the partner (male or female) is also a parent of the child. A sperm or ovum donor is not a parent unless he or she is the partner of the woman at the time of conception or unless the woman was single at the time of conception, and the donor later became the woman's partner.

Under the Births, Deaths, Marriages and Relationships Registration Act 1995, a preliminary notice of birth must be sent to the Registrar within five working days of the child's birth,[13] and full notification of birth within two years.[14] There are two versions of the notification form, an online version and a hardcopy version.[15] Interestingly, an earlier version of the online form contained

[13] Section 5A of the Births, Deaths, Marriages and Relationships Registration Act 1995.

[14] Section 16 of the Births, Deaths, Marriages and Relationships Registration Act 1995.

[15] Both are found on the New Zealand government website: <https://www.govt.nz/browse/family-and-whanau/having-a-baby/registering-a-new-baby-and-getting-a-birth-certificate/#how-to-register-your-baby> accessed 21.01.2019.

preliminary notes which stated in bold that 'if any of these circumstances apply you must obtain and fully complete a hardcopy form ...'. The applicant must then click on a link to view the circumstances, one of which is 'd) The child born as a result of a woman acting alone in an assisted human reproduction procedure ...'.[16]

There is no reference to assisted reproduction in the sections of the online form relating to the child or the mother, and as a result, if commissioning parents believe that they are the legal parents, they would likely provide their own information rather than that of the surrogate and her partner. The form does ask for the ethnicity of the child as well as the ethnicity of the mother and the father, and it is possible that commissioning parents might list the ethnicity of the surrogate mother for the child, and if that differs from the ethnicity listed for the named mother and father this might indicate the involvement of a third party. This information does not, however, appear on the birth certificate itself.

Under the section relating to the father, the online form asks whether 'the child [is] born as a result of an assisted human reproduction procedure' with the choice of selecting 'yes' or 'no'. If 'yes' is selected, the person is then asked to:

> 'select one of the following to describe your relationship. The option you select will change how the father/other parent details are completed.
>
> - The mother is in a legal relationship ... with a man, who consented to the procedure. Complete the father questions using his details.
> - The mother is in a legal relationship with a woman, who consented to the procedure. Complete the other parent questions using her details.
> - The mother is not in a legal relationship. You do not complete the father/other parent or parental relationship questions.'

While these options reflect the language in the Status of Children Act, they do not address surrogacy as neither this section, nor the previous section, defines 'mother'.[17]

The hardcopy version contains more extensive explanations than the online version, although there is again no reference to assisted reproduction in the

16 This language appeared on the author's viewing of the form in December 2016.

17 When previously viewed in December 2016, these options were not present. After selecting 'yes', no further information was asked for, nor was there an explanation of how this might affect parentage. This information did not appear on the birth certificate.

sections relating to the child or the mother. Under the section relating to the father, it advises that:[18]

> 'if a child was born as a result of an assisted reproductive procedure (such as artificial insemination), the details ... should be completed as follows:
>
> (a) If the mother married, or entered into a civil union or de facto relationship with, a man who consented to the mother undergoing the procedure, that man's details should be entered. Note: the Donor is generally not the father or other parent.
> (b) If the mother married or entered into a civil union or de facto relationship with a woman who consented to the mother undergoing the procedure, tick the following box, enter the details of the mother's partner, and complete the details in the rest of the form wherever details of "Father" are indicated. Her details will be shown on the child's birth registration and birth certificates as either "Mother" or "Parent" (instead of "Father"). If situation (b) applies, tick one box for her preference: Mother/Parent'

If the child is subsequently adopted by the commissioning parents (as is required in surrogacy cases to transfer legal parenthood), a second birth certificate is issued listing the adoptive parents as the mother and father. This post-adoption birth certificate is generally indistinguishable from the original (although if the adoptive parents wish, the wording 'adoptive parents' can be used).

If the surrogate mother is not the legal mother of the child, there is no law that requires the preservation of the information concerning the surrogate as the person who gave birth to the child. This can be contrasted with the law in relation to donors of embryos or cells under Pt 3 of the HART Act, which requires specific information to be preserved indefinitely by providers. In the case of a traditional surrogacy, the information preserved would identify her only as an ovum donor and not as a surrogate.

4. ELIGIBILITY FOR SURROGACY

The eligibility criteria for surrogacy are found in the ACART Guidelines. The only reference to the surrogate is that ECART must 'take into account' whether the intending surrogate has completed her family.[19] The independent medical reports required as part of the application will consider whether she has given

---

18 The final two sentences were added in May 2018 following a complaint to the Human Rights Commission in late 2017 that a female same-sex couple could not both be listed on the birth certificate as 'Mother'. The Department of Internal Affairs agreed in May 2018 to change its systems to allow for two 'Mothers' to be listed.

19 Advisory Committee on Assisted Reproductive Technology, New Zealand, above n. 3, Guideline 2(c).

birth previously and whether there were any complications arising from any prior births. There have been examples of ECART deferring applications until further medical evidence has been provided if a concern has arisen about potential health issues during the pregnancy. There has been no research in New Zealand on the characteristics of women acting as surrogates.

In relation to the commissioning parents, the Guidelines require that they show:

1. A genetic link between at least one of the commissioning parents and the resulting child;[20]
2. That the proposed surrogacy be 'the best or only opportunity' for at least one commissioning parent to be a genetic parent.[21]
3. That the surrogacy is not for personal or social convenience.[22]

The previous requirements under the 2007 Guidelines that the commissioning parents be a 'couple' (thus not permitting a sole applicant), and that at least one of the couple be a female, have been removed under the current Guidelines.

In addition, it must be shown that any risks to the adult parties and resulting child are justified in the proposal.[23] These specifically include risks to the health and wellbeing of the parties, risks associated with pregnancy, and risks associated with the relinquishing of the child by the surrogate or the accepting of parenting responsibility of the child by the commissioning parents.

Finally, Guideline 2(a) requires that both parties must have received independent legal and medical advice and counselling, and that there has been 'discussion, understanding, and declared intentions between the parties about the day-to-day care, guardianship and adoption of any resulting child, and any ongoing contact.' Although not specifically required to do so, ECART appears to be increasingly requiring that the commissioning parents have a plan to adopt the resulting child as a condition of approval of the application (as found in the minutes of ECART meetings on the website). This requirement of adoption therefore incorporates the criteria in the Adoption Act 1955 for becoming adoptive parents into the surrogacy application. One such criterion is that the

---

20 Advisory Committee on Assisted Reproductive Technology, New Zealand, above n. 3, Guideline 2(a), although note the discussion above at n. 5 that ACART is reviewing this requirement.

21 Advisory Committee on Assisted Reproductive Technology, New Zealand, above n. 3, Guideline 2(b). This might be because a female commissioning parent is unable to conceive, gestate or give birth or that there will be significant physical or psychological risks in doing so, or that the child is unlikely to survive the pregnancy or birth or is likely to have his or her health significantly impacted by this.

22 Advisory Committee on Assisted Reproductive Technology, New Zealand, above n. 3, Guideline 2(b).

23 Advisory Committee on Assisted Reproductive Technology, New Zealand, above n. 3, Guideline 2(b).

applicant cannot be a single male wishing to adopt a female child, unless 'the applicant is the father of the child or there are special circumstances which justify the making of an adoption order'.[24] It appears to be accepted in the Family Court that being the genetic father under a surrogacy arrangement will be considered such a special circumstance.[25] A second criterion is that if the application is made by a couple they must be 'spouses',[26] therefore requiring the applicants to be married. Until 2010 this language prevented applications to ECART from heterosexual couples who were not married, and from same-sex couples (who were not legally permitted to marry until 2013). In 2010 it was determined by the Family Court that 'spouses' could include heterosexual de facto couples, but that there were 'formidable barriers' to extending this definition to include same-sex de facto couples.[27] In 2013 the Marriage (Definition of Marriage) Amendment Act allowed same-sex couples to marry, and in 2015 the extension of the definition of 'spouses' to include same-sex de facto couples was made in *Re Pierney*.[28]

As regards rules in New Zealand concerning gametes used in surrogacy arrangements, the commercial supply of gametes is prohibited under s. 13 of the HART Act.

The Act and various ACART Guidelines[29] set out additional rules about both the collection and the use of gametes. In relation to collection of gametes, this cannot occur if the donor is under the age of 16, or is comatose, or deceased. In relation to use of gametes, genetic, social and cultural issues with inter-generational familial donation must be considered. Donor egg or sperm cannot be used by a member of the donor's family if there is an inter-generational link between donor and recipient (i.e. father-daughter). If both donor egg and sperm are to be used, there must also not be an inter-familial link between the donors (for example father/daughter or brother/sister), and both commissioning parents must demonstrate a medical diagnosis of unexplained infertility, or a medical condition affecting their reproduction. If an embryo is donated, the commissioning parents must satisfy the criteria for donation of both egg and sperm as well as two additional criteria: the embryo must have been created as part of the donor's own IVF treatment and be surplus to requirements, and no other couple can have received an embryo from this same source.

---

24 Section 4(2) of the Adoption Act 1955.

25 *Re BWS* [2011] NZFLR 611; *Re Kennedy* [2014] NZLFR 367.

26 Section 3(2) of the Adoption Act 1955.

27 *Re AMM and KJO* [2010] NZFLR 629.

28 *Re Pierney* [2015] NZFC 9404.

29 Advisory Committee on Assisted Reproductive Technology, New Zealand, *Guidelines on Donation of Eggs or Sperm between Certain Family Members (2013)*, *Guidelines on the Creation and Use, for Reproductive Purposes, of an Embryo created from Donated Eggs in conjunction with Donated Sperm (2010)* and *Guidelines on Embryo Donation for Reproductive Purposes (2008)* <https://acart.health.govt.nz/publications-and-resources/guidelines-and-advice-issued-ecart> accessed 21.01.2019.

5. TRANSFERRING PARENTHOOD

5.1. LEGAL PROCESS

There is no specific mechanism for the acquisition of parenthood by commissioning parents in New Zealand law. The commissioning parents must therefore either adopt the child or obtain a guardianship or parenting order. An adoption order is the only option that transfers legal parentage from the surrogate and her partner to the commissioning parents. Guardianship and parenting orders grant legal rights in relation to the child to the commissioning parents, but do not remove legal parentage from the surrogate and her partner. As has previously been mentioned, if an application is made to ECART there must have been a 'discussion, understanding and declared intentions between the parties about the day-to-day care, guardianship, or adoption of the resulting child.'

In relation to domestic adoption cases (where the adopting parents live in New Zealand and the child was born in New Zealand), the Adoption Act will apply. Under this Act, following the adoption the child will be deemed to be the child of the adoptive parent(s) and will cease to be the child of the surrogate and her partner.

In relation to international adoption cases (where the adopting parents live in New Zealand and the child was born overseas) the situation is more complicated. Under the Adoption (Intercountry) Act 1997, New Zealand has adopted the Hague Convention of 29 May 1993 on Protection of Children and Co-operation in Respect of Intercountry Adoption ('Hague Adoption Convention'). This sets out a specific process to be followed where a child is 'habitually resident' in one contracting state and is to be moved to another country in which the adoptive parents are habitually resident. It is unclear whether a child who is born in one country as a result of an international surrogacy arrangement, but who all parties intend to be moved to another country shortly after birth, can be considered to be 'habitually resident' in the country of birth. If the Hague Adoption Convention applies, a specific procedure must be followed. Once this is completed, the adopting parents will be deemed the parents of the child, but the surrogate and her partner will remain as parents until the New Zealand Family Court issues an order terminating this relationship. If the Hague Adoption Convention does not apply, the adoption will be treated as a domestic application. Once completed, the adopting parents will be deemed to be the parents of the child, and the surrogate and her partner will have their parental status terminated. It appears that the judges have reached a consensus that a child born as a result of a surrogacy arrangement either has no habitual residence, or has the habitual residence of the commissioning parents. Therefore, where it is intended by both parties that the child travels shortly after birth to New Zealand with the commissioning parents, the Hague Adoption Convention will not apply: *Re BWS*.[30] *Re BWS* also suggested that for this to apply there must be a genetic link between at least one commissioning parent and the child. However, this was not considered to be necessary in *Re Clifford*,[31] where the (sole) commissioning mother had used both an egg and sperm donor. The only case in which the Hague Adoption Convention has been held to apply was *Re DMW*.[32] In this case, a laboratory mix-up meant that the child was not biologically related to the commissioning father (as intended). The judge in this case felt that the facts, and the lack of cooperation from the Thai hospital, raised a concern as to whether the biological parents of the child were looking for their son, and whether the commissioning father had a biological son in Thailand. As the parties had not intended that this specific child (being a child not biologically related to the commissioning parents) leave Thailand soon after birth, this child was to be treated as habitually resident in Thailand, and the Hague Adoption Convention needed to apply to safeguard all those involved.

A second option is to apply for guardianship of the child. Under the Care of Children Act 2004, the Family Court can appoint any person as an additional guardian of a child. According to s. 15, a guardian has 'all duties, powers, rights, and responsibilities that a parent of the child has in relation to the upbringing of the child.' This does not terminate the parental status of the surrogate and her partner. There are only two New Zealand cases in which guardianship was sought instead of adoption, *Minkov v Caldwell*[33] and *Re CGL and SJP*.[34] In *Minkov*, the New Zealand commissioning parents were planning to move to Australia for the commissioning father's employment. They therefore sought a guardianship order in New Zealand, and planned to undertake the adoption process in Australia. In *Re CGL* (discussed further below) Australian commissioning parents sought parenting and guardianship orders to return to Australia with the child. It was unclear whether adoption would follow in the Australian courts (since surrogacy had only been de-criminalised in the commissioning parents' home state of Tasmania three months prior to this decision).

The final option is a parenting order under s. 48 Care of Children Act. This is an order determining 'the time or times when specified persons have the role of providing day-to-day care for, or may have contact with, the child.' It was designed to grant particular rights to caregivers or partners of parents, but does not terminate the parental rights of the surrogate and her partner. A parenting order was sought in *Re CGL and SJP*[35] in addition to a guardianship order.

---

30 *Re BWS* [2011] NZFLR 621.
31 *Re Clifford* [2016] NZFC 1666.
32 *Re DMW* [2012] NZFC 2915.
33 *Minkov v Caldwell* [2014] NZFC 3587.
34 *Re CGL and SJP* [2012] NZFC 9828.
35 *Re CGL and SJP* [2012] NZFC 9828.

5.2. RESPONSIBILITY FOR OVERSEEING THE TRANSFER OF PARENTHOOD

This is a judicial procedure. An adoption order is normally made by the Family Court, but the District Court and the High Court (acting in its jurisdiction on appeal) can also make such an order.

In order for an adoption order to be made, s. 4 of the Adoption Act requires certain criteria to be met by the applicants. First, an application can only be made by one person, unless the co-applicants are spouses.[36] Second, at least one applicant must (unless special circumstances exist) either be over the age of 25 and at least 20 years older than the child; or be over the age of 20 and a relative of the child; or be the mother or father of the child. Third, an order cannot be made in relation to the adoption of a female child by a sole male applicant unless special circumstances exist.[37] In addition, under s. 6 the applicants cannot keep the child in their home prior to the adoption if the child is under 15 years of age, unless an interim order is in force or a social worker has given prior approval (such approval lasting for only one month). Finally, under s. 11 the court must also be satisfied that each applicant is 'a fit and proper person to have the role of providing day-to-day care for the child and of sufficient ability to bring up, maintain, and educate the child' and under s. 11 the adoption must promote the welfare and interests of the child.

Sections 6 and 11 were considered in an international surrogacy context in *Re SCR*.[38] The commissioning parents filed the necessary application under s. 6 well in advance of the child's birth, and approval was granted on 18 January 2012. The male applicant and the child were overseas until 13 March, and argued that the one-month period in fact started then (when the child began living in the home), and not from the date of the approval. Judge Walsh found that any alleged breach 'could only be considered as "technical" and [did] not impede the court' in its decision making. Nor did it reflect adversely on the applicants, or suggest that they were not fit and proper persons under s. 11. They had 'done all they could in the circumstances to comply.'

The parents or guardians must consent to the adoption. Under s. 7, any document signifying consent by the mother is not admissible unless the child was at least 10 days old on the date of execution of the document. By s. 8(1)(a) of the Adoption Act, the requirement of consent may be dispensed with, inter alia:

> 'if the court is satisfied that the parent or guardian has abandoned, neglected, persistently failed to maintain, or persistently ill-treated the child, or failed to exercise the normal

---

36 Although see above nn. 26–27 for a discussion of how this has been read down.

37 As stated above n. 25 the fact that there is a genetic link and the child is born following a surrogacy arrangement will satisfy this: *Re BWS* [2011] NZFLR 611; *Re Kennedy* [2014] NZLFR 367.

38 *Re SCR* [2012] NZFC 5466.

> duty and care of parenthood in respect of the child; and that reasonable notice of the application for an adoption order has been given to the parent or guardian where the parent or guardian can be found ...'

If these requirements are met, the court may, in its discretion, grant an adoption order. Under s. 5, an interim adoption order is to be made in the first instance, unless special circumstances exist. This will remain in force for one year, unless it is revoked or a final order is made. An application for a final adoption order can be made after six months, although again special circumstances allow for an earlier application. Before any order is made, a social worker must furnish a report, which the court must consider. Between 2012–14 half of the reported judgments involved the grant of a final order at first instance for the sole reasoning that this was a surrogacy arrangement. From 2015 onwards, whether this could occur became a standard question presented to the judges for consideration, and in all reported cases a final order was granted at first instance.

Although not a condition to be met before an adoption order can be granted, it is important to emphasise that it is an offence to give or receive, or agree to give or receive, any payment in consideration of the adoption unless this payment has received the consent of the court.[39] It is also an offence to advertise that the parent or guardian of a child wishes to have the child adopted, or that a person desires to adopt a child, or that a person is willing to arrange an adoption.[40] A breach of one of these offences will result in conviction and imprisonment for a term not exceeding three months, or a fine not exceeding NZ$15,000 or both. It should not affect the ability to adopt the child.

There is no mechanism in place for the adjudication of disputes concerning surrogacy arrangements. Under s. 14(1) of the HART Act a surrogacy arrangement 'is not of itself illegal, but is not enforceable by or against any person.' A court would not, therefore, have jurisdiction to hear any application relating to enforcement of the agreement. There has yet to be a reported case in New Zealand involving a dispute between surrogate and intended parents.

The surrogate, as the legal mother at birth, will have her details recorded on the child's birth certificate. Should adoption then occur, a new birth certificate will be issued showing the commissioning parents as the legal parents, but a copy of the original birth certificate will be kept by the Registrar of Births.[41] For a discussion of the information contained on a birth certificate, see above Section 3 ('Legal Parenthood at the Time of Birth'). As also discussed in

---

39 Section 25 of the Adoption Act 1955.

40 Section 26 of the Adoption Act 1955.

41 For a discussion of the information contained on a birth certificate, see above Section 3 ('Legal Parenthood at the Time of Birth').

Section 3, providers are required under the HART Act to collect certain information about donors, but there is no equivalent provision for surrogates.

5.3. RIGHTS OF CHILDREN

Due to the fact that it was drafted in 1955, there are no guiding principles in the Adoption Act as to what extent the child's rights or interests are relevant to a determination of whether a transfer of parenthood will be permitted (in contrast to the 2004 Care of Children Act which contain reference to these in ss. 3, 4 and 5). Section 11 does, however, require that before making an adoption order, the court must be satisfied that 'the welfare and interests of the child will be promoted by the adoption …'.

New Zealand has ratified the United Nations Convention on the Rights of the Child. This includes Art. 21, which states that 'States Parties that recognize and/or permit the system of adoption shall ensure that the best interests of the child is the paramount consideration.' New Zealand courts must therefore read statutory provisions in a way that is consistent with this.

6. AGENCIES AND CRIMINALISATION

6.1. THE ROLE OF MEDIATORS, AGENCIES AND MIDDLEMEN

Under s. 14(3) of the HART Act, a person commits an offence if they 'receive or agree to receive valuable consideration … for another person's participation in a surrogacy arrangement'. The only exceptions to this are payments for specific medical, counselling and legal expenses for the surrogate which can be paid directly to the professional by the commissioning parents. It should be noted that the language relating to legal advice covers a woman who 'is, or might become, pregnant', allowing for advice to be given throughout the pregnancy, but the language in relation to the medical expenses appears restricted to attaining pregnancy, and not to care during the pregnancy. The language of s. 14 therefore heavily restricts the involvement of third parties on a commercial basis. Whether non-profit organisations who receive payments that cover only their reasonable expenses are also caught by the language of 'valuable consideration' is unclear, and has yet to be tested. None of the reported domestic surrogacy cases appear to have involved any such third parties operating on a commercial basis.

In addition, s. 15 contains a broad prohibition on advertising in relation to surrogacy, which applies to both the potential parties to a surrogacy arrangement and to any third parties. With the exception of this section, there are no specific rules regulating actions taking place prior to entering into a surrogacy arrangement, for example the provision of advice or information or the arranging of introductions, unless these actions contravene ss. 14 or 15.

6.2. PENALTIES

A breach of s. 14 of the HART Act prohibition on commercial surrogacy can result 'on conviction to imprisonment for a term not exceeding 1 year or a fine not exceeding NZ$100,000, or both.' A breach of the s. 15 prohibition on advertising can result 'on conviction to imprisonment for a term not exceeding 3 months or a fine not exceeding NZ$2,500, or both.' The Act does not have extraterritorial effect.[42]

The provisions in the HART Act impose liability on any 'person' who breaches these sections. The wording in s. 14(3), which refers to the giving or receiving of valuable consideration in relation to either 'their participation' or 'another person's participation' makes clear that both the parties to the agreement and third parties can be liable. There is also no differentiation in levels of penalty imposed on the parties or on third parties.

It should also be remembered that the Adoption Act contains certain relevant offences, including keeping a child in the home of any person for the purpose of adoption without prior approval, and giving or receiving payment in consideration of adoption. These have been discussed above. The penalty for breach is imprisonment for a term not exceeding three months or a fine not exceeding NZ$15,000, or both. A breach of these sections will not prevent the adoption order being granted.[43]

It does not appear that any of these penalties have been imposed. As discussed above, Family Court judges have noted that when they are faced with the competing policy objectives of acting in the best interests of the child and of prohibiting commercial surrogacy, it is the best interests of the child which should take precedence, and not the enforcement of criminal sanctions. As examples of this, in *Re BWS*[44] Judge Walker commented that 'despite policy considerations, I am prepared to exercise my discretion to grant the adoption order as I think this is the best outcome for the children.' More strongly, in *Re KR and DGR*[45] Judge Ryan concluded 'policy considerations are not within the role of this court to impose ... my role is to determine this particular application in front of me.'

---

42 For a discussion of how the impact of this on international surrogacy arrangements, see below Section 7, 'International Surrogacy Arrangements'.

43 *Re ALH* Family Court North Shore, FAM-2011-044-000371, Judge Walker.

44 *Re BWS* [2011] NZFLR 611.

45 *Re KR and DGR* [2011] NZFLR 429.

7. INTERNATIONAL SURROGACY ARRANGEMENTS

7.1. FOREIGN SURROGACY ARRANGEMENTS

The ECART application is designed to be made by a New Zealand-based fertility clinic and the requirement of joint counselling sessions between the potential surrogate and commissioning parents implies that both parties are resident in New Zealand.

The HART Act does not have extraterritorial effect, and is silent on international surrogacy. The extent to which this has resulted in international surrogacy is unclear. Of the 31 reported adoption decisions, 17 were international surrogacy cases (although three of these were inter-family arrangements where one member happened to live in Australia). This author's empirical research with lawyers, however, makes it clear that the number of reported decisions represent only a small fraction of applications for adoption being made to court, or advice being given to clients, so these numbers may not be representative. In the last few years, both lawyers and government departments have reported noticing a rapid and exponential increase in the number of inquiries about international surrogacy. It should be recognised, however, that a large number of these inquiries would have come from people who felt that the language of the Adoption Act meant that domestic surrogacy was not an option for them. The recent decision in *Re Pierney*[46] which now permits adoption by gay de facto couples, might result in a decrease in numbers looking to international surrogacy. Where international surrogacy is considered by New Zealanders, the destination of choice has been overwhelmingly the United States, with California being the most common state. The second most common destination (until rumours of a ban emerged) was Thailand.[47]

There have been two cases in which jurisdiction to hear applications for adoption resulting from international surrogacy arrangements involving foreign commissioning parents been heard by a New Zealand court. In *Re KJB*[48] the surrogate was the sister of the commissioning father. The commissioning parents lived in Sydney, Australia, and implantation had occurred there following the Sydney equivalent of the ECART process. The surrogate had then returned to New Zealand to care for her own children, and the child was born in New Zealand. The reported judgment dealt with the preliminary question of whether a New Zealand court had jurisdiction to hear the adoption application. The court determined that it did, based on the wording of the Status of Children Act

46 See above n. 28.

47 It is interesting to note that New Zealanders do not seem to be choosing the same countries (India, Cambodian, Vietnam, Laos) as our close neighbours Australia, who are regarded as one of the highest user countries of international surrogacy.

48 *Re KJB* [2010] NZFLR 97.

which deemed the New Zealand surrogate to be the mother of the child, and also based on the need to resolve the issue of parentage as soon as possible in the child's best interests. In *Re CGL v SJP*,[49] the commissioning parents lived in Tasmania, Australia, and the surrogate (who had previously acted as a surrogate for them) lived in New Zealand. The child was born in New Zealand. This was again a preliminary hearing to determine if the Family Court had jurisdiction to hear an application, this time for parenting and guardianship orders. Despite the issue of the legality of the application being raised by the Family Court (on the grounds that surrogacy had been illegal in Tasmania until three months previously), the court decided that it did have jurisdiction. Further affidavits would need to be supplied before the application could be determined.

As regards parenthood arising out of a surrogacy arrangement in another jurisdiction, s. 11 of the Adoption (Intercountry) Act 1997 provides that any adoption by the commissioning parents in accordance with the Hague Adoption Convention will be recognised in New Zealand. In all other cases, the commissioning parents must obtain parentage through the New Zealand Family Court. Under the Status of Children Act, the commissioning parents are not the legal parents of the child and must apply to a New Zealand court for a transfer of parentage. This is regardless of whether or not they are considered to be the legal parents in the country of the child's birth.

7.2. THE RETURN OF A CHILD BORN UNDER AN INTERNATIONAL SURROGACY ARRANGEMENT

If the Hague Adoption Convention applies and the intercountry adoption process has been completed, New Zealand law will recognise the commissioning parents as the legal parents, enabling the child to apply for a New Zealand passport and therefore travel to New Zealand.

If the Hague Adoption Convention does not apply, the situation becomes complicated. To enter New Zealand a person is generally required to have a passport. As the child will not be the legal child of the commissioning parents until an adoption order is granted in a New Zealand court (and the child must be present in New Zealand for some of the adoption criteria to be determined), the child will not be considered to be a New Zealand citizen at the time of the intended travel from the country of birth and will therefore not be entitled to a New Zealand passport. The child may be entitled to a passport from the country of birth, but this will depend on rules as to parentage and citizenship in that country.

[49] *Re CGL v SJP* [2012] NZFC 9828.

An exit visa may also be necessary. Obtaining an exit visa may require negotiation with relevant authorities in the country of birth. In relation to the New Zealand entry visa, a joint information task sheet issued by four government departments states that:[50]

> 'There is no immigration policy to facilitate the entry of children into New Zealand who have been born as a result of a surrogacy arrangement overseas. Any decision to grant a temporary visitor visa to a child born via a surrogacy arrangement is made by the Minister of Immigration.'

In determining whether to grant this visa, the Minister of Immigration may be guided by a set of non-binding Guidelines, which have been agreed by Cabinet. These Guidelines state that:[51]

'1. Minister may consider:
2. Whether there is a genetic link between at least one of the commissioning persons and the child.
3. The outcome that is in the best interests of the child.
4. New Zealand's international obligations.
5. The nature of the surrogacy arrangement, i.e., is it altruistic or commercial?
6. Whether the commissioning persons intend to or have taken steps to secure legal parenthood or other legal rights in respect of child in NZ.
7. What the commissioning persons have done in the child's country of birth to secure legal parenthood or other legal rights in respect of the child.
8. Whether the applicants have demonstrated respect for the laws of the jurisdiction in which the surrogacy was carried out.
9. Whether there is satisfactory evidence of informed consent from the:
   - gamete (egg/sperm donor (if relevant))
   - surrogate mother for the surrogacy arrangement to take place (was she a willing party?)
   - surrogate mother (and her partner if relevant) for the child to depart the country of birth and enter New Zealand
   - surrogate mother (and her partner if relevant) for the child's adoption.
10. Steps taken by the commissioning persons to preserve the child's identity, e.g. do the commissioning persons intend to retain information about the child's origins?

[50] Oranga Tamariki, Immigration New Zealand, Department of Internal Affairs, and New Zealand Ministry of Foreign Affairs and Trade, Information Sheet: International Surrogacy (March 2018), <https://www.orangatamariki.govt.nz/assets/Uploads/Documents/information-sheet-international-surrogacy.pdf> accessed 21.01.2019.

[51] Ibid, at Appendix A.

11. Whether the recognised authority of the birth country has agreed or objects to the child leaving the country permanently.
12. Any other considerations that the Minister wishes to take into account.'

Under the Citizenship Act 1977, citizenship in New Zealand is acquired in four situations: citizenship by birth (s. 6: generally, being born in New Zealand with at least one parent who is a New Zealand citizen or permanent resident); citizenship by descent (s. 7: generally, being born outside New Zealand after January 1978 to a parent who is a New Zealand citizen other than by descent, or to a parent who was a New Zealand citizen by descent and the person would otherwise be stateless); citizenship by grant of Minister (s. 8); and citizenship in special cases (s. 9).

In relation to international surrogacy, citizenship by birth will not be available as the child is born outside New Zealand. Citizenship by grant is unlikely to be available. The person seeking citizenship must make the application themselves and cannot do so until the age of 16 years. While this might appear to simply delay an application for citizenship until then, the person must also have been present in New Zealand for 1,350 days in the five years preceding the application, and be legally entitled to remain in New Zealand indefinitely under the Immigration Act 2009. The duration of a temporary visitor visa (the only way the child can enter New Zealand legally) is generally a maximum of 12 months, meaning these criteria cannot be met. Citizenship by descent may be available once an adoption order is granted, provided one of the commissioning parents to whom the adoption order has been granted is a New Zealand citizen or permanent resident.

Citizenship in special cases may be available. The Minister may authorise the grant of citizenship to a person:[52]

'(a) Who has not yet attained the age of 16 years; or
(b) Whose father or mother was, at the time of that person's birth, a New Zealand citizen by descent; or
(c) If the Minister is satisfied that granting a certificate of New Zealand citizenship to the applicant would be in the public interest because of exceptional circumstances of a humanitarian or other nature relating to the applicant; or
(d) If the person would otherwise be stateless.'

In exercising his or her discretion, the Minister may have regard to any of the requirements for citizenship by grant as the Minister thinks fit, and must have regard to specific requirements listed in s. 9A if the applicant has a criminal conviction.

52 Section 9(1) of the Citizenship Act 1977.

Of the four options, only the first would be clearly applicable in a case of international surrogacy. The second option would not apply due to New Zealand parentage laws designating the surrogate (and possibly her partner) as the legal parent(s). In relation to option four, the potential for 'statelessness' in international surrogacy is well known. This can arise where New Zealand law and the law of the country of birth apply different tests for legal parenthood, resulting in neither country recognising the child as one of their citizens. The third option is complicated. It could potentially be argued that the lack of citizenship following being born from an international surrogacy agreement is an 'exceptional circumstance of a[n] other nature relating to the applicant' justifying the grant of citizenship.

It is not clear whether an application for citizenship in special cases has been successfully made for a child born as the result of a surrogacy arrangement, but it is believed that some applications have been made. The obvious issue with an application of this nature is that it grants only citizenship, and not legal parentage. The intended parents will still need to adopt the child, and provided the commissioning parents are New Zealand citizens or permanent residents, the child can acquire citizenship through the adoption process. It may well be the case that the underlying motivation for the applications made for citizenship in special cases is that the applicant commissioning parents feel strongly that they should not have to adopt 'their child'. While this is understandable, ensuring that the child has both New Zealand legal parents and citizenship should be the objective.

8. CONCLUSION

Surrogacy is regulated in New Zealand under legislation that was drafted between 1997 and 2004. There are only two specific provisions, and both received only minimal discussion or debate during the legislative process. Notably absent from the Act are any provisions relating to altruistic surrogacy or providing for a surrogacy specific means of transferal of legal parentage, despite the fact that such provisions can be found in legislation enacted at a similar time in other jurisdictions. While it seems to have been intended that these would be revisited at a later date, this has yet to occur.

In relation to domestic surrogacy, the use of an ethics committee, ECART, to consider applications for surrogacy is an innovative approach utilised in few other jurisdictions (Israel and some Australian states being the only known examples) and should be regarded as a successful approach to domestic surrogacy regulation. The relevant Guidelines allow for consideration of the best interests of all parties concerned (and their broader families), and ensure that both surrogate and commissioning parents have obtained medical and legal advice and have attended separate and joint counselling sessions. The Guidelines do, however, require certain criteria to be met before ECART can consider the application. Notably, these include that it cannot be a commercial surrogacy arrangement, that there be a genetic link between at least one commissioning parent and the child and until recently, that there be a commissioning 'mother' with a specific medical condition affecting pregnancy or gestation. For any potential commissioning parent(s) who cannot meet these criteria the only options are private surrogacy (without the involvement of a fertility clinic) or international surrogacy.

In relation to international surrogacy, the Act is silent. A commissioning parent or parents entering into an international surrogacy arrangement therefore rely on the discretionary grant of visas from both New Zealand and the country of birth in order to bring the child back to New Zealand, which can be a lengthy and uncertain process. Four government departments in New Zealand play a role in advising the Minister of Immigration in the exercise of this discretion to grant a visa, and have issued a joint fact sheet providing some basic information. It should be acknowledged that the approach of these government departments demonstrates a clear commitment to working together to achieve a result that is in the best interests of the child.

The regulation of surrogacy in New Zealand can probably therefore be regarded as workable, albeit not optimal, and in need of reconsideration. Judges in particular report struggling with the use of the Adoption Act to transfer parentage, and often mention in judgments the difficulties resulting from being faced with the potentially inconsistent policy objectives of prohibiting commercial surrogacy and of acting in the best interests of the child. Thus far they have taken a pragmatic and child-focussed approach, which arguably achieves the best outcome in the circumstances, but does so by de-prioritising the application of the provisions in the HART Act.

At the present time there is no indication that a reconsideration of surrogacy laws is on the government's legislative agenda. Should ACART advise the Minister to reconsider the biological link policy, however, this might trigger a broader discussion on surrogacy regulation.

SURROGACY IN PORTUGAL

Rute Teixeira PEDRO

1. GENERAL LEGAL FRAMEWORK

1.1. STATUTORY FRAMEWORK

In Portugal, specific legal rules allowing surrogacy were introduced very recently. Law no. 25/2016, dated 22 August 2016, which introduced amendments to Law no. 32/2006, dated 26 July 2006 ('the Medically-Assisted Procreation Law'), created a legal framework for surrogacy in Portugal in 2016. A specific Regulatory Decree was enacted in 2017 (Regulatory Decree no. 6/2017, dated 31 July 2017) to supplement Law no. 25/2016, governing surrogacy.

In 1997, a change to the Constitution of the Portuguese Republic mandated the Portuguese State to regulate access to medically assisted procreation techniques 'in such a way as to safeguard the dignity of the human person', as is stated in its Art. 67 no. 2(e).[1] But it took almost 10 years before the constitutional mandate was finally fulfilled: the law governing Medically-Assisted Procreation Law no. 32/2006, dated 26 July 2006 was enacted in 2006.[2] According to its first version, although the use of medically assisted techniques to procreate was authorised (as long as certain requirements were met) surrogacy was not permitted in any circumstances. Another 10-year period elapsed before surrogacy was accepted by the Portuguese legal system: this happened with the enactment of Law no. 25/2016, dated 22 August 2016, which created many particular safeguards and envisaged the use of surrogacy as exceptional, and only possible when certain strict conditions were fulfilled.

Article 3 of this law expressly referred to the need for regulation of surrogacy, stating that the government had to approve the corresponding Regulatory Decree[3] of the abovementioned Law no. 25/2016 within 120 days after the date of its publication in the Portuguese Official Journal which was 22 August 2016. The deadline was not met as Regulatory Decree no. 6/2017 was published almost one year later, on 31 July 2017. As a consequence, the legal regime governing surrogacy only entered into force on 1 August 2017.[4]

Less than nine months later, on 24 April 2018, the Portuguese Constitutional Court has declared that rules of the statutory framework regarding surrogacy, as they were enacted in 2016, violated provisions of the Constitution of Portuguese Republic.[5] Nevertheless, in the following the legal framework as it

---

1 Paragraph e) was added to Art. 67 no. 2 of the Constitution of the Portuguese Republic in 1997.

2 Law no. 32/2006, 26.07.2006 is still in force today with amendments introduced by Law 59/2007, dated 04.09.2007, Law no. 17/2016, dated 20.06.2016, Law no. 25/2016, dated 22.08.2016 and Law no. 58/207, dated 25.07.2017. Hereafter, Law no. 32/2006, dated 26.07.2006 with the subsequent amendments will be referred to as the Medically-Assisted Procreation Law. Furthermore, from this point on, whenever we refer to an article without a reference to the law it belongs to, it is an article of the Portuguese Medically-Assisted Procreation Law as it was amended and is in force at the moment.

3 According to Art. 112, no. 6 of the Constitution of Portuguese Republic, Regulatory Decrees are normative instruments that contain government regulations about a subject that needs to be regulated in detail, as is required by the law that governs that specific subject.

4 As stated in Art. 4 of Law no. 25/2016, dated 22.08.2016, in conjunction with Art. 8 of the Regulatory Decree no. 6/2017, dated 31.07.2017.

5 Regarding this decision, see especially below Section 1.3.

was enacted in 2016 will be described and analysed, but highlighting the aspects that were declared unconstitutional by the Constitutional Court.

1.2. REGULATORY FRAMEWORK

According the legal framework as it was enacted in 2016 and supplemented in 2017,[6] the use of surrogacy is controlled, in a case-to-case assessment, by two authorities, which are involved in different ways in the process of authorising and implementing it.

On the one hand, the National Council for Medically-Assisted Procreation[7] (‘*Conselho Nacional de Procriação Medicamente Assistida*’, ‘CNPMA’) has the power to grant authorisation for the surrogacy arrangement to be concluded, and this has to happen before the beginning of the process. Afterwards, the Council supervises the whole process of surrogacy.[8] On the other hand, this entity has to hear the Portuguese Medical Association prior to the decisions that are to be taken. Thus, with regard to each individual surrogacy application, the National Council for Medically-Assisted Procreation has the decisional power and the Medical Association the consultative power (Art. 8 no. 2 of Medically-Assisted Procreation Law).

Accordingly, the application for surrogacy is submitted to the National Council for Medically-Assisted Procreation using a form that is available on its website[9] and which must be signed jointly by the commissioning parents and the surrogate (Art. 2 no. 1 of the Regulatory Decree no. 6/2017). Specific information and documents must accompany the application, according to Art. 2 no. 2 of the Regulatory Decree no. 6/2017.[10] These include the medical

6 As it will be highlighted below (Section 1.3.), the Portuguese Constitutional Court considered that the terms of this case-to-case assessment as they were (insufficiently) designed in Art. 8 of Medically-Assisted Procreation Law violated the Constitution of Portuguese Republic.

7 It is composed of nine experts with special qualifications in the areas of ethical, scientific, social and legal matters related to medically assisted procreation. Five of them are nominated by the Portuguese Parliament (‘*Assembleia da República*’) and the remaining four by the government members responsible for the areas of health and science (Art. 31 of the Medically-Assisted Procreation Law). Currently, its members are specialised in medicine, genetics, biology, physics and law. The Council's work is performed within the Portuguese Parliament, which covers its costs and offers technical and administrative support.

8 The National Council for Medically-Assisted Procreation, in its plenary meeting on 08.09.2017, established the three phases (preliminary phase, instruction phase and decision phase) of this process, which will be explained below.

9 Its website is accessible at: <http://www.cnpma.org.pt/> accessed 07.09.2018.

10 Other information and documents that have to be enclosed are: the identification of the commissioning couple and of the surrogate; their acceptance of the surrogacy contract model; a statement by a psychiatrist or psychologist in favour of the surrogacy; and a statement by the Director of the medically assisted procreation centre, where the medically assisted techniques that are required for the surrogacy shall be performed, expressing acceptance of the procedure.

documents issued by the medically-assisted procreation centre where the medically-assisted technique that is required for the surrogacy shall be carried out. These documents must attest that the conditions for surrogacy stated in Art. 8 no. 2 of Medically-Assisted Procreation Law are met.

Within 60 days of the application there must be a preliminary assessment of the application by the National Council for Medically-Assisted Procreation, who may accept or reject it. If it is accepted, the application and the abovementioned medical documents are sent to the Portuguese Medical Association who is obliged to express its technical opinion within 60 days.[11] Subsequently, the National Council for Medically-Assisted Procreation has to decide whether the surrogacy should be authorised. This decision must be adopted before another period of 60 days elapses.[12] According to the rules set out in Art. 2 of the Regulatory Decree no. 6/2017, the commissioning parents and the surrogate should not have to wait for more than six months to learn of the final decision concerning the planned surrogacy.

In addition to this case-to-case assessment, the National Council for Medically-Assisted Procreation was assigned not only the task of creating the model of the application form through which the request for surrogacy is expressed (Art. 2 no. 1 of the Regulatory Decree no. 6/2017),[13] but also the task of approving the model of the surrogacy contract in accordance with Art. 3 of Regulatory Decree no. 6/2017.[14] These tasks are in line with its general responsibility of expressing its views regarding the ethical, social and legal issues raised by medically-assisted procreation (Art. 30 no. 1 of Medically-Assisted Procreation Law) and its special powers described in the 16-paragraph Art. 30, no. 1 of the Medically-Assisted Procreation Law.[15]

---

11 The technical opinion expressed by the Portuguese Medical Association does not bind the National Council for Medically-Assisted Procreation (Art. 2 no. 5 of the Regulatory Decree no. 6/2017).

12 In order to adopt the final decision, National Council for Medically-Assisted Procreation shall adopt the measures it considers appropriate and necessary for the final decision. In particular, a meeting with the surrogate and the commissioning parents has to take place. Additionally, a complete and independent evaluation of the surrogate and the commissioning parents must be undertaken by a technical and multidisciplinary team, particularly in the area of maternal and mental health (Art. 2 no. 9 of the Regulatory Decree no. 6/2017).

13 The form can be accessed at: <http://www.cnpma.org.pt/Docs/CNPMA_formulario_DR_6_2017.pdf> accessed 07.08.2018.

14 The models of the document used by the beneficiaries of the medically-assisted techniques (including the commissioning parents and the surrogate) to give their consent to the technique were also approved by the National Council for Medically-Assisted Procreation (Art. 30 no. 2, h) of the Medically-Assisted Procreation Law). There are different models according to the technique that will be performed. They were approved in 2008 and revised in 2012, 2015 and 2016. They are available at: <http://www.cnpma.org.pt/profissionais_modelos.aspx> accessed 07.09.2018.

15 Among those powers it should be highlighted that the National Council for Medically-Assisted Procreation is charged with the following tasks: to define the conditions that must

1.3. DEBATES LEADING UP TO THE DECISION NO. 225/2018 OF THE PORTUGUESE CONSTITUTIONAL COURT

The need for a specific legal framework regarding surrogacy emerged from the abovementioned Art. 67 no. 2(e) of the Constitution of the Portuguese Republic. As a consequence, when the Medically-Assisted Procreation Law was enacted in 2006, two special rules covered surrogacy. Article 8 stated that surrogacy agreements were always void as they were considered contrary to the principles of 'public order' and *bonos mores*.[16] Hence they had no legal effect, irrespective of whether they were commercial agreements or not.

In order to strengthen the effectiveness of this prohibition, Art. 8 no. 3 stressed that the surrogate would be regarded as the mother of the child for all intents and purposes. Additionally, taking into consideration Art. 39, criminal penalties should be applied to anyone who concluded or promoted surrogacy agreements, either directly or indirectly.[17]

Ten years after the enactment of the law, a revision was deemed to be needed. Law no. 17/2016, dated 20 June 2016, and Law no. 25/2016, dated 22 August 2016, significantly reshaped the rules regarding the use of medical techniques for procreation. These two laws represented an important landmark in the legal treatment of the subject as they implied a shift in emphasis compared to the previous framework.[18] One of the key changes implemented by Law no. 17/2016, dated 20 June 2016, is that medically-assisted procreation techniques may now be used by any woman, irrespective of a diagnosis of infertility (Art. 4 no. 3 of the Medically-Assisted Procreation Law)[19] and

be met by the centres where medically-assisted procreation techniques are performed and by the centres where gametes or embryos are preserved; to monitor the activities of those centres, supervising their compliance with the Medically-Assisted Law; to express its decision regarding the authorisation of new centres, as well as on the suspension or revocation of such authorisation; to evaluate research projects involving embryos in order to approve or reject them; and to take a decision, on a case-by-case basis, about the use of PMA techniques for selection of Human Leukocyte Antigen compatible group for the treatment of serious disease.

16 Contracts that violate the 'public order' or the *bonos mores* are void and with no effect because of the rule defined in Art. 280 of the Portuguese Civil Code. Despite the existence of this general rule, in Law no. 32/2006, dated 26 July 2006, lawmakers expressly stipulated this for surrogacy contract. Furthermore, if there was payment of any amount of money, entering into a surrogacy contract constituted a criminal offence according to Art. 39 of the original version of the 2006 Law.

17 The agent held liable for those conducts could be imprisoned for two years.

18 Cf. in R. Teixeira Pedro, 'The dawn of a brave new world in Portugal? – A critical overview of the new legal framework applicable to medically-assisted procreation', in M. Brinig (ed.), *The International Survey of Family Law: Edition 2017*, Jordan Publishing, Bristol 2017, p. 274.

19 As a consequence, at present, in Portugal 'no medical justification is required for access to medically-assisted procreation, in the sense that any woman, even if she is able to procreate naturally, may choose to materialize her parental project by means of medically assisted techniques, instead of opting for the practice of sexual intercourse. The subsidiarity

regardless of her civil status and her sexual orientation.[20] As a consequence of the amendments introduced to the law, now any single woman over 18 years, and female couples (married or cohabiting) are allowed to use medically-assisted procreation techniques Art. 6 no. 1 of the Medically-Assisted Procreation Law.

In addition, Portuguese Lawmakers also changed their approach to surrogacy agreements. They will be discussed in detail later,[21] but it must be highlighted that the use of surrogacy was allowed in 2016 only 'in cases of the absence of a uterus, injury or disease of this organ that absolutely and definitively prevents the woman's pregnancy or in clinical situations that justify it' (Art. 8 no. 2 of the Medically-Assisted Procreation Law). As a consequence, the principle of subsidiarity (of surrogacy to natural procreation) fully applied as far as surrogacy was concerned. Also, in the light of the legal framework enacted in 2016, no genetic connection may exist between the surrogate and the baby, and it therefore cannot be conceived using the eggs of the woman who carries the pregnancy. Thus only gestational surrogacy was allowed.

This shift in the legal approach regarding surrogacy gave rise to a number of legal questions that were formulated by the National Council of Ethics for Life Sciences ('*Comissão Nacional de Ética para as ciências da vida*', 'CNEV').[22] When the President of the Republic first received the Decree of the Portuguese Parliament regarding surrogacy (Decree no. 27/XIII) for enactment as a law, he exercised the right of veto, granted by Art. 136 no. 1 of the Constitution of the Portuguese Republic. Accordingly, he sent a message to Parliament setting out the grounds for his veto and requesting that the legislative act be reconsidered. In this message he referred to the technical judgment of the National Council of Ethics for Life Sciences and pointed out the objections formulated by this entity. The major doubts concerned the lack of a proper solutions concerning:

- the provision of information to the commissioning parents and the surrogate about the meaning and consequences of the influence of the latter in the embryonic and foetal development;

---

principle was partially replaced by the (thus yet limited) acceptance of the complementary or alternative principle of these medical reproduction methods', R. Teixeira Pedro, above n. 18, pp. 274–75.

20 It must be stressed that this possibility of single parenthood is afforded only to women and is denied to men.

21 See below Section 2.

22 The objections were expressed in its technical judgment about the proposed law presented to Parliament by groups of deputies, which led to the two laws approved in 2016 and referred to in text. The technical judgement is called '*Parecer 87/CNEV/2016*', dated 11.03.2016 and is available at: <http://www.cnecv.pt/admin/files/data/docs/1461943756_P%20CNECV%2087_2016_PMA%20GDS.pdf> accessed 07.09.2018. The Council declared that the proposed rules did not properly safeguard the rights of the unborn child or the rights of the surrogate. Concurrently it was considered that the proposed legal framework had not taken into account some objections that were formulated in a previous judgment of the same Council ('*Parecer 63/CNECV/2012*').

- the possibility of the revocation of consent, the terms of its exercise and the consequences that emerge from it;
- the inclusion in the surrogacy agreement of details regarding potential cases of malformations or foetal diseases and the possibility of interruption of pregnancy, and the decisions about any health intercurrences – both concerning the foetus and the surrogate – occurring during pregnancy and the non-imposition of behavioural restrictions on the surrogate.[23]

Even if only some of these objections were overcome, – as will be discussed in the following – the President, in accordance with Art. 116 no. 2 of the Constitution of the Portuguese Republic, was bound to enact the legislative act since it was confirmed by the vote of an absolute majority of all the Members of the Assembly of the Republic in full exercise of their office. Therefore, Law no. 25/2016, dated 22 August 2016 was enacted.

A group of members of the Portuguese Parliament immediately asked the Portuguese Constitutional Court to declare, with general binding force, the unconstitutionality of the new law.[24] Their request was based on the violation of the rights of the unborn child and the surrogate which deserved protection under the Constitution of the Portuguese Republic. On 24 April 2018, the Portuguese Constitutional Court handed down its decision.[25] While recognising that the 'Portuguese model of surrogacy', per se, was not incompatible, 'in principle', with the Constitution of Portuguese Republic,[26] the court stated that certain aspects of the newly introduced solutions violated Constitutional provisions. As a consequence, the court declared, with general binding force, the unconstitutionality of eight of the 12 paragraphs that compose the article that governs surrogacy (Art. 8 of the Medically-Assisted Procreation Law).[27]

In line with the perspective of the President of the Republic and with the technical judgment of the National Council of Ethics for Life Sciences,

23 The message of the President of the Portuguese Republic is available at: <http://www.presidencia.pt/?idc=10&idi=108689> accessed 07.09.2018.

24 According to Art. 281 no. 2, f) of the Constitution of the Portuguese Republic, one-tenth of the Members of the Portuguese Parliament ('Assembly of the Republic') may ask the Portuguese Constitutional Court for a declaration of unconstitutionality or illegality with generally binding force.

25 The Decision no. 225/2018 was published in the Portuguese Official Journal ('*Diário da República*') on 07.05.2018 and can be accessed at: <https://dre.pt/application/conteudo/115226940> accessed 07.09.2018. Quotations and references to this decision will be made taking into account this publication.

26 Paragraphs 51–53 of the decision, pp. 1928–31.

27 As will be explained below, this Decision has also declared, with general binding force, the unconstitutionality of other rules of the Medically-Assisted Procreation Law, namely rules concerning the anonymity of the donor and of the surrogate.

the major issues that Portuguese Constitutional Court criticised in the legal framework approved in 2016 were:

- the lack of determinability of the legal framework applicable to the surrogacy arrangements:[28] the law does not establish neither criteria for the authorisation of the conclusion of the surrogacy arrangement to be awarded by the National Council for Medically-Assisted Procreation, nor criteria for the control of the content of the agreement. The legal determination of standards for the decision to be taken by that Authority is of paramount importance as the conclusion of surrogacy arrangements was allowed only on an exceptional basis. Since the content of this kind of agreement concerns the exercise of fundamental rights (the right to the development of personality as well as the right to form a family, enshrined in Arts 26 no. 1 and 36, no. 1 of the of the Constitution of the Portuguese Republic) it cannot solely be dependent only on the will of the individuals. The Constitutional Court highlighted the need for the definition by the lawmaker of more detailed terms and conditions for the conclusion of the surrogacy arrangements, in order to guarantee the respect for the fundamental rights involved in the process, for the principle of equality (Art. 13 of the of the Constitution of the Portuguese Republic) and for the principle of proportionality of any restriction to rights, freedoms and guarantees enshrined in the Constitution (Art. 18 of the of the Constitution of the Portuguese Republic). According to the court, the deficit of density of the normative framework regarding surrogacy arrangements generated the breach of the principle of determinability of laws that is a corollary of the principles of the democratic rule of law (Art. 2 of the of the Constitution of the Portuguese Republic), and of the reservation of law (Art. 18 and Art. 165 no. 1, b) of the Constitution of the Portuguese Republic).[29]
- the irrevocability of the consent of the surrogate after the beginning of medically-assisted procreation. The Portuguese Constitutional Court considered that the surrogate should have the right to revoke her consent until the moment she delivers the baby to the commissioning parents, as the only means to safeguard 'the continuity of her consent for the entire duration of the contract'.[30] As a consequence, in the perspective of the court, the preclusion of the possibility of the surrogate of revoking her consent before that moment constitutes the violation of her right to the development of the personality,

---

28 Paragraph 38 of the Decision, p. 1919.

29 Bearing in mind these objection rules inserted in nos 4, 10 and 11 of Art. 8, and as a consequence, in nos 2 and 3 of the same article were declared unconstitutional. All these rules governed the process leading to the conclusion of the surrogacy arrangement and its content.

30 Paragraphs 39–47 of the Decision, pp. 1920–26. The quoted sentence is on p. 1921.

interpreted in accordance with the principle of the human dignity and right to form a family, as a result of excessive restriction of those fundamental rights (Arts 1, 26 no. 1, 36 no. 1 and 18 no. 2, all of the Constitution of the Portuguese Republic).[31] Consequently, the court rejected the rule that determines that the commissioning parents are the legal parents of the child born through surrogacy from birth. Instead, their legal parenthood can be established only after the delivery of the baby to the commissioning parents by the surrogate.[32]

- the inadequacy of the legal consequence applicable to the contracts when any of the legal conditions demanded for allowing surrogacy is not met.[33] In that situation, as will be discussed below, irrespective of the specific condition not met, the contract is void. As a consequence, no effects can be derived from it and the declaration of the lack of legal effects can be judicially requested with no time limits. As stated by the Constitutional Court, the application of this 'rigid' solution gives rise to a significant degree of uncertainty regarding the legal parenthood already established, 'which is not compatible with the legal certainty required regarding the status of persons'.[34]

The declaration of unconstitutionality,[35] with general binding force, of the rules governing surrogacy arrangements necessarily forecloses the possibility of validly concluding such agreements in Portugal, but only 'until the Parliamentary legislator establishes a constitutionally adequate regime', as it is stressed by the Portuguese Constitutional Court in its decision.[36] As a matter of fact, the court explicitly stated that surrogacy per se does not infringe constitutional provisions. Surrogacy itself does not give rise to the violation of the human dignity of the unborn child[37] or of the surrogate (provided that the continuity of her consent is safeguarded as it was explained above).[38] It does not create a specific danger to the children[39] and does not collide with the concept

---

31 Number 8 of Art. 8, was declared unconstitutional.

32 Number 7 of Art. 8, was declared unconstitutional.

33 Paragraphs 48–50 of the Decision, pp. 1926–28.

34 Paragraph 50 of the decision, p. 1928. Number 12 of Art. 8 was declared unconstitutional.

35 Taking into account the fundamental rights that could be affected with the immediate application of the decision, and the need for the respect for the health and physical integrity of those who could already have been subject to medical acts corresponding to the use of Medically-Assisted Procreation techniques, the Portuguese Constitutional Court, limited the effects of its decision, saving the contracts previously authorised if the treatments had already begun. The National Council for Medically-Assisted Procreation, in its plenary meeting on 27.04.2018, declared extinct the seven pending procedures for authorising the conclusion of the surrogacy contracts for having ceased its legal ground. See <http://www.cnpma.org.pt/Docs/CNPMA_ATA04-III.pdf> accessed 07.09.2018.

36 Paragraph 53 of the Decision, p. 1931.

37 Paragraphs 31–33 of the Decision, pp. 1914–16.

38 Paragraphs 28–30 of the Decision, pp. 1911–13.

39 Paragraphs 34–36 of the Decision, pp. 1916–18.

of family.[40] According to the perspective of the court, not only there is no incompatibility with the Constitution, but also surrogacy has 'positive constitutional relevance' and its permission 'corresponds to an option of the legislator that, besides being not arbitrary, favours constitutionally protected interests and, as such, should not be dismissed without strong reasons'.[41] Furthermore, the Constitutional Court expressed its approval of what was called the 'Portuguese model of surrogacy' which was characterised by the following elements: the subsidiary, exceptional and purely gestational nature; the demand for autonomous consent of the involved parties to guarantee their free and sustained consent; the formalisation of the agreement by means of a written and non-commercial contract which is previously authorised by a competent authority.[42]

It is unclear how Parliament will reshape the legal framework of surrogacy within the margin of evaluation and appreciation awarded by the Constitution set by the Constitutional Court. At the time of writing Parliament has not yet prepared a new set of rules governing surrogacy. As a consequence, in the following the legal framework as it was enacted in 2016 will be presented, and whenever the provisions were declared unconstitutional by the Constitutional Court this will be made explicit.

1.4. STATISTICS

As the law allowing surrogacy only entered into force at the beginning of August 2017 and as it was in force for less than nine months there is no statistical information concerning surrogacy and no birth has taken place in Portugal as a consequence of a surrogacy arrangement abiding by this law. Nevertheless, by 15 December 2017 according to the National Council for Medically-Assisted Procreation more than 100 couples[43] had informally expressed the intention of using surrogacy; however, only a dozen formal applications were made. Two of these were already approved by the date the previously mentioned decision of the Constitutional Court was issued (24 April 2018), and as a result of this decision then declared extinct.[44]

---

40 Paragraph 37 of the Decision, pp. 1918–19.

41 Paragraph 27 of the Decision, p. 1911.

42 Paragraph 9 of the Decision, p. 1898.

43 The couples who have expressed informal intention and have sought information from National Council for Medically-Assisted Procreation are composed of Portuguese and non-Portuguese (mainly Spanish) individuals.

44 The first contract was approved on 15 December 2017 (see <http://www.cnpma.org.pt/Docs/CNPMA_ATA56-II.pdf> accessed 10.09.2018). The second contract was approved on 13.04.2018 (see <http://www.cnpma.org.pt/Docs/CNPMA_ATA03-III.pdf> accessed 10.09.2018). Regarding the latter, no treatments had begun when the Constitutional Court issued

According to the information provided by the Council on its website,[45] there are 26 clinics (10 that are public and 16 that are private) in which surrogacy may take place in Portugal.

2. SURROGACY ARRANGEMENTS IN GENERAL

Surrogacy contracts[46] were permitted in Portugal in exceptional circumstances by Law no. 25/2016, dated 22 August 2016, which amended the Medically-Assisted Procreation Law. According to the new version of Art. 8, surrogacy contracts would be binding if several strict conditions were met cumulatively, as many safeguards were built into the revised law.[47] As mentioned above, the Portuguese Constitutional Court has approved this model (the 'Portuguese Model' as the court called it), but mandated clarification of the criteria that have to be applied when a specific contract and its content are being evaluated.[48] In the following the traits of the Portuguese Model will be explained.

Firstly, the surrogacy contract can only be concluded 'in cases of the absence of a uterus, injury or disease of this organ that absolutely and definitively prevents the woman's pregnancy or in clinical situations that justify it' (Art. 8, no. 2 of the Medically-Assisted Procreation Law). Thus there must be medical reasons for seeking access to surrogacy. Portuguese law therefore does not allow parentage through the use of the body of another woman when the intended mother is able to carry the child herself.

Secondly, the surrogate may not be remunerated for her participation in the surrogacy contract. Commercial contracts are absolutely forbidden and only gratuitous/altruistic contracts are permitted. No reward in money or in kind is allowed. An exception is made for the reimbursement of the amount

its decision and consequently it was declared void. Concerning the former, treatments had already taken place, but the surrogate (in the case the mother of the woman of the commissioning couple) the pregnancy was not successfully achieved and as the surrogate would become 51 soon (over the age limit allowed), the process was declared extinct too.

45 See the list available at <http://www.cnpma.org.pt/centros_lista.aspx> accessed 10.09.2018.

46 Portuguese Law expressly qualifies the surrogacy arrangements as contracts (Art. 8 of the Medically-Assisted Procreation Law), namely as 'gestational surrogacy contracts' ('*contratos de gestação de substituição*').

47 If a surrogacy contract would be concluded, in the absence of any of those cumulative requirements, criminal penalties may be applied to the commissioning parents and the surrogate who enter into the surrogacy agreement and to the persons who, directly or indirectly, promote those contracts, according to Art. 39, no. 3, no. 4 and no. 5 of the Medically-Assisted Procreation Law. The penalties applied to the commissioning parents and to those who promote the contracts are more severe than those which are applicable to the surrogate. As for the criminal penalties linked to the economic advantages obtained with the conclusion of a surrogacy contract, see below Section 6.

48 Regarding the decision of the Portuguese Constitutional Court see Section 1.3.

corresponding to the healthcare expenses actually provided to the woman, including expenses for transportation, if these expenses are duly certified in a specific document (Art. 8, no. 2 of the Medically-Assisted Procreation Law). Besides the list of the types of expenses that qualify for reimbursement, there are no additional guidelines nor any limits to the total amount reimbursed. According to Art. 39, criminal penalties may be applied to the commissioning parents and the surrogates who conclude surrogacy contracts in contravention of the abovementioned requirements, and to other persons who, directly or indirectly, promote those agreements or take economic advantage from them.[49]

Thirdly, the contract must be concluded in writing. The declarations of the parts must be expressly formulated in a written document. The consent of the commissioning parents and the surrogate must comply with the provisions of Art. 14 of the Medically-Assisted Procreation Law, which, in a general way, regulates the consent of the beneficiary(ies) of medically-assisted procreation. As a consequence, the commissioning parents and the surrogate must be informed in advance of 'all known benefits and risks' arising from the use of those techniques, as well as of their ethical, social and legal implications (Art. 14, no. 2 of the Medically-Assisted Procreation Law) and of the importance of the influence of the surrogate on embryonic and foetal development (Art. 14, no. 6 of the Medically-Assisted Procreation Law). The demanded information is included in a document approved by the National Council for Medically-Assisted Procreation, through which the beneficiaries give their consent (Art. 14, no. 3 of the Medically-Assisted Procreation Law). After the provision of that information, the commissioning parents and the surrogate must expressly give their free, informed, written consent to the doctor responsible for the medically-assisted procreation technique that is required for the surrogacy to be carried out (Art. 14, no. 1 of the Medically-Assisted Procreation Law).

Fourthly, as stated above in Section 2, the conclusion of the surrogacy contract depends on the prior authorisation granted by the National Council of Medically-Assisted Procreation, which must be issued after the technical opinion of the Portuguese Medical Association (Art. 8, no. 4 of the Medically-Assisted Procreation Law and Art. 2 of the Regulatory Decree no. 6/2017). According to the Portuguese Constitutional Court, the lack of definition of detailed criteria for these judgments constitute the violation of constitutional provisions as it was explained in Section 1.3. above.

Fifthly, when a surrogacy contract is concluded, the gametes of at least one of the commissioning parents must be used. It follows, therefore, that the

---

49 In line with what was stated in n. 47, the penalties applied to the commissioning parents and to those who promote the contracts or obtain economic benefit from the conclusion of those contracts are more severe than those which are applicable to the surrogate. See below Section 6.

medically-assisted procreation technique that is needed for the surrogacy to be performed may only be partially heterologous. For the conception of the baby, donation of gametes is possible regarding only one part of the genetic material: either eggs or spermatozoids, but not both. Besides, in case of the need for egg donation, the surrogate herself cannot be the donor of any oocyte used in the particular procedure in which she participates (Art. 8, no. 3 of the Medically-Assisted Procreation Law). As a consequence, as mentioned above, a genetic link – by virtue of the donation of eggs[50] or otherwise – between the surrogate and the child is absolutely excluded.

Finally, Portuguese law forbids the conclusion of a surrogacy contract if there is a relationship of economic subordination between the parties, namely a labour/employment relationship (Art. 8, no. 6 of the Medically-Assisted Procreation Law). The aim of this condition is to safeguard the protection of freedom of will when someone decides to enter into a surrogacy contract.

With regard to the content of surrogacy contracts, there is a model of contract approved by the National Council for Medically-Assisted Procreation that must be used by the parties. They can merely add additional clauses to it. But for those additions, certain limitations have been stipulated, namely against the inclusion of clauses that either impose 'behavioural restrictions'[51] on the surrogate or 'violate her rights, freedom and dignity' (Art. 8, no. 11 of the Medically-Assisted Procreation Law).

According to Art. 8, no. 11 of the Medically-Assisted Procreation Law and from the 13 paragraphs of Art. 3, no. 3 of the Regulatory Decree no. 6/2017, there is a minimum content that must be included in the surrogacy contract concluded by the parties. As *essentialia negotii*, it is mandatory to include provisions concerning the following aspects:

1. the obligations of the surrogate regarding the compliance with medical guidelines defined by the obstetrician who follows the pregnancy, and the duty to undergo the examinations and therapeutic acts needed for appropriate clinical follow-up of the pregnancy, which safeguard the normal evolution of the pregnancy and the well-being of the child;
2. the right of the surrogate to 'participate' in the decisions concerning the choice of obstetrician who will follow the pregnancy, the type of delivery and the place where it will take place;

50 The genetic link may exist when the surrogate is genetically linked with one of the commissioning parents. This actually would be the case in the first request presented and approved in Portugal, as the intended surrogate is the mother of the commissioning mother. No baby will be born from this process as it was already declared extinct. See n. 44.

51 However, the surrogate is obliged to adopt conduct which respect medical guidelines, according to Art. 3, no. 3, a) of Regulatory Decree no. 6/2017, as will be referred to in the text.

3. the right of the surrogate to psychological support before and after the childbirth;
4. other obligations and rights of the surrogate, for instance the possibility of refusing to undergo diagnostic tests, such as amniocentesis, and the possibility of travelling on certain means of transport or out of the country in the third trimester of gestation;
5. the provision of complete and appropriate information on clinical techniques and their potential health risks;
6. the provision of information to the commissioning parents and the surrogate regarding the meaning and consequences of the influence of the surrogate's lifestyle on the embryo and foetal development;
7. the provisions to be observed in the event of the occurrence of malformations or any health matters occurring during pregnancy, both to the foetus and to the surrogate;
8. the provisions to be observed in the case of possible voluntary termination of pregnancy, in accordance with the criminal legislation in force (Art. 8, no. 11 of the Medically-Assisted Procreation Law);[52]
9. the possibility of termination of the surrogacy contract by either party in the event of a number of failed attempts of pregnancy and the terms upon which such termination may occur;
10. the terms of revocation of both the consent[53] and the contract and the corresponding consequences;
11. the gratuitous/altruistic nature of the legal transaction and the absence of any type of payment or donation made by the commissioning parents for the benefit of the surrogate due to the child's gestation, except for the amount corresponding to the expenses resulting from the effectively provided health assistance and transport;
12. the health insurance or other kind of financial system that may be associated with the object of the contract;
13. the type of conflict resolution to be adopted by the parties in case of disputes arising from the interpretation or execution of the surrogacy contract.

---

[52] In Portugal, voluntary termination of pregnancy by choice of the woman is possible within the first 10 weeks of pregnancy, as stated in Art. 142, no. 1, e) of the Portuguese Criminal Code. The recognition of this possibility in the case of the surrogate is clearly expressed in Art. 4 of Regulatory Decree no. 6/2017.

[53] Article 14, no. 4 of the Medically-Assisted Procreation Law states that consent may be freely revoked by any party to the contract 'until the beginning of the therapeutic processes of medically-assisted procreation'. The application of this rule to surrogate is unconstitutional as the Portuguese Constitutional Court has declared in its Decision no. 225/2018. See above Section 1.3. and below Section 3.3.

3. LEGAL PARENTHOOD AT THE TIME OF BIRTH

3.1. LEGAL PARENTHOOD OF THE COMMISSIONING PARENTS AT THE TIME OF BIRTH

The rule regarding the establishment of the legal parenthood of the commissioning parents, as enacted in 2016, was declared unconstitutional with general binding force by the Decision no. 225/2018 of the Portuguese Constitutional Court. In the following, the rule will be considered first, and afterwards the objections of the Constitutional Court will be explained.

As is stated in Art. 8, no. 7 of the Medically-Assisted Procreation Law, the commissioning parents are the legal parents of the child born through surrogacy. This solution is in line with the rule that governs the establishment of parenthood of any child born as a result of the use of medically-assisted techniques (Art. 20 of the Medically-Assisted Procreation Law): its parent(s) is/are the person/couple who decides/decide to materialise a parental project by means of medically-assisted techniques and has/have given consent to the use of those techniques under the terms of Art. 14 of the Medically-Assisted Procreation Law.[54] Accordingly, when a child is born as a consequence of a surrogacy contract, its legal parent are the two persons – who must be either a married couple or a cohabiting couple – who, as commissioning parents, have concluded the contract with the surrogate. Neither the surrogate, nor the possible donor of gametes used to conceive the child will be considered as legal parents of the child. There will be two parents: a mother and a father if the contract involves a heterosexual couple, or two mothers (co-motherhood), if it involves a same-sex couple.[55]

The solution as stated in Art. 8, no. 7 deviates from the general rules governing the establishment of parenthood in the Portuguese legal system,[56] which are

[54] Portuguese law calls that person/those people the beneficiary(ies) of the medical technique.

[55] The right to use medically-assisted procreation techniques is not afforded to same-sex couple composed of two men. Regarding couples formed by two women, the possibility of using those techniques is expressly recognised in Art. 6 of the Medically-Assisted Procreation Law. The use of surrogacy is not excluded by law. So if the conditions set out in Art. 8 are met (e.g. a case where neither of the two women can carry the pregnancy or there are clinical grounds supporting that solution), there are no grounds to deny recourse to surrogacy. No argument in favour of that exclusion can be derived from Regulatory Decree no. 6/2017. See below Section 4.2.

[56] Arguably the recently increasing deviations from the general rules governing the establishment of affiliation mean that a 'revolution' is taking place in the Portuguese legal system, see R. Teixeira Pedro, 'An ongoing (r)evolution unfolded step by step: redefinition of the legal concept of parentage and promotion of children's autonomy. An overview of the current developments in the Portuguese Law regarding Children's rights and affiliation' in B. Atkin (ed.), *The International Survey of Family Law 2016 Edition*, Jordan Publishing, Bristol 2016, p. 391 and G. Oliveira, 'Critérios Jurídicos da Parentalidade'

included in Art. 1796 and ff of the Portuguese Civil Code.[57] According to those rules, the mother is the woman who gave birth to the child and the father is the man whose spermatozoid fertilised the egg.

The legal solution stated in Art. 8, no. 7 of the Medically-Assisted Procreation Law in principle only would apply to situations in which surrogacy takes place as a result of a valid surrogacy contract. The application of this rule would raise some difficulties when one or several of those legal conditions are not met and consequently the contract is void. Indeed, questions had arisen as to whether the rules on the establishment of parenthood should apply in a situation in which the contract is void. As the text of the statute does not make a distinction between valid and void contracts, it is arguable that the person interpreting the law should not make such a distinction either ('*ubi lex non distinguit nec nos distinguere debemus*'). If this would be the accurate interpretation of the norm, the commissioning parents would be the legal parents of the newborn, even if the contract is void and as a contract has no legal effect.

Some scholars[58] opposed this conclusion as the persons who would be the child's legal parents may face criminal charges for their behaviour. This would mean that they would succeed in legally achieving the aim pursued through criminal activity and a void contract. If this view was followed, this would exclude the application of Art. 8, no. 7 of the Medically-Assisted Procreation Law and would lead to the application of the aforementioned general rules regarding the establishment of parenthood. As a consequence, the surrogate would be the legal mother of the child. As far as fatherhood is concerned, if the genetic material came from the male member of the couple, he would be the legal father as he had provided the genetic material used in the conception of the child. However, if the child was conceived using donor sperm, Art. 10, no. 2 of Medically-Assisted Procreation Law would apply. This rule states

---

in G. Oliveira (ed.), *Textos de Direito da Família para Francisco Pereira Coelho*, Imprensa da Universidade de Coimbra, Coimbra 2016, at pp. 278–306.

57 On the legal framework governing affiliation of children born through natural procreation, see the comments on those rules of Portuguese Civil Code by E. Chaby, in A. Prata (ed.), *Código Civil Anotado*, vol. II, Almedina, Coimbra 2017, pp. 716–75 and also P. Coelho and G. Oliveira, *Direito da Família*, G. Oliveira (coordinator), Coimbra, Imprensa da Universidade online, 2017, accessible at: <http://www.guilhermedeoliveira.pt/resources/Estabelecimento-da-Filiac%CC%A7a%CC%83o.pdf> accessed 10.09.2018.

58 As could be understood in the first congress about the subject after the 2016 amendments to the Medically-Assisted Procreation Law that took place in April 2017 at the Law Faculty of the University of Porto, Portugal. The papers presented in that Congress have been published in L. Neto and R. Teixeira Pedro (eds), *Debatendo a Procriação medicamente assistida*, Universidade do Porto, Porto 2018. See, especially considering the problem of the validity or invalidity of the contract, M. Raquel Guimarães, 'Subitamente, no verão passado»: a contratualização da gestação humana e os problemas relativos ao consentimento', pp. 121–24.

that the donor can in no circumstances be considered the father of the child. In this case, the newborn would be the son/ daughter of a single parent: the surrogate, even though she has no intention of actually becoming the mother. In my point of view this solution is not in accordance with the promotion of the best interests of the child, which must be the basis for the regime applicable to affiliation. As a consequence, even if none of the solutions seemed to provide the ideal protection to the child, the application of Art. 8, no. 7 of the Medically-Assisted Procreation Law is preferable, as this means that the persons who really intend to become parents would be legally recognised as such and would perform that role.[59] Although this solution has its critics,[60] it would promote the 'best interest of the child' more effectively, irrespective of unlawful nature of the behaviour of the (adults) commissioning parents.

On 24 April, the Portuguese Constitutional Court declared Art. 8, no. 7 of the Medically-Assisted Procreation Law unconstitutional with general binding force.[61] This declaration was made as a consequence of a previous statement of the court. The court held that the possibility of revoking the consent has to be awarded to the surrogate until after the birth of the child.

3.2. DOCUMENTATION OF SURROGACY ON THE BIRTH CERTIFICATE

In the Portuguese legal system there is no indication on the birth certificate that the child was born as a result of a surrogacy arrangement as Art. 15, no. 5 expressly forbids this.

3.3. RETENTION OF INFORMATION ON THE SURROGATE

The information concerning surrogacy, including information on the surrogate collected by the National Council for Medically-Assisted Procreation who has the duty to preserve it.

The information about all the persons who intervene in the medically-assisted procreation process – including donors – also has to be preserved. The data regarding each process is kept in the medically-assisted procreation centre that performs the technique for a period of 30 years after the end of

59 This is the interpretation proposed by the National Council for Medically-Assisted Procreation, as is accessible at: <http://www.cnpma.org.pt/Docs/CNPMA_Declaracao Interpretativa_SET2016.pdf> accessed 10.09.2018.

60 See footnote 58.

61 §47 of the decision, pp. 1925–26.

their clinical use.[62] The National Council for Medically-Assisted Procreation centralises the information regarding the application of the medically-assisted procreation techniques in every centre, namely the registration of donors, beneficiaries and children born and keeps that information for a period of 75 years (Art. 17, no. 1 and 2 of the Regulatory Decree no. 6/2016, dated 29 December 2016). Personal data relating to the medically-assisted procreation may be deleted in four situations:

1. by the expiry of the storage period;
2. by judicial decision;
3. at the request of the beneficiary who revokes the consent until the beginning of the therapeutic processes of medically-assisted procreation; and
4. in other situations stated in the law[63] (Art. 20 of the Regulatory Decree no. 6/2016).

The collection or storage of this information (Art. 16) is legally required. The possibility of having access to this information was governed by Art. 15 of the Medically-Assisted Procreation Law, but was the object of an important change due to the already mentioned decision no. 225/2018 of the Portuguese Constitutional Court.

According to Art. 15, no. 1 a principle of confidentiality would apply, as 'anyone who, in any way, becomes aware of the use of Medically-Assisted Procreation techniques, including surrogacy, or of the identity of any of the participants in the respective processes, is obliged to maintain secrecy on the identity of the same and on the Medically-Assisted Procreation process itself'. Relevant information could only be provided in three situations. Firstly, the person who has been born through surrogacy in which donated gametes or embryos were used may obtain genetic information, except for the identification of the donor (Art. 15, no. 2). Secondly, the same person, when he/she decides to marry, may obtain information on the possible existence of a legal

62 In the event that a medically-assisted procreation centre ceases its activity before completing the period of time referred to in the text, the person responsible shall communicate the situation, six months in advance, to the member of the government responsible for health, who determines the fate of the cryopreserved data on the medically-assisted procreation, gametes and embryos. The entity that receives the data and information guarantees their protection and security under the same conditions required for the centre that ceased the activity (Art. 17, no. 3 and no. 4 of the Regulatory Decree no. 6/2016, dated 29.12.2016). Access to data on medically-assisted procreation has a medical purpose, namely prophylactic, diagnostic and therapeutic. For the purposes of medical research, access to personal data that directly or indirectly allows identification of any of the persons involved is forbidden, except if they express consent in writing (Art. 19 of the same Regulatory Decree).

63 At this moment no other specific situation is set out in the law. This is a general safeguard clause.

impediment to that planned marriage, in order to assess if he/she meets the legal requirements to marry a specific person (Art. 15, no. 3); the purpose of this obviously is to prevent persons who are closely related from marrying. The identity of the donor will not be disclosed unless he/she has expressly allowed that disclosure (Art. 15, no. 3 *in fine*).[64] Thirdly, the law foresees the possibility of information regarding the identity of the donor being obtained, even if the donor has not expressed his/her consent in very specific situations. In this case, the request must be based on an important reason and a court ruling is required (Art. 15, no. 4).[65] The law made no exception regarding the surrogate. As a consequence, according to the law her identity could never be disclosed.

Decision no. 225/2018 of the Portuguese Constitutional Court has declared the unconstitutionality, with general binding force, of nos 1 and 4 of Art. 15 as the court considered that they violated the rights to the personal identity and to the development of the personality of persons born through medically-assisted procreation techniques. Therefore, the principle of confidentiality has been suppressed but nos 2 and 3 remain in force, which created a very complex situation to be dealt with. Parliament has to intervene urgently, especially to define which regime – perhaps a transitory regime – should apply to the situations that have already materialise (donations, embryos created, children already born and who may be grown ups now, etc.).

4. ELIGIBILITY FOR SURROGACY

4.1. ELIGIBILITY CRITERIA FOR WOMEN ACTING AS A SURROGATE

The Portuguese Medically-Assisted Procreation Law does not provide any eligibility criteria for women acting as surrogates. Nonetheless, in a plenary meeting that took place on 24 November 2017, the National Council for Medically-Assisted Procreation, exercising the powers,[66] established age limits: the surrogate may not exceed the age of 45 years in general or 50 years if she is the mother or the sister of one of the commissioning parents.

---

64 The legal regime applicable to adoption, after the reform that took place in 2015, provides a greater protection of adoptees' right to know their origins. For further information, see R. Teixeira Pedro, n. 56, pp. 398–400.

65 Besides those three situations referred to in the text, the director of the medically-assisted procreation centre or the health staff designated by him/her are allowed to access the data on the medically-assisted procreation, after the end of their clinical use. Additionally, within inspection actions that have to occur every two years, the auditors who perform the inspection are authorised to access the data (Art. 18 of Regulatory Decree no. 6/2016, dated 29.12.2016).

66 See above Section 1.2.

Even if there are no criteria related to the financial status of the surrogate, as pointed out above, the law forbids surrogacy when the surrogate is economically subordinate to the commissioning parents, namely as a consequence of a labour/employment relationship (Art. 8, no. 6 of the Medically-Assisted Procreation Law) that exists between them.

Since the Portuguese law permitting surrogacy was only in force for a short period of time there is no information available concerning either the characteristics of women acting as surrogates, or their reasons for doing so.

4.2. ELIGIBILITY CRITERIA FOR COMMISSIONING PARENTS

4.2.1. Personal Characteristics of the Commissioning Parents

As far as commissioning parents are concerned, the Medically-Assisted Procreation Law only lays down very few eligibility criteria. Since the amendments introduced to the Medically-Assisted Procreation Law by Law no. 17/2016, 20 June 2016, access to medically-assisted methods of procreation is allowed for any single woman irrespective of her civil status and sexual orientation, and to (married or cohabiting) couples composed of different sex individuals or of same-sex female individuals (Art. 6, no. 1). In any of these cases, a minimum age of 18 years old is stipulated.

Based on this, it at first glance would seem that this regime would also fully apply to surrogacy. But taking Regulatory Decree no. 6/2017 into account, a different conclusion must be drawn as the norms included in this decree always refer to the 'couple' that enters into the contract with the surrogate.[67] It never refers to a single person. So it appears inferable from this decree that a single woman who has access to medically-assisted methods of procreation cannot use surrogacy if she cannot carry the pregnancy even if the conditions stated in Art. 8, no. 2 take place. Only couples are allowed to enter into surrogacy contracts as commissioning parents. But it is unclear whether this also includes same-sex couples, provided the latter are composed of two women. Neither in the Medically-Assisted Procreation Law nor in the abovementioned Regulatory Decree is the exclusion of same-sex couples clearly expressed, even if Art. 2, no. 2, c) of Regulatory Decree no. 6/2017 refers to 'the woman who is the member of the commissioning couple'; the wording could be understood to imply that only different-sex couples are being considered for surrogacy because in same-sex couples composed of women there obviously is more than one 'woman who is the member of the commissioning couple'. However, the wording does not preclude the other person in the couple also being a woman.

[67] On this see Art. 2 no. 1, Art. 2, no. 2, a), b), c), Art. 2, no. 9 and Art. 3, no. 3, f) and k).

The National Council for Medically-Assisted Procreation, in its plenary meeting that took place on 10 October 2017 came to a similar conclusion, namely that only couples – either different-sex couples or same-sex couples composed of women[68] – may have recourse to surrogacy.[69] Time will tell how the norms are interpreted by courts.

Irrespective of the interpretation adopted, no minimum duration of the marriage or of the cohabitation is required to allow access to medically-assisted procreation. As far as the commissioning parents are concerned, the only additional condition formulated at a legal level is the occurrence of one of the situations described in Art. 8, no. 2: the absence of a uterus, the injury or disease of the uterus that absolutely and definitively prevents the woman's pregnancy or the existence of a clinical situation that justifies surrogacy.

The existence of a familial relationship between the commissioning parents and the surrogate does not eliminate the possibility of concluding a contract between the parties. They may be genetically linked, when, for instance, the surrogate is the mother or the sister of one of the commissioning parents. Only economic subordination would be an obstacle to surrogacy.

Even if the aforementioned law and Regulatory Decree are silent about age criteria,[70] in a plenary meeting that took place on 24 November 2017, the National Council for Medically-Assisted Procreation[71] has established age limits: a commissioning parent cannot be older than 60 if he is male and 50 years old if she is female. These limits are intended to serve the best interest of the child, preventing the existence of parents who are too old to properly play the parental role. No explanation was given for the difference in age limit.

4.2.2. *Use of Gametes of at Least One of the Commissioning Parents*

As was previously mentioned, gametes of at least one of the commissioning parents must be used in the surrogacy. A genetic relationship between the commissioning parents and the child is always required. Therefore, surrogacy may only be partially heterologous.

---

68 Couples composed of men are excluded. This solution may be challenged in the light of the principle of equality enshrined in Art. 13 of the Constitution of Portuguese Republic. As a consequence no person may be privileged, favoured, prejudiced, deprived of any right or exempted from any duty for reasons of gender. See R. Teixeira Pedro, above n. 18, p. 275.

69 See Decision 20-II, 20.10.2017 ('*Deliberação 20-II, de 20 de outubro de 2017*').

70 The absence of age limits is subject to criticism, especially as there are such age limits for adoption (Art. 1979, 1–3 of the Portuguese Civil Code): the maximum age limit for adoption is 60. On this see R. Teixeira Pedro, above n. 18, pp. 279–81 and R. Teixeira Pedro, 'Uma revolução na conceção jurídica da parentalidade? – breves reflexões sobre o novo regime jurídico da Procriação Medicamente Assistida', in L. Neto and R. Teixeira Pedro (eds), *Debatendo a Procriação medicamente assistida*, Universidade do Porto, Porto 2018, p. 160.

71 See above Section 1.2.

Sperm and egg donation is permitted in the Portuguese legal system, but it must concern only one of the gametes.[72] No payment may be made by the commissioning parents for the donations (Art. 18 of Medically-Assisted Procreation Law). The rule of anonymity of the donor applied (Art. 15) until the Decision no. 225/2018 of the Portuguese Constitutional Court. Only if there was a judicial ruling recognising the existence of a significant reason, his/her identity would be disclosed (Art. 15, no. 4 of the Medically-Assisted Procreation Law).[73] The Constitutional Court in its recent decision radically changed the rule and no special reason nor a judicial decision seems to be needed anymore to have access to the identity of the donor. The solution that should apply, in the absence of an intervention of the legislator (which is urgently demanded by the practitioners and the scholars) is unclear.

5. TRANSFERRING PARENTHOOD

Regarding the transfer of parenthood to commissioning parents, a distinction has to be drawn, considering the solution introduced in 2016 in Art. 8, no. 7 of the Medically-Assisted Procreation Law, on one hand, and the content of the Decision no. 225/2018 of the Constitutional Court that declared that rule unconstitutional, on the other hand.

According to Art. 8, no. 7 of the Medically-Assisted Procreation Law the commissioning parents automatically were the legal parents of the child born through surrogacy from birth. Their parenthood is recorded in the civil register and the birth certificate. Therefore, no specific mechanism for transferring parenthood to the commissioning parents was stipulated by law. Their parenthood would be automatically established by means of the legal recognition of the intent that underlies access to medically-assisted procreation (Art. 20 of the Medically-Assisted Procreation Law), which is displayed through the consent that must be expressed in the terms of Art. 14 of the Medically-Assisted Procreation Law. Their parenthood would be recorded in the civil register (Arts 2 and 3 of the Portuguese Civil Registry Code) and consequently could be immediately invoked against third parties.

According to the legal framework introduced, except at the time when a surrogacy contract is concluded and therefore the National Council for Medically-Assisted Procreation is involved, no other public authority would ever be involved in the process, meaning that no public authority would be

---

72 As was mentioned above, the surrogate cannot be the donor of the oocyte used to conceive the child she will carry (Art. 8, no. 3).

73 See above Section 3.3.

aware whether the child was delivered to the commissioning parents.[74] Thus the child's rights/interests were not relevant at this stage, as there was no transfer of parenthood. As said before, the commissioning parents automatically are the legal parents of the child from birth.

The Decision no. 225/2018 of the Constitutional Court changed this state of law.[75] According to the court, even if the surrogate is therefore legally bound to hand over the baby to the commissioning parents, she must have the possibility to reconsider and revoke her consent, in order to guarantee the respect for her fundamental rights (namely the right of development of personality) and her human dignity. As a consequence, the surrogate may revoke her consent until the moment she delivers the baby to the commissioning parents. According to the content of the Decision no. 225/2018 of the Constitutional Court, if she does not revoke it and if she delivers the baby to the commissioning parents, the latter will be the legal parents of the child and their legal parenthood will be established. Conversely, if the surrogate revokes her consent, the rules included in the Portuguese Civil Code that govern the establishment of parenthood (Arts 1796 ff.) will apply. The surrogate, as she is the woman who gives birth to the child, will be the legal mother; if she is married, her husband will be the legal father. In this case, commissioning parents, could bring the case to a court that will decide in a case-to-case approach, who should be legally considered her/his parents taking into account the best interests of the child. The mechanism and the process to materialise the transfer of parenthood needs to be defined and shaped by the law.

Due to the fact that surrogacy has only very recently become legal in Portugal, there is no information yet about the number of disputes that have arisen following surrogacy, and the outcomes of such disputes.

As mentioned in Section 3, the information concerning the surrogate – as the person who gave birth – is preserved by the relevant authorities, even if she is not legally the mother of the child and the rule of confidentiality applies. Potential access to this information is governed by Art. 15, considering the content of the Decision of the Portuguese Constitutional Court 225/2018.

6. AGENCIES AND CRIMINALISATION

Portuguese Medically-Assisted Procreation Law does not recognise any particular role for mediators or agencies in the Portuguese legal system. There are no special rules or regulations concerning their involvement in the

---

74 In the case of adoption, a succession of administrative and judicial entities intervene in the process and adoption is created through a judicial decision (Art. 1973 of the Portuguese Civil Code).

75 See above Section 1.3. and 3.1.

surrogacy process, besides the criminal sanctions for misconduct that will discussed in the following.

In order to strengthen compliance with the conditions that have to be met for the authorisation of a surrogacy process, criminal and administrative penalties may apply according to Arts 39 and 45 of the Medically-Assisted Procreation Law.

According to Art. 39, any breach of a legal provision concerning surrogacy may lead to the application of criminal penalties, which differ depending on the person who breaches the law[76] and the type of behaviour perpetrated by him/her.

If the surrogacy contract is of a commercial nature, criminal penalties may be applied to both the commissioning parents and the surrogate who have entered into it: the former may face either imprisonment up to two years or be liable to pay a criminal fine[77] of up to 240 days; the latter may only incur a criminal fine of up to 240 days (Arts 39 nos 1 and 2 of the Medically-Assisted Procreation Law). If the surrogacy contract is gratuitous but one of the other legal conditions demanded for its conclusion is not met, criminal penalties may also apply: the commissioning parents may face either a prison sentence of up to one year or may be liable to pay a criminal fine of up to 120 days and anyone who promotes the contracts may face a prison sentence of up to two years. These criminal penalties are more severe than those which are applicable to the surrogate: to her only a criminal fine of up to 120 days may be applied (Arts 39 nos 3 and 4 of Medically-Assisted Procreation Law).

Furthermore, any person who, by any direct or indirect means, including by direct invitation or through a personal or public announcement, promotes the conclusion of a surrogacy contract outside the limits legally established for it in Art. 8, from no. 2 to no. 6 of the Medically-Assisted Procreation Law, shall be punished with a prison sentence of up to two years. Additionally, any person who, in any circumstance, derives economic benefit from the conclusion of a surrogacy contract or from the promotion thereof, by any means, namely by direct invitation or through an intermediary or by public announcement, shall be punished with a prison sentence of up to five years (Art. 39, no. 5 and no. 6 of the Medically-Assisted Procreation Law).

---

76 Whether if the agent is a commissioning parent, the surrogate or another person who, directly or indirectly, promoted those agreements or has derived economic advantage from the conclusion of the surrogacy contract.

77 A criminal fine is defined considering a number of days that is ascertained by the court based on the fault of the agent and the prevention goals that should be pursued through the application of that penalty. For that purpose, the court shall take into account all circumstances which are in favour of the agent or against him/her, according to Art. 71 of the Portuguese Criminal Code. Each day of fine corresponds to an amount between €5 and €500, which the court sets according to the economic and financial situation of the person sentenced and his/her personal expenses (Art. 41 of the same code).

Article 43-A of the Medically-Assisted Procreation Law states that legal persons and similar entities are criminally responsible, in general terms applicable in the Portuguese legal system,[78] for the crimes set out in that law.

All these criminal penalties may apply even if the intended result is not achieved. Indeed, even an attempt to engage in that kind of conduct may be a criminal offence (Art. 39, no. 7 of the Medically-Assisted Procreation Law).

In addition to the criminal penalties, administrative fines (from €10,000 to €50,000 in the case of natural persons, and up to a maximum of €500,000 in the case of legal persons) of an administrative punitive (quasi-criminal) nature may also apply,[79] in four situations:

1. application of any medically-assisted procreation technique without the conditions laid down in Art. 4 being met;
2. the application outside the authorised centres of any medically-assisted procreation technique, including those carried out in the context of surrogacy situations provided for in Art. 8;
3. the application of any medically-assisted procreation technique without the requirements laid down in Art. 6[80] being met; and
4. the application of any medically-assisted procreation technique without the consent, in accordance with the requirements laid down in Art. 14, of any of the beneficiaries.

If the above actions take place without intent (i.e. by negligence), the maximum amount of the administrative fines will be reduced by half.

When a person is sentenced to a criminal penalty or to an administrative fine, additional accessory penalties may be applied to them according to Art. 45 of the Medically-Assisted Procreation Law, as follows:

1. judicial injunction;
2. temporary prohibition of the exercise of their professional activity;
3. deprivation of any financial support granted by public entities or services;
4. temporary closure or termination of the authorisation to operate of the medically-assisted procreation centre; or
5. the conviction being made public.

---

78 The general conditions on which the legal persons may be held criminally liable are set out in Art. 11 of the Portuguese Criminal Code.

79 The determination of the administrative fine shall be made by reference to the seriousness of the administrative offence, the fault of the agent, his/her economic situation and the economic benefit which he/she has derived from the practice of that offense (Art. 18, no. 1 of the Portuguese General Regime of Punitive Administrative Responsibility set out in the Executive Law no. 433/1982, dated 27.10.1982).

80 Article 6 defines the circle of beneficiaries of the medically-assisted procreation techniques.

These rules regarding criminal responsibility do not apply extra-territorially, according to the general principle applicable to Portuguese criminal law as stated in Art. 4 of the Portuguese Criminal Code: Portuguese criminal law shall apply to acts committed on Portuguese territory, regardless of the nationality of the agent, or on board Portuguese vessels or aircrafts.[81] The rules regarding the rules of the administrative punitive responsibility apply the principle of territoriality, with no exceptions, according to the general principle stated in Art. 4 of the General Regime of Punitive Administrative Responsibility set out in the Executive Law no. 433/1982, dated 27 October 1982.

7. INTERNATIONAL SURROGACY ARRANGEMENTS

7.1. APPLICATION OF THE GENERAL PRIVATE INTERNATIONAL LAW RULES AND DOMESTIC LAW

In Portugal there are no specific rules concerning surrogacy contracts that take place in other jurisdictions, nor are there specific rules regarding surrogacy that occurs in Portugal involving foreign persons. Therefore, general international private provisions and the Medically-Assisted Procreation Law apply respectively.[82]

The determination of the law applicable to the establishment of parenthood derives from the application of a general rule stated in Art. 56 of the Portuguese Civil Code. In accordance with this article, the personal law of the parent should apply. Personal law, as set out in Art. 31 of the Portuguese Civil Code is the law of the nationality of the individual. Regarding fatherhood, the national law that should be applied is the law of the biological father or, in cases of the use of heterologous medically-assisted procreation techniques, the law of the beneficiary who has expressed his consent to the use of those techniques according to Art. 14. Regarding the mother, in the specific context of surrogacy, the law is not clear. Portuguese doctrine has not given an undisputed answer to the question as to whether it should be the national law of the surrogate, the national law of the commissioning mother or commissioning mothers (if a couple composed of two women were the commissioners of the surrogacy) or a complex solution that combines those laws (for instance, the national law of the

[81] Exceptions to this rule are set out in Art. 5 of the Portuguese Criminal Code.

[82] For further developments regarding matters raised in Sections 7.1. and 7.2., see H. Mota, 'A gestação de substituição no Direito Internacional Privado português', in L. Neto and R. Teixeira Pedro (eds), *Debatendo a Procriação medicamente assistida*, Universidade do Porto, Porto 2018, pp. 63–82.

commissioning mother or commissioning mother(s), if the national law of the surrogate accepts that she renounces motherhood).[83]

7.2. RECOGNITION OF FOREIGN SURROGACY

As for the recognition of parenthood arising from a surrogacy arrangement in another jurisdiction, two issues need to be looked at separately.

On the one hand, the birth and corresponding parenthood recorded in a foreign registry and the resulting certificates should be registered at the Portuguese Civil Registry, in accordance with Art. 6 of the Portuguese Civil Registry Code,[84] if that registration was undertaken by the competent foreign authority under the terms of that law and if there is no violation of the international *ordre public* of the Portuguese State (Art. 22 of the Civil Code).

On the other hand, when there is a foreign judicial decision regarding the civil status (namely concerning its affiliation) of the child born through surrogacy, the registration of the child requires prior revision and confirmation (Art. 978 and ff. of the Portuguese Code of Civil Procedure and Art. 7, no. 1 and no. 2 of the Portuguese Civil Registry Code). The registration according to Art. 980, f) must not violate the international *ordre public* of the Portuguese State (Art. 22 of the Civil Code). Additionally, if the commissioning parents are Portuguese, it is also possible to challenge the confirmation of the foreign judicial decision if the decision of the case according to Portuguese substantive law would be more favourable to them and under the Portuguese rules of conflicts of laws Portuguese law would be considered competent (Art. 938, no. 2 of the Portuguese Code of Civil Procedure).

Considering Law no. 25/2016, dated 22 August 2016, and its acceptance of surrogacy, the invocation of international *ordre public*[85] of the Portuguese State has been reshaped. However, issues may arise if the foreign law is significantly more liberal than Portuguese law.[86]

---

83 See H. Mota, above n. 82.

84 This inscription is mandatory for every person who has been born in Portugal, even if he/she is a child of foreign citizens and for the Portuguese citizens, even if they were born abroad and is optional for foreign citizens when they have been born abroad (Art. 1, no. 1, a) and b)) of the Portuguese Civil Register Code). In the latter situation it is demanded the proof of a legitimate interest in that inscription (Art. 6, no. 4 of the Portuguese Civil Register Code).

85 On the application of this concept to surrogacy in the Portuguese doctrine, see H. Mota, above n. 82, D. Moura Vicente, 'Maternidade de substituição e reconhecimento internacional', in *Estudos em homenagem ao Prof. Doutor Jorge Miranda*, vol. V, Coimbra Editora, Coimbra 2012, p. 620, L. Lima Pinheiro, *Direito Internacional Privado, Vol. II. Direito de Confl itos. Parte Especial*, 4th ed., Almedina, Coimbra 2015, p. 673.

86 This may be the case when surrogacy is accepted, in the foreign legal system, without the strict conditions stated in Art. 8 of the Portuguese Medically-Assisted Procreation Law and

7.3. NATIONALITY AND ENTRY INTO PORTUGAL

Portuguese law does not state the need for any special authorisation for the return of a child born under an international surrogacy arrangement.

As far as acquisition of nationality is concerned, the general rules will apply. As a consequence, a child born through an international surrogacy arrangement, even if born abroad, automatically acquires Portuguese nationality according to Art. 1 of Law 37/81, dated 3 October (also known as 'Law of Nationality') either if the child is legally considered the child of a Portuguese mother or a Portuguese father; or if the birth of the person born through surrogacy is registered in the Portuguese Civil Register. Additionally, the person born through surrogacy, whose father or mother is Portuguese, may declare that he/she wishes to be Portuguese and will be considered Portuguese. The same result will be achieved if individuals born abroad have at least a Portuguese grandmother or a grandfather, apply for Portuguese citizenship, and have effective ties to the national community and their birth is registered at the Portuguese Civil Registry Office (Art. 1, no. 1, b), c) and d)).

Individuals born in Portuguese territory who are children of foreigners will be considered Portuguese if at least one of the parents was also born in and has residence in Portugal at the time of the birth, or if at that moment at least one parent has been a legal resident in Portugal for at least five years (Art. 1, no. 1, e) and f)).

8. CONCLUSION

Altruistic surrogacy was legally accepted in Portugal in 2016 for a certain number of exceptional situations and only if required for medical reasons. Considering the array of legal and ethical problems that surrogacy gives rise to, Portuguese law demanded strict and cumulative conditions to be met. Nevertheless, this recognition of surrogacy was a major step for the Portuguese legal system, as previously surrogacy was considered as being contrary to the principles of 'public order' and '*bonos mores*' and surrogacy contracts were without any legal effect, whether of a commercial nature or not. Despite the merits of the new law, some parts of the adopted legal framework were somewhat incomplete, and other parts were unclear and even contradictory. Furthermore, some months after the entry into force of the Law, the Portuguese Constitutional Court has issued a decision stating that for the most part of the legal solutions concerning

that characterise the 'Portuguese Model of surrogacy'. For example, when the surrogacy is of a commercial nature, or when it constitutes an alternative to natural procreation, or if it is available to a single person or to couples composed of two men.

surrogacy violated the constitutional provisions. Therefore the court has declared, with general binding force, their unconstitutionality. As a consequence, no surrogacy may be implemented in Portugal until a new set of rules is adopted by the lawmaker.

It must be stressed that the Constitutional Court has recognised 'positive constitutional relevance' to surrogacy and it has approved the so-called 'Portuguese model of surrogacy'. This model is characterised by some traits, such as the subsidiary, exceptional and purely gestational nature, the demand for autonomous consent of the involved parties to guarantee their free and sustained consent and the formalisation of the agreement by means of a written and non-commercial contract which is previously authorised by a competent authority.

An intervention by Parliament is being awaited in order to amend the law in the light of the Constitution as interpreted by the Constitutional Court. Among the aspects that need to be reshaped is the attribution of affiliation. A specific mechanism for transferring parenthood to the commissioning parents is necessary as the Constitutional Court declared that the surrogate may reconsider and revoke her consent until the moment she delivers the child to the commissioning parents. Another aspect to be clarified is the legal consequences applicable when the surrogacy contract is void, in order to adequately pursue the best interests of the child. Finally, even if the Constitutional Court has not addressed the issue, the recognition of surrogacy to couples composed of two women and the exclusion of that possibility to couples composed of two men may be a violation of the principle of equality set out in Art. 13 of the Constitution of the Portuguese Republic which states that no person may be privileged, favoured, prejudiced, deprived of any right or exempted from any duty for reasons of sex.

Therefore, work remains to be done by the legislature, academia and the courts.[87]

[87] Regarding not only surrogacy, but also concerning the use of medically-assisted procreation in general, as I have already written in R. Teixeira Pedro, above n. 18, p. 282.

SURROGACY IN ICELAND

Hrefna FRIÐRIKSDÓTTIR

1. GENERAL LEGAL FRAMEWORK

1.1. BAN ON SURROGACY IN ICELAND

Popular Icelandic folklore has numerous stories of women bearing children and giving them to others to raise, undoubtedly for different reasons and under various circumstances.[1] The emergence and development of the science

[1] Surrogacy has been named one of the oldest solutions to infertility, H.S. OLAFSDOTTIR, 'Counselling and ART' in H. ÁSGEIRSSON and S. NORDAL (eds), *Reproductive Technology and Surrogacy*, TemaNord 2015:561, p. 18.

of human biology, reproduction and genetics has steadily increased the focus on how and to what extent reproductive technologies should be used to help persons desiring to create a family.

The use of artificial technologies in Iceland has been growing steadily for the last decades. Though a general legal framework was lacking, procedures using artificial insemination started in 1980 and in vitro fertilisation in 1991.[2] The Act on Children from 1992 incorporated articles on paternity for children born through the use of artificial fertilisation. In 1996 Iceland passed the Act no. 55/1997 on Artificial Fertilisation and use of Human Gametes and Embryos for Stem-Cell Research. This Act sets out certain criteria for the use of different reproductive technologies, for example opened up the possibility of egg donation. The Act also marks the first formal discussion on whether or not to allow for the use of surrogacy in Iceland.

According to Art. 5 of the Act on Artificial Fertilisation, surrogacy is prohibited in Iceland. The Act defines surrogacy as 'artificial fertilisation performed on a woman who intends to carry a child for another woman, and has agreed before the pregnancy to give up the child immediately after the birth.' The preparatory comments on the issue of surrogacy were brief, first and foremost underlining that various ethical issues surround the question of allowing surrogacy. The preparatory comments specifically mention the issue of the maternity of the child, particularly after the use of egg donation, and emphasise the *mater semper certa est* (*mater est*) principle as the most widely acknowledged.[3] The minority of the Parliamentary Standing Committee dealing with the Bill in 1995 issued a separate opinion agreeing with the majority on the ban on surrogacy while emphasising that surrogacy raised very many ethical and legal questions and particularly stated the view that commercial surrogacy was the worst form of female repression possible.[4] Following the 1995 Act on Artificial Fertilisation, the revised Act on Children from 2003 also explicitly states that a woman who gives birth to a child conceived by artificial fertilisation shall be regarded as its mother.

1.2. LEGISLATIVE DEBATES ON SURROGACY IN RECENT YEARS

Interest in surrogacy increased significantly after the turn of the century and Iceland, as many other countries in the region, has been faced with

2 Þ. Óskarsson, 'Tæknifrjóvganir á Íslandi: Þróun starfseminnar' [Reproductive technologies in Iceland: Developments] (2001) 87(6) *Læknablaðið [The Icelandic Medical Journal]* 509–10.

3 Parliamentary Assembly 120, 1995–96, Case 154, Doc. 184.

4 Parliamentary Assembly 120, 1995–96, Case 154, Doc. 824.

two crucial questions: Should surrogacy services be made available domestically? How should cases of cross-border surrogacy be dealt with?

The 1995 Act on Artificial Fertilisation was amended in 2006 allowing women in same-sex relationships access and again in 2008 allowing single women access to reproductive technologies. The working group preparing the Bill for the 2008 amendments specifically discussed the issue of surrogacy. The preparatory comments mention various concerns relating to the status and interests of persons involved, firstly the commissioning parents, secondly the surrogate and thirdly the child. The main issue was considered to be the maternity of the child, and changes to the *mater est* principle were seen as inevitable when allowing surrogacy. Concerns were raised regarding possible attachments between the surrogate and the child with general references to unspecified examples of difficult and complicated cases having arisen elsewhere. Surrogacy was considered putting a lot of physical and often emotional pressure on the surrogate possibly endangering her existing familial relationships. Permitting surrogacy was also thought to require a careful consideration of the interests of the child, calling for specific counselling for parents to be able to give the child information to facilitate understanding and acceptance. The conclusion of the working group was that a comprehensive and thorough discussion in society at large was needed before legal amendments allowing for surrogacy could be introduced by Parliament. Such discussions were again encouraged in the preparatory comments.[5]

In September 2008 a request was raised in Parliament urging the Minister of Health to facilitate the discussion on surrogacy. The Minister of Health commissioned a multi-professional working group in January 2009 to deliberate on the ethical, legal and medical issues concerning surrogacy and whether the practice should be allowed in Iceland. In November 2009 a voluntary organisation, Staðganga, was formed, actively supporting legislation on the issue. The working group submitted an interim report in 2010, outlining multiple concerns and stressing the need for further informed discussions on the matter, particularly for whom surrogacy services should be made available, the criteria for allowing surrogacy, the legal status and rights of the child, and who should bear various costs involved.[6] In November 2010 a multi-partisan group of parliamentarians proposed a Parliamentary Resolution calling for the legalisation of surrogacy in Iceland. Around the same time the case of a child born by a surrogate in India for Icelandic parents received extended media coverage. The focus was on the lack of a legal framework and open questions as to citizenship and filiation.

---

5 Parliamentary Assembly 135, 2007–08, Case 620, Doc. 992.

6 *Áfangaskýrsla vinnuhóps heilbrigðisráðherra um staðgöngumæðrun 2010* [Interim report of the Ministry of Health Working Group on Surrogacy 2010] <https://www.stjornarradid.is/media/velferdarraduneyti-media/media/Skyrslur/Afangaskyrsla-vinnuhops-um-stadgongumaedrun.pdf> accessed 17.10.2018.

The case affected public opinion; in January 2011 a poll suggested that there was 85 per cent support for the legalisation of surrogacy in Iceland.[7] The multi-partisan proposal was resubmitted in Parliament in October 2011 after some discussions and important changes and in January 2012 the Parliament passed a Resolution requiring the Minister of Health to commission a working group with the direct mandate to prepare a bill allowing for altruistic surrogacy in Iceland.

According to the Parliamentary Resolution the working group in framing the bill should firstly prioritise the rights and interests of the child born through surrogacy, secondly protect the rights, autonomy and welfare of the surrogate and her family and thirdly to secure the successful involvement and outcome for the commissioning parents. The mandate was to introduce a solid legal framework, strict conditions and comprehensive guidelines on the practices and supervision of surrogacy services.[8]

1.3. BILL ON ALTRUISTIC SURROGACY IN ICELAND

A working group was commissioned in September 2012 and the group submitted a draft Bill with comprehensive preparatory comments to the Minister of Health in February 2015. A Bill allowing for altruistic surrogacy was introduced in Parliament in March 2015 and resubmitted in October 2015. The aim of the Bill was to realise the objectives of the 2012 Parliamentary Resolution. Surrogacy was introduced not as a right but as a method to help involuntarily childless persons to create a family. The preparatory comments specifically discuss the impact on gender and gender equality, emphasising that surrogacy provides means to fulfil the wish to have a child regardless of sex, gender or sexual orientation. An important aspect of the Bill was thus to counteract insidious links between gender and parental fitness and to advance equal opportunities for men and women.[9]

It was evident from the first reading of the Bill that Parliament was divided on the issue, the majority (middle to right-wing) government was mostly favourable but some members of the minority parties (middle to left-wing) voiced strong opposition. The Bill was referred to a Parliamentary Standing

7 *Markaðs- og miðlarannsóknir, fréttatilkynning January 28, 2011* [Market and media research, press announcement 2011] <http://mmr.is/images/stories/PDF/1101_tilkynning_stagngumur.pdf> accessed 11.09.2018.

8 Parliamentary Assembly 140, 2011–12, Case 4, Doc. 702.

9 Parliamentary Assembly 145, 2015–16, Case 229, Doc. 245; Proposal to legalise surrogacy in Iceland *Iceland Monitor* 14.10.2015 <https://icelandmonitor.mbl.is/news/politics_and_society/2015/10/14/proposal_to_legalise_surrogacy_in_iceland/> accessed 11.09.2018.

Committee for consultation and examination. In the course of its examination the committee requested written opinions from various interested parties. The opinions were overwhelmingly negative. Some rejected the idea of allowing surrogacy in Iceland altogether, such as The Icelandic Directorate of Health, The Centre for Gender Equality, The Icelandic Human Rights Centre, The Institute for Gender, Equality and Difference at the University of Iceland, The Icelandic Women's Rights Association, The Icelandic Nurse's Association, The Icelandic Medical Association and The Icelandic Social Workers Association. Others voiced various concerns and advocated caution, such as The Government Agency for Child Protection, Save the Children Iceland and The Centre for Ethics at the University of Iceland. Some were neither for nor against but offered opinions on certain provisions, such as The Icelandic Psychological Association and The National Queer Organization. The support organisation Staðganga and The Icelandic Infertility Association advocated for the acceptance of the Bill on surrogacy in Iceland and recommended easing some of the strict criteria that the Bill relied on.[10] Reasons for the considerable opposition were first and foremost concerns for the best interests of children, the danger of increasing cross-border surrogacy, covert commercial transactions and the vulnerability, exploitation and objectification of women.[11]

Before the Standing Committee finished its examination of the Bill in preparation of the third reading and final Parliamentary vote there was a governmental crisis in Iceland. The prime minister resigned and all focus turned to preparations for elections held in October 2016. The next government collapsed and elections were held yet again in October 2017.

The Bill on altruistic surrogacy has not been reintroduced in Parliament and its fate is uncertain. The following Sections 2 to 6 will nonetheless outline important elements of the Bill to offer insights into this possible pathway forward. To facilitate this, Figure 1 presents an overview of the proposed process for altruistic surrogacy in Iceland.

As seen in Figure 1, the Bill on altruistic surrogacy in Iceland frames surrogacy arrangements as a highly regulated activity. The surrogate (and her spouse) and the commissioning parents would apply jointly for a licence from a special Committee on surrogacy. The application process involves a thorough assessment of fitness and mandatory counselling on medical, legal, ethical and social implications of surrogacy. Applicants would then sign a mutual declaration of intent. If the Committee approves the application the fertility treatment could begin. The period of pregnancy would also involve further mandatory counselling. Transfer of care and custody would be possible at birth but transfer

10 Parliamentary Assembly 145, 2015–16, Case 229, Doc. 245. Written opinions <http://www.althingi.is/pdf/erindi_mals/?lthing=145&malnr=229> accessed 11.09.2018.

11 S. Kristinsson, 'Legalizing altruistic surrogacy in response to evasive travel? An Icelandic proposal' (2016) 3 *Reproductive BioMedicine and Society Online* 111.

of parenthood would not be possible until at least two months after birth. The best interests of the child would be the primary concern in all cases of conflict.

Figure 1. Overview of the process

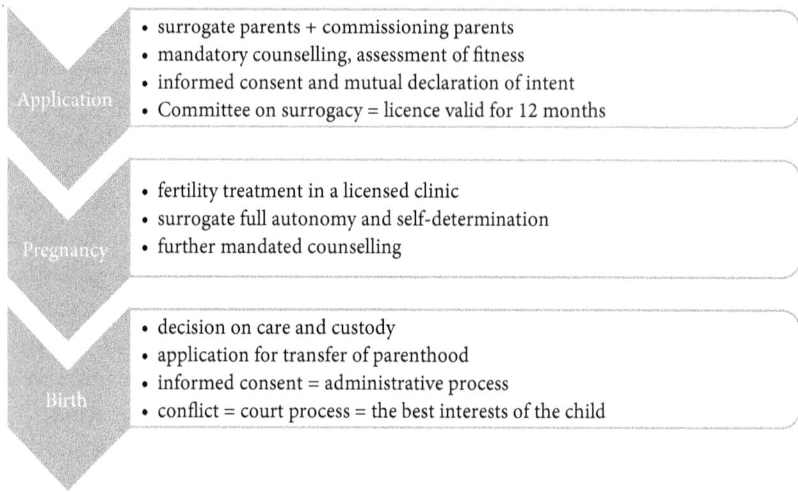

Source: Produced by the author.

1.4. THE NORDIC COUNTRIES

One of the key themes for those opposing the Bill on altruistic surrogacy in Iceland was the lack of a Nordic consensus and contrary legislation in the other Nordic countries. It is thus interesting to quickly examine Nordic legal characteristics and note recent developments in the Nordic region on the issue of surrogacy.

Iceland is one of the Nordic countries, alongside Denmark, Finland, Norway and Sweden. Based on their commonalities, the Nordic countries have a long history of legislative cooperation, prominently in core private law areas such as family law, where the specific aim has been to exchange information and to attain the greatest possible uniformity. The Nordic countries are all characterised as civil law countries where core principles and concrete practical rules are codified to serve as the primary source of law. Their systems of government have unique characteristics which are often embodied using the terms Nordic welfare state model or Nordic model. Historically, the Nordic model is moulded on principles of actively encouraging strong social cohesion based on core values of equality, social solidarity, security and opportunities for all.[12] The Nordic model pursues

[12] The Nordic Council, <www.norden.org> accessed 11.09.2018.

to balance social and individual justice and it has been argued that a distinctive model of political decision making has evolved in the Nordic countries with a particular emphasis on compromise and pragmatic solutions.[13]

Surrogacy through the use of reproductive technologies is prohibited by law in all the other Nordic countries: in Norway since 1987, Sweden since 1988, Denmark since 1997 and Finland since 2007.[14] There has been a growing debate on the issue among various political and professional actors in each country. While the common denominator has been a rejection of commercial surrogacy, opinions have differed on altruistic surrogacy but no active proposals for change have been introduced.[15] Iceland is thus the first of the Nordic countries to introduce a comprehensive proposal allowing for the use of surrogacy.

A government-appointed committee in Sweden was recently given the overall remit to consider different ways to increase the possibilities for involuntarily childless people to become parents, including whether to permit altruistic surrogacy in Sweden. A comprehensive report was published in 2016.[16] The Swedish committee did not consider that altruistic surrogacy should be permitted in the Swedish healthcare system. The committee did admit that the procedure would have some advantages, most importantly enabling involuntarily childless people to become parents. A procedure in Sweden would also offer better security and guarantees than provided in many of the countries presently offering surrogacy services. Permitting the procedure in Sweden would furthermore guarantee the prospective child the right to information about its origins and alleviate complicated legal problems relating to cross-border surrogacy arrangements. The committee then went on to point to numerous

---

13 T. Persson and M. Wiberg, 'The Nordic Model of Parliamentary Government and its Challenges' in T. Persson and M. Wiberg (eds), *Parliamentary Government in the Nordic Countries at a Crossroads: Coping with Challenges from Europeanisation and Presidentialisation*, Santérus Academic Press, Stockholm 2011, p. 17.

14 Parliamentary Assembly 145, 2015–16, Case 229, Doc. 245. Before the Finnish law on reproductive technologies banned surrogacy in 2007 private clinics could perform altruistic surrogacy services and it has been estimated that between 1991–2006 around 20 such arrangements were made, see *Olika vägar till föräldraskap [Different pathways to parenthood]*. SOU 2016:11 [Swedish Government Official Reports], p. 195.

15 *Surrogacy treatment in Finland*. ETENE [The National Advisory Board on Social Welfare and Health Care Ethics in Finland] 2011, <http://etene.fi/documents/1429646/1561478/2011+Statement+concerning+surrogacy+treatment+in+Finland.pdf/37082250-0120-4e7f-82d2-a8c114924955/2011+Statement+concerning+surrogacy+treatment+in+Finland.pdf.pdf> accessed 11.09.2018; *International handel med menneskelige æg, rugemoderskap og organer [International handling of human eggs, surrogacy and organs]*. Det Etiske Råd [The Danish Ethical Board] 2013; *Bør surrogati være tillatt i Norge? [Should surrogacy be allowed in Norway?]*. Bioteknologirådet [The Norwegian Biotechnology Advisory Board] 2015, <http://www.bioteknologiradet.no/filarkiv/2015/06/Uttalelse-om-surrogati.pdf> accessed 11.09.2018; *Olika vägar till föräldraskap [Different pathways to parenthood]*. SOU 2016:11 [Swedish Government Official Reports].

16 *Olika vägar till föräldraskap [Different pathways to parenthood]*. SOU 2016:11 [Swedish Government Official Reports].

disadvantages, the first relating to serious gaps in knowledge regarding the consequences for a child born through the use of surrogacy services. According to the committee, this lack of knowledge made it difficult to assess risk factors in the short and long term and therefore made it impossible to draw any definite conclusions as to whether the procedure was consistent with the principle of the best interests of the child. The committee concluded that in 'such circumstances, the precautionary principle indicated that surrogacy should not be permitted'.[17] Another disadvantage was thought to be the risk for pressure on a potential surrogate and the risk for covert commercialisation. The third disadvantage mentioned relates to the transfer of parenthood. The committee underlined the necessity of respect for the *mater est* principle and the surrogate mother's autonomy and self-determination. This subsequently created a need for special decisions on the transfer of parenthood that could result in serious problems and conflicts potentially having adverse effects on the child. Further disadvantages were mentioned, such as difficulties in framing acceptable regulations regarding costs involved. The overall conclusion was that 'disadvantages outweigh the advantages and that surrogacy should not be permitted in the Swedish health system.'[18]

The Swedish committee also had the role of examining and analysing surrogacy arrangements abroad with the intent to remove the current uncertainty about the legal positions of those involved while deterring circumvention of a ban or restrictions on domestic surrogacy. On the best interest principle the committee concluded:

> 'The principle of the best interests of the child cannot be held to demand that we, in Sweden, make extensive amendments to legislation in this area or that we take other far reaching measures to solve all the problems that may arise when individuals from Sweden receive children through a surrogacy arrangement abroad. But this principle must be held to demand that we in Sweden have good regulations for the children who are here and for the children abroad who are Swedish citizens. In addition, the principle must, of course, be taken into account in various contexts that concern a child, for instance when amending legislation. Our view is thus that there may be a need to introduce special rules to deal with the problems that have arisen in Sweden after a surrogacy arrangement abroad. There may also be a need to introduce such rules to counter the emergence of other problems.'[19]

The committee went on to place great emphasis on the conclusion not to recommend domestic surrogacy in any form and to deter the use of commercial surrogacy services abroad. Logically the committee rejected any proposals on

17 Ibid, p. 58.
18 Ibid, p. 59.
19 Ibid, pp. 63–64.

introducing transfer of paternity or parenthood after a surrogacy arrangement abroad or rules about blanket recognitions of such transfers. The conclusion was to follow the *mater est* principle as regards maternity, excluding the possibility of establishing the commissioning mother as the legal mother. Therefore, on the conditions that his sperm was used, only a commissioning father could be established as the legal father of the child. Parenthood for commissioning parents other than the genetic fathers would continue to presuppose a stepchild adoption or an ordinary adoption.[20]

1.5. STATISTICAL ESTIMATES

There are a few reported cases in Iceland where people seem to have tried or succeeded in manipulating the procedures regulated in the Act on Artificial Fertilisation with the intent to enforce private/informal surrogacy arrangements. One such case was reported in the media in 2015. The actual commissioning parents were a different-sex couple. They got divorced and the woman pretended to cohabit with the woman that had agreed to be their surrogate. In this case the artificial insemination was unsuccessful.[21] In another case a woman agreed to carry a child for her relative and his husband. According to her story she tried artificial insemination as a single mother without revealing her intent, but the procedure failed. She then got pregnant after a casual sexual encounter but decided to pretend that the artificial insemination had been successful. After giving birth she pointed to her relative as the father, he accepted paternity under Icelandic law and later his husband adopted the child as a stepparent. The story came out later when they argued over her role in the child's life.[22]

It is also unknown whether and to what extent private arrangements relying on informal insemination of a surrogate mother and later adoption may have occurred. It is estimated that cases like these are very rare as adoptions of newborn Icelandic babies are extremely rare. A Supreme Court case from 2012 involved a dispute over an inheritance in which a woman tried to invalidate her father's admission of the paternity of her sister. The woman claimed that their mother had gotten pregnant and given birth to her sister in 1955 with the intent to give the child to another couple to adopt. Her mother had allegedly changed her mind after birth and soon thereafter married a man who claimed paternity.

---

20 Ibid, p. 65.

21 Þóttust vera lesbískt par til að reyna staðgöngumæðrun [Pretended to be a lesbian couple to try surrogacy] *Vísir* 18.02.2015 <http://www.visir.is/g/2015150218907/thottust-vera-lesbiskt-par-til-ad-reyna-stadgongumaedrun> accessed 11.09.2018.

22 Hefur ekki séð dóttur sína í tvö ár [Hasn't seen her daughter in two years] *Morgunblaðið [The Morning paper]* <https://www.mbl.is/frettir/innlent/2015/09/24/hefur_ekki_sed_dottur_sina_i_tvo_ar/> accessed 11.09.2018.

The case was dismissed and DNA tests therefore not done as the woman did not have standing in such a dispute on paternity according to Icelandic laws.[23]

Discussions on the issue of surrogacy have been based on an estimated demand of some 10 cases per year, but since surrogacy has been illegal there may be a hidden, accumulated extra demand.[24]

The number of instances involving cross-border surrogacy is unknown. During the preparation of the draft Bill on altruistic surrogacy in Iceland only five known cases were discussed.[25]

2. SURROGACY ARRANGEMENTS IN GENERAL

2.1. SURROGACY CONTRACTS

Currently surrogacy contracts are not binding or enforceable in Iceland. It is worth mentioning that if an informal arrangement ends in adoption, then according to the Adoption Act from 1999 an adoption decree is final.

According to the Bill on altruistic surrogacy, applicants for surrogacy services would be expected to sign a mutual declaration of intent (Bill Art. 16). This declaration of intent would clarify various aspects of the arrangements, such as communication during pregnancy, reimbursement of costs, attendance at birth, care and custody until transfer of parenthood and communication after birth. The declaration of intent would not be enforceable by law, apart from the surrogate being able to claim reimbursement of costs agreed upon and already realised or paid by her.[26]

2.2. REMUNERATION

The Icelandic Bill only creates a legal framework for altruistic surrogacy and expressly rejects commercial surrogacy arrangements. The Bill bans the offering, paying, accepting or enjoying any benefits of any monetary or other compensations in relation to the surrogacy arrangement (Bill Art. 30). This would cover the commissioning parents, the surrogate and her family and anyone acting or enjoying benefits on their behalf or in relation to them.[27]

According to the Bill, reimbursements of costs are permissible. Costs are not defined in monetary terms but can stem from the fertility procedures

23 Supreme Court of Iceland 27.04.2012, case no. 211/2012.

24 *Proposal to legalise surrogacy in Iceland* <https://icelandmonitor.mbl.is/news/politics_and_society/2015/10/14/proposal_to_legalise_surrogacy_in_iceland/> accessed 11.09.2018.

25 Parliamentary Assembly 145, 2015–16, Case 229, Doc. 245.

26 Ibid.

27 Ibid.

and pregnancy and birth, such as travel costs, costs of medicine and medical assistance, clothing and general healthcare (Bill Art. 17). Costs are otherwise to be specified through government regulation.

3. LEGAL PARENTHOOD AT THE TIME OF BIRTH

According to the Bill on altruistic surrogacy the surrogate would always be the mother of the child at the time of birth. If she is married, or in an unmarried cohabitation according the National Registry Iceland, her spouse would be the father or co-parent of the child (Bill Art. 22).[28] This is in line with general rules on maternity and paternity according to the Act on Children from 2003.

The surrogate would enjoy full autonomy regarding all decisions relating to the pregnancy and birth as any other pregnant women in the Icelandic healthcare system (Bill Art. 4). She would also be eligible for maternity leave according to The Act on Maternity/Paternity and Parental Leave from 2000.[29]

The Bill defers to the Ministry of Justice in deciding whether birth certificates, issued after the transfer of parenthood in cases of surrogacy, would thereafter reflect the name of the birth (surrogate) parents.[30]

4. ELIGIBILITY FOR SURROGACY

4.1. ELIGIBILITY FOR SURROGATE PARENTS

The Bill on altruistic surrogacy has strict eligibility criteria for both the surrogate mother (and her spouse/partner, if applicable). In order for surrogacy to be permitted in a particular case, an investigation into the circumstances of the surrogate and her spouse would have to confirm, as the main criterion, that their mental and physical health, financial and social conditions are good and that circumstances are conducive to a good, nurturing environment for the child (Bill Art. 4).

Further criteria involve (Bill Art. 8):

- legal capacity for surrogate and her spouse;
- legal domicile and continuous lawful residency of surrogate in Iceland for the preceding five years;

---

28 Iceland adopted same-sex marriage in 2010.

29 Upon transfer of care after birth the commissioning parents would also be eligible for leave payments.

30 Parliamentary Assembly 145, 2015–16, Case 229, Doc. 245.

- consent of surrogate. If she is married or in an unmarried cohabitation relationship, her spouse/partner must also consent and they must have lived together for at least three years;
- neither the surrogate nor her spouse can be siblings or in direct lineage with the commissioning parent that supplies any gametes;
- surrogates must be 25–39 years old;
- surrogates must have at least one child following a normal pregnancy and birth, her youngest child must be at least two years old and her last pregnancy may not have terminated unexpectedly or with stillbirth;
- surrogates must have sufficient mental and physical health to be able to undertake fertility treatment, pregnancy and birth with only standard risks for herself and/or the child;
- surrogates and/or their spouse/partner may not have lost a child in two years prior to the application.

The abovementioned criteria are based on the fundamental concern for the child's best interests. The emphasis on parental fitness assessments thus takes into consideration the possibility that transfer of parenthood might not happen. There are various other justifications for the strict criteria. The residency requirement is both to deter possible surrogacy travel to Iceland and to try to ensure that all persons involved are informed of social conditions and attitudes in Iceland and are more likely to fully comprehend all elements of the surrogacy arrangement. The residency requirement is also a prerequisite for a realistic assessment of fitness. Criteria concerning age, family status and family relations are considered enhancing the likelihood of a well-balanced decision and to decrease the probability of undue pressure and conflict.[31]

4.2. ELIGIBILITY FOR COMMISSIONING PARENTS

The Bill on altruistic surrogacy also has strict eligibility criteria for commissioning parents. As is the case with the surrogate and her spouse/partner, an investigation into the circumstances of the commissioning parents would have to confirm as overall criteria that their mental and physical health, financial and social conditions are good and that circumstances are conducive to a good, nurturing environment for the child (Bill Art. 4).

The Bill does not limit surrogacy to married couples. In case of marriage or a legally recognised cohabitation relationship, the couple has to apply together, and they must have lived together for at least three years preceding the application. An individual can apply for surrogacy services only under special circumstances if the interests of the child are evidently secured.

[31] Ibid.

Further criteria for commissioning parents involve (Bill Art. 9):

- legal capacity;
- legal domicile and continuous lawful residency in Iceland for the preceding five years;
- consent and an obligation to apply for the transfer of parenthood after birth;
- commissioning parents must be 25–45 years old;
- commissioning parents may neither have a child, or have legal responsibility for a child, under the age of two;
- it must be impossible for commissioning parents, for medical or biological reasons, to have a child through their own pregnancy.

The abovementioned criteria again first and foremost are based on the fundamental concern for the child's best interests. Further justifications are otherwise similar as for the criteria for surrogate parents mentioned above in Section 4.1.[32]

4.3. USE OF GAMETES

The Bill on altruistic surrogacy introduces various restrictions when it comes to the origin of gametes. These restrictions involve both the surrogate parents and the commissioning parents (Bill Art. 10).

As for the surrogate parents, according to the Bill it would be prohibited to use the surrogate's own ova. It would also be prohibited to use gametes from the surrogate's spouse/partner or anyone in direct lineage to the surrogate or her spouse/partner.

As for the commissioning parents the bill makes it obligatory to use gametes from at least one of the commissioning parents. The use of donor gametes would only be permissible for individuals or, in case of couples, if serious medical or biological reasons prevent one of the commissioning parents from supplying gametes. If using donor gametes, according to the Bill it would be prohibited to use gametes from anyone in direct lineage to the commissioning parents. The same prohibition applies to siblings of the commissioning parent that supply the necessary gametes.

The justifications for the abovementioned criteria first and foremost are to avoid complex emotional conflicts and pressures and thus to strengthen the prospects for a successful outcome of the surrogacy arrangement, both short term and long term. On the one hand it can be argued that familial ties may make it more likely for someone to offer to carry a child or to offer to supply

32 Ibid.

gametes. On the other hand, certain familial and/or biological links are thought to have the potential to cause undue pressure and precipitate deeply complicated conflicts both before and during pregnancy, after birth, and for an unforeseeable future.[33]

5. TRANSFERRING PARENTHOOD

5.1. LEGAL PROCESS

The Bill on altruistic surrogacy in Iceland introduces a unique way of transferring parenthood after the birth of the child, only applicable to surrogacy. According to the Bill such transfer of parenthood would be incorporated in the Act on Children, either as an administrative procedure through the District Commissioner or as a judicial procedure through the regular court system. The primary aim of the proposed changes to the Act on Children is to provide a clear and concise process while managing possible complications, for example due to conflicts, death or divorce of the parties involved.[34]

As mentioned before, the surrogate (and her spouse/partner if applicable) are the legal parents of the child at birth. The proposed process requires that no later than two months after birth the commissioning parents apply to a District Commissioner for the transfer of parenthood. If either one of them has passed away the surviving commissioning parent can apply alongside a special guardian appointed to safeguard the interests of the child. Even if both commissioning parents have passed away the legal parents can apply for the transfer of formal parenthood alongside a specially appointed guardian for the child, thereby establishing the rights to inheritance and new familial ties which could have an impact on the choice of foster or adoptive parents for the child. If the commissioning parents disagree on the transfer of parenthood the case can be brought to the courts.

The legal parents, that is the surrogate (and her spouse/partner, if applicable) have to give their informed consent to the transfer of parenthood. This consent can be given no earlier than two months after birth. If the surrogate and/or her spouse/partner refuse to give consent the case can be brought to the courts.

This means that the Bill authorises an administrative process in cases of no conflict. But if there is conflict, the transfer of parenthood requires a judicial procedure. According to the Bill the primary consideration for the courts would be the best interests of the child. The Bill explicitly states that the courts would be able to grant the transfer of parenthood without the consent of the legal parents

33 Ibid.

34 Ibid.

(the surrogate and/or her spouse/partner) if the child is or has been in the care of the commissioning parents and the transfer would be highly in the child's favour. It is also worth noting that upon request of the surrogate the court even would be able to transfer parenthood to the commissioning parents against their will. They would thus become legal parents and be responsible for all further actions that might be necessary to safeguard the interests of the child, such as foster care or adoption. The court's decision could either be to deny transfer of parenthood leaving both the surrogate and her spouse/partner as legal parents, or to transfer parenthood to both of the commissioning couple. If either couple has separated or divorced, the courts would be authorised to concurrently decide on custody, residence, contact and maintenance.

When and if eventually issued, the transfer of parenthood would apply retrospectively from birth. According to the Bill the transfer of parenthood severs all ties between the child and the legal birth parents and the child instead acquires the status of the legal child of the commissioning parents (Bill Art. 40).

It is worth noting that according to the Bill a child born through surrogacy will have a right to be informed about its origins. Parents are thus obliged to inform the child of the surrogacy arrangement before the child reaches the age of six. At the age of 16 the child can request information about the arrangement, including information on possible gamete donors. In order for this to succeed, all information must be preserved by the relevant authorities.

5.2. RIGHTS OF CHILDREN

As mentioned above, the best interests of the child would be the primary consideration in all matters of the transfer of parenthood according to the Bill on altruistic surrogacy. The District Commissioner would be able to deny transfer of parenthood if transfer would be considered contrary to the best interests of the child. Such cases, as other cases of conflict, would be dealt with in the courts applying the best interest principle.

6. AGENCIES AND CRIMINALISATION

As mentioned in Section 1.1. above, surrogacy currently is prohibited in Iceland. A breach of the current law is punishable by a fine or prison up to three months.

According to the Bill on altruistic surrogacy all advertising in relation to surrogacy and all mediation services would be banned. The aim of the ban is to prevent all commercial aspects of the surrogacy arrangement. As mentioned in Section 2.2. above, the Bill also bans the offering, paying, accepting or enjoying any benefits from any monetary or other compensations in relation to the surrogacy arrangement, beyond permissible reimbursements (Bill Arts 30–32).

The Bill would not prevent the organisation of interest groups providing a platform for sharing general information and knowledge on issues relating to surrogacy.

According to the Bill any breach of the rules banning commercial surrogacy, advertising and/or mediation would be punishable by a fine or prison for up to three years. The penalties would not apply extra-territorially.

7. INTERNATIONAL SURROGACY ARRANGEMENTS

At the moment there are no special rules in Iceland concerning surrogacy arrangements that take place in other jurisdictions. As mentioned in Section 1.5. above, the number of cases involving cross-border surrogacy is unknown and these have been dealt with on a case-by-case basis according to applicable domestic legislation, such as on maternity, paternity and citizenship.[35] The domestic legislation in principle is based on the *mater est* and *pater est* principles. Only a commissioning biological father can thus be established as the legal father of the child. Parenthood for commissioning parents other than the genetic fathers would presumably continue to presuppose a stepchild adoption or an ordinary adoption. No such full adoption decree seems yet to have been issued in Iceland.

In 2017 there was a landmark case on cross-border surrogacy, the first of its kind materially adjudicated by the Supreme Court of Iceland.[36] The Supreme Court rejected the recognition of a foreign decision on parenthood after surrogacy arrangements. The facts of the case concerned a lesbian couple that hired a US surrogate mother to carry their child, using both donor egg and sperm. A boy was born in 2013 and a court in California confirmed the commissioning parents as the boy's legal parents. The couple brought the child to Iceland and requested registration of parenthood and subsequent Icelandic citizenship with the National Registry of Iceland. The National Registry rejected the request and the Ministry of the Interior confirmed the rejection. The case was reported to the Child Protective Services (CPS) in Iceland as is mandated in situations where a child is without formal legal guardians. The CPS as formal legal custodians went through the proper channels to secure the boy Icelandic citizenship and with regards to the best interests of the child a decision was made to place the boy in foster care with the commissioning parents. The couple filed suit demanding recognition of the US court decision on parenthood.[37] The Supreme Court

---

35 Parliamentary Assembly 145, 2015–16, Case 229, Doc. 245.

36 Supreme Court of Iceland 30.03.2017, case no. 367/2016.

37 It is worth mentioning that the couple also applied for adoption with Icelandic authorities but the adoption petition was dismissed when the couple got divorced. After the divorce the foster care decree was amended, placing the boy in foster care with one of them and giving the other contact rights.

emphasised the *ordre public* exception, highlighting that Icelandic courts will not recognise or enforce foreign decisions on personal status that contravene fundamental laws and norms of the country. The Supreme Court went on to state that the US decision on parenthood directly violated Icelandic laws on the *mater est* principle and the ban on surrogacy. The Supreme Court then analysed rights under Art. 71 of the Icelandic Constitution no. 33 from 1944, as amended in 1995, corresponding to Art. 8 of the European Convention on Human Rights on the right to respect for private and family life. Citing the European Court of Human Rights' (ECtHR) judgment in *Paradiso and Campanelli v Italy* from 2017 and the non-existence of a genetic link, the Supreme Court found no violation of the applicant's right to respect for family life.[38] The Supreme Court went on to interpret Art. 71 of the Constitution in conjunction with Art. 8 of the UN Convention on the Rights of the Child where states undertake to respect the right of the child to preserve his or her identity, including family relations, as recognised by law. According to the Supreme Court these articles protect family relations that originate legally in a manner conforming with Icelandic laws. Rejecting the recognition of the US judgment of parenthood was therefore not considered to have constituted unlawful interference with legal family relations. Interestingly the Supreme Court does not refer to the child's right to respect for private life and identity apart from family relations. The lower court, reaching the same material conclusion, argued that the rejection of transfer of parenthood constituted an interference with the rights of the child to private and family life, citing ECtHR *Mennesson v France* from 2014, but concluded that the restrictions were justified and necessary in the interests of public order.[39] The lower court emphasised the steps taken by Icelandic authorities in order to protect the interests of the child, such as obtaining citizenship and providing formal care through the foster care system, effectively secured the child's status and rights in society. The lower court also noted that adoption would normally be the legal avenue for the commissioning parents.

The Bill on altruistic surrogacy provides a new channel for dealing with cross-border surrogacy arrangement. Firstly, it would be prohibited to actively seek, make arrangements or mediate in Iceland for the use of commercial surrogacy arrangements in other countries (Bill Art. 33). Secondly, all cases concerning children brought to Iceland following surrogacy arrangements abroad would be referred to the Committee on surrogacy authorised to recognise foreign transfers of parenthood. The key issue would be to examine whether the foreign decision was against the fundamental principles stipulated in the Icelandic legislation, first and foremost to make the distinction between altruistic and commercial surrogacy.[40] The Bill specifically states that the Committee would deny the

---

38 *Paradiso and Campanelli v Italy* 24 January 2017 no. 25358/12.

39 *Mennesson v France* 26 June 2014 no. 65192/11.

40 Parliamentary Assembly 145, 2015–16, Case 229, Doc. 245.

recognition of foreign decisions on parenthood not in consistence with the best interests of the child involved or in violation of fundamental principles of law.

8. CONCLUSION

Iceland has been considered having progressive public policies when it comes to reproductive rights.[41] In the case of surrogacy it is safe to say that attitudes are polarised, both socially and to some extent politically. It is interesting to contrast the decision of Parliament to work towards legalising altruistic surrogacy, mainly fuelled by public and political opinions, with the overwhelming opposition from professional interest groups, both before and during the drafting of the Bill on altruistic surrogacy and after the Bill was introduced in Parliament.

The Bill on altruistic surrogacy in Iceland presents an interesting regulatory framework that aims to secure and navigate the complicated rights at stake. The aim of the proposed framework is to accept some form of surrogacy as a way to help involuntarily childless people while addressing legal, social and ethical concerns or disadvantages. It is important to note that the Bill frames surrogacy as a method to create a family more than as an infertility treatment.[42] The Bill first and foremost aims at securing the best interests of the child. This is reflected firstly in the strict regulatory process, strict criteria and assessment of fitness before fertility treatment, mandatory counselling and declaration of intent. Secondly, the best interests of the child would be a key premise in solving conflicts that may arise after birth. Thirdly, the child would have a right to be informed about its origin and right to information on the surrogacy arrangement.

The Icelandic Bill on altruistic surrogacy has the potential to serve as a model for furthering the discussions in the Nordic countries as a region. As the Nordic countries strive for conformity or a common understanding, the Swedish governmental report from 2016 rejecting surrogacy in all forms on the other hand has the potential to serve as a deterrence on further developments. Looking more closely at the reported disadvantages, only time will provide further research filling in the gaps in knowledge regarding the consequences for the child. In alleviating certain risks relating to vulnerability, undue pressures and covert remuneration, the Icelandic Bill relies heavily on the strict centralised regulation, criteria and mandated counselling spread over time. The Bill obviously strikes a delicate balance, the strict criteria on family ties as regards the surrogate and the origin of gametes may on the one hand reduce pressures

---

41 S. Kristinsson, 'Legalizing altruistic surrogacy in response to evasive travel? An Icelandic proposal' (2016) 3 *Reproductive BioMedicine and Society Online* 110.

42 Á Stefánsdóttir, 'Is "surrogacy" an infertility treatment?' *Clinical Ethics* 27 October 2017 <https://doi.org/10.1177/1477750917738113> accessed 11.09.2018.

and short/long-term familiar conflicts but may on the other hand potentially diminish altruistic motives and sentiments and thereby increase the risks for commercial overtures. Another sensitive issue is that while domestic surrogacy services may better secure respect for the rights of all involved and to some extent reduce cross-border surrogacy, legitimising surrogacy could also raise hopes that may turn out to be hard to realise domestically due to strict criteria and lack of surrogates – which subsequently may result in increasing interest in cross-border surrogacy. As regards conflicts with transfer of parenthood, such risks can never be completely circumvented. Here again the comprehensive regulation, including assessment of fitness before treatment, counselling and the formal declaration of intent are seen as playing a pivotal role alongside detailed procedures for the transfer *ex post* and the ultimate application of the best interest principle.

Ongoing medical advances and cross-border travel will continue to present complex questions of domestic and private international law that implicate children's fundamental human rights.[43] The Nordic focus on welfare, gender equality and children's rights increase the prospects of a re-examination of the issue of surrogacy. But currently it is uncertain when and how the issue of surrogacy will be revisited in Iceland and the other Nordic countries.

[43] The Report of the Special Rapporteur on the sale and sexual exploitation of children, including child prostitution, child pornography and other child sexual abuse material, 15 January 2018, A/HRC/37/60, focuses specifically on surrogacy and notes the need for clear and comprehensive laws addressing the complex issues involved.

THE FREE MARKET APPROACH

SURROGACY IN RUSSIA

Olga A. KHAZOVA

1. GENERAL LEGAL FRAMEWORK

1.1. SOME INTRODUCTORY COMMENTS

The first time Russian law introduced provisions on assisted reproduction was in 1990, when Russia was still part of the Soviet Union.[1] Although there were

[1] The USSR Law 'On Amendments to Some USSR Legislative Acts concerning Women, Family and Childhood' no. 1501-I of 22.05.1990, s. 6.2.

just two legal rules in that law, they were important and still exist in the current Russian legal regulation, albeit with a slightly modified wording. The first one stated that a husband who consented to assisted reproduction with donor insemination of his wife should be registered as the father of a child born to his wife. Under the second one, a person, who was registered as a child's father by that person's application or joint application with the child's mother, should not be able to contest that person's paternity at a later stage provided, if, at the moment of presenting a paternity application, that person knew that he actually was not the child's biological father.

These provisions established that assisted reproduction should be understood as an imitation of natural procreation and to a significant extent shaped a general approach of future Russian regulation in the area of assisted reproduction, including surrogate motherhood. This approach, in turn, derived from understanding of assisted reproduction as fertility treatment. It was first formally stated in the Fundamental Principles of Legislation on Protection of Citizens' Health 1993 that stipulated the 'right of every adult woman of childbearing (procreative) age to assisted reproduction and embryo implantation' (s. 35). It was further developed in the Law on Protection of Citizens' Health 2011 (s. 55), which is currently a standing law and which will be dealt in more detail later. Here, it is just important to note two points. Firstly, the 2011 Law says that a man and a woman, married as well as not married, have the right to have access to assisted reproduction technologies, provided they gave their mutual informed consent to medical interference. Secondly, the 2011 Law defines assisted reproduction technologies as methods of fertility treatment when some or all stages of conception and early development of an embryo are performed outside the mother's body (including with the use of donor's and (or) frozen gametes, tissues of reproductive organs, and embryos, as well as surrogate motherhood). Therefore, if a person or a couple cannot have a child, they should be able to ask for medical assistance, if such a service is available. In other words, in order to get access to medical treatment, there should be medical indications for it.[2]

Under a 'normal' scenario, ideally, when children are conceived naturally, social and biological parentage coincide, and, until recently, the only exception to this in Russian law was adoption where adoptive parents replaced natural parents both legally and socially. Biomedical advances in assisted reproduction have brought a new dimension to the regulation of parentage. In accordance with an understanding of assisted reproduction as an 'imitation of natural procreation', a non-biological parent who agreed to participate in an assisted

2 There is one exception to a general rule on medical indications for access to assisted reproduction technologies. In accordance with the Ministry of Health Regulations 2012 (as it was before), if a single woman does not have a sexual partner, this is considered as an indication for artificial insemination with a donor's sperm (para. 63), and should be interpreted not as a medical but a 'social' indication.

reproduction programme with a goal to have a child should to be considered as a social parent and, with the use of a legal fiction, also as a biological parent, and consequently registered as a legal parent. As will be described further, legal regulation of surrogacy does not quite fit into this approach and is predominantly targeted to protecting motherhood, i.e. the surrogate mother.

Surrogate motherhood was first mentioned in the Family Code 1995, and, technically, this legalised surrogate motherhood in Russia. The same year the first case of full (gestational) surrogacy took place when two children were born to a surrogate in Saint-Petersburg's IVF clinic.[3] Since then, surrogacy has been flourishing in the country. In 2015, there were 89 assisted reproduction centres where 1,539 cycles with participation of surrogates ended in embryo transfers (in 2014 – 1,318 cycles in 78 centres).[4] As a result, 712 pregnancies occurred (46.4 per cent) (in 2014 – 42.9 per cent), of which 508 resulted in timely births (80.9 per cent) (in 2014 – 73.1 per cent).[5]

Russia is considered as a 'surrogacy friendly' jurisdiction.[6] Indeed, legislation has been either very permissive, or lacking; surrogacy programmes are also cheaper in Russia than in many other 'surrogacy friendly' jurisdictions. All this, despite certain restrictions and confusing provisions that will be discussed further, attracts many foreigners to Russia. There are no official statistics available but it is known that IVF centres have clients from the Netherlands, Germany, Austria, Italy, Lithuania, Latvia, China, Uzbekistan, Pakistan, United Arab Emirates – just to show the variety of countries.[7]

1.2. LEGAL RULES DEALING WITH SURROGACY

At present, Russian legal regulation on assisted reproduction in general and surrogacy specifically, although being permissive on the whole, is fragmentary and not always consistent. There are many gaps, and those legal rules that exist

---

3 V.S. Korsak, E.V. Isaakova, O.A. Vorobjeva et al., 'The First Experience in Russia of Conducting of a Program of Surrogate Motherhood' (in Russian), (1996) 2 *Problems of Reproduction* 46.

4 The 2015 Report of the Register of the RAHR (2017) 5 *Problems of Reproduction* 10. The figures include the centres that participated in the Register of the Russian Association of Human Reproduction (RAHR). Under the 2013 Report of the Register of the RAHR, the number of the IVF centres-participants of the Register constituted 74.5 per cent and was the highest among European countries with voluntary participation in the national registers. See: '2013 Report of the Register of the Russian Association of Human Reproduction' (2015) 6 *Problems of Reproduction* 19.

5 2015 Report of the Register of the RAHR (2017) 5 *Problems of Reproduction* 10.

6 K. Trimmings and P. Beaumont, 'General Report on Surrogacy' in K. Trimmings and P. Beaumont (eds), *International Surrogacy Arrangements. Legal Regulation at the International Level*, Hart Publishing, Oxford 2013, p. 443.

7 Information received from a private talk with the head of one the Moscow IVF clinics.

often contradict each other. There is no specialised authority set up with the goal of overseeing surrogacy in Russia. Moreover, different ministries deal with different aspects of surrogacy, and this inevitably leads to adoption of overlapping or contradictory legal acts.

The Russian legal sources with rules related to surrogacy currently are as follows.

- Family Code 1995 (as amended), especially ss. 51–52 (hereinafter – 'FC');
- Federal Law on the Basics of Protection of Citizens' Health 2011, s. 55 (hereinafter – 'the 2011 Law');
- Federal Law on the Acts of Registration of Civil Status 1997 (as amended), s. 16 (hereinafter – 'Registration of Civil Status Law');
- The Ministry of Health Order of 13 August 2012 no. 107н 'On the Order of Use of Assisted Reproduction Technologies, Contraindications to Them, and Their Limitations' (thereinafter – 'the Ministry of Health Regulations 2012'); and
- Decree of the Plenum of the Supreme Court of the Russian Federation no. 16 of 16 May 2017 'On application of legislation by the courts when considering cases on establishing filiation of children' (hereinafter – 'the Supreme Court Decree').[8]

In accordance with the FC:

> 'A married couple, that has agreed to implantation of an embryo to another woman for the purpose of its gestation, can be registered as the child's parents only if this woman (surrogate mother) gives her consent to such a registration.' (s. 51 (para. 4, pt 2)).

This provision, firstly, introduced the notion of surrogate motherhood into Russian law. Secondly, by using the word 'implantation' the legislator meant to indicate (though, as will be indicated below, not quite convincingly) that it legalised gestational surrogacy only, which means a surrogate should be genetically unrelated to a child born as a result of surrogacy arrangements. Thirdly, this provision gave the surrogate the right to keep the baby she gestated and gave birth to.

1.2.1. Gestational Surrogacy Only

Thus, only full, or gestational, surrogacy is allowed in Russia. As has been mentioned earlier, the word 'implantation' (*implantatsija* – in Russian) in the text of the FC meant to restrict the use of surrogacy in Russia to gestational

8 <http://www.supcourt.ru/documents/own/15888/> accessed 11.09.2018.

surrogacy only.[9] This wording meant to assume that an embryo that was created as a result of in vitro fertilisation and, thus, was genetically unrelated to a surrogate is transferred into her body. This, however, disregarded another possible, though rare, scenario of extra-corporeal fertilisation where a surrogate is a genetic mother of a child she gestates. In such a case, this would rather be a 'partial' or traditional surrogacy because a surrogate, despite IVF procedure, remains a genetic mother, although 'traditional' surrogacy is, as a rule, just an artificial insemination with a donor's sperm (whether anonymous or not) without any in vitro fertilisation at all.[10] In either case, therefore, under a traditional surrogacy scenario, a birth mother is not a 'surrogate' but a true mother.[11] This lack of clarity in the FC wording, although it might have created confusion, should not have been interpreted as permitting traditional surrogacy in any case. Under Russian law, if a woman (genetic and birth mother) wants to get rid of her child, she may do so only by placing the child for adoption. The adoption procedure is very strict, not applicable in case of surrogacy,[12] and a violation of this procedure is a serious offense.

With the enactment of the new 2011 Law all ambiguities in that regard were eliminated. This Law introduced a clear prohibition of traditional surrogacy, when it stated that 'a surrogate mother shall not be an oocytes donor' (s. 55(10)).

1.2.2. The Right of a Surrogate to Keep a Child

The FC gave a surrogate the right to keep the child she had gestated. This follows from the FC (s. 51 (para. 4, pt 2)) that stipulates, as noted above, that spouses can be registered as the child's parents only if a surrogate gives her consent to such registration. This provision is based on the concept that a woman who gives birth to a child is considered at law as a mother of this child, and is a modern modification of the old Roman law principle '*mater semper certa est*'

---

9 The term 'implantation' is not quite correct and needs clarification; 'embryo transfer', and not 'embryo implantation', would be a more appropriate expression. However, the FC followed the terminology used in the previous 1993 Law (the Fundamental Principles of Legislation on Protection of Citizens' Health), where it was stated that every adult woman of reproductive age had the right to access 'to artificial fertilization and embryo implantation' (s. 35).

10 See for inst.: J.D. Arras and B. Steinbock, *Ethical Issues in Modern Medicine*, 5th ed., California 1999, pp. 407–44; M. Garrison, 'Law Making for Baby Making: An Interpretive Approach to the Determination of Legal Parentage' (2000) February *Harvard Law Review* 835.

11 The word 'traditional' in the context of surrogate motherhood refers us to the Old Testament when Sarah, Rachel, and Leah due to infertility had to seek the assistance of their handmaids (Genesis 16:1–4,15; 30:1–10). The term was rightly called a 'misnomer' as in such a case a woman serving as a 'surrogate' is a natural mother of a child, and in some sense she acts as a 'surrogate wife' for a sperm donor for whom she gestates the child. M. Field, *Surrogate Motherhood. The Legal and Human Issues*, Cambridge (Mass.) 1990, pp. 4–5.

12 Although such incidents were known to take place in practice. See: 'Theme Issue: Surrogate Mothers' (2010) 4(4113) *Ogonyek* 30, 33.

('the mother is always certain').[13] It aims at protection of motherhood and childhood even though there is no genetic link between the surrogate and a child she delivered.[14] If she gives birth to a child, she is the mother, therefore, she can keep a child. It is also considered to be one of the main safeguards against exploitation of women involved in surrogacy arrangements. Finally, this provision was inspired by the recommendations made by a group of European experts in biomedical science in 1989.[15]

The right of a surrogate to keep a child if she wants had been under constant attack until very recently, and there had been many unsuccessful attempts to withdraw this right from her by making corresponding amendments to the law. The very last one was made in the autumn of 2016 but did not receive enough support.[16] In 2017 the Plenum of the Supreme Court of the Russian Federation, in its Decree noted above, in fact changed the law in this regard (to be discussed in Section 1.2.4.). Before that, however, there was a Constitutional Court ruling, which cannot be omitted.

1.2.3. The Right of a Surrogate to Keep a Child vs. the Rights of Commissioning Parents: Constitutional Court Ruling

It is obvious that the right of a surrogate to keep a child clashes with the rights of commissioning parents. The question on whether the legal rule that gives a surrogate the right to keep a child she gestated for commissioning parents contradicts the Russian Constitution and should be, therefore, declared unconstitutional was raised before the Russian Constitutional Court in a case *Ch.P. and Ch.Yu.* in 2012.[17]

---

[13] This postulate has been challenged by the recent advances of reproductive science that allow a child to have two genetic mothers (three parents). See: I. Sample, 'First UK baby with DNA from three people could be born next year' 2016 *The Guardian* 15.12.2016 <https://www.theguardian.com/science/2016/dec/15/three-parent-embryos-regulator-gives-green-light-to-uk-clinics?CMP=Share_iOSApp_Other> accessed 11.09.2018; <https://www.vox.com/2018/7/24/17596354/mitochondrial-replacement-therapy-three-parent-baby-controversy> accessed 09.12.2018.

[14] However, there is a biological link between a surrogate and a child she gestates, and this link is probably much more complicated and significant than we used to think. See for instance: R. Martone, 'Scientists Discover Children's Cells Living in Mothers' Brain: The connection between mother and child is ever deeper than thought' 2012 *Scientific American* 4.12.2012 <https://www.scientificamerican.com/article/scientists-discover-childrens-cells-living-in-mothers-brain/> accessed 11.09.2018.

[15] Council of Europe. Report on human artificial procreation. Principles set out in the report of the Ad hoc Committee of Experts in the Biomedical Science (CAHBI, 1989). Principle 14. See: <www.coe.int/t/dg3/healthbioethic/texts_and_documents/default_en.asp> accessed 11.09.2018.

[16] See: 'Gave birth to a child – not a mother yet' (in Russian), *Rossiiskaya gazeta* 20.09.2016 <https://rg.ru/2016/09/20/v-rossii-predlozhili-propisat-pravila-surrogatnogo-materinstva.html> accessed 11.09.2018.

[17] RF Constitutional Court Ruling of 15.05.2012 No. 880-O.

According to the facts of this case, the commissioning genetic parents and a surrogate made a surrogacy contract in 2010. Under the terms of that contract, the surrogate, after the implantation of an embryo created by in vitro fertilisation, in case of her pregnancy, undertook to deliver a child she gestated and gave birth to to the commissioning parents. However, after the birth of the child, upon her application to a civil status registry, she was registered as the child's mother; her former husband was registered, with his consent, as the legal father of the child. The commissioning parents filed an application to the court to establish their parentage with regard to the child, to annul a birth registration entry in the birth registration books, and to order a civil status registry to register them as the legal parents of that child. The court refused to satisfy their claim because the surrogate did not give her consent to their registration as legal parents; their appeal was not allowed either. The commissioning parents applied to the Constitutional Court claiming that this rule contradicts the constitutional principle of equality and of state protection of motherhood, childhood and the family, as well as the rule on equal parental rights and duties on taking care of children and their upbringing, because the law permits their registration as legal parents exclusively with the surrogate's consent. The Russian Constitutional Court did not find that the legal rule under discussion contradicted the Russian Constitution and refused to consider the application. It stated that the model of legal regulation chosen by Russian legislation, although it 'was not the only possible, did not exceed the legislative authority of a federal legislator'.

One of the judges of the Constitutional Court[18] issued a dissenting opinion, in which he analysed in detail the issue before the court. Among other arguments against the Constitutional Court ruling, he stated that the legislator while establishing 'an exclusive prerogative of a surrogate' in making a decision on commissioning genetic parents' parental rights 'remained indifferent to the interests' of those whose gametes were used for the child's conception. That created, in his opinion, a legal soil for the violation of a balance of constitutional values and denial not only of the rights and legal interests of genetic parents but also of a child born as a result of assisted reproduction. The judge did not reject that gestation process inevitably creates a biological link between a child and a surrogate. At the same time – as the judge argued – it is important to take into account that initial basis of the life of a human being born as result of in vitro fertilisation was an embryo created with the commissioning parents' gametes. That is why 'an absolute parental priority of a surrogate is far from being indisputable and at least requires assessment of its compliance with the rules' of the Russian Constitution.

---

18 Judge S.D. Knyazev.

1.2.4. The Right of a Surrogate to Keep a Child vs. the Best Interests of the Child: Supreme Court Decree

Apart from the interests of commissioning parents, it seems obvious that the wording of the FC Art. 51(4) nowadays needs to be adjusted to the interests of the child born as a result of surrogate motherhood. In its current wording, this article recognises the absolute priority of a surrogate in deciding who will be registered as the child's legal parents and does not take into account either the interests of genetic parents or, what is fundamentally important, the interests of the child him- or herself. It should be recognised that the main consideration that the developers of the FC were guided by in 1994 when intensive work on revision of family legislation was under way, was to protect the interests of the surrogate rather than the child she gave birth to. Therefore, the law should obviously be changed in favour of a more balanced approach, according to which the court could, in case of a dispute, while recognising in principle the right of a surrogate to give her consent to registration of commissioning parents as the legal parents, recognise the commissioning parents as the legal parents, provided there is a genetic link between them (or one of them) and a child born by a surrogate mother and this would be in the best interests of that child. This would allow the court to thoroughly examine the situation and make a judgment where the main considerations would be protection of the child and his or her best interests.

Such an approach has apparently served as the basis for explanations given to the Russian courts by the Supreme Court Decree. In this Decree, it is noted that the fact that a surrogate refused to give her consent to 'potential parents'' registration as legal parents should not serve as an unconditional ground for refusal of these persons' claim on their recognition as the child's parents and transfer the child to them (para. 31). In order to ensure correct consideration of a case – as the Plenum of the Supreme Court highlighted – the courts should in particular check whether the parties concluded a contract on surrogate motherhood and what the terms of the contract are, whether the petitioners are genetic parents of a child, why the surrogate refused to give her consent to register the petitioners as the child's legal parents, and, 'taking into consideration all the circumstances of a case, as well as provisions of Article 3 of the Convention on the Rights of the Child, resolve a dispute in the interests of the child' (para. 31).

It is known that there were already cases where the courts, in accordance with the explanations of the Plenum of the Supreme Court, made decisions that recognised the intending parents who had genetic links with a surrogate-born child as the legal parents of that child and ordered, accordingly, the child to be transferred to them.[19] In 2018, there was a Ruling of the Russian Constitutional

---

19 See: <https://rg.ru/2017/08/21/sudy-nachali-zabirat-detej-u-surrogatnyh-materej.html> accessed 09.12.2018.

Court where the Court refused to accept the application, in which a surrogate mother unsuccessfully tried to contest the constitutionality of the Russian legal rules on surrogacy that allowed a broad interpretation of the provision on the right of a surrogate to consent to the intending parents being registered as the legal parents of a surrogate-born child. The Constitutional Court noted that, as it followed from its legal position expressed earlier in a case *Ch.P. and Ch.Yu.* in 2012 (discussed above, in Section 1.2.3.), the model of legal regulation chosen by the Russian legislator was not the only possibility from the point of proper protection of such values as family, motherhood and childhood guaranteed by the Russian Constitution. As explained in the Ruling, in this case a surrogate mother abused her rights not only acting in violation of the terms of the contract, but also to the detriment of the interests of both surrogate-born children, whose genetic parents are intending parents, and children born in her marriage before. In its reasoning, the Constitutional Court also referred to the Plenum of the Russian Supreme Court explanations on the application of these legal provisions by courts.[20]

2. SURROGACY ARRANGEMENTS IN GENERAL

Until recently, the notion of a surrogacy contract was absent in Russian law, although, as has been noted, surrogate motherhood was permitted by law in 1995, and such contracts were known to take place in practice. At the same time, the fact that surrogacy contracts remained unregulated brought uncertainty in the issue of their validity in general. On the one part, as surrogacy was permitted by law and there was no clear prohibition of surrogacy contracts, such contracts should have been recognised as legitimate. This conclusion followed from one of the basic principles of civil law on the freedom of contract fixed in the Russian Civil Code: 'everything which is not forbidden is allowed'.[21] On the other part, there was a risk that a court might invalidate a surrogacy contract on the basis of its contradiction to the fundamental principles of public order and morality.[22]

To a significant extent, this uncertainty was resolved by the 2011 Law, which clarified the legislator's position on surrogacy in general, defined a surrogacy contract, and filled some gaps in the legal regulation.

20 RF Constitutional Court Ruling of 27.09.2018 No. 2318-O <http://legalacts.ru/sud/opredelenie-konstitutsionnogo-suda-rf-ot-27092018-n-2318-o/> accessed 09.12.2018.

21 In accordance with the Russian Civil Code s. 421 titled 'Freedom of contract', 'persons … are free to conclude contracts' (1), and 'the parties may conclude a contract which is contemplated as well as one which not contemplated by law or other legal acts …' (2).

22 The Russian Civil Code s. 169. Such risk, of course, still exists, and it depends on how the terms of a surrogacy contract are formulated.

Thus, the 2011 Law gave a definite positive answer to the question on whether it is possible to make a surrogacy contract, thus legalising these contracts in Russian law. It defines surrogate motherhood as:

> 'gestation of and giving birth to a child (including premature birth) under a contract made between a surrogate mother (a woman who carries a foetus after transfer of a donor's embryo) and potential parents, whose germ cells were used for fertilization, or a single woman, for whom it is impossible to gestate and give birth to a child by medical reasons'.

Many questions, however, remained unanswered, and many issues that had arisen earlier due to shortcomings of previous regulation remained unsolved. One of them is whether a surrogate may receive payments for her services. There is nothing in the 2011 Law about any consideration or at least compensation under a surrogacy contract, not to mention any prohibition to receive such payments. There is no regulation on payments to surrogates anywhere else in Russian law either. Besides, since the surrogacy contract is legal under the law, it is reasonable to assume that at least some kind of consideration for the services rendered by a surrogate is supposed to be legal as well. Therefore, we may say that contracts on surrogate motherhood in Russia can be altruistic and non-altruistic (in other words, commercial or for-profit).

There is no clear understanding what kind of payments transform altruistic surrogacy to a commercial one, and what is actually meant by 'commercial surrogacy'. Russian economists interpret commercial surrogacy as 'a form of female employment', what is evidenced 'by increase in the number of proposals to become a surrogate mother'.[23] As to the surrogate themselves, they refer to their service as 'a normal job for which they receive a satisfying payment and are often ready to fulfil it repeatedly'.[24] What payment could be recognised as 'satisfying' can be obviously defined on a case-by-case basis, and there is no clear understanding of what is meant by 'reasonable expenses' either. In practice, medical expenses[25] of surrogates are known to be covered by commissioning parents or reimbursed by them if a surrogate paid for some medical tests or services. Usually, loss of earnings and/or monthly allowance are also compensated or paid, and, as a rule, these provisions are included in a contract. However, as to the payment per se for the services rendered, the parties may try to make it hidden and interpret it as a compensation for the need to restore health and for moral and physical sufferings caused by pregnancy and

---

23 N. Rusanova, 'Assisted Reproductive Technologies in Russia: History, Problems, Demographic Perspectives' (in Russian) (2013) 1(11) *The Journal of Social Policy Studies* 75, 83.

24 Ibid. 75.

25 Those that are not covered by mandatory medical insurance.

child delivery. In practice, it is known that the services of surrogate mothers in Russia were estimated approximately between US$15,000–20,000,[26] although sometimes might reach US$100,000.[27]

Until recently, it was hard to predict what would happen in case of a dispute if, for instance, the commissioning parents failed to pay money to a surrogate, and she tried to get her money through the court. In 2016, there was a case covered by mass media about a successful claim of a surrogate to receive money under a surrogacy contract from a commissioning parent who refused both to take a child and pay the money. A court that rendered a judgment recognised the validity of that contract and ordered a commissioning parent to pay a surrogate the amount indicated in the contract.[28]

The surrogacy contract is a civil law contract, and shall, therefore, meet all the transactions' mandatory requirements in accordance with the Civil Code (those related to the subject-matter, purpose, and the form of a contract, parties' legal capacity, consent, etc.). As there are no reported cases, it is possible to speculate only on the conditions of a surrogacy contract that a court may find inconsistent with the legal requirements. Whether a surrogacy contract may be invalidated or found unenforceable will depend on the terms of the particular contract and the facts of the particular case. However, it seems possible to state that in any case a surrogacy contract shall not contain provisions prohibiting a surrogate from terminating her pregnancy. Under Russian law, every woman has the right to decide issues of maternity on her own,[29] and a contract provision restricting this right will interfere with the individual's autonomy.[30] There could also be problems with the provisions requiring a surrogate to live in a particular place and not visiting her home city as it will interfere with her constitutional right to travel freely and freely choose the place of temporary or permanent residence[31] (although, in practice, such provision is often included in surrogacy contracts). Validity of a surrogacy contract may also not be recognised because of conditions that the court may find extremely unfavourable for a surrogate;

---

26 See 'Theme Issue: Surrogate Mothers' (2010) 4(4113) *Ogonyek* 32–33 (in Russian); 'Russian Surrogate Moms Attract Foreigners' (2012) 1726(37) *The Moscow Times* 25.09.2012 <https://themoscowtimes.com/articles/russian-surrogate-moms-attract-foreigners-18051> accessed 11.09.2018.

27 J.G. Schenker, *Ethical Dilemmas in Assisted Reproductive Technologies*, Berlin/Boston, Walter de Gruyter GmbH & Co. KG. 2011, p. 156.

28 A surrogate decided to keep that child in her family. See 'Chuzhaya rodnja' (Someone Else's Kin), no. 7132 (264), no. 7132 (264) *Rossiiaskaya gazeta*, 21.11.2016 г. <https://rg.ru/2016/11/21/surrogatnaia-mat-otsudila-u-zakazchika-25-milliona-rublej.html> accessed 11.09.2018.

29 The Law on Protection of Citizens Health 2011 (s. 56).

30 Russian Constitution 1993 states: 'Everyone shall have the right to freedom and personal inviolability' (Art. 22(1)).

31 Russian Constitution 1993 Art. 27(1).

depending on the circumstances, it may decide that a surrogate was forced to conclude the transaction, for instance, as a result of concurrence of grave circumstances under conditions which are extremely unfavourable for her, which another party took advantage of.[32] The parties to a surrogacy contract tend to include in it a provision that obliges the surrogate to deliver a child to the commissioning parents. Such provision may help the commissioning parents psychologically feel more secure and certain about the outcome of 'the deal'. However, such provision has no sense under the law and is legally unenforceable because, as has been explained in a previous part, a surrogate is entitled to keep the child if she wants. The inclusion in a surrogacy contract of provisions such as those described above, in combination with the lack of proper legal regulation, often turns a surrogacy contract just into 'an unimportant "piece of paper"'[33] with all the consequences thereof.

To repeat, many questions arising from the definition of a surrogacy contract given in the 2011 Law remain unanswered and many issues unsolved. Moreover, some provisions of this Law turned out to be formulated in a way that raised new serious questions and created the consequent uncertainty of their application in practice. In the context of a surrogacy contract, among these areas of concern is also a question on who may be the parties to such contract that will be discussed later, in the Section 4 'Eligibility for Surrogacy'.

3. LEGAL PARENTHOOD AT THE TIME OF BIRTH

Legal parenthood at the time of a child's birth, under Russian law, is based on the children's filiation, established in the order stipulated by law:[34] in other words, on the fact of registration of a man and a woman as a child's legal parents in a child's birth certificate and a birth registry book in a civil status registry. The law requires the child be registered within one month of his or her birth.[35] As a rule, provided there is no dispute over the child's origin, no court judgment is required to finalise parental rights with regard to a child born by a surrogate; although there are situations when it still might be necessary to get a court order to register the birth of a child.

If a surrogate mother gave her consent to the registration of the commissioning parents as the legal parents of a child she gestated for them, the birth registration procedure is the same as in case of registration of the birth of a child conceived in a natural way, with one exception. The law requires that,

32 The Civil Code s. 179.

33 A.T. Bonner, 'Legislation on Artificial Fertilisation and Practice of Its Application by the Courts' (in Russian) (2015) 9 *Zakon* 173.

34 The FC s. 47.

35 The Registration of Civil Status Law s. 16(6).

apart from other documents that should usually be presented to the civil status registration body (for instance, parents ID/passports and a medical statement on child's birth), the commissioning parents also present an 'official note' issued by a medical clinic that confirms that a surrogate has agreed to the commissioning parents being registered as the legal parents.[36] The child's birth certificate looks the same as a 'normal' birth certificate where both commissioning parents are indicated as legal parents, respectively, in the lines 'the mother' and 'the father'. However, information about a surrogate is kept in the birth registry books, and it is possible to trace the circumstances of the child's conception and birth.

If the commissioning parent is a single woman, and the surrogate consented to her registration as the child's legal mother, the child's birth registration procedure is the same as described above. The main difference is that there is a blank space left in the line 'the father'. The law also permits that information about the child's father is indicated 'under the mother's instructions', i.e. a false entry about the father's first name and patronymic name is made in the child's birth certificate. The surname of the child's father, in such a case, is the same as the mother's one.[37] This rule covers all cases when a single mother registers the birth of her child, irrespective of how the child was conceived. The fact that information about the child's father was made 'under mother's instructions' is reflected in the registry books of the birth registration body.

In those rare cases when a commissioning parent is a single man, he is registered as a legal father, and the line 'the mother' left blank.[38]

It should be noted, however, that due to the discrepancy between the federal laws dealing with surrogacy and registration of birth of children conceived with assisted reproduction technologies, the civil status registries often refuse to register birth of children whose commissioning parents are not married to each other or are single parents. This results from a contradiction between the 2011 Law and the FC.[39] As discussed above, under the 2011 Law, a man and a woman, married and not married, as well as single women, have the right to access to assisted reproduction technologies, including surrogacy.[40] The FC, on the contrary, requires the commissioning parents to be married to each other, thus excluding those that are not spouses or are single.[41] Many cases are known to take place in practice where civil status registration bodies refused to register commissioning parent(s) who did not meet that requirement as legal parent(s) of children born for them by surrogates.[42] Moreover, the civil status

36 The Registration of Civil Status Law s. 16(5).
37 FC s. 51(3); the Registration of Civil Status Law s. 17(3).
38 See also below Section 4. Eligibility for Surrogacy, Section 4.2.3.
39 The FC and the Registration of Civil Status Law have similar provisions in this regard.
40 Section 55(3)(9).
41 Section 51(4)).
42 See <http://surmama-donor.ru/surrogatnoe-materinstvo-dlya-odinoki-2/> accessed 09.12.2018. See also below Section 4. Eligibility for Surrogacy, Sections 4.2.1 and 4.2.2.

registries often literally interpret the FC provision that 'a married couple, that *has agreed to implantation of an embryo* to another woman for the purpose of its gestation ...' (emphasis added) and require commissioning parents not only be married at the time when they asked to register the birth of their child but to be already married at the time they gave their consent to 'implantation of an embryo to another woman',[43] i.e. before the child was conceived.

In all such cases commissioning parent(s) have had to apply to the court to get a judgment that would order the civil status registry to register the child's birth. Such applications are known, at least until recently, to have been granted, and birth of children registered under the court's order.[44] To decide otherwise would mean to leave the children gestated by surrogates for non-married or single commissioning parent(s) without parents and to place these children for adoption or under foster care or even worse – with the state institutions – while there are persons who are eager to take care of them. Sometimes, however, the court proceedings take a long time, and the legal status of a child in such a situation remains uncertain during this period with all the consequences thereof. In recent times, there have been several draft laws in the Russian Parliament that aimed to amend the FC and the Registration of Civil Status Law with provisions that would allow an unmarried commissioning couple and a single woman to be registered as legal parent(s) of a child born by a surrogate on the same basis as those stipulated for a married couple.[45] None of them, so far, has reached the upper chamber of Parliament.

If a surrogate exercises her right to keep the child, if she refuses to deliver a child and to give her consent to the commissioning parents' registration as the child's legal parents, she is registered as the child's mother in the birth registry book and child's birth certificate in accordance with the ordinary procedure. If she is married her husband is registered as the child's father. Except her ID/passport and a medical clinic 'statement' certifying that she delivered the child, a surrogate presents to the civil status registry no documents that reveal the story of the child's conception and birth. Therefore, a civil status registry has no information about the commissioning parents, even if they are genetic parents, and no information about them is reflected in the birth registry books.

---

43 This is at least a situation in Moscow.

44 See, for instance RF Supreme Court Ruling of 08.09.2008, case no. 78-Ф08-1314; Judgment of Kalininskyi district court of Saint-Petersburg of 05.08.2009, case no. 2-4104; Judgment of Smolninsky district court of Saint-Petersburg of 06.10.2010, case no. 2-3927/10. About single men being registered as legal fathers, see: Judgment of Smolninsky district court of Saint-Petersburg of 04.06.2012, case no. 2-2470/12; <www.jurconsult.ru/news/news40.php> accessed 11.09.2018 and <www.jurconsult.ru/news/news39.php> accessed 11.09.2018.

45 See, for inst., Draft Law no. 473140-7 – <http://sozd.parliament.gov.ru/bill/473140-7> accessed 11.09.2018. In case of unmarried commissioning couples, this will, however, require a special regulation on recognition of paternity, different from that established for married ones.

Accordingly, it will be very difficult, if possible at all, for a child to know the truth about his or her origins at a later stage if the child's mother (the surrogate) prefers to keep it secret.

The original documents related to the acts of legal status are kept by the registries of the acts of civil status for 100 years; thereafter, they will be transferred to the state archives.[46] A child (until 18 years of age) may not have access to the information related to his or her birth. Only a child's parent (legal representative) has the right to apply to a legal status registry with a request to issue a copy of a document certifying the child's birth or to provide other relevant information.[47]

The legal status of a child conceived through ART is absolutely the same as the status of a child conceived in a natural way (including, in particular, inheritance rights).

4. ELIGIBILITY FOR SURROGACY

4.1. ELIGIBILITY CRITERIA FOR SURROGATES

The main requirements that a woman that is going to serve as a surrogate should meet, are fixed now in the 2011 Law.[48] Thus, it is required that such a woman:

1. give her written informed consent to medical intervention;
2. be between 20 and 35 years old;
3. have at least one healthy child;
4. receive a medical statement that she is healthy (has a 'satisfactory state of health');
5. receive a written consent of her husband to her acting as a surrogate, if she is married; and
6. shall not be an oocyte donor.[49]

The requirement on consent of a surrogate's husband, although it might look as an intrusion into the surrogate's rights and restriction of her freedoms, is explained by the presumption of paternity, where a husband of a child's mother is considered by law as the child's father. Because a surrogate has the right to keep a child, her husband, if she is married, will be the father of that child.

46 The Registration of Civil Status Law s. 77.
47 Ibid. s. 9.
48 Previously they were stipulated at the governmental level, in the Ministry of Health Regulation 2003.
49 Section 55(10).

Therefore, it is necessary that a surrogate's husband be aware in advance about such a scenario and has an opportunity to either agree to it or not.[50]

There are no other legal requirements regarding a surrogate stipulated in the Russian law.

There has been no reliable research in Russia on the characteristics of women acting as surrogates. In the opinion of a manager of one of the Saint-Petersburg's firms working in this area, the surrogates 'are young, lower- or lower-middle-class women with no higher education. They generally do not have enough money to support their family and no education to find a good job'.[51] It is also noted that 'they are typically single, divorced or widowed women from small towns'.[52]

4.2. COMMISSIONING PARENT(S)

As has been noted in the beginning of this chapter, the 2011 Law defines assisted reproduction technologies as methods of fertility treatment, which include surrogate motherhood. The Russian Constitution 1993 stipulates that 'a man and a woman shall enjoy equal rights and freedoms and have equal opportunities for their realization' (Art. 29(3)), that 'everyone has the right to protection of health and health care' (Art. 41(1)), and that 'in the Russian Federation state support of the family, maternity, paternity and childhood is ensured' (Art. 7). From these statements, it logically follows that, first, surrogacy motherhood is interpreted as a method of fertility treatment, and to get access to it one should have a fertility problem and certain medical indications, and, secondly, that everyone who has a fertility problem, provided corresponding medical treatment is available (including with participation of a surrogate), shall have the right to have access to it. Other legislative provisions that will be discussed below suggest, however, another, more restrictive approach, and their application creates confusion in practice.

4.2.1. Commissioning Parents: Married or Not?

As discussed above, the 2011 Law says that a man and a woman, married as well as not married, have the right to access assisted reproduction technologies, provided they gave their mutual informed consent to medical interference.

50 Before the 2011 Law was enacted, the IVF clinics usually asked for such a written consent of a would-be surrogate's husband to her serving as a surrogate.

51 'Russian Surrogate Moms Attract Foreigners', (2012) 1726(37) *The Moscow Times* 25.09.2012 <https://themoscowtimes.com/articles/russian-surrogate-moms-attract-foreigners-18051> accessed 11.09.2018.

52 Ibid.

Although the wording of this provision is not quite clear, it is obvious that the legislator meant here, apart from a married couple, also a man and a woman that are not married to each other. The same Law names 'potential parents' as a party to a surrogacy contract, without specifying whether they are married to each other or not. At the same time, according to the FC, this can only be a married couple, and the wording of the Law leaves no doubt about that. Similar provision can be found in the Registration of Civil Status Law (s. 16). As has been noted earlier, the only solution for commissioning parents for the problems that arise due to the described discrepancy between the laws, until it is eliminated by the legislator, is to get a court order (see above Section 3).

4.2.2. A Commissioning Parent: A Single Woman

Under the law, a single woman can be admitted to a surrogacy programme, and she can also be a party to a surrogacy contract, although she may face the same problems when trying to register the birth of a child born by a surrogate, as commissioning parents that are not married to each other do (see above Section 3).

There was a case widely covered in the Russian press about a 58-year-old woman who, after she had lost her son, made arrangements with two surrogates, with the use of the son's genetic material and donor's oocytes. Each of the surrogates delivered two children.[53] As a result, she became a grandmother of four children (one girl and three boys). However, the courts at all levels refused to make a decision that would instruct the civil status registry to register her as a legal mother of these children. All in all, the court proceedings took about one year and three months. Eventually, all four children received birth certificates, but there were blank spaces in the lines 'the mother' and 'the father', which meant they were orphans. Fortunately, the grandmother became the legal custodian for her grandchildren. The grandmother's status as custodian, however, although it provides children with a certain level of security, is not comparable with legal parentage.

4.2.3. A Commissioning Parent: A Single Man

As for single men, it appears as if they are almost completely excluded from the surrogacy context, despite the constitutional provisions on gender equality, on everyone's right to protection of health and health care, and on state support

53 See for instance <http://www.aif.ru/society/people/32322> accessed 11.09.2018. For a detailed legal analysis of this case (in Russian), see: S.F. Afanasiev, 'The Legal Aspect of the Initiation and Court Review of Cases on Application of Assisted Reproductive Technologies' (2013) 1(16) *Law. Legislation. Persons. Research Journal*, Saratov. 7–12 <http://xn--80af5bzc.xn--p1ai/documents/pzl/files/pzl-01-2013.pdf> accessed 11.09.2018.

for the family, maternity, paternity and childhood. A single man is mentioned neither in the paragraph of the 2011 Law that stipulates the right of a man and a woman (meaning, a couple) and the right of a single woman to have access to assisted reproduction technologies, nor as a party to a surrogacy contract in the definition of surrogate motherhood in another paragraph of the same Law (see above Section 2). Whether it means that a single man is deprived of the right to have access to surrogacy arrangements is a question to which there is no clear answer yet.

Before the enactment of the 2011 Law that excluded single men from surrogate motherhood contracts,[54] they were generally in the same position as single women. That means that formally a single man could participate in surrogacy as a commissioning parent but might have (and often did have) problems when trying to register the birth of his child born for him by a surrogate. Nevertheless, these problems seemed to have been sorted out, at least when single men are the biological fathers of the children (with the use of donor's oocytes). Enactment of the 2011 Law made a single man's access to surrogacy arrangements more complicated as it did not, to repeat, name a single man as a party to a surrogacy contract. The IVF clinics prefer to avoid contracting with single men due to the restrictive rule of the 2011 Law, despite it still being unclear whether it means complete prohibition of participation of single men in surrogacy arrangements. Nevertheless, such cases are still known to take place in practice. The courts have no choice but to order a civil status registry to register the birth of a child and his biological father as the child's only legal parent.[55]

In this connection a question arises: why does Russian legislation – either the current Law of 2011, or the previous one of 1993 – not mention single men? Does it mean that men with fertility problems are intentionally excluded and may not get access to IVF treatment? Regarding the 1993 Law, the answer should be certainly negative. We could hardly assume that the drafters of the 1993 Law pursued a goal to restrict access of men to assisted reproduction; there was no reasonable explanation for this, and moreover, methods of medical treatment of male infertility had already been widely applied in medical practice at the time the Law 1993 was elaborated. Taking into account the time when the draft law was elaborated – early 1990s, when extramarital cohabitation was not as widespread as it is nowadays, and open same-sex cohabitation was a rare case – this explanation would be rather simple. Fertility treatment was conventionally associated with medical treatment of women even if male infertility was a problem. In practice, these were usually married couples, who would come to medical clinics, irrespective of which of the spouses had problems. This explanation, however, does not sound that convincing in the year of 2011 when

54 Section 55 of the Law on Citizens' Health was in force since 01.01.2012.

55 See for instance RF Supreme Court Ruling of 21.10.2014, case no. 5-КГ14-93; Judgment of Smolninsky district court of Saint-Petersburg of 28.07.2014, case no. 2-3767/14.

the Law on Protection of Citizens Health was adopted. Although, we can hardly assume that the 2011 Law meant to close access to medical treatment for single men who had fertility problems – that would mean its contradiction to several principles of Russian Constitution that were mentioned earlier – it is tempting to state that now it has acquired a completely different connotation, particularly in the light of restrictive definition of a surrogacy contract.

4.3. GAMETES AND EMBRYO DONATION

Gamete and embryo donation for fertility treatment with assisted reproduction technologies is permitted under Russian law. Whether it is permitted in surrogacy, and in which situations, is a question to which current law does not give a clear answer, and this will be discussed below in Section 4.3.1.

As to gamete donation per se, whether male or female, under current regulation, it may be anonymous or non-anonymous. To be a donor of gametes one should be between 18 and 35 years of age, be physically and mentally healthy, and go through a medical and genetic examination.[56] There is currently no regulation regarding payments to donors of gametes; and, in practice, they are usually compensated. Payments to oocyte donors have not been, as a rule, interpreted as a purchase of genetic material but as a compensation for the harm caused to health, and payments to sperm donors as a compensation for a discomfort connected with the service.[57] It is also possible to use donors' embryos, provided they were left from other patients' fertility treatment, and both patients agreed to embryo donation.[58] Other restrictions on the use of donors' material that were stipulated in the previous Ministry of Health Regulations 2003 were not included in the current regulation. In particular, neither the 2011 Law nor the Ministry of Health Regulations 2012 contain the former rule that birth of 20 children from the same donor in a region with 800,000 population is a basis to terminate the use of that donor in that region.[59] Another important provision of the previous Regulations that was not included in the current legal text required an oocyte donor to be between 20 and 35 years of age and have her own healthy child.[60] Current law, regrettably, does not contain such requirements.

---

56 The Ministry of Health Order 2012, paras 54 and 62.

57 See: O. Khazova, 'Genetics and Artificial procreation in Russia' in M.-Th. Meulders-Klein, R. Deech and P. Vlaardingerbroek (eds), *Biomedicine, the Family and Human Rights*, Kluwer Law International, The Hague 2002, p. 386. At present, the amount of payments varies significantly and may reach, in case of an oocyte donor, US$700–1,000, or more, if there are special requirements regarding a donor (for instance, level of education), and in case of a sperm donor – about US$50.

58 The Ministry of Health Order 2012, para. 71.

59 The RF Ministry of Health Regulation of 26.02.2003 no. 67 'On application of assisted reproductive technology (ART) in therapy of female and male infertility' para. 6.

60 Ibid. Para. 6.1.

In cases of anonymous donation of gametes or embryos, the patients may receive information about the results of the donor's medical and genetic tests, his/her nationality, ethnicity, education and profession, as well as phenotypic traits.[61] Accordingly, in the future, a child will not be able to have access to the information about the donor's identity.

The 2011 Law states that gametes, human reproductive tissues and human embryos cannot be used for industrial purposes.[62]

4.4. COMMISSIONING PARENT(S): GENETIC LINKS

The 2011 Law is confusing on another important issue, that is, whether it is possible to use donated genetic material for IVF treatment in a surrogacy arrangement, or whether the commissioning parent(s) must be necessarily genetically related to a child that a surrogate gestates. Before its enactment, there were no legal restrictions on the use of donated gametes in surrogacy arrangements, if there were medical indications to it. Legal regulation on this matter was limited to the rules on donation of gametes and requirements that donors should meet.

Turning to surrogacy, to recall, the 2011 Law defines surrogate motherhood as 'gestation of and giving birth to a child … under a contract made between a surrogate mother … and potential parents, *whose germ cells were used for fertilization*, or a single woman, for whom it is impossible to gestate and give birth to a child by medical reasons' (emphasis added). According to the literal interpretation of this provision, the donor's genetic material is available for a single woman only but not for couples, whether married or not. Therefore, in case of a single woman, both oocyte and sperm donation is permitted for the purpose of surrogacy, and it may happen that a child born by a surrogate for a single woman will have no genetic links with his or her legal parent at all. As to a couple-commissioning parents, the situation is the opposite: under this provision, they shall be genetic parents of a child that a surrogate will gestate for them; more than that, literal wording of this provision suggests that both the commissioning parents shall have genetic links with the child. It is hardly possible to find any reasonable explanation to such an inconsistency, and it is unclear what the idea behind such wording was, as there are still no comments or official explanations of this rule. The only thing that is clear is that this provision significantly restricts the application of surrogate motherhood as a type of fertility treatment, and there are doubts if it is actually observed in practice.

There was an 'interesting', and ethically and legally dubious, attempt to interpret the expressions 'their gametes' and gametes 'belonging to them'

61 Ibid. Para. 73, Individual map of a sperm donor, Individual map of an oocyte donor.
62 Section 55(6).

as meaning that the gametes that commissioning parents had acquired ('purchased') from the donors became 'their own' gametes (or 'their own' embryos), therefore enabling them to be considered as parents (almost equalising them with genetic parents). That kind of interpretation was, for example, given by a lawyer representing the applicants in a case of *Paradiso and Campanelli v Italy*,[63] where Italian commissioning parents entered into a gestational surrogacy agreement with a Russian firm, and two embryos 'belonging to them' were implanted in the womb of a surrogate, and where male and female donated gametes were used.[64] After the birth of a child, the surrogate gave her consent to the commissioning parents being registered as the child's legal parents in the birth registry. In her written declaration, she stated that:

> 'I, the undersigned … gave birth to a boy … The child's parents are an Italian married couple … who expressed in writing their wish to have *their embryos* implanted in my womb ….'[65] (emphasis added).

The Italian authorities, however, refused to recognise the child's birth certificate issued by the Russian birth registry, and enter the appropriate information in the Italian register of births, marriages and deaths, and removed the child from the commissioning parents because neither of them had a genetic link to the child, as the Italian law required.

The European Court of Human Rights did not go into the discussion of 'ethical consideration' of the actions of a lawyer who 'indicated that it was entirely possible to circumvent the requirement to have a genetic link with one of the future parents by purchasing the embryos, which thus became "one's own" embryos'. '[T]he consequences of those actions', however, – as the court stated – 'have been very serious for the applicants ….'[66]

5. TRANSFERRING PARENTHOOD

In principle, Russian law does not contain any rules on transference of parenthood in the context of surrogacy after the child's birth was registered. After the commissioning parents have been registered as the legal parents of a child born by the surrogate, she is considered to be a legal stranger to this child and does not have any legal right to claim to maintain contact with this child.

---

63 *Paradiso and Campanelli v Italy*, no. 25358/12, [2nd Section] 27 January 2015; [Grand Chamber] 27 January 2017. (referred to the Grand Chamber).
64 *Paradiso and Campanelli v Italy*, [2nd Section] 27 January 2015, paras 6 and 65.
65 *Paradiso and Campanelli v Italy*, [Grand Chamber] 27 January 2017, para. 14.
66 *Paradiso and Campanelli v Italy*, [2nd Section] 27 January 2015, para. 76.

Accordingly, under the opposite scenario, after a surrogate who decided to keep a child has been registered as the legal mother of that child, the commissioning parents have no rights in relation to this child.

At the same time, because it is hardly possible to predict all scenarios that the life may offer, the law contains specific rules on contesting parentage in case of surrogacy. Thus, the FC stipulates that:

> 'a married couple who has agreed to implantation of an embryo to another woman, as well as a surrogate mother ... when contesting paternity or maternity, cannot refer to these circumstances after registration of the child's parents in a birth registration book.'[67]

By 'these circumstances', FC means that a child was conceived through IVF with a surrogate's participation. In other words, those who participate in surrogacy arrangements (commissioning parent(s) and a surrogate) cannot contest parentage in court if it is based on the circumstances related to the use of assisted reproduction technologies. Thus, in such cases, non-genetic paternity or maternity, once recognised, cannot be revoked later on ART grounds.

In the previous Ministry of Health Regulations 2003, there was a provision that clearly stated that the donors 'provide their gametes ... to other persons to overcome infertility and do not undertake parental obligations towards a future child' (para. 6). That means that the use of donors' genetic material in the course of assisted reproduction had no legal consequences for the donors with regard to parentage. Interestingly, there was a case considered by the Russian Supreme Court in 2011 upon application by a woman (N.T.V.), in which she claimed on her behalf and on behalf of her daughter that para. 6 of the Ministry of Health Regulations mentioned above, which excluded any possibility of establishing paternity of a sperm donor, should be annulled. She claimed that this provision contradicted the Russian Constitution and Russian Family Code, and violated her and her daughter's rights as a child born as a result of ART to establish paternity with regard to a sperm donor. By this very fact – she also claimed – her daughter was placed in an unequal position in comparison with the children born as a result of natural conception.[68] The Supreme Court refused to satisfy the claim of N.T.V. and in particular stated that a woman by applying to a medical institution with the goal of artificial fertilisation entered into legal relations with this institution, which warned her in advance that a donor would not undertake parental obligations toward a future child. The court also noted that a donor, too, entered into legal relations with a medical institution, which after it received donor's genetic material became its owner and was responsible for its use for

67 FC s. 52(3(2)).

68 Russian Supreme Court judgment of 13.01.2011, case no. ГКПИ10-1601.

medical purposes. Therefore, as the Supreme Court concluded, a woman that gave birth to a child as a result of artificial fertilisation and a donor did not enter into any legal relations with each other. For this reason, the FC provision on establishment of paternity (s. 49) was not applicable in that case, and that donor could not be recognised as a father of a child conceived with ART.

However, the new Ministry of Health Regulation 2012 that is currently in force does not contain any provisions on the possible legal parentage of the donors of genetic material. It is silent on the issue of donor's relation to a future child conceived with the use of donor's gametes. Whether it is a mistake, and now there is a gap in the legal regulation on ART, or whether there are any particular reasons behind such 'omission', remains unclear. It nevertheless has obviously created problems in practice because the Supreme Court had to react to that situation recently. In the Supreme Court Decree already mentioned above, it is explained that according to the meaning of family law (clause 4 of Article 51 of the FC), the birth of a child conceived with the use of donor's genetic material does not entail the establishment of parental rights and obligations between the donor and the child, regardless of whether the intending parents of the child knew that donor or not (para. 32).[69]

6. AGENCIES AND CRIMINALISATION

There is no specific regulation regarding the advertisement of surrogacy services and the work of agencies in this area. As to the former, numerous advertisements may be found on the internet. As to the latter, there are actually not that many law firms or agencies that openly advertise their work on surrogacy arrangements.

Russian criminal legislation does not contain any provisions that specifically address issues regarding surrogacy.

7. INTERNATIONAL SURROGACY ARRANGEMENTS

As international surrogacy is developing in Russia, additional problems connected with taking a child born by a surrogate mother abroad or settling disputes between the parties of international surrogacy arrangements will increasingly become topical.

As far as taking a child born in Russia abroad, getting entry visa for a child and further legalisation of the child in a home country of the child's parents may be a problem. Thus, in many jurisdictions, it is necessary to have a court

[69] This part of the text of the Decree has been slightly reworded in order to translate it into English without changing the meaning of the provision.

judgment in order to finalise parent-child relations. In Russia, however, these issues, as has been noted, are routinely administratively regulated – by registration of a child's birth in a state body for registration of civil status, and no court order is, as a rule, required. To give an example, this was particularly a problem with an Australian couple who expected a child to be born in Moscow by a Russian surrogate. To get an Australian entry visa for their child the couple was supposed to present a court order which would stipulate their parental rights with regard to their newborn.[70]

In the opposite situation, when, for instance, Russian commissioning parents want to bring their child born abroad as a result of international surrogacy arrangements, a birth certificate issued in a country of the child's birth should be automatically recognised in Russia, provided it was issued by a competent body and was apostilled.[71] Depending on from which country a child in such a situation is going to be brought to Russia, he or she may require a Russian entry visa.

As to the private international law context, Russian law does not contain any specific rules that directly address international surrogacy arrangements or cross-border disputes related to surrogacy. The Family Code, in part dealing with family relations with 'foreign participation', refers to nationality/citizenship as a connecting factor with regard to legal parenthood. It is stated in the FC that establishment and contest of paternity (maternity) is determined under the law of the state whose citizenship a child has by birth (s. 162 (1)). Parental rights, however, in accordance with the FC, shall be determined under the law of the state where parents and children have a common place of residence. The law of the country of the child's nationality/citizenship is used as a connecting factor in such cases only if there is no common place of residence. With regard to child maintenance and other parent-child relations, the law also allows, upon the petitioner's request, application of the law of the country where a child permanently resides (s. 163).

There are no specific rules with regard to nationality of a child born as a result of a surrogacy arrangement. In such cases general rules on citizenship apply, and the main principle of Russian law concerning a child's citizenship is that a child shall not be left stateless. Thus, the Federal Law on Citizenship 2002[72] states that a child shall acquire Russian citizenship by birth if one of the child's parents has

---

70 See: O. Khazova. 'Russia' in K. Trimmings and P. Beaumont (eds), *International Surrogacy Arrangements. Legal Regulation at the International Level*, p. 320, n. 31, see above n. 6, p. 2.

71 Under the Registration of Civil Status Law, 'the documents that were issued by the competent authorities of foreign states to certify the civil status acts committed outside the territory of the Russian Federation in accordance with the laws of the relevant foreign states with regard to Russian citizens, foreign citizens and stateless persons are recognized as valid in the Russian Federation provided they were legalised, unless otherwise established by the international treaty of the Russian Federation.' (s. 13).

72 Section 12.

Russian citizenship and the other parent is a foreign citizen, provided that the child has been born in the territory of the Russian Federation or if otherwise the child becomes a stateless person. In case both of the child's parents or the child's only parent residing in the territory of the Russian Federation are foreign citizens or stateless persons, a child shall acquire Russian citizenship by birth on condition that the child has been born in the territory of the Russian Federation, while the state where the child's parents are citizens does not grant its citizenship thereto. As to a child whose parents both have, or the child's single parent has, Russian citizenship, a child shall acquire Russian citizenship by birth irrespective of the child's place of birth.

8. CONCLUSION

It is obvious that there are gaps and contradictions in the Russian law on surrogacy. Many of them have been analysed in this chapter. Among those that have not been discussed are the issues related to responsibility of commissioning parent(s) for the fate of a child that has been conceived by their 'request', gestated and born by a surrogate. What happens if the commissioning parents change their mind and refuse to take a child? Who will take care of this child? There are no answers to that question in Russian law. As a *de lege ferenda* proposal, it seems to be reasonable to make the commissioning parent(s) responsible for maintenance of 'their' child, at least, until the child is adopted and such responsibility shifts to adoptive parents. There are also other questions that should have been necessarily addressed but so far no answers have been given to them either. To name just a few: Shall there be any age limits for commissioning parents?; How far does the child's right to know his or her origins extend?; Should post mortem conception be permitted, and if 'yes', on what terms? Apart from domestic issues, there is a whole set of questions related to private international law, and among them those of most importance are the legal status of a child born as a result of international surrogacy arrangements and recognition of the child's birth certificate across borders.

The most disturbing in the context of surrogacy, however, is the fact that a child has not been placed at the forefront of surrogacy regulation, not only in Russia but also in many other countries, at least until very recently. The explanation for this, as far as is Russia concerned, seems to be connected with the fact that assisted reproductive technologies, including surrogacy, emerged and have been developing as a fertility treatment, which could be offered, due to advances in reproductive medicine, to people who were not able to conceive in a natural way. These were and still are relations exclusively between the patients and a medical clinic, with a surrogate or intermediary involved, as the case may be. There are still almost no child-related considerations at the initial stage when a decision on the treatment is made. There has been little attention, if any, drawn to the question of whether there should be any criteria, apart from medical indications, that the commissioning parent(s) should meet in order to be admitted to a surrogacy programme. Should there be any 'filters' in access to surrogacy? Should commissioning parent(s) go through a kind of a 'testing' of their 'fitness' as would-be parent(s), before a decision on their participation in a surrogacy programme has been approved? At first impression, it may sound odd, especially taking into account that surrogacy, being a method of assisted reproduction, is a fertility treatment; accordingly, commissioning parent(s) are supposed to have fertility problems and, therefore, medical indications to such a treatment. At the same time, particularly taking into account the recent cases reported in the mass media about commissioning parent(s) being involved in child sexual abuse,[73] such considerations become increasingly topical. There are countries where a system of 'pre-approval' of a surrogacy programme by a court or a special committee is stipulated by law.[74] Depending on how the pre-approval system operates and how the terms of such pre-approval are formulated, it may help to evaluate to what extent a child that will be born as a result of a surrogacy arrangement will be protected against any harm that may be caused to him.

---

73 See, for instance <http://www.thejc.com/news/israel-news/108352/israeli-horror-sex-abuser-adopts-girl-4> accessed 11.09.2018; <http://www.smh.com.au/world/australian-surrogate-father-allegedly-abused-twins-from-thailand-20140901-10b7m3.html> accessed 11.09.2018; <http://www.smh.com.au/national/man-pleads-guilty-to-sexually-abusing-his-twin-surrogate-babies-20160421-goc83m.html> accessed 11.09.2018.

74 See K. Trimmings and P. Beaumont 'General Report on Surrogacy', pp. 458–59, see above, n. 6, p. 2.

SURROGACY IN THE UNITED STATES OF AMERICA

Naomi Cahn and June Carbone

1. AN OVERVIEW OF SURROGACY ACROSS THE UNITED STATES

1.1. INTRODUCTION

In the United States, the law of surrogacy reflects a combination of state law, with the majority of states having adopted no direct legislation or definitive appellate precedents; and private law, with contracts of uncertain enforceability shaping the courts' and the parties' expectations about the outcomes in the event of a dispute. While this creates substantial uncertainty about surrogacy law, the states that enjoy the most robust surrogacy practices do have comprehensive legal standards, and jurisdiction shopping within the United States is relatively easy to do. In addition, established commercial agencies, which draft standardised contracts, develop practices that set industry norms. As a result, American surrogacy law is more robust than a review of statutes and reported decisions might suggest.

Surrogacy law in the United States has developed in the context of a federal system, which entrusts family law, the licensing of medical professionals, and private contract law to the individual states. At the federal level, Congress has some power to address surrogacy on a national basis, but it has not chosen to exercise it.[1] The states are therefore free to adopt their own approaches to the legality of surrogacy and to the determination of the children's parents. In the majority of the states that lack explicit statutes on surrogacy, however, many courts have yet to address surrogacy at all or have done so only in decisions that do not constitute binding precedent. Complicating matters further, commissioning parents who live in a jurisdiction that prohibits surrogacy may contract with a surrogate in another state where such contracts are enforceable, and the determination of parentage may then depend on the child's residence at the time of the order (typically the state where the surrogate gives birth). The US Constitution then requires that other states accord 'full faith and

---

1 In addition, the Supreme Court has not addressed the validity of surrogacy agreements, though the court has supported equal rights for same-sex couples in accordance with state law that applies to different-sex parents in cases that involve artificial insemination. See *Pavan v Smith* 137 S. Ct. 2075 (2017). Some lower courts, however, have held state statutes to be unconstitutional where they refuse to recognise an intended parent who supplies a gamete as a legal parent in a surrogacy arrangement. *See J.R. v Utah* 261 F. Supp. 2d 1294, 1296–1298 (D. Utah 2002); *T.M.H. v D.M.T* 79 So. 3d 787 (Fla. App. 2011); *Soos v Super. Ct. ex rel. County of Maricopa* 897 P.2d 1356 (Ariz. Ct. App. 1994).

credit' to the parentage judgments.[2] The states are similarly free to regulate international surrogacy arrangements on whatever terms they choose; the fact that the commissioning parents come from outside the United States does not affect state power to determine parentage or the validity of contracts.

State differences reflect in part differences in the timing of regulation. Many of the first state statutes were a response to the *Baby M* case,[3] which attracted intense publicity in the late 1980s and raised concerns about baby selling, the potential exploitation of women and the role of commercial brokers. These statutes, with as many as 20 states enacting laws by 1992, tended to restrict the availability of surrogacy or to ban the commercial brokers who facilitated it. As surrogacy practices changed from traditional surrogacy, which used the surrogate's own eggs, to gestational surrogacy, which used in vitro fertilisation to implant embryos created through the use of eggs either from the intended mother or a donor, public acceptance of the practice increased, and later statutes tended to be more likely to authorise the practice. Still, many states that viewed surrogacy as ethically permissible sought to limit it to heterosexual couples or to intended mothers who were unable to give birth because of physical limitations. Other states, whose legislatures could not agree on the acceptability of the practice or the appropriate scope of the restrictions did nothing, allowing surrogacy arrangements to develop in these states without state oversight. As a result of these differences, states vary significantly in their approaches to the issue and in many, the absence of state legislation or definitive judicial decisions makes the resolutions of disputes that may arise uncertain. Nonetheless, reputable agencies use detailed contracts in an attempt to shape the parties' expectations, and many courts have deferred to those contracts in the absence of alternative sources of state law.

This chapter first provides an overview of the framework for surrogacy in the United States before focusing on California, which is one of the most surrogacy friendly jurisdictions in the country.

1.2. GENERAL LEGAL FRAMEWORK

1.2.1. The Legal Status of Surrogacy in the United States

In the United States generally, parties are free to pursue any practice if no law forbids it. In the significant number of states that have enacted no legislation

2 The United States Constitution requires every state to recognise valid judgments from other states, and the courts have held that this doctrine applies to parentage determinations, with the state in which the child is born ordinarily having jurisdiction to determine parentage. See, e.g., *Berwick v Wagner* 509 S.W.3d 411, 414 (Tex. App. 2014) (according full faith and credit to California judgment recognising the parentage of two Texas residents for child born to a surrogate in California).

3 *In re Baby M* 537 A.2d 1227 (N.J. 1988).

or that have no binding case law on surrogacy, doctors therefore are free to engage in the practice and the state's general parentage laws (which vary from state to state) apply. In addition, contract law, which is more uniform than family law across the 50 states, determines the validity of individual contractual provisions. Nonetheless, the very idea of surrogacy, that is, the validity of an agreement to exchange money for the willingness to carry a child to term, is sufficiently controversial that in the absence of a definitive judicial ruling, the enforceability of the contracts may be in doubt. Even in jurisdictions that explicitly authorise surrogacy, the determination of the enforceability of the individual contract provisions may vary from state to state. A third of the states have explicit statutes on surrogacy and an increasing number have addressed surrogacy through judicial decisions without explicit statutory direction. Still, a number have yet to address surrogacy at all in any official way, posing dilemmas not just for state residents who enter into surrogacy contracts to be performed within the state but also for interstate surrogacy contracts. Parentage decisions in the contracting state, if that state has jurisdiction over the parties, will be entitled to full faith and credit in other states, but jurisdiction may depend on which state is treated as the child's residence. Regulation of international surrogacy arrangements similarly varies, though American courts in states that recognise commissioning parents as legal parents are generally willing to issue parentage orders for foreign nationals who arrange for a surrogate birth in the United States.

In regulating surrogacy, two distinct bodies of laws apply. First, all states have statutes establishing legal parentage and these laws can be applied to surrogacy arrangements, whether or not the legislatures expressly considered surrogacy agreements at the time that they enacted the legislation. These statutes provide a framework for determining whether the genetic or the gestational connection confers maternity, whether legal parentage can be determined before birth, whether adoption procedures are necessary to transfer parentage from the surrogate to one or both of the commissioning parents after birth, and what standards apply in determining custody. Second, all states employ a mix of statutory and common law principles in determining the enforceability of surrogacy agreements. Applying these principles, all states agree that certain provisions, such as those governing abortion, will not necessarily be subject to orders of specific performance, but they vary in determining which parts of surrogacy contracts may give rise to damage awards or other types of enforcement.

Generalisations about the practice of surrogacy in the United States are, consequently, impossible. Given that family law is state law in the United States, the states are free to develop their own distinct approaches to the entire range of issues involving surrogacy. The states that have addressed surrogacy operate on a continuum that ranges from outright prohibition to liberal enforcement of surrogacy contracts. At one end of the continuum, some states prohibit surrogacy outright. Michigan, for example, imposes criminal penalties on anyone involved in surrogacy, providing that a woman who agrees to become a surrogate can be prosecuted for a misdemeanour and fined up to US$10,000 and/or imprisoned for up to a year, while anyone involved in making a surrogacy arrangement is subject to a penalty five times greater. Michigan, together with New York and Indiana, further treat surrogacy contracts as unenforceable, with New York explicitly declaring that: 'Surrogate parenting contracts are hereby declared contrary to the public policy of this state, and are void and unenforceable.' In these states, residents can still access surrogacy by going to another state to arrange the birth or by arranging for it privately and trusting that the surrogate will voluntarily surrender the child. Since the contract is unenforceable, an adoption proceeding may be necessary to secure the intended parents' parental rights. At least one state, Washington, enacted a statute to determine the parentage of its residents even if the child was born in another state, but Washington repealed the statute, and the validity of the provisions has not yet been tested.[4]

By contrast, as discussed below, California is at the other end of the continuum, a surrogacy friendly state that enforces individual contracts for surrogacy, as are others, including Illinois, Arkansas and New Hampshire. In between are a variety of approaches. In some states, surrogacy is permissible so long as the woman is not paid for her services or for an agreement to relinquish custody; for example Washington State, until recently, declared that a surrogacy agreement 'entered into for compensation, whether executed in the state of Washington or in another jurisdiction, shall be void and unenforceable in the state of Washington as contrary to public policy.' In Virginia, surrogate brokers cannot accept compensation for arranging gestational contracts, although lawyers are permitted to be paid for providing legal advice with respect to a surrogacy agreement. In other states, surrogacy contracts are subject to judicial pre-authorisation. Under this model, after individuals enter into a parentage agreement, they must submit that agreement to court prior to moving forward with the surrogacy arrangement. Some of these states restrict these pre-authorisation procedures to intending parents who are married or who suffer from a medical ailment that precludes giving birth.

Even a proposed uniform law on parentage reflects these differing approaches. In 2002, the Uniform Law Commission adopted a Uniform Parentage Act[5] that validated surrogacy. On the other hand, it took the unusual step of 'bracketing' the provisions, clarifying that omitting the surrogacy section would not affect states' enactment of the remainder of the act, out of 'of a concern that state

---

4 See *Family and Community Property Law Handbook 26.26.021* 2016 ed. (Washington Practice), p. 22.

5 The Uniform Parentage Act (2000) (revised December 2002).

legislatures may decide that they are still not ready to address gestational agreements, or that they want to treat them differently.'

The second body that governs surrogacy involves the enforceability of the contracts. In all states, general contract principles apply. These principles include the prohibition of unconscionable agreements, a view of 'baby selling,' that is, explicit payment for a child as opposed to the labour involved in carrying a child to term, as void as against public policy, and a presumption against specific performance of personal services contracts, particularly intrusive terms such as those involving abortion. In addition, a number of states have examined specific surrogacy terms. Nevada allows for enforcement of an agreement that requires the surrogate 'to abstain from any activities that the intended parent or parents or the physician providing care to the gestational carrier during the pregnancy reasonably believes to be harmful to the pregnancy and the future health of any resulting child, including, without limitation, smoking, drinking alcohol, using non-prescribed drugs, using prescription drugs not authorized by a physician aware of the pregnancy, exposure to radiation or any other activity proscribed by a health care provider.' Utah explicitly allows for the payment of compensation to the surrogate, but also provides that the agreement 'may not limit the right of the gestational mother to make decisions to safeguard her health or that of the embryo or fetus.' Even in states that might permit a provision concerning abortion or selective reduction, there is 'consensus that specific performance of such provisions would never occur but disagreement about whether a surrogate could be liable in damages for breach of contract.'

No national regulatory agency exists overseeing surrogacy or other aspects of assisted reproduction, nor do such entities exist within individual states. The only national regulations concern the obligation to report success rates for assisted reproductive technology and federal laws on citizenship of children born overseas.

1.2.2. Reasoning Behind the Law on Surrogacy

As noted earlier, part of the American patchwork stems from the timing of surrogacy regulations and later political division about the ethical acceptability of surrogacy. Many of the first state statutes were a response to the *Baby M* case, which attracted intense publicity in the late eighties. That case involved an agreement between William Stern and Mary Beth Whitehead to produce a child who would be raised by William and his wife, Elizabeth. Mr Stern was the only child of Holocaust survivors and he wished to carry on the family line. Mrs Stern had multiple sclerosis, and had been advised that a pregnancy might worsen her condition. The Infertility Center in New York matched willing surrogates with commissioning parents, and they brokered the contract between Whitehead and the Sterns. The contract provided that Mrs Whitehead would be inseminated with Mr Stern's sperm, producing a child genetically related to both of them. When the child (whom the Sterns would name 'Melissa') was born, Mrs Whitehead would deliver custody to Mr Stern, and do whatever was necessary to facilitate Mrs Stern's ability to adopt the child. After the birth, however, Mrs Whitehead became distraught and fled with the child to Florida, touching off a media storm of publicity. The police recovered the child and delivered it to the Sterns and the trial court upheld the validity of the contract, but the New Jersey Supreme Court reversed, finding such contracts to be void as against public policy because they circumvented New Jersey adoption law, which would have allowed the birth mother a period of time after the birth to change her mind. The courts nevertheless provided Mr Stern with custody, and Mrs Whitehead with visitation.

The publicity surrounding the case raised concerns about baby selling, the potential exploitation of women and the role of commercial brokers. New York responded in 1992 by adopting legislation restriction outlawing the commercial brokering of surrogacy contracts and severely restricting the practice. The New York law turned out, however, to be the high-water mark of the anti-surrogacy movement. While state legislation from that era restricts the process, with about a third of the states adopting such acts, surrogacy has won greater acceptance thereafter, with more jurisdictions moving towards acceptance. For example, the District of Columbia, which formerly banned surrogacy agreements, enacted a new law in 2017 that permits 'collaborative reproduction and surrogacy agreements.'[6] In addition, in 2018, Washington adopted the Uniform Parentage Act provisions authorising commercial surrogacy.[7]

The most important source of the change was the shift from traditional to gestational surrogacy. Traditional surrogacy, as in the *Baby M* case, uses the surrogate's own eggs, which means that the child to whom she gives birth is in every sense her own child. With the advent of in vitro fertilisation, embryos could be created in the lab, using egg and sperm from the commissioning parents or from donors, and then implanted into a surrogate. The 'gestational surrogate' would thus not be carrying a child to whom she was genetically related. Support for surrogacy increased with the case of *Johnson v Calvert*[8] in California. The Calverts wished to have a child, but Mrs Calvert could not become pregnant because she had had a hysterectomy. Anna Johnson, who heard about the Calverts from a co-worker, volunteered to be a surrogate. The Calverts were able to create an embryo using their own egg and sperm, and Johnson gave birth to the child. Relations between them deteriorated during the pregnancy, however, touching off litigation about the child's parentage.

---

6 The new law will be codified at Chapter 4 of Title 16.

7 See Uniform Parentage Act 2018 Wash. Legis. Serv. Ch. 6 (S.S.B. 6037) (West).

8 *Johnson v Calvert* 5 Cal. 4th 84 (1993).

The California Supreme Court held that under that state's version of the Uniform Parentage Act of 1973, both women had standing to assert maternity: Mrs Calvert because of her genetic connection to the child and Ms Johnson because she had given birth. The court ruled that intent was the tiebreaker, and that between two otherwise fit adults with parental standing, the contract should control.

Gestational surrogacy has almost completely replaced traditional surrogacy in the United States, and it contributed to the greater acceptance of surrogacy practices. In the *Calvert* case, the fact that Anna Johnson bore no genetic connection to the child made it a much easier case legally, and a more sympathetic case politically. The California Court effectively ruled that the child had been the Calverts' child from the beginning; no adoption was needed. Other states, ruling without legislation, could reach the same conclusion under their parentage statutes. Most allow a man, on the basis of the genetic connection to a child, to assert paternity. Applying that principle to women on a gender-neutral basis would allow a genetic mother like Mrs Calvert to assert maternity on the basis of the genetic tie. And if donor eggs were used, the intended father's assertion of a biological tie would be enough in many states to establish parentage to the exclusion of a surrogate with no genetic connection to the child. In the absence of a state policy discouraging surrogacy, this made it relatively easy for state courts to grant custody of the child to the commissioning parents in the event of a dispute.

Particularly where the commissioning parents provide the gametes, both the public and surrogates have come to see the child as the offspring of the commissioning parents. Legislation following the *Calvert* case has thus been more supportive of surrogacy, and more likely to recognise the commissioning parents as legal parents without adoption. Still, there have been two continuing sources of opposition.

First, some religious groups oppose surrogacy. The Catholic Church, for example, objects to in vitro fertilisation, along with contraception and abortion, as inconsistent with human dignity and church teachings about sexuality. It opposes surrogacy altogether. Such religious groups, which rarely have enough support to enact restrictions, often have sufficient clout to block legislation, which contributes to the large number of states without legislation at all.

Second, some groups, who do not necessarily oppose surrogacy, wish to affirm the traditional married family. They object to the growing recognition of same-sex couples or reproduction by single parents, and do not wish to authorise recognition of such families. At the same time, many groups who favour surrogacy wish to provide equal access irrespective of sexual orientation or marital status. In some states, this has led to surrogacy legislation that restricts recognition of the commissioning parents to married couples, or to those who cannot have children because of medical issues, thus excluding gays and lesbians who cannot have children because they do not wish to engage in a sexual relationship with a member of the opposite sex. In other states, these controversies contribute to the difficulties of drafting legislation that can win broad legislative support.

The US Supreme Court's embrace of marriage equality may change receptivity to such legislation, but it is too early to predict what effect the decision will have. In the meantime, legislative gridlock advances the agenda of many groups. Those who favour surrogacy often prefer no legislation to legislation that restricts the freedom of action of doctors and patients. Those opposing surrogacy also may prefer no legislation to legislation that approves surrogacy as a legitimate option. They are willing to look the other way as surrogacy exists in the shadows, but oppose state legitimisation of the practice or of the resulting families.

1.2.3. Statistics

Federal law requires that US clinics report annual data on their assisted reproductive technology (ART) cycles to the Centers for Disease Control and Prevention (CDC), and the CDC estimates that it is able to collect information on more than 95 per cent of all such cycles. From 1999–2013, there were 30,927 gestational carrier cycles in the United States, which resulted in 13,380 deliveries; because more than a third of the deliveries resulted in multiple infants, there were 18,400 babies born through gestational surrogacy during this time period.[9] The number of gestational carrier cycles increased by a factor of almost five, from 727 in 1999 to 3,432 in 2013, and, in 2013, these cycles constituted 2.5 per cent of all assisted reproductive technology cycles. The CDC does not appear to collect information separately on non-gestational carrier surrogacy cycles (that is, cycles in which the surrogate's own egg is used), but it is estimated that most surrogate births involve gestational arrangements.

During this same time period, the number of 'non-U.S. residents among gestational carrier cycles' increased from 68 in 1999 (constituting under 10 per cent of all such cycles) to 619 in 2013 (almost 20 per cent of all cycles).[10]

More than two-thirds of all clinics which reported their ART results to the CDC performed at least one gestational carrier cycle during 2013.[11]

Despite the increase in surrogacy, litigation is rare. And fears that surrogacy arrangements would disproportionately involve poor or minority women have

---

9 See CDC, *ART and Gestational Carriers* (2016), <https://www.cdc.gov/art/key-findings/gestational-carriers.html>.

10 See K. Perkins, et al., Trends and Outcomes of Gestational Surrogacy in the United States, 106 Fert. & Steril. 435 (2016), <https://www.sciencedirect.com/science/article/pii/S0015028216610579?via%3Dihub>.

11 Ibid.

not proven to be the case. American surrogates are usually white, and in their late twenties and early thirties. They typically have at least a high school education and children of their own. While they are not as well off as commissioning couples, they are not desperate. They often use the use the money to supplement family income while staying home to raise children or working part-time. And gestational carriers typically state that they view the child as the offspring of the commissioning parents. Their satisfaction with the surrogacy process often depends on the quality of the relationship they develop with the commissioning parents, rather than the relationship with the child.

1.3. LEGAL PARENTHOOD AT THE TIME OF BIRTH

The determination of parenthood in the context of surrogacy decisions depends on whether the state has legislation that specifically addresses surrogacy and, if not, the background law of parentage in the state. Each state has developed its own means for recognising – or not recognising – the status of the commissioning parents and the surrogates in accordance with these principles. The states split in their recognition of the parental status of the surrogate in the following ways:

1. Some states prohibit surrogacy or try to discourage it by recognising the woman giving birth as a legal mother in all cases, irrespective of the parties' intent and the source of the egg and sperm that produce the child. In Michigan, for example, the state both recognises the woman who gives birth as a legal parent and may also presume that her husband is a legal parent, with a relatively high bar to rebutting the marital presumption.[12] In these states, the commissioning parents are likely to receive recognition as legal parents only if the woman who gives birth consents and they are able to arrange an adoption. In the event of a dispute, the surrogate will be deemed the legal parent, and efforts to challenge that result could expose a commissioning couple to prosecution for violation of state law prohibiting surrogacy. A less draconian Utah law, which also recognised a gestational surrogate as a legal parent in circumstances where the intended mother had supplied the egg, was declared unconstitutional.[13] The constitutional validity of the Michigan law has not been tested in a context where the woman who supplies the egg is also the intended mother.

---

12 See C. VanWormer, 'Outdated and Ineffective: An Analysis of Michigan's Gestational Surrogacy Law and the Need for Validation of Surrogate Pregnancy Contracts' (2012) 61 DePaul L. Rev. 911, 916 (describing Michigan's law as the most anti-surrogacy legislation in the country).

13 *J.R. v Utah* 261 F. Supp. 2d 1294, 1296–1298 (D. Utah 2002).

2. Some states provide that the woman who gives birth is the legal parent absent adoption.[14] The surrogate who agrees to surrender her child can do so, 72 hours after the birth. New Jersey may also recognise the man who provided the sperm as a legal parent, even if the gestational carrier is married. In these cases, the courts could award the birth mother and the biological father shared custodial responsibility for the child. Even if the birth mother agrees to an adoption, New Jersey allows her a period after the child's birth in which she can change her mind, building uncertainty into the process. In states with no applicable legislation, many commissioning parents similarly use adoption procedures to insure the parental status of one or both of the commissioning parents.
3. Some states, such as Texas and Florida, authorise recognition of the commissioning parents only if they participate in a pre-implantation judicial proceeding; otherwise, the woman who gives birth will be recognised as the legal mother absent adoption.[15] In some of these states, the pre-implantation proceedings are limited either to married couples or men and women, and have traditionally excluded same-sex couples and single parents from recognition. In addition, states such as Illinois limit the availability of these procedures to parties suffering from a physical condition that precludes pregnancy. Some of these statutes were specifically written to exclude same-sex couples while others simply intended to limit recognition to married couples at a time when same-sex marriage did not seem possible. It is unclear how the courts will treat these statutes today, though to the extent that their primary purpose was to prevent recognition of married same-sex couples in circumstances where other married couples would receive parental status, they should be unconstitutional under *Obergefell v Hodges*.[16]
4. Some states, like California and Connecticut, confer parental status on the commissioning parents who arrange for surrogate births.[17] In these states, the commissioning parents may be treated as legal parents from the time of conception forward, and their names will ordinarily be entered on the birth certificate. Nonetheless, parents in these states typically choose to obtain a court order recognising their legal status that will be recognised in other states in the event of a dispute.
5. Some states, like Missouri and Minnesota, have almost no laws directly addressing surrogacy. In these states, surrogacy still takes place, and the

---

[14] See *A.H.W. v G.H.B.* 772 A.2d 948, 954 (N.J. Ch. 2000). New Jersey enacted new surrogacy legislation in 2018.

[15] See *A.H.W. v G.H.B.* Ibid.

[16] *Obergefell v Hodges* 576 US (2015).

[17] See, e.g. Conn. Gen. Stat. Ann. ss. 7–48a(b) (West 2011); Cal. Fam. Code s. 7962 (2016).

> courts have had to resolve disputes, though often without producing reported opinions with precedential value. Intended couples in these states are likely to be able to secure parental recognition through an adoption proceeding that terminates the parental status of the birth mother where she consents to the proceeding after birth.[18]

While the states enjoy considerable latitude in their approach to surrogacy, it is not unlimited. Two statutes that recognised a gestational carrier as a legal parent to the exclusion of an intended mother who supplied the child's eggs have been declared unconstitutional by state supreme courts. As a general matter, courts have refused to recognise the parental status of an commissioning parent who donates genetic material that led to the creation of a child only where state law is explicitly designed to discourage surrogacy, and the constitutional validity of such provisions, while they remain on the books in a number of states, is in doubt.

1.4. ELIGIBILITY FOR SURROGACY

1.4.1. Eligibility Criteria for Women Acting as a Surrogate

States vary, with many states having no legislation, leaving it to the discretion of the agencies. Among those with legislation, Illinois, for example, requires that the carrier must be at least 21, have already given birth to at least one child, completed a medical and mental health evaluation, consulted with an independent lawyer about the surrogacy agreement, and obtained health insurance. Other states require a court to find that the carrier's pregnancy would not be an 'unreasonable risk' to either the mother or the baby.

While there is little sustained research on the characteristics of women acting as surrogates, or their reasons for doing so, there have been some studies. Those studies that exist indicate that surrogates are typically motivated by altruistic considerations; they feel good about producing a child for someone who cannot do so on her own. But the studies also indicate that, given the risk and inconvenience, gestational carriers would not agree to do so absent payment.

Even without state regulation, agencies typically have their own standards for gestational carriers. They prefer women who have already given birth, are between the ages of 21 and under 41, have no sexually transmitted diseases,

---

[18] See, e.g. *In re Baby Boy A.* no. A07-452, 2007 WL 4304448, at *1 (Minn. Ct. App. Dec. 11, 2007) (applying a choice of law clause referring to Illinois law in the absence of applicable Minnesota law).

cancer, substance abuse, or other disqualifying medical conditions, be financially secure, have a supportive environment, and be capable of handling pregnancy's physical and emotional issues. Ideally, clinics psychologically screen prospective surrogates, even if state law does not require doing so.

1.4.2. Eligibility Criteria for Commissioning Parents

Again, states vary as to eligibility. The states without legislation generally have no restrictions on access to surrogacy, though commissioning parents without a biological tie to the child may have difficultly securing legal recognition as parents and may need to go through an adoption. Some states with legislation require that the intending parents be a married husband and wife. Others have different requirements and may, for example, specify that the intending parent be unable to carry the pregnancy to term, or be unable to do so without 'unreasonable' risk to her health. Illinois imposes a list of requirements for the intending parents, such that they must certify that:

> '(1) he, she, or they contribute at least one of the gametes resulting in a pre-embryo that the gestational surrogate will attempt to carry to term;
> (2) he, she, or they have a medical need for the gestational surrogacy as evidenced by a qualified physician's affidavit attached to the gestational surrogacy contract and as required by the Illinois Parentage Act of 2015;
> (3) he, she, or they have completed a mental health evaluation; and
> (4) he, she, or they have undergone legal consultation with independent legal counsel regarding the terms of the gestational surrogacy contract and the potential legal consequences of the gestational surrogacy.'[19]

1.5. TRANSFERRING PARENTHOOD

1.5.1. The Legal Process

States vary in how they assign parenthood, and they also vary as to whether expedited procedures apply only to gestational surrogacy or also include traditional surrogacy. Some states allow courts to issue pre-birth orders such that the intending parents are the legal parents. In other states, so long as a gestational surrogacy arrangement has complied with statutory requirements, the intending parents are the parents as soon as the child is born. Washington state provides that its law applies to determine legal parenthood,

19 750 Ill. Comp. Stat. Ann. 47/20(b) (2017).

regardless of where the child was born, though there have been no cases testing the validity of the provision.

Third, some states establish a post-birth process. For example, in Texas, once a child is born, the commissioning parents then file a notice of the birth with the court, which will issue an order confirming that the intending parents are the legal parents. Finally, in the absence of a state-established procedure, the intending parents may need to adopt the child, typically with the consent of the surrogate mother.

Many states also legislate concerning jurisdiction to determine parentage and custody over children born in their state, regardless of the residence of the commissioning parents. Jurisdiction may be based on the residency within the state of either the surrogate or the commissioning parent or on the birth of the child in the state. A few states have much broader provisions that, for example, extend to include jurisdiction if the agreement is executed there.

Other states have not comprehensively addressed the jurisdictional issues involved in adjudicating the parentage of a child born through surrogacy.

1.5.2. Children's Interests

Children's rights are not considered in the determination of parenthood when there is a legally enforceable agreement. In these cases, there is no transfer of parentage; the commissioning parents are viewed as legal parents from the time of conception forward and the law that governs their relationship to their children is the same as for any other parents. Where the parties arrange for a post-birth adoption, the courts have the power to consider the child's interests, but rarely conduct an independent inquiry where all of the parties are in agreement on the adoption.

1.6. INTERNATIONAL SURROGACY ARRANGEMENTS

Under federal law, children born in the United States are viewed as American citizens irrespective of the nationality of their parents. If the commissioning parents are from the United States, and the child is born to a surrogate outside of the United States, then the child's citizenship is a question of federal law. Even if local law recognises a surrogacy agreement and finds that US parents are the legal parents of a child conceived through artificial reproductive technologies (ART), then the child will not be a US citizen at birth if the US citizen parents do not have a biological connection to the child. Parents can apply for a US passport for the child at the US Embassy or Consulate in country where child was born, and must comply with applicable regulations for issuing a US passport to a minor. The burden of demonstrating citizenship of minor's legal parents rests with passport applicant.

1.7. CONCLUSION

When the New Jersey court that decided the *Baby M* case in 1988 labelled surrogacy as essentially 'illegal baby selling', the New York Times proclaimed that the court had 'reinforce[d] sound values for all who aspire to parenthood.'

Yet, while many states initially outlawed or imposed severe restriction on surrogacy – close to 20 had done so by 1992 – regulation and public attitudes have changed. To be sure, California is one of the most surrogacy-friendly states in the United States, but it is not alone. Practitioners understand that their clients who want to use surrogacy can find a hospitable jurisdiction, even if is not the state of residence. For example, they know whether states will recognise the rights of both members of a same-sex couple to be listed on a birth certification, or whether the state will record only the names of the biological progenitors on a birth certificate, regardless of the sex of the intending parents. And even New Jersey now permits surrogacy.

Foreign countries that wish to police international surrogacy more closely could work with American agencies. Practically, agency contracts shape both the parties' expectations about surrogacy arrangements, and influence judicial determinations in the event of a dispute in the absence of other governing law. A nation whose citizens access American surrogacy arrangements could take measures to influence the development of this form of private ordering that has had an enormous influence on surrogacy development in the United States.

A foreign country ('the home country'), for example, could pass laws indicating that the home country will recognise the parentage of children born through surrogate services without a separate adoption proceeding in the home country if the parents enter into a contract with an agency on the home country's approved list of surrogacy providers. The home country could specify standards for the approval, including supervision of the agency's treatment of the gestational carriers, recruitment practices, availability of counsel, and security for medical or other payments. The home country could also establish screening procedures for commissioning parents and require pre-conception approval of the contract. By guaranteeing recognition of parentage, the home country would create a powerful incentive for agencies to comply with the required procedures and for parents to use only those agencies that have received approval.

Two problems should be considered. First, the home country might not be able to bind the state in which the child is born. The pre-conception determination could therefore not ordinarily override a later, post-birth determination of parentage in the state in which the surrogate lives, if the law in that state does not recognise the validity of the preconception agreement. In such a case, the intended parents would not be able to obtain a passport allowing the child to leave the United States and the child's place of residence would ordinarily determine jurisdiction over parentage and custody issues. To prevent such a scenario, the home country could require that the commissioning parents and international agencies secure surrogates only in jurisdictions that will ratify the result of the contract. Or it could make the home country's approval contingent on also securing a parentage order in the child's place of birth.

Second, while the home country could condition its parentage order on contract terms that limit surrogacy payments, the country may find that few parents will use the procedure if the payment limits are too strict. As a practical matter therefore, the proposal is likely to work only if it allows reasonable payments. The payments could be characterised as compensation for medical expenses, lost employment opportunities, or discomfort and inconvenience.

National regulation of surrogacy in the United States is unlikely, and states such as California appear committed to allowing the practice to continue. In addition, the principle of equal recognition for same-sex couples has increased support for surrogacy in a number of states. To the extent the states have had misgivings about international visitors' access to surrogacy, the concerns have involved specific practices, such as the age of the commissioning parents, rather than surrogacy itself. The surrogacy friendly jurisdictions in the United States, such as California, are accordingly likely to remain open to international surrogacy, at least for those who can afford the high prices of the services. Within this framework, a major concern involves recognition of the parental status of the commissioning parents in the home country, where the parental status of other parties has been severed in the United States, or the potential difficulties that may arise if international visitors access surrogacy services in those states without clear regulation. The interplay between domestic and foreign laws on surrogacy is therefore likely to remain subject to significant uncertainty about the resolution of potential disputes, particularly where the parties disagree after the birth of a child.

2. THE CASE OF CALIFORNIA

California has one of the most comprehensive systems in the United States for regulating surrogacy. In this section, the specific regime governing surrogacy in that state is examined in detail by way of an example.

2.1. GENERAL LEGAL FRAMEWORK

In 2012 (effective 2013), California enacted a comprehensive statutory approach to gestational surrogacy. Prior to that time, California regulated surrogacy through statutes that applied more generally to any form of assisted reproduction and judicial decisions interpreting the statutes and applying them to surrogate arrangements. Those statutes and decisions continue to control the practice of traditional (although not gestational) surrogacy. The 2013 statute (subsequently amended) includes extensive instructions for what an assisted reproduction contract must include, such as details on how commissioning parents will pay for the surrogate's medical bills and discussion of insurance policies. It mandates execution of the surrogacy agreement before any procedure occurs. Prior to the baby's birth, the parties can petition the court for a judgment establishing the intending parents as the legal parent. There is no requirement for a hearing or evidence, unless either the court or one of the parties has a good faith, reasonable belief that the surrogacy agreement does not comply with the surrogacy law.

This section focuses on California's regulation of gestational surrogacy rather than traditional surrogacy, providing details on the California system.

2.2. SURROGACY ARRANGEMENTS IN GENERAL

2.2.1. General

To be enforceable, the parties to the surrogacy agreement must be represented by independent legal counsel. The agreement must include the following: (1) the persons from whom the gametes originated (unless anonymous); (2) the identity of the commissioning parents; and (3) disclosure of how commissioning parents will cover surrogate's medical expenses. The contract must be notarised (or equivalent as required by the jurisdiction in which the agreement is executed). A contract that complies with these (and a few other) requirements is presumptively valid; California law appears to apply to any such contract, regardless of whether it concerns an in-state or interstate agreement.

The state does not establish a scheme for remuneration, and the costs vary by the type of surrogacy.

2.2.2. Basic Forms of Surrogacy

There are three basic forms that surrogacy arrangements assume.

2.2.2.1. Commercial Surrogacy

The surrogacy is arranged through an agency that provides all screening and matching services as well as counselling, case management and support groups. The agency may include a benefit package for the surrogate. The financial arrangements involve a base fee as well as additional compensation for various factors (procedures, complications, level of experience, travel, miscellaneous expenses).

2.2.2.2. Independent Surrogacy

In this form of surrogacy, there is no agency involvement; the commissioning parents themselves arrange for a contract with a surrogate. Although it is generally less expensive than going through an agency, independent surrogacy is often more complicated and riskier for all parties because no one may have screened the surrogate for health risks concerning the pregnancy or psychological issues that may affect her willingness to surrender the child, the parties may not have consulted professionals in entering into the arrangements, and they may have conflicting expectations about what may happen in the event of complications with the pregnancy.

2.2.2.3. Known Surrogacy

The surrogate is a friend or relative of the commissioning parents, and this can be referred to as 'altruistic surrogacy.' This typically does not involve financial compensation outside of medical expenses.

2.2.3. Payment or Compensation

When payment is involved, the surrogate is usually paid an agreed-upon base fee (averaging approximately US$30,000 to US$60,000) for gestational services as well as additional compensation for any invasive procedures or multiple pregnancies (twins or triplets) as well as supplies (maternity clothes, pre-natal vitamins, etc.), travel expenses, legal fees, lost wages, health and life insurance provided either as part of benefit package through agency or by the commissioning parents.

Surrogacy funds must be held by either a licensed attorney or bonded escrow company, *not* the surrogate company. The parties' attorneys act as mediators to make sure both parties comply with the agreed-upon compensation terms spelled out in the contract. Agencies also can act as intermediaries between parties (more often between the parents and outside parties, such as doctors), all in compliance with the terms of the contract.

2.3. LEGAL PARENTHOOD AT THE TIME OF BIRTH

Under California law, the commissioning parents are the legal parents at the time of birth, if all agreements were executed in accordance with statutory requirements. Once the surrogacy contract is signed and notarised, an attorney files in court to make the commissioning parents the legal parents at the time child is born; this is often referred to as the parental rights confirmation process.

Once commissioning parents complete this process, they will be listed on the child's birth certificate. Barring any extraordinary circumstance, judgment is usually issued the same day as the hearing. As a result of the court judgment, it is also clear that the surrogate (and partner/spouse, if applicable) will not be held legally responsible for the child after birth.

The creation of parenthood through surrogacy is an exception to general California law. Under the Uniform Parentage Act, motherhood is established through either genetic relation or the physical act of giving birth; like adoption, surrogacy and its parental rights confirmation process create an alternative means of obtaining parenthood. The surrogacy parental rights confirmation differs from adoption because it: (1) does not require home study; and (2) it is completed much more quickly than adoption. California is one of the few states where the names of the commissioning parents can be on the birth certificate, eliminating the need for second-parent adoption in order for an commissioning parent without a biological connection to the child to receive legal recognition. However, for births occurring in the state of California, the Office of Vital Records requires that the surrogate's address be listed on the confidential portion of the birth certificate for statistical purposes, tracking the number of births in different regions of California. This information will not be reflected on the copy of the birth certificate the commissioning parents receive.

2.4. ELIGIBILITY FOR SURROGACY

California law does not establish requirements concerning who is eligible for surrogacy. The only implicit requirement appears to be that the parties are capable of entering into a contract (and able to pay). Instead, agencies set out their own criteria.

2.4.1. Eligibility for Surrogates

Common requirements include: that the surrogate be between the ages of 21–40 years old, a US citizen, a non-smoker, non-drug user, in 'excellent health' with a healthy BMI, show a good reproductive history, have given birth to at least one child, had all births at 36+ weeks gestation without complications, and be self-supporting/not receiving federal financial aid. Agencies typically require that surrogates undergo a full background check and pass a psychological consultation, and some agencies require the surrogate's spouse or partner to undergo the same. The surrogates must also provide all official medical records and a current pap smear as well as undergo medical screening/testing. Once matched with commissioning parents, sent to their reproductive physician for disease and drug screening. Most agencies do not impose any limits on sexual orientation, race, or marital status.

2.4.2. *Eligibility for Commissioning Parents*

Specific requirements vary by agency but each typically uses screening process to make sure the commissioning parents are financially and psychologically prepared for the surrogacy process. Because California law does not require a home visit (as it would for adoptive parents), there is, however, no baseline for the commissioning parents.

2.4.3. *Issues Concerning Donor Gametes*

Sperm, egg, and embryo donation and sale are permitted in California, and can be anonymous, unless both the commissioning parents and the donor sign an agreement stating otherwise. While California law does not permit children to access identifying information, some gamete providers (such as The Sperm Bank of California) have an identity release program, giving sperm donors the option to sign a release that a child born of their gametes may access donor's information.

There are no limits on whose gametes can be used in the surrogacy process – those of the donor, surrogate, or commissioning parents are permissible – so the parties can decide for themselves. There is no requirement that there be a genetic relationship between commissioning parents and child.

2.5. TRANSFERRING PARENTHOOD

2.5.1. *The Legal Process*

For gestational surrogacy, the commissioning parents can obtain a pre-birth – or post-birth – order that confers parenthood. Such births do not use the general adoption procedure, but instead undergo a process called parental rights confirmation (a court order pursuant to the terms of a legal and binding surrogacy contract which meets all of the statutory terms).

For traditional surrogacy, the commissioning parents can obtain a declaration of legal parentage either through a second-parent adoption or a court judgment granting parenthood.

For gestational surrogacy, the parties' attorneys bring the motion for parenthood to a court for final judgment; parties may or may not be required to appear in court. The court documents, including the agreement between the surrogate and the commissioning parents and related documents are not open to inspection, except by the parties to the proceeding and their attorneys, as well as the California Department of Social Services, other than when ordered by a judge under 'exceptional circumstances.'

Any dispute concerning the surrogacy arrangement is adjudicated through the courts and the parties' legal counsel; there is no central authority that regulates and makes decisions.

The surrogacy contract typically sets out the various protections for confidentiality.

2.5.2. Rights of Children

Although not legally required to do so, many surrogacy agencies conduct thorough background checks and psychological screening as part of the application process to ensure a financially and emotionally stable home for the child.

In non-gestational surrogacy cases, courts have looked to the intentions of commissioning parents and the surrogate (both in conduct and in written contract) to determine parenthood.

2.6. AGENCIES AND CRIMINALISATION

California permits attorneys and agencies to act as mediators between the commissioning parents, the surrogate, insurance companies, hospitals, and courts. Depending on the type of surrogacy (known, commercial, independent), the level of involvement varies. There are few rules/regulations concerning their involvement, although California law does require that the surrogate and commissioning parents be represented by separate counsel of their choice.

If the requirements for a legal surrogacy contract under the California Family Code are not met,[20] the contract may not hold up in a court of law as valid and the commissioning parents are not the legal parents of the child. Additional court hearings must then take place to determine financial settlements as well as child custody (varies by circumstance; considered on a case-by-case basis). If there is evidence of bad faith execution by any involved party (lawyer, doctor, surrogate, commissioning parents), then this may result in legal penalties and further court proceedings.

3. CONCLUSION

Ultimately, while there is relatively little regulation of the commercial surrogacy agencies that engage in surrogacy, the states do oversee the determination of

---

[20] Cal. Fam. Code §7962.

parentage and the commercial aspects of surrogacy agreements. In addition, surrogacy in the United States is moving towards greater popular and legal acceptance. With recognition of marriage equality and greater use by gay men, in particular, the practice of surrogacy is becoming more routinised and institutionalised across the fifty states, and more open to international and domestic cross-border arrangements.

THE INFLUENCE OF INTERNATIONAL COURTS

SURROGACY BEFORE THE EUROPEAN COURT OF HUMAN RIGHTS

Paul BEAUMONT and Katarina TRIMMINGS*

* The authors are grateful for the comments of Justin Borg-Barthet, their colleague in the Centre for Private International Law, University of Aberdeen, on an earlier version of this contribution.

1. INTRODUCTION

The issue of how cross-border surrogacy should be regulated has been a significant strand of the present authors' research for several years. The Nuffield Foundation funded them from 2010 to 2012 to work on this topic and the main fruit of that labour was a substantial edited book that set out how surrogacy was being dealt with in many legal systems and presented the arguments for a new hard law solution of a Treaty regulating cross-border surrogacy arrangements along the lines of the highly successful Hague Convention on Intercountry Adoption.[1] As a follow up to that work the present authors have systematically analysed the law on cross-border surrogacy from a comparative perspective in Europe[2] and have recently analysed how the European Court of Human Rights ('ECtHR') has decided cases where a cross-border surrogacy arrangement was involved. The most recent work considered the case of *Paradiso and Campanelli v Italy*[3] at the stage when the Chamber had taken its decision and the decision of the Grand Chamber was pending.[4] In this contribution the authors intend to analyse the Grand Chamber decision in *Paradiso and Campanelli* and to consider the possible use of international soft law to help move states closer to achieving the consensus needed to regulate cross-border surrogacy arrangements in a Hague Convention.

2. FACTS OF *PARADISO AND CAMPANELLI*

In 2010, Ms Donatina Paradiso and Mr Giovanni Campanelli ('the applicants' or 'the commissioning parents'), both Italian nationals and a married couple, entered into a surrogacy arrangement with a Moscow-based clinic called Rosjurconsulting whom they paid €49,000 for their services. A surrogate was implanted with two embryos on 19 June 2010 and she gave birth to a child in Moscow on 27 February 2011. On the same day the surrogate gave her written consent to the child being registered as the applicants' son. In accordance with

1 K. Trimmings and P. Beaumont (eds), *International Surrogacy Arrangements*, Hart Publishing, Oxford 2013 (549 pages and prelims).

2 K. Trimmings and P. Beaumont, 'Parentage and Surrogacy in a European Perspective' in J. Scherpe (ed.), *European Family Law*, vol. III, Edward Elgar, Cheltenham 2016, pp. 232–83.

3 *Paradiso and Campanelli v Italy*, no. 25358/12, ECHR 2015/12. The Chamber decision was given on 27.01.2015 and the Grand Chamber decision was given on 24.01.2017.

4 P. Beaumont and K. Trimmings, 'Recent jurisprudence of the European Court of Human Rights in the area of cross-border surrogacy: is there still a need for global regulation of surrogacy?' in G. Biagioni (ed.), *Migrant Children in the XXI Century: Selected Issues of Public and Private International Law*, Editoriale Scientifica, Italy 2016, Ch. 5. Available as a Centre for Private International Law Working Paper no. 2016/4 <http://www.abdn.ac.uk/law/documents/CPIL_2016-4.pdf> accessed 11.09.2018.

Russian law, the applicants were registered as the child's parents. There was no indication in the Russian birth certificate that the child had been born through surrogacy. The Italian consulate in Russia issued travel documents for the child, allowing the commissioning parents to remove the child to Italy. In Italy, the commissioning parents applied to the municipal authority for the registration of the birth. Their request was, however, refused on 4 August 2011 by the Registry Office after the mother had conceded that the ova that was used was from a donor and a DNA test had revealed that Mr Campanelli was not the genetic father of the child. On 20 October 2011 the Youth Court decided that the child should immediately be removed from the commissioning parents, not only given the lack of any genetic relationship between the commissioning parents and the child, but also because the authorities had doubts over the commissioning parents' capabilities to raise the child as they had acted contrary to the law.[5] The decision to remove the child from the applicants was upheld by the Campobasso Court of Appeal on 28 February 2012. The baby was placed in a children's home, without the commissioning parents being informed of the child's location or permitted to see him. Afterwards the baby was entrusted to foster parents, whilst being left without a formal identity. Following the revelation that there was no genetic link between the child and the commissioning parents, the Italian authorities viewed the case as one of international adoption rather than a cross-border surrogacy arrangement. On 5 June 2013 the Youth Court declared that the applicants no longer had capacity to act in the adoption proceedings brought by them given that they were neither the child's parents nor members of his family. The commissioning parents then lodged an application with the ECtHR, relying on Arts 6 (right to a fair trial), 8 (right to respect for private and family life) and 14 (non-discrimination) of the Convention. In particular, they complained that the refusal to recognise the legal parent-child relationship established through the Russian birth documents, and the removal of the child by Italian authorities from their care violated the applicants' right to respect for private and family life.

3. DECISION OF THE CHAMBER

The court dismissed the complaint regarding the refusal by Italian authorities to register the child's birth certificate, finding that the applicants had not exhausted available domestic remedies as they had not appealed to the Italian Court

[5] In this context, the court made a rather harsh statement that the commissioning parents had purposively circumvented the adoption law and 'it could be thought that the child resulted from a narcissistic desire on the part of the couple or indeed that he was intended to resolve problems in their relationship.' *Paradiso*, para. 22.

of Cassation.[6] The court also dismissed the applicants' attempt to bring an action on behalf of the child because in the absence of any biological ties with the child or any authorisation from a lawful representative of the child the applicants did not have legal standing to represent the child's interests in the context of judicial proceedings.[7]

Nevertheless, the court decided to deal with the case entirely under Art. 8 and decided that the second complaint fell within the scope of that Article on the basis that there had been a de facto family life between the child and the applicants.[8] Although the court found that the removal of the child had been in accordance with law and served the legitimate aim of 'preventing disorder' and protecting the 'rights and freedoms of the child',[9] it concluded that the actions of the Italian authorities were not necessary in a democratic society.[10] Indeed, the removal of a child from the family setting is 'an extreme measure, which should only be resorted to as a very last resort. Such a measure can only be justified if it corresponds to the aim of protecting a child who is faced with immediate danger'.[11] The court also criticised the Italian court's rationale that the commissioning parents, who had been assessed as suitable to adopt in 2006, were later held to be unfit as prospective adopters on the sole ground that they had breached domestic adoption laws, 'without any expert report having been

---

6 *Paradiso and Campanelli v Italy* above n. 3, paras 62 and 90.

7 *Paradiso and Campanelli v Italy* above n. 3, paras 48–50. Very surprisingly, the second section found the applicants' objection to the decision that they had no standing to contest the adoption proceedings to be admissible even though the applicants could have appealed that decision at two levels and did not appeal the decision at all, see *Paradiso and Campanelli v Italy* above n. 3, para. 64.

8 *Paradiso and Campanelli v Italy* above n. 3, paras 54 and 67–69. This complaint was admissible because the decision to remove the child from the applicants and place him under guardianship was confirmed by the Campobasso Court of Appeal and could not be appealed on a point of law to the Italian Court of Cassation because it was a non-final decision, see *Paradiso and Campanelli v Italy* above n. 3, para. 63. De facto family life was established in this case on the basis of the period of six months the child spent with the applicants in Italy from the age of three months to nine months and the first few weeks of the child's life spent with the female applicant in Russia, para. 69, and this was agreed with rather reluctantly by the two dissenting judges in their opinion, see *Paradiso and Campanelli v Italy* above n. 3, cit., dissent para. 2, but with a critique that the majority did not apply a 'proportionality' test given that the de facto family life was based on a 'tenuous link' between the applicants and the child, see *Paradiso and Campanelli v Italy* above n. 3, dissent para. 3.

9 *Paradiso and Campanelli v Italy* above n. 3, paras 72–73 and dissent para. 6.

10 *Paradiso and Campanelli v Italy* above n. 3, para. 81.

11 *Paradiso and Campanelli v Italy* above n. 3, para. 80. The court noted that a high standard had been set in previous ECtHR case law in this respect. It highlighted in particular the case of *Wagner and J.M.W.L. v Luxembourg* no. 76240/01, judgment of 28 June 2007, where the national authorities refused to recognise the parent-child relationship established abroad through adoption on the grounds of public policy. The situation in *Wagner*, however, differed from the present case as family life had not been interfered with through a physical removal of the child from the adoptive mother.

ordered by the courts'.[12] Moreover, following the removal of the child from the commissioning parents, he was left without any formal identity for over two years.[13] The child's lack of identity until April 2013 may have been contrary to Art. 7 of the United Nations Convention on the Rights of the Child,[14] as no child should be 'disadvantaged on account of the fact that he or she was born to a surrogate mother, especially in terms of citizenship or identity'.[15] Consequently, the court held by five votes to two that the Italian authorities had failed to strike the correct balance between the interests of the state and those of the commissioning parents, whilst also having failed to take account of the paramountcy of the child's best interests.[16] Nevertheless, this finding was not to be understood as obliging Italy to return the child to the physical care of the commissioning parents as in the meantime the boy had undoubtedly developed emotional ties with his foster family.[17]

In a powerful dissent Judges Raimondi and Spano accused the majority of acting as a 'fourth-instance' by substituting its own assessment for that of the domestic authorities even though the decision of the relevant domestic authorities to remove the child from the care of the applicants was not arbitrary.[18] Their final conclusion about the impact of the majority judgment is compelling:

> 'In addition, the majority's position amounts, in substance, to denying the legitimacy of the State's choice not to recognise gestational surrogacy. If it suffices to create, illegally, a link with the child abroad in order for the national authorities to be obliged to recognise the existence of 'family life', then it is clear that the States' freedom not to give legal effect to gestational surrogacy, a freedom that has nonetheless been acknowledged by the Court's case-law (see *Mennesson v. France*, ... §79, and *Labassee v. France*, ... §58), is reduced to nought.'[19]

---

12 *Paradiso and Campanelli v Italy* above n. 3, para. 84. Clearly the lack of an expert report may be seen to make the removal of the child appear 'arbitrary' but as the dissent point out, para. 12, this was not enough to make the decisions of the domestic courts to remove the child from the applicants arbitrary because they were dealing with a sensitive and urgent case where 'the suspicions hanging over the applicants were serious.' Although the majority acknowledged the risk that leaving the child with the applicants would have 'developed closer emotional ties', para. 82, between the child and the applicants, the majority did not give enough weight to the legitimate interest of the Italian authorities in preventing such harm to the child in forming these deeper emotional links if the child was not to be adopted by the applicants because of their breach of Italian adoption law.

13 *Paradiso and Campanelli v Italy* above n. 3, para. 85.

14 United Nations Convention on the Rights of the Child, 20 November 1989, see *Paradiso and Campanelli v Italy* above n. 3, para. 85. However, the dissent, para. 14, correctly says that this argument about the child's identity did not have an impact on the 2011 decision to separate the child from his parents and was therefore irrelevant to the applicants' case.

15 *Paradiso and Campanelli v Italy* above n. 3, para. 85.

16 *Paradiso and Campanelli v Italy* above n. 3, paras 80 and 86.

17 *Paradiso and Campanelli v Italy* above n. 3, para. 88.

18 *Paradiso and Campanelli v Italy* above n. 3, dissent paras 12–14.

19 *Paradiso and Campanelli v Italy* above n. 3, dissent para. 15.

4. THE SUGGESTIONS BY THE PRESENT AUTHORS MADE PRIOR TO THE GRAND CHAMBER DECISION

When the case was pending before the Grand Chamber of the ECtHR the present authors made the following analysis.[20]

4.1. GENETIC LINK

Although the Court in *Paradiso* did not address the problem of the recognition of legal parentage, it did touch upon the issue of genetic link. This was, however, in relation to the question of whether 'family life' for the purposes of Art. 8 existed between the child and the commissioning parents of whom neither was the child's genetic parent but who had acted as parents and cared for the child for a substantial part of the first nine months of his life. The court held that a genetic link was not a necessary pre-requisite for the existence of 'family life' for the purposes of Art. 8 as a de facto family had been established. Judges Raimondi and Spano in their joint partly dissenting opinion argued that in the absence of a biological link between the applicants and the child if the custody of the child was obtained through an illegal act that was contrary to public policy (i.e. in the present case commercial surrogacy or an illegal adoption), the relationship does not constitute 'family life' as protected by Art. 8(1).[21]

The present authors urged the Grand Chamber in *Paradiso* to take the opportunity to restrict the notion of de facto family life in Art. 8 of the ECHR.[22] They suggested that is not for the ECtHR to effectively create 'family rights' for any couple in Europe who want to have a baby by hiring a surrogate anywhere in the world even when neither commissioning parent has a genetic relationship with the child.[23] This has to be a matter on which countries in Europe are allowed to have different views. Therefore, intention to be a parent coupled with under nine months of de facto parenting – the situation in *Paradiso* – should not be regarded as a de facto family for the purposes of Art. 8 of the ECHR. The Grand Chamber was encouraged to respect democracy and subsidiarity by exercising restraint and saying that the case falls outside the scope of the Convention as the applicants had no right to family life to protect.[24] Were the Grand Chamber to decide that there was a de facto family life (or an interference

20 K. Trimmings and P. Beaumont, above n. 4.

21 *Paradiso and Campanelli v Italy* above n. 3, dissent para. 3.

22 See K. Trimmings and P. Beaumont, above n. 4, p. 123.

23 Ibid.

24 Ibid.

with private life) in this case within the scope of the Convention, it was exhorted to resist the temptation to act as a 'fourth-instance' court.[25] The present authors advised against the Grand Chamber second guessing the view of the national courts on the best interests of the child.[26] It was well within Italy's margin of appreciation (especially on an issue like the assessment of the best interests of a child which turns on the facts of the individual case and an appraisal of the suitability of the applicants to exercise parental responsibility which it is hard for any appellate court to do but particularly hard for a human rights review court to do years after the event) for the Italian authorities to remove the child from the applicants when the child had been with them for less than nine months, the applicants had no genetic link with the child, the applicants had not been approved by the Italian authorities to adopt a very young child[27] when they had earlier gone through an adoption process in Italy, and the longer the child remained in the applicants' care the more emotionally damaging it would be to the child to remove him from that care.

4.2. THE STATE'S CHOICE TO OUTLAW SURROGACY

The present authors noted that the problem raised by Judges Raimondi and Spano, in their dissenting opinion in the Chamber decision in *Paradiso*, had attracted wider attention among commentators.[28] Critics had rightly observed that the ECtHR's approach, although not directly challenging the state's choice to outlaw surrogacy,[29] compelled states to accept the effects of cross-border commercial surrogacy arrangements by requiring them not to remove a child from the care of the commissioning parents established through surrogacy

25 See *Paradiso and Campanelli v Italy* above n. 3, dissent para. 13 and a similar critique of the ECtHR's tendency to act as a fourth instance in family cases by P. Beaumont, K. Trimmings, L. Walker and J. Holliday, 'Child Abduction, Recent Jurisprudence of the European Court of Human Rights' (2015) 64 *ICLQ (International and Comparative Law Quarterly)* 39, 45–48, 62–63.

26 K. Trimmings and P. Beaumont, above n. 4, p. 124.

27 *Paradiso and Campanelli v Italy* above n. 3, para. 12. It is also worth noting that the Italian government argued before the ECtHR that the applicants could have adopted an older child in Russia making use of the bilateral agreement between Italy and Russia, see *Paradiso and Campanelli v Italy* above n. 3, para. 66.

28 K. Trimmings and P. Beaumont, above n. 4, p. 124.

29 In *Mennesson v France*, no. 65192/11, 26 June 2014, *Labassée v France*, no. 65941/11, 26 June 2014, and *Paradiso and Campanelli v Italy* above n. 3, the Chambers acknowledged that the states had the freedom to outlaw surrogacy arrangements. In the first two cases the ban pursued the legitimate aim of 'the protection of health' and the 'protection of the rights and freedoms of others', and in the last case it pursued the legitimate aim of the 'prevention of disorder' and the 'protection of the rights and freedoms of others'.

abroad unless the child is in immediate danger.[30] An unintended but likely consequence of this approach is that it will encourage commissioning parents to circumvent national legislation prohibiting surrogacy.

The present authors also noted the risk that the ECtHR jurisprudence will become a vehicle for the pro-surrogacy lobby groups that have commercial interests in the area of surrogacy in the receiving countries.[31] This was another reason why they urged a cautious approach to be taken by the Grand Chamber in *Paradiso*.

4.3. THE BEST INTERESTS OF THE CHILD

In *Paradiso*, the best interests of the child were examined in relation to the physical removal of the child from the commissioning parents' care. The Chamber observed that the reference to public policy could not be used as giving 'carte blanche' for any measure as states have to take account of the best interests of the child, irrespective of the existence of a genetic link between the child and the commissioning parents.[32] This observation was in principle favourable to the commissioning parents as neither of them were genetically related to the child. Nevertheless, the best interests' principle compelled the court to conclude that, although the removal of the child violated the applicants' Art. 8 rights, the child could not be returned to the applicants as he had in the meantime settled with his foster parents.[33]

4.4. COMMERCIAL SURROGACY

Payments beyond reasonable expenses in surrogacy are often the determinative characteristic when it comes to states deciding whether to allow or ban surrogacy arrangements. Some jurisdictions allow altruistic surrogacy but ban

30 G. Puppinck and C. De La Hougue, 'ECHR: Towards the Liberalisation of Surrogacy: Regarding the *Mennesson v France* and *Labassee v France* Cases' <http://papers.ssrn.com/sol3/papers.cfm?abstract_id=2500075> accessed 11.0.2018 (originally published in French in [2014] *Revue Lamy de Droit Civil* 78).

31 K. Trimmings and P. Beaumont, above n. 4, p. 126.

32 *Paradiso and Campanelli v Italy*, above n. 3, para. 80.

33 It has been critically observed that this outcome did not secure the protection of 'real human rights' as in practical terms the judgment did not result in any change for the commissioning parents, see European Centre for Law and Justice (ECLJ), 'Comments on the ECHR case of *Paradiso and Campanelli v. Italy*', 30 January 2015, <http://eclj.org/Releases/Read.aspx?GUID=ec4d5af3-db22-4b01-8b44-2ab3846b770e&s=eur> accessed 11.09.2018. However, the child's best interests must trump those of the commissioning parents and therefore leaving the child with the foster family he had been with for two years is a protection of 'real' human rights.

commercial surrogacy arrangements on ethical grounds as they seek to prevent the commercialisation of conception.[34] Other jurisdictions ban surrogacy in both its forms.[35] In either scenario, the undesirable consequence of the ECtHR jurisprudence is that states are expected to undermine their moral objections against surrogacy where their citizens circumvent national laws by obtaining a child through commercial surrogacy abroad and seek recognition in their home country of the legal parent-child relationship established in the foreign jurisdiction. Should the ECtHR have the authority to, albeit in an indirect way, interfere with a country's choice not to allow its citizens to reproduce through surrogacy, especially through commercial surrogacy?

The present authors noted that commercial surrogacy raises serious concerns over the exploitation of women and commodification of children.[36] Indeed, there have been numerous reports of cases involving serious human rights abuses, including child abandonment, problems with the consent of surrogates and difficulties with intermediaries.[37] The failure of the ECtHR to distinguish between commercial and altruistic surrogacy in its jurisprudence is worrying as it implies an acceptance on the part of the Court of commercial surrogacy with all its risks and the ethical concerns that are associated with this practice.

5. GRAND CHAMBER DECISION

On 24 January 2017 the Grand Chamber gave its judgment. It is lamentable that it took the court so long to reach a judgment. The decision of the Chamber was delivered on 27 January 2015, the Italian government asked that the case be referred to the Grand Chamber on 27 April 2015, a panel of the Grand Chamber granted that request on 1 June 2015 and a hearing took place in the Grand Chamber on 9 December 2015. However, it took the Grand Chamber over 13 months from the hearing to give its judgment. This of course has the effect that the ECtHR is not in a position to rectify human rights breaches in

---

34 E.g. the United Kingdom (UK) where commercial surrogacy is banned but altruistic surrogacy is allowed. For more information on the issue of payments in surrogacy arrangements in the UK see M. Wells-Greco, 'United Kingdom' in K. Trimmings and P. Beaumont, above n. 1, pp. 377–80, and M. Wells-Greco, *The Status of Children Arising from Inter-Country Surrogacy Arrangements*, Eleven, The Hague 2016, pp. 166–74.

35 Such countries can be referred to as 'anti-surrogacy jurisdictions'. For more information, see K. Trimmings and P. Beaumont, 'General Report on Surrogacy' in K. Trimmings and P. Beaumont, above n. 1, pp. 463–64.

36 See for example, Hague Conference On Private International Law, 'The Parentage/Surrogacy Project: An Updating Note, February 2015' paras 5–12 <http://www.hcch.net/upload/wop/gap2015pd03a_en.pdf> accessed 11.09.2018; and K. Trimmings and P. Beaumont, 'General Report on Surrogacy', above n. 1, pp. 528–31.

37 For a detailed analysis see Hague Conference On Private International Law, 'The Parentage/Surrogacy Project', ibid, Annex II.

individual cases, particularly where young children are involved because their de facto position should almost always not be disrupted after a year never mind after several years, but rather is effectively giving opinions which it hopes will help states to determine how they treat individuals in future cases. The Grand Chamber decided by 11 votes to six that there had been no violation of Art. 8 in this case. This reversal of the Chamber decision is to be greatly welcomed.

5.1. DE FACTO FAMILY LIFE

As mentioned above, the present authors had argued that the Chamber were wrong to find that de facto 'family life' existed in this case. The majority of the Grand Chamber acknowledged that in certain situations de facto family life can exist between an adult or adults and a child in the absence of biological ties or a recognised legal tie 'provided that there are genuine personal ties'.[38] The majority accepted that 'the applicants had developed a parental project and had assumed their role as parents *vis-à-vis* the child ... had forged close emotional bonds with him in the first stages of his life, the strength of which was, moreover, clear from the report drawn up by the team of social workers following a request by the Minors Court'.[39] The majority found that the couple had spent about six months together with the child in Italy and that the commissioning mother had spent about two months before that with the child in Russia.[40] The majority were not willing to establish a minimum period of shared life which would be necessary to constitute de facto family life 'given that the assessment of any situation must take account of the "quality" of the bond and the circumstances of each case'.[41] The majority acknowledged that the court had accepted the existence of family life protected by Art. 8 in *D and Others v Belgium*[42] in which a Belgian couple had been together with a child born to a Ukrainian surrogate for only two months. It distinguished that case on the grounds that there was a biological tie with at least one of the parents in that case and no biological tie with either parent in the *Paradiso* case and because the cohabitation had subsequently resumed.[43] The majority concluded that:

> 'Having regard to the above factors, namely the absence of any biological tie between the child and the intended parents, the short duration of the relationship with the child and the uncertainty of the ties from a legal perspective, and in spite of the existence

38 *Paradiso and Campanelli v Italy*, Grand Chamber, above n. 3, para. 148.
39 Ibid, para. 151.
40 Ibid, para. 152.
41 Ibid, para. 153.
42 *D and Others v Belgium*, no. 29176/13, 8 July 2014.
43 *Paradiso and Campanelli v Italy*, Grand Chamber, above n. 3, para. 154.

of a parental project and the quality of the emotional bonds, the Court considers that the conditions enabling it to conclude that there existed a *de facto* family life have not been met.'[44]

In the view of a joint dissenting opinion of five judges,[45] de facto family life did exist in this case. The minority argued that it is essentially a 'question of fact'[46] whether the close personal ties between the applicants and the child constituted de facto family life. The reason why they reached a different conclusion to the majority was as follows:

> 'For us it is important that the cohabitation started from the very day the child was born, lasted until the child was removed from the applicants, and would have continued indefinitely if the authorities had not intervened to bring it to an end. The majority dismiss this argument on the ground that the intervention was the consequence of the legal uncertainty created by the applicants themselves "by engaging in conduct that was contrary to Italian law and by coming to settle in Italy with the child" ... We fear that the majority thus make a distinction between a "legitimate" and an "illegitimate" family, a distinction that was rejected by the Court many years ago ..., and do not give full weight to the long-established principle that the existence or non-existence of "family life" is essentially a question of fact. Although the period of cohabitation was in itself relatively short, we consider that the applicants had acted as parents towards the child and conclude that there existed, in the particular circumstances of the present case, a *de facto* family life between the applicants and the child.'

One problem with this conclusion of the minority is that it does not really explain why from a factual point of view the eight-month cohabitation of one parent with the child, six months of which also involved the other parent, is sufficient to constitute de facto family life. It is an assertion rather than a reasoned opinion. The more normative problem with the approach of the dissent is that it does not seem to allow any analysis of the illegality of the formation of family life to come into the picture of determining the 'factual' question as to whether there is de facto family life. If one were to apply the approach of the dissenters what would prevent the formation of de facto family life when a couple kidnap a baby from an orphanage and look after the baby for eight months before they are caught by the police?

It is surely correct for the majority to treat the question of whether there is de facto family life as a mixed question of fact and law. It is permissible to take into account, as the majority does, 'the uncertainty of the ties from

---

44 Ibid, para. 157.

45 Joint dissenting opinion of Judges Lazarova, Trajkovska, Bianku, Laffranque, Lemmens and Grozev. It is not clear who the sixth dissenting judge was and what opinion he or she had in this case.

46 *Paradiso and Campanelli v Italy*, Grand Chamber, above n. 3, dissent, para. 3.

a legal perspective'. A couple who have created a connection with a child unlawfully, and know that the connection with the child could be severed by the relevant authorities at any time, should not have the status of a human right to respect for family life conferred on their relationship as quickly as a couple who tried to act legally in establishing their family. De facto family life should not depend simply on the fact that a person cares for a child for a few months but must take account of the legal context in which that came about. This means that a couple who are looking after a child, who was born to a surrogate in another country as part of an altruistic surrogacy arrangement, and who was willingly handed over by the surrogate to the commissioning parents could be treated as being in de facto family life with the child in a country that, in principle permits altruistic surrogacy, in the period before the authorities have legally conferred parental status on the commissioning parents. Whereas on the same facts in a country where even altruistic surrogacy arrangements are banned no such de facto family life would be created.

5.2. PRIVATE LIFE

5.2.1. Private Life v Family Life

Although the majority of the Grand Chamber did not find that there was de facto family life in *Paradiso and Campanelli* the court did find that there was an interference with the 'private life' of the applicants by the authorities taking away the child from them.[47] The court is not very clear on what the dividing line between 'family life' and 'private life' is. The latter seems to encompass 'the emotional bonds created and developed between an adult and a child in situations other than the classic situations of kinship.'[48] The court seems to want to include 'informal' parenting arrangements within the category of 'private life' rather than 'family life'. In doing so it cited *X v Switzerland*[49] in which a friend of a couple looked after their child for several years before the parents asked for the child back and the European Commission of Human Rights regarded the friend's rights to care for the child as falling within her private life under Art. 8 of the Convention. It seems much more logical to view that case as a de facto 'family life' case because the friend had been conferred the right to look after the child by the parents (no hint of unlawfulness) and had been doing so for such a long period that 'genuine personal ties' had developed between the friend and the child. The issue was surely whether after such a long period of time

---

47 See *Paradiso and Campanelli v Italy*, Grand Chamber, above n. 3, paras 161–63.
48 Ibid, para. 161.
49 *X v Switzerland* no. 8257/78, Commission Decision of 10 July 1978, Decisions and Reports 5.

the parents could just unilaterally insist on the child coming back to them. The Grand Chamber in *Paradiso* also seems to confuse 'private life' and 'family life' by arguing that the reason why there was an 'interference with the applicants' private life' was as follows:

> '[...] what is at issue is the right to respect for the applicants' decision to become parents ... and the applicants' personal development through the role of parents that they wished to assume *vis-à-vis* the child ... the Court concludes that the facts of the case fall within the scope of the applicants' private life.'[50]

In the present authors' view if the 'close personal ties' between an adult and a child are not enough to constitute de facto 'family life' then the removal of the child from the care of an adult should not be treated as an interference with their 'private life'.

5.2.2. Interference with the Private Lives of the Applicants

The Grand Chamber went on to consider whether there was an interference with the private lives of the applicants. It said:

> 'The Court considers that the measures taken in respect of the child – removal, placement in a home without contact with the applicants, being placed under guardianship – amounted to an interference with the applicants' private life.'[51]

The four judges in the majority that issued a Joint Concurring Opinion were critical of the lack of clarity from their colleagues in the Grand Chamber majority judgment as to why the applicants' private life was found to be interfered with in this case.[52]

In relation to the question whether this interference was 'in accordance with the law' the Grand Chamber said that this:

> '[...] not only requires that the impugned measure should have some basis in domestic law, but also refers to the quality of the law in question, requiring that it should be accessible to the person concerned and foreseeable as to its effects ...
>
> In the present case the domestic courts applied the Italian rule on conflict of laws which provides that the legal parent-child relationship is determined by the national law governing the child at the time of his or her birth (Private International Law Act ...). However, as the child had been conceived from the gametes of unknown donors, his nationality was not established in the eyes of the Italian courts.

50 *Paradiso and Campanelli v Italy*, Grand Chamber, above n. 3, paras 163–64.
51 Ibid, para. 166.
52 *Paradiso and Campanelli v Italy*, Grand Chamber, above n. 3, Joint Concurring Opinion of Judges De Gaetano, Pinto de Albuquerque, Wojtyczek and Dedov, para. 5.

> Section 37bis of the Adoption Act provides that, for the purposes of adoption, placement and urgent measures, Italian law is applicable to foreign minors who are in Italy … The situation of the child T.C., whose nationality was unknown, and who had been born abroad to unknown biological parents, was equated with that of a foreign minor.
>
> In such a situation, the Court considers that the application of Italian law by the national courts, giving rise to the finding that the child was in a "state of abandonment", was foreseeable.
>
> It follows that the interference with the applicants' private life was in accordance with the law.'[53]

The Grand Chamber also decided that the action of Italy in this case had a legitimate aim:

> 'In so far as the applicants' conduct ran counter to the Adoption Act and the Italian prohibition on heterologous artificial reproduction techniques, the Grand Chamber accepts the Chamber's view that the measures taken in respect of the child pursued the aim of "preventing disorder". Moreover, it accepts that those measures were also intended to protect the "rights and freedoms" of others. The Court regards as legitimate under Article 8 §2 the Italian authorities' wish to reaffirm the State's exclusive competence to recognise a legal parent-child relationship – and this solely in the case of a biological tie or lawful adoption – with a view to protecting children.'[54]

In relation to whether the measures taken by Italy were necessary in a democratic society the Grand Chamber said the following:

> 'According to the Court's established case-law, the notion of necessity implies that the interference corresponds to a pressing social need and, in particular, that it is proportionate to the legitimate aim pursued, regard being had to the fair balance which has to be struck between the relevant competing interests … In determining whether an interference was "necessary in a democratic society" the Court will take into account that a margin of appreciation is left to the national authorities, whose decision remains subject to review by the Court for conformity with the requirements of the Convention …
>
> While the authorities enjoy a wide margin of appreciation in the area of adoption (see Wagner …) or in assessing the necessity of taking a child into care …, in particular where an emergency situation arises, the Court must still be satisfied in the particular case that there existed circumstances justifying the removal of the child …'[55]

53 *Paradiso and Campanelli v Italy*, Grand Chamber, above n. 3, paras. 169–74.
54 Ibid, para. 177.
55 Ibid, paras 180–83.

5.2.3. *The Margin of Appreciation*

On the margin of appreciation the Grand Chamber stated that:

> 'The Court observes that the facts of the case touch on ethically sensitive issues – adoption, the taking of a child into care, medically assisted reproduction and surrogate motherhood – in which member States enjoy a wide margin of appreciation ...
>
> In contrast to the situation in the Mennesson judgment ... the questions of the child's identity and recognition of genetic descent do not arise in the present case since, on the one hand, any failure by the State to provide the child with an identity cannot be pleaded by the applicants, who do not represent him before the Court and, on the other, there are no biological links between the child and the applicants. In addition, the present case does not concern the choice to become genetic parents, an area in which the State's margin of appreciation is restricted.'[56]

The contrast with *Mennesson* is very important because it implies that the Grand Chamber may accept the decision of the Chamber in that case that if one of the commissioning parents is also a genetic parent that greatly narrows the margin of appreciation of the State and makes it difficult for the State to remove the child from their genetic parent without violating the child's human rights, even when the child came into the world through a commercial surrogacy arrangement. However, four judges in the majority in the Grand Chamber issued a joint concurring opinion arguing that commercial surrogacy is contrary to human dignity and is illegal under international law.[57]

5.2.4. *Relevant and Sufficient Reasons*

On relevant and sufficient reasons, the Grand Chamber observed that the Italian authorities had relied on the illegality of the applicants' behaviour and the need to take urgent measures in relation to the child, who was considered to be 'in the state of abandonment'.[58] The Grand Chamber acknowledged these reasons as being relevant and directly connected with 'the legitimate aim of preventing disorder'.[59] With regard to the question of sufficiency of these reasons, the Grand Chamber reiterated that, given its conclusion in respect of 'family life' in the given case, the application was to be examined from the perspective of the applicants' right to respect for their private life, 'bearing in mind that what was at stake was their right to personal development through their relationship with

---

56 Ibid, paras 194–95.

57 Judges De Gaetano, Pinto de Albuquerque, Wojtyczek and Dedov JJ, De Gaetano, Pinto de Albuquerque, Wojtyczek and Dedov.

58 *Paradiso and Campanelli v Italy*, Grand Chamber, above n. 3, para. 196.

59 Ibid, para. 197.

the child'.[60] Without further analysis, the Grand Chamber concluded that the reasons given by the Italian courts 'were sufficient'.[61]

The Grand Chamber reached the correct decision on reviewing the relevance and sufficiency of the reasons why the national authorities took the child away from the applicants but the Grand Chamber's reasoning on 'sufficiency' could be said to be rather minimal if not even 'insufficient'.

5.2.5. *Proportionality*

In relation to proportionality, the Grand Chamber acknowledged that the laws which had been breached by the applicants[62] and the measures which the Italian authorities took in response to the applicants' conduct 'served to protect very weighty public interests'.[63] The domestic courts 'had to make a difficult choice between allowing the applicants to continue their relationship with the child, thereby legalising the unlawful situation created by them as a fait accompli, or taking measures with a view to providing the child with a family in accordance with the legislation on adoption.'[64] The Grand Chamber noted that, before concluding that the separation of the child from the applicants would not cause the child 'grave or irreparable harm', the Italian courts properly assessed the child's specific situation, and their reasoning in this respect was not 'automatic or stereotyped'.[65] In contrast, the domestic courts did not expressly address the effect of the separation from the child on the applicant's private life; however, this has to be considered in the context of the illegality of the applicant's behaviour and the lack of a biological link between the child and either of the applicants.[66] The applicants also complained that the procedure before Italian authorities had suffered from a number of deficiencies, in particular that the Italian courts did not accept an expert opinion submitted by the applicants, and that the courts did not explore alternatives to the separation from the child. The Grand Chamber, however, disagreed with both submissions. In relation to the former it pointed out that the 'Minors Court is a specialised court which sits with two professional judges and two expert members'.[67] As to the latter the Grand Chamber highlighted the fact that the proceedings were urgent and '[a]ny measure prolonging the child's stay with the applicants, such as placing him in their temporary care, would have carried the risk that the mere passage of

---

60 Ibid, para. 198.
61 Ibid, para. 199.
62 In particular, the prohibition of surrogacy arrangements and private adoptions based on contract under Italian law. Ibid, paras 202 and 203.
63 Ibid, para. 204.
64 Ibid, para. 209.
65 Ibid, para. 210.
66 Ibid, para. 211.
67 Ibid, para. 212.

time would have determined the outcome of the case'.[68] Accordingly, the measures taken by the Italian authorities were held proportionate to the legitimate aims pursued, i.e. that they have struck a fair balance between the competing public and private interests.

5.2.6. *Conclusion*

The Grand Chamber's final conclusion was:

> 'The Court does not underestimate the impact which the immediate and irreversible separation from the child must have had on the applicants' private life. While the Convention does not recognise a right to become a parent, the Court cannot ignore the emotional hardship suffered by those whose desire to become parents has not been or cannot be fulfilled. However, the public interests at stake weigh heavily in the balance, while comparatively less weight is to be attached to the applicants' interest in their personal development by continuing their relationship with the child. Agreeing to let the child stay with the applicants, possibly with a view to becoming his adoptive parents, would have been tantamount to legalising the situation created by them in breach of important rules of Italian law. The Court accepts that the Italian courts, having assessed that the child would not suffer grave or irreparable harm from the separation, struck a fair balance between the different interests at stake, while remaining within the wide margin of appreciation available to them in the present case.
>
> It follows that there has been no violation of Article 8 of the Convention.'[69]

6. THE WAY FORWARD

6.1. INTERNATIONAL CONVENTION ON SURROGACY

There is a need for a truly multilateral approach whereby an international Convention on surrogacy, which would depart from the traditional method of the unification of the conflicts rules, would be developed.[70] This would help to solve the problem at its source in countries which permit commercial

[68] Ibid, para 213.

[69] Ibid, paras 215–16.

[70] For a detailed outline of a potential Convention on surrogacy see K. Trimmings and P. Beaumont, 'General Report on Surrogacy', above n. 35, pp. 531–49. Other commentators advocating a hard law Treaty solution along the lines of the 1993 Hague Adoption Convention have taken a slightly more restrained approach towards the utility of the Adoption Convention in the surrogacy context. See e.g. H. Van Loon, 'The Global Horizon of Private International Law' (2016) 380 *Recueil des Cours* 76; and H. Baker, 'A Possible Future Instrument on International Surrogacy Arrangements: Are There "Lessons" to be Learnt from the 1993 Hague Intercountry Adoption Convention?' in K. Trimmings and P. Beaumont, above n. 1, p. 411 (See K. Smith Rotabi and N. Bromfield, *From Intercountry*

surrogacy and are happy for foreign commissioning parents to take advantage of this service. Rather than focusing on traditional rules on jurisdiction and applicable law, the Convention should establish a framework for international cooperation with emphasis on the need for substantive safeguards and on procedures for courts, administrative authorities and private intermediaries. The Convention would be based on a pre-approval system and would not only seek to tackle the problem of legal parenthood but also to protect the people involved (notably commissioning parents, surrogates, and, above all, the intended child(ren)) and to regulate the cross-border surrogacy market. The Convention should draw inspiration from the highly successful 1993 Hague Intercountry Adoption Convention which is also based on the principle of cooperation between the country of origin and the receiving country and on the need to regulate international adoptions to protect the people involved, especially the children.[71] Regulation has the benefits of: reducing the risks of

Adoption to Global Surrogacy A Human Rights History and New Fertility Frontiers, Routledge, London 2017, for a detailed social science-oriented analysis of the differences and similarities between intercountry adoption and cross-border surrogacy). Yet other commentators have highlighted the need for an approach rooted primarily in the human rights perspective. See e.g. M. Wells-Greco, *The Status of Children Arising from Inter-Country Surrogacy Arrangements*, above n. 34; C. Fenton-Glynn, 'Review Article: Human Rights and Private International Law: Regulating International Surrogacy' (2014) 10 *JPIL (Journal of Private International Law)* 157; R. Blauwhoff and L. Frohn, 'International Commercial Surrogacy Arrangements: The Interests of the Child as a Concern of Both Human Rights and Private International Law' in C. Paulssen et al. (eds), *Fundamental Rights in International and European Law – Public and Private Law Perspectives*, Asser Institute, The Hague 2016, pp. 211–41; and B. Stark, 'Transnational Surrogacy and International Human Rights Law' (2012) 18 *ILSA Journal of International and Comparative Law* 369. Alternative proposals have centred either around a complete global ban on surrogacy (see e.g. U. Smerdon, 'Crossing Bodies, Crossing Borders: International Surrogacy Agreements between the United States and India' (2009) 60 *Cumberland Law Review* 81; and S. Allan, 'Governing Transnational Surrogacy Practices: What Role Can National and International Regulation Play?' in M. Davies (ed.), *Babies for Sale? Transnational Surrogacy, Human Rights and the Politics of Reproduction*, Zed Books, London 2017), or the need for a domestic regulation of surrogacy that would deter commissioning parents from seeking to commission surrogacy abroad (see e.g. C. Fenton-Glynn, 'Outsourcing Ethical Dilemmas: Regulating International Surrogacy Arrangements' (2016) 24 *Medical Law Review* 59). For an exploration of regulatory options at the EU level see European Parliament, 'A Comparative Study on the Regime of Surrogacy in EU Member States' 2013, <http://www.europarl.europa.eu/RegData/etudes/STUD/2013/474403/IPOL-JURI_ET(2013)474403_EN.pdf> accessed 11.09.2018. See also C. Thomale, 'State of Play of Cross-Border Surrogacy Arrangements – Is There a Case for Regulatory Intervention by the EU?', <http://www.ipr.uni-heidelberg.de/md/jura/ipr/personen/weller/europaparlament_policy_hub_statement.pdf> accessed 11.09.2018, wisely suggesting that the EU should refrain from regulating on the problem of cross-border surrogacy and instead support relevant global initiatives.

71 Hague Convention on Protection of Children and Co-operation in Respect of Intercountry Adoption 1993. The Convention is one of the most successful family law instruments that has been developed under the auspices of the Hague Conference on Private International Law. As of March 2017, there were 98 Contracting States to the Convention. See Hague Conference on Private International Law, 'Convention of 29 May 1993 on Protection of Children and

exploitation of surrogates by middlemen (e.g. those operating fertility clinics) and sometimes by commissioning parents; of creating mechanisms to screen out commissioning parents who are a potential danger to children; of ensuring that commissioning mothers, whether genetically linked to the child or not, are treated equally with genetically linked commissioning fathers as the legal parents; and ensuring that children will be able to trace their surrogate and understand their complex identity when they become adults.

Recent developments at the Hague Conference on Private International Law demonstrate the pressing need for global regulation of cross-border surrogacy.[72] At the Council on General Affairs and Policy meeting in March 2015, it was decided that an Experts' Group be set up to explore the feasibility of further work in the area of international surrogacy arrangements.[73] The first meeting of the Experts' Group was held in February 2016[74] and the work of the Group is still ongoing.[75]

The work of the Hague Conference on Private International Law was noted by the Grand Chamber in *Paradiso*:

> 'The Hague Conference thus considered that there is now a pressing human rights requirement, including from the perspective of children's rights, for its work in "this area"'.[76]

Co-operation in Respect of Intercountry Adoption: Status Table' <https://www.hcch.net/en/instruments/conventions/status-table/?cid=69> accessed 11.09.2018. K. Trimmings and P. Beaumont, 'General Report on Surrogacy', above n. 35, and following and developing that approach see Y. Margalit, 'From Baby M to Baby M(anji): Regulating International Surrogacy Arrangements' (2016) 24 *Journal of Law and Policy* 41 <https://works.bepress.com/hezi_margalit/14/> accessed 11.09.2018.

72 See Hague Conference website, section 'Parentage/Surrogacy Project' <https://www.hcch.net/en/projects/legislative-projects/parentage-surrogacy> accessed 11.09.2018.

73 Hague Conference on Private International Law, 'Council on General Affairs and Policy of the Conference: Conclusions and Recommendations', March 2015, para. 5, <http://www.hcch.net/upload/wop/gap2015concl_en.pdf> accessed 11.09.2018.

74 The Group concluded that work should continue, whilst its focus should be primarily on recognition. Hague Conference on Private International Law, 'Report of the February 2016 Meeting of the Experts' Group on Parentage / Surrogacy', February 2016, para. 16, <https://www.hcch.net/en/news-archive/details/?varevent=470> accessed 11.09.2018. This view was endorsed by the Hague Council on General Affairs and Policy in its Conclusions and Recommendations at the March 2016 Council, see no. 15 <https://assets.hcch.net/docs/55122e44-d132-441f-a1f3-d4c543c99e97.pdf> accessed 11.09.2018. It is suggested here that this is a rather narrow approach, focusing on 'recognition', which does not adequately address the complex nature of a cross-border surrogacy arrangement. For an overview of possible future approaches as considered prior to the Experts' Group meeting, see Preliminary Document no. 3 of March 2014, Hague Conference on Private International Law, 'The Desirability and Feasibility of Further Work on the Surrogacy/Parentage Project', paras 44–47 and 52–60 <http://www.hcch.net/upload/wop/gap2015pd03b_en.pdf> accessed 11.09.2018.

75 The next meeting of the Expert Group is scheduled to take place in February 2019. See Hague Conference on Private International Law, 'Council on General Affairs and Policy of the Conference: Conclusions & Recommendations', March 2018, para 6, <https://assets.hcch.net/docs/715fc166-2d40-4902-8c6c-e98b3def3b92.pdf> accessed 15.10.2018.

76 *Paradiso and Campanelli v Italy*, Grand Chamber, above n. 3, para. 80.

It is to be hoped that the Experts' Group and the Hague Council on General Affairs and Policy quickly come to realise that an *ex post facto* solution based on recognition of parentage is not a satisfactory way forward for surrogacy and instead bite the bullet and press forward with a regulatory solution in order to protect the rights of the vulnerable (notably the putative child and the surrogate). However, the early signs are not encouraging. The Experts' Group met from 31 January to 3 February 2017 and reached the following conclusions and recommendations as to its future work.

[T]he Group agreed:

> 'a) in principle, on the feasibility of developing a binding multilateral instrument dealing with the recognition of foreign judicial decisions on legal parentage. Further consideration and discussion are needed on how such an instrument could operate;
>
> b) that owing to the diversity of approaches with respect to the determination of legal parentage and the recognition of the legal parentage when recorded in a public document, further consideration and discussion are needed in relation to this issue;
>
> c) that owing to the complexity of the subject and the diversity of approaches by States in cases of ISAs, definitive conclusions could not be reached at this meeting as to the feasibility of the possible application of future agreed general PIL rules on legal parentage to ISAs and the possible need for additional rules and safeguards in these cases and in cases of ART. The Group concluded that further consideration and discussion of these matters are needed.
>
> The Group therefore recommends to Council that its mandate be continued to work on these matters, noting the urgency already identified. In this regard, the Group also recommends that Council direct the Permanent Bureau to undertake the necessary work with a view to preparing a next meeting of the Group and to allocate resources accordingly.'[77]

However, a recognition of parentage Convention would probably leave most of the important issues open and not resolve the human rights issues referred to by the ECtHR. The fundamental problem with a recognition Convention in this context is that for many states this will only be possible in relation to foreign judgments (see the conclusion from the Experts' Group above). In that limited context the question of whether to recognise the parentage of the commissioning parents in a surrogacy arrangement (especially any parent with no genetic link to the child) would ultimately be left to the decision of individual national courts in each Contracting State determining whether the recognition of that particular

---

[77] See Hague Conference on Private International Law, 'Report of the Experts' Group on the Parentage/Surrogacy Project', February 2017, para. 38 <https://assets.hcch.net/docs/ed997a8d-bdcb-48eb-9672-6d0535249d0e.pdf> accessed 11.09.2018.

foreign judgment granting parentage is contrary to the receiving state's public policy. The further question as to whether the child should be removed from his or her commissioning parent(s) if the foreign judgment was not recognised on grounds of public policy would not be regulated by the Convention either. It will probably not be possible to agree to recognition of foreign status documents or to harmonised applicable law rules regarding parentage.[78]

Given that reaching consensus in The Hague Conference on Private International Law on the need for a Convention providing for a regulatory solution to the problem of cross-border surrogacy seems like a medium to long-term objective the present authors will explore below the value of a project seeking to develop global soft law principles for the handling of cross-border surrogacy arrangements.

6.2. PRINCIPLES FOR BETTER PROTECTION OF THE HUMAN RIGHTS OF CHILDREN IN CROSS-BORDER SURROGACY

In July 2013, the International Social Service (ISS) issued a call for action titled 'International Surrogacy and Donor Conceived Persons: "Preserving the Best Interest of Children"', where it noted an increasingly frequent occurrence of surrogacy cases within its casework and called for a coordinated action to tackle the legal and ethical problems inherent in this practice.[79] The document suggested that such an action should take account of a variety of perspectives by involving specialists from diverse backgrounds, in particular 'international legal, social service, psycho-social and child advocacy communities'.[80] Building on this proposal, in February 2016 the ISS issued a second call for action in respect of cross-border surrogacy titled 'Urgent need for regulation of international surrogacy and artificial reproductive technologies'.[81] In this document, the ISS pointed out that unregulated cross-border surrogacy paved the way for 'very lucrative business opportunities' as well as 'potentially worrying activities and practices of intermediary agencies, specialized clinics and candidates for parenthood'.[82] It called for a regulatory initiative embedded in the children's rights perspective, in particular 'the rights of children to be protected from

[78] Ibid.

[79] International Social Service, General Secretariat, 'International Surrogacy and Donor Conceived Persons: "Preserving the Best Interest of Children": Call for Action by the International Social Service Network', July 2013 <http://www.iss-ssi.org/images/Surrogacy/Call_for_Action2013_ANG.pdf> accessed 11.09.2018.

[80] Ibid.

[81] International Social Service, 'Call for Action 2016: Urgent Need for Regulation of International Surrogacy and Artificial Reproductive Technologies', February 2016 <http://www.iss-ssi.org/images/Surrogacy/Call_for_Action2016.pdf> accessed 11.09.2018.

[82] Ibid.

being sold', referring to the specific circumstances of unregulated cross-border surrogacy.[83] This approach finds its starting point in relevant human rights treaties, in particular, the United Nations Convention on the Rights of the Child[84] (UNCRC) and its Optional Protocol to the Convention on the Rights of the Child on the sale of children, child prostitution and child pornography.[85]

Following the 2016 call, the ISS established a group of experts from a variety of backgrounds to develop a set of principles that would provide a much-needed international human rights framework, comprehensively addressing a wide range of relevant issues from a multi-disciplinary perspective.[86]

The project, which is purely literature based, aims to target two key research questions:

1. What considerations (human rights/legal/psycho-social/medical/political and ethical) should be taken into account to protect children's rights born through cross-border surrogacy?
2. How should these considerations be translated into concrete principles to safeguard the human rights protection of children born through cross-border surrogacy?

In order to answer the above research questions, the project coordinates a process of multidisciplinary research, analysing the various aspects of cross-border surrogacy. The main objective is to establish a set of approximately 20 principles for the concrete protection of the human rights of children born through cross-border surrogacy. These could be considered as minimum

---

83 Ibid. The document refers to the following finding by the Committee on the Rights of the Child: 'Commercial use of surrogacy, which is not properly regulated, is widespread, leading to the sale of children and the violation of children's rights.' Committee on the Rights of the Child, 'Convention on the Rights of the Child: Concluding Observations on the Combined Third and Fourth Periodic Reports of India', 2014 <http://tbinternet.ohchr.org/_layouts/treatybodyexternal/Download.aspx?symbolno=CRC%2fC%2fIND%2fCO%2f3-4&Lang=en> accessed 11.09.2018.

84 United Nations Convention on the Rights of the Child, 2 September 1990, available at <http://www.ohchr.org/EN/ProfessionalInterest/Pages/CRC.aspx> accessed 11.09.2018.

85 Optional Protocol to the Convention on the Rights of the Child on the sale of children, child prostitution and child pornography, 18 January 2002 <http://www.ohchr.org/EN/ProfessionalInterest/Pages/OPSCCRC.aspx> accessed 11.09.2018. See D. Smolin, 'Surrogacy as the Sale of Children: Applying Lessons Learned from Adoption to the Regulation of the Surrogacy Industry's Global Marketing of Children', Samford University, Selected Works, 2015 <https://works.bepress.com/david_smolin/19/> accessed 11.09.2018. More generally, see UNICEF, 'Handbook on the Optional Protocol on the Sale of Children, Child Prostitution and Child Pornography', 2009 <https://www.unicef-irc.org/publications/pdf/optional_protocol_eng.pdf> accessed 11.09.2018.

86 'Principles for a better protection of children's rights in cross-border reproductive arrangements, in particular international surrogacy'. See International Social Service, 'Call for Action 2016', above n. 81.

elements for the development and implementation of relevant domestic, regional and international instruments, policies and practices in this regard.

Each principle will be supported by an explanatory text, focusing on the following considerations:

1. Human rights considerations: with a focus on the approaches and/or opinions expressed by the various United Nations bodies and instruments, as well as at regional level, such as within the European Union and the European and Inter-American human rights systems;
2. Legal considerations: with a focus on how different jurisdictions have responded to surrogacy. As a part of this element, the differences between domestic legislation, relevant case law and existing good practices as well as customary international standards will be explored;
3. Psycho-social and medical considerations: with a focus on the identification of risks throughout the whole process, its follow-up and with an emphasis on promising practices that may provide useful practical and ethical responses to the identified risks (including a review and comparative study of the lessons learned from intercountry adoption);
4. Political considerations: with a focus on the (shared) responsibility and cooperation needed amongst the various actors involved (governmental bodies, specific institutions, intermediary agencies, civil society organisations, etc);
5. Ethical considerations: with a focus on the dignity of the human person, commercialisation and commodification of persons and of the processes of human procreation, exploitation and inequality, ethical evaluation of claimed rights to procreate, and ethical aspects of splitting biological motherhood and of legal parenthood regimes based on intent or contract.

The project is coordinated by the ISS, with the research work being carried out jointly by the ISS and a core group of experts. In order to ensure the inclusion of a variety of opinions, a platform to foster constant exchanges has been established in the form of the project advisory group. This platform serves as a consultative and advisory body where complex issues are shared and discussed. In order to galvanise support for the principles at international level, several expert consultations have been planned to disseminate preliminary findings and consider eventual commentary.[87] This will be followed by advocacy efforts

[87] The first expert consultation was held between the 18.05.2017 and 20.05.2017 at the University of Verona, Italy. This was followed by the second expert consultation which was held at the University of Zürich, Switzerland between the 31.01.2018 and 02.02.2018.

undertaken at the United Nations Human Rights Council[88] and through the United Nations treaty body system,[89] facilitated by the fact that some members of the advisory group are members of United Nations bodies or already closely working with them. A launch event to disseminate final principles at an international arena will also be arranged. Advocacy efforts will then be undertaken to promote international endorsement.

7. CONCLUSION

Although the ECtHR has provided useful guidance on certain aspects of cross-border surrogacy arrangements, there is still an urgent need for a multilateral solution in the form of an international Convention on surrogacy. In order for such a Convention to be able to truly tackle the pressing problems inherent in cross-border surrogacy, it must depart from traditional rules on jurisdiction, applicable law and recognition. Instead, the Convention should follow the model of the 1993 Hague Intercountry Adoption Convention, in particular, through establishing a framework for international cooperation with emphasis on the need for substantive safeguards and on procedures for courts, administrative authorities and private intermediaries. The solution currently under consideration at the Hague Conference on Private International Law, i.e. a Convention aimed solely at the recognition of parentage, is likely to leave most of the important issues open and not resolve the relevant human rights issues, referred to also by the ECtHR in *Paradiso and Campanelli*. In any case, whatever the form of the future Convention, given the variety of domestic legal approaches to surrogacy reaching consensus at the Hague Conference is likely to be a lengthy process. Therefore, there is a need to develop global soft law principles, guided by multidisciplinary considerations, which would serve as a framework for the protection of children born from cross-border surrogacy. The principles would provide guidance and inform legislators, judges and policymakers in different jurisdictions to ensure that legal problems arising from cross-border surrogacy are adequately addressed and children's and women's rights are protected.

---

88 The UN Human Rights Council is an inter-governmental body within the United Nations responsible for the worldwide promotion and protection of human rights. See <http://www.ohchr.org/en/hrbodies/hrc/pages/hrcindex.aspx> accessed 11.09.2018.

89 Such as a UN General Assembly resolution or a General Comment. See, generally, United Nations, 'General Assembly Resolutions' <http://www.un.org/en/sections/documents/general-assembly-resolutions/index.html> accessed 11.09.2018; and United Nations Human Rights Office of the High Commissioner, 'Human Rights Treaty Bodies – General Comments' <http://www.ohchr.org/EN/HRBodies/Pages/TBGeneralComments.aspx> accessed 11.09.2017.

PART II

EASTERN PERSPECTIVES

THE PROHIBITIVE APPROACH

SURROGACY IN CHINA

Lei SHI*

1. GENERAL LEGAL FRAMEWORK

1.1. LEGAL RULES AND REGULATIONS

There is currently no specific law regulating surrogacy in China. One important judicial interpretation concerning artificial reproductive technology (hereinafter referred to as 'ART') is the Reply on How to Determine the Legal Position of the Child Born Through Artificial Insemination after Divorce (《关于夫妻离婚后人工授精所生子女的法律地位如何确定的复函》) issued on 8 July 1991 by the Supreme People's Court (hereinafter referred to as the Reply of the Supreme Court in 1991). According to this judicial interpretation, if both parties to a marriage agree to have a child through artificial insemination before the marriage ends, such a child should be regarded as the legitimate child of both parents. Relevant provisions of the Marriage Law should be applied regarding the rights and obligations between parents and children. But it is clear that this Reply can only be applied in legal artificial insemination procedures where the birth mother is married to the father, so in judicial practice this is not

* This is an initial result of a social science planned project in Chongqing, China (2016BS097) and the research project 'Regulation of Surrogacy and Its Related Problems' (2015XZQN-21). The author adopts a restrictive meaning of 'law', not including administrative rules and regulations.

applied when deciding the parent-child relationship concerning a child born from surrogacy.

Since surrogacy cannot be accomplished without medical assistance, the Ministry of Health[1] addressed this area first and issued the Procedures on the Administration of Human Assisted Reproductive Technology (《人类辅助生殖技术管理办法》) on 1 August 2001. This document imposes restrictions on the application of ART. It states that ART can only be implemented in medical institutions approved by the administrative department of health, and only for medical purposes in accordance with national family planning policies, ethical principles and provisions of the relevant laws. Meanwhile, Art. 3 in this regulation stipulates that the sale of gametes, zygotes and embryos in any form is prohibited and medical institutions and medical personnel cannot perform any form of surrogate technology. This document therefore makes clear that any medical staff should not be involved in surrogacy. Article 22 further stipulates that any health institution involved in surrogacy would be given an admonition and a 30,000 RMB fine by the provincial health authorities.

In the same year, the Ministry of Health also issued a Code of Practice of Human Assisted Reproductive Technology (《人类辅助生殖技术规范》), Basic Standards for Human Sperm Banks (《人类精子库基本标准》), a Code of Practice of Technology Concerning Human Sperm Banks (《人类精子库技术规范》), as well as Ethical Principles of Performing Human Assisted Reproductive Technology (《实施人类辅助生殖技术的伦理原则》) (hereinafter referred to as Code of Practice, Basic Standards and Ethical Principles) on 14 May. Two years later, the Ministry of Health then revised the Code of Practice, Basic Standard and Ethical Principles. These rules continue to prohibit any performance of surrogacy as well as other controversial technologies such as stimulating ovulation to achieve multiple births and providing eggs for commercial purposes.

Notably, the Procedures on the Administration of Human Assisted Reproductive Technology and the Code of Practice, Basic Standards and Ethical Principles are only medical administrative documents regulating doctors and medical institutions. Therefore it is difficult to impose punishment on agencies introducing surrogacy and surrogates in accordance with these documents.

Lack of a specific law leads to social chaos in reality. Surrogacy agencies have sprung up in big cities. With media reports on this problem, the legislature tried to deal with this. When amending the Population and Family Planning Law of PRC (《中国人口与计划生育法》) at the end of 2015, lawmakers added Art. 5 in this amendment draft which expressly stipulates that any medical or health institutions with qualified doctors and technicians, facilities and

1 On 17 March 2013, the Ministry of Health was replaced by the National Health and Family Planning Commission.

equipment, ethics review panel and relevant supervising regulations can carry out ART with the approval of province-level health administrative agencies, but surrogacy expressly is prohibited. A new Art. 6 further provides criminal sanctions for those violating Art. 5.[2] However, the no-surrogacy article led to heated debate. Some lawmakers argued that the present problems of surrogacy should be examined thoroughly, the public should be consulted, and only afterwards the law on ART should be drafted. Social chaos on surrogacy thus could be controlled by specific rules. Others point out that although the sale of gametes, zygotes and embryos in any form should be completely prohibited, there is reasonable social need of surrogacy by infertile women or those losing their chance of giving birth to babies in other ways. It was argued that it would be inhuman to deny these people access to medical techniques, including surrogacy, to become a mother. The legal committee of National People's Congress (hereinafter referred to as NPC) later concluded that this article is not directly relevant to the family planning policies and surrogacy needs further study.[3] Therefore, this article and Art. 6 were finally repealed and the status quo of no legal provisions in statutory laws regarding surrogacy still exists.

1.2. REGULATORY AUTHORITY

At present, no specialised authority has been set up to oversee surrogacy in China. The supervision is mainly conducted by the health authorities. But due to its terms of reference, local health departments only have authority to regulate the doctor's professional conduct, that means any doctor assisting with the surrogacy procedure would be punished under professional regulations, and his or her professional license would be cancelled due to this violation. The local administration bureaus for industry and commerce would not do anything since no laws and rules prohibit surrogacy agency. Neither would the bureau of public security take any measures to delete surrogacy advertisements

---

2 This provision provides that those carrying out ART without a licence, sale of gametes, zygotes and embryos, performing surrogacy, etc. should be given an admonition, and asked for correction by relevant family planning departments or health departments in accordance with their power. The illegal income from these activities should be seized. If the illegal gains exceed 10,000 yuan, the responsible party should be fined no less than twice but not more than six times the sum of the illegal gains. If there are no illegal gains or the gains are less than 10,000 yuan, the responsible party should be fined over 10,000 yuan but not more than 30,000 yuan. If the circumstances are serious, the medical practice certificate shall be revoked by the original issuing institution. If there is a criminal offence, the criminal responsibility shall be borne according to law.

3 NPC Legal Committee's Report on the Results of Reviewing the Draft of the Population and Family Planning Law of PRC, 2016(1) *Bulletin of the Standing Committee of National People's Congress* <全国人民代表大会常务委员会公报> 75.

from the internet.[4] However, in order to deal with illegal surrogacies under the present Procedures on the Administration of Human Assisted Reproductive Technology, the relevant authorities took some measures. The latest one is from April 2015, in which the National Health and Family Planning Commission, as a leader, with the help of the other 12 ministries such as the Ministry of Public Security, the Ministry of Civil Affairs, the Ministry of Industry and Information Technology, etc., carried out a special mission to shut down surrogacy nationwide till the end of that year.

It is important to note that surrogacy continues to be considered prohibited by health professionals. Chunsheng Zhang, head of the National Health and Family Planning Commission, said that despite the amendment legislation to the Population and Family Planning Law of PRC (in effect since the beginning of 2016) which deleted a clause that made surrogacy illegal, surrogacy is still not allowed because of a ban of the service in two central government documents overseeing other infertility treatment technology and sperm banks.[5]

1.3. RELEVANT STATISTICS

National statistics on surrogacy do not exist. The estimated number of surrogate births in China was reported to be a number between 5,000 to 10,000 per year according to American news sources. The estimated number of surrogacy agencies in 2014 reached around 1,000.[6] It is further estimated that about 1,000 commissioning parents went to the United States to use surrogacy services each year.[7]

2. SURROGACY ARRANGEMENTS IN GENERAL

In China, those willing to find a surrogate usually enter into surrogacy contracts through an intermediary such as a surrogacy agency. However, if the People's Court had to decide a dispute concerning such a surrogacy contract, the contract would be deemed to be invalid based on basic principles stipulated in the General Principles of the Civil Law of PRC (hereinafter referred to as

---

4 Y. Luo, 'How to Regulate Surrogacy Agency, Relevant Authorities Said They Have No Control', *Changjiang Times* <长江商报>, 15.10.2009.

5 J.Y. Liu, 'Crackdown on Surrogacy 'to Continue' Even as Ban Idea Dropped', Caixin Online <财新网>, <http://english.caixin.com/2015-12-29/100894062.html> accessed 13.09.2018.

6 Y.Y. Wang (ed.), 'Black Market of Surrogacy Uncovered by New York Times, Demand of Surrogate Exceeds Supply', *Reference News* <参考消息>, 17.08.2014.

7 Y.L. Sun, 'Around Thousand Couples in China Found Surrogate in USA per Year', *Yangcheng Evening News* <羊城晚报>, 31.03.2015.

'GPCL', 《中国民法通则》) since it involves personal rights and duties which cannot be freely agreed, and because it violates public policy.[8] Therefore, there are no legal remedies for any breach of surrogacy contracts. Thus, a surrogate mother cannot get her payment by law if the commissioning parents do not pay. Similarly, if the surrogate breaks the contract and does not hand over the child, the commissioning parents cannot demand that she does so.

While it can be said that to some extent surrogacy agencies play an important role to make the surrogacy arrangement work, given that they are working in an unregulated, almost 'black market' environment means that the surrogacy contracts are illegal and the basic rights and interests of surrogates and commissioning parents are poorly protected, if at all. That is why some Chinese couples choose to go abroad for a surrogate, for example, the United States. While there is no data on the total number of Chinese who have sought or used US surrogates, agencies in both countries say demand has risen rapidly in the first two years of the 2010s.[9]

3. LEGAL PARENTHOOD AT THE TIME OF BIRTH

The Marriage Law of PRC (《中国婚姻法》) in China has only 51 articles. In order to get the law understood by as many people as possible (especially in a country with a big population like China), the law uses simpler words and comparatively less articles than other laws. With regards to parent-child relationship, Art. 25 stipulates that an illegitimate child shall have the same rights as a legitimate child, and shall not be harmed or discriminated against by any person. This is the only provision which has express reference to legitimacy. No definition of a legitimate child can be found, and thus there is no guidance on which basis a child can acquire its position as legitimate in law. Although the statute is not satisfactory, the judicial practice uses other guidelines issued by the People's Supreme Court to hear such cases. In 1956, the People's Supreme Court issued a reply, that is the Reply on How to Determine the Paternity of Xiao Miao born to Xu Xiu Mei (《关于徐秀梅所生的小苗应如何断定生父问题的复函》). This reply expressly proposes a principle to identify the legal father of a child, that is, a child born during a marriage should be a child to the husband and the wife in this marriage. The husband is the child's legal father. Any husband willing to deny paternity must prove that there is no cohabitation when the wife

---

8 The principle of public policy can be found at Art. 10 of the General Rules of the Civil Law ('GRCL') in force since 01.10.2017. However, this new law does not make the GPCL void.

9 A. Harney, 'Rich Chinese Hire American Surrogate Mothers for up to $120,000 a Child', *The Telegraph*, 23.09.2013, <http://www.telegraph.co.uk/news/worldnews/asia/china/10328132/Rich-Chinese-hire-American-surrogate-mothers-for-up-to-120000-a-child.html> accessed 13.09.2018.

gets pregnant. The People's Court may also commission professional institutes to carry out paternity tests.[10] Considering the high accuracy of a paternity test, this technology is widely used in China now. But, in judicial practice, the court will sometimes encounter difficulties when persons refuse such a test. Thus, No. 3 Interpretations of the Supreme People's Court of Several Issues on Application of the Marriage Law of PRC (《最高人民法院关于适用〈中华人民共和国婚姻法〉若干问题的解释（三）》) (hereinafter referred to as the 'No. 3 Interpretations of the Marriage Law') issued in 2011 provides at para. 2 of Art. 2 that where there is convincing evidence to prove paternity, and the current legal father who cannot prove that the petitioner's claim is untrue but refuses to do a paternity test would bear the adverse consequences, resulting in confirmation of the petitioner's paternity.

No children were born through artificial insemination in China until the late 1980s. The first relevant legal disputes can be found in 1991. Again, the People's Supreme Court issued the Reply of the Supreme Court in 1991. This reply stipulates that any child born through artificial insemination during the marriage is the child of both parents if both of them agreed to undergo the relevant procedures. The Marriage Law will be applied to regulate the rights and duties between parents and child. That means that if the husband does not agree to carry out this procedure and the wife secretly undergoes it herself, the child would not be regarded as the father's legal child unless he acknowledges to be the child's father afterwards.[11]

To summarise, the basic rules on parent-child law applied in judicial practice are as follows: 1) A child born in a marriage is a legitimate child, thus the couples in this marriage are his or her legal parents. 2) A child born out of marriage is an illegitimate child. The legal mother is the woman giving birth to the child. The legal father then either is a man who acknowledges paternity or who is shown to be the genetic father of the child by a DNA test.[12] 3) A child born through artificial insemination in a marriage when both couples agree is a child to the husband and the wife.

Based on these legal principles of parent-child law, the People's Court tends to conclude that the legal mother of a child born through a surrogacy arrangement is the surrogate who gave birth to the child, even if this surrogate has no genetic relation with the child. Thus, if the child's custody is awarded to the legal father, she can be awarded the visitation right accordingly.[13]

---

10 C.Z. Wu (ed.), *New Research on the Marrriage and Family Law* <婚姻家庭法新论>, China University of Political Science and Law Press, 2002, p. 237.

11 W. Zhang, 'Tentative Research on Legal Position of Children Born Through Artificial Insemination' (2003) 6 *CLR (Contemporary Law Review)* <当代法学> 81–82.

12 On this see further W. Chen (ed.), *Marriage, Family and Succession Law*, 2nd ed., <婚姻家庭继承法学>, Qunzhong Press, Beijing 2012, pp. 166–76.

13 *Yao v Tan* (2011) Zeng Min Yi Chu Zi No. 838 ((2014) 增民初字第564号), The People's Court in the Chengzhong District of Liuzhou City, Guangxi Province, 2011, See M. Zhao (ed.),

As regards household (i.e. Hukou) registration of this baby, new rules on population registration give opportunities for these babies to be registered as a Chinese permanent resident. On 14 January 2016, Opinions on Resolving the Problem of Registering Household for The Unregistered People Issued by General Office of the State Council (《国务院办公厅关于解决无户口人员登记户口问题的意见》) was promulgated. Thus, any child born outside of marriage can be registered. However, according to this document the relevant party needs to apply for a paternity test first. Once a paternity certificate is acquired, they then can apply for a birth certificate at the local health department. The child or his or her guardian then can apply for permanent residence registration with this birth certificate, the household book of a parent and the marriage certificate or an explanation of this out-of-wedlock birth. Obviously, no information on the surrogate will be registered into the household book in cases of surrogacy. But she might be recognised as the legal mother of the child if the court gives such a judgment as mentioned above.

4. TRANSFERRING PARENTHOOD

Regarding the commissioning mother, according to the Marriage Law, there are two options for a commissioning mother to establish legal parenthood. First, Art. 14 of the Adoption Law of PRC stipulates that the stepfather or the stepmother can adopt the stepchild if the birth mother or the birth father consents. Therefore, if the commissioning mother goes through the adoption procedure, she acquires the status as legal parent; this also terminates the surrogate mother's legal status as the mother. Second, if the commissioning parents raise the surrogate child for a period of time, such a support relationship can be held as a factor to determine that the stepparent and the stepchild have the presumed legal parent-child relationship according to Art. 27 of the Marriage Law. Crucially, the second relationship between the commissioning mother and the surrogate child does not mean that the parent-child relationship between the surrogate mother and the surrogate child terminates. In other words, this means that the surrogate child actually has two legal mothers. The birth mother has no automatic priority to win a custody if the birth father dies and the child has been living in the birth father's family where the stepmother raises and educates the child.[14]

Visitation Right Dispute of Yao v. Tan, the China Institute of Applied Jurisprudence of the Supreme People's Court, *Case Comment of the People's Court* <人民法院案例选> 2012 (2), Beijing: 80, 89.

14 See *Chen v Huang* (2014) Xun Ming Chu Zi No. 564 ((2014)寻民初字第564号). In this case, the birth father petitioned for custody when the birth mother died. The local court

But the commissioning mother faces an insurmountable barrier if the surrogate after birth wants to keep this baby since the surrogate will be deemed to be the legal mother in judicial practice.[15] However, there was one case in which the surrogate lost the dispute about custody in Foshan, Guangdong province, in 2010. In this case, the surrogate mother was the genetic mother of the child as well, and the child had been living with the father since it was born. The court based its judgment on the fact that the father had better economic status to raise this child rather than its biological mother, i.e. the surrogate.[16]

Obviously, this kind of surrogacy is the exception, and usually surrogates are not the genetic mother of the child. Therefore, it is probable that these surrogate mothers now will not keep the child themselves and the surrogacy agencies will ensure that the contract is enforced with other, non-legal measures since the surrogacy contract is illegal in accordance with the basic principles of the civil law.

To conclude, while nominally in cases regarding custody the decision is based on the best interest of the child, in practice the cases mentioned above show that the central consideration to determine the custody of a child born through surrogacy is with whom the child lives when the case is heard. So, if the surrogate keeps the child, she will be awarded custody, and the genetic father would be ordered to pay child support in accordance with the Marriage Law.[17] However, if the father has already taken the child away, the mother usually cannot win the custody battle, particularly if (as usually will be the case) she is in a weaker economic position.

If the commissioning father is not the genetic father because donor sperm was used, the rules on children born via ART will apply. That means that the

---

in Kunming, Yunnan province confirmed that Mr Huang had raised and educated the two children. They can be presumed to have a legal parent-child relationship. The children were willing to live with Mr Huang. Therefore, the court rejected Mr Chen's petition to claim custody.

15 See M. Qu, 'Dispute Arose, the Surrogate Won Child Custody Case', *Jiangsu Legal News* <江苏法制报>, 15.05.2014. In this case, the surrogate has a sexual relation with the husband so that the child was genetically related to the surrogate. Even if the surrogate has no sexual relation with the husband, the court tends to regard her as the child's legal mother, see Judge Q. Jiang and S.H. Zhong, 'Borrowing a Womb, Who Has the Custody Right?', Fuzhou Court Online <抚州法院网>, <http://fzzy.chinacourt.org/article/detail/2014/07/id/1339400.shtml> accessed 13.09.2018.

16 Further details see J.B. Lin and H. Yang, 'Borrowing a Womb to Give Birth to a Baby Results in a Custody Battle', *The People's Court News* <人民法院报>, 12.08.2010.

17 Another case was reported in Xiamen, Fujian province in 2012. See J.X. Zheng and C.P. Yang, 'Finding a Surrogate Leads to a Custody Battle', *The People's Court News* <人民法院报>, 02.12.2012, <http://rmfyb.chinacourt.org/paper/html/2012-12/02/content_54418.htm> accessed 18.11.2016.

donor will not be held as the legal father of the child while the party consenting to this medical treatment would be the legal father of the child.

5. AGENCIES AND CRIMINALISATION

At present, despite surrogacy contracts being illegal, surrogacy agencies play a central role in helping commissioning parents to find surrogates. Since there is no clear prohibition of surrogacy itself stipulated in laws, the industrial and commercial administration departments cannot impose administrative sanctions on these agencies. Even the recent document named the Circular on Printing and Distributing the Program of Special Action against Surrogacy (《关于印发开展打击代孕专项行动工作方案的通知》) issued in April 2015 only stipulates that the industrial and commercial administration departments and the internet information regulation departments should prohibit surrogacy advertisement posts issued by these agencies and delete any information concerning surrogacy agencies. However, even these measures are largely ineffective.

Due to the current circumstances both in law and in reality, surrogacies are being carried out secretly. This actually creates great risks to the surrogate and the commissioning parents, and also the children born through surrogacy. In terms of criminal offences, the present criminal law in China does not stipulate any offence directly relevant to surrogacy, but the following offences might be committed:

1. An offence of abandonment is committed if the child born through surrogacy is abandoned due to his disability or because the commissioning parents get divorced and neither of them wants to raise this child. The surrogate could also commit this offence if she also does not want to raise this child under these circumstances (Art. 261 of the Criminal Law of PRC (《中国刑法》)).
2. If the child born through surrogacy is unwanted by both commissioning parents and the surrogate, the surrogacy agency might attempt to sell the child. Of course, selling a child is a criminal offence, namely the offence of trafficking children (Art. 240 of the Criminal Law of PRC). If the surrogate would not give this baby to anyone else unless she receives a payment, she would also commit this offence.
3. Any doctor carrying out surrogacy procedures for commissioning parents and surrogate mothers might commit an illegal medical practice (Art. 336 of the Criminal Law of PRC). But in practice, it is difficult to say whether an actual prosecution and/or conviction is likely, given that it is a requirement of the law that the illegal medical practice under the circumstances is

considered 'serious', which is unlikely in the case of surrogacy.[18] However, some administrative punishment probably is unavoidable for the medical staff involved.

4. If a surrogacy agency posts advertisements on the internet or asks for deposits, making-pair fees,[19] transplanting fees, surrogacy fees, miscarriage prevention fees, etc. from commissioning parents without providing these services, this agency may commit the offence of fraud (Art. 266 of the Criminal Law of PRC).

In some recent cases, agents and medical institutes were prosecuted in China. For instance, in 2011, a couple were convicted of fraud for providing fraudulent surrogacy services.[20] In 2015, it was found that a hospital in Wuhan, Hubei province, rented out one of its departments to a commercial company where illegal surrogacies were carried out. The licences of medical practice of the doctors involved were revoked. In addition, the licences for diagnosis and treatment of infertility and for obstetrics and gynaecology in this hospital were revoked, and fines were imposed as well. Furthermore, the cases of those suspected of committing criminal offences were transferred to the public security departments.[21]

6. INTERNATIONAL SURROGACY ARRANGEMENTS

The present law treated international surrogacy arrangements in the same way as domestic surrogacy arrangements. No special law addresses this issue. However, as the General Principles of the Civil Law of PRC stipulates at Art. 150 where foreign law or international custom is applied in accordance with this chapter, there must not be a violation of the public interest of the People's Republic of China. Likewise, the reservation of public policy principle is reflected in the Law of the Application of Law for Foreign-related Civil Relations of PRC (《中国涉外民事关系法律适用法》) (hereinafter referred as the Law of the Application of Civil Law) as well. Article 5 of the Law of the Application of Civil Law stipulates that if the application of foreign laws is against the public policy of the People's Republic of China, the laws of the

---

18 Some scholars suggest that a new offence should be stipulated for this illegal surrogacy. See B.Y. Huang, 'Illegal Surrogacy Should Be Convicted', China Court Online <中国法院网>, <http://www.chinacourt.org/article/detail/2014/05/id/1298743.shtml> accessed 13.09.2018.

19 I.e. finding a surrogate whom the commissioning parents are satisfied with.

20 J. Yu, 'Couples Opened a Surrogacy Center, Convicted for Their Cheating Clients of Millions of Yuans', *Beijing Times* <京华时报>, 15.07.2011.

21 Y.J. Lin and Y. Xu, 'Four Departments Collaborating, A Surrogacy Den Destroyed', *Chutian News* <楚天都市报>, 02.10.2014.

People's Republic of China shall apply. Surrogacy contracts are deemed as being against the public policy. Therefore, issues regarding surrogacy would be dealt with in accordance with Chinese substantive law.[22] In practice, this means that such arrangements are invalid. It is important to note that the parties also cannot choose the applicable law in their contract with a view to circumventing prohibitive regulations.

Regarding regulatory rules on parent-child relations arising from international surrogacy, Art. 25 of the Law of the Application of Civil Law stipulates that the laws at the common habitual residence shall apply to the personal and property relations between parents and children. If there is no common habitual residence, among laws at the habitual residence of one party or of the state of nationality of one party, the laws in favour of protecting the rights and interests of the weak shall apply. It is safe to conclude that this article shall apply when dealing with an illegitimate child (where the commissioning parents are not in a marriage, otherwise the child is legitimate) since the present law in China treats legitimate child and illegitimate child equally.[23] Accordingly, if the child born through surrogacy is taken back to China and lives with the commissioning parents for a period of time, the Chinese law should apply to regulate the parent-child relations arising from international surrogacy. The commissioning parents are likely to be Chinese nationals while the surrogate in case of international surrogacies usually will not be.[24] In these circumstances, the People's Court tends to determine that the commissioning parents would be the legal parents of a child born through surrogacy based on Art. 27 in the Marriage Law of PRC and that they have the custody of the child. This legal reasoning can be found in the famous case of *Chen v Luo*[25] heard by the Shanghai Municipal First Intermediate People's Court closed on 17 June 2016.

As regards to recognition and enforcement of foreign judgement given in a different jurisdiction concerning parenthood arising from a surrogacy arrangement, Art. 282 of the Civil Procedure Law of PRC (《中国民事诉讼法》) provides that in the case of an application for recognition and enforcement of an effective judgment or an effective order issued by a foreign court, the People's Court shall examine it in accordance with the international treaties concluded or acceded to by the People's Republic of China, and in accordance with the principle of reciprocity. If the court finds that the decision does not contradict the basic principles of the law of the People's Republic of China, and neither

22 T. Du (ed.), *Theory on Private International Law* <国际私法原理>, Fudan Press, Shanghai 2014, pp. 105–06.

23 Article 25 of the Marriage Law of PRC. See X.S. Liu (ed.), *Private International Law* <国际私法>, Law Press, Beijing 2011, p. 250.

24 There are few reports on the opposite position where the commissioning parents are foreigners and the surrogate is Chinese.

25 *Chen v Luo* (2015) Hu Min Shao Zhong Zi No. 56. ((2015) 沪一中少民终字第56号).

violates State sovereignty nor public interest of the country, then it will recognise the validity of the judgment or the order, and if required, issue a writ of execution to enforce it in accordance with the relevant provisions of this Law. But if the application contradicts the basic principles of the law of the People's Republic of China, violates State sovereignty or public policy of the country, the People's Court shall not recognise its validity. Assuming that the commissioning parents will have been recognised as the legal parents or been given custody by a foreign court, such decisions would probably be recognised in China. The People's Court usually will hold the child's best interest principle as the paramount principle when hearing child custody disputes.

Practically speaking, when a child is born through surrogacy in a foreign country where the surrogacy is legal (as for example in California in the United States), the first question usually is how to return to China with the child. In that scenario, they can get a birth certificate showing the commissioning parents to be the legal parents already. If a child of a Chinese national is born aboard, it will acquire Chinese nationality immediately. The child's parents can therefore apply for a travel document for their child at the Chinese embassy.[26] With this travel document, this child can go back to China with his or her commissioning parents. Afterwards, these parents can apply for registering him or her as their families, i.e. acquiring an entry in the census register (Hukou) which is important for this child's future and their life and education in China.

7. CONCLUSION

As mentioned above, China has a ministry level regulation on surrogacy now which leads to difficulties on strictly prohibiting this practice. There is no consensus regarding surrogacy in legislature. Legislators are divided as to whether to impose a ban on surrogacy in law instead of the current ministry level regulation. Thus, the efforts of adding a surrogacy prohibition article are of no effect in terms of changing the legal position at the time of writing, but it obviously brings the topic back to the centre of public discussion.

Generally, the People's Court still deals with disputes concerning children born via surrogacy in a traditional way applying the child's best interest principle as the main consideration to give its judgment when the child born

[26] See notice on the website of the Embassy of the People's Republic of China in the United States of America, <http://www.china-embassy.org/chn/ywzn/lsyw/lszj/hzlxz/blxz/lxz/> accessed 13.09.2018. Article 5 of the Nationality Law of PRC stipulates that any person born abroad whose parents are both Chinese nationals and one of whose parents is a Chinese national shall have Chinese nationality. Therefore, a surrogate with a birth certificate indicating that one commissioning parent is its parent, the officer in the embassy will issue a travelling document to the surrogate child.

via surrogacy is involved. However, local judges may have different opinions on what is in the child's best interests in the specific circumstances of the case.

Legal academic opinions also vary over the surrogacy problem. As a response to the argument that ART might bring about lots of bad consequences, proponents of surrogacy argue that banning surrogacy is unacceptable. They think that it is unfair for women with uterine fertility issues to completely prohibit surrogacy. It is argued that every woman should have the right to have a child that is genetically related to her. Surrogacy indeed protects these women's right to procreation. Women with fallopian tube issues are allowed to have access to ART, but those with uterine issues are denied access to available techniques including surrogacy. Arguably this amounts to discrimination against these patients. Besides the argument of right to procreation,[27] some also argue that surrogacy is beneficial to protect the marriages of those infertile women; also, it is argued that there is no evidence that the children born via surrogacy would suffer disadvantages.[28]

Opponents, however, argue that legal responses and regulations of surrogacy should be based on ethical analysis of surrogacy. Surrogacy, they say, essentially is an ART completely against the principal ethical concepts on human nature, since this medical practice actually would lead to objectification of humans and degrading the basic human nature of being a mother.[29] Thus, it is deemed against public policy and good morals. Furthermore, they maintain that infertile women can have children through adoption rather than surrogacy. But the current adoption system has shortcomings in terms of fairness as well as effectiveness. The problem of imbalance between supply and demand of child adoption still exists, which conversely reinforces the infertile couple's desire to have a baby by surrogacy.[30] But opponents completely disagree with this argument. In their view, society cannot meet each desire of a person. One scholar argues that the 'right to procreation' is not a true human right because this right comes from their biological structures. So, if people have infertility issues, they just lose their right to procreation.[31] Others raise concerns of exploitation and discrimination, as only economically disadvantaged women would want to act as surrogates, and thus any surrogacy contract would not

27 P. Xiao and Z.Y. Ye, 'How to Regulate Surrogacy by Law' (2014) 4 *PAL (Public Administration and Law)* <行政与法> 108, 110.

28 X.J. Zhang, 'Research on Legal Problems of Partial Surrogacy' (1997) 3 *SL (Science of Law)* <法律科学> 53–54.

29 C.Q. Liu, 'Debates on Surrogacy Legalization and its Regulation' (2016) 1 *SE* (*Studies in Ethics*) <伦理学研究> 115, 118.

30 B. Yang, 'The Problem of Enforceability of Surrogacy Contract' (2015) 7 *TPSL (Tribunal of Political Science and Law)* <政法论坛> 34, 40.

31 C.Q. Liu, 'On Administrative Regulation Mode of Surrogacy' (2013) 4 *ALR (Administrative Law Review)* <行政法学研究> 64, 66.

be based on their true free will but forced upon them by their economic situation.[32] Finally, some also criticise surrogacy because the surrogate child would be harmed due to its personal relationship disorder with more than one mother or father and it would be discriminated.[33]

Xiaomei Qu, a member of the public policy advisory committee in the National Health and Family Planning Commission, clearly stated that at present, ART is being abused and a crackdown on illegal surrogacy is necessary. As regards the voice of permitting surrogacy for medical reasons, she reiterated that such a public policy needs to be carefully investigated and studied before enactment. At current, there is no such study of surrogacy, including the ethical and legal issues, the supervisory role of the State, etc. It therefore was still too early to talk about the possibility of a statutory or other regulation.[34] To some extent, her voice stands for the official position of health authorities towards surrogacy. However, some doctors treating infertility have different opinions. Admitting the present problems resulting from illegal surrogacy, Doctor Liu, a deputy director of the Reproductive Medicine Center of the 3rd Hospital of Beijing University,[35] said that 'infertility actually causes great suffering for the infertile women. And medical surrogacy[36] indeed can help them. Legalising medical surrogacy can bring them happiness.'[37]

In the present author's opinion, it is apparent that to leave surrogacy to the health department cannot resolve relevant social problems. Although reports in the beginning of 2016 emphasised again and again that deleting the no-surrogacy article in the draft of the Population and Family Planning Law amendment does not indicate that surrogacy is legal now and the attitude of the health authority indeed has not changed either, it is obvious that the movement of crackdown on illegal surrogacy cannot be an effective avenue to resolve surrogacy problems. Surely it cannot curb the infertile couple's intention to get their own, genetically related child since they can turn to foreign surrogates (provided they can afford this). Surrogacy websites still exist on the internet now. The present legal

---

32 G.S. Wang, 'On the Mode Choice of Surrogacy Regulation' (2009) 4 *LSD* (*Law and Social Development*) <法制与社会发展> 118, 124.

33 C.Q. Liu, 'Jurisprudential Comments on Limited Access to Surrogacy and Surrogacy Regulation' (2016) 3 *RRL* (*Research on Rule of Law*) <法治研究> 143, 144.

34 C. Ying, 'Is It Time to Legalize Medical Surrogacy?' (2015) 31 *Xinmin Weekly* <新民周刊> 24.

35 This hospital is ranked the no. 1 hospital specialising in artificial reproductive technology in China where the first IVF procedure was carried out in 1984 by a research team led by Professor Lizhu Zhang, and the first test-tube baby was born there in 1988, too. Many infertile couples seek treatment there.

36 According to these doctors' views, medical surrogacy refers to surrogacy as a kind of medical treatment option for the infertile couple. Thus, it is unavailable for those without medical infertility, such as same-sex couples or single women.

37 J. Tan, 'Surrogacy Is Not "Prohibited", What does This Mean?', *Health News* <健康报>, 15.01.2016.

framework does not deal with surrogacy appropriately. A specific law is needed for surrogacy regulation and protection of all parties involved.

It is suggested here by the author that the present legal situation actually proves that a ban on surrogacy is not a good option. The law should differentiate altruistic surrogacy and commercial surrogacy. Because of the current situation in China, altruistic surrogacy should be legalised, and commercial surrogacy should be prohibited instead. First, there is a reproductive right of the infertile women with womb diseases leading to infertility. Denying their reproductive right and access to medical surrogacy actually discriminates against them. Indeed, altruistic surrogacy has been regarded as a special medical treatment for the infertile woman since the early 1990s. Professor Lizhu Zhang successfully carried out the first medical surrogacy in China which was regarded as a significant breakthrough in medicine. The patient's sister-in-law (cousin's wife) offered to act as surrogate, and with the help of doctors, the women with the fertility issues finally had her own child.[38] Secondly, to protect the infertile woman's right surely is conducive to protecting her family. As a famous Chinese sociologist explains, division of labour between two sexes and the task of raising a child must require cooperation between two sexes. Only division of labour between two sexes plus child raising lead to stable long-term relationships, a male and a female become a couple, and a family is established.[39] The genetic relation between the parents and the child would strengthen family cohesion. Even if the child born via surrogacy has no genetic relation with the commissioning mother, the biological relation between the father and the child also help protect the present family. The abovementioned cases proved that the commissioning father did not end his marital relationship because of the woman's infertility. Thirdly, regarding the surrogate, it is self-evident that the sister-in-law in the abovementioned case did not suffer exploitation. Neither should she be punished because of providing help for others. This would be against basic social morals. The surrogate has the right to her own body and to use it to help other infertile women. Fourthly, in terms of public policy which worries the public most, altruistic surrogacy has no adverse impact on the common good. The State's role to safeguard the common good for the society requires that if an act is against the common good and is a threat to public order. Thus, the State in principle can intervene even the party concerned is willing to make sacrifices for others. But the act in question may be justifiable as long as such self-harm shows respect to other's life and social good. Unlike commercial surrogacy where a woman's reproductive organs may merely be regarded as

---

38 J. Tan, 'Surrogacy Is Not "Prohibited", What does This Mean?', *Health News* <健康报>, 15.01.2016.

39 Emphasis is added by this author. X.T. Fei, *Reproduction System* <生育制度>, Tianjin People's Press, Tianjin 1981, p. 26.

a commercial tool and thus violates the person's human dignity,[40] altruistic surrogacy greatly reduces ethical risks by limiting it to non-profit circumstances and does not subvert the public order or go against public policy. It just helps infertile women realise their dreams of being a mother. Surrogates in altruistic surrogacy usually demonstrate their selfless love. Altruistic surrogacy therefore should be legalised.

Regarding legal motherhood, the present traditional way to recognise the surrogate as the legal mother of the child born via surrogacy should be revised accordingly. The blood test for confirming motherhood and the parenting intention test should be combined.[41] Since the circumstances concerning surrogacy vary greatly, the rules to give a woman legal motherhood should not be simplified to one rule. Firstly, if the child has a genetic relation with the commissioning mother, then the commissioning mother should be given the legal motherhood at birth. Secondly, if the child has no genetic relation with the commissioning mother or the surrogate but was conceived with donor ova, the commissioning mother also should be recognised as the legal mother at birth when the commissioning parents both agree with the surrogacy, and the surrogacy is carried out in a clinic licensed by health departments. The reasons for this is that this scenario is similar to a child born through ART where the Letter of the Supreme Court in 1991 already applies: the parents both willing to undergo the ART should be legally recognised as the child's parents from birth and that sperm donors or egg donors would have no parent-child relations with the child born via ART. Thirdly, regarding any disputes arising from illegal surrogacy where the child born from surrogacy has a genetic relation with the surrogate (so a 'traditional surrogacy'), then the surrogate should be the legal mother of the child born via surrogacy. She then may or may not transfer the parenthood after birth.

As regards to the fatherhood, this is much easier since the People's Court in most cases can confirm the parentage using the basic genetic relation standard. If the child is genetically related to the commissioning father, which is the common case concerning surrogacy, the commissioning father's parentage can be proved through a paternity test. In the present law, China does not have rules to limit the biological father to claim his right as a legal father.[42]

---

40 Y.S. Zheng, 'Punishment for Self-Harm Acts Defences Based on Legal Paternalism and Its Practice' (2016) 3 *LSD (Law and Social Development)* <法制与社会发展> 181, 187.

41 B.T. Tan and Y. Duan, 'Parent-child Relation Concerning Surrogacy' (2010) 13 *PJA (People's Judicature (Application))* <人民司法(运用)> 66, 69.

42 But in theory, consent from the mother or the child involved is a precondition for any claims of being a child's father put before the court. See W. Chen (ed.), *Marriage, Family and Succession Law*, 2nd ed., <婚姻家庭继承法学>, Qunzhong Press, Beijing 2012, p. 173. In practice, a family facing a third party claiming to be their child's biological father, once confirmed, would usually end in divorce and this biological father then becomes the legal father.

However, if the child has no genetic relation to the commissioning father either and the surrogate has a husband during pregnancy, it is therefore possible that the surrogate's husband would be held as the legal father of the child born via surrogacy. When the surrogate's husband has no intention of raising this child, he may petition to renounce his fatherhood according to para. 1 of Art. 2 of the No. 3 Interpretations of the Marriage Law, since he will be able to show that he is not the genetic father. The child born through surrogacy therefore would not have a legal father, as would be the case if the surrogate was not married. Therefore, this author argues that the parent-child rule concerning ART should apply since the sperm comes from a donor without any intention to raise this child. Thus, the intended commissioning father should be put into the legal father's shoes. This is undoubtedly beneficial to the child born via surrogacy, too.

Given that commercial surrogacy ought to be illegal, surrogacy agencies should be prohibited since at present these agencies only conduct commercial surrogacies. The law should expressly stipulate that providing commercial surrogacy services are a criminal offence in order to protect the weaker parties including surrogate mother, resulting child and egg donor/seller in some cases.

As regards international surrogacy, some scholars concluded that states have little success in preventing international surrogacy where there is a genetic connection, even if it is contrary to their own law.[43] This author agrees. Although any law prohibiting commercial surrogacy is of no effect considering the child's best interests principle stipulated in the Convention on the Right of the Child, the law has multiple functions, not only including disputes resolution but also provision of direction and incentive within society.[44] Within China's context, international commercial surrogacy cannot be legalised due to violation of public policy. Adopting a compromise approach to this problem is a more realistic and acceptable option. Therefore, to make a sacrifice in efficacy but provide direction and incentive is a last resort.

To bring the policy of international surrogacy in line with national surrogacy policy, the law should, on the one hand, admit the child's Chinese nationality based on the child's best interest principle. Its filiation can be established by the genetic relationship with one parent. On the other hand, international commercial surrogacy still should be stated as illegal in the present law. With inherent flaws, the proposed surrogacy system cannot punish the commissioning parents and surrogate mothers based on protection of the child's right. But the law can stipulate other measures to make the surrogacy

43 C. Fenton-Glynn, 'International surrogacy before the European Court of Human Rights' (2017) 13 *JPIL (Journal of Private International Law)* 546, 566.

44 K.N. Llewellyn, 'The Normative, the Legal and the Law-Jobs: The Problem of Juristic Method' (1940) 49 *YLJ (Yale Law Journal)* 1355–1400.

law more effective. What we need to do is as follows: First, to provide as many authorised health institutes or clinics as possible where the infertile couple may have the chance to get special treatment. With a cheaper alternative, the demand for international commercial surrogacy would decrease greatly. Second, to strengthen the regulation of those agencies engaging in international surrogacy. These agencies should be punished in accordance with the same standard applied when regulating national surrogacy agencies. For surrogacy agencies based outside of China, the law should expressly state its position that no international commercial surrogacy agencies can do business in China. Any dealings between the agency and the client should be a criminal offence. No advertisement and relevant information should be allowed to be posted on the internet. Any offender should be punished in administrative way including compulsory administrative detention if needed. Ultimately, it is to be hoped that a convention on surrogacy could be drafted and signed by as many countries as possible to resolve the issues arising from international surrogacy.

SURROGACY IN TAIWAN

Chih-Hsing Ho

The legal approaches to surrogacy vary widely around the globe. In Asia, commercial surrogacy is prohibited in many countries, though in several jurisdictions surrogacy is merely unregulated. Taiwan falls into the latter group, despite legalising altruistic surrogacy being discussed for more than a decade. The legal vacuum on the issue forces infertile couples who wish to have their own biological child into the global commercial surrogacy market to seek a possible resolution. Challenges exist in seeking to reach a consensus in Taiwan over controversial aspects of regulating surrogacy and balancing the rights and interests of surrogates, would-be parents commissioning this service, and children born via surrogacy. This chapter discusses the legal and ethical concerns on legalising surrogacy. It first introduces the historical background, statistics and general legal framework on assisted reproduction in Taiwan. It then illustrates the prolonged legislative trajectory on surrogacy in Taiwan and analyses recent draft amendments relating to surrogacy, such as eligibility criteria for commissioning parents, and surrogates, surrogacy contracts, agencies, and the arrangement of legal parenthood. Finally, the chapter elucidates issues concerning international surrogacy arrangements and the socio-legal causes behind the debates over amendments on regulating surrogacy in Taiwan.

1. GENERAL LEGAL FRAMEWORK

1.1. HISTORICAL BACKGROUND

Demand for assisted reproduction has been growing rapidly around the world as people seek to take advantage of the medical and technical advances in assisted reproductive technologies ('ART'). Statistics published by the Taiwan Health Promotion Administration ('HPA') of the Ministry of Health and Welfare ('MOHW') demonstrate that in the past decades, the share of test-tube baby births as a percentage of overall births in Taiwan has risen from 1.38 per cent to 3.24 per cent, the equivalent of a rise from 2,500 to 5,800 infants.[1] Since 1985, when Taiwan's first test-tube baby was successfully delivered at the Veterans General Hospital in Taipei, further debates and discussions in the Taiwanese society on legal and ethical issues of the application of ART, such as in vitro fertilisation ('IVF') and surrogate motherhood emerged. Even though the demand of assisted reproduction has been increasing, nonetheless, the process of legislative enactment in the jurisdiction to regulate surrogacy has never been smooth. In 1986, the Department of Health ('DOH', the former MOHW) issued ethical guidelines to regulate human assisted reproduction.[2] These guidelines prohibited surrogacy in principle, but allowed for exceptions conditional on professional evaluations made by individual medical doctors. Three years later, further revisions to the guidelines took a much stricter position, prohibiting surrogacy entirely in Taiwan.

In 1994, the DOH started to enact the Administrative Measures on Assisted Reproduction Technology ('the Measures') to address emergent ethical issues on ART.[3] The Measures were revised in 1997 and 1999, but the government's position on prohibiting surrogacy remained unchanged. In Arts 5 and 7 of the Measures, surrogacy was explicitly prohibited though the application of in vitro technology was allowed. In Taiwan the Civil Code restricts access to in vitro fertilisation to married couples, specifically a 'husband and wife'. As a result, after a successful fertilisation process takes place in petri dishes in scientific laboratories, those fertilised oocytes were required to be implanted

1 M. Huang, 'Taiwan has highest success rate of test tube babies in world', *Taiwan News*, 15.11.2016, <http://www.taiwannews.com.tw/en/news/3029669> accessed 13.09.2018.
2 Ethical Guidelines on the Use of Assisted Reproduction Technology (1986).
3 The Administrative Measures on Assisted Reproduction Technology (1994).

back into the 'wife's uterus', according to the Measures. This requirement excluded single people or gay and lesbian individuals who may wish to avail themselves of ART to have a child.[4] Nevertheless, as there was neither a statute nor a formal legislation enacted to regulate surrogacy, the administrative measures prohibiting surrogacy were regarded as a violation of legal preservation, a fundamental principle deemed to be the basis of the rule of law in a democratic society. In response to this concern, the government later decided to draft specific legislation to address emerging legal and ethical issues regarding the application of ART.

The first meeting of the advisory committee for this legislative endeavour was held in January 1996.[5] At that meeting, advisory committee members suggested that due to the complexity of surrogacy policies and the lack of a consensus in Taiwanese society regarding how to regulate assisted reproduction, the draft law should consider entirely excluding provisions on surrogacy in order to avoid further delay of the overall legislative process on ART. The DOH then commissioned Grand Justice Tai Tung-Hsiung (戴東雄), a renowned legal scholar in Family Law, to take charge of drafting the legislation.[6] In June 1997, Grand Justice Tai proposed two parallel versions of the draft law on ART. The first explicitly banned all forms of surrogacy, while the second took a relatively compromised position and conditionally permitted altruistic surrogacy instead. After the two draft versions were proposed, the DOH then initiated a series of 13 advisory committee meetings during the years 1997–98 to further debate and discuss the draft legislation.[7] In 1998, the newly appointed Director General of the DOH, Chan Chi-Shean (詹啟賢) proposed his policy blueprints, one of which recommended taking a deregulated approach to the overall rules on medical affairs in Taiwan. These claims had been interpreted as a subtle sign that the government may be willing to consider loosening the regulations on surrogacy.

Ultimately, rather than opening up further room for surrogacy, the DOH decided to withdraw the draft bill that set conditions for partially allowing altruistic surrogacy in Taiwan. In October 2010, the DOH submitted to the Legislative Yuan (the Parliament) the revised draft legislation on ART, in which

---

4 Article 972 of the Civil Code in Taiwan restricts that marriage shall be made by the male and female parties in their own concord. Although in recent years, there have been discussions about the possibility to revise the Civil Code to make same-sex marriage legal. The revision is not yet fulfilled and therefore same-sex marriage has not yet been legalised in Taiwan at the time of writing.

5 Y. Chiu, 'The Controversies of Legalising Surrogacy' (2004) 47 *Taiwan Medicinal Journal* 7 (in Chinese).

6 Y. Hsien, 'The Impact of the Matter of Surrogate Mothers on Laws and Ethics' (2008) 3 *Kuang Tien Medical Journal* 6, 57 (in Chinese).

7 The China Post News Staff, 'Legalisation of surrogacy requires careful planning', *The China Post*, 23.11.2012, <https://chinapost.nownews.com/20121123-115535> accessed 13.09.2018.

rules on surrogacy were removed entirely. The rationale behind this decision – to separate surrogacy from the general legislation on ART – speaks to several considerations. First, it reflects the complexity of the issue of surrogacy and that Taiwanese society has encountered real difficulties in trying to reach a consensus on whether to legalise it, and if so, under what conditions surrogacy could be permitted and how it would be regulated. Practical concerns provide another important reason for the government to take this position. The newly enacted Administrative Procedure Law was scheduled to take effect in 2001, which imposed a tight deadline on the passage of legislation on ART. Indeed, while drafting legislation on ART, the government began to worry that there would be insufficient time to pass it through the Legislative Yuan, and that existing administrative measures on the use of ART would be invalidated by the new Administrative Procedure Law. In order to avoid a period of legal vacuum, the DOH ultimately decided to propose only the draft bill on assisted reproduction in general and to exclude entirely the provisions dealing with surrogacy in particular.[8]

1.2. STATISTICS AND PUBLIC OPINIONS ON SURROGACY

In the early 2000s, Taiwan was reported to have one of the world's lowest birth rates.[9] Due to long working hours and the challenges to balancing work and family life, many young adults were opting to postpone marriage and having their first child. Recently, due to improvements in fertility policies on childbirth subsidies and maternity leave, birth rates have rebounded from a historical low of 0.91 children per woman in 2010, to about 1.20 in 2016.[10] Recent statistics from the Ministry of Interior show that the average age of women in Taiwan giving birth to their first child was over 30 years in 2015, with women in Taipei having their first child at an average of 32.44 years.[11] These figures illustrate the reasons behind the rise of the demand for infertility treatment, which afflicts roughly one out of seven couples in Taiwan according to statistics published by the MOHW. It is estimated that in Taiwan the percentage of infertile women aged 22–40 years old is about 10 per cent–15 per cent, meaning

8 I. Lin, 'Taiwan women divided over surrogacy', *Taipei Times*, 19.01.2001, <http://www.taipeitimes.com/News/local/archives/2001/01/19/0000070389> accessed 13.09.2018.

9 N. Tso, 'Why has Taiwan's birthrate dropped so low?', *TIME Magazine*, 07.12.2009, <http://content.time.com/time/world/article/0,8599,1945937,00.html> accessed 13.09.2018.

10 W. Chen, 'Nation's birth rate rising despite poor conditions', *Taipei Times*, 16.05.2016, <http://www.taipeitimes.com/News/taiwan/archives/2016/05/16/2003646390> accessed 13.09.2018.

11 Reporter, 'Taipei women give birth to first baby at 32.44 years old on average', *China Post*, 24.06.2016, <https://chinapost.nownews.com/20160624-18505> accessed 13.09.2018.

that approximately 300,000 women might have been diagnosed as infertile.[12] Among these infertile women, about 10–20 per cent, or 5,000–10,000 women have been diagnosed as suffering from uterus infringement; these statistics speak to the potential market for surrogates among infertile couples. However, as the draft provisions on surrogacy were entirely removed from the Law of Assisted Reproduction ('LAR') when passed by the Legislative Yuan in 2007, surrogacy remains prohibited in Taiwan. After 2004, the DOH convened several public hearings and consensus meetings seeking to reach common ground on regulating surrogacy.

In 2010, the government carried out a poll of the general public, aged 20 years or above, on surrogacy in Taiwan; the poll garnered 1,068 valid samples from 23 cities and counties.[13] The polling results demonstrate that 85 per cent of the Taiwanese population have heard of the term 'surrogacy', and about 53.5 per cent of the general public agrees that in cases in which the wife's uterus has been diagnosed as the reason for a couple's infertility, the infertile couples should be permitted to seek a surrogate. Among those who supported the legalisation of surrogacy for infertile couples, about 95.6 per cent agree that surrogates should be remunerated for their expenses or losses.[14] In 2013, the government ran the poll again, collecting a total of 1,075 valid samples from individuals aged 20 years old or above, from 22 cities and counties.[15] The polling results reveal that 68 per cent of the Taiwanese population do not support an ongoing blanket prohibition of surrogacy, and 86 per cent of the general public agrees that under specific conditions, which include a medical examination, surrogacy should be legally permitted for infertile couples. In this poll, 88.26 per cent of the respondents agree that couples commissioning a surrogate should remunerate the surrogate for nutritional support and to compensate them for the attendant health risks. Furthermore, 78 per cent of the respondents support the proposal that the reproductive cells – both sperm and egg – must be provided by the commissioning parents; 47 per cent think that having reproductive cells provided by only one party of the couple is sufficient, and 14 per cent of the respondents support the proposal that both of the reproductive cells can be acquired by donation, meaning that there will be no genetic connection between the commissioning parents and the baby borne by the surrogate.

12 Legislators – Chiang Huei-Chen (江惠貞) and Su Chin-Quan (蘇清泉)'s proposal to revise the Law of Assisted Reproduction. See Legislative Yuan General Document no. 1586, Legislators' proposal no. 15405, 02.10.2013.

13 A MOST Response Report for the Revisions of the Law of Assisted Reproduction proposed to the General Meeting of the Social Welfare and Environmental Hygiene Committee at the Legislative Yuan, 16.12.2013, p. 7.

14 Ibid.

15 Ibid. p. 8.

In September 2012, the DOH initiated a public deliberative meeting in which the following consensuses on surrogacy was reached:

1. The government shall permit surrogacy as soon as possible under the circumstances when the commissioning parents are able to provide healthy sperm and egg cells for surrogates, and shall also permit surrogacy in the circumstances that the commissioning parents may only provide either healthy sperm or egg cells to surrogates, but not both.
2. In terms of the complex and mingled relations of rights and responsibilities of surrogates, commissioning parents and the child born through surrogacy, the government shall play an active role in the operation of surrogacy. One of the commissioning parents must be the national of the R.O.C. (Taiwan), and the child who was born as a result of surrogacy arrangement needs to be taken good care of before and after the birth. In addition, surrogacy contracts shall not infringe the fundamental right of women acting as surrogates.
3. Surrogacy shall be altruistic, so even though a surrogate may be remunerated for her participation in the surrogacy arrangement, such remuneration shall cover necessary cost only as a means to recognise surrogates' altruistic behaviour, and shall not be used as a means of earning profits. There is a need to recognise the role of agencies and mediators in order to make the rights of surrogates, commissioning parents and child born through surrogacy can all be better protected.

2. THE LAW OF ASSISTED REPRODUCTION

Except for providing rules on surrogacy, the LAR enacted in 2007 was a comprehensive legislation addressing the application of assisted reproduction in Taiwan. The LAR was a legislative attempt to balance the rights and interests of different stakeholders regarding the use of ART and to ensure that the practice is carried out in an ethical and appropriate manner. According to its legislative purpose, the LAR was enacted in order to satisfy the following goals: fostering the sound development of assisted reproduction; maintaining social ethics and health, and protecting the rights and interests of infertile couples, children conceived through assisted reproduction, and donors.[16]

Like earlier administrative measures, the LAR restricts the use of assisted reproduction to married couples only. In the clause on terminology interpretation in Art. 2, the term 'recipient couple' is defined as 'a husband

[16] Article 1 of the LAR.

and wife receiving assisted reproduction, where the wife's uterus can carry a fetus and give birth to a child.'[17] This narrow definition of who is qualified to access assisted reproduction excludes the possibility of surrogacy, which involves a surrogate mother carrying a pregnancy to term. As a result, when the government's position gradually changes from maintaining a blanket prohibition to conditionally permitting surrogacy, it requires proposing amendments to the LAR in order to put surrogacy under regulation.

2.1. CRITERIA FOR REPRODUCTIVE CELLS DONATION

The LAR establishes eligibility criteria for reproductive cells donation. Besides the age limit – men at least 20 and less than 50 years of age; women at least 20 and less than 40 years of age, the donor needs to satisfy the following conditions: agrees to donate without compensation,[18] and has never donated sperm or egg cells before, or the donor's previously donated reproductive cells never helped any recipient couple complete live birth and were not stored.[19] The rationale behind these very restrictive criteria is to prevent commercialisation of eggs and sperm for reproduction and to avoid possible ethical dilemmas associated with complex kinship relations. Even though there is a global market activity around sperm donation, concerns over commercialisation arise mainly from the potential exploitation or commodification of female body parts due to the scarcity of egg cells and growing demand for regenerative medicine research and infertility treatment.

In order to ensure the quality of donated sperm and eggs, and the suitability of both parties to carry out ART, the law requires that assisted reproduction institutions carry out the following testing and assessment of donors and recipient couples before accepting donated reproductive cells or performing assisted reproduction:[20]

1. General psychological and physiological state.
2. Family disease history, including records of hereditary diseases of the person in question and blood relatives within the fourth degree of kinship.

---

17 Article 2 of the LAR.

18 However, according to the LAR a recipient may commission the assisted reproduction institution to provide a nutrition allowance or nutrition products to the donor, or may pay for the donor's necessary testing, medical and transportation expenses and loss of working time, within the monetary amount or price limit set by the competent authority. See Art. 8 para. 2.

19 Article 8 para. 1 of the LAR. In addition, an assisted reproduction institution is required to check with the competent authority concerning this condition and it is not allowed to use the donor's sperm or egg cells until the competent authority provides confirmation. See Art. 8 para. 3 of the LAR.

20 Article 7 para. 1 of the LAR.

3. Suspected hereditary or infectious diseases affecting ability to give birth.
4. Other matters designated and announced by the competent authority.

Before accepting donated reproductive cells, written consent is always required for the assisted reproduction institutions to make sure that the donors have been informed and understood their relevant rights and responsibilities.[21] In addition to keeping records of testing and assessment, assisted reproduction institutions are also required to keep records of the information on the donated items, quantity and date, as well as the following information about the donor: donor's name, address, national ID card number or passport number, date of birth, height, body weight, blood type, skin colour, hair colour and ethnicity.[22]

According to the LAR, donors shall not request the return of any donated reproductive cells.[23] However, an exception applies when a donor is diagnosed or proven as having a functional impairment of reproduction by a physician, and under this circumstance, the donor may request the return of any reproductive cells that have not yet been destroyed.[24] The law also allows reproductive cells which are donated to an assisted reproduction institution to be transferred to another for carrying out assisted reproduction so long as the donor has given his or her written consent.[25]

2.2. DESTRUCTION OF REPRODUCTIVE CELLS

There are several conditions established by the LAR for an assisted reproduction institution to compulsorily destroy donated reproductive cells. For example, the recipient couple has completed one live birth using the donated cells or the reproductive cells have been preserved for more than 10 years.[26] In addition, the donated reproductive cells are also required to be destroyed once it has been discovered after the donation that they are unsuitable for use in assisted reproduction.[27] The LAR requires an assisted reproduction institution to destroy the reproductive cells when the providers of the reproductive cells have asked for their destruction or the providers of the reproductive cells have died.[28] The destruction rule also applies in cases in which the reproductive cells have been preserved for more than 10 years. However, an exception applies when

[21] Article 9 para. 1 of the LAR.
[22] Article 9 para. 2 of the LAR.
[23] Article 19 of the LAR.
[24] Ibid.
[25] Article 20 of the LAR.
[26] Article 21 para. 1 of the LAR.
[27] Ibid.
[28] Article 21 para. 2 of the LAR.

written consent is obtained such that the preservation period may be extended to the date assigned by the providers of the reproductive cells.[29]

According to the law, an assisted reproduction institution shall destroy an embryo created for a specific recipient couple when the embryo has been preserved for more than 10 years, or the recipient couple has given up their attempts to carry out assisted reproduction.[30] The same rule applies when the marriage of the recipient couple is invalid or annulled, the couple divorces, or one spouse dies.[31] In general, an assisted reproduction institution shall destroy its preserved reproductive cells or embryos when the institution terminates its business operation.[32] However, with written consent from the donor, such donated reproductive cells may be transferred to another assisted reproduction institution for preservation or carrying out ART.[33] As for the recipient couple's reproductive cells or embryos, it is also permissible for them to be transferred to another assisted reproduction institution for continued preservation so long as the recipient couple's written consent has been obtained.[34]

2.3. PERFORMING ASSISTED REPRODUCTION

The LAR stipulates several eligibility criteria and restrictions for performing assisted reproduction. First, according to Art. 15 of the LAR, assisted reproduction shall not be carried out among a certain range of kinship relations – direct blood relatives, direct relatives by marriage, and collateral blood relatives within fourth degrees of kinship – in order to avoid potential kinship dilemmas and ethical and legal issues through assisted reproduction. Moreover, the law enumerates limitations for performing assisted reproduction based on the circumstances or methods. According to the LAR, medical institutions are prohibited from carrying out ART using reproductive cells or embryos provided exclusively for research purposes, or creating a human embryo other than by fertilisation.[35] In addition, sex selection is not permissible in the course of assisted reproduction, with the sole exception of reasons connected to hereditary disease. Additionally, the LAR does not allow for using mixed semen or the importation of donated reproductive cells from outside of Taiwan. More restrictions apply to using embryos cultivated in vitro for more than seven days, and the

[29] Ibid.
[30] Article 21 para. 3 of the LAR.
[31] Ibid.
[32] Article 21 para. 4 of the LAR.
[33] Ibid.
[34] Ibid.
[35] Article 16 of the LAR.

implantation of more than five embryos at a time.[36] An assisted reproduction institution, according to the LAR, is not allowed to provide reproductive cells donated from a single donor to two or more recipient couples at the same time.[37] After a recipient couple successfully achieves pregnancy, assisted reproduction institutions are required to immediately cease providing reproductive cells from the same donor and must destroy donated reproductive cells when the recipient couple completes a live birth.[38]

It is worth repeating that in Taiwan, access to assisted reproduction is restricted to married couples (of the opposite sex). Article 11 of the LAR sets several conditions and eligibility criteria for a married couple seeking assisted reproduction:[39]

1. The results of testing and assessment confirm suitability to receive assisted reproduction.
2. The husband or wife of the married couple has been diagnosed as suffering from infertility, or has been diagnosed as suffering from a major hereditary disease designed by the competent authority and it is suspected that natural conception and birth will cause abnormal children.
3. At least one member of the married couple possesses healthy reproductive cells, and that person has no need accepting donated sperm or egg cells.

When the condition prescribed in point (2) above is not met but the married couple has a legitimate medical reason, the LAR provides an exception which would allow the married couple to receive assisted reproduction after reporting to, and obtaining approval from, the DOH.[40]

Like the requirement for reproductive cell donation, written consent is also required from both parties of the recipient couple before performing assisted reproduction. A medical care institution must explain carefully the necessity of assisted reproduction, the implementation technique, the success rate, any possible complications or hazards and possible alternative treatment methods to the recipient couple and make sure that they understand fully the described information before the implementation of ART.[41] In circumstances when the implementation of assisted reproduction involves the recipient couple's acceptance of sperm donated by a third party, the performing medical care

---

36 Ibid.
37 Article 10 of the LAR.
38 Ibid.
39 Article 11 of the LAR.
40 Ibid.
41 Article 12 of the LAR.

institution shall obtain the husband's written consent before performing assisted reproduction.[42]

Furthermore, the LAR prohibits a medical care institution from performing assisted reproduction while using a specific donor's reproductive cells as requested by the recipient couple.[43] The same rationale applies to the donor, who is prohibited from requesting his or her reproductive cells be used by a specific recipient couple.[44] With the exception of the limitation on specific use stated above, a medical care institution shall provide information concerning the donor's ethnicity, skin colour, and blood type for the reference of the recipient couple.[45] A medical care institution which carries out assisted reproduction shall also record the following information:[46]

1. The name, address, national ID card number or passport number, date of birth, height, body weight, blood type, skin colour, and hair colour of the husband and wife of the recipient couple.
2. The donor's national ID card number or passport number and case history number at the medical care institution.
3. Progress of assisted reproduction performance.

According to the LAR, an assisted reproduction institution is not allowed to use donated reproductive cells, the reproductive cells of the recipient couple, or an embryo produced by a recipient couple for any purposes other than assisted reproduction.[47] The only exception lies in the circumstance when both written consent from the donor and recipient couple have been obtained and the DOH also grants its permission that the reproductive cells or embryos which should otherwise be destroyed may be reserved for research purposes.[48] In addition, according to the LAR, a medical care institution is required to apply for, and then obtain, a permit from the competent authority – the DOH – before it can perform assisted reproduction, including accepting, storing or providing donated reproductive cells.[49] The permit is usually valid for three years and renewal of the permit must be filed with DOH within three months prior to expiration if continued performance of assisted reproduction is desired.

---

42 Ibid, para. 2; the written consent is required to be notarised by a public notary when using the reproductive cells donated from the third party.
43 Article 13 of the LAR.
44 Ibid.
45 Ibid.
46 Article 14 of the LAR.
47 Article 22 of the LAR.
48 Ibid.
49 Article 6 of the LAR; according to para. 3 of this article, the competent authority needs to set up implementation rules, including regulations which govern the conditions of permits, application procedures, and other binding matters.

3. DRAFT AMENDMENTS ON SURROGACY PROPOSED BY LEGISLATORS

3.1. ELIGIBILITY CRITERIA FOR COMMISSIONING PARENTS AND SURROGATES

In recent years, some legislators have proposed revisions to the LAR in order to include surrogacy under the general regulations on assisted reproduction. The draft amendments cover several legal aspects of surrogacy, including eligibility criteria for surrogates and commissioning parents, surrogacy contracts, agencies, and the arrangement of legal parenthood.[50] In the draft amendments proposed by legislators Yang and Chiang in 2014, the eligibility criterion for commissioning parents remains restricted to couples among whom the wife was born without a functional uterus, or has been diagnosed with potentially life-threatening diseases due to pregnancy or childbirth and who therefore has difficulty in carrying a child to term.[51] Like the LAR, the draft amendments do not make surrogacy available as an option for singles, non-married couples, or married couples who have not yet been diagnosed as having uterine-related or immune disease. In addition, it requires that at least one of the commissioning parents be an R.O.C. (Taiwan) national. Furthermore, when the commissioning parents require donated sperm and eggs, the draft amendment stipulates that the surrogates' eggs not be used, meaning that only gestational surrogacy is permissible; if the surrogate is married, the draft amendment also prohibits the use of the sperm of the surrogate's spouse.[52]

As for the eligibility criteria for women who might act as surrogates, the draft amendments require that they be women who are R.O.C. nationals no older than 45 years old, who have given birth to a child, and have undergone psychological and social evaluations to determine their suitability to act as surrogates.[53] In addition, they need to be physically fit to act as a surrogate, meaning free of infectious disease or other illness that would make them a poor candidate for pregnancy or unable to give birth to a child.[54] If a surrogate is married, their partner must also pass a physical evaluation to ensure that there is no possibility of an infectious disease adversely influencing the health of a child born through surrogacy.[55] Moreover, in order to avoid turning surrogacy into

50 The draft amendments to the LAR on surrogacy proposed from legislators Yang Yu-Hsin, Chiang Hui-Chen and Chen Shu-Huei. See The Legislative Yuan Agenda Related Document, the Yuan no. 1586; the legislators proposed no. 16360. (Published on 30.04.2014.)

51 The draft amendments, Art. 18-1, I.

52 The draft amendments, Art. 18-1, II.

53 The draft amendments, Art. 18-2, I, II, III.

54 The draft amendments, Art. 18-2, IV.

55 The draft amendments, Art. 18-2, V.

a means of exploiting women's wombs, the draft amendments set a limit of two surrogate pregnancies per woman.[56]

3.2. SURROGACY CONTRACTS

According to the draft amendment proposal, a surrogacy contract must be signed between the commissioning parents and a surrogate after the surrogacy plan has been approved by the competent authority, and both parties have undergone a professional consultation process.[57] Such consultations should cover overall assessments of the physical and psychological impacts on both commissioning parents and surrogates, and, should assisted abortion be required, the potential risks to, and impacts on, the family and society. The surrogacy contract shall be acknowledged before an officer or other person authorised by law to act as a notary public. For surrogates who are married, their spouses are also required to sign the contracts.[58] However, under circumstances in which commissioning parents do not know that the surrogates are married, and such ignorance of that fact is not due to negligence, the surrogacy contract will remain valid even without the signature of the surrogate's spouse.

The draft amendments enumerate the following contents that are required to be covered in the surrogacy contract to protect rights and interests of surrogates.[59]

1. Respect for the right to privacy and for private life and health information not to be interfered.
2. Respect for the autonomy to decide health and physical condition-related matters during the period of pregnancy.
3. The right to visitation within two years after the birth of the child.
4. When the pregnancy is not successful, the right to terminate contracts or refuse to renew surrogacy contracts.
5. The right for life insurance being arranged from commissioning parents.

As for the right to visitation, the draft amendments preserve that courts may, based either on their independent authorities or requests from commissioning parents or other interested persons, alter the contents of the right to visitation if carrying out such right would be harmful to the interests of the child.

In addition, according to the draft amendments, surrogacy should be altruistic. However, surrogates may receive nutritional support and reimbursement from

---

[56] The draft amendments, Art. 18-2, VI.
[57] The draft amendments, Art. 18-3, II.
[58] The draft amendments, Art. 18-3, III.
[59] The draft amendments, Art. 18-4.

commissioning parents within certain limits set by the competent authority for necessary health checks, consultations, medical care, transportation, lost wages, and other related benefits.[60]

Furthermore, in the draft amendment Art. 18-10, it is permissible for voluntary assisted abortion to be carried out by the surrogate under the circumstances that a fetus has been diagnosed as having serious genetic diseases or that due to medical considerations,[61] for example that the pregnancy or childbirth may cause a life-threatening risk or be detrimental to the surrogate's physical and mental health as stipulated by the Genetic Health Act in Taiwan. The rationale behind this legal mechanism is to recognise surrogates' autonomy to decide whether, under circumstances stipulated by the Genetic Health Act, they would be willing to continue or terminate pregnancy; this is necessary in order to protect the interests of surrogates, especially as in the draft amendments the law would recognise commissioning parents rather than surrogates as the legal parents of the child born through surrogacy.

3.3. AGENCIES

In order to minimise the possibility of disputes arising from surrogacy, the draft amendments recognise accredited agencies as a means of mediating related surrogacy arrangements, and assist in the signing of surrogacy contracts between commissioning parents and surrogates.[62] The agencies are required to be recognised by competent authorities, which shall stipulate further measures regarding the qualifications of agencies, the application procedure for, and termination of, accreditation, and other related matters. The rationale behind this mechanism is to echo the results of public consultations held in 2012, which found that there is a need to recognise the function of agencies in hopes of ensuring that the interests of all three parties involved – surrogate, commissioning parents and child born through surrogacy – are well protected, and that the agencies are also under the supervision of the government.

3.4. LEGAL PARENTHOOD AT THE TIME OF BIRTH

According to the draft amendments, at the time of birth, it is commissioning parents, rather than the surrogate, who are regarded as legal parents of a child

60 The draft amendments, Art. 18-5.

61 However, it is still not clear and under debate whether this assisted abortion may apply to the circumstances under which that if the fetus is found to be seriously disabled, and the commissioning parents wish to abort but the surrogate does not.

62 The draft amendments, Art. 18-7.

born through surrogacy.[63] In proposed amendment Art. 18-9, a child born through surrogacy is deemed to be born in wedlock to the commissioning parents, and therefore the child is entitled to any rights and duties stipulated for a legitimate child under the Civil Law. In Taiwan, Art. 1061 of the Civil Law defines a legitimate child as one conceived in marriage. The draft amendments recognise only gestational surrogacy, the rationale being that legal parenthood reflects the original genetic link between commissioning parents and the child born through surrogacy. As such, commissioning parents do not need to apply to adopt in order to be regarded as legal parents of a child born through surrogacy as their parental status will commence automatically at the time of birth of the child.

During the surrogate's pregnancy, the draft amendment decrees that the commissioning parents are the legal custodians of the child not yet born.[64] Should the commissioning parents pass away before the child is born, and if the child therefore would be given up for adoption, priority is to be given to the surrogate should she wish to apply to adopt.[65] It is worth noting that under the draft amendment, other relatives, for example the commissioning parents' parents or siblings cannot step in and take custody of the child. Additionally, in order to protect the best interests of the child, the draft amendments stipulate that it is not permissible for commissioning parents to file a claim to deny the parent-child relationship even if it were later proven that no genetic link existed between the commissioning parents and the child born through surrogacy. The only exception applies when either party of the commissioning parents is able to prove that his or her consent to surrogacy was obtained through fraud or coercion, or it is proven that the child was conceived using the surrogate's egg.[66] In such a case, a claim to deny the parent-child relationship must be filed by the commissioning parents within a year of the birth of the child.[67] Even though the draft amendments recognise only gestational surrogacy, the legislators acknowledge that there is still a possibility that the child born through surrogacy may prove to be without a genetic link to a commissioning parent, for example, due to doctors' negligence, such that the surrogate may bear a child who has no genetic relationship with commissioning parents. Under such circumstances, in order to protect the interests of the child under the Civil Law, the commissioning parents are deemed to be the beneficiaries of the surrogacy arrangement and to bear the preponderance of the risk.

In addition, under the draft amendment, assisted reproduction institutions would be required to provide written certificates proving that the implantation

---

63 The draft amendments, Art. 18-9, I.
64 The draft amendments, Art. 18-9, II.
65 The draft amendments, Art. 18-9, III.
66 The draft amendments, Art. 18-9, IV.
67 The draft amendments, Art. 18-9, V.

of a couple's IVF embryos into a surrogate mother were successful, and that the embryo was implanted at the commissioning parents' request.[68] This documentation could be used for delivery hospitals to register the commissioning parents as legal parents of a child born through surrogacy as a means of simplifying the birth registration procedure.

4. DRAFT AMENDMENTS PROPOSED BY THE MINISTRY OF HEALTH AND WELFARE

In addition to the draft amendments proposed by the legislators, the Ministry of Health and Welfare ('MOHW') also proposed several draft amendments to the LAR that must be reviewed by the Ministry's Law and Regulation Commission before the draft amendments can be submitted to the Executive Yuan (the Cabinet) for further review and then sent to the Legislative Yuan for legislative action. The draft amendments demonstrate the MOHW's intention to ease certain restrictions on surrogacy in Taiwan even though the complementary measures and the implementing rules are subject to further discussions. Similar to the draft amendments proposed by the legislators, the MOHW's amendments stipulate that surrogacy must be altruistic and no financial compensation would be allowed. In addition, the amendments set a ceiling for the reimbursement of medical services, nutrition, examination costs and the loss of wages.

According to the amendments, surrogates must be Taiwan (R.O.C.) nationals and have previously given birth to a child. The age limit set by the MOHW for surrogates is between 20 and 40, and surrogacy is limited to three times per woman. However, unlike the legislators' proposed amendments, there is no need to obtain the consent of a surrogate's spouse to enter into a valid surrogacy agreement. Furthermore, the MOHW's amendments allow surrogates to change their minds during pregnancy and permit assisted abortion during the first 24 weeks of gestation without due cause.[69] The MOHW also recognises only gestational surrogacy, so a surrogate may not donate her eggs to be used in surrogacy in order to avoid greater complexity in the recognition of a genetic relationship. Identical to the draft amendments proposed by the legislators, the MOHW's proposed amendments do not require the commissioning parents to go through adoption procedures to be regarded as legal parents of a child born through surrogacy. However, under the circumstances that see the commissioning parents' divorce, or decide not to have the child after more than

---

68 The draft amendments, Art. 18-8, I.

69 Central News, 'Surrogate Motherhood to be allowed under Certain Conditions', 17.12.2013, <http://www1.kmt.org.tw/english/page.aspx?type=article&mnum=112&anum=13867> accessed 13.09.2018.

24 weeks of gestation, the proposed amendments give preference to the surrogate in the right of adoption.[70] If, in the end, neither the commissioning parents nor the surrogate is willing to care for the child, the amendments stipulate that the government would need to become involved and take responsibility for caring for the child born through surrogacy.

5. INTERNATIONAL SURROGACY ARRANGEMENTS

Although discussion and debate on the draft amendments on surrogacy have never ceased, reaching a consensus on regulating surrogacy remains challenging in Taiwan, especially in regards to the need to balance a couple's interest in having a biological child with rights and interests of the surrogate and the child born through surrogacy. For infertile couples, seeking surrogacy abroad has become an alternative as the procedure currently remains illegal at home. Across the globe, the market for international surrogacy continues expanding. So are the complex legal problems associated with the cross-border surrogacy arrangements, such as legal parenthood and the nationality of the child. As domestic legal responses to surrogacy vary widely among different countries, forum shopping turns to be an emergent phenomenon for infertile couples who seek surrogacy and choose surrogacy friendly jurisdictions as their destinations.

In general, it appears there are three approaches – the gestational test, the genetics test, and the intent test – being developed for the recognition of legal parenthood in international surrogacy arrangements.[71] According to the gestational test, a surrogate mother will be viewed as the legal mother of the child, no matter whether she is biologically related to the child. By contrast, if the genetics test applies, a surrogate mother can only be regarded as the legal mother of the child when she and the child are genetically related. In the case of the intent test, it is the intent of the parties that counts, so the legal parenthood is determined by what is expressed in the surrogacy agreement.

In Taiwan, when courts decide legal parenthood, they usually take into consideration two basic principles – the best interests of the child and the principle of biological connection. Even though it is not always easy to reach a balance among the interests of all parties to a surrogacy arrangement, the child's best interest is a paramount consideration. In addition, courts would ensure that at least one of the commissioning parents is biologically related to the child. In fact, a child born under an international surrogacy arrangement will not automatically acquire R.O.C. (Taiwan)'s nationality. The commissioning

70 Ibid.

71 K. Trimmings and P. Beaumont, 'International Surrogacy Arrangements: An Urgent Need for Legal Regulation at the International Level' (2011) 7 *Journal of Private International Law* 3, 630.

parents will be required to undertake adoption procedures under which the commissioning mother will be recognised as the adoptive mother, while the commissioning father registers the child as his though born out of wedlock.[72] In addition, in Taiwan, although there is no penalty for commissioning parents, mediators and agencies who broker such arrangements and gain financially from them face the possibility of a two-year jail term and/or a fine of between NTD$200,000 to NTD$1 million if convicted.[73]

6. THE GENETIC LINK AND THE IMAGE OF THE FAMILY: AN ANALYSIS OF THE PROPOSED AMENDMENTS ON SURROGACY

Looking into the contents of the draft amendments proposed by legislators and the MOHW, it is not difficult to discern an inclination towards greater protection of the rights and interests of the commissioning parents than the surrogate or child born though surrogacy. This may be reflective of cultural familial norms in Taiwanese society, in which the traditional preference for biological offspring to carry on the family line, especially the paternal line, remains strong. This also speaks to why many people would prefer to seek surrogates abroad, despite the considerable expense, rather than adopt a child. In some jurisdictions where surrogacy is legal, at the time of birth a surrogate may be automatically regarded as the legal mother of a child born through surrogacy, especially when traditional surrogacy is involved and the surrogate is artificially inseminated with the commissioning father's sperm. In such cases, commissioning parents must transfer legal parenthood for children born to surrogates, either through adoption or other specific legal mechanisms. Under such arrangements, the law establishes the necessary conditions that must be met before the transfer of parenthood can be recognised in order to protect the interests of surrogates. Some jurisdictions even stipulate that, under certain circumstances, if the child is biologically related, the surrogate has the right, for a certain period of time after the birth of the child, to rescind the contract.[74] The rationale behind these

---

72 Reporter, 'Feature: Couples suffer as long as surrogacy remains illegal', *Taipei Times*, 20.07.2013, <http://www.taipeitimes.com/News/taiwan/archives/2013/07/20/2003567762/1> accessed 13.09.2018.

73 Reporter, 'Woman prosecuted for brokering surrogacy', *The China Post*, 04.05.2016, <http://www.chinapost.com.tw/taiwan/local/hsinchu/2016/05/04/465110/Woman-prosecuted.htm> accessed 13.09.2018.

74 For example, in Florida in the United States, a surrogate has the right to rescind the contract up to 48 hours after the birth of the child if the child is biologically related to her. See A. Finkelstein et al., 'Surrogacy Law and Policy in the U.S.: A National Conversation Informed by Global Lawmaking', a research paper carried out by *Columbia Law School Sexuality & Gender Law Clinic* (2016), p. 10.

legal mechanisms is to ensure that surrogates will not be compelled, against their will, to relinquish their parental rights.

In Taiwan, the proposed legal amendments would only recognise gestational surrogacy. The draft legal mechanisms view the genetic link as prevailing over a non-genetic relationship between surrogate and a child born through surrogacy. The legal mechanisms in the draft legislation are designed to recognise the legal parenthood of the commissioning parents, and are derivative of the rationale that puts greater weight on kinship and genetic relationships. This also illustrates the government's concerns with the complicated ethical and legal issues involved in legalising surrogacy. Although the general public is willing to see the government adopt a more permissive attitude on surrogacy, several polls show that the majority of the public (78 per cent) still supports maintaining the genetic link in surrogacy arrangements. This position is reflected in the proposed legal mechanisms for regulating ART and surrogacy, which would require that both reproductive cells – sperm and egg – be provided by the commissioning parents. Under such proposed amendments, surrogacy could provide an important alternative means for infertile couples to have their own genetic children.

Surrogacy will inevitably redefine the traditional meaning of family even though surrogacy may take place in a number of ways, and different types of surrogacy may have different implications for the genetic relationship between the surrogate and the child. Compared to traditional surrogacy, gestational surrogacy ensures that there is no genetic link between the surrogate and the child.[75] In Taiwan, the draft legal mechanism recognising only gestational surrogacy illustrates the government's attitudes toward the maintenance of the genetic link in order to minimally reconfigure established notions of family. The greater protections granted to commissioning parents' interests have caused unease among women's rights groups in Taiwan. Concerns have been raised that the draft legal amendments may provide means for the rich to exploit the poor insofar as the surrogate's role is restricted to gestation only. Currently, under the proposed amendments, there is a lack of comprehensive mechanisms for regulating the preservation of information concerning the surrogate. Under the present draft amendments, the transferring of legal parenthood is not a precondition for commissioning parents to be regarded as legal parents at birth; whether the child will later be able to access information on their conception and birth, and if so under what conditions, is as yet unclear. Avoiding a situation in which the legalisation of surrogacy benefits only the rich and renders a

75 Because gestational surrogacy arrangement requires the use of assisted reproductive technology, the advances in ART have made this type of surrogacy far more common than the traditional surrogacy nowadays.

woman's body a commodity has emerged as the main issue yet to be resolved in the Taiwanese context.[76]

7. CONCLUSION

Although legalising surrogacy has been discussed in Taiwan for more than a decade, it has not yet been realised. The enactment of the Law of Assisted Reproduction in 2007 provides comprehensive legislation addressing the application of assisted reproduction, but surrogacy was excluded entirely from the LAR. The latest opinion polls carried out by the government show that over 85 per cent of respondents support legalising surrogacy so long as necessary complementary measures are in place. Recently, draft amendments were again proposed that would include altruistic surrogacy under the regulation. Concerns remain for the women's rights groups that the proposed amendments give the rich means to exploit the poor by regarding a surrogate as a gestational carrier only, and some consider the protections extended to protect the rights and interests of surrogates and children to be adequate. As the issue of surrogacy remains controversial in Taiwanese society, reaching a consensus on this contentious issue appears to be imperative if the government is to move forward the legislation.

---

76 The comments proposed by Huang Sue-ying (黃淑英), then chairperson of Taiwan Women's Link, the advocacy group for women's rights development in Taiwan. See 'Taiwan couples seek surrogacy abroad to escape ban,' *Fox News*, 17.07.2013, <http://www.foxnews.com/world/2013/07/17/taiwan-couples-seek-surrogacy-abroad-to-escape-ban.html> accessed 13.09.2018.

SURROGACY IN SINGAPORE

Terry KAAN

1. GENERAL LEGAL FRAMEWORK

1.1. THE GENERAL LEGAL FRAMEWORK AND SOCIAL BACKGROUND

Singapore has no legislation that deals directly with surrogacy by that name. But the lacuna is not an oversight. The Singapore Parliament is well aware of the issues, given that the formal regulation of surrogacy has been urged upon the government of the day in recent Parliamentary debates.[1] This does not, however, mean that surrogacy is beyond the reach of regulation or formal law in Singapore. As will be explained later in this chapter, Singapore does however have a number of legislative enactments that, together with executive instruments having the force of subsidiary legislation, impose clear and enforceable legal restrictions on the conduct of surrogacy arrangements *within* Singapore. Further, some of these legal provisions have extra-territorial reach,

1 Singapore Parliamentary Reports (*Hansard*), Parliament no. 12, Session no. 1, vol. 90, Sitting 21, 12.08.2013, the speech of Ms Tan Su Shan, NMP; and the response of the Minister for Law, Mr K. Shanmugam on the Second Reading of the Status of Children (Assisted Reproduction Technology) Bill ('STATUS OF CHILDREN ACT', *Hansard*).

and have the potential to affect surrogacy arrangements involving a party or parties having a sufficient connection to Singapore as defined by the law.

It may be useful at this point to set out briefly the key features of the constitutional and legal framework in Singapore in order to understand the development of the regulatory regime for surrogacy in Singapore, and in particular, the impact of English common precedents on local judicial decisions. From 1819 to 1963, Singapore was a British colonial possession before its merger with the new state of Malaysia in 1963. In 1965, Singapore became an independent country after peaceful secession from Malaysia by mutual agreement. Like many former British colonies, it inherited a constitutional system of the Westminster model, but with an elected President replacing the monarch, and a unicameral Parliament instead of a bicameral one. More than half a century after ceasing to be a British Crown Colony, the English common law continues to play the dominant role in its constitutional and legal system.

The habit of adherence to the English common law has deep historical roots some two centuries old in the form of the Second Charter of Justice 1826 by which the Crown decreed that English law should be applied to its new possessions in the Straits of Malacca, including Singapore. Formal legal links between the United Kingdom and Singapore continued after independence with the Judicial Committee of the Privy Council being constituted as the highest court of appeal within the legal system. This link was only finally broken in 1993 with the constitution of the present Court of Appeal of the Supreme Court of Singapore as the apex court in place of the Privy Council.[2] In 1994, Parliament moved to pass the Application of English Law Act.[3] By this Act, the continued application of English statutes was restricted to a short list spelt out in the Act. More significantly, s. 3 of the Act specified that while the English common law ('including the principles and rules of equity') was to continue to apply, a cut-off date of 12 November 1993 was to be applied. The formal effect of the Act is that English common law developments after 1993 can no longer be regarded as a source of binding precedents. The real effect, however, has been that the highest court of the land, the Singapore Court of Appeal, was from that date free to consider sources of jurisprudence from a much wider range of jurisdictions. Common law jurisdictions such as the United Kingdom, Australia, Canada, New Zealand, Malaysia (of which country Singapore was once part) and the United States are the sources of foreign jurisprudence most commonly considered by the local courts, but in practice, current English common law precedents continue to be the most frequently applied body of foreign jurisprudence, especially in tort and contract (both areas of law relevant to surrogacy) although the decisions themselves are no longer binding.

2 With the passage of the Supreme Court of Judicature (Amendment) Act 1993 (no. 16 of 1993).

3 The Application of English Law Act (Cap. 7A).

Freed from the constraints of being bound by English precedents, the Court of Appeal has not hesitated to reverse long-established principles of English common law, or establish altogether novel legal concepts of its own, such its recent formulation of a right to damages for the loss of 'genetic affinity' in *ACB v Thomson Medical Pte Ltd* which will be discussed below.[4]

The first 'test-tube baby born in Asia' was born in Singapore on 19 May 1983. The baby, Samuel Lee, had been conceived in vitro in an artificial reproductive technologies ('ART') fertilisation programme which was the first of its kind in Asia.[5] Three decades on, fertility has assumed an even greater urgency in the national consciousness, with the low fertility rate meriting numerous mentions in Parliament as well as in the media. Singapore has the dubious distinction of having one of the lowest Total Fertility Rates ('TFR') in the world at just 1.20.[6] Singapore has a tiny population of just 5.6 million, of which just 3.4 million people are citizens.[7] The median age of first marriage for both men and women at 30.3 and 28.2 are high for an Asian society, and on a steadily rising trend.[8] This trend has become a matter of increasing concern to the government, which has in recent years introduced subsidy and incentives such as the Marriage and Parenthood Package, which has been announced will cost the state some S$2 billion (US$1.4 billion) a year.[9] This largesse, it must be remembered, is for a population in which there were just 27,971 marriages in 2017.[10]

Given the relatively small window of remaining fertile years for women, the lateness of marriage has inevitably led to an increased demand for ART services, to the extent that the state established a subsidy scheme for couples seeking ART treatment in 2008. This scheme was subsequently expanded, so that couples seeking ART treatment may now apply for a subsidy of up to 75 per cent of the cost of ART treatment and may use a further S$6,000 (approximately US$4,350 at mid-2017 exchange rates) from their Medisave accounts.[11]

---

4 *ACB v Thomson Medical Pte Ltd and others* [2017] SGCA 20.

5 'Made in Singapore: Asia's first test-tube baby', *Straits Times*, 18.06.2015.

6 Data for 2017, Department of Statistics, Singapore, <https://www.singstat.gov.sg/modules/infographics/total-fertility-rate> accessed 25.04.2017; 'The World Factbook', 'World Development Indicators: Reproductive Health', 'The World Bank', <http://wdi.worldbank.org/table/2.14#> accessed 13.09.2018.

7 'Population Trends 2016', Department of Statistics, Singapore, Table 1.1, p. 3.

8 'Statistics on Marriage and Divorces, 2015', Department of Statistics, Singapore, Chart 1.5, p. 6; 'Trend Towards Older Grooms and Brides', *Statistics Singapore Newsletter*, September 2011, Department of Statistics, Singapore, p. 10.

9 'Government releases new measures to promote marriage and parenthood', *Straits Times*, 21.01.2013. The subsidies include a 75 per cent subsidy for ART procedures.

10 Department of Statistics, Singapore, <https://www.singstat.gov.sg/find-data/search-by-theme/population/marital-status-marriages-and-divorces/latest-data> accessed 28.04.2017.

11 Medisave Accounts are accounts held by Singaporeans with the Singapore Central Provident Fund from which payments can be made to cover the expenses of in-hospital treatment and some kinds of outpatient treatment. The Medisave scheme is mandated by law under s. 13

There are however restrictions: the subsidy is only available for a maximum of three fresh and three frozen ART cycles, and the fertility treatment must be carried out at government hospitals. The subsidy is available to men and women alike but women seeking the ART subsidy must be below the age of 40, and the ART procedures do not extend to the freezing of eggs (as opposed to embryos).[12] There are no publicly available statistics of the demand for fertility treatment, but a figure of 1,308 births in 2010 resulting from ART procedures has been cited in Parliament.[13] The very low birth rate has resulted in a shortfall that has not been fully met by immigration, given a population growth rate of just 0.8 per cent annually.[14] For most couples with fertility problems, adoption is an unlikely alternative: just 387 babies were adopted in 2016.[15] But with surrogacy services being unavailable to them legally in Singapore, the only remaining option is surrogacy procedures carried out abroad. No reliable data or even estimates are available for the number of couples resorting to surrogacy arrangements carried out abroad. This is not surprising, given the questions about the legality of such procedures both in countries where these arrangements are carried out, as well as in Singapore, but media reports indicate that would-be parents 'have gone to countries such as Malaysia, India, the United States and Thailand and paid six-figure sums for a stranger to carry their baby'.[16]

---

of the Central Provident Fund Act (Cap. 36). Under this scheme, employees in Singapore are required to contribute a portion of their monthly salary (ranging from eight per cent to 10.5 per cent, depending on the age of the contributor) to their personal Medisave accounts, with self-employed persons contributing on a different scale. There is a limit to the amount to be held in Medisave accounts: as at 1 January 2018, the maximum amount to be held in a Medisave account was S$54,500 (about US$39,700 as at July 2018). Once this amount is reached, account holders are not liable for further contributions until the balance falls again through outgoing payments for medical services. The Medisave scheme allows for the reimbursement of expenses for medical treatment not only at government hospitals, but also private hospitals and private clinics and outpatient providers. Medisave accounts may also be used to pay for approved medical expenses of immediate family members who may not have a sufficient balance in their own Medisave account – a contributor using her or his own Medisave account to pay for the medical expenses of an elderly parent or of a child are common scenarios. On the death of the account holder, the entire balance in the Medisave account forms part of the disposable estate of the account holder. For more information, see the Central Provident Fund, 'What is Medisave?' <https://www.cpf.gov.sg/Members/Schemes/schemes/healthcare/medisave> accessed 13.09.2018.

12 Ministry of Health, Singapore, <https://va.ecitizen.gov.sg/CFP/CustomerPages/MOH/explorefaq.aspx> accessed 13.09.2018.

13 Singapore Parliamentary Reports (*Hansard*), Parliament no. 12, Session no. 1, vol. 90, Sitting 21, 12 August 2013, the speech of Mr Hri Kumar Nair, MP.

14 'Population Trends 2016', Department of Statistics, Singapore, Table 1.1, p. 3.

15 Ministry of Social and Family Development, Singapore, <https://www.msf.gov.sg/Adoption/Pages/Adoption-Statistics.aspx> accessed 13.09.2018. The data does not disclose what proportion of this figure related to adoption of babies from abroad.

16 T. Tan, 'Singaporeans pay big bucks to rent a womb', *Straits Times*, 10.08.2014.

1.2. HISTORICAL DEVELOPMENT LEADING TO THE CURRENT LAW

In 1997, the Law Reform Committee of the Singapore Academy of Law commissioned a review of the state of the law relating to the status of children born through ART procedures (the 'SAL Report').[17] Among the points made in the SAL Report was the observation that despite the popularity and ready availability of ART, there were no specific legislative provisions dealing with the legal status of children born through ART procedures: Singapore did not have the equivalent of the then UK Human Fertilisation and Embryology Act 1990 ('HFEA 1990') with the result that issues like legitimacy and parenthood of such children were left to the uncertainties and legal vacuum of the very common law considered by the Warnock Report[18] which led to the enactment of the HFEA 1990.[19] A particular concern was that the principal legislative provision governing presumptions of legitimacy (and thereby parenthood) was an 'obsolete' statutory presumption dating back to the late nineteenth century.

Section 114 of the Evidence Act[20] then provided for a statutory presumption for a child to be presumed to be a child of the marriage if the child was born in wedlock, or within 280 days of the dissolution of the marriage 'unless it can be shown that the parties had no access to each other at any time when he could have been begotten'. This provision in effect statutorily crystallises the long-standing English law common presumption in favour of the legitimacy of a child born in wedlock.[21] But this presumption takes no account of advances in medical technologies, particularly of ART procedures and blood and genetic tests which can now determine with certainty biological paternity (and it must be added, maternity as well, in the case where the gestational mother has received an embryo that has resulted from an egg not her own). While the public policy intent behind the presumption is clear, the presumption could operate to create injustice in some circumstances even when ART procedures are not involved. Thus the Singapore courts have had to consider cases such as *WX v WW* in which a man ('H') who had entered into marriage under the mistaken impression that the woman was carrying his child.[22] DNA tests subsequently confirmed that he could not have been the father of the

---

17 The Law Reform Committee, Singapore Academy of Law, 'Report of The Sub-Committee on the Status of Children Born Through Artificial Conception', 26.09.2007.

18 'Report of the Committee of Inquiry into Human Fertilisation and Embryology' (Cmnd. 9314: 1984, reprinted HMSO 1988).

19 The SAL Report, 2.6–2.10.

20 Currently the Evidence Act (Cap. 97), originally based on the Indian Evidence Act (no. 1 of 1872).

21 See, for example, 'Blood Tests and the Proof of Paternity in Civil Proceedings', The Law Commission (HMSO: 1968), at para. 11.

22 *WX v WW* [2009] 3 SLR 573; [2009] SGHC 70.

child, and the court had to consider whether the appellant (the true biological father) ought be made liable for the maintenance of the child. The appellant argued that s. 114 of the Evidence Act created an irrebuttable presumption that H was the lawful father, DNA tests results notwithstanding. The High Court disagreed, noting that just as the presumption of legitimacy and fatherhood was based on public policy, it was also public policy that the court should not permit the presumption to be used in a way that 'offends both justice and commonsense'.[23]

But the point here is simply that this seemingly obvious issue of paternity, as well as the admissibility of blood tests and other medical technologies, raised sufficient issues of ambiguity and uncertainty in the law that it had to go through two levels of courts before being resolved.[24] What, then, of the situation if a man sought to challenge the paternity of a child born in wedlock, but through ART using sperm donated by a third party? Would it make a difference if he had actually consented (or known about, but had not raised objections) to the procedure? What if the mother, with the consent or knowledge of her partner, had had an embryo implanted in her which was fertilised with the sperm of an unknown and anonymous sperm donor? In this situation, even decisions such as *WX v WW* would be of no assistance, as the result might be that the child might be left without a legal father.[25] More directly relevant to surrogacy, s. 114 failed altogether to address the situation where the embryo implanted in the mother is the result of a donated egg (i.e. not her own egg), and third-party donor sperm – in this case there would be no biological connection at all between the 'parents' and the child: there was no statutory presumption that the woman who gives birth to a child is the lawful mother of the child.

For these reasons, the SAL Report made the recommendation that a provision along the lines of the then s. 27 of the HFEA 1990 (now s. 33 of the HFEA 2008) should be implemented, namely that the gestational mother of a child, regardless of the source of the egg, should be regarded as the lawful mother of the child, and no other.[26]

The SAL Report also noted that there were no statutory provisions relating to the legal protection for (or responsibilities of) third-party sperm donors – there was nothing in the statutes to guarantee their anonymity, or preserve them against potential claims for maintenance, and recommended that these protections be put in place. The SAL Report did not, however, specifically address surrogacy issues, despite that many of its recommendations would have a direct impact on surrogacy arrangements: would, for example, a surrogate

23 Ibid., at para. 6.

24 The action was commenced in the first instance in the District Courts, and went on appeal to the High Court.

25 The SAL Report, 3.11.

26 The current s. 33(1) of the UK Human Fertilisation and Embryology Act 2008.

mother who had been implanted with an embryo created from the egg and sperm of a commissioning couple be entitled to claim exclusive rights to legal motherhood in contravention of a surrogacy agreement between her and the commissioning couple?

Despite the steep rise births resulting from ART procedures as described above, the remarkable thing is that the recommendations advanced in the SAL Report were not taken up for another decade and a half. It was only in early 2011 that these issues were brought back into sharp focus before the public eye when the events leading to the *ACB v Thomson* case (discussed at the end of this chapter) involving a sperm mix-up was reported in the media. Two years later, by the end of 2013, a new statute was passed for the comprehensive regulation of the status of children born through ART procedures: the Status of Children (Assisted Reproduction Technology) Act ('Status of Children Act').[27] This new statute has profound implications for surrogacy arrangements entered into by persons who are Singapore citizens (or have a connection with Singapore as determined by the Act), and for the legal parentage of the child – whether the child was conceived or born in Singapore, or abroad.

2. SURROGACY ARRANGEMENTS IN GENERAL

2.1. LEGALITY AND ENFORCEABILITY

There is currently no legislation directly addressing surrogacy arrangements in Singapore. The assumption must be that questions of legality and enforceability (which are of course not the same thing) are left to be governed by common law. The question, as explained above, is *whose* common law, and what part of it. Even if English common law is to be assumed to be applicable, the Application of English Law Act clearly requires a cut-off date of 13 November 1993. This means in effect that the courts would have to look at the English common law as it stood at that date. Both the common law and statutory law of England have moved on since. Singapore has not had the advantage of the certainty provided by the UK Surrogacy Arrangements Act 1985, which does not apply in Singapore. Instead, it is left to the devices of the uncertainties of a body of English common law left obsolete and grandfathered in 1985 by the advent of the UK Surrogacy Arrangements Act.

In the absence of legislation, it therefore technically is *not* unlawful (in the sense of contravening a statutory provision) for parties to enter into a surrogacy agreement. As far as legislation is concerned, all that can be said is that the parties entering into such an agreement will not be committing a criminal

27 Cap. 317A (originally Act 16 of 2013).

offence. But finding a doctor or a medical establishment in Singapore to give effect to the agreement will be an entirely different matter. What the law *does* say is that no party may provide the necessary medical services: it is against the law for any hospital, clinic or medical professional to carry out any surrogacy procedure *in Singapore*. This prohibition comes about in a somewhat convoluted and indirect way. By s. 5 of the Private Hospital and Medical Clinics Act ('PHMCA'), all hospitals, medical clinics, clinical laboratories and healthcare establishments are required to operate within the terms of licenses granted by the Director of Medical Services ('DMS'), and to comply with the directions of the DMS.[28] The subsidiary legislation gazetted under the PHMCA then goes on to provide that 'specialized procedures or services' may not be carried out without a specific licence from the DMS.[29] The relevant Schedule to the rules define 'specialized procedures or services' as including 'Assisted reproduction services'.[30] Pursuant to its powers under s. 6(5) of the PHMCA, the Ministry of Health publishes a document detailing the licensing terms and conditions for any medical establishment granted a licence to carry out ART procedures ('ART Licence Terms').[31] Paragraph 5.48 of the ART Licence Terms provide as follows (emphasis in the original):

> '5.85 AR Centres shall **not** carry out any of the following activities:
>
> *(a)* …
> *(b)* Surrogacy (surrogacy is where a woman is artificially impregnated, whether for monetary compensation or not, with the intention that the child is to be given or adopted by some other person or couple); …'

The net result of all these layers of rules and regulations is that any AR Centre (and the individuals who staff that centre) that carries out or facilitates surrogacy will be guilty of a criminal offence under s. 5 of the PHMCA, and be liable on conviction of a fine of up to S$2,000, or to a jail term of up to two years, or both. On the other hand, the rules do not bind persons not subject to the jurisdiction of the DMS under the Act. Commissioning parents (unless of course they are physicians themselves) do not come under the jurisdiction of the PHMCA, and so are presumably free to enter into surrogacy agreements. There is still the possibility of a surrogacy arrangement being effected through a DIY intrauterine insemination procedure, so long as no medical personnel was involved in facilitating it.

---

28 Cap. 248.

29 Regulation 18 of the Private Hospitals and Medical Clinics Regulations (Cap. 248, Rg 1).

30 Second Schedule.

31 Ministry of Health, Singapore, *Terms and Conditions on Assisted Reproduction Services Imposed Under Section 6(5) of the Private Hospitals and Medical Clinics Act (Cap 248)* – the latest version as of 04.25.2017 is dated 26.04.2011.

On 17 December 2018 the High Court of Singapore, sitting in its Family Division appellate jurisdiction, delivered its decision in the case of *UKM v Attorney-General.*[32] Space permits only a brief consideration here of this decision, which has implications for some of the issues discussed in this chapter. In *UKM*, the applicant was a gay man in a long-term relationship with another man. Both were Singaporeans, and both wanted a child together. At the beginning of 2013, they entered into a surrogacy arrangement with a surrogate mother and her husband in the United States for a child conceived through the fertilisation of an egg from an anonymous donor with the applicant's sperm to be brought to term and to be delivered to the applicant and his partner. The applicant paid a total of around 'US$200,000, including medical fees, insurance, legal costs, agency fees and a payment to M [the surrogate mother] of US$25,000'.

The same-sex relationship in this case is significant, as homosexual acts (but not the relationship itself) between men (but not between women) remain a crime, with a jail term of up to two years.[33] But as the High Court in *UKM* noted, 'Although s 377A is not enforced, it has not been repealed' despite much public debate and legal challenges brought before the courts in recent years as to the constitutionality of the provision.[34]

The child was born an American citizen by virtue of American *jus soli* constitutional provisions, so the complication of statelessness of the child in cases like *X & Y (Foreign Surrogacy)* was not in issue.[35] Shortly after birth, the child was brought back to Singapore to live with the applicant and his partner. But the applicant decided to make an application for the adoption of his biological son with a view to eventually obtaining Singapore citizenship or permanent residency for the long term.

In the District Court below, the application for adoption was refused on various grounds, including that since 'gestational surrogacy was not legally available here to anyone, whether homosexual or heterosexual, married or single', to allow the adoption would be to allow the applicant to walk 'through the back door of the system when the front door was firmly shut'.[36] This view was firmly overturned by the High Court, which confirmed that surrogacy of itself was not unlawful in Singapore, nor was it unlawful for intending commissioning couples to seek surrogacy services abroad. The High Court rejected the view that there was a strong 'public policy against obtaining surrogacy services, whether in or outside Singapore'.[37]

---

32 [2018] SGHCF 18.
33 Section 377A, Penal Code (Cap. 224).
34 Most recently in *Lim Meng Suang v Attorney-General* [2015] 1 SLR 26.
35 [2008] EWHC 3030 (Fam).
36 *UKM v Attorney-General* [2018] SGHCF 18, at paras. 16–21.
37 Ibid., at para. 178–179.

2.2. EXTRA-TERRITORIALITY

Until the *UKM* decision, there was no certainty as to whether it was lawful for commissioning couples to seek surrogacy services abroad. All that could be said was that the rules were silent altogether on this point.

With the *UKM* decision, all uncertainty was removed: the High Court held that commissioning parents were indeed free to seek surrogacy services abroad. It noted that, during the hearing, the Guardian disclosed that in the 10 years to 2018, the Ministry of Social and Family Development had overseen '14 applications for adoption which involved the use of surrogacy. Ten were supported by the Guardian, and the remaining four were, at the time of the hearing, pending investigation. And in all 14 cases, surrogacy had been resorted to overseas because the couple were infertile'. The High Court concluded that given the Guardian's support for these applications, it was 'difficult to hold … that there is a strong and clear public policy against surrogacy'.[38]

The net position is that, while surrogacy services are all but impossible to obtain *within* Singapore, it is perfectly lawful for Singaporeans to resort to such services abroad – even where significant payments are involved, as will be seen in the discussion of the *UKM* decision in Section 4 below.

3. LEGAL PARENTHOOD

3.1. GENERAL STATUTORY PRESUMPTIONS

Since 1 October 2014,[39] the Status of Children Act has been the controlling legislation governing the status of children born through any ART procedure.[40] Of necessity, this would cover all kinds of surrogacy arrangements where ART is used but would exclude contracts for the adoption (or parenthood or 'ownership') of a naturally conceived child. The basic rule is set out in s. 6:

> '**Gestational mother treated as mother**
>
> **6.** Subject to section 9, where a woman has carried a child as a result of a fertilisation procedure, the woman shall be treated as the mother of the child from the date of the birth of the child, whether she was in Singapore or elsewhere at the time she underwent the fertilisation procedure.'

---

38 Ibid., at paras. 176–177.

39 Status of Children (Assisted Reproduction Technology) Act 2013 (Commencement) Notification 2014.

40 Section 2 of the Status of Children Act sets out the definition of 'fertilisation procedure'. There is uncertainty as to whether the definition would in fact cover DIY intrauterine insemination, as it speaks of 'the placing of an embryo or of sperm and eggs in a woman' – note sperm and eggs are mentioned in the conjunctive.

This provision is essentially the same as the current s. 33 of the HFEA 2008.[41] The question then is to what kind of fertilisation procedures might s. 6 apply. For instance, would the provisions of the Status of Children Act bind commissioning couples who go abroad to country X (it having been established that a Singaporean couple may by the laws of Singapore lawfully go abroad to commission a surrogate child) to commission a surrogate child to which either the commissioning husband or the wife or both have contributed their sperm or egg? To this, s. 3 of the Status of Children Act provides the answers. If the child is born in Singapore, then regardless of the citizenship of the gestational mother, the Act applies. But if the child is born abroad, the situation is rather more complicated. The Act applies if any of the following parties to the surrogacy arrangement is domiciled in Singapore: the gestational mother, the husband of the gestational mother, the 'de facto partner' of the gestational mother, 'the person whose sperm or egg the child was brought about with', or 'the person who consented to the fertilisation procedure'.

For the purposes of surrogacy arrangements, it is the reference to 'the person whose sperm or egg the child was brought about with' that may cause difficulties for the commissioning parents if either or the both of them have contributed towards the child with their own gametes. In such a situation, the foreign gestational mother would be assumed in Singapore law to be the mother of the child, and no other, even if she has never stepped foot in Singapore, and has no other connection to Singapore.

3.2. APPLICATION TO SURROGACY ARRANGEMENTS

There is a fundamental problem in construing the provisions of the Status of Children Act in the context of surrogacy arrangements. Although the provisions clearly cover surrogacy arrangements given that ART procedures are invariably employed, the Act refrains from specifically addressing surrogacy arrangements. This is neither a mistake nor an oversight. In the Parliamentary debates on the Second Reading for the passage of the Bill, the government was urged to consider the plight of:

> 'the growing trend of Singaporean couples resorting to surrogacy abroad. … If a woman is not medically able to carry a pregnancy, the couple may choose to have a gestational surrogate overseas as surrogacy is not allowed here. The Bill in its current

---

41 The 'and no other woman' provision in s. 33(1) of the HFEA 2008 is taken up separately in s. 3(3) of the Singapore Status of Children Act, which uses the phrase 'no other person' to define the exclusive right not only of the mother, but also of any man treated as the father under the Status of Children Act to be identified and treated as the mother or father, as the case may be. In short, therefore, a child born of ART procedures (including a child born of surrogacy arrangements) has only one mother and one father in law (this is discussed further below).

> form leaves unclear the status of this child in relation to the Singaporean couple using a gestation carrier abroad. The outcome could be harsh for the couple if the child is, in fact, genetically the child of the couple.'[42]

The point being here is that the commissioning mother would be precluded by ss. 3 and 6 of the Act from asserting a claim to legal motherhood despite her genetic link to the child. This may well have the unfortunate effect of leaving the child in a legal limbo if the foreign gestational mother insists on surrendering the child to the commissioning parents in accordance with the terms of the surrogacy arrangement. Conversely (and arguably perversely) a set of commissioning parents who arranged for the implantation of an embryo created from egg and sperm from non-Singaporean third parties, would stand a better chance of being recognised in Singapore law as the legal parents, at least in the sense that they would not be statutorily and prima facie excluded as parents by the Status of Children Act, as the provisions of the Act would have no application to such an arrangement. They would of course still face an uphill task in persuading the Singapore courts to recognise the validity and effect of the surrogacy arrangement in the gestational mother's jurisdiction. But the concerns here are clear. One is that the commissioning parents who have a genetic link to the child will be presumptively denied the possibility of legal parenthood. The other is that the child will be cast into legal and nationality limbo if the laws of the gestational mother's jurisdictions refuses to treat such surrogate children as being entitled to citizenship. This of course has profound consequences for any attempt at obtaining Singaporean residency and citizenship for the child. The alternative of course is adoption, but this avenue may be foreclosed to the commissioning parents by virtue of their having contravened the laws of Singapore relating to adoption (this is further discussed below) by having paid for the surrogacy arrangement. In the same vein, the legal limbo of the child (potentially stateless, and without a legal parent) will not help matters.

The response of the Minister of Law to the plea for the law to address specifically the situation of commissioning surrogate parents and the resulting child was categorical: 'It is not intended through this Bill to address the larger question of surrogacy'.[43] In short, commissioning parents who go abroad to enter into surrogacy arrangements must take their chances in arranging for the adoption of their own genetic child under circumstances which may involve a breach of the provisions of the adoption laws in Singapore.

Given that surrogacy arrangements although theoretically legal are all but impossible to implement in Singapore since the involvement of any medical

42 Ms Tan Su Shan, NMP, above n. 1.

43 Above n. 1.

professional would constitute a criminal act, commissioning parents have no choice but to look abroad. As explained above, this the law allows, if only through omission and silence. But as argued above, the Status of Children Act now operates to create a presumption of motherhood for the gestational mother, and the gestational mother only. No other woman can be the mother, and a child may only have one mother and one father as far as the law is concerned.[44] As the Minister for Law put it: '... the real point of this Bill is to make sure that Children who are conceived through the ART process are not left in a legal limbo'.[45] This rule applies even if the biological reality is that both of the commissioning parents are the biological parents of the child. Even in such a case, the Status of Children Act will operate to hold the gestational mother the legal and sole mother of the child, regardless of the fact that she may have no genetic connection with the child at all.

The only exception made by the Status of Children Act is for circumstances in which 'by reason of any mistake, negligence, recklessness or fraud, any egg, sperm or embryo used in a fertilization procedure undergone by a gestational mother' was not the intended gamete or embryo.[46] This is unlikely to be of any use to commissioning mothers in surrogacy arrangements, as the wording of s. 9 appears to preclude any attempt by a commissioning mother to apply for an order declaring herself the mother of the child even if the child has been abandoned by the gestational mother because no fraud or mistake would have been involved. The Act is clearly focused principally on the identity of the legal mother, and less on that of the father. Under the Act, a child born of ART procedures *has to have* a legal mother, but not necessarily a legal father – as is the case for natural births where the natural father is unknown or has not been identified as such to the authorities responsible for registering the birth.[47] Compared to the rigid presumption of motherhood for the gestational mother, there is somewhat more wiggle room for the presumption of paternity under the Status of Children Act. The general rule is that the husband *of the gestational mother* is to be presumed to be the father if the pregnancy of the gestational mother was brought about with his sperm, or (as would be much more likely the case in surrogacy arrangements) if the pregnancy was brought about with his consent using sperm from a third-party donor (e.g. the commissioning father).[48] If the gestational mother is unmarried, a 'de facto partner' (a man 'living in a relationship as if he were her spouse') may under the circumstances defined in the Act be presumed as the father of the child.[49]

44 Section 3 of the Status of Children Act.
45 Above n. 1.
46 Section 9 of the Status of Children Act.
47 Under the Registration of Births and Deaths Act (Cap. 267) and the Legitimacy Act (Cap. 162).
48 Section 7(1), (2) of the Status of Children Act.
49 Section 7(3)–(6) of the Status of Children Act.

The Act itself recognises that because of the complexity of the rules relating to the determination of the legal father, it is entirely possible that more than one man may qualify for the presumption of fatherhood. But, again, the Act takes a firm stand against multiple parentage by specifying that in such cases, 'only the man who is to be treated as the father of the child earlier in time by virtue of a provision in this section shall be treated as the father of the child, and no other man ...'.[50] The upshot of this is that a commissioning father who has contributed his sperm stands little chance of being recognised as the legal father under the Act, notwithstanding his genetic connection to the child.

There is one final possibility for commissioning parents confronted with the general presumptions in the Status of Children Act. Section 9(3) of the Act provides that:

> '... the court may, in its discretion and upon an application made under section 10 by a person other than the person to be treated as the parent of a child under subsection (2), declared that the person shall be the parent of the child.'

Such an application must be made within two years. At first sight, this provision may seem to offer hope for commissioning parents who have commissioned a surrogate child abroad. Under s. 10 of the Act, the courts are enjoined to consider as the 'first and paramount consideration of the court' the 'welfare and best interests of the child'. Section 10 goes on to set out the matters which the courts may take into account 'in considering the welfare and best interests of the child': these would include 'the child's biological relationship with any party in the proceedings', 'the intention of the parties to the proceedings with regard to the parenthood of the child', 'the respective abilities of the parties ... to provide for the child's physical, emotional, developmental and other needs'.[51] But all these 'matters' may be taken into account only for the purpose of determining 'the welfare and best interests of the child'. The strongest kind of case for such an application might occur in the context of a surrogacy arrangement by Singaporean commissioning parents who contribute both egg and sperm for the embryo to be implanted in the foreign gestational mother, and which child is then not just surrendered but abandoned by the gestational mother to the commissioning parents. In such a case, there may be an argument that it would be in the 'welfare and best interests of the child' (the child coming within the jurisdiction of the Singapore courts under s. 3 of the Status of Children Act by virtue of the commissioning parents having contributed the egg and sperm) for the Singapore courts to exercise its discretion to confer legal motherhood on the commissioning mother, for otherwise

---

50 Section 7(7) of the Status of Children Act.
51 Section 10(7) of the Status of Children Act.

the child would effectively be left motherless and stateless, which would be contrary to the express public policy purpose of the Act. Whether such an application might succeed is unknown, as no application by commissioning parents on this basis have yet come before the Singapore courts. Difficult questions of conflict of laws would have to be settled by the courts (the legality of surrogacy arrangements in the surrogate country versus that of Singapore's, presumptions of nationality and citizenship, and so forth).

In summary, the provisions of the Status of Children Act would appear to generally prevent any claim to parenthood by Singapore citizens of any surrogate child born abroad through ART procedures, even if either of them or both have donated the egg or sperm for the embryo to be implanted in the gestational mother. Singapore law would insist on the gestational mother and her husband (or de facto partner) being treated as the lawful mother and father to the exclusion of all others.[52]

4. TRANSFERRING PARENTHOOD

If the provisions of the Status of Children Act effectively means that transfer of parenthood from the gestational mother is all but impossible, what other option or options might there be for commissioning parents? Adoption might appear to be the obvious answer at first sight. But again, this is not as simple as it may seem. Adoptions in Singapore are governed by the Adoption of Children Act.[53] Intending adoptive parents are required to attend a Pre-Adoption Briefing by the Ministry of Family and Social Development, and all applications for adoptions are heard by the Family Court. Of special concern to commissioning parents will be the requirement that a Home Study Report be commissioned and carried out. A Home Study Report is required for the adoption of any child from abroad, and is 'a comprehensive investigation into the circumstances surrounding the adoption and the circumstances of your family. It also assesses whether you and your spouse are eligible and ready to adopt a child' – a worrying prospect indeed for commissioning parents who may not be particularly eager to shed light on the true circumstances of the underlying arrangement![54]

Worse, s. 11 of the Adoption of Children Act states in categorical terms that:

> '... it shall not be lawful for any adopter or any parent or guardian except with the sanction of the court to receive and payment or other reward in consideration of the

52 This interpretation was confirmed in the case of *UKM v Attorney-General* [2018] SGHCF 18, at paras. 171–172. The High Court noted that, unlike in the HFEA 1990, there was no mechanism for 'parental orders' for the transfer of parenthood to commissioning parents.

53 Cap. 4.

54 Ministry of Social and Family Development, <https://www.msf.gov.sg/Adoption/Pages/Apply-for-Home-Study-Report.aspx> accessed 13.09.2018.

adoption of any infant under this Act or for any person to make or give or agree to make or give to any adopter or to any parent or guardian any such payment or reward'.

In the *UKM* case, one of the principal arguments (which the District Court below had accepted) against the grant of the adoption order was that the US$200,000 payment made to the surrogate mother ran afoul of s. 11. The High Court, however, took a more nuanced interpretation of s. 11: it held that while s. 11 indeed provided for a rebuttable presumption of illegality where a payment had been made, it also at the same time conferred on the courts the power to sanction such payments.[55] It took the view that 'the kind of payment described in s 11 is usually made in circumstances where the child in question is being trafficked or otherwise exploited'[56] and held that the legislative intention 'was that the court may sanction a payment caught by s 11 if it is satisfied that the payment was made for the purpose of adopting the child with a sincere desire to benefit and promote his welfare.'[57]

5. CONCLUSION

The insistence on the presumption of motherhood for the gestational mother, regardless of her actual biological connection (or lack thereof) in the Status of Children Act is curious, given the background to the passage of the Act. The clear preference was for the certainty offered in the person of the gestational mother, as opposed to allowing a substantive inquiry into who might be the actual genetic parents of the child. It will also be remembered that the government declined to make explicit provisions for surrogate children and commissioning parents in the Act. Less than four years after the passage of the Act, the highest court in Singapore, the Court of Appeal, delivered its judgment in the case of *ACB v Thomson Medical Pte Ltd and others* (the '*Thomson* case').[58] The public consultation on the proposed bill for the Status of Children Act, as well as the passage of the Act took place in the short period between the facts of the case coming into the media spotlight, and the final disposition of the claims arising from it in 2017. Although the passage of the Act came too late to affect the parties in the *Thomson* case, there is little doubt that the publicity given to the circumstances of the case was one of the drivers behind the passage of the Act.[59]

---

55 *UKM v Attorney-General* [2018] SGHCF 18, at paras. 211–215.

56 Ibid., at para. 215.

57 Ibid., at para. 227.

58 *ACB v Thomson Medical Pte Ltd and others* [2017] SGCA 20. The judgment was delivered on 22.03.2017.

59 The *Thomson* case was alluded to in the Parliamentary debates: see above n. 1.

In the *Thomson* case, the appellant and her husband had sought to conceive a child through IVF. A first attempt in 2006 was successful and resulted in the birth of a boy in 2007. A second IVF procedure was undertaken in 2010, using egg and sperm taken from the appellant and her husband. A girl, 'Baby P' was born as a result. But the parents soon realised that 'Baby P's skin tone and hair colour were different from their own, and were also markedly different from those of their first child, who had also been conceived through IVF'.[60] The appellant was a Singaporean Chinese woman, while her husband was ethnically and by nationality German. Tests subsequently showed that the appellant was indeed the biological mother of the child, but her husband was not the father. There had been a mix-up: the appellant's egg had been fertilised not with her husband's sperm but with that of 'an unknown male Indian donor'.[61] The first respondent subsequently plead guilty to a charge under the Private Hospitals and Medical Clinics Act for breaching the terms of its licence for conducting ART procedures, and was fined the maximum amount of S$20,000 permitted at that time. In June 2012, the appellant commenced her action against the respondents in negligence, claiming for among other things, the cost of upkeep of the child until she was 'financially self-reliant'. This part of the appellant's claim the respondents resisted, arguing that a claim for the upkeep of a healthy child (the 'upkeep claim') was legally unsustainable.

Examining the authorities from a wide range of common law jurisdictions, the court observed that there were essentially three kinds of claims for 'reproductive wrongs': wrongful life (claims brought by children themselves for an act of negligence that has resulted in a disability or disadvantage for them); wrongful birth (claims brought by a parent of the child on the basis of the negligent failure of the doctors to inform them that the child might be born with a disability); and wrongful conception (claims brought by parents for negligent performance of sterilisation operations that result in an unexpected pregnancy and child). The present situation, however, did not fall into any of these three common categories. It noted that while there had been reports of 'wrongful conception' resulting from the negligent handling of sperm or egg, few had ever come before the common law courts. The only case that they could discover on the point of an upkeep claim in such circumstances was a case decided in 2007 by the New York Supreme Court in *Andrews v Keltz*.[62] In that case, the upkeep claim was rejected. After an exhaustive survey of the common law precedents on reproductive wrongs in the United Kingdom and Australia, the court decided to follow the policy reasoning in

---

60 *ACB v Thomson Medical Pte Ltd and others* [2017] SGCA 20, para. 8.

61 Ibid., at para. 8.

62 *Andrews v Keltz* 15 Misc 3d 940. The Singapore Court of Appeal did consider the English decision of *Leeds Teaching Hospitals NHS Trust v Mr A* [2003] EWHC 259 (QB) but held it irrelevant to the present inquiry as upkeep was not an issue before the court.

McFarlane and another v Tayside Health Board ('*McFarlane*'), on the grounds that it would be against public policy to allow a claim for the upkeep of a child born healthy and normal (as Baby P happily was). In the view of the court, recognising such a claim would 'be inconsistent with, and deleterious to, the health of the institution of parenthood and would be against the public interest'.[63]

The significance of this decision is that the court did not stop there. Instead, it went on to consider whether there was any justification for an altogether novel head of claim for damages in negligence: that of the loss of 'genetic affinity'. While it was clear that the appellant was precluded by public policy for claiming for the incidents of bringing up a healthy baby which she and her husband had unreservedly accepted into their family, the court asked whether the appellant and her husband had suffered a 'real loss' in the loss of 'genetic affinity' to the child. Yes, it was true that she had her wish for a second healthy child fulfilled. But she had not wished for *any* child: she had wanted (and her husband had wanted) a child by her husband, and no other man: her 'desire … was for "genetic affinity"', and not just any child.[64] The court held that:

> '… what is clear is that the Appellant would be ill-served by a judicial refusal to fully engage with these issues in order to recognize the true loss which has been suffered. In our judgment, the Appellant's interest in maintaining the integrity of her reproductive plans in this very specific sense – where she has made a conscious decision to have a child *with her Husband* to maintain an intergenerational genetic link and to reserve "affinity" – is one which the law should recognise and protect.'[65]

The court therefore allowed a claim for damages on the head of 'loss of genetic affinity'.

What is interesting about this case is the court's recognition of the importance of biological connection and genetic affinity between the intending parents and the child born. As the court itself noted, this is probably the first decision of its kind in the common law world in which a court has allowed such a claim for loss of genetic affinity. This defence by the court of the importance of biological connectedness sits uneasily against the insistence on the presumption of motherhood for the gestational mother in the Status of Children Act. There is now the possibility, therefore, that the fact of biological connectedness or 'genetic affinity' may operate as a powerful argument for commissioning parents seeking a determination of parenthood in their favour under ss. 9(3) and 10 of the Status of Children Act, particularly bearing in mind the Act's provision for 'the child's biological relationship to any party to the proceedings' being taken

---

63 *ACB v Thomson Medical Pte Ltd and others* [2017] SGCA 20, para. 101.
64 Ibid., at para. 127, citing F. Norton, 'Assisted Reproduction and the Frustration of Genetic Affinity: Interest, Injury and Damages' (1999) 74 *NYU L Rev* 793.
65 Ibid., at para. 135.

into account in considering the 'paramount consideration' of the 'welfare and best interests of the child'.

It should not be assumed that the door is closed to specific legislation governing surrogacy and setting out the rights and status of the various parties. In his speech to Parliament during the debate on the Status of Children Act, the Minister of Law noted that surrogacy would 'continue to be regulated by the Ministry of Health' and that it was 'an issue within the purview of the Ministry of Health. It has also been raised with them before'.[66] Whether this was a hint that a formal legislative regime will eventually be set up for surrogacy remains to be seen: what seems clear is that indirect partial regulation of surrogacy through the machinery of the Private Hospitals and Medical Clinics Act (last substantially amended in 1999, and long overdue for an overhaul) leaves surrogate children born abroad to Singaporean commissioning parents who have contributed their own gametes in a severely disadvantaged position with the advent of the Status of Children Act.

Going forward, the Singapore government will have to tread a fine line between allowing desperate Singaporean parents to go abroad to commission a child (by not explicitly outlawing surrogacy arrangements, and prohibiting only the conduct of ART procedures for surrogacy within Singapore), and perhaps exacerbating tensions with nearby countries in Asia with more permissive legal regimes (or enforcement of such regimes) for surrogacy. Taken together, the current legal regime governing ART and surrogacy procedures *in* Singapore, and the Parliamentary pronouncements on surrogacy reveal a certain degree of ambivalence: while surrogacy is all but impossible in Singapore, the state is prepared (as the evidence in the *UKM* case revealed) to support adoption of children born abroad of surrogacy procedures commissioned by Singaporeans. What next steps Parliament may take is unknown. It could, of course, like Hong Kong, explicitly make it unlawful for persons to enter into a surrogacy arrangement for payment *anywhere*, and to declare all such arrangements unenforceable.[67] But that would merely have the effect of pushing desperate intending parents further into the shadows of the black market beyond the pale of regulation, and to deny or ignore the fundamental human drive to have children of one's own, and for that all-important genetic link, which the court in the *Thomson* case described as 'a basic human impulse, and its loss is keenly and deeply felt, even if it is difficult to put into words'.[68] In keeping with the spirit of the Status of Children Act, which directs the court to take as 'the first and paramount consideration' the welfare and best interests of the child, perhaps the first step would be clarify the status of surrogate children

---

66 Above n. 1.

67 Sections 17 and 18 of the Human Reproductive Technology Ordinance (Cap. 561).

68 *ACB v Thomson Medical Pte Ltd and others* [2017] SGCA 20, para. 127.

born abroad of gametes contributed by Singaporean parents and to relieve them of the legal limbo which they now find themselves in as a result of the current presumptions of motherhood and fatherhood under the Act.[69] This, if nothing else, because the child has had no choice about where and to whom it was born. To merely treat it as an incident of a legally doubtful arrangement would not be right. The decision in *UKM* shows the way forward: the welfare of the child should be 'the first and paramount' consideration.[70]

69 The Adoption of Children Act also directs, in s. 5(b) the courts to grant an adoption order only if it is satisfied that it 'will be for be for the welfare of the infant'.

70 *UKM v Attorney-General* [2018] SGHCF 18, at para. 248.

A TOLERANT APPROACH?

SURROGACY IN HONG KONG

Daisy CHEUNG

In 2010, the Hong Kong public was shocked by media reports of Peter Lee, son of renowned tycoon Lee Shau Kee, and the triplets born to him in the United States through a surrogate mother. Surrogacy was catapulted to the forefront of public discussion. The particular controversy surrounding Peter Lee's triplets was due to multiple factors. For example, there was the fact that Peter Lee was a single father and that the triplets would thus grow up motherless,[1] as well as speculation that he had undergone sex selection to ensure that the triplets would be sons.[2] Given that the triplets had been born pursuant to a commercial surrogacy arrangement in the United States, there was also a question as to whether Peter Lee may have contravened any prohibition contained in the relevant legislation and committed an offence (discussed further below).

The following chapter aims to provide an overview of the regulation of surrogacy in Hong Kong. It begins with the general legal framework, tracing the historical development of the relevant legislation and then setting out its main provisions and prohibitions in relation to surrogacy. This is followed by an examination of the Council on Human Reproductive Technology and the Code of Practice it publishes, together with the eligibility requirements contained within. The latter half examines parenthood in Hong Kong and how it is transferred for the purposes of surrogacy arrangements.

1. GENERAL LEGAL FRAMEWORK

The legal framework for surrogacy in Hong Kong is largely contained within the Human Reproductive Technology Ordinance (Cap. 561) ('HRTO').

---

1 See for example, 'Public upset with Peter Lee renting womb: "Poor Motherless Triplets"' (translated), *Apple Daily*, Hong Kong, 28.10.2010. Web. <http://hk.apple.nextmedia.com/news/art/20101028/14600431> accessed 11.08.2018.

2 See for example, Z. Li, 'Lee Shau-kee triplet grandsons affirm traditional values', *CNN Travel*, Hong Kong, 29.10.2010. Web. <http://travel.cnn.com/hong-kong/life/lee-shau-kee-triplet-grandsons-affirm-traditional-values-774281/> accessed 11.08.2018.

1.1. HISTORY OF THE HUMAN REPRODUCTIVE TECHNOLOGY ORDINANCE

1.1.1. Background

The historical development of the HRTO can be traced back to the 1980s. The first donor insemination service in Hong Kong was established in 1981, which led to the birth of the first baby conceived using in vitro fertilisation ('IVF') technology in 1986.[3] In response to these developments, the Secretary for Health and Welfare at the time set up a multidisciplinary Committee on Scientifically Assisted Human Reproduction in 1987.[4] This Committee was tasked with advising the government on social, moral, ethical and legal issues arising from reproductive technology. To that end, it conducted two public consultation exercises in 1989 and 1993, and from these came to a consensus that reproductive technology should be regulated by statute through a licensing system.[5]

To advise on the drafting of the legislative provisions and a code of practice, the Secretary for Health and Welfare further appointed a Provisional Council made up of a body of multidisciplinary professionals and government representatives in 1995. The Provisional Council conducted further consultation, as well as identifying other areas requiring further consideration.[6]

The government then introduced the Human Reproductive Technology Bill into the Legislative Council in September 1998.[7] The Human Reproductive Technology Bill had previously been put before the Legislative Council in January 1997, but because issues surrounding the 1997 handover had priority, it was not enacted at the time.[8] After the Human Reproductive Technology Bill was introduced, it was suggested that a Bills Committee be formed for members to study the important issues involved.[9]

1.1.2. The Debates

The topic of surrogacy generated debate both at the Bills Committee meetings and the Council Meeting on the second reading of the Bill. The content of some of these debates will be discussed below.

---

3 E. Ng et al., 'Regulating Reproductive Technology in Hong Kong' (2003) 20 *Journal of Assisted Reproduction and Genetics* 281, 281.
4 Ibid.
5 Hong Kong, *Report of the Bills Committee on Human Reproductive Technology Bill*, Legislative Council Paper no. CB(2)2296/99-00, p. 1.
6 Ibid.
7 Ibid.
8 Ng et al., above n. 3, p. 281.
9 See above n. 5, p. 2.

1.1.2.1. Surrogacy at All?

To begin with, there was some opposition to the idea that surrogacy should be allowed at all. When presenting his views to the Bills Committee, Professor Chan Ho Mun of the City University of Hong Kong argued that surrogacy should be banned because it would 'break up the bond' between parent and child, as well as distort the relationship between mother and child. Furthermore, given that surrogacy arrangements were to be legally unenforceable, all parties involved would be vulnerable. In particular, the child's welfare would be at risk because the commissioning parents and the surrogate mother could both decide to fight for the child or give the child up.[10]

In response to the suggestion that surrogacy may be the only means for some infertile couples to reproduce, Professor Chan argued that the focus should be on the risks of surrogacy, namely the possibility of trauma for the surrogate mother who is giving up a child and the deprivation of parenthood for the commissioning parents if the surrogate mother refuses to do so.[11] Members of the Bills Committee also pointed out that banning surrogacy would not be an effective measure because commissioning parents could easily go abroad for similar arrangements. Professor Chan did not consider this to be relevant; if the assessment was that surrogacy involved too many risks, it should be prohibited in Hong Kong regardless of any opportunities for surrogacy abroad. As to whether difficulties would then arise in relation to disputes involving such overseas surrogacy arrangements, Professor Chan was of the view that the court should deal with each case individually and adjudicate based on the child's best interests.[12] Professor Chan's views were recorded but the Bills Committee proceeded on the basis that surrogacy was not to be prohibited entirely.

1.1.2.2. Surrogacy in the Human Reproductive Technology Bill

Although she was in support of surrogacy generally, Legislative Council member Chan Yuen Han was strongly of the view that no provisions about surrogacy should be included in the Human Reproductive Technology Bill due to a lack of consultation and lack of awareness about the issue. She thus proposed an amendment to remove all surrogacy related provisions.[13] Most of the members, however, considered the removal of all such provisions problematic because

---

10 Hong Kong, *Bills Committee on Human Reproductive Technology Bill: Minutes of the ninth meeting held on Tuesday, 23 February 1999 at 8:30 am in Conference Room A of the Legislative Council Building*, Legislative Council Paper no. CB(2)2089/98-99, paras 15–18.

11 Ibid.

12 Ibid.

13 Hong Kong, *Hansard*, Official Record of Proceedings of the Legislative Council, 22.06.2000, p. 8029.

it would mean that there would be no regulation of surrogacy at all.[14] It was suggested that legislation regarding surrogacy be introduced, and amendments be passed later if necessary.[15] The motion to pass Legislative Council member Chan Yuen Han's amendments was accordingly negatived.[16]

1.1.2.3. Limitations to the Provision of Reproductive Technology

Another issue that was discussed involved the limitations that should be placed on the provision of surrogacy and other reproductive technology services.

One of the proposed limitations was to provide reproductive technology procedures to married couples only. It was argued that this was both for the welfare of the child and for better social order generally.[17] It was also brought up that the mainstream opinion in society, as demonstrated by the consultation exercise, was that children born as a result of reproductive technology procedures should have both parents and be brought up in a proper family.[18] Cohabiting couples were considered unsuitable because they had no legal status and it would be difficult to determine the number of years of cohabitation that would be required for reproductive technology services to be provided to them.[19]

In response to the concern that such a limitation would be discriminatory,[20] the Senior Assistant Law Draftsman present confirmed that such a limitation would not be problematic under the Sex Discrimination Ordinance (Cap. 480) and the Family Discrimination Ordinance (Cap. 527), although he could not advise on compliance with the Hong Kong Bill of Rights.[21] The problems that may be associated with this limitation will be explored in further detail below.

Another proposed limitation was to provide reproductive technology procedures to infertile couples only.[22] There was general agreement that this should be the case, and the discussion focused on the definition of infertility and how best the infertility requirement should be laid out.

---

14 See for example, ibid, pp. 8047 and 8049.

15 See for example, ibid, pp. 8072 and 8090.

16 Ibid, p. 8094.

17 See for example, Legislative Council Member Chan Yuen Han's comments (Hong Kong, *Bills Committee on Human Reproductive Technology Bill: Minutes of the tenth meeting held on Wednesday, 3 March 1999 at 8:30 am in Conference Room B of the Legislative Council Building*, Legislative Council Paper no. CB(2)1782/98-99, para. 10).

18 See Dr Leong Che Hung's comments (Hong Kong, *Bills Committee on Human Reproductive Technology Bill: Minutes of meeting held on Wednesday, 23 September 1998 at 8:30 am in Conference Room B of the Legislative Council Building*, Legislative Council Paper no. CB(2) 507/98-99, para. 47).

19 See Deputy Secretary for Health and Welfare's comments, above n. 17, para. 48.

20 Hong Kong, *Bills Committee on Human Reproductive Technology Bill: Minutes of meeting held on Thursday, 29 October 1998 at 8:30 am in Conference Room B of the Legislative Council Building*, Legislative Council Paper no. CB(2) 904/98-99, para. 29.

21 Ibid, para. 30.

22 See above n. 17, para. 3.

The primary concern was the difficulty in defining infertility. For example, the Deputy Secretary for Health and Welfare appearing on behalf of the government raised the issue of whether there was a consensus among the medical profession on how infertility should be defined, given that there were conditions such as psychological impotency which may not be considered infertility.[23] After consultation with medical specialists, the government raised an additional concern. If the definition of infertility generally used by the medical profession was adopted into the Human Reproductive Technology Bill, it would be necessary to further provide a list of exceptions to cover all the circumstances in which a reproductive technology procedure might be provided to a couple that did not fall within the definition of infertile.[24] This might include a scenario, for example, where a couple was not infertile but had an otherwise justifiable need for the procedure to avoid the birth of a child with severe genetic disease.[25] Although there was some support for an explicit provision in the legislation to specify infertility as an eligibility requirement,[26] the government considered it more appropriate and flexible to reflect the infertility requirement in the Code of Practice and licensing conditions, given the impracticality of listing all the exceptions exhaustively.[27]

After several deliberations on the matter, it was agreed that the infertility requirement would be placed in the long title of the Human Reproductive Technology Bill, with further specifications in the Code of Practice.[28]

1.1.2.4. Surrogacy by Natural Means?

The final issue that will be briefly discussed here is the possibility of surrogacy by natural means, a discussion which arose in the context of the definition of 'surrogate mother'. In an earlier draft of the legislation, the government had included in the definition the possibility of a surrogate mother conceiving a baby

23 See above n. 17, para. 5.

24 Hong Kong, *Bills Committee on Human Reproductive Technology Bill: Minutes of the eleventh meeting held on Friday, 19 March 1999 at 4:30 pm in Conference Room B of the Legislative Council Building*, Legislative Council Paper no. CB(2) 1811/98-99, para. 3.

25 Ibid, para. 9.

26 Ibid, para. 12.

27 Hong Kong, *Bills Committee on Human Reproductive Technology Bill: Minutes of the twenty-first meeting held on Wednesday, 22 December 1999 at 10:45 am in Conference Room B of the Legislative Council Building*, Legislative Council Paper no. CB(2)1117/99-00, para. 8.

28 Hong Kong, *Bills Committee on Human Reproductive Technology Bill: Minutes of the 22nd meeting on Thursday, 23 December 1999 at 8:30 am in Conference Room B of the Legislative Council Building*, Legislative Council Paper no. CB(2)2161/99-00, para. 2. While there is currently no definition of infertility either in the HRTO or the Code of Practice, infertility in the surrogacy chapter of the Code of Practice is widely construed as including the situation where the wife is unable to carry a pregnancy to term (see below Section 1.4.1. for further information).

by means other than a reproductive technology procedure.[29] The intention had been to define 'surrogate mother' as broadly as possible, so as to cover all unlawful commercial surrogacy arrangements.[30] For example, if surrogacy by natural means were excluded from the definition, a surrogacy arrangement whereby the commissioning parents place a newspaper advertisement offering payment to a surrogate mother to produce a child via sexual intercourse with the husband would not be in contravention of the relevant provisions.[31]

Members of the Bills Committee were generally against this, however. They were of the view that only a woman who had conceived a child with the gametes of the commissioning parents as a result of a reproductive technology procedure could be a 'surrogate mother'. In particular, they were concerned that a definition that included surrogacy by natural means would give the impression that such a form of surrogacy was permitted by the law.[32] After discussion, it was agreed that the definition of 'surrogate mother' should be restricted, and the current definition in the HRTO includes the requirement that the child must have been conceived by a reproductive technology procedure.[33]

1.1.2.5. Enactment and Implementation

After lengthy debates in the Bills Committee and at the second reading debate in the Legislative Council, the Bill was enacted in June 2000. It took another seven years before the HRTO came into effect. Since 2007, subsidiary legislation about licensing and fees have also come into force.[34]

1.2. THE LEGAL FRAMEWORK

The main provisions regulating surrogacy, which are set out below, are contained in Pt III (Prohibitions) of the HRTO.[35]

---

29 Hong Kong, *Bills Committee on Human Reproductive Technology Bill: Minutes of the 12th meeting held on Wednesday, 14 April 1999 at 8:30 am in Conference Room A of the Legislative Council Building*, Legislative Council Paper no. CB(2)72/99-00, para. 25.

30 Ibid, para. 26.

31 Ibid, para. 27.

32 Hong Kong, *Bills Committee on Human Reproductive Technology Bill: Minutes of the 13th meeting held on Monday, 26 April 1999 at 8:30 am in Conference Room B of the Legislative Council Building*, Legislative Council Paper no. CB(2)73/99-00, para. 24.

33 Section 2 of the HRTO.

34 Specifically, the Human Reproductive Technology (Licensing) Regulation (Cap. 561A) and the Human Reproductive Technology (Fees) Regulations (Cap. 561B).

35 Certain provisions of the HRTO were amended on 03.01.2017, when the Human Reproductive Technology (Amendment) Ordinance came into operation. The amendments are not related to surrogacy and are confined to the provision of an additional offence in relation to the publication or distribution of advertisements to promote sex selection services.

1.2.1. Donated Gametes

Section 14 prohibits the use of donated gametes in a surrogacy arrangement. This means that only the genetic material of the commissioning parents can be used, and that partial or traditional surrogacy is not permitted in Hong Kong.

1.2.2. Persons Not Party to a Marriage

Section 15(5) prohibits the provision of reproductive technology procedures, including surrogacy, to persons who are not parties to a marriage. Surrogate mothers are an exception to this prohibition. This is the statutory provision that reflects the limitation on the provision of reproductive technology to unmarried couples discussed in Section 1.1.2.3. above. It also entails that if one of the parties to the marriage dies, reproductive technology procedures cannot be provided to the other to have a child posthumously.

As briefly mentioned in Section 1.1.2.3. above, the provision of reproductive technology procedures, including surrogacy, to married couples only arguably is discriminatory in nature due to its exclusion of cohabiting couples and same-sex couples. The starting point of the discussion is s. 56B of the Sex Discrimination Ordinance (Cap. 480) ('SDO'), which states that none of the prohibitions against discrimination contained in Pt 4 (Discrimination and Sexual Harassment in Other Fields) and Pt 5 (Other Unlawful Acts) of the SDO renders discrimination between persons of different marital status arising from the provision of reproductive technology procedures unlawful. This means that the limitation of reproductive technology procedures to married couples is expressly permitted under the SDO.

Even though such a limitation is permitted under the SDO, however, there are still human rights concerns with denying reproductive technology procedures to cohabiting couples and same-sex couples. For example, there are at least two sources of constitutional rights that such couples can rely on. Article 37 of the Basic Law protects the right to raise a family:

> 'The freedom of marriage of Hong Kong residents and their right to raise a family freely shall be protected by law.'

Article 14 of the Hong Kong Bill of Rights contains the right to protection of family:

> '(1) No one shall be subjected to arbitrary or unlawful interference with his privacy, family, home or correspondence, nor to unlawful attacks on his honour and reputation.
> (2) Everyone has the right to the protection of the law against such interference or attacks.'

If the restrictions on these rights of unmarried couples (due to the denial of reproductive technology procedures) do not pass the proportionality test,[36] such a limitation on the provision of reproductive technology procedures may be found to be unconstitutional. This, however, has yet to be tested in the Hong Kong courts.

1.2.3. Commercial Dealings

Section 16 contains a prohibition against commercial dealings in a prescribed substance (namely a gamete, embryo, fetal ovarian tissue or fetal testicular tissue) intended to be used for a surrogacy arrangement. Section 17 contains a prohibition against the negotiation of surrogacy arrangements and the compiling of information for the purposes of such negotiations on a commercial basis.[37] The provisions prohibit the publication or distribution of advertisements related to (i) commercial dealings or negotiations for commercial dealings in a prescribed substance and (ii) surrogacy arrangements respectively.

It is worth noting that the prohibitions contained in ss. 16 and 17 are expressly extra-territorial in nature.[38] The provisions use the phrase 'whether in Hong Kong or elsewhere', language that extends the prohibitions beyond the geographical borders of Hong Kong. In December 2010, in response to the abovementioned case of Peter Lee and his triplets, Legislative Council member Cyd Ho put a question to the then Secretary for Food and Health Dr York Chow regarding the application of s. 17 of the HRTO.[39] While refusing to comment on any individual case, Dr Chow reiterated the extra-territorial nature of s. 17, drawing upon the legislative intent (as demonstrated by discussion in the Bills Committee) to fill the loophole in cases where payment is made or received outside Hong Kong. It appears, however, that no prosecutions have

---

36 A four-step proportionality test was recently laid down in the case of *Hysan Development Co Ltd and Others v Town Planning Board* [2016] HKCFA 66, a decision concerning planning restrictions imposed by the Town Planning Board upon companies in the Hysan Development Co Ltd group, and whether such restrictions constituted an unconstitutional infringement of its property rights in contravention of the Basic Law.

37 While beyond the scope of this chapter, it is this author's view that there are deficiencies in the drafting of s. 17 that need to be further explored.

38 Extra-territorial legislation on surrogacy is rare, and arguably should be. While it is beyond the scope of this chapter to go into this issue in detail, I note that various scholars have pointed out problems with imposing an extra-territorial criminal offence in areas such as commercial surrogacy (see for example A. Stuhmcke, 'Extra-Territoriality and Surrogacy: The Problem of State and Territory Moral Sovereignty' in P. Gerber and K. O'Byrne (eds), *Surrogacy, Law and Human Rights*, Routledge, Abingdon 2015; and I.G. Cohen, *Patients with Passports: Medical Tourism, Law and Ethics*, Oxford University Press, Oxford 2014). Ultimately, we need to think about what our justification for the criminalisation of the practice is, and whether such a justification warrants the extra-territorial reach.

39 Government of the HKSAR, 'LCQ2: Human Reproductive Technology Ordinance' (Press Release, 01.12.2010).

been made under these sections so far,[40] and no court decisions interpreting the extra-territorial application of these sections exist. Apart from what appears to be a lack of appetite to prosecute, this may also be because of the difficulties associated with enforcement outside of Hong Kong's borders.

1.2.4. Enforceability

Section 18 provides that surrogacy arrangements are unenforceable. This means that neither the surrogate mother nor the commissioning parents can sue to compel the other party to fulfil the terms of the surrogacy arrangement.

1.2.5. Offences

Contraventions of the prohibitions contained in the sections mentioned above are criminal offences, and the offences are created by s. 39 in Pt VI (Enforcement and Offences) of the HRTO. Pursuant to s. 39(1), an individual who contravenes such prohibitions commits an offence and is liable on first conviction to a fine at level 4 and to imprisonment for six months. On subsequent conviction, the individual is liable to a fine at level 6 and to imprisonment for two years.[41]

It should be noted that both the commissioning parents and the surrogate mother can be convicted of these offences. This is unlike the position in the United Kingdom, where in relation to the offence of negotiating surrogacy arrangements on a commercial basis, s. 2(2) specifically provides that neither commissioning parents nor surrogate mothers are caught by the provision (see the England and Wales chapter in this collection for further information). Looking back at the relevant English *Hansard* records, it appears that this is because the aim of the offence was primarily to ban the commercial agencies, and not to punish the commissioning parents (who may be compelled into making a surrogacy arrangement because of their predicament) or surrogate mothers (who may genuinely be trying to assist an unfortunate infertile couple or may have been exploited by the commercial agencies).[42] A further consideration in excluding surrogate mothers from the offence was to avoid the possibility of the 'taint of criminality' on the child that would be born.[43]

These considerations arguably are very important and do not seem to have been brought up in Hong Kong during the deliberations on the Human

---

40 It was reported that the police had declined to press charges after a 10-month investigation into the Peter Lee case. For further details, please see 'Surrogates here to stay', *South China Morning Post*, Hong Kong, 03.04.2012. Web. <http://www.scmp.com/article/997316/surrogates-here-stay> accessed 11.08.2018.

41 A fine at level 4 is equivalent to HK$25,000 and a fine at level 6 is equivalent to HK$100,000.

42 HC Deb 15.04.1985 vol 77 cc23-56, col. 24.

43 Ibid.

Reproductive Technology Bill at the various Legislative Council meetings. Although prosecutions have yet to be made under the provisions discussed above, it is imperative that the current position be reviewed in light of such considerations to determine whether the potential criminalisation of commissioning parents and surrogate mothers actually is desirable.

1.3. COUNCIL ON HUMAN REPRODUCTIVE TECHNOLOGY

The authority that oversees surrogacy practices in Hong Kong is the Council on Human Reproductive Technology (the 'Council'). The Council was established in April 2001 pursuant to s. 4 of the HRTO to, among other things, regulate surrogacy arrangements.[44] It is made up of 22 non-official members and four public officers appointed by the Secretary for Food and Health.[45]

The functions of the Council are laid out in s. 5 of the HRTO. These functions include, but are not limited to, (i) keeping under review information about, among other things, surrogacy arrangements; (ii) regulating and issuing licenses on reproductive technology procedures; (iii) publishing lists of licensed premises and relevant statistics relating to reproductive technology activities; and (iv) providing general information about reproductive technology to service providers and the public.[46]

Pursuant to s. 6 of the HRTO, the Council is also authorised to establish committees to better perform its functions and exercise its powers. There are currently three established committees, the Ethics Committee, the Inspection Committee and the Investigation Committee.[47] The functions of the Ethics Committee include consulting the public on the various social, moral, ethical and legal issues arising from reproductive technology procedures and providing advice to the Council on these issues.[48] The Inspection Committee is responsible for conducting inspections of centres in order to grant them licenses under the HRTO, as well as making recommendations to the Council about the granting of such licenses.[49] The Investigation Committee conducts investigations related

44 Long Title, HRTO.

45 'About Us: Council on Human Reproductive Technology', *Council on Human Reproductive Technology*, 13.09.2016. Web. <http://www.chrt.org.hk/english/aboutus/aboutus_mem_chrt.html> accessed 11.08.2018.

46 'About Us: Objectives and Functions', *Council on Human Reproductive Technology*, 12.04.2010. Web. <http://www.chrt.org.hk/english/aboutus/aboutus_obj.html> accessed 11.08.2018.

47 'About Us: Membership', *Council on Human Reproductive Technology*, 11.04.2013. Web. <http://www.chrt.org.hk/english/aboutus/aboutus_mem.html> accessed 11.08.2018.

48 'About Us: Ethics Committee', *Council on Human Reproductive Technology*, 11.04.2016. Web. <http://www.chrt.org.hk/english/aboutus/aboutus_mem_ec.html> accessed 11.08.2018.

49 'About Us: Inspection Committee', *Council on Human Reproductive Technology*, 11.04.2016. Web. <http://www.chrt.org.hk/english/aboutus/aboutus_mem_ins.html> accessed 11.08.2018.

to matters which may result in the Council exercising its powers to revoke, vary or temporarily suspend a license granted under the HRTO.[50]

1.4. CODE OF PRACTICE

The Council is also responsible for the Code of Practice on Reproductive Technology and Embryo Research (the 'Code of Practice'), which it prepares and maintains pursuant to s. 8 of the HRTO. The Code of Practice provides guidance regarding the standards of practice that reproductive technology service providers are expected to comply with. The compliance with such standards, or the lack thereof, are matters that will be considered when the Council decides whether to grant, renew, vary, revoke or suspend a licence.[51] The revised Code of Practice has been in effect since 1 January 2013.[52]

Chapter 12 of the Code of Practice, entitled 'Surrogacy', contains the standards of practice in relation to surrogacy arrangements.[53]

1.4.1. Infertility

As mentioned above, the long title of the HRTO provides that reproductive technology procedures can only be provided to infertile couples. Paragraph 12.2(b) of the Code of Practice expands this to include a wife who is unable to carry a pregnancy to term and has no other practicable treatment option. Thus, the Code of Practice suggests that the wife of a fertile couple may nonetheless be able to receive a reproductive technology procedure pursuant to a surrogacy arrangement, provided she cannot carry the pregnancy to term and there is no other practicable option.

1.4.2. Suitability to be a Surrogate Mother

Paragraphs 12.3 and 12.4 address the suitability of a woman to be a surrogate mother.

---

50 'About Us: Investigation Committee', *Council on Human Reproductive Technology*, 28.09.2016. Web. <http://www.chrt.org.hk/english/aboutus/aboutus_mem_inv.html> accessed 11.08.2018.

51 'For Service Providers: Code of Practice on Reproductive Technology & Embryo Research', *Council on Human Reproductive Technology*, 04.02.2013. Web. <http://www.chrt.org.hk/english/service/service_cod.html> accessed 11.08.2018.

52 'Publications and Press Releases: Revised Code of Practice', *Council on Human Reproductive Technology*, 04.02.2013. Web. <http://www.chrt.org.hk/english/publications/publications_code.html> accessed 11.08.2018.

53 Council on Human Reproductive Technology, 'Code of Practice on Reproductive Technology and Embryo Research', 01.01.2013. Web. <http://www.chrt.org.hk/english/publications/files/code.pdf> accessed 11.08.2018, p. 29.

Paragraph 12.3 provides that the suitability of a woman to be a surrogate mother should be assessed by a registered medical practitioner (one who is not responsible for performing the procedure), and the factors that should be considered include the surrogate mother's marital status, her history of pregnancy and her physical and mental fitness to carry a baby. It should perhaps be questioned whether a registered medical practitioner would be the most appropriate candidate to assess the suitability of a woman to be a surrogate mother, given that some of the considerations involved do not appear to be medically related.

Paragraph 12.3 further states that a woman at higher risk of suffering pregnancy related complications should not be permitted to be a surrogate mother. Paragraph 12.4 provides a minimum age for surrogate motherhood: a woman under 21 is not to act as a surrogate mother.

1.4.3. Informed Consent

Paragraph 12.5 of the Code of Practice requires the consent of both the woman intending to be a surrogate mother and her husband, if she is married. Both the commissioning parents and the surrogate mother should be informed that surrogacy arrangements are not enforceable under the law.[54]

Counselling must also be provided. Paragraph 12.7 provides that counselling by a multi-disciplinary team must be provided to the commissioning parents and the surrogate mother (together with her husband, if any) to ensure that they understand all the implications of surrogacy. The team should at least comprise the following members: (i) two registered medical practitioners to explain the medical aspects; (ii) a legal advisor to explain the legal aspects; and (iii) a social worker to explain the social and moral aspects. A clinical psychologist should also be brought into the team when it is appropriate to assess the commissioning parents and surrogate mother (together with her husband, if any).

1.4.4. Welfare Assessment

The counselling mentioned in the above Section 1.4.3. is to be followed by an assessment of the parties involved. Paragraph 12.8 provides that in conducting this assessment, the welfare of the child is to be of 'paramount importance'. The factors that should be considered in this assessment include the following:

1. commitment to having and bringing up the child;
2. ability to provide a stable and supportive environment;
3. medical histories (including that of family);

---

[54] Ibid, para. 12.6.

4. ages and likely future ability to care for the child;
5. any risk of harm to the child (including inherited disorders, problems during pregnancy and neglect or abuse); and
6. attitudes of other family members towards the child.

It should be noted that the welfare assessment provided in para. 12.8 of the Code of Practice is not a legal requirement in Hong Kong, although it does have licencing implications. In addition, the assessment makes no mention of the welfare of any other child or children who may be affected by the birth of the child resulting from the surrogacy arrangement, unlike jurisdictions like the United Kingdom where the welfare of any other child in the family is also considered.

1.5. STATISTICS

There do not appear to be complete and accurate records of surrogacy procedures in Hong Kong. Despite reports in the media of surrogacy arrangements being carried out,[55] none of the centres in the Council's 'List of Licensed Centres' are listed as providing surrogacy services.[56] None of the Reports and Statistics, which are available between 2009 and 2017 and based on the information in data collection forms received from licensed centres up to 31 December of the year in question, contain records of any patients receiving surrogacy procedures.[57]

2. LEGAL PARENTHOOD AT THE TIME OF BIRTH

2.1. THE LEGAL FRAMEWORK

The main provisions concerning parentage in Hong Kong are contained in the Parent and Child Ordinance (Cap. 429) ('PCO'). The PCO, brought into effect in June 1993, was enacted in response to the concerns raised by a Law Reform

---

55 See for example, 'HK has two surrogate mothers', *South China Morning Post*, Hong Kong, 10.03.2008. Web. <http://www.scmp.com/article/629375/hk-has-two-surrogate-mothers> accessed 11.08.2018, which reports at least two surrogate births and two further requests for surrogacy procedures.

56 'List of Licensed Centres – Treatment (as at 12 October 2018)', *Council on Human Reproductive Technology*, 15.10.2018. Web. <http://www.chrt.org.hk/english/licensed/files/treatment_eng.pdf> accessed 15.10.2018.

57 The official figure in each of the reports from 2009 to 2017 is zero patients. The full list of reports is accessible at 'Publications and Press Releases: Reports and Statistics', *Council on Human Reproductive Technology*, 25.10.2018. Web. <http://www.chrt.org.hk/english/publications/publications_rep.html> accessed 01.12.2018.

Commission report in October 1991 that illegitimate children were being unfairly disadvantaged by the law.[58] In the specific context of births resulting from medical treatment, Pt V (Determination of Parent Where Birth or Pregnancy Results From Medical Treatment) of the PCO sets out how motherhood and fatherhood are to be determined at the time of birth.[59]

2.1.1. *Motherhood at the Time of Birth*

Section 9 of the PCO provides that the woman who carries a child as a result of the placing in her of an embryo or of sperm and eggs, and that woman only, is to be regarded as the mother of the child. This means that the mother of the child is the gestational mother, to the exclusion of other candidates (for example the genetic mother).

2.1.2. *Fatherhood at the Time of Birth*

In the case of a child born of a surrogacy arrangement, s. 10(2) of the PCO provides that if the surrogate mother is married, the husband of the surrogate mother is to be regarded as the father of the child,[60] unless he did not consent to the procedure.[61] If the surrogate mother is not married, but obtained services with a male partner, s. 10(3) provides that the male partner is to be regarded as the father of the child in the first instance. If an individual is identified as the father of the child pursuant to ss. 10(2) or 10(3), s. 10(4) states that no other individual is to be regarded as the father of the child.

2.2. ACCESS TO INFORMATION

The HRTO contains access to information provisions in relation to children who are born of reproductive technology procedures. Pursuant to s. 33 of the HRTO, the Council is to keep and maintain a register, Register A, containing information that fulfils two conditions: (i) the information relates to a reproductive technology procedure where the child would not be created solely from the gametes of the intended parents and (ii) the child, any of the parties

58 L. Course and V. Yu, *The Annotated Ordinances of Hong Kong: Parent and Child Ordinance (Chapter 429), Part 429*, Butterworths Asia, Hong Kong 1996, p. 1.

59 Although commissioning parents will not be regarded as the mother and father at the time of birth, they can acquire parenthood according to the procedure described in Section 4.1. below.

60 What is also known as the legal fiction of fatherhood.

61 It is unlikely that the husband of the surrogate will not be regarded as the father because the Code of Practice requires that both the surrogate mother and her husband, if any, consent before surrogacy can be recommended. See above Section 1.4.3. for further detail.

to the marriage and/or any individual whose gametes have been used can be identified from the information.

It should be noted, however, that such access to information provisions do not extend to surrogate motherhood. This is because the information kept in Register A only relates to reproductive technology procedures where the child born would not be created from the gametes of the commissioning parents, and there is a prohibition on the use of donated gametes for the purposes of surrogacy arrangements in Hong Kong.[62]

As to why access to information provisions do not cover children born of surrogate mothers, this appears to be because the primary concern Register A seeks to address is the possibility of incest. This is demonstrated by the fact that the information that is to be provided upon a request made pursuant to s. 33(4) of the HRTO is (i) whether any other person might be a parent of the individual but for ss. 9, 10 and 11 of the PCO, and, if so, (ii) whether the individual and the person s/he wishes to marry is or might be related.[63]

3. ELIGIBILITY FOR SURROGACY

This section will briefly summarise the various requirements for surrogate mothers and commissioning parents described above.

3.1. SURROGATE MOTHERS

To act as a surrogate mother, a woman must be over 21 years of age. She should not be at high risk of pregnancy related risks, and must generally be deemed suitable by a medical practitioner, taking into account such factors as her marital status, history of pregnancy and fitness to carry a baby. She and her husband, if any, must both consent to the procedure. She must also be subject to a welfare assessment, which will consider such issues as her commitment to having the child, her medical history and any risk of harm to the child that may be caused by problems during pregnancy, for example.[64]

3.2. COMMISSIONING PARENTS

To be eligible as commissioning parents, the couple must be married (and thus in Hong Kong of the opposite sex).[65] The couple must either be infertile,

---

62 See above Section 1.2.1. for further information.

63 Section 33(4) of the HRTO.

64 For further detail, please refer to Sections 1.4.2. to 1.4.4. above.

65 For further detail, please refer to Section 1.2.2. above.

or the wife must be unable to carry a pregnancy to term.[66] The couple must also be subject to a welfare assessment, which will consider such issues as their commitment to bringing up the child in a stable and supportive environment, their medical histories, their future ability to take care of the child, any risk of harm to the child that may be caused by inherited disorders, neglect or abuse and the attitudes of any other family member toward the child.[67] Following the procedure, the couple must be over 18 years of age in order to be granted a parental order pursuant to s. 12 of the PCO (see below Section 4.1. for further information).

4. TRANSFERRING PARENTHOOD

4.1. ACQUIRING PARENTHOOD

As demonstrated in Section 2.1. above, the commissioning parents will not be the legal parents at the birth of the child born as a result of a surrogacy arrangement. Instead, they will need to acquire parenthood.

The mechanism for the transfer of parenthood for surrogate births is a judicial procedure, namely a parental order granted by the court pursuant to s. 12 of the PCO. Under s. 12(1) of the PCO, if a child was carried by a surrogate mother and the gametes of the husband or wife or both[68] were used to create the embryo, the court can make an order providing for the child to be regarded in law as the child of the commissioning parents, subject to certain conditions. The conditions are as follows:

1. the commissioning parents must apply for the parental order within six months of the birth of the child;
2. at the time of application and the making of the order, the child's home must be with the commissioning parents or either of them, and the commissioning parents or either of them must have a connection with Hong Kong;[69]
3. at the time of the making of the order, the commissioning parents must both be at least 18 years of age;

---

66 For further detail, please refer to Section 1.4.1. above.

67 For further detail, please refer to Section 1.4.4. above.

68 Pursuant to s. 14 of the HRTO (which was enacted *after* the PCO), the gametes of both the husband and wife must be used to create the embryo.

69 Specifically, the commissioning parents or either of them must be domiciled in Hong Kong, habitually resident in Hong Kong throughout the immediately preceding one-year period or have a substantial connection with Hong Kong.

4. the court must be satisfied that both the surrogate mother and the father at the time of birth (if any) have freely, and with full understanding of what is involved, agreed unconditionally to the order (the surrogate mother's agreement having been given at least six weeks after the child's birth[70]);[71] and
5. the court must be satisfied that no money or benefit[72] was given or received for the making of the order, the unconditional agreement required in condition (4) above, the handing over of the child or the making of any arrangements related to the making of the order, unless the money or benefit was authorised or subsequently approved by the court.[73]

4.2. ACCESS TO INFORMATION

As mentioned in Section 2.2. above, the access to information provisions in the HRTO do not extend to surrogate births.

5. AGENCIES AND CRIMINALISATION

Agencies and other middlemen do not play a visible role in surrogacy arrangements in Hong Kong. As mentioned in Section 1.2.3. above, s. 17 of the HRTO prohibits the negotiation of surrogacy arrangements and the compiling of information for the purposes of such negotiations on a commercial basis. It also prohibits the publication or distribution of advertisements related to surrogacy arrangements.

Contravention of the s. 17 prohibitions is a criminal offence with extra-territorial effect. Please see Section 1.2.5. above for further details regarding the penalties for contravening s. 17.

6. INTERNATIONAL SURROGACY ARRANGEMENTS

Hong Kong does not have specific laws concerning surrogacy arrangements that take place in other jurisdictions. As mentioned in the section above, however, several of the prohibitions contained in the HRTO have extra-territorial effect (for example, ss. 16 and 17 of the HRTO).

---

70 Otherwise the agreement of the surrogate mother would be considered ineffective.
71 This condition does not require the agreement of a person who is unable to be found or incapable of giving agreement.
72 Apart from expenses that have been reasonably incurred.
73 Sections 12(2) to 12(7) of the PCO.

Parenthood that has been assigned in another jurisdiction does not appear to be automatically recognised in Hong Kong, and thus commissioning parents are still required to obtain a parental order pursuant to s. 12 of the PCO (see above Section 4.1. for further information). In the case of *Re D (Parental Order: s.12 Parent and Child Ordinance (Cap. 429))*,[74] the commissioning parents had entered into a surrogacy agreement with a surrogate mother in California. Prior to the birth of the child, a Pre-Birth Order was obtained from the Superior Court of the State of California, and the commissioning parents were declared as the legal parents of the child. Subsequently, the commissioning parents brought their child back to Hong Kong. To regularise their legal relationship with the child and apply for residency, they applied for a parental order under s. 12 of the PCO.[75]

The case was heard by the Family Court and the main question before the court was whether the case should be transferred to the High Court pursuant to s. 16 of the PCO due to the difficulty or importance of the issues involved.

There were three main legal issues involved in the application. The first concerned whether the commissioning parents were qualified to make an application under s. 12 of the PCO given that they had not been married at the time of birth of the child.[76] The second issue concerned whether the Pre-Birth Order granted by the Superior Court of the State of California was an adoption order for the purposes of s. 17 of the Adoption Ordinance (Cap. 290). The third issue concerned whether the payments the commissioning parents made under the surrogacy agreement should be sanctioned by the court, in light of the abovementioned s. 12(7) of the PCO which allows 'expenses reasonably incurred or otherwise authorised or subsequently approved by the court' and the prohibitions contained within s. 17 of the HRTO.

The court concluded that the case should be transferred to the High Court because it was the first of its kind in Hong Kong and the issues involved were thus novel. Ultimately, however, the case was settled and there was no judicial determination on the important issues raised.

In the recent case of *S v J*,[77] the commissioning parents entered into surrogacy arrangements with two surrogate mothers in India, who then gave birth to two children. The commissioning parents brought the children back to Hong Kong, where they were granted permanent resident status.[78] Subsequently, the wife

---

74 *Re D (Parental Order: s.12 Parent and Child Ordinance (Cap. 429))* [2015] 1 HKLRD 229.

75 The alternative ground of the application was that the court grant a declaration that the child was their lawful child pursuant to s. 17 of the Adoption Ordinance (Cap. 290).

76 Section 12 of the HRTO states that the court may make an order providing for a child to be regarded as a child of the 'parties to a marriage'. The commissioning parents in this case were married *after* the birth of the child (but prior to the parental order application).

77 *S v J* [2017] 5 HKC 288.

78 Interestingly, the Department of Immigration granted the children permanent resident status on the basis of the fact that the children were considered 'born of' his or her alleged parents,

filed for a petition for divorce and sought custody of the children. The judge in the divorce proceedings pointed out that they did not have a parental order, which led to the husband initiating proceedings for a parental order. The case was ultimately disposed with on the basis that the wife would not join in the proceedings, which meant the husband was applying for a parental order on his own. The court made clear that this was not possible pursuant to s. 12(2) of the PCO, which requires the husband *and* wife to apply for the order within six months of the birth of the child.[79] The children were made wards of the court until better arrangements could be made with regard to their legal identities.[80] No mention was made of the payments that presumably had been made under the surrogacy arrangements in India.

7. CONCLUSION

We have seen in the above that Hong Kong permits a form of surrogacy (namely full surrogacy), which it regulates using a statutory regime, with the Council on Human Reproductive Technology overseeing its operation and its Code of Practice specifying standards of practice in further detail. After a child is born of a surrogacy arrangement, the legal mother of the child is the surrogate mother, and the legal father is the surrogate mother's husband or male partner (if any). In order to transfer parenthood to themselves, the commissioning parents can apply to the court for a parental order, provided certain conditions are met.

While there appear to be relatively comprehensive rules regulating surrogacy in Hong Kong, the application of these rules has yet to be fully litigated or even understood, as demonstrated by the lack of judicial determination on key issues arising from the facts in *Re D* and *S v J* discussed above. In addition, this chapter has also identified areas in which difficulty may arise, namely the possibly unconstitutional denial of reproductive technology procedures to unmarried couples, the criminalisation of surrogate mothers and commissioning parents and the extra-territorial nature of some of the criminal offences under the HRTO. It is hoped that these issues will be further explored in the near future to ensure a principled and fair regime for surrogacy in Hong Kong.

---

which was interpreted as a genetic relationship, rather than one based on the method of delivery of the child. This is a position contrary to that contained in the PCO, as discussed above. This results in the paradox that the court highlighted in this case – even though the children's relationship with the HKSAR had been established, they could not establish a legal relationship with their parents (see para. 42 of the judgment).

79 *S v J*, above n. 77, para. 12. Presumably the parents would not have been able to apply within the six-month period, even if the wife had joined in the proceedings.

80 Ibid, para. 30. An adoption order was suggested by the court as a long-term solution for the children.

REGULATION THROUGH PROFESSIONAL MEDICAL BODIES

SURROGACY IN JAPAN

Shinichiro HAYAKAWA

1. INTRODUCTION

Japan has not yet enacted any laws to regulate medically assisted reproduction ('MAR').[1] While several guidelines issued by the Japan Society of Obstetrics and Gynecology ('JSOG') deal with MAR, including surrogacy,[2] these guidelines are merely self-imposed rules by the JSOG addressed to its members.

Japan also has no laws to specifically regulate the parentage of children born by MAR, but there have been several court cases where issues of such parentage were at stake.

Of course, not all of the cases of MAR raise questions on legal parentage. Some cases can be treated exactly the same way as natural reproduction. For example, artificial insemination with the husband's sperm ('AIH') does not cause any specific new legal problems as long as the husband is alive when the artificial insemination is conducted. However, for surrogacy, Japan has faced some difficult issues concerning legal parentage.

2. JAPANESE LAW OF PARENTAGE IN GENERAL

The Japanese Civil Code was enacted in 1898. Part IV (Family Law) of the Civil Code was drafted under considerable influence of the French Civil Code at

---

1 Cloning of a human being is prohibited by the Act on Regulation of Human Cloning Techniques (enacted on 5 December 2001).

2 According to the guidelines of JSOG, surrogacy and donation of egg/embryo are prohibited while artificial insemination with donor's sperm ('AID') is permitted subject to certain conditions.

that time. Although Pt IV was amended extensively after World War II under the American occupation, particularly in order to introduce new principles such as equality between men and women, the provisions concerning parentage remain fairly untouched. Therefore, Japanese law of parentage has much in common with old French law (i.e. the original French Civil Code).[3] Thus the Japanese Civil Code still retains the distinction between a legitimate child and an illegitimate child.

When a married woman gives birth to a child, legitimate parentage (father-child relationship) is automatically established between the woman's husband and the child. Such legitimate parentage can be denied only under very restrictive circumstances.[4] Although there is no relevant provision on the legitimate mother-child relationship in the Civil Code, such a relationship is considered to be automatically established once a married woman has given birth to a child.

When an unmarried woman gives birth to a child, an illegitimate father-child relationship is established only by recognition. The father can recognise the child voluntarily or could be forced to recognise the child by a court order.[5]

---

3 We should note, however, that the Japanese rules of parentage differed from the French Civil Code (of 19th Century) on several substantial points: for example, (1) Japanese Civil Code allowed, from the beginning, an illegitimate child and its mother to seek in the court a forced recognition by its 'father'; (2) Japan has not adopted the system of '*possesion d'état*'.

4 The relevant articles in the Civil Code read as follows nb:
'Article 772 (Presumption of Child in Wedlock)
(1) A child conceived by a wife during marriage shall be presumed to be a child of her husband.
(2) A child born after 200 days from the formation of marriage or within 300 days of the day of the dissolution or rescission of marriage shall be presumed to have been conceived during marriage.'
'Article 774 (Rebutting Presumption of Legitimacy)
Under the circumstances described in Article 772, a husband may rebut the presumption of the child in wedlock.'
'Article 775 (Action to Rebut Presumption of Legitimacy)
The father's right to rebut the presumption of child in wedlock under Article 774 shall be exercised by an action of denial of child in wedlock against the child or a mother who has parental authority. If there is no mother who has parental authority, the family court shall appoint a special representative.'
'Article 777 (Limitation upon Action of Rebutting Presumption)
A husband shall bring an action to rebut the presumption of the child in wedlock within one year of knowing of the child's birth.'
English translation is quoted from the website of 'Japanese Law Translation' offered by the Japanese government <http://www.japaneselawtranslation.go.jp/?re=02> accessed 14.09.2018.

5 The relevant articles in the Civil Code read as follows:
'Article 779 (Recognition)
A father or a mother may recognize his/her child out of wedlock'

While the Civil Code prescribes the recognition of the child by the mother,[6] the Supreme Court has decided that an illegitimate mother-child relationship nevertheless is automatically established, so without the recognition, once an unmarried woman has given birth to a child.[7]

3. PARENTAGE OF CHILDREN BORN THROUGH SURROGACY

The guidelines of JSOG prohibit all types of surrogacy. Since the guidelines are quite well respected by JSOG members, almost all the Japanese physicians with expertise in this field, there have been very few surrogacy cases in Japan.

However, an obstetrician named Yahiro Nezu, who had performed the first surrogacy procedure in Japan in 2001, openly protests against the guidelines and has been continuing to perform such procedures. The children born by surrogacy in the clinic of Dr Nezu are said to have been registered first as the child of the surrogate mother and then have been adopted by the couple who had requested the surrogacy. Such adoptions have been permitted without difficulties in Japanese courts.[8]

Most of the Japanese couples who seek to have a baby by surrogacy travel abroad to a country where surrogacy is permitted. The couple then brings the child back to Japan and registers it with the municipal office as their own child born abroad. When the couple applies for registration of child birth with a birth certificate certifying that the woman of the couple is the mother, the municipal office usually does not check whether she really gave birth to the child. It is estimated that far more than 100 children have been registered in this way as a legitimate child of the commissioning couple. However, should the municipal office somehow happen to learn that the child was not born by the commissioning 'mother', it refuses the registration. In a case where a couple

---

'Article 787 (Action for Recognition)
A child, his/her lineal descendant, or the legal representative of either, may bring an action for recognition; provided that this shall not apply if three years have passed since the day of the death of the parent.'
The English translation is quoted from the website of 'Japanese Law Translation' offered by the Japanese government, <http://www.japaneselawtranslation.go.jp/?re=02> accessed 14.09.2018, with some alterations by the author of this note.

6 Above n. 5, Art. 779.

7 Supreme Court Decision on 27.04.1962 (*Minshu* vol. 16, no. 7, p. 1247).

8 There is no Supreme Court decision on this point, but there are several lower court decisions which admitted the adoption of the child born through surrogacy by the intended couple: for example Kobe Family Court Himeji Branch Decision on 26 December 2008 (*Katei Saiban Geppo* vol. 61, no. 10, p. 72).

brought a lawsuit against the municipal office that had refused the registration on such ground, the Supreme Court, in its Decision on 19 March 2007,[9] affirmed the refusal of the registration.

That case involved a surrogate birth in Nevada, United States. The commissioning couple (a Japanese celebrity couple living in Japan, who had extensively publicised their surrogacy project through mass media) brought back the children (twins) and applied for the birth registration as their own children. Having been refused the registration, the couple brought the case before the courts. The Tokyo Family Court, the court of first instance, upheld the refusal of registration, denying the legal parentage between the couple and the children. The couple appealed to the Tokyo High Court, which overturned the Family Court decision and ordered the Municipal Office to accept the registration. According to the Tokyo High Court, the Nevada court's judgment ('Nevada judgment'), which established the parentage between the couple and the children, should be recognised in Japan. The Municipal Office then appealed to the Supreme Court.

The Supreme Court decided that the Nevada judgment could not be recognised in Japan. The Nevada judgment was, according to the Supreme Court, against the public policy (*ordre public*) of Japan in that it is incompatible with a fundamental principle of Japanese Family Law: a woman who has given birth to a child should be identified as the mother of the child.[10] The crucial part of the decision reads as follows:

> 'A natural parent-child relationship is the most fundamental relationship concerning a person's status. It is the foundation for various relationships in social life, and in this respect, it does not only concern matters between private persons but is also deeply involved in the public interest, and it has a material impact on child welfare. The eligibility for a natural parent-child relationship is an issue concerning the fundamental principle or fundamental philosophy that serves as the basis of the rules of law on personal status in each country. Therefore, the criteria for the eligibility for a natural parent-child relationship should be definite and clear, and the existence or nonexistence of a natural parent-child relationship should be determined uniformly according to such criteria. Consequently, it should be construed that the Civil Code, which forms the rules of law on personal statuses in Japan, will acknowledge a natural parent-child relationship only in the cases set forth therein, while denying the establishment of a natural parent-child relationship in other cases. In conclusion, a judgment rendered by a foreign court acknowledging the establishment of a natural parent-child relationship between the persons who are not eligible for such relationship under the Civil Code, is incompatible with the fundamental principle or fundamental philosophy of the rules

9 Supreme Court Decision on 19.03.2007 (*Minshu* vol. 16, no. 7, p. 1247).

10 A case note in English on this decision is published in Y. Nomura and J. Ribeiro (eds), *Japanese Yearbook of International Law, No.51*, 2008, p. 552 (edited by, and translated by K. Anderson).

of law in Japan, and therefore it should be deemed to be contrary to public policy as prescribed in Article 118, item 3 of the Code of Civil Procedure. This conclusion would not be affected even if there is room, as a matter of legislative policy, to acknowledge the establishment of a natural parent-child relationship in cases other than those prescribed in the Civil Code.'[11]

In this case, three of the Supreme Court Justices suggested, in their concurring opinions, that the commissioning parents would be allowed to adopt the children. In fact, it is reported that the commissioning parents, having been refused the registration of the children as their natural children by the Supreme Court decision, indeed applied for adoption successfully.

Thus, the current rules under Japanese law concerning the parentage of children born by surrogacy can be summarised as follows:

1. The legal mother is the woman who delivered the child, both for domestic surrogacy and overseas surrogacy;
2. The legal father-child relationship is determined according to the rules on paternity for children by natural reproduction;[12] and
3. The commissioning parents can adopt the child.

4. PREPARATIONS FOR LEGISLATION

There is great need for comprehensive legislation regulating the issues arising from MAR including surrogacy in Japan, and the government indeed has been trying to introduce such legislation. It has set up several committees to discuss relevant issues to prepare legislation. These committees have delivered detailed reports, essentially recommending restrictions on surrogacy.

The most recent and most comprehensive report was issued by a special committee formed Science Council of Japan. The conclusions of the report of this committee, called the Assisted Reproductive Technologies Review Committee, are as follows:[13]

'In Japan, the actual state of surrogate pregnancy has not been objectively ascertained, and the medical safety, certainty and the long-term prognosis of children born

11 This translation is quoted form the website of the Supreme Court of Japan <http://www.courts.go.jp/app/hanrei_en/detail?id=883> accessed 14.09.2018.

12 If the surrogate mother is married, a legal father-child relationship is automatically established between her husband and the child. This parentage can only be denied under very restrictive circumstances. If the surrogate mother is not married, a father-child relationship can be established by recognition (see also above n. 4 and n. 5).

13 Assisted Reproductive Technologies Review Committee, Science Council of Japan 'Report on Issues Related to the Assisted Reproductive Technologies Centered on Surrogate

through surrogate pregnancy is unclear, and it would be fair to say that there is a lack of medical information on surrogate pregnancy. Meanwhile, there have been various arguments related to surrogate pregnancy such as issues related human dignity and ethics of placing physical and psychological burdens and risks of pregnancy and childbirth onto a third person, and the legal aspects regarding legal status of children. Despite these arguments, it would be hard to say that a social consensus has yet been reached. Although reviews on these problems have been advanced by administrative government agencies, academic societies and specialists, the result of these reviews has not been enshrined into law. Amid these circumstances, some medical doctors have proceeded to assist in surrogate pregnancy, and there have also been an increasing number of cases in which people travel overseas for this purpose. The Committee hereby makes the following proposals based on the results of examination over a period of one year and three months described in this report;

(1) Regulation of surrogate pregnancy is needed as it is unacceptable that the issue of surrogate pregnancy be left as it currently stands. Regulation should be based on the law, and new legislation, for instance, the Assisted Reproductive Technologies Act (provisional name) is thought to be needed. Further, in principle, surrogate pregnancy should be prohibited in accordance with this regulation.
(2) Surrogate pregnancy arranged for profit should be dealt with by the imposition of punishments. Punishments should apply to the medical doctors providing the treatment, the mediators, and the commissioning persons.
(3) While respecting the protection of maternal health and the rights and welfare of the child, bearing in mind the need for long-term observations related to the medical issues surrounding surrogate pregnancy – specifically, checks on the risks to the gestational mother and to the fetus/child, and in particular, the postnatal mental development of the child –, and bearing in mind the need to identify ethical, legal and social issues and other possible harmful effects, consideration may be given to the trial implementation of surrogate pregnancies (clinical trials) under strict control, with exclusively limiting the targets to the women with congenital absence of the uterus and to the women who have undergone a hysterectomy as a form of treatment (these are examples of absolute indication).
(4) In conducting the trial of surrogate pregnancies, a public administrative organization which fairly conducts duties such as registration, follow-up studies, guidance, and evaluation should be established. The organization should be comprised of medical, welfare, legal, counseling and other specialists. After a certain period of time, the medical safety and the social and ethical validity of surrogate pregnancy should be fully examined. When no problems are found, the law should be amended and surrogate pregnancy will be permitted under certain guidelines. If numerous harmful effects are found, the trial should be discontinued.

Pregnancy – Toward a Social Consensus', 08.04.2008, available at <http://www.scj.go.jp/ja/info/kohyo/pdf/kohyo-20-t56-1e.pdf#page=1> accessed 14.09.2018; the conclusions quoted here can be found on pp. 39–40.

(5) With respect to the legal status of the born child as a result of surrogate pregnancy, the surrogate mother shall be regarded as the mother. The same shall also hold during the trial. Further, this shall also apply to instances where a surrogate pregnancy is conducted overseas.
(6) With respect to a married couple commissioning a surrogate pregnancy and the child born as a result of that pregnancy, parenthood is established by way of an adoption or special adoption. The same shall also hold during the trial. Further, this shall also apply to instances where the surrogate pregnancy is conducted overseas.
(7) The right to obtain identifying information should be respected as much as possible from the perspective of emphasizing the welfare of the child. This child's right attached to the surrogate pregnancy, however, should be assessed only after full examination on the same right of the child in the cases of AID and the like, which have been practiced for many years. This is an important issue for future examination.
(8) There remain issues which have not been thoroughly discussed, such as the cases using donor eggs and the cases using the frozen sperm of a dead husband, and further, there is a possibility that new problems emerge in the future. Thus, the examination of ART needs to be ongoing.
(9) Concerning the various problems related to bioethics, in view of the importance of a new public research institute should be founded, and a new public standing committee should be established in order to deal with these problems including policy planning.
(10) When discussing surrogate pregnancy and other ART, the welfare of the child should be given the highest priority.'

5. CONCLUSION

Without having clear and comprehensive legislation to regulate MAR operations, including surrogacy, little can be said about parentage issues resulting from MAR, and introducing any legislation to resolve such issues will face considerable difficulties.

Although the government has been trying to introduce legislation to regulate MAR, preparation of the legislation has been shelved for a long time because of various reasons, including strong opposition by some politicians against restrictive regulations in this field. In the meantime, the Liberal Democratic Party (LDP), which is currently the ruling party, established its own project team (LDP-PT) for legislating MAR regulations. The LDP-PT has been discussing matters intensively but has not yet reached any final conclusion on surrogacy. Therefore, for the time being, it is quite unpredictable whether, when and how surrogacy will be regulated by legislation in Japan.

SURROGACY IN SOUTH KOREA

Ock-Joo KIM and Byung-Hwa LEE

Korea has a traditional culture that highly values the patriarchal bloodline and emphasises the family relationship. Thus, an infertile couple often has a strong desire to establish a family with their own child.[1] As the number of infertile people and availability of artificial reproductive technology is increasing, the number of surrogate arrangements presumably is high, but no official statistical data is available.

In South Korea, there are no statutes or laws on surrogacy. Because of the culture that emphasises blood relations, it is the surrogate mother who goes to the medical institution in the name of the commissioning mother to enter the family registration as a child of the commissioning mother. In the absence of legal regulation of surrogacy, the problems raised from surrogacy contracts must be solved by the application and interpretation of the general law. Until recently, the prevailing opinion among legal scholars was that such contracts would be void. But as artificial reproductive technology including the surrogate arrangement are used more widely, calls for specific legislation on surrogacy get more support from legal scholars as well as the general public.

1. GENERAL LEGAL FRAMEWORK

In South Korea, neither statutes nor regulations address surrogacy despite the increasing practice of surrogacy, as revealed by the South Korean news reports and broadcasting media. Given that there are not even legal cases at courts generally, nor any decisions made on surrogacy by the Supreme Court, surrogacy contracts are neither illegal nor regarded as legal. Traditionally the bloodline of a family is of paramount importance in South Korea, and

[1] Y.G. Paik, 'Return of the Sibaji?: Rethinking the Issue of Surrogacy in Contemporary South Korea' (2010) 26 *Asian Women* 73.

the commissioning parents generally hide the history of the child born to a surrogate by registering the baby as if born to the commissioning mother. Although not addressing surrogacy expressly, the Bioethics and Safety Act (in force since January 2005) indirectly affected surrogacy by regulating IVF clinics (on which see below Section 1.1.). Several bills have been proposed to regulate surrogacy in South Korea, but all were aborted (on which see below Section 1.2.). Meanwhile the South Korean Society of Obstetrics and Gynaecology issued Ethical Guidelines on Assisted Reproduction in January 2011, but they are non-binding and not enforceable.

1.1. BIOETHICS AND SAFETY ACT

The first IVF baby in South Korea was born in 1985, but there was no law on assisted reproductive technology in South Korea at the time, leaving gamete trafficking and commercial surrogacy largely unregulated. The Bioethics and Safety Act, enacted on 29 January 2004, and implemented on 1 January 2005, allows IVF procedures to be performed only by government-designated Embryo Production Institutions with a specific workforce and facilities. The Act includes prohibition of monetary transaction for gametes, but contains no provisions on surrogacy and on the rights of babies born from IVF. Although the Bioethics and Safety Act does not deal with surrogacy, the effect of the Act will have been a decrease in surrogacy arrangements by regulating IVF clinics and gamete donation.[2]

1.2. LEGISLATIVE TRENDS

After the implementation of the Bioethics and Safety Act in 2005, several bills were proposed to regulate surrogacy in South Korea, but none were enacted. A brief account of each bill demonstrates the legal issues on surrogacy addressed in South Korea in the past.

1.2.1. Bill (no. 4331) on In Vitro Fertilization (April 2006)

This Bill proposed to legalise altruistic surrogacy, and prohibit commercial surrogacy. By securing the safety and ethics of in vitro fertilisation (IVF),

---

2 J.O. Ha, 'Gestational Surrogacy in Korea' in E. Scott Sills (ed.), *Handbook of Gestational Surrogacy: International Clinical Practice and Policy Issues*, Cambridge University Press, Cambridge 2016, pp. 181–88.

this bill aimed to clarify the status of a child born from artificial reproductive technology including surrogacy. The Bill required registrations of egg and sperm donors and recipients; a surrogate childbirth would have to be approved by the In Vitro Fertilization and Control Division. The Bill defined the eligibility of a surrogate mother, requiring previous childbirth experience, a specific age, health status, and consent of spouse; and also regulated the frequency of surrogate births permitted. Only infertile couples who could generate fertilised eggs by their own reproductive cells could have been a commissioning couple for surrogate birth. This Bill also clarified the legal status of a child born to a surrogate birth: a child born to a surrogate mother would have been regarded as a child of commissioning parents from birth. A surrogate mother therefore could not recognise a child born to her under a surrogacy arrangement as her own child.

1.2.2. Bill (no. 5175) on Medical Assisted Reproduction (October 2006)

This Bill proposed making surrogacy contracts void in principle. However, it also stated that the parts of the contracts should be effective in part, thus requiring some of the payment agreed upon and amounts set by the Ordinance of the Ministry of Health and Welfare to be paid to the surrogate mother, such as medical expenses for the surrogate mother during the surrogacy period. Medical corporations or doctors should not perform assisted reproductive procedures if they know that it is a case of surrogacy. The Bill further proposed to strengthen the requirements of the IVF process: couples who wanted to use medical assisted reproduction would have had to agree to become parents of the child born from sperms or eggs (including germ cells) provided by the donor, and they would have to confirm this in writing before a family court judge.

1.2.3. Bill (no. 5000) on Revision of Bioethics and Safety Act (June 2009)

This Bill banned facilitation of surrogacy contracts. It also declared void any surrogacy contracts: 'a surrogate mother brokerage shall be nullified regardless of the form or name of the contract.' The Bill also prohibited doctors to perform artificial reproductive treatment for the pregnancy and delivery of a surrogate mother through the brokerage of the surrogate mother.

1.2.4. Bill (no. 1814659) on Assisted Reproduction (February 2012)

This Bill simply prohibited a surrogacy including brokerage or intermediation of surrogacy arrangement.

1.3. THE REASONS FOR THE ABSENCE OF LAWS ON SURROGACY IN SOUTH KOREA

No laws or regulations on surrogacy exist in Korea, and this is not an oversight, but rather intentional. In April 2007, the Health and Welfare Committee of the National Assembly of Korea issued two reports evaluating two bills on surrogacy (both discussed briefly above):[3] Bill (no. 4331) on In Vitro Fertilization which would permit altruistic surrogacy, and Bill (no. 5175) on Medical Assisted Reproduction, which would make surrogacy contracts void by law. These reports documented well the reasons why legislating on surrogacy so far has been avoided.

The reports recognise the lack of laws on surrogacy is set against the backdrop of an increasing number of assisted reproductive technologies such as artificial insemination, in vitro fertilisation, and surrogate birth. The Bill (no. 4331) on In Vitro Fertilisation entailed permissions needing to be sought for surrogacy arrangements, prohibits commercial surrogacy, and contains rules on who the legal parent is in the case of surrogate birth. The Bill (no. 5175) on Medical Assisted Reproduction proposed to make all types of surrogacy contracts void, and indirectly prohibited surrogate births by not defining the legal family relations arising from surrogate births. The Committee provided opinions for and against this.

1.3.1. Opinions Favouring the Legislation to Make Surrogacy Contracts Void

Opposition to surrogacy was based on three main arguments. First, surrogacy contracts were thought to contradict human dignity, value and public order; because both the reproductive function of the woman and the resulting child are regarded as the object of the monetary benefit. Second, the relationship between the surrogate mother and the fetus is different from the common relationship between ordinary mother and the fetus; the surrogate mother might have chances to behave in ways which harm the fetus. Third, the surrogate mother often is economically and socially disadvantaged without proper means to protect her legal rights. The surrogate mother therefore can be easily exploited by a contract drafted in a disadvantageous manner to the surrogate.

---

3 Senior Expert Health and Welfare Committee, Review on In Vitro Fertilization, 2007, p. 4; Senior Expert Health and Welfare Committee, Review on Medical Assisted Reproduction, 2007, p. 4.

1.3.2. Opinions Disagreeing with the Legislation to Make Surrogacy Contracts Void

Other took a different view. Firstly, surrogate birth was increasingly widely practiced as medical technology developed. Therefore, there was a need to prevent cases where commissioning parents refuse to accept a child, for example if there were disabilities. Secondly, surrogate childbirth can be an altruistic act where the surrogate makes a sacrifice for others. Making surrogacy contracts void would prevent the contract from being enforceable, making it unclear whether the parties will fulfil the contract, thereby effectively suppressing even altruistic surrogate births. Moreover, if the surrogacy nevertheless takes place (or has taken place already), since the contract is void this would mean the surrogate mother then legally becomes the mother of a child, and the sperm donor the father – which under the circumstances may be detrimental for the well-being of the child.

1.3.3. Reasons Not to Implement Legislation on Surrogacy

The Committee raised concerns over the possible promotion of surrogate birth by legislation. If surrogacy contracts became valid by law in South Korea, the legal relations between the parties to the surrogacy contract would become stable, surrogate birth may become socially acceptable and this may lead to promotion of surrogacy. But whether the surrogacy contract should be declared void by the law required the balancing of interests, namely between the need to suppress surrogate births on the one hand and the need to protect children born through surrogacy on the other. The Committee concluded that the need of legislation on surrogacy should be discussed after the public of South Korea reaches a social consensus, citing a telephone survey in 2004, where 66.1 per cent of respondents opposed legislation on surrogacy.[4]

The Committee suggested that, until the law on surrogacy based on social consensus in South Korea, such cases should be solved by taking subsequent steps following the general law, taking into account the case law of other jurisdictions. The Committee pointed out that even if surrogacy and in vitro fertilisation are carried out without legal regulation, society does not have the policy means to control it without law.

1.3.4. Women's Groups Facing Dilemmas Regarding Legislation on Surrogacy

As with the Special Committee of the National Assembly, South Korean society has an ambiguous position on legislation of surrogacy. Particularly feminist

---

[4] I.Y. Lee, 'Examination of problems related to surrogate mother and seeking legislative policy plan legislative policy. Report to the Ministry of Health, Welfare and Family Affairs, Office of Women Policy' (2005), p. 123. <http://www.nibp.kr/xe/info4_6/1400> accessed 14.09.2018.

groups in South Korea cannot escape from this ambivalent attitude. A reporter said that women's groups have not yet to set a clear position on the issue of legislation of surrogate birth. Son Bong-hee, the head of the health team at the Korean Women's Welfare Association said:

> 'It's true that we have a dilemma. Through surrogacy contracts, women's bodies become subject to commercial trade. In a situation like this, we cannot allow the surrogate mothers to continue to be the victims of exploitative contracts without protection. On the other hand, the situation of infertile couples cannot be ignored. Unjustified legalization, however, risks increase of indiscriminate surrogacy. The dilemma continues. In the South Korean society, where blood relation is so strong, the legalization of surrogacy can cause pressure upon other women in the infertile families to serve as a surrogate for the sake of preserving the bloodline of the family.'[5]

1.4. STATISTICAL INFORMATION ON SURROGACY

1.4.1. Statistics on Infertility Treatment in South Korea

Statistics on infertility treatment in South Korea show a constant increase. The number of infertility patients published by the Health Insurance Review and Assessment Service increased from 186,027 in 2010 to 195,999 in 2013 and 21,114 in 2014, up 13.5 per cent over the past five years. In 2015, there were 218,144 infertility patients, with 16,480 women and 48,704 men (3.3 times more). By age, the number of people aged 30–34 was the highest with 93,821, followed by 65,775 people aged 35–39, 23,510 people aged 40–44, and 22,262 people aged 25–29.[6] According to statistics from the South Korea Institute for Health and Social Affairs (published 26 November 2012), 13.5 per cent of all couples in South Korea were infertile, which means one couple out of eight couples is infertile.[7] The steady increase of infertility treatments is partly due to the National Support Program for Infertile Couples in South Korea. This program provides infertile couples with financial support for assisted reproductive technologies ('ART'), and started in 2006 as a part of the 'First Basic Plan on Low Fertility and the Aging Society' to counter low birth rates.[8] In the case of in vitro

---

5 <http://h21.hani.co.kr/arti/cover/cover_general/19864.html> accessed 03.02.2017. 'Surrogate contracts that involve various illegal activities and human right violations' (2007) *Hangyerye 21* 662.

6 'Surrogate mother and agency illegal sites skyrocketed 45%.' *Medical Newspaper* 08.09.2015 <http://www.bosa.co.kr/news/articleView.html?idxno=592889> accessed 14.09.2018.

7 J.R. Park, 'The Legislative Directions about Surrogacy Contract in the Civil Code' (2013) 18(4) *Journal of the Korea Society of Computer and Information* 161–69.

8 J. Ha, 'Familialism and Pro-natalism to Respecting New Kinds of Family Values and Improving' (2015) 31(2) *Health Journal of Korean Women's Studies* 257–97.

fertilisation, 21,154 cases of assisted reproductive technology were performed in 2005, and 971 cases were made using eggs or sperm of non-spouses.[9]

1.4.2. Statistics on Illegal Surrogate Agency Sites in South Korea

Online monitoring of illegal websites that provide embryos, ova or spermatozoa for money, or act as a broker for providing them, identified a total of 4,076 violations of illegal germ cell sales and agency activities, totalling 2,025 in 2012, 902 in 2013, 401 in 2014, and 748 in 2015.[10] For surrogacy arrangements, the broker places the homepage address and his or her contact information for facilitation of surrogacy. This will be posted with the aim of recruiting both the clients and the applicant of surrogacy at the same time; totalling 249 cases in 2013, 89 cases in 2014 and 155 cases in 2015. In the case of surrogate mother issues, it is difficult to prove illegality if the monetary purpose on the individual homepage is not clearly revealed.[11]

Further data on illegal sites for surrogate mothers and agents published by the Health and Welfare Committee of the National Assembly Health and Welfare Committee on 7 July 2015 revealed 62 surrogacy sites in 2013, and 90 sites in 2014, an increase of more than 45 per cent in one year. For two years, the number of illegal broker sites for surrogate fathers was 95 (62.5 per cent), surrogate mothers 76 (50 per cent), both surrogate father and surrogate mother five (3.3 per cent), and egg sales one (two per cent).[12]

1.4.3. Statistics on Surrogacy in South Korea

Professionals in obstetrics and gynaecology, as well as reporters in South Korea, agree that gestational surrogacy is currently practiced, although no official statistics are available on this in South Korea.[13] Since gestational surrogacy is not illegal in South Korea given there are no definite regulations, surrogacy is practised secretly by both commissioning parents and surrogates. In addition to social prejudice against surrogacy, several unlawful acts involved in the practice of surrogacy prevent parties from coming forth about their surrogacy arrangement. For example, the surrogate mother uses commissioning mother's name at the birth clinic to get the birth certificate of the resulting child.[14]

---

9 Ministry of Health and Welfare, '2005 Survey on the status of embryo storage and provision' (19.05.2006).

10 H. Moon, S. Park and M. Kim, 'Online Monitoring about Illegal Surrogacy Arrangement on a Commercial Basis in Korea' (2016) 19(1) *Korean J Med Ethics* 36.

11 Ibid.

12 See above n. 6.

13 J.H. Seo, 'The study on surrogacy agreement' (2009) 23(3) *Korean Journal of Family Law* 45–106.

14 J.O. Ha, above n. 2, pp. 181–88.

Several authors have speculated that the number of surrogacy arrangements ranged from 10 cases per year,[15] to several hundred per year in South Korea. A legal scholar presumed about 70 to 80 cases per year nationwide.[16] The Congressman proposing the bill to regulate surrogacy said, 'It is estimated that hundreds of cases are performed annually nationwide, considering the number and the conditions of surrogacy facilitation given through the internet sites.'[17]

There are about 150 medical institutions practicing IVF infertility treatment in South Korea. In 2012, 200,000 infertile people visited IVF clinics. 65,000 cases of infertility treatment (artificial insemination, test-tube treatment) were performed, and an estimated 34,000 cases of in vitro fertilisation (test-tube treatment). This is a 3.4-fold increase compared to the number seven years ago. On the other hand, in South Korea, an average of 430,000–450,000 babies are born per year, and about 8–10 per cent of them are born through the artificial reproductive technology (artificial insemination, IVF, etc.).

Hankyoreh 21 published a survey on the practice of surrogacy in South Korea. The reporter, pretending to be a client seeking IVF and surrogacy procedures, asked whether a surrogacy arrangement would be possible at 41 hospitals, excluding university hospitals, all of which were institutions for the Infertile Couple Support Program designated and supported by the Ministry of Health of South Korea in metropolitan cities like Seoul, Daegu, Busan, Gwangju, Daejeon and Incheon. Out of the total 41 hospitals, 30 hospitals replied, 'we can do it', nine said 'we do not do it', and two were not confirmed. Among the 30 hospitals which said surrogacy was possible, only two hospitals said that only relatives can be a surrogate. One of the hospitals said to the reporter, 'you only need to find a surrogate. For we are not the police, we won't check whether the surrogate is your relative or not. If someone asks you, reply that she is your relative.'[18]

2. SURROGACY ARRANGEMENTS IN GENERAL

2.1. WHETHER THE SURROGACY CONTRACT IS VALID IN SOUTH KOREA[19]

In South Korea, even where a surrogacy contract has been entered into, there are no express legal rules that directly govern it. Therefore, various theories have

---

15 J.R. Park, above n. 7, 161–69.

16 D.J. Park, 'Surrogate Motherhood in Korea; Legislative Theoretical Research' (2010) 51(4) *Law Review* 337–58.

17 See above n. 5.

18 See above n. 5.

19 B.H. Lee, 'A Study on the International Surrogacy Arrangement' (2016) 22(1) *Korea Private International Law Journal* 145–48.

been argued among legal professionals in South Korea about the validity of the surrogacy contract. If these theories are broadly classified, they can be divided into void, effective, and of limited effect.

First, the invalidity theory is the view of the majority of legal scholars in South Korea. The theory argues that the surrogacy contract itself is invalid based on the infringement of *bonos mores* and public order according to Civil Code Art. 103. Article 103 (Juristic Acts Contrary to Public Order) says, 'A juristic act which has for its object such matters as are contrary to good morals and other public order shall be null and void.'[20] Particularly, surrogacy contracts, which promise the surrogate the payment of money as a compensation, are no different from the case of buying or selling a child, and thereby it instrumentalises women as pregnancy machines and commercialises the uterus.

By contrast, the theory of effectiveness of surrogacy contracts states that there is no law prohibiting the surrogacy contract explicitly under the present law in South Korea, and therefore it cannot be regarded as a violation of Art.103 of the Civil Code. According to current family law, the parents can recognise the surrogacy contract as an act in the identification law, because family law recognises the legal adopting system. Furthermore, surrogacy is the only means for overcoming the infertility of some women that would still allow them to have children of their own. Thus, this theory suggests that surrogacy contracts should be recognised, when the surrogacy is the only way for the infertile couples in a stable marriage to have a child of their own.

Finally, the theory of limited effect states that the effectiveness of surrogacy contracts should be limited to the case where the contract is free from financial transactions. In other words, commercial surrogacy is invalid, but altruistic surrogacy is not. However, considering contract law, women's human rights, and social aspects, it is difficult to recognise the validity of the surrogacy contract even for altruistic surrogacy. Given that surrogacy contracts exist in South Korean society, the contract should not be regarded as null and void because of the need to protect the surrogate and the commissioning couple. This view has gained support from more scholars recently: from a legal policy point of view, they argue, it is reasonable to move toward recognising a surrogacy contract under certain conditions.

2.2. LEGAL BINDINGNESS OF SURROGACY CONTRACTS

It is reasonable that the preliminary agreement on parenthood cannot be enforced. The transferral of parental rights under the surrogacy contract is null

---

20 Civil Code Art. 103. <http://law.go.kr/engLsSc.do?menuId=0&subMenu=5&query=#liBgcolor0> accessed 14.09.2018.

and void, but can be converted into a preliminary agreement on parenthood that is valid by the so-called legal act of invalid act conversion – but impossible to enforce.[21] As a result, surrogacy contracts, with the exception of the part relating to parenthood, can be viewed as an effective contract. According to this view, it cannot be argued that the surrogacy contract commercialises the uterus, ignores the special relationship between the surrogate mother and the child, and is contrary to the public orders of the Art. 103 of the Civil Code. This is because some considerations are already given to the special relationship between the surrogate mother and the child through the impermissibility of enforcement of the prearrangement of the transfer of parenthood.

2.3. REMUNERATION FOR PARTICIPATION IN THE SURROGACY ARRANGEMENT

The surrogate sites for recruiting and providing surrogate mothers can be easily accessed in South Korea. The total cost of surrogate arrangements vary, but are usually around 80 to 90 million Korean Won (US$70,000 to US$78,800). The websites claim that birth by a foreign surrogate, not a domestic surrogate, is legal. A report written after consulting with a surrogate agency in South Korea revealed the total cost for the commissioning parents to receive a child from a surrogacy arrangement is about 65 million Korean Won (US$58,500).[22] The total sum of money paid to the surrogate mother is about 33 million Korean Won (about US$28,800), and 15 million Korean Won (US$13,500) is to be paid in advance. The remaining balance will be paid after delivery, and a broker will be paid a commission of 3 million Korean Won (US$2,700), which is 10 per cent of the reward. The contract stipulates that all risks of pregnancy and childbirth are the responsibility of the surrogate mother, and that the commissioning parents will not be liable for any civil or criminal damages.

According to newspaper articles, there are additional rewards if the surrogate mother gives birth to a son.[23] Remuneration is greatly reduced if a child is born with a deformity or disability. The payment to the surrogate varies depending on the age and condition of the surrogate mother. In reality, the

21 D. Eom, 'Surrogate Mother Contract' (2001) *The Justice* 34, 88 (in Korean).

22 'Uterine lending surrogate market to track the uncomfortable truth. One hundred million per baby ... imagine the business for children in the shadows' [Tracking Issue Focus 1] *Saguninnews* 23.09.2014. <http://www.sagunin.com/sub_read.html?uid=3473> accessed 14.09.2018.

23 'Surrogate mother ... Is it a necessary evil in society? Infertile couples do not mind surrogate to get kids.' *Sunday Seoul* 20.07.2015. <http://www.ilyoseoul.co.kr/news/articleView.html?idxno=115789> accessed 14.09.2018.

surrogacy brokers in South Korean society have a wide range of payments from international surrogacy arrangements:

> 'Depending on nationality, age, academic background, appearance, and birth experience, you can meet a variety of surrogate mothers starting from 25 million Korean Won ($22,500 USD). Southeast Asian women are the cheapest, Chinese Koreans are 30 million Korean Won ($27,000 USD), and Korean women are 40 million ($36,000 USD) to 60 million Korean Won ($54,000 USD). Special A grade is about 100 million Korean Won ($90,000 USD), and the clients cannot get these surrogate mothers with only money because they choose the couple of clients.'[24]

2.4. GUIDELINES CONCERNING APPROPRIATE LEVELS OF PAYMENTS

There is no guidance on the level of payment to surrogate mothers. However, the most similar criteria to refer to is the compensation for the egg donors listed in the Enforcement Decree of the Bioethics and Safety Act in South Korea. Based on this, guidelines made by the Obstetrics and Gynecology Society are as follows:

1. The practicing physician and the medical institution shall not be entitled to any financial or property benefit or other countervailing benefit. They must not use or provide eggs or induce or arrange them as a financial transaction.
2. In the procedure of donating eggs, the donation by the donor to the recipient should be free in principle. However, the actual costs used to collect or donate eggs can be paid, and the recipient of eggs shall pay to the donor of the eggs.
3. The calculation of the expenses to be paid to the donor includes payments for items such as transportation expenses, food expenses, accommodation expenses, etc. The cost calculation standard should be prepared and reviewed by the Institutional Bioethics Committee, and the amount of actual expenses paid should be reported to the Institutional Bioethics Committee.

2.5. LIMITS ON PAYMENTS

In order to prevent economic incentives to the egg donors, the actual expense compensation is suggested based on the travel expenses and the daily expenses

24 See above n. 5.

and transportation expenses of government officials. The limit is about 100,000 (US$90) to 150,000 Korean Won (US$135) per day. A total of 1,500,000 Korean Won (US$1,350) per egg retrieval cycle therefore roughly is the upper limit. The donation of the egg donor is reviewed by the Institutional Bioethics Committee. The cost assessment criteria should be reviewed, and the details of the payment should be reported afterwards. According to these standards, the estimated money received by the surrogate mother during the 270 days of gestation will be from 2.7 million (US$27,000) to 40 million Korean Won (US$36,000), which is fairly close to the actual payments made for surrogacy in South Korea.

3. LEGAL PARENTHOOD AT THE TIME OF BIRTH

3.1. MATERNITY

Following the Roman law principle '*mater semper certa est*', the maternal relationship in South Korea arises from giving birth to the child, regardless of the effect of the surrogacy contract. The relationship between the surrogate mother and the child therefore according to South Korean law is determined by the fact that the legal mother-child relationship arises from the childbirth, so the legal mother of the child is the gestational mother.

3.2. PATERNITY

If the surrogate mother is unmarried, the surrogate-born child will be a child out of wedlock, and the problem of presumptions of fatherhood will not arise. But if the surrogate mother is married, according to Civil Code Art. 844 her husband is presumed to be the father of the child, even he is not the genetic father. However, this paternity can be contested by legal action. If the commissioning father is the genetic father, he can bring such an action with the aim of becoming the legal father according to Art. 865 of the Civil Code.

Provided the commissioning father's sperm was used, he therefore can be the legal father either by recognition if the surrogate is unmarried, or by taking the appropriate legal action if she is married at the time of birth. However, according to the view that the surrogacy contract is void, the latter path is only open if the surrogate's husband denies paternity.

4. ELIGIBILITY FOR SURROGACY

Given the lack of laws on surrogacy in South Korea, Ethical Guidelines on Assisted Reproduction issued in January 2011 by the Korean Society of

Obstetrics and Gynaecology provide eligibility criteria for women acting as surrogates, although they are non-binding and not enforceable. The guidelines define 'pregnancy through gestational surrogacy', referring to transplanting embryos formed from sperms and eggs of married couples into the womb of another person and attempting pregnancy. Thus, only legally married couples who can produce embryos from their own eggs and sperms are eligible for surrogacy arrangements. Therefore, according to the Ethical Guidelines on Assisted Reproduction, only a genetic father and a genetic mother can be commissioning parents for surrogacy arrangements. Surrogacy procedures should be reviewed by the Institutional Bioethics Committee before the procedure.

4.1. ELIGIBILITY CRITERIA FOR WOMEN ACTING AS A SURROGATE

1. Surrogate mothers must be healthy women who have no physical or other obstacles to pregnancy maintenance and childbirth. However, in principle, women who have no experience of birth should be excluded.
2. The surrogate mother must be under 45 years of age considering the complications of pregnancy and birth.
3. The surrogate mother must receive appropriate tests for embryo transfer, pregnancy and birth.
4. The surrogate mother must not be naturally pregnant during the procedure.
5. The doctors and the medical institutions must give the following information and obtain consent from the surrogate mother and her spouse:
   a. Procedures and related complications and their treatment.
   b. The fact that the genetic parents are intended to be the parents and the surrogate mother consents to this.
   c. The fact that there is no financial relationship with the genetic parents in relation to a surrogate arrangement.
   d. The surrogate mother must follow advice and medical treatment through the entire process of pregnancy and childbirth, and avoid drinking, smoking, or taking any medication.

4.2. ELIGIBILITY CRITERIA FOR COMMISSIONING PARENTS

1. Genetic parents must be in a legal valid marriage.
2. Genetic parents must not arrange financial remuneration for the surrogate for carrying and giving birth to the child.
3. Genetic parents must understand the process of IVF-induced ovarian hyperstimulation and general complication and must agree in writing.

4. Genetic parents must undergo the basic tests required for in vitro fertilisation procedures.
5. Eligibility criteria for commissioning mothers:
   a. When there is no uterus congenitally.
   b. Hysterectomy performed due to cancer, uterine bleeding, or other diseases.
   c. Severe risks to the mother's health during pregnancy due to major organ diseases.
   d. Endometrial damage due to severe endometriosis or uterine tuberculosis.
   e. Repetitive failure in maintaining pregnancy, and thereby the possibility of pregnancy retention is very low.

5. TRANSFERRING PARENTHOOD

As explained above, according to the South Korean Civil Code the legal parents of a child born through surrogacy are the surrogate mother who gave birth to the child and her spouse. There is no indication on the birth certificate or other documents that the child was born because of a surrogacy arrangement.

Parenthood can be transferred to commissioning parents from a surrogate mother and her husband through the following procedures.

1. The surrogate mother and her husband bring a civil action for denial of paternity.
2. The commissioning genetic father files confirmation of existence of biological parental relation.
3. The commissioning genetic mother undergoes the process of adoption to become a legal mother.
4. The record shows who the legal mother (the surrogate) and father was before the adoption.

6. AGENCIES AND CRIMINALISATION

As said several times, South Korea has no specific rules or regulations on surrogacy. The Bioethics and Safety Act regulates only the selling and buying of gametes. Article 66 (Penal Provisions) of the Act says 'any of the following persons shall be punished by imprisonment with prison labor for not more than three years: a person who provides or uses an embryo, ovum, or spermatozoon for money, an interest in property, or any other consideration, who solicits another person to provide or use an embryo, ovum, or spermatozoon for such consideration, or who acts as a broker for providing or using an embryo, ovum, or spermatozoon, in violation of Article 23 (3)'.[25]

There are no further provisions imposing criminal liability in cases of surrogacy.

7. INTERNATIONAL SURROGACY ARRANGEMENTS

7.1. INTERNATIONAL SURROGACY CONTRACTS, RECOGNITION OF FOREIGN ORDERS AND INTERNATIONAL PUBLIC POLICY ISSUES IN GENERAL

In general, if the outcome of the application of the foreign law specified by the governing law is contrary to the national public policy (*ordre public*), the application of the foreign law is excluded.

This follows from Art. 10 of the South Korean Private International Law (the provisions of foreign laws contrary to social order) which stipulates that 'where the application of the provisions is required by the foreign law, it does not apply when it clearly violates the good customs and other social order of the Republic of Korea.' General and abstract standards of 'good customs and other social order' are also defined. 'Application of the provisions' means the result of applying foreign law; 'good customs' means the ethics of South Korean society, and 'other social order' means the spiritual purpose of Korean law. In addition, in order to prevent the abuse of the provision of public order, it was stated that the application of foreign law would be excluded only if it was 'clearly' in violation of good customs and social order.

If the commissioning parents have been declared to be the legal parents by a foreign court order, the question of the recognition of that order and of the international public policy arise. Therefore, the issues of surrogacy being contrary to public policy and the order concerning parenthood must be separated, as the former necessarily leads to a finding that the recognition of the foreign order is against public policy.

Foreign judgments are recognised and enforced under certain conditions. In South Korea the recognition of foreign judgments is regulated by Art. 217 of the Civil Procedure Act and Arts 26 and 27 of the Civil Execution Act. Article 217 of the Civil Procedure Act stipulates that a final judgment of a foreign court requires that the court had international jurisdiction, that certain procedural standards were adhered to, mutual recognition and that there is no violation of the public order.

[25] Article 66 (Penal Provisions) of the Bioethics and Safety Act.

The central question in case of parenthood through surrogacy is whether or not this contradicts the public order of South Korea. Considering the fact that the internal relevance should be taken into consideration in determining the issue, if the couple is resident in South Korea, it may be contrary to public order to acknowledge the establishment of parental relations. On the other hand, a foreign court approving the establishment of parenthood by a surrogate mother contract may be approved in cases of lack of domestic relations with South Korea.

7.2. NATIONALITY OF CHILDREN BORN TO FOREIGN SURROGATE MOTHERS

The South Korean Nationality Act adopts parental hereditary lineage, and a person whose father or mother is a national of the Republic of Korea at the time of birth is a citizen of South Korea, because she or he acquires the nationality of the Republic of Korea through birth (Art. 2 para. 1, Item 1 of the Nationality Act). The term 'father or mother' means a legal parent. Hence the legal parentage must be established, which can also happen through adoption, as the child can then be naturalised and acquire South Korean nationality accordingly (Art. 4 of the Nationality Act).

8. CONCLUSION

If a child is already born through surrogacy, in South Korea or elsewhere, immediate legal action is necessary in order to secure the rights of the commissioning couple, the surrogate mother and the child. If the law prohibits or restricts surrogacy in South Korea, couples will seek to have a child through international surrogacy. This may lead to diplomatic frictions and difficult private international law cases. Currently surrogacy contracts according to the view of the majority view are simply void, but permitting altruistic surrogacy for couples with fertility issues certainly is interesting from a public policy perspective.

Under the current law the only way for both commissioning parents to gain legal parenthood is to adopt the child born by a surrogate mother. Whether this is necessarily the best approach should be examined with regard to the best interests of the child and the human rights of the surrogate and the commissioning couple.

In the past, the law and the courts (not only in South Korea but globally) have generally taken a negative position with regard to surrogacy. However, there appears to be a tendency to allow the surrogate contracts with certain limitations. This requires careful thought, not only on whether such contract should be valid or not, but also with regard to enforceability and potential damages in case of breach of contract and particularly who should be regarded as the parent of the child at birth.

The question here is what should be given greater importance, gestation or genetics, or intention or the willingness to 'be a parent' and raise the child? As a society, it is irresponsible not to take any legislative action. Surrogacies happen, and everyone involved at the very least deserves legal certainty. If we do not make an effort to minimise the gap between reality and the law, we are doomed to remain in the vicious cycle of an ever-increasing demand for surrogacy and the problems arising from operating in the shadow of the law. Ignoring surrogacy or expressly making it illegal is not a realistic answer. What is required is a form of institutional framework with a focus on the best interests of the child.

FROM FREE MARKET TO REGULATION

SURROGACY IN INDIA

Prabha KOTISWARAN

1. GENERAL LEGAL FRAMEWORK

1.1. THE LEGAL FRAMEWORK FOR SURROGACY

There is no specific statute at the federal level or provincial state level on surrogacy in India as of February 2019. The Surrogacy (Regulation) Bill 2016 (hereafter 'SRB') has been approved by the Union Cabinet of Ministers at the federal government and was introduced in Parliament in late 2016. It was referred to a Parliamentary Standing Committee in January 2017, which submitted its report in August 2017. The revised Bill, the Surrogacy (Regulation) Bill 2018 based on the SRB, was passed by the lower house of Parliament in December 2018 but is yet to be considered by the upper house. The SRB has been quite controversial; details of the SRB will be discussed later in this chapter in Sections 2–6.

In the absence of any statutory framework, two sets of guidelines and rules currently apply to surrogacy in India. The first are the National Guidelines for Accreditation, Supervision and Regulation of ART Clinics in India, published by the Ministry of Health and Family Welfare and drafted by the Indian Council of Medical Research ('ICMR') in 2005 (hereafter 'ICMR Guidelines').[1] These guidelines are not considered to be binding but several Indian fertility clinics, particularly the well-known clinics claim to abide by them.

Apart from the ICMR guidelines there are executive orders issued by various Indian federal ministries. In 2012, the Ministry of External Affairs issued a circular to regulate the use by foreign couples of surrogacy services in India, including the need to obtain a surrogacy visa prior to commencing their treatment using assisted reproduction techniques (hereafter 'ART') and an exit visa after the surrogacy transaction was concluded.[2] In 2015 however, this 2012 circular was superseded by an order of the Ministry of External Affairs and Health[3] – which banned surrogacy by foreigners and details of which are set out later in this section. Since 2015, therefore, only foreign couples who had commenced their ART treatment prior to the ban have continued to use the services of fertility clinics and Indian surrogates. Commercial surrogacy however continues to be undertaken by commissioning parents who are Indian citizens although in far fewer numbers when compared to foreign commissioning parents. Once the Surrogacy (Regulation) Bill 2018 comes

1 <https://www.slideshare.net/ovary2009/guidelines-for-art-clinics-in-india> accessed 30.11.2018.

2 No. 25022/74/2011/F.I. dated 09.07.2012, 07.03.2013, 16.07.2013 and 14.10.2013.

3 Government of India Ministry of Home Affairs (Foreigners Division) no. 25022/74/2011-F.I (vol. III) dated 03.11.2015; Government of India Ministry of Health & Family Welfare (Department of Health Research), no. V. 25011/119/2015-HR dated 04.11.2015.

into force however, commissioning parents who are Indian citizens cannot commission commercial surrogacy anymore. During this interim period, the ICMR Guidelines continue to apply to domestic commissioning parents.

There is no explicit right to reproduction protected under the Indian Constitution. However, in *B.K. Parthasarthi v Government of Andhra Pradesh*,[4] the Andhra Pradesh High Court upheld the 'right of reproductive autonomy' of an individual as a facet of his 'right to privacy' which is protected under Art. 21 of the Indian Constitution. This reading was reiterated by the Supreme Court in the right to privacy judgment *Puttaswamy v Union of India*, where it held that 'a woman's freedom of choice whether to bear a child or abort her pregnancy are areas which fall in the realm of privacy' (Justice Chelamaswar, para. 38).[5] The majority also noted that 'the sanctity of marriage, the liberty of procreation, the choice of a family life and the dignity of being are matters which concern every individual irrespective of social strata or economic well-being. The pursuit of happiness is founded upon autonomy and dignity. Both are essential attributes of privacy, which makes no distinction between the birth marks of individuals' (majority, para. 157). In another case *Javed v State of Haryana*[6] however, dealing with electoral laws that bar individuals with more than two children from contesting elections to local bodies (*panchayats*), the Supreme Court upheld this effective restriction on the right to reproduce on the basis that it was justified for 'socio- economic welfare and health care of the masses' and 'consistent with the national population policy'.

Another constitutional provision that is likely to be implicated by the practice of commercial surrogacy is the prohibition of forced labour under Art. 23. Article 23 prohibits 'traffic in human beings and begar and other similar forms of forced labour' and states that any contravention of Art. 23 shall be an offence punishable in accordance with the law.[7] Although unlawful compulsory labour has been criminalised under the Indian Penal Code 1860, a more comprehensive provision was introduced to the Indian Penal Code 1860 in 2013 by the Criminal Law (Amendment) Act 2013. Section 370 prohibits trafficking and involves three elements – an act element relating to recruitment, transportation, harbouring, transferring or receiving persons. The second element is the means by which any of the above acts are achieved; these means include the use of threats, the use of force, or any other form of coercion, abduction, the use of fraud, or deception, or the abuse of power, or inducement, including the giving or receiving of payments or benefits, in order to achieve the

---

4 *B.K. Parthasarthi v Government of Andhra Pradesh* 2000 (1) ALD 199.

5 *K. S. Puttaswamy v Union of India*, Writ Petition (Civil) no. 494/12 of 2017.

6 *Javed v State of Haryana* AIR 2003 SC 3057.

7 Indian courts find 'begar' requires showing 'that the person has been forced to work against his will and without payment.' *See*, *Ram Khelwan Pathak vs State of U.P.* (1998) 2 A.W.C. 1171 (India).

consent of any person having control over the person recruited, transported, harboured, transferred or received. The third element of the offence under s. 370 is the purpose for which the said person is trafficked, namely, for purposes of exploitation. The term 'exploitation' is however not defined in s. 370 and is said to include at a minimum, 'any act of physical exploitation or any form of sexual exploitation, slavery or practices similar to slavery, servitude, or the forced removal of organs.' Further where any of the said means are used, the consent of the victim is immaterial. Although s. 370 has not been invoked in the context of commercial surrogacy to my knowledge, the broad scope of the offence and the lack of a definition of the term 'exploitation' means that the prosecution of stakeholders where a woman is coerced into commercial surrogacy is possible. Indeed, a proposed statute, which builds upon s. 370, titled the Trafficking of Persons (Prevention, Protection and Rehabilitation) Bill 2018 was passed by the lower house of the Indian Parliament in July 2018. It incorporates a specific offence of aggravated trafficking punishing any person who traffics a woman for the purpose of bearing a child by natural means or through ART. The punishment is imprisonment for a minimum of 10 years, which can extend up to life. Other provisions, which criminalise commercial surrogacy in the SRB will be discussed in Section 6.

Although there is no statute per se on surrogacy as of February 2019, the Surrogacy (Regulation) Bill 2018 was passed by the lower house of Parliament in December 2018 but is yet to be passed by the upper house and receive Presidential assent before it becomes law. In addition to the ICMR Guidelines and Ministry circulars detailed later in this section, Indian professional bodies have articulated non-binding ethical guidelines that they expect their member clinics to abide by. Thus the Indian Society for Third Party Assisted Reproduction ('INSTAR')[8] lists its key recommendations, which include prioritising the 'welfare and well being' of surrogates. The recommendations specify minimum rates of compensation, providing for the health care of the surrogate in various scenarios and the need for including certain contractual terms between the commissioning parents and surrogates. The Federation of Obstetric & Gynaecological Societies of India ('FOGSI') is similarly in favour of legalisation of commercial surrogacy in India and recommends that certain criteria be met both in terms of eligibility for commissioning parents as well as surrogates, terms of the contract between the stakeholder parties as well as the need to institute a special court with members from the judiciary, FOGSI and society in general to handle disputes arising from the commercial surrogacy transactions.[9] The Indian Medical Association, while registering its protest against the SRB, suggests certain eligibility criteria for commissioning parents and calls on the

---

8 <http://instar.co.in/highlights.html> accessed 14.09.2018.

9 <http://www.fogsi.org/fogsi-policies/> accessed 14.09.2018.

government to reconsider the regulation of ART Banks and liability of doctors so that 'a liberal and ethical ART law' formulated in consultation with various medical bodies can offer ethical and regulated surrogacy for both Indian nationals as well as foreign nationals including Persons of Indian Origin ('PIO') and Overseas Citizens of India ('OCI').[10] Finally, there is a whole range of laws that governs medical practice in India including laws relating to the *qualifications and conduct of professionals*, storage and *sale of drugs, law governing the management of patients*, laws governing the safety of patients, public and staff within hospital, laws relating to environmental protection, laws relating to employment matters, laws relating to professional training and research and regulations relating to the business aspects of the hospital. There are also laws on abortion (the Medical Termination of Pregnancy Act 1971) and pre-natal diagnosis (The Pre-Natal Diagnostic Techniques (Regulation and Prevention of Misuse) Act 1994, as amended in 2003).

1.2. SPECIALISED AUTHORITY TO OVERSEE SURROGACY

There is no specialised authority set up to oversee surrogacy in India although ART clinics have generally looked to the ICMR which is 'the apex body in India for the formulation, coordination and promotion of biomedical research, (and) is one of the oldest medical research bodies in the world' for guidance in the area of ART.[11] The ICMR Guidelines did envisage the creation of state accreditation authorities to oversee the accreditation, supervision and regulation of ART Clinics as well as appropriate authorities for the implementation of its 2005 Guidelines. These were however not set up.

Sections 14 through 31 of the Surrogacy (Regulation) Bill 2016 meanwhile envisage the creation of a National Surrogacy Board and State Surrogacy Boards. Under s. 14, the National Surrogacy Board will be set up at the national level consisting of members in charge from the relevant ministries (health, women and child development, law, home affairs), members of Parliament, representatives from the IVF sector and civil society and chairpersons of State Surrogacy Boards. Sections 15 through 21 specify the term of the Board, meetings of the Board and the process by which it will conduct its meetings. The main purpose of the National Surrogacy Board is to advise the central government on policy matters relating to surrogacy, review the implementation of the SRB, to lay down a code of conduct for surrogacy clinics, set out minimum standards in terms

10 See <http://emedinews.in/ima/Press_Release/august/26.pdf> accessed 14.09.2018; 'IMA opposes ART Bill; says the Bill lacks humanistic approach', *India Medical Times*, 29 November 2015, <http://www.indiamedicaltimes.com/2015/11/29/ima-opposes-art-bill-says-the-bill-lacks-humanistic-approach/> accessed 18.10.2018.

11 <https://icmr.nic.in/content/about-us> accessed 30.11.2018.

of physical infrastructure and oversee the performance of the various bodies constituted under the SRB including the State Surrogacy Boards. Sections 23–31 have mirroring provisions for the constitution of the State Surrogacy Boards. Section 23 in particular specifies that the State Surrogacy Boards will review the activities of the appropriate authorities set up under the SRB, monitor the implementation of the provisions of the SRB and send consolidated reports about activities in the state to the central government. Chapter VI of the SRB also requires the constitution of 'appropriate authorities' in all the states and union territories, whose primary role is to manage the registration of surrogacy clinics, enforce standards within them, investigate complaints of the breach of the SRB and undertake legal action (including *suo motu*) under the SRB, recommend any modifications to the rules and regulations to the surrogacy boards and make decisions on applications for certificates of essentiality and eligibility from the commissioning parents and surrogates.

1.3. HISTORIC DEVELOPMENT LEADING UP TO THE CURRENT LAW

In the Indian context given the cultural dominance of its Hindu majority, there is a spiritual premium to having one's genetic progeny to complete end-of-life religious rituals. This has meant that infertile couples have for long used other methods to complete their families including insemination by someone other than a spouse, intra-family and inter-family adoption, altruistic surrogacy undertaken by family members, and indeed illegal practices such as the selling and buying of babies. ART in India developed against the backdrop of an anti-natalist context in which the coercive state apparatus controlled women's bodies and reproductive choices in its pursuit of population control and an aggressive two-child policy, which even led to a brief period during the Emergency years in the 1970s of forced sterilisation. Surrogacy was developed in India initially by the government as a means to reverse sterilisation. Commercial surrogacy services provided by private fertility clinics is however of relatively recent vintage and developed in leaps and bounds from the late 1990s and early 2000s when entrepreneurial medical professionals like Dr Nayna Patel of the Akanksha Fertility Clinic in Anand, Gujarat assisted a grandmother to deliver the children of her own infertile UK-based daughter. Commercial surrogacy over the past 15 years has taken the form of gestational surrogacy; the 2005 ICMR Guidelines do not permit the egg donor to be the surrogate.

Although there is no binding statute to date, which specifically permits or prohibits surrogacy, several Bills have been proposed specifically in relation to surrogacy and in allied areas of regulation such as criminal law (relating to trafficking) over the past 15 years. They are best understood as belonging to three phases of development of the surrogacy market and the Indian state's attempts to regulate it. These include an emergent medico-liberal phase from the late 1990s up to 2008; a highly contested but regulatory phase between 2008–12 and a contracting and normative phase between 2012 and 2016. In other words, if we were to plot the trajectory of the *proposed* regulation of the Indian surrogacy industry between the late 1990s and 2016, these *proposed* laws have gone from being highly favourable to fertility clinics (and less so to surrogates) to severely restricting parties who could avail of ART on the basis of marital status, sexual orientation and the nationality/citizenship of commissioning parents. Almost correspondingly, the levels of protection offered to the surrogates under the proposed legislative bills have increased over time. Each phase is dealt with in turn.

1.3.1. Medico-Liberal Phase Late 1990s–2008

It is during the medico-liberal phase, that we find the first attempts at regulating surrogacy. In 1999, the ICMR constituted a committee of experts to develop national standards for ART clinics. After extensive national consultations and considerable feedback from medical professionals, patients, bureaucrats, and the public, the ICMR drafted in 2005 the National Guidelines for Accreditation, Supervision and Regulation of ART Clinics in India. The ICMR estimated that there were 250 ART clinics in India.

The ICMR guidelines had three main components – regulation of the industry through the institution of administrative bodies; regulation of the political economy of the industry and finally regulation of the relations between the various stakeholders who are party to any given surrogacy transaction. These Guidelines have formed the basis for subsequent legislative proposals. In terms of regulating the surrogacy industry, the ICMR Guidelines provided for the accreditation of ART clinics and provided guidelines for informed consent, confidentiality, counselling and the need to publicly display charges and the success rates of fertility treatments. The ICMR outlined the need to maintain information about donors and recipients and the need for confidentiality. Under these Guidelines, the child had the right to know about his or her genetic parents and surrogates except for their names and addresses. The ICMR Guidelines also outlined permissible roles for the different stakeholders in the surrogacy industry including the ART Clinic and the ART Bank, the qualifications of the sperm and egg donors and the surrogate as well as the commissioning parents. More detail on these aspects is provided in Section 4. The ICMR also referred to several aspects of the medical process itself offering model consent forms as appendices to the Guidelines. The regulatory thrust of the ICMR Guidelines was to permit commercial gestational surrogacy whereby commissioning parents could commission a surrogacy transaction by payment of compensation to gamete donors as well as surrogates. The sensibility of these regulations is informed by a public health view of infertility, which is liberal when it comes to highly contested normative questions over whether the private life process of reproduction typically undertaken within a nuclear family unit can be commercialised by third parties in the market.

1.3.2. Contested and Regulatory Phase 2008–12

Between 2008–12, the surrogacy industry flourished with the emergence of different business models largely catering to international commissioning parents. There were full service clinics like the Anand-based Akanksha Fertility Clinic, Delhi-based SCI Healthcare and the Hyderabad-based Kiran Infertility Center which offered comprehensive package deals – from identifying the egg donor and surrogate to performing IVF treatment, to maintaining a surrogate hostel, to delivering the baby to facilitating local travel and obtaining the exit visa before leaving the country. Then there were agencies, which liaised with the commissioning parents, the egg donor and surrogate and looked after the surrogates (either by maintaining a hostel or otherwise) while the medical processes were separated into the IVF component performed by the fertility clinic and the delivery being conducted at a hospital of choice. Then, there were intermediate models wherein an agency was run by a medical professional who liaised with the various stakeholders to provide the commissioning parents comprehensive services from start to finish.

It was around 2008 that intra-industry disputes arose. Unlike in the United States or United Kingdom, it was not surrogates who litigated because they had decided to keep the babies they had borne. Surrogates in India have a collective action problem even in places like Anand where the sector assumed small industrial proportions and several surrogates stayed together. Access to formal state institutions was a huge barrier for individual surrogates. Due to the highly medically mediated nature of the sector and surrogates' own desire to access clinics for a repeat transaction, they were loathe to antagonise fertility clinics or approach the courts for any relief when the terms of their surrogacy agreements were violated. Instead, it was the commissioning parents who went to court either due to differences in how national jurisdictions regulated surrogacy or parentage or because of a change in their own personal circumstances (e.g. divorce). The Indian judiciary had to adjudicate these complex decisions in the face of legislative inaction. As Justice Hedley has observed in the context of English surrogacy cases, 'the developing law of surrogacy is almost entirely made up of first instance decisions'.[12] India was no different.

The well-known *Baby Manji* case arose in 2008.[13] In this case, the Japanese commissioning parents got divorced after they commissioned the surrogate to carry the baby. The wife did not want the baby. Since Japanese law only

12 *G v G* [2012] EWHC 1979 (Fam), para. 48.

13 *Baby Manji Yamada v Union of India (UOI) and Anr* AIR 2009 SC 84.

recognises the birth mother as the legal mother the baby could not obtain a Japanese passport; under Indian law, the husband could not adopt the baby as he was single. Indian authorities refused to issue her an Indian passport; the birth certificate was finally issued with the name of the father only, which posed obstacles to his ability to take the baby back to Japan. The baby's grandmother finally approached the Indian Supreme Court and took temporary custody of her and travelled back to Japan.

Another case of cross-border surrogacy which ran into legal difficulties is the *Jan Balaz* case.[14] Here the Registrar of Births and Deaths registered the twins born to German commissioning parents with the commissioning mother as the mother on the birth certificate. When they revised the certificate to indicate the correct birthdate, they inserted the name of the surrogate instead. Indian passports were issued to the twins on this basis. However, the Regional Passport Office ('RPO') pending litigation before the Gujarat High Court in the matter requested the surrender of the passports. The father complied with this request. However, since the commissioning parents desired a UK visa, Balaz and his lawyer Dushyant Dave appealed the decision of the RPO and approached the Gujarat High Court seeking Indian passports for the twins. The High Court decided that:

> 'In the absence of any legislation to the contrary, we are more inclined to recognize the gestational surrogate who has given birth as the natural mother, a view prevailing in Japan.'

Since the surrogate was the legal mother, the children were Indian citizens under s. 3(1)(c) of the Indian Citizenship Act 1956, so the reasoning was that they should be issued Indian passports. The Union of India appealed this decision and the Indian Supreme Court while awaiting legislative action on the matter, vigorously sought a pragmatic solution to the predicament of the Balaz twins. As the German embassy would not issue German passports to the twins due to the German law prohibiting surrogacy, the Solicitor-General and Supreme Court explored the possibility of an inter-country adoption. The Central Adoption Regulation Authority issued a no-objection certificate. The Indian government provided identity documents and the Ministry of External Affairs issued an exit visa while the German embassy issued the twins with visas to enable them to travel to Germany. Balaz initiated proceedings in Germany to adopt them under German law so that they could avail of German passports. Pending the outcome of these proceedings, he undertook to update the Supreme Court of progress in the case and on the children's welfare.

---

14 *Union of India & Anr v Jan Balaz and others*, Special Leave to Appeal (Civil) no. 31639 of 2009 Supreme Court of India; *Union of India & Anr v Jan Balaz and others*, Civil Appeal no. 8714 of 2010 Supreme Court of India.

Meanwhile, as a result of the *Baby Manji* case, the Law Commission of India submitted Report 228 in August 2009. The gist of its approach to surrogacy is as follows:

> '... prohibition on vague moral grounds without a proper assessment of social ends and purposes which surrogacy can serve would be irrational. Active legislative intervention is required to facilitate correct uses of the new technology i.e. ART and relinquish the cocooned approach to legalization of surrogacy adopted hitherto. The need of the hour is to adopt a pragmatic approach by legalizing altruistic surrogacy arrangements and prohibit commercial ones.'

The Law Commission also made several recommendations for the protection of the rights of the surrogate and the surrogate child, the need for a genetic link between at least one commissioning parent and the surrogate child as well as clear legislative provisions that required the birth certificate of the child to contain the names only of the commissioning parents and clarification that no adoption or declaration of guardianship was necessary to establish the parentage of the commissioning parents.

As business boomed, the ICMR went back to draft the ART Bill with the help of lawyers. The ART Bill 2008 was very similar to the 2005 ICMR guidelines. The Bill introduced offences; placed restrictions on egg donation; reiterated that ART was available to all, irrespective of marital status and introduced stringent requirements that the baby be accepted, that a local guardian be appointed by foreign commissioning parents and that they be able to establish that the baby could be taken back home. Sample forms of the surrogacy agreement indicated that the surrogate should be paid 75 per cent of her remuneration at the time of the embryo transfer and remaining payments later.

The ART Bill 2008 was followed by the ART Bill 2010, which made further refinements to the previous draft. The definition of the term 'couple' was changed to cover two persons living in India and having a sexual relationship that was legal in India. Surrogacy continued to be available to all single persons, married couples and unmarried couples. The Bill added additional requirements for foreign commissioning parents to ensure that they were no stateless babies. Hence the foreign commissioning parent needed documentation that their home country permitted surrogacy and that the baby would be able to enter their home country. If the commissioning parents failed to take the baby, the local guardian would be legally obliged to take delivery of the child and hand him or her over to adoption within a month or keep the baby who was then entitled to become an Indian citizen. For the first time, individual brokers and paid intermediaries obtaining gamete donors or surrogates were punishable by imprisonment of up to three years and a fine. The model surrogacy agreement modified the suggested payment schedule from the ART Bill 2008 such that the surrogate would be paid 75 per cent of the remuneration only after delivery.

1.3.3. *Contracting and Normative Phase 2012–17*

As the surrogacy sector became well developed and courts' repeated exhortations to the legislature to enact a specific law on surrogacy fell on deaf ears, the government used administrative procedures (including under immigration law) to regulate the sector. In 2012, the Ministry of Home Affairs (Foreigners Division) issued circulars directed at foreign commissioning parents. The gist of these circular[15] is that they required foreign commissioning parents to travel to India on a surrogacy visa. The pool of eligible commissioning parents was restricted on the grounds of their marital status and sexual orientation. Hence only a foreign man and woman married for at least two years could become commissioning parents. They required a letter from their embassy or their foreign minister that their country recognised surrogacy and that the child would be permitted entry as a biological child. The couple had to furnish an undertaking that they would take care of the child. They could avail of treatment only at an ICMR-registered ART Clinic. They had to produce a notarised agreement between the applicant couple and surrogate. They could travel on a tourist visa to conclude an agreement with the surrogate but could give no biological samples to the clinic on that visit. When the baby was born, they would need to secure exit visas from the Foreigners Regional Registration Officer ('FRRO') or Foreigners Registration Officer ('FRO') for which they had to obtain a certificate from the ART clinic that the babies had been duly taken custody of and that the parents' liabilities towards the surrogate had been fully discharged as per the agreement. A copy of the birth certificates and passports would be retained by FRO or FRRO. Non-resident Indians ('NRI') and Persons of Indian Origin ('PIO') meanwhile did not need a medical visa and only had to obtain special permission from the concerned FRO or FRRO on arrival provided they satisfied all the above conditions applicable to foreign commissioning parents in general; they would also need to approach the FRO/FRRO before exiting the country.[16]

The immigration orders of 2012 brought some regulation into the sector. After years of working in the shadows, fertility doctors felt secure that the government was monitoring the sector and that they were not doing anything illegal; moreover it offered them some security against recalcitrant commissioning parents. The legislative fine-tuning in relation to a surrogacy specific statute meanwhile continued. A 2013 version of the ART Bill restricted the number of surrogacies a woman could undertake (three live births including her own children) and there had to be two-year intervals between deliveries. Children were required to be insured up to the age of 21 and at

---

15 25022/74/2011/F.I. dated 09.07.2012, 07.03.2013, 16.07.2013 and 14.10.2013.

16 An additional letter dated 19–21 February 2014 was issued with respect to OCI/PIO cardholders. Government of India Ministry of Home Affairs (Foreigners Division), Notification dated 19.02.2014 (stamped 21.02.2014) no. 25022174/2011-F.1 (vol. III).

least one commissioning parent had to be genetically linked to the child. The commissioning parents had to pay for insurance for the surrogate's health until the child was handed over and she was free of complications.

The ART Bill 2014 confirmed earlier restrictions when it explicitly excluded LGBT commissioning parents. It excluded foreign commissioning parents as well. The stringent requirements under the immigration circulars of the Ministry of External Affairs were now made applicable to NRIs, OCIs, PIOs and foreigners married to an Indian citizen who commissioned surrogacy. It proposed different levels of compensation for surrogates depending on whether the commissioning parents were based in India or abroad. There were several provisions for the protection of surrogates including insurance in the event of her death, medical emergency or medical complications for life. She was required to be ever married, be between the ages of 23–35 with at least one live child (who was at least three years old) and could only have one surrogate baby who was born alive. She could only be subject to three IVF cycles in total. The ART Bank was required to act as the legal representative of the surrogate and represent her in her legal cases free of cost. At the time of delivery, the life of the surrogate was to be prioritised over that of the baby and she was to get paid the remuneration due to her, irrespective of the outcome for the baby. Where she died or became disabled, it was presumed to be due to the negligence of the ART clinic. Similar provisions were contemplated in relation to the egg donor.

Even as the government of India refined its legislative mandate on surrogacy, a public interest petition was filed in 2015 in the Supreme Court inviting the court to respond to several of the vexed moral and normative questions that arose from surrogacy.[17] The petitioner Jayasree Wad's prayers to the court were to prohibit commercial surrogacy and the import of embryos into the country given the rampant subordination, exploitation and commodification of women and children. However, the day before the government was set to answer these questions in court, it decided to ban commercial surrogacy for foreigners. The ICMR as part of the Department of Health Research, Ministry of Health and Family Welfare sent out a circular to ART clinics that surrogacy would be limited only to Indian married couples; they were 'requested not to entertain any foreigners for availing surrogacy services in India.'[18]

The import of human embryos except for research (on which guidelines were said to be forthcoming) was prohibited under the 26 October 2015 notification of the Ministry of Commerce and Industry (whereas earlier such import was permitted subject to procuring a no-objection-certificate from the ICMR).[19] The Ministry of

---

17 *Mrs Jayashree Wad v Union of India & Ors* Writ Petition no. 95 of 2015.

18 Indian Council of Medical Research (Division of Reproductive Biology and Maternal Health), Notification, 'Foreigners for availing surrogacy services in India', dated 27.10.2015.

19 Government of India, Ministry of Commerce & Industry, Department of Commerce, Directorate General of Foreign Trade, Notification no. 25/2015–2020, dated 26.10.2015.

Home Affairs then issued instructions on 3 November 2015 which withdrew the 2012 circulars and set forth that no visas were to be issued to foreign nationals to commission surrogacy; no permission was to be issued by FRROs/FROs to OCIs; and no exit permission was to be given to foreign nationals except for those who had already commissioned surrogacy and in relation to whom decisions would be made on a case-by-case basis.[20] Any visas or permissions, which were granted after the issue of the circular, but before its receipt by the concerned officials were to be cancelled. This was followed up by a circular dated 4 November 2015 from the Director of the Department of Health Research of the Ministry of Health and Family Welfare.[21] This specified very clearly that until the ART Bill was passed, the instructions listed therein as well as the ICMR Guidelines would prevail (unless contrary to the circular) and be applicable to all clinics offering surrogacy and ART services. The circular itself summarised the provisions of the circulars relating to visas issued to foreign commissioning parents and the ban on import of embryos but also clarified that cases where medical treatment had already commenced (i.e. where embryos had already been imported and implantation had occurred) would be allowed to be completed provided they approached state health authorities for permission which would be decided on a case-by-case basis.

Close on the heels of these developments, the Prime Minister appointed a working group of union ministers to consider surrogacy law reform. They proposed this time to split the ART Bill into two Bills – one which dealt with the regulatory aspects of the ART industry and the other specifically with surrogacy. In a highly publicised media event in August 2016, the Minister for External Affairs Sushma Swaraj unveiled the provisions of the Surrogacy (Regulation) Bill 2016. Upholding what she called the 'ethos of the Indian people', she explained that the proposed Bill would ban commercial surrogacy altogether irrespective of whether it was undertaken by domestic or non-resident Indian parents. Rather than ban all surrogacy outright however, the Bill would allow for altruistic surrogacy only. The provisions of the SRB will be discussed in detail in Sections 2–6. At the time of writing, a revised version of the SRB has been passed by the lower house of Parliament but is yet to be considered by the upper house.

1.4. STATISTICAL INFORMATION CONCERNING SURROGACY IN INDIA

India has participated in the transnational commercial surrogacy market primarily as a destination country rather than as a source of commissioning

[20] Government of India Ministry of Home Affairs (Foreigners Division), Notification no. 25022/74/2011-F.I (vol. III), dated 03.11.2015.

[21] Government of India Ministry of Health & Family Welfare (Department of Health Research), Notification no. V. 25011/119/2015-HR, dated 04.11.2015.

parents who travel to other jurisdictions. While this does not preclude a select few from travelling outside India for commercial surrogacy, there is no data on this phenomenon. Media coverage and academic research are instead focused on babies born and delivered within India. In terms of the size of the market, the surrogacy market as of 2008 was said to be worth US$445 million and in 2011 worth US$20 billion.[22] The ICMR predicted that commercial surrogacy would grow into a US$6 billion-per-year industry.[23] Another commonly cited figure is that surrogacy would generate US$2.3 billion annually by 2012.[24] The Confederation of Indian Industry meanwhile estimated that in 2012 nearly 10,000 foreign clients visited India for reproductive services; 30 per cent were queer or single. However, my own empirical work including interviews of leading fertility clinics in 2012 and more recently in 2016 suggests that the highest number of babies delivered by any Indian clinic is around 1,500. Therefore, between the most successful fertility clinics, the total number of babies delivered is likely to be around 6,000. The estimates of fertility clinics in India range between 300 and 3,000 with the ICMR suggesting that there are 700–800 IVF clinics throughout the country.[25] Even accounting for the lower numbers of babies delivered by smaller clinics, the number of surrogacy transactions to date does not seem to generate the revenue that statistics on the size of the market suggest. Since 2015 however, there has been a slump in the market. As of August 2016, when I visited Akanksha Fertility Clinic, the last foreign commissioning couple, who had obtained permission for surrogacy in India pre-2015 were leaving with their baby. Only a handful of surrogates who were carrying babies for domestic couples remained in the surrogacy hostel.

2. SURROGACY ARRANGEMENTS IN GENERAL

2.1. ENFORCEABILITY OF SURROGACY CONTRACTS

As of February 2019, surrogacy contracts are legal in India.[26] Under s. 10 of the Indian Contract Act 1872, 'all agreements are contracts if they are made by the

---

22 P. Nayak, 'The Three Ms of Commercial Surrogacy in India: Mother, Money and Medical Market', in S. DasGupta and S. Das DasGupta (eds), *Globalization and Transnational Surrogacy in India*, Lexington Books, UK 2014, pp. 1–22, 2.

23 M. Chang, 'Womb for Rent: India's Commercial Surrogacy' (2009) 31 *HLR (Harvard Law Review)* 11, 12.

24 S. Rudrappa, *Discounted Life: The Price of Global Surrogacy*, Orient BlackSwan, New Delhi 2015, p. 5.

25 D. Deomampo, *Transnational Reproduction: Race, Kinship, and Commercial Surrogacy in India*, NYU Press, New York 2016, p. 238.

26 Law Commission of India, *Need for Legislation to Regulate Assisted Reproductive Technology Clinics as well as Rights and Obligations of Parties to a Surrogacy*, Report no. 228, New Delhi 2009, <http://lawcommissionofindia.nic.in/reports/report228.pdf> accessed 14.09.2018.

free consent of parties competent to contract, for a lawful consideration and with a lawful object, and are not hereby expressly declared to be void.' So far no Indian court has declared a contract for commercial surrogacy void. The Gujarat High Court has held that 'commercial surrogacy is never considered to be illegal in India.'[27] The Indian Supreme Court has in fact observed that:[28]

> '"Commercial surrogacy" is a form of surrogacy in which a gestational carrier is paid to carry a child to maturity in her womb and is usually resorted to by well off infertile couples who can afford the cost involved or people who save and borrow in order to complete their dream of being parents. This medical procedure is legal in several countries including in India where due to excellent medical infrastructure, high international demand and ready availability of poor surrogates it is reaching industry proportions.'

The Law Commission of India has further commented that surrogacy is legitimate in India as no Indian law prohibits it.[29] A writ petition filed in 2015 by Jayashree Wad however explicitly requested the Supreme Court to comment on the validity of such contracts as they were in the view of the petitioner void for being immoral and against public policy under s. 23 of the Indian Contract Act 1872. The Supreme Court is yet to decide on the petition.

2.2. SURROGATE REMUNERATION

Before the Surrogacy (Regulation) Bill 2016 was proposed, payments to surrogates were regulated solely by the ICMR guidelines. The Guidelines under clause 3.10.3 of Chapter 3 specify that payments to surrogates should cover all genuine expenses associated with the pregnancy. Clause 3.5.4 specifies that the surrogate is 'entitled to a monetary compensation from the couple for agreeing to act as a surrogate'; the exact value is to be determined by discussion between the commission couple and the surrogate. The sample Agreement for Surrogacy, which is part of Chapter 4 of the ICMR Guidelines includes a clause where the surrogate represents that she 'has worked out the financial terms and conditions of the surrogacy with the couple in writing.'

There are no official guidelines on the appropriate levels or limits of payments. The ICMR guidelines under clauses 3.9.2, 3.10.3 and 3.5.3 clarify that the ART Bank and ART Clinic must not play a role in the monetary aspect of the compensation, which is to be determined independently between the surrogate and the commissioning parents. The ICMR does not indicate how payments can be monitored. The ART Bill in 2008 and 2010 offered a payment

---

27 *Jan Balaz v Anand Municipality & 6 Ors* AIR 2010 Guj 21.

28 *Baby Manji Yamada v Union of India (UOI) and Anor.*

29 Law Commission of India 2009, p. 21.

schedule, which have been detailed in Section 1. However, no monitoring system was envisaged. Although the leading ART clinics performing surrogacy claim to be in compliance with the ICMR Guidelines, they in fact set the levels of remuneration and often matched the surrogate with the commissioning parents based on the former's financial needs. Clinics in other words played a central role in negotiating transactions between these key stakeholders. Clinics also claimed to credit surrogate's remuneration to bank accounts set up in the names of surrogates themselves so that it did not get misused by husbands and other family members. The only informal guidance on minimum payments is from INSTAR which recommends a minimum compensation of 2.25 lakhs for (GBP£2,329) surrogates and that full compensation be paid after 28 weeks irrespective of the outcome.[30]

There are no publicly available statistics on the payments that surrogates receive given the fragmented, marginal and stigmatised nature of surrogates' labour. Journalistic accounts and empirical data from ethnographers alike suggest that remuneration for commercial surrogacy varies considerably around India and depends on the nature of the transaction and whether it is facilitated by a full-service fertility clinic or by a surrogacy agency. Thus where surrogates in Anand were being paid US$8,000 per delivery, in Bangalore they were paid US$4,000.[31] Deomampo reports that most of the women that she interviewed in Mumbai earned between US$4,400 and $5,500; they would earn US$550–$650 more if they had twins and US$1,000 to $3,000 if they had a caesarean section.[32] Pande similarly estimates that surrogates in Anand, Gujarat got paid between US$2,500 to $7,000.[33] In Gujarat, the average payment was between US$3,000 and $6,200.[34] Sangari notes that although US agencies claimed that surrogates were paid US$7,000, in reality, this varied between US$4,000 and $7,000 and in the movie *Made in India*, the protagonist surrogate was paid less than US$3,500.[35] Some surrogates particularly in smaller cities and depending on their financial situation are known to undertake surrogacy for US$1,500 to $2,300.[36] The rates payable to surrogates have also changed over time. Where in 2012 surrogates in Akanksha Fertility Clinic, run by Dr Nayna Patel were paid close to US$4,600 for a single delivery, in 2016, the rates were closer to US$8,500. In fact one surrogate in Anand claimed that women get even

30 <http://instar.co.in/highlights.html> accessed 14.09.2018.

31 S. Rudrappa, above n. 24, p. 104.

32 D. Deomampo, *Transnational reproduction: Race, kinship and commercial surrogacy in India*, New York University Press, New York 2016, p. 183.

33 A. Pande, *Wombs in Labor: Transnational Commercial Surrogacy in India*, Columbia University Press, New York 2014, p. 213, endnote 12 to Ch. 1.

34 K. Sangari, *Solid: Liquid, A (Trans)National Reproductive Formation*, Tulika Books, New Delhi 2015, p. 205, endnote 68 to Ch. 3.

35 Ibid., p. 81.

36 Ibid., p. 205, endnote 68 to Ch. 3.

up to US$10,000.[37] One can also safely say that the supply of surrogates generally outstripped the demand from commissioning parents with clinics claiming prior to the 2015 ban, that they had long waiting lists of interested parties.

Under the Surrogacy (Regulation) Bill 2016, s. 35(1) prohibits any person, organisation or clinic from undertaking or providing commercial surrogacy or any related components or services in any form to select surrogates or use brokers or intermediaries to arrange for surrogate and surrogacy procedures. Any violation of this section is punishable by 10 years' imprisonment and a fine, which may extend to 10 lakh rupees. Section 2(f) defines 'commercial surrogacy' as the commercialisation of surrogacy services or procedures including the sale and purchase of embryos, gametes or services of a surrogate by giving payment in cash or kind except for the payment of medical expenses and the insurance coverage for the surrogate.

Although commercial surrogacy is prohibited under the SRB, under s. 47, the central government may make rules pertaining to the required insurance coverage in favour of the surrogate. There is no corresponding provision on rules relating to medical expenses that might be incurred for purposes of altruistic surrogacy.

3. LEGAL PARENTHOOD AT THE TIME OF BIRTH

3.1. LEGAL PARENTS OF A CHILD BORN THROUGH SURROGACY AT THE TIME OF BIRTH

There are a few relevant legal provisions under Indian law relating to the question of parentage although they do not necessarily shed light on parentage in the context of surrogacy. These provisions include s. 112 of the Indian Evidence Act of 1872. The section presumes the legitimacy of any person born during the continuance of a valid marriage between the child's mother and any man, or within 280 days after its dissolution (them remaining unmarried). The presumption is conclusive proof of legitimacy unless it can be shown that the parties had no access to each other during that time. According to s. 4 of the Act, this presumption is not rebuttable. The Registration of Births and Deaths Act 1969 requires notification of the relevant government officer of the birth or death of a person. It only mentions the terms 'parent' and 'guardian' in the context of their registering the name of a child within a specified period of time. There is no definition of the term 'parent' or indeed who might be designated as such under the Act. Another statute, The Maintenance and Welfare of Parents and Senior Citizens Act 2007 defines the term 'parent' under s. 2(d) as the father

37 A. Pande, above n. 33, p. 181.

or mother whether biological, adoptive, stepfather or stepmother, as the case may be, whether or not the father or the mother is a senior citizen.

The Law Commission of India notes that biological parents can move an application under the Guardians and Wards Act 1890 for appointment or declaration as the guardian of the surrogate child.[38] Section 3(1)(c) of the Citizenship Act, 1955 meanwhile stipulates the conditions under which a person can be a citizen of India. Under the section, every person born in India shall be a citizen at birth where both of his parents are citizens of India or where one of his parents is an Indian citizen and the other is not an illegal migrant at the time of his birth. It does not however define the term 'parent'.

The ICMR Guidelines under clause 3.5.4 require that the birth certificate be in the name of the commissioning parents. Clause 3.10.1 also clarifies that where a child is born through surrogacy, he or she must be adopted by the commissioning parents unless they can establish that the child is theirs through genetic fingerprinting. A child born through ART is also presumed to be the legitimate child of the couple under clause 3.12.1. Clause 3.16.1 also makes clear that the sperm and egg donor shall have no parental right or duties in relation to the child. It further requires third-party donors and surrogates under clause 3.5.5 to relinquish in writing all parental rights concerning the child. Although the ICMR Guidelines have been followed when it comes to registration of births of surrogate babies, complications tend to arise in international surrogacy cases where either the commissioning parents get divorced and the destination country recognises only the birth-mother as the legal mother (as in the *Manji* case) or where the laws of the home jurisdiction of the commissioning parents prohibit surrogacy so that passports are unable to be issued to enable the commissioning parents to take children out of the country (as in the *Jan Balaz* case).

The Law Commission of India in its 2009 report commented that the ICMR Guidelines needed improvement. Particularly in relation to parentage, the Law Commission recommended that at least one parent have a genetic link to the child born out of surrogacy, that the birth certificate contain the names of the commissioning parents only and that Parliament recognise the child to be the legitimate child of the commissioning parents without having to undergo any formal process of adoption or declaration of guardianship.[39]

The Surrogacy (Regulation) Bill 2016 attempts to ameliorate the uncertain legal environment in relation to parentage. Several conditions have to be satisfied by the commissioning parents in order to obtain a certificate under s. 4(iii)(a) of the Bill. They have to obtain an order concerning the parentage

[38] Law Commission of India 2009, p. 21.
[39] Law Commission of India 2009, p. 26.

and custody from a Magistrate of the first class on an application made by the commissioning parents and the surrogate. Section 7 further provides that the child born out of a surrogacy transaction shall be deemed to be a biological child of the commissioning parents and that the child will be entitled to all the rights and privileges available to a natural child. Section 2(ze) defines the 'surrogate mother' as the woman bearing the child that is genetically linked to the commissioning couple. However there is no specific provision elaborating on the nature of this genetic link.

3.2. INDICATION REGARDING SURROGACY ON THE BIRTH CERTIFICATE

Under clause 3.5.4 of the ICMR Guidelines the birth certificate of the baby born out of surrogacy is required to list the names of the commissioning parents but does not require the disclosure of the fact that the baby was born out of a surrogacy arrangement. The Surrogacy (Regulation) Bill 2016 makes no mention of such a requirement either.

3.3. PRESERVATION OF INFORMATION ON THE SURROGATE

According to the ICMR Guidelines (clause 3.3.7), details of the surrogate are to be maintained by the ART Clinic for at least 10 years, after which the records must be transferred to a central depository to be maintained by the ICMR. The child has the right to seek information (except for information on the name and address, i.e. the persons' individual identity) about the surrogate under the ICMR Guidelines (clause 3.4.8) upon reaching the age of 18. The commissioning couple is not obliged to provide this information to the child but must not hide this information from a child when the occasion arises and the issue becomes important for the child.

Under s. 34(2) of the Surrogacy (Regulation) Bill 2016, the appropriate authority is required to maintain the details of registration of surrogacy clinics and the grant of certificates of essentiality and eligibility to the commissioning couple and surrogates. Under s. 43, records under the Act are required to be maintained by surrogacy clinics for a period of 25 years. There is however no provision as to the right of the child to access this information. Note however that under s. 4(iii)(b)(II), only a close relative of the commissioning parents can act as a surrogate. The term 'close relative' is not defined in the SRB. However, given this requirement, it is more likely than before that a child born out of surrogacy will learn that a close relative gave birth to him or her.

4. ELIGIBILITY FOR SURROGACY

4.1. ELIGIBILITY CRITERIA FOR WOMEN ACTING AS SURROGATES

Under the ICMR Guidelines (clause 3.10.5), a surrogate could not be over 45 years of age. Clause 3.10.6 specifies that she could be a relative, a known person or a person unknown to the commissioning parents. In case a relative acted as surrogate, she had to belong to the same generation as the commissioning mother. The ART clinic must ascertain that she is medically fit to undergo the surrogacy. Clause 3.10.7 required that the surrogate be sero-negative. She also had to provide a written certificate that she had not had a drug intravenously administered into her through a shared syringe, that she had not undergone blood transfusion and that she and her husband (to the best of their knowledge) had had no extra-marital relationship in the last six months. This was meant to ensure that the person would not come up with symptoms of HIV infection during the period of surrogacy. The prospective surrogate also had to declare that she would not use drugs intravenously, and not undergo blood transfusion excepting of blood obtained through a certified blood bank. Finally, clause 3.10.8 required that no woman act as a surrogate more than thrice in her lifetime.

Under s. 4(iii)(b)(II) of the proposed Surrogacy (Regulation) Bill 2016, only a close relative can act as a surrogate. The term 'close relative' has not been defined. Sub-clause (I) requires that the surrogate be between the ages of 25 and 35 on the day of the implantation and that she must have been ever married and had a child of her own. Sub-clause (III) requires that she cannot act as a surrogate more than once in her lifetime. Sub-clause (IV) requires that she be issued a certificate of medical and psychological fitness for surrogacy from a registered medical practitioner.

4.2. CHARACTERISTICS OF SURROGATES

Several recent ethnographies of the surrogacy sector in India reveal some surprising facts about the characteristics of surrogates. Although it is easy to assume that they are resorting to surrogacy out of desperation, empirically speaking, highly deprived women are not in sufficiently good health to meet clinics' requirements for healthy surrogates. Surrogacy agencies therefore do not recruit poverty stricken women.[40] Instead surrogates tend to be working-class women who are in prime reproductive age, married, already have children, have sympathetic husbands to help with the household and have adequate resources

40 S. Rudrappa, above n. 24, p. 42.

for taking care of the surrogate's children without making demands on the surrogate when she is in the surrogates' hostel.[41] They are typically women who were garment workers, construction workers and makers of incense-sticks.[42] Most were in their 20s and 30s but not older than 45.[43] Kumkum Sangari notes that they often stand below the poverty line and occasionally at a lower-middle-class fringe. If employed, they tend to work as domestic maids, child minders, seasonal commercial cooks, midwives, nurses, cleaners, garbage sorters, rural and urban daily wage labourers in home-based stitching, embroidery or other piece work as well as in factories, farms, clinics, shops, schools, construction sites, beauty parlours, hotels and restaurants.[44] Many have husbands who are unemployed or have irregular low-income work in the informal economy.[45] Although surrogates are not destitute, they are financially desperate.[46] Amrita Pande who conducted an ethnographic study of surrogates in Anand, reports that amongst her surrogates, the median family income was US$50 in 2006 and that all but one of the surrogates reported acute financial desperation as the reason for undertaking surrogacy.[47] For most surrogates, income from surrogacy equals approximately five years' worth of the total family income.[48] Surrogates are typically married because although this is not a requirement under any law, surrogacy clinics in India require proven fertility of their surrogates and having children outside the institution of marriage is rare.[49] Given the sensitivities around caste, most empirical studies are unable to gather the caste profiles of surrogates. However, one researcher claims that 30 per cent of the surrogates she interviewed were Buddhist suggesting that they were dalit;[50] caste was certainly a consideration for certain commissioning parents.[51]

4.3. ELIGIBILITY CRITERIA FOR COMMISSIONING PARENTS

The ICMR Guidelines do not specify any particular eligibility criteria for commissioning parents other than that 'surrogacy by assisted conception should

41 Ibid.

42 Ibid., p. 57.

43 A. Pande, above n. 33, p. 20.

44 K. Sangari, above n. 34, p. 73. Most of the surrogates in Tambe's sample were housewives, the others worked at schools, clinics, farms and stores; essentially in informal or contract work with low, irregular incomes. p. 109. Deomampo's surrogates shared a similar work profile, see D. Deomampo, above n. 32, p. 236.

45 Ibid., p. 73.

46 S. Rudrappa, above n. 24, p. 78; D. Deomampo, above n. 32. p. 236.

47 A. Pande, above n. 33, p. 20.

48 Ibid.

49 D. Deomampo, above n. 32, p. 236, where she notes that only surrogate she interviewed had been childless.

50 Ibid., p. 237.

51 K. Sangari, above n. 34, p. 198, endnote 28 to Ch. 3.

normally be considered only for patients for whom it would be physically or medically impossible/undesirable to carry a baby to term' (clause 3.10.2). Further under clause 3.14.1, the ICMR Guidelines specify that the minimum age for ART for a woman is 20 years. For a woman between 20 and 30 years, she would need to have spent two years in cohabitation and/or marriage without the use of a contraceptive before she can avail of ART services. This two-year period does not apply where the man is infertile or she cannot physiologically conceive. If the woman is above 30 years of age, the inability to have children after one year of co-habitation or marriage without the use of contraceptive meant that she could use ART services.

The Surrogacy (Regulation) Bill 2016 however has more stringent requirements for prospective commissioning parents. Section 2(g) defines a 'couple' as a legally married Indian man and woman above the age of 21 years and 18 years respectively. This excludes any gay, lesbian, or transgender commissioning parents. Section 2(p) further defines 'infertility' as the inability to conceive after five years of unprotected coitus or other proven medical condition preventing a couple from conception. Section 2(r) defines an 'intending couple' as a couple who have been medically certified to be an infertile couple and who intend to become parents through surrogacy. In addition, s. 4(ii)(a) specifies that surrogacy can only be undertaken when either or both members of a couple is suffering from proven infertility. Further, as per s. 4(iii)(a)(I), the intending couple needs to obtain a certificate of essentiality, which in turn requires a certificate of infertility in favour of either or both members from a District Medical Board. The commissioning parents are required under s. 4(iii)(c) to obtain an eligibility certificate from the appropriate authority satisfying certain conditions, namely, that the age of the intending couple is between 23 to 50 years in case of the female and between 26 to 55 years in case of the male on the day of certification; that the couple are married for at least five years and are Indian citizens; and that they have not had any surviving child biologically or through adoption or through surrogacy earlier. The only exception to the last requirement is where the commissioning parents do have a child but the child is mentally or physically challenged or suffers from a life-threatening disorder or fatal illness with no permanent cure and this has been approved by the appropriate authority on the basis of a medical certificate from a District Medical Board. The commissioning parents must also be 'close relatives' of the surrogate under s. 4(iii)(b) but the term 'close relative' has not been defined under the SRB. These stringent guidelines are to prevent the further commercialisation of the surrogacy sector where celebrity couples with biological children (and complete families) resorted to 'social surrogacy' by commissioning a surrogate's services for a third child. At the same time, policy makers want to make sure that couples desperate to have their own genetically related families could use surrogacy as an option.

4.4. RULES REGARDING GAMETES FOR SURROGACY

The ICMR Guidelines do not permit pre-existing relationships between the gamete donors and the commissioning parents; donations are to be anonymous and facilitated by ART Banks and donors can be compensated by the ART Bank; the ART Bank in turn can be remunerated by the commissioning parents.

Under clause 3.5.13 the use of sperm or eggs donated by a relative or a known friend or either the wife or the husband shall not be permitted. The ART Bank is allowed to charge the couple for the semen and eggs. The commissioning couple is allowed to obtain information on several parameters including height, weight, skin colour, educational qualification, profession, family background, medical condition, ethnic origin and the DNA fingerprint of the donor. However, they do not have the right to know the identity and address of the donor. Donors of sperm and eggs can be suitably compensated by the ART Bank (clauses 3.9.1.3 and 3.9.2). Under clause 3.5.4 an oocyte donor cannot act as a surrogate for the couple to whom the oocyte is being donated. There is no requirement in the ICMR Guidelines that the child be genetically related to his or her parents; in fact it requires commissioning parents to adopt the child resulting from ART unless they can prove that they are genetically related. The requirement for a genetic link emerges in later legislative proposals including in the report of the Law Commission of India.

Under clause 3.3.6, the information about the gamete donor is required to be confidential but can be revealed only to the child and only if he/she asks after he/she reaches the age of 18 years or as and when specified for legal purposes. It can never be revealed to the parents (except when directed by a court of law). Clause 3.4.8 clarifies that the commissioning couple should be made aware that a child born out of ART has the right to seek information about his genetic parent and surrogate on reaching 18 years excepting information on the name and address of the concerned individual. Although the couple is not obliged to provide this information to the child the couple must not hide this information when the information becomes important to the child.

There are a few other related provisions under the ICMR Guidelines. Gametes produced by a person under the age of 18 cannot be used in ART treatments under clause 3.5.8. The accepted age for a sperm donor is between 21 and 45 years and for the egg donor between 18 and 35 years. Further, clause 3.2.7 requires that no more than three embryos are placed in a surrogate in any one cycle excepting under exceptional circumstances and that no woman should be treated with embryos derived from the gametes of more than one man or woman during any one treatment cycle.

Unlike previous legislative proposals which addressed both the ART sector in general and surrogacy in particular, the Surrogacy (Regulation) Bill 2016 only deals with surrogacy. A separate law on ART is expected to be drafted on the heels of the SRB. Without reading the two legislations together, it is not possible to answer the questions relating to gamete donation in definitive terms. However, the SRB in general is less liberal about the sale and purchase of gametes for the purposes of surrogacy than the ICMR Guidelines. Section 2(f) of the SRB defines 'commercial surrogacy' as the 'commercialisation of surrogacy services or procedures or its component services or component procedures including selling or buying of human embryo or *trading in the sale or purchase* of human embryo or *gametes* or selling or buying or trading the services of surrogate motherhood, except the medical expenses incurred on the surrogate mother and the insurance coverage for the surrogate mother.' Commercial surrogacy is prohibited under s. 35 of the SRB; s. 35(e) in particular prohibits the sale of gametes for purposes of surrogacy. That said, s. 4(iii)(b)(III) specifies that no woman 'shall act as a surrogate mother or help in surrogacy in any way, by providing gametes or by carrying the pregnancy, more than once in her lifetime' which implies that a woman other than the surrogate could potentially donate an egg. However the term 'altruistic surrogacy' defined in s. 2(b) includes a surrogacy where only medical expenses and insurance costs are paid; 'surrogacy' in turn is defined under s. 2(zb) as a practice whereby one woman bears and gives birth to a child for an intending couple with the intention of handing over such child to the intending couple after the birth; the altruistic donation of gametes is not included here. Further, the SRB is not explicit about the genetic link between the commissioning parents and the child although s. 2(ze) of the SRB defines 'surrogate mother' to mean a 'woman bearing a child who is genetically related to the intending couple, through surrogacy from the implantation of embryo in her womb.'

5. TRANSFERRING PARENTHOOD

5.1. ACQUIRING PARENTHOOD

The ICMR Guidelines under clause 3.5.4 require that the birth certificate be in the name of the commissioning parents. Furthermore, the clinic must also provide a certificate to the genetic parents giving the name and address of the surrogate. Clause 3.10.1 also clarifies that where a child is born through surrogacy, he or she must be adopted by the genetic parents unless they can establish that the child is theirs through genetic fingerprinting. A child born through ART is also presumed to be the legitimate child of the couple under clause 3.12.1. Clause 3.16.1 makes clear that the sperm and egg donor shall have no parental right or duties in relation to the child. It further requires third-party donors and surrogates under clause 3.5.5 to relinquish in writing all parental rights concerning the child. The ICMR Guidelines have been followed when it comes to registration of births of surrogate babies.

For foreign commissioning parents, the ease with which they became legal parents depended on the laws of their home countries. The embassies of the countries where commissioning parents came from refined over time, certain procedures for dealing with transnational surrogacy cases. These procedures varied for different countries; some required DNA testing and a genetic link. Others didn't. The US and Australian embassies were considered to offer less cumbersome procedures while the UK was considered more cumbersome because of the waiting period required under the Human Fertilisation and Embryology Act 2008. Complications however tended to arise in international surrogacy cases where either the commissioning parents got divorced and the destination country recognised only the birth-mother as the legal mother (as in the *Manji* case) or where the laws of the home jurisdiction of the commissioning parents prohibited surrogacy so that passports were unable to be issued to enable the commissioning parents to take children out of the country (as in the *Jan Balaz* case). There is little information on how parentage has been transferred for domestic commissioning parents who are Indian citizens and resident in India when they have sought to complete their families through commercial surrogacy.

The Law Commission of India in its 2009 report commented on the ICMR guidelines as being in need of improvement. Particularly in relation to parentage, the Law Commission recommended that at least one parent have a genetic link to the child born out of surrogacy, that the birth certificate contain the names of the commissioning parents only and that Parliament recognise the child to be the legitimate child of the commissioning parents without having to undergo any formal process of adoption or declaration of guardianship.[52]

The Surrogacy (Regulation) Bill 2016 attempts to ameliorate the uncertain legal environment in relation to parentage. Several conditions have to be satisfied by the commissioning parents in order to obtain a certificate of essentiality under s. 4(iii)(a). They have to obtain an order concerning the parentage and custody from a Magistrate of the first class on an application made by the commissioning parents and the surrogate. Specific details on the process for obtaining this parentage order are not set out in the SRB nor is there any information on whether details of the surrogate will be maintained by the relevant authorities. Section 7 further provides that the child born out of a surrogacy transaction shall be deemed to be a biological child of the commissioning parents and that the child will be entitled to all the rights and privileges available to a natural child. Section 2(ze) defines the 'surrogate mother' to be the woman bearing the child that is genetically linked to the commissioning couple. However, there is no specific provision elaborating on the nature of this genetic link.

---

52 Law Commission of India 2009, p. 26.

5.2. DISPUTES REGARDING SURROGACY

There is no data on the frequency of disputes around transnational surrogacy arrangements that have arisen since the late 1990s. The ICMR Guidelines do require ART clinics to have procedures for acknowledging and investigating complaints and to have a nominated person to deal with them. The clinics are also obliged to inform the accreditation authority of the number of complaints made in any given year and those that are outstanding. However, accreditation authorities are yet to be set up under these Guidelines hence the information on the number of disputes is not available yet. Disputes have therefore been taken to the courts if they cannot be resolved through informal mechanisms. The Statement of Objects and Reasons for the Surrogacy (Regulation) Bill 2016 notes that 'India has emerged as a surrogacy hub for couples from different countries for past few years. There have been reported incidents of unethical practices, exploitation of surrogate mothers, abandonment of children born out of surrogacy and import of human embryos and gametes.' The Director General of the ICMR Dr Soumya Swaminathan has also attributed the urgency with which the SRB has been formulated to 'a number of complaints [which] had come to the notice of the government and also to the notice of the National Commission for Women.'[53]

5.3. RIGHTS OF CHILDREN

The ICMR Guidelines have a separate section on the rights of children born through various ART technologies. These relate to the legitimacy of the child (3.12.1, 3.16.1, 3.16.4, 3.16.5) and children's right to information (including medical and genetic) (under clauses 3.12.2, 3.12.3, 3.4.8) about their genetic parents that may be relevant to their health. See Section 4 for more details on these provisions.

The Surrogacy (Regulation) Bill 2016 on the other hand has no provisions on the rights of the child. It is possible that this is because the surrogate under the SRB must be a 'close relative' of the commissioning parents and that therefore the child is likely to find out about his or her birth mother within a family context. Section 7 provides that 'any child born out of surrogacy procedure, shall be deemed to be a biological child of the intending couple and the said child shall be entitled to all the rights and privileges available to a natural child under any law for the time being in force.'

---

53 T.K. Rajalakshmi, 'Surrogacy a Hot Topic', Interview with Dr Soumya Swaminathan, Director General, Indian Council of Medical Research, *Frontline*, 14.10.2016.

6. AGENCIES AND CRIMINALISATION

The ICMR Guidelines make no mention of agents, intermediaries or middlemen. The Guidelines envisage a functional separation between ART banks and ART clinics whereby only banks are supposed to be involved in some commercial aspects of ART and surrogacy but not clinics. The only penalties mentioned in the Guidelines are those that a State Accreditation Authority might impose on clinics which do not satisfy guidelines as to ethics and operating procedures. The first provisions criminalising intermediaries therefore only emerge in the ART Bill 2010.

While the ICMR Guidelines permitted commercial surrogacy, the Surrogacy (Regulation) Bill 2016 seeks to prohibit it. Hence the Bill has an entire Chapter (VII), which creates several offences. Section 35 prohibits commercial surrogacy and the prohibition extends to any person, organisation, surrogacy clinic (broadly defined under s. 2(zc)), laboratory or clinical establishment. It covers a range of activities under various sub-sections including undertaking or providing commercial surrogacy and 'related component procedures or services'; but also where such an actor might 'run a racket or an organised group to empanel or select surrogate mothers or use individual brokers or intermediaries to arrange for surrogate mothers and for surrogacy procedures' (s. 35(1)(a)). The section also prohibits advertisement (s. 35(1)(b)), abandoning, disowning or exploiting a child born out of surrogacy (s. 35(1)(c)), exploiting the surrogate or the child (s. 35(1)(d), selling or buying embryos or gametes for surrogacy (s. 35(1)(e)) or importing embryos or gametes for surrogacy (s. 35(1)(f)). This offence is punishable with imprisonment for not less than 10 years and with a steep fine of up to 10 lakh rupees (£10,363). Medical professionals who contravene provisions of the Act (other than the offence under s. 35) can be subject to imprisonment for not less than five years and a fine extending up to 10 lakh rupees. Section 37 states that commissioning parents who initiate commercial surrogacy transactions are also liable for imprisonment for a period of not less than five years and subject to a fine of 5 lakh rupees (£5,181) with higher penalties for subsequent offences. Section 38 is a residual clause which renders any violation of the provisions of the Act for which there is no specified penalty, punishable with three years' imprisonment and heavy fines. Where cases under the Act might be brought to court, s. 39 creates a rebuttable presumption that a woman or surrogate was compelled by her husband, the commissioning parents or any other relative to render surrogacy services; these actors are viewed as abetting the initiation of surrogacy which is punishable under s. 37. All these offences are cognisable, non-bailable and non-compoundable. These provisions do not apply extra-territorially.

7. INTERNATIONAL SURROGACY ARRANGEMENTS

Neither the ICMR nor the SRB envisage Indians leaving the country for obtaining surrogacy services abroad. Intermediate drafts of the ART Bill however did require that the surrogate be an Indian citizen and that she reside in India. The ART Bill 2014 further required that no ART bank or clinic receive or send an Indian woman for surrogacy abroad.

8. CONCLUSION

Within a period of 13 years the policy framework for surrogacy in India has gone from a medico-liberal model to a socially conservative prohibitionist model. Through these years, the categories of who could avail of commercial surrogacy progressively narrowed, first excluding gay, lesbian and transgender individuals and couples (2012), then foreigners and then even persons of Indian origin who were foreigners (2015). Commercial surrogacy finally came to be prohibited (2016) and is now being sought to be replaced by a model of altruistic surrogacy under the Surrogacy (Regulation) Bill 2016, wherein the surrogate has to be a close relative of the commissioning parents. In a sense, the practice of surrogacy is sought to be brought back full circle; recollect Dr Nayna Patel's first foray into surrogacy when a woman delivered her own grandchildren for the sake of her daughter. One could however argue that the discursive shift is less stark than the policy shift. After all, if it was the logic of furthering the hetero-patriarchal institution of marriage and its primary goal of biological reproduction that permitted the commercialisation of surrogacy in the first place, the very same logic also provided a rationale for limiting the sites for biological reproduction to the domestic familial space where women will now only be allowed to reproduce for the family (albeit extended family) rather than for the market.

That said, there has been considerable criticism of the Surrogacy (Regulation) Bill 2016 from liberals and feminists alike. While liberals cringe at the Hindu nationalist mindset of the SRB which deprives single men and women and gay and lesbian couples from resorting to surrogacy, feminists are concerned that the requirement that close relatives of commissioning parents become surrogates will place undue pressure on women within extended Hindu families to conform to the wishes of their elders and childless relatives.

Not unsurprisingly when the Surrogacy Regulation Bill 2016 was introduced in Parliament, it was referred to a Parliamentary Standing Committee in January 2017. Based on extensive consultations with numerous stakeholders (governmental and otherwise), the Committee in its August 2017 report reversed literally every key feature of the Surrogacy Regulation Bill 2016. In an extraordinary analysis, the Committee stated that imposing altruism on women was a paternalistic form of exploitation and that the 'real' exploitation that surrogates suffered arose from the lack of proper regulation of the surrogacy sector and from the poor and even lower-paying alternatives they had to commercial surrogacy. It instead proposed a 'compensated' model for surrogacy whereby women's reproductive labour would be compensated at a rate fixed by the state taking into consideration numerous factors.[54] Their exploitation under this model could be 'minimized through adequate legislative norm-setting and robust regulatory oversight'.[55]

The Committee confirmed that only gestational surrogacy should be permitted. The Committee opined that the Bill's requirement for a surrogate to be a close relative would translate into high levels of familial coercion. Hence, the surrogate need not be related to the commissioning parents. Surrogates instead ought to be empaneled. The surrogate could bear only one live child through surrogacy. The Committee proposed strengthening the informed consent provisions of the SRB so that the surrogate received extensive counselling from a competent authority consisting of independent functionaries including NGOs before she gave consent. The Committee also recommended comprehensive insurance cover for the surrogate for one year from the date the surrogacy procedure starts and for six years from the date of confirmation of pregnancy. Life insurance must be provided for the surrogate and child. It also advocated for maternity benefits for the commissioning mother and the surrogate. It favourably referred back to the 2014 Bill on this issue and other drafting matters (including the definition of surrogacy, storage of embryos, composition of the National Surrogacy Board and the registry of ART clinics).

The Committee liberalised the eligibility criteria for commissioning parents extending the surrogacy option to live-in couples, divorced women, widows, NRIs, PIOs and OCIs but not other foreign nationals. Also one year of proven infertility was sufficient to be able to avail of surrogacy; where the need for surrogacy was absolute due to medical reasons, even the one-year period was to be waived.[56] Medical documentation was sufficient for proceeding with surrogacy and a certificate of infertility was not required. The Committee suggested that the SRB offer clarification on the role of gamete donors and include a provision on birth certificates. Furthermore, a parentage order was inadequate to spell out the obligations of the various stakeholders; a comprehensive legally binding agreement between the commissioning parents, the surrogate and the clinic,

---

54 R. Sabha, *One Hundred Second Report on the Surrogacy (Regulation) Bill 2016.* <http://www.prsindia.org/uploads/media/Surrogacy/SCR-%20Surrogacy%20Bill,%202016.pdf> accessed 14.09.2018, p. 30.

55 Ibid., p. 27.

56 Ibid., p. 38.

registered with the state was necessary. Babies born from surrogacy had to be provided breast milk through banks for six months.

Significantly, the Committee advised reworking the highly carceral framework of the Bill calling instead for punishments to be proportionate to the nature of the infraction, always keeping in mind the best interests of the child born through surrogacy. Finally it called for setting up an independent agency with quasi-judicial powers to resolve disputes between parties and for the ART Bill to be passed prior to the Surrogacy Regulation Bill 2016.

The government ignored the suggestions made by the Parliamentary Standing Committee when it proposed the Surrogacy (Regulation) Bill 2018 based on the SRB. The 2018 Bill introduced some minor modifications. It clarified that a surrogate cannot provide her own gametes for surrogacy, that she could withdraw from surrogacy before the embryo was implanted in her womb and that she should be provided with insurance cover for 16 months to cover any postpartum complications. Further, the Bill amended the minimum mandatory punishments prescribed in the SRB to render them as the maximum period of punishment. This Bill was passed by the lower house of Parliament in December 2018 but must be passed by the upper house and receive the assent of the President before it becomes law.

If the SRB is passed in its 2018 form, some anticipate that the surrogacy sector will go underground. However, this is unlikely to occur on a large scale given the highly medically mediated nature of the practice. It is more likely however that Indian surrogacy clinics will now share their expertise of performing surrogacy transactions with overseas clients. As countries around the world ban transnational surrogacy (e.g. Nepal and Thailand), the various processes involved in transnational commercial surrogacy transactions are becoming fragmented and are likely to be performed at different stages in various jurisdictions thus not attracting any particular country's legislation. It could well be that Indian doctors and lawyers alike who have invested a decade in perfecting the practice of surrogacy will become transnational economic actors even while Indian surrogates will have fewer livelihood choices.

SURROGACY IN THAILAND

Soraj HONGLADAROM*

1. GENERAL LEGAL FRAMEWORK

Thailand was a favourite target for international surrogacy arrangements as the country is famous for the quality of its healthcare facilities and personnel. These arrangements tend to avoid the limelight and are low key. However, in recent years there have been a number of very high-profile cases where these arrangements were burst out in the open, creating international uproars which led to the country introducing new legislation designed to stamp out unregulated, commercial surrogacy once and for all. Perhaps the most famous of these high-profile cases is the *Baby Gammy* case. In July 2014, a news story broke where a Thai surrogate mother, Pattaramon Janbua, sought an amount of money to help her critically ill surrogate son, Gammy, who was born with Down syndrome. The baby boy was a twin brother of a baby girl, Pipah, who had already been taken away to Australia by a commissioning Australian couple, who had previously contacted Janbua through agents to act as their surrogate mother. The surrogacy arrangements were done in Thailand and Janbua gave birth to the twins in December 2013. However, during her pregnancy it was discovered that Janbua was carrying twins and one of them, Gammy, had Down syndrome, and also

* The author wishes to thank Terry Kaan, Claire Fenton-Glynn and Jens Scherpe for inviting him to the Hong Kong conference and for their hospitality. This chapter has been partially supported by a grant from Chulalongkorn University, under the Research Fellow Project under the Ratchadapisek Fund.

congenital heart and lung disorders. The agency that ran the surrogacy requested that Janbua allow an abortion of the defective foetus, which she refused. The news story caused a huge amount of uproar not only in Thailand but also throughout the world. According to Janbua the commissioning couple took away only the healthy twin girl and left Gammy in Thailand. Janbua became attached to Gammy and tried to raise him along with her own children. However, the cost of raising Gammy became too much for her and soon afterwards the story was publicised in the international media. However, the Australian commissioning couple initially claimed that they did not know about the existence of Gammy because the truth was hidden from them by the agency. Later they conceded that they had known about Gammy's existence at the earliest stage. David Farnell, the commissioning father, claimed afterwards that no couple would want to have a baby with Down syndrome. Janbua then tried to raise Gammy with the money raised for her via the internet and put in a trust by an international charity organisation only for taking care of Gammy. However, Janbua then claimed that she did not receive her full surrogate fee, while the Farnells, the commissioning couple, sought to get a refund from the agency.

The international outcry caused by the story prompted the military government which ruled Thailand at that time to start the process of drafting a new law which was intended to put an end to commercial surrogacy altogether. A team of experts was set up to draft the law. It was presented to the National Legislative Assembly in 2014 and was signed into law by the King in April 2015. The process was much faster than normal, presumably because of the intense attention of the international community on Thailand because of Gammy's case. The law, directly translated as Protection of Children Born through Assisted Reproductive Technologies Act, B.E. 2558,[1] was primarily aimed at banning

1 Thailand uses Buddhist Era (B.E.) instead of the Common Era to tell the years. Buddhist era is 543 years earlier than Common Era; thus B.E. 2558 corresponds to 2015 C.E. The Thai text of the law can be obtained at <http://rh.anamai.moph.go.th/download/pdf/%E0%B8%9E%E0%B8%A3%E0%B8%9A.%E0%B9%80%E0%B8%97%E0%B8%84%E0%B9%82%E0%B8%99%E0%B9%82%E0%B8%A5%E0%B8%A2%E0%B8%B5%E0%B8%8A%E0%B9%88%E0%B8%A7%E0%B8%A2%E0%B8%81%E0%B8%B2%E0%B8%A3%E0%B9%80%E0%B8%88%E0%B8%A3%E0%B8%B4%E0%B8%8D%E0%B8%9E%E0%B8%B1%E0%B8%99%E0%B8%98%E0%B8%B8%E0%B9%8C.pdf> accessed 14.09.2018. An English translation of a preliminary draft of the law is available at <http://www.thailawforum.com/thailand-draft-surrogacy-law/>; however, this is not a translation of the actual law which was signed by the King, though many provisions remained the same. A summary of the law can also be found in J.M. Caamano, 'International, Commercial, Gestational Surrogacy through the Eyes of Children Born through Surrogates in Thailand: A Cry for Legal Attention' (2016) 96 *Boston Law Review* 571, 607. A review of the transnational business on gestational surrogacy in Thailand and Asia can be found in D. Macer, 'Ethical Conditions for Transnational Gestational Surrogacy in Asia' (2014) 14 *The American Journal of Bioethics* 1, 2. A rather scathing criticism of the whole practice in Thailand detailing the event that led of the passing of the PCA law is E. Cohen, 'Surrogacy as international business and national disgrace of Thailand' (2015) *Asian Anthropology* 115, 132.

commercial surrogacy, that is, surrogacy arrangements as business transactions through middlemen where surrogate mothers are procured to serve the needs of the commissioning parents. However, there are other provisions in the law including allowing researchers to conduct experiments on human embryos during the first 14 days, not including the time when the embryos are frozen. A provision on artificial insemination, where the sperm comes from a donor, is also included – in this case the commissioning couple must be legally married, and both the husband and wife must provide written consent. However, the main intent of the law is to prohibit commercial gestational surrogacy and leave all forms of technology assisted reproduction services to the hands of the medical professionals.

The introductory section of the Protection of Children Act (henceforth 'PCA') starts with a definition of key terms, followed by a stipulation that the Minister of Public Health and the Minister of Social Development and Human Security will be jointly responsible for enforcing it. The first Ministry, Public Health, deals with medical matters, and the Ministry of Social Development and Human Security is responsible for protection of vulnerable people, including children. The next section establishes a new commission, the Commission on Protection of Children Born through Assisted Reproductive Technologies, with the Undersecretary of Public Health as Chair. Its members include the following: President of the Medical Council as Deputy Chair, Representative from the Ministry of Social Development and Human Security, Representative from the Department of Health, Ministry of Public Health, Representative from the National Commission on Protection of Children, President of the Royal College of Pediatrics, President of the Royal College of Psychiatry, President of the Royal College of Obstetrics and Gynecology. Furthermore, there are three experts, one each on law, women's rights and children's rights, appointed by the Minister of Social Development and Human Security, and three further experts, one each on assisted reproductive technology, medical genetics and research, appointed by the Minister of Public Health. The Commission has a four-year term, and no commissioner can serve for no more than two terms (Art. 8). In addition, the Head of the Department of Health Service Support will be a member and secretary of the Commission.

Article 7 of the Protection of Children Act stipulates the powers of the Commission as follows:

'(1) Propose views to the Minister regarding policies to protect children born through assisted reproductive technologies,
(2) Propose views to the Minister regarding development or solution of problems concerning assisted reproductive technologies,
(3) Recommend to the Minister to pass regulations in order to comply with this Act,

(4) Announce rules, procedures or conditions related to how to seek permission and permission regarding surrogacy according to Art. 23,
(5) Permit procedures regarding surrogacy arrangements according to Art. 23,
(6) Announce rules, procedures or conditions related to how to seek permission regarding to the use of extranumerary embryos for research according to Article 37,
(7) Permit procedures regarding the use of extranumerary embryos according to Article 37,
(8) Approve publication of announcements of the Medical Council regarding technology assisted reproduction services according to this Act, where said announcements shall be only enforceable when they are published in the Royal Gazette,
(9) Control, investigate and regulate technology-assisted reproduction services so as to comply with this Act,
(10) Promote and support research on ethical, legal and cultural aspects of technology-assisted reproduction services,
(11) Prepare reports containing results of the work of the Commission at least once a year to be submitted to the Minister,
(12) Perform other duties assigned by the Minister.'

As for the relevant statistical information, it is hard to come by because the surrogacy arrangements are usually kept secret. Before the passing of the PCA, regulation of surrogacy arrangements was under the responsibility of the Medical Council, which is the main authority for licensing and regulating the practice of medical doctors. However, lax enforcements have resulted in a proliferation of commercial surrogacy practices, at least operating under the radar screen of media attention. It is reported in some media websites in Thailand that surrogate mothers usually receive around 300,000 baht, which is around US$10,000, for their services in gestational surrogacy. This does not include 2,000 baht a month (around US$67) for food during her pregnancy, and the middleman receives around 10,000 to 20,000 baht (US$334 to US$667).[2] The numbers of women seeking and obtaining surrogacy services are also difficult to obtain. A report in a reputable online news website in 2015 says that there are around 30 IVF clinics in Thailand performing 3,000 to 4,000 cases a year.[3] The article also reports a number of websites advertising surrogacy services to potential commissioning couples all around the world such as weneedbaby.com and vibhavadi.com, though a look at these websites do not appear to contain

---

[2] 'Cutting Open Surrogacy Business,' *Manager Daily*, 05.08.2014, available at <https://mgronline.com/daily/detail/9570000089096> accessed 10.12.2016 (in Thai).

[3] Sumonman Singna, 'Surrogate Mother: Womb Labor, Ultrasound, the Image of Biomedicine in Thailand,' *Prachatai.com*, 22.07.2015, available at <http://prachatai.com/journal/2015/07/60480> accessed 14.09.2018 (in Thai).

any information concerning gestational surrogacy arrangements, though many services are advertised.

2. SURROGACY ARRANGEMENTS IN GENERAL

According to the new law, only licensed medical professionals are allowed to perform the medical procedures related to gestational surrogacy, and they must be qualified according to the regulations of the Medical Council (Art. 15). Furthermore, Art. 16 requires that before surrogacy can be performed, the medical professional has to conduct a test to monitor readiness of all those involved in terms of their bodies, mental health and the environment. These include the commissioning couple, the potential surrogate mother and the egg or sperm donor if necessary. The test also must include a measure to prevent hereditary and other diseases. Procedures and details about all these measures will be announced by the Medical Council.

Then Art. 17 stipulates measures concerning creation, storage, use and destruction of frozen embryos. The Medical Council has the power to introduce measures regulating this field under recommendation by the PCA Commission. However, use of embryos older than 14 days is not permitted. Article 18 says that in performing assisted technologies reproduction services, the medical professional may undertake a diagnosis of the embryo before it is implanted, but sex selection is expressly forbidden. The PCA Commission will issue announcements regulating these pre-implantation diagnoses. Article 19 covers artificial insemination. This can only be done to legally married women, under the standard to be issued by the Medical Council and approved by the Commission. The next article (20) then states that artificial insemination using donated sperm must be approved in writing by both the legally married husband and wife who desire such procedure. Again, the Commission has the power to issue rules and regulations on this matter.

Then the next article, Art. 21, specifically covers gestational surrogacy. A direct translation of this important article is as follows:

> 'Under the provisions of Articles 15, 16, and 18, surrogacy arrangements have to comply at least the following criteria:
>
> (1) The legally married couple, where the wife is not able to carry a child to term and where the couple desire to have a child through a surrogate mother, must be Thai citizens. In case one of them is not a Thai citizen, they must be legally married for not less than three years.
> (2) The woman wanting to act as surrogate mother must not be a parent or a child of the husband or the wife.

(3) The surrogate mother must be related to either the husband or the wife by blood. In case where such blood relative cannot be found, another woman can only act as a surrogate mother according to the rules, regulations, procedures and conditions to be issued by the Minister of Public Health under the recommendation of the Commission.

(4) The surrogate mother must already have had at least a child of her own. If such woman already has a legally married husband, or a husband which is publicly recognized, the husband has to approve such procedure.'

The next article, Art. 22, stipulates that there are only two permitted methods of surrogacy, namely (1) using sperm and eggs of the legally married couple who want to have a child, or (2) using embryos born from the sperm of the husband and donated eggs obtained from the third person, or from the eggs of the wife and donated sperm of a third person. The latter option therefore means that the child must be genetically related to at least one of the commissioning parents. Article 23 states that any person who provides gestational surrogacy services according to Art. 21(1) must be given permission to do so by the Commission specifically to perform only for that particular commissioning couple. This means that a new permission needs to be obtained for each provision of surrogacy service. Again, the Commission retains the power to issues rules and regulations on this matter.

Article 24 merely states: 'It is forbidden to conduct surrogacy services for commercial purposes.' Article 25 then stipulates that the Minister of Public Health, under recommendation of the PCA Commission, will specify rules, regulations, procedures and conditions related to surrogacy services as well as all the expenses involved, including expenses for maintaining the health of the surrogate mother both before and after giving birth. These expenses also include those for taking care of the health of the baby for the period of no less than 30 days after birth.

Article 26 concerns termination of pregnancy, and it says that termination of pregnancy can only be performed by a licensed medical professional and with the express written consent by the commissioning couple and the surrogate mother. However, if the surrogate mother does not give her consent, no termination can be performed. When the surrogate mother does not consent to termination, the article stipulates that the surrogacy contract will be null and void, and the surrogate mother does not have to pay for any possible damage that might occur as a result of her denial of consent to the termination proposal. It is worth noting that the purpose of Art. 26 is to give power to the surrogate mother to stop any act which leads to termination of her pregnancy. This has a strong relation to the *Baby Gammy* case, where the commissioning couple wanted to abort one foetus and keep another, but this was not allowed by Janbua, who was the surrogate mother.

Article 27 prohibits the middleman approach to the procedure: 'It is forbidden for anyone to act as a middleman who calls for, accepts, or consents to accept any kind of benefits as a remuneration for arranging or linking up interested parties to perform surrogacy.' Then the next article, Art. 28, bans any kind of publicisation of availability of surrogate women, or of the fact that there are couples who want a woman to act as their surrogate mother, no matter whether the surrogacy service is done for commercial purposes or not.

So in conclusion, surrogacy contracts are considered legally binding as they are legal contracts. According to the new law, the contract has to be drawn up between the surrogate mother and the commissioning parents under the terms specified in the law. Since no middleman is allowed the contract can only be made in the context of the infertility clinic under the supervision of licensed medical professionals. Furthermore, remuneration of the surrogate mother is not allowed under the law, as commercialisation is forbidden. However, since the surrogate mother has to be related by blood to either of the commissioning parents, it is assumed that they will undergo surrogacy out of love for their relative and expect nothing in return, except for expenses concerning her health during pregnancy which is allowed by the law. However, details about all types of permitted payments are to be decided upon and announced by the PCA Commission and the Medical Council at some point.

3. LEGAL PARENTHOOD AT THE TIME OF BIRTH

The next chapter in the Act concerns legal parenthood of children born through assisted reproductive technologies. Article 29 states that children born through assisted reproductive technologies, no matter if they are born from the legally married wife or a surrogate mother, will be considered legal offspring of the commissioning couple, even if by the time when the child is born one of the commissioning parents has died. Another clause in this article also says that donors either of sperm or egg have no claim whatsoever concerning the parenthood of the child. Article 30 stipulates that in case both the commissioning parents are dead before the child is born, the surrogate mother will be the legal guardian until new legal parents are established. In this case the surrogate mother and the official according to child protection law can request to the court to establish new parents for the child. Articles 31 and 32 concern the requirements that the parents need to notify the hospital about the surrogacy arrangements and to declare the birth of the child to the district office within specified time. Article 33 forbids the commissioning parents from refusing the child born through assisted reproduction technologies. Then Art. 34 says that the relevant provision of the Civil Code shall be applied to this case in so far as it does not violate the stipulations of the Act.

Then in the next section, Art. 35 states that those who perform assisted reproduction technologies procedures must be licensed medical professionals. This includes storage, usage and receiving sperm, eggs and embryos as well as destruction of embryos. Article 36 forbids creation of embryos for other purposes except for therapy of infertility of the commissioning parents, and Art. 37 requires that those who would like to obtain such embryos for research purposes must be permitted to do so by the Commission, who will issue rules and regulations for this purpose. Article 38 holds that no other method of human reproduction apart from conception through sperm and egg is allowed. Article 39 forbids anyone from inserting egg, embryo or any part of their cells in the body of an animal, or to insert animal reproductive cells or cells created through conception of animal cells into the body of a human. Article 40 bans anyone from creating, storing, selling, exporting or otherwise using embryos containing genetic material of more than two human beings, or embryos containing genetic material of humans and other species of animals.

Article 41 forbids anyone from buying, proposing to buy, importing and exporting sperm, egg or embryo. Article 42 stipulates that in the case of assisted reproductive technologies services to a legally married couple, if one of the intended parents is dead, no sperm, egg or embryo of the dead can be used, unless one of the commissioning parents has consented to such use in writing before he or she died, and such use can only be performed for treating infertility of the surviving spouse only.

Article 44 says that any licensed medical professional who violates the standard of practice laid out in case of assisted reproduction services according to Art. 35 will be considered to have violated the code of ethics according to the law on medical practice. Thus, the Medical Council has the authority to suspend or to revoke the license of those professionals who are found to violate the Code.

In conclusion, then, the law is clear in specifying who is going to be the legal parents of the child. In this case the surrogate mother can claim nothing regarding parenthood and guardianship, unless privately agreed upon with the commissioning parents. This is a new development in Thai law because traditionally only the 'mother,' namely the woman who is pregnant and who bears the child will be considered the legal mother according to the Civil Code. Thus, the new law stipulates that the commissioning parents notify the relevant public authorities about the provisions in the law so that they realise that the baby belongs to them and not to the surrogate mother who gives birth to the child. The new law is also clear that birth certificates will indicate that the baby's parents are the commissioning parents. However, the new law does not require that the birth certificates indicate that the baby is born through surrogate arrangements. The new law is silent on whether the information about surrogacy is to be preserved. It is presumed that this will be a private matter of the commissioning parents and the surrogate mother. Thai law does not recognise the right to know one's genetic origins on the part of the child yet.

4. ELIGIBILITY FOR SURROGACY

Eligibility for surrogacy is covered in Art. 21, as mentioned earlier. Generally, both the commissioning parents need to be Thai citizens. In case one of the couple is not a Thai citizen, they have to be legally married for no fewer than three years. The surrogate mother has to be blood related to one of the commissioning parents, but cannot be either a parent or a child of the husband or the wife. However, there is one important exception. As mentioned earlier, Art. 21(3) allows that the surrogate mother does not have to be blood related in cases where neither of the commissioning parents have blood relatives; for such cases regulations to be announced later on by the Minister of Public Health, under recommendation of the PCA Commission, will be enforced. What this means is that, during this interim period where the regulation on the exception has not been promulgated, consideration of this exception will be done on a case-by-case basis. As for the woman who is eligible to become a surrogate mother, if the exception clause applies, then she does not have to be blood related to one of the commissioning parents, but she has to have at least one child (Art. 21(4)) and in case she is married, her husband has to give consent to the procedure.

As for the commissioning parents, the only requirements are that they are legally married and are Thai citizens. In cases where one of them is not a Thai citizen, the couple have to be legally married for at least three years prior to the surrogacy arrangement. There are no other legal requirements. Sperm and egg donation are permitted in the law, as they are mentioned in the text (Art. 22) and are not specifically forbidden. Thus, apparently sperm and egg donation are allowed, and owing to another article mentioning the fees, it is to be presumed that fees and expenses regarding sperm and egg donation will be set up by the Ministry of Public Health. This means that the hospital can arrange for sperm and egg donation and it is still a grey area pending the regulations that have yet to be established. However, sperm and egg donation can only be used for treatment of infertility (Art. 36), and Art. 41 specifically forbids commercialisation of sperm and egg donation, which means that in the context of the fertility clinic only sperm and egg donation can be allowed, and given the pending regulation on fees and expenses, it is to be presumed that the fertility clinic will operate under a certain grey area where the money that changes hands will be considered expenses for the 'loss of health' or the 'troubles' that the egg or sperm donor has to undergo for their donation. There is, however, no requirement either way whether the donor of sperm or egg has to be anonymous or not, which means that as of the present time the issue of whether the baby has the right to know their genetic origin/the identity of his or her donor is an entirely private matter.

5. TRANSFERRING PARENTHOOD

The new law makes it clear that the legal parents of the baby born through assisted reproductive technologies are the commissioning couple from birth. This is an automatic matter. The hospital needs to notify the public authorities that the baby was born through this procedure in order for the latter to issue a birth certificate accordingly. The surrogate mother has no claim of parenthood at all, except in the case where both the commissioning parents are dead, which is unlikely. In such cases the surrogate mother assumes temporary legal parenthood, and she can work with the relevant public officials to request the court to declare who is going to be the permanent legal parent. In effect, then, the surrogate mother can claim the baby to be her own only if both the commissioning parents are dead and no one from the side of the commissioning parents claim otherwise. However, in cases where the surrogate mother does not want the baby and when both the commissioning parents are dead, the court has to establish the legal parents for the child.

As for the rights of the child, he or she has the same rights as other children born in Thailand. However, the law does not say anything about the child's right to know or right not to know who their surrogate mother is, or even whether he or she was born by a surrogate mother. As previously mentioned, this is a private matter between the commissioning parents, the surrogate mother and perhaps the healthcare professionals.

6. AGENCIES AND CRIMINALISATION

A section in the PCA Law specifies penalties for violating certain provisions of the law. Article 46 says that anyone found violating Art. 15 (requiring the one who performs the surrogacy procedure to be a licensed medical professional) is liable to no more than one-year imprisonment or 20,000 Baht fine, or both. In practice, since the regulations concerning how to license medical professionals in this area have not been issued by the Medical Council, only qualified obstetricians and gynaecologists will be able to undertake the procedure. Article 47 states that those found violating Art. 23 (requiring those who perform surrogacy services to be specifically permitted to do so by the Commission) will be liable to no more than six months' imprisonment, or 10,000 Baht fine, or both. Those found violating Art. 24 (banning commercialisation of surrogacy) will be liable to no more than 10 years in prison, or 200,000 Baht fine, or both (Art. 48). Then Art. 49 stipulates that those found violating Arts 27 (acting as middleman), 28 (advertising a surrogacy service), 33 (refusing a baby born through assisted reproductive technologies) and 40 (creating and storing hybrid embryos) will be liable to no more than five years' imprisonment, or 10,000 Baht fine, or both.

Article 50 stipulates that those found violating Art. 35 (only licensed medical professional can perform assisted reproductive technologies services) will be liable to no more than 10 years' imprisonment or 200,000 Baht fine, or both. Article 51 then holds that anyone found violating Arts 36 (creating embryos for purposes other than therapy), 41 (buying or proposing to buy sperm, egg or embryo) and 43 (using the sperm, egg or embryo of a dead person unless permitted) will be liable to no more than three years' imprisonment or 60,000 Baht fine, or both. Then Art. 52 states that anyone who is not a licensed medical professional found violating Art. 37 (which requires that those who can conduct research on embryos must be a licensed medical professional) will be liable to no more than three years imprisonment, or 60,000 Baht fine, or both. This means that only medical doctors can conduct research involving human embryos, which may be too restrictive and could hinder progress of research in this area in Thailand. Then Art. 53 says that anyone found violating Arts 38 (attempting to reproduce humans apart from conception of sperm and egg) and 39 (creating cross-species embryos) will be liable to three to 10 years' imprisonment, or 60,000 to 200,000 Baht, or both.

In conclusion, then, what happens as a result of the law is that surrogacy arrangements will be strictly a matter for the healthcare facilities and the couple who go there to have their infertility problem treated. No middleman or private agencies will be permitted, as this would mean commercialisation of the practice, which is expressly banned by the law. In this case the hospital and other fertility clinics which are licensed by the Royal College of Obstetrics and Gynecology will be able to conduct advertisements of their own, which does not have to violate Art. 28 because the advertisement is for treatment of infertility only and not a publicisation of availability of surrogate women. In other words, the intent of the new law is that the entire operation of surrogacy arrangements will be given to the care of medical professionals, and since the Medical Council, which oversees ethical conduct of doctors, is composed entirely of medical doctors themselves, the whole thing appears to be a closed loop where the medical profession takes care of itself in all areas.

7. INTERNATIONAL SURROGACY ARRANGEMENTS

The new law here in effect puts an end to international surrogacy arrangements for foreigners in Thailand. This is because of the requirement that the commissioning couple have to be Thai citizens, or if one of the parents is not a

Thai citizen, they have to be legally married for no less than three years. Another requirement is that the surrogate mother has to be blood related to either one of the commissioning parents. While the law here only is enforceable in Thailand, children born through surrogacy arrangements in other countries are accepted as legal children provided that the parents can provide documentation that the children are accepted as legal in their own country. This is a normal practice according to the Civil Code. The child born through surrogacy arrangements will be a Thai citizen provided that one of his or her parents is a Thai citizen; this applies whether the child is born in Thailand or not. Thus, since the PCA law allows that children born through surrogacy arrangements will be the legal offspring of the commissioning parents, in case where one of the parents is a Thai citizen, then the child receives Thai citizenship automatically.

8. CONCLUSIONS

The context in which the PCA law was passed was that Thailand was under military dictatorship. The intention that the junta declared to the Thai people was that they wanted to clean up the political scene that they said were entirely corrupt. This is a way for the junta to justify their usurping of the power – they kept on saying that they staged the coup d'état to get the elected politicians out of power whom they said were corrupt. In this atmosphere, only a few months after the coup, the *Baby Gammy* scandal broke onto the scene. The junta felt that they needed to do something fast to shore up the image of the country and more importantly of themselves. And as the junta is in fact an arm of the bureaucracy (all the army personnel in the junta were bureaucrats who aimed to hold on to power and did not want to share it with the elected politicians), other bureaucrats, especially the medical doctors in the Ministry of Public Health, joined in and helped in drafting the PCA law with remarkable speed. Hence it is no surprise that many of the provisions in the law leave it open for the groups of medical doctors, especially those in the Medical Council and the specialists in the field, to have their way in drafting the new law. Leaving the details of the regulations of surrogacy to announcements and regulations of the Medical Council appears to be a convenient way for the doctors to do things as they like because regulations are much easier to pass and amend than the law. Thus, it is no surprise that to date (the law was passed in April 2015) no regulation mentioned in the law has been passed by the Medical Council. In the eyes of the medical profession the advantage of this reluctance may be that surrogacy arrangements are still a 'grey area' where there are no specific regulations, leaving room for (wide) interpretation. As mentioned earlier in the paper, many of the arrangements which in other jurisdictions are strictly regulated, such as whether the baby has a right to know who their surrogate mother is, is not mentioned at all in the law. This apparent monopoly by the medical profession is clear in Art. 52, which forbids anybody who is not a medical professional to do research on the embryo under stiff penalty.

As a result, given the rather loose nature of the PCA law, it should be workable only because the difficult details are not mentioned and regulations which the law says will be passed by the Medical Council are not yet available. What became apparent immediately is that the surrogate mother in reality does not actually have to be blood related to either of the commissioning parents, even though the law appears to be based on the intention that the surrogate mother has to act out of her altruism toward the commissioning parents. In practice, however, a foreign couple can in fact come to Thailand and have their infertility problem treated. If the doctor prescribes gestational surrogacy for the couple, arrangements can then be made within the hospital itself – no middleman would be needed. In this case, since there is the exception clause in Art. 21 allowing for an unrelated surrogate mother, a Thai woman can then act as surrogate mother to the foreign commissioning couple. The only requirement is that the commissioning couple do not have any blood relatives. Consequently, the new law does not actually ban foreign surrogacy arrangements as mentioned in many articles on the topic.

A way toward possible reform of the new law would be that the doctors at the Medical Council and the Royal Colleges collaborate more with people in other professions and especially with the general public. More urgently, the regulations that are mentioned in many places in the law need to be passed and widely publicised. The procedure leading up to the drafting and passing also needs to be fully transparent. Whether this actually will happen remains to be seen.

PART III

COMPARATIVE PERSPECTIVES ON SURROGACY

SURROGACY IN A GLOBALISED WORLD

Comparative Analysis and Thoughts on Regulation

Claire Fenton-Glynn and Jens M. Scherpe

What was said in the introduction to this volume remains valid, as transpires very clearly from every preceding chapter of this volume: the issues arising out of surrogacy are global ones. As the contributions in this book show, there is a huge disparity in the way different jurisdictions deal (or indeed do not deal) with surrogacy. The aim of this final chapter is to examine the different aspects of regulation present in the 21 Eastern and Western jurisdictions discussed in this volume. Sections 1 to 7 therefore first provide a comparison and overview of the features of the various legal frameworks (or lack thereof), identifying similarities and trends. The concluding Section 8 then undertakes a critical analysis of the current state of the law of surrogacy throughout both Eastern and Western jurisdictions, and in doing so addresses the strengths and weaknesses of the current approaches.

Given the vastly different social, ethical, political, cultural, traditional and legal views on surrogacy, it would be highly inappropriate (to say the very least) to draft firm recommendations or concrete conclusions on what every jurisdiction ought to do, as this would inevitably be coloured by the authors' own views, which by necessity are embedded in their own social and legal cultures. Thus the aim of this chapter is not to prescribe adherence to any one framework, but to point out issues that will inevitably have to be dealt with or addressed, and show how other jurisdictions have done this. That said, the chapter concludes by identifying five key features that must define any legal framework for surrogacy and therefore must be considered by any jurisdiction, irrespective of which approach ultimately is taken.

1. GENERAL LEGAL FRAMEWORK

1.1. STRUCTURE OF THE REGIME

The jurisdictions canvassed in this book can be divided into five main categories: prohibitive; tolerant; regulatory; free market; and regulation by the medical profession. While there will of course be some systems that will blur the boundaries between these categories, they hopefully serve to show the different approaches taken by the legislature (or not taken, as the case may be), and how the vastly differing starting positions may affect the ability of the international community to come to a consensus concerning cross-border surrogacy.

In the first group, six of the jurisdictions considered – *France, Germany, PR China, Singapore, Spain* and *Taiwan* – prohibit surrogacy domestically, in any form. For some of these jurisdictions, this is simply the case because the relevant authorities have not yet decided what the most appropriate legislative approach should be (e.g. *Singapore*, *Taiwan*).[1] But in jurisdictions such as *France* and *Germany*, a deeper antipathy to the practice of surrogacy can be seen. For example, in *France*, surrogacy is seen as violating the dignity of the surrogate, as it commodifies the human body, and treats it as a means for others, rather than an end in itself. Further, it is argued that changes in civil status must derive from law, rather than from private arrangements, and surrogacy is merely a way to circumvent adoption.[2]

For those jurisdictions that do allow surrogacy, at least in some form, the choice then becomes between toleration, regulation, free market, or a legal lacuna regulated only by the medical profession.

Australia, *England*[3] and *Hong Kong* represent a (somewhat) tolerant approach – jurisdictions that do not regulate surrogacy itself, but exercise control over its effects, in the form of regulating the transfer of parenthood from the surrogate to the commissioning parents through surrogacy specific mechanisms. In each of these jurisdictions, only altruistic surrogacy is permitted, and commercial surrogacy is prohibited. In *England*, this form of regulation is intended to protect women from exploitation – commercial surrogacy is seen as inconsistent with human dignity, as a woman's womb should not be used for financial profit, but only in a 'gift relationship' between the surrogate and commissioning parents.[4] In *Australia*, the choice of a 'tolerant' approach was pragmatic – intended to balance an unwillingness to

---

1 T. Kaan, Singapore, in this volume, p. 397; C. Ho, Taiwan, in this volume, p. 377.

2 W. Pintens, France, in this volume, p. 18.

3 For the purposes of this chapter any reference to 'England' or 'English law' is to be understood as referring to the jurisdiction of England and Wales.

4 C. Fenton-Glynn, England and Wales, in this volume, p. 116.

give effect to surrogacy arrangements, given their potentially exploitative nature, but an acknowledgement that they will inevitably take place and the consequences will have to be dealt with.[5]

A number of jurisdictions – *Greece*, *Israel*, *New Zealand*, *Portugal*, *South Africa* and the proposed *Icelandic* law – go one step further, and not only tolerate surrogacy, but actively facilitate it. In contrast to the 'tolerant' approaches, these jurisdictions regulate surrogacy *before* the conception of the child, with permission needing to be sought from the appropriate authorities before the medical procedures can take place. The reasons for taking such an approach are varied. In *Israel*, this is a reflection of pro-natalist policies, and the right to procreation, as recognised by the national courts.[6] In *Greece*, the basis of the law is more pragmatic: the authorities recognised that a prohibition of surrogacy could never be enforced entirely, so determined that it would be in the best interests of children to have certainty and control through a regulatory framework.[7]

The most liberal jurisdictions discussed in this volume, however, are *California* and *Russia*, both of which practice a 'free market' model. This is so called because they do not regulate who can enter into surrogacy arrangements, or on what grounds, and instead allow for private commercial arrangements between the parties to be enforced.

Thailand[8] and *India*[9] also previously followed this 'free market' approach, but then shut down their previously booming (international) surrogacy markets, instead adopting very restrictive regimes. This change came about following a series of high-profile scandals, including the infamous Baby Gammy case.[10] These jurisdictions are interesting from a comparative perspective, as it is possible to track legislative changes in response to specific concerns raised regarding the practice – and in particular, the exploitation of women in commercial surrogacy arrangements.

The final structure identified in this volume is not a legislative one, but the regulation of surrogacy by the medical profession. This is the case in *Japan* and *South Korea*, where access to surrogacy is controlled by medical/ethical guidelines, which are non-binding and unenforceable. In *South Korea*, this has been a deliberate decision not to legislate, given the diversity of views surrounding the practice,[11] whereas in *Japan*, there has been consideration of legislation, but likewise an inability to decide on the best way forward.[12]

---

5 M. Keyes, Australia, in this volume, pp. 87–89.
6 R. Schuz, Israel, in this volume, pp. 168–169.
7 E. Zervogianni, Greece, in this volume, p. 148.
8 S. Hongladarom, Thailand, in this volume, pp. 499–501.
9 P. Kotiswaran, India, in this volume, pp. 470–481.
10 S. Hongladarom, Thailand, in this volume, pp. 499–500.
11 O-J. Kim and B-H. Lee, South Korea, in this volume, pp. 453–455.
12 S. Hayakawa, Japan, in this volume, pp. 441, 445–447.

1.2. RESPONSIBLE AUTHORITIES FOR REGULATING SURROGACY

In prohibitive jurisdictions, there is obviously no responsible authority for regulating surrogacy, and instead the criminal law is invoked in instances where it occurs. However, for (almost) all the other jurisdictions considered in this volume, regulation is achieved through either administrative, judicial or medical authorities.

In some regulatory systems, control is exercised over surrogacy through administrative bodies. In *New Zealand*, an Ethics Committee is responsible for approving surrogacy arrangements before they take place,[13] while in *Portugal*, the new legislation allocates this responsibility to a National Council for Medically-Assisted Procreation.[14] In *Israel*, this role falls to an 'Approvals Committee', which includes two doctors with expertise in gynecology and obstetrics; one doctor with expertise in internal medicine; a clinical psychologist; a social worker; a lawyer; and a religious cleric (according to the religion of the parties).[15]

Where the responsible authority is judicial, this can occur at two different stages. In *California*, *Greece*, *Israel*, *South Africa* and the *Australian* states of *Victoria* and *Western Australia*, the courts are involved pre-birth – requiring that eligibility for surrogacy be proven before authorisation is given for the fertilisation to take place.[16] On the other hand, in *England*, *Hong Kong* and the rest of *Australia*, the courts are not involved until after the child has been born, and are responsible only for deciding whether to transfer parenthood from the surrogate to the commissioning parents.[17] The difficulties involved in a post-birth determination of a surrogacy, and in particular how it is affected (and arguably determined) by an evaluation of the best interests of the child, will be discussed below in Section 5.1.

In *Japan* and *South Korea*, as discussed above, the appropriate authority is not administrative or judicial, but medical. The difficulty with this approach can be seen in their advisory, rather than compulsory, nature – and indeed in *Japan* one practitioner openly refuses to follow them and conducts surrogacies despite their prohibition.[18] Such an approach is also problematic when it comes to the allocation of legal parenthood: where the law does not recognise

---

13 D. Wilson, New Zealand, in this volume, pp. 204–205.

14 R. Teixeira Pedro, Portugal, in this volume, pp. 231–232.

15 R. Schuz, Israel, in this volume, pp. 166–167.

16 E. Zervogianni, Greece, in this volume, p. 149; R. Schuz, Israel, in this volume, p. 166; J. Sloth-Nielsen, South Africa, in this volume, p. 192; N. Cahn and J. Carbone, United States of America, in this volume, p. 323; M. Keyes, Australia, in this volume, pp. 94, 97.

17 C. Fenton-Glynn, England and Wales, in this volume, p. 125; M. Keyes, Australia, in this volume, p. 97; D. Cheung, Hong Kong, in this volume, pp. 435–436.

18 S. Hayakawa, Japan, in this volume, p. 443.

surrogacy, parties are forced to resort to general law provisions, which may not be appropriate for the specific issues that surrogacy presents.

The final jurisdiction to mention in this context is *Russia*, which does not exercise any control over surrogacy arrangements – judicial, administrative or medical. Instead, the arrangement is left to the parties, who can organise their affairs as they see fit, with the court only intervening if there is a dispute.[19]

1.3. INFLUENCES ON REGULATION

The influence of culture, history, and religion on the regulation (or lack thereof) of surrogacy cannot be underestimated – particularly when trying to draw lessons from the experience of other jurisdictions in a comparative analysis.

The clearest example of this is *Israel*, where Jewish laws concerning marriage, parenthood and the status of children are central to the way the system has been developed. *Israel* is one of the few jurisdictions that permit commercial surrogacy, motivated not by a free market ideology, but by the fact that altruistic surrogacy was not a realistic option since a close family relationship between the surrogate and one of the commissioning parents raises doubts about the status of the child in Jewish law. Similarly, restrictions on the gametes used, and the religion of the surrogate, can be traced to the need to ensure the child's status. Israeli society also places great emphasis on supporting procreation – given its historical and geo-political context – which can be seen in the judicial recognition of the right to become a parent.[20]

The right to parenthood can also be seen influencing the *Russian* approach to surrogacy. In that jurisdiction, assisted reproduction is seen as an imitation, and extension, of natural reproduction, which all individuals have the right to take part in. Consequently, the role of the government is to facilitate the formation of a family, reflected in the legislative right of adult women to assisted reproduction and embryo implantation, including surrogacy.[21]

Judaism is not the only religion to influence the regulation of surrogacy. In *India*, the importance to the Hindu majority of having one's genetic progeny to complete end-of-life rituals had long meant that infertile couples used other methods to complete their families, and was significant in the former relaxed laws surrounding surrogacy. History too has also been influential in *India* – artificial reproductive technology developed in that jurisdiction in response to previous aggressive anti-natalist policies in pursuit of population control, and was encouraged by government as a means of reversing forced sterilisation.[22]

---

19 O. Khazova, Russia, in this volume, pp. 281–306.
20 R. Schuz, Israel, in this volume, p. 168.
21 O. Khazova, Russia, in this volume, pp. 281–282.
22 P. Kotiswaran, India, in this volume, p. 474.

1.4. STATISTICS

One of the ongoing difficulties in coming to grips with the phenomenon of surrogacy is that we have no real idea of the extent and scope of the practice. Statistics on surrogate births are available in only a handful of jurisdictions, and even then, these are mostly gathered by independent researchers rather than by the government itself.

In *France*, *Germany*, *Hong Kong*, *Iceland*, *Japan*, *Portugal*, *Singapore*, *South Africa*, *South Korea*, *Spain* and *Taiwan*, no statistics are available – either official, or unofficial.

In *PR China*, *Thailand* and *India*, the only statistics that can be obtained are gross estimates, often without reliable sources. In *PR China* and *Thailand*, media estimates are all that can be referred to. In relation to *PR China*, American media sources estimate between 5,000 and 10,000 domestic surrogate births per year, with a further 1,000 commissioning parents going to the *United States* to undertake surrogacy there.[23] In *Thailand*, an online news website reported that in 2015 there were around 30 IVF clinics performing 3,000 to 4,000 surrogacies a year.[24] In *India*, the Confederation of Indian Industry meanwhile estimated that in 2012 nearly 10,000 foreign clients visited *India* for reproductive services; however, according to research conducted by Prabha Kotiswaran and reported in this volume, this number is likely to be closer to 6,000 per year.[25]

In *Russia*, on the other hand, the Russian Association of Human Reproduction collects statistics on clinics and surrogacy arrangements, giving a more accurate picture. In 2015, there were 89 assisted reproduction centres where 1,539 cycles with participation of surrogates ended in embryo transfers (in 2014 – 1,318 cycles in 78 centres).[26] Of course, this does not indicate how many surrogate births resulted from such procedures.

In jurisdictions where the process must be authorised by a court or other official body, statistics are likely to be more reliable. In the *United States*, federal law requires clinics to report the number of surrogacy arrangements they oversee. From 1999–2013, there were 30,927 gestational carrier cycles in the *United States*, which resulted in 13,380 deliveries.[27] In *New Zealand*, from 2005–2017, the Ethics Committee on Assisted Reproductive Technology heard 253 applications – at a rate of 16–29 per year. Of these, 157 were approved outright, 41 approved with conditions, and 10 approved with recommendations.[28]

---

23 L. Shi, China, in this volume, p. 362.

24 S. Hongladarom, Thailand, in this volume, pp. 502–503.

25 P. Kotiswaran, India, in this volume, pp. 481–482.

26 O. Khazova, Russia, in this volume, p. 283.

27 N. Cahn and J. Carbone, United States of America, in this volume, p. 315.

28 D. Wilson, New Zealand, in this volume, p. 209.

In *Israel*, there were 1,042 applications for surrogacy submitted between 1996 and 2014, resulting in 408 births.[29]

In *Greece* and *South Africa*, despite court authorisation being required before a surrogacy can take place, statistics are not centrally collected or published. In *Greece*, independent researchers have delved into court records, with the result that they are able to estimate that numbers of applications are in their hundreds.[30] In *South Africa*, on the other hand, this task has not been undertaken, and therefore information is not available.[31]

It should also be noted that even where the government does record its own statistics, these are not always internally consistent or reliable. For example, in the *United Kingdom*, the Ministry of Justice indicated that in 2013, 162 children were the subject of Parental Orders following surrogacy, with 240 in 2014. However, the General Register Office reported 185 in 2013, and 258 in 2014. While it may be argued that some of the confusion arises from international surrogacy arrangements, even with children born within the *United Kingdom*, the Ministry of Justice records 102 in 2013 and 163 in 2014, as opposed to the Registrar's 116 and 151.[32]

2. SURROGACY ARRANGEMENTS IN GENERAL

2.1. ENFORCEABILITY OF CONTRACTS

Some jurisdictions have no legislation on surrogacy, sometimes deliberately so, resulting in the legal situation being unclear. For example, in *South Korea*, three academic theories were put forward as to how a surrogacy agreement might be interpreted by the authorities: it might be seen as void (as contrary to public morals), effective (as it is not explicitly prohibited), or of limited effect (for example, only if altruistic).[33] While it was clear that such a surrogacy agreement would not be enforceable for handing over the child, in all other respects this leaves commissioning parents and surrogates in a state of uncertainty.

In *Singapore* the lack of legislation is deliberate (see above).[34] The result of this, however, is that while we know that surrogacy contracts are not illegal, as no domestic cases have yet come before the courts, we do not know the extent to which such agreements will be enforced.

---

29 R. Schuz, Israel, in this volume, pp. 169–170.
30 E. Zervogianni, Greece, in this volume, pp. 148–149.
31 J. Sloth-Nielsen, South Africa, in this volume, p. 186.
32 C. Fenton-Glynn, England and Wales, in this volume, pp. 117–118.
33 O-J. Kim and B-H. Lee, South Korea, in this volume, pp. 453–455.
34 C. Ho, Taiwan, in this volume, p. 397.

Jurisdictions that choose not to regulate – either deliberately, or as a result of a lack of consensus – or who leave regulation to medical bodies and guidelines rather than the law, thus are leaving commissioning parents, surrogates and children in a state of legal uncertainty, which can only have detrimental effects. On the one hand, while this may deter people from entering into surrogacy arrangements in those jurisdictions (and presumably means that commissioning couples are going to resort to international surrogacy), on the other hand it may even encourage couples to 'just give it a try' or to have surrogacies in the shadow of the law, which ultimately may lead to great legal problems. It therefore appears that not taking a position on surrogacy by not legislating is, at best, avoiding the problem and, at worst (and more likely), creating more legal problems.

2.1.1. *Jurisdictions where an Agreement is Unenforceable*

Unsurprisingly, in most jurisdictions where surrogacy is prohibited, or even simply tolerated, purported surrogacy contracts are null and void under the law. This is the case, for example, in *France*, *Germany*, *Spain*, *PR China*, *Hong Kong*, *England* and *New Zealand*.[35]

While some jurisdictions go further than this, declaring the contracts themselves illegal (for example, *France*, *Germany* and *Spain*), in others they are legal, but simply unenforceable (as in *England* and *New Zealand*).

The new *Portuguese* law, on the other hand, imposes criminal penalties for entering into a commercial surrogacy agreement, but an altruistic agreement is (partly) enforceable (see below).[36]

2.1.2. *Jurisdictions where an Agreement is (Partly) Enforceable*

2.1.2.1. Procedural Requirements

In *Greece*, *South Africa*, *Israel*, and *California*, a surrogacy agreement must be approved by the relevant authority to be legal (be that administrative or judicial).[37] By contrast, in *Russia*, there is no oversight of the terms of the arrangement, thus earning it its moniker as a 'free market' jurisdiction.

---

[35] W. Pintens, France, in this volume, p. 18; A. Dutta, Germany, in this volume, p. 37; E. Farnós Amorós, Spain, in this volume, p. 62; L. Shi, China, in this volume, pp. 362–363; D. Cheung, Hong Kong, in this volume, p. 428; C. Fenton-Glynn, England and Wales, in this volume, p. 118; D. Wilson, New Zealand, in this volume, p. 209.

[36] R. Teixeira Pedro, Portugal, in this volume, pp. 239–240.

[37] E. Zervogianni, Greece, in this volume, p. 150; J. Sloth-Nielsen, South Africa, in this volume, p. 187; R. Schuz, Israel, in this volume, p. 170; N. Cahn and J. Carbone, United States of America, in this volume, pp. 323–324. This was also the proposal for the Portuguese law, but this provision was struck down as unconstitutional (R. Teixeira Pedro, Portugal, in this volume, pp. 239–242).

Apart from this requirement (and the requirement that the agreement be in writing), procedural requirements are generally very slim, with the focus being on the substantive provisions. The exceptions to this are that in both *Israel* and *California* it must be confirmed that the parties had independent and separate legal advice before the contract can be confirmed and enforced, and in *South Africa*, details of the agency and the sums paid to it must be put before the court.[38]

One jurisdiction that stands out from the rest with regard to procedural requirements is *California*. While for most jurisdictions the procedure is overshadowed by substantive requirements, in *California*, procedural requirements are all there is. In this respect, it is notable for its simplicity – and commercial perspective. As long as the parties have had independent legal advice, and there are satisfactory details concerning how the commissioning parents will cover the surrogate's medical expenses, then the agreement will be authorised. There is no further confirmation needed concerning the eligibility of the surrogate or commissioning parents, nor of the interests of the child. Autonomy is put at the forefront of the transaction – as long as the parties want to enter into this contract, and have the money to do so, then they are free to contract as they like.[39]

In *Greece* and *California* providing the contract meets the procedural requirements set out in law, and contains the appropriate substantive clauses (as discussed below), then the authority must authorise the agreement.[40] However, in *Israel* and *South Africa*, the investigation goes deeper. In *South Africa*, the High Court must consider the child's best interests before an agreement is confirmed.[41] In *Israel*, an agreement can only be approved if the Approvals Committee is satisfied that there is no risk to the health of the surrogate or the welfare of the child to be born, and that the surrogacy agreement does not contain conditions which harm or prejudice the rights of the child to be born, or those of one of the parties.[42]

---

38 R. Schuz, Israel, in this volume, p. 170; N. Cahn and J. Carbone, United States of America, in this volume, p. 323; J. Sloth-Nielsen, South Africa, in this volume, p. 190.

39 N. Cahn and J. Carbone, United States of America, in this volume, pp. 323, 326.

40 E. Zervogianni, Greece, in this volume, p. 149; N. Cahn and J. Carbone, United States of America, in this volume, p. 323.

41 *Ex Parte CJD and others (Centre for Child Law intervening as amicus curiae)* (case no. 53131/2017, North Gauteng High Court). Interestingly, New Zealand requires that the surrogate receive independent legal advice, even though the contract is not enforceable: see D. Wilson, New Zealand, in this volume, p. 215.

42 R. Schuz, Israel, in this volume, pp. 165–166.

2.1.2.2. Substantive Requirements

2.1.2.2.1. Payments to Surrogates

In *Israel* and *California* the contract is enforceable in relation to payments.[43] However, this is hardly surprising, since in these jurisdictions, surrogacy arrangements in general are enforceable, including the obligation to hand over the child at birth (subject to some restrictions).

But there are also hybrid systems such as *Russia*, where the surrogacy contract is enforceable with respect to payment – and commercial surrogacy is permitted – but is *not* enforceable in relation to the handing over of the child to the commissioning parents. It is only with the surrogate's consent that this can occur. Commissioning parents can thus be left in a situation where they can be contractually obliged to make significant payments – with average payments for the services of surrogate mothers being estimated between US$15,000–20,000 – but have no remedy if the surrogate decides not to hand over the child.[44]

Likewise, in *Australia*, altruistic surrogacy arrangements are enforceable with respect to payments for medical expenses, etc., but not with respect to any other terms.[45] This is also what was proposed by the *Icelandic* Bill, where the contract would be seen as a statement of intent, which enables surrogates to claim a reimbursement of her costs, but not otherwise enforceable.[46]

2.1.2.2.2. Obligation to Hand Over the Child

California is the only jurisdiction canvassed in which the obligation to hand over the child is unconditionally enforceable.[47] All other jurisdictions, even those which have approved the parenthood of the commissioning parent(s) pre-birth, have some exceptions.

For example, in *South Africa*, as long as the surrogacy arrangement has been approved by the High Court, the child is to all intents and for all purposes the child of the commissioning parent(s) from birth, and the surrogate must hand over the child as soon as reasonably possible after the birth. However, there is an exception where the surrogate is genetically related to the child, in which case she can terminate the agreement within 60 days of birth, and, as a result, parental

---

43 R. Schuz, Israel, in this volume, pp. 171–172; N. Cahn and J. Carbone, United States of America, in this volume, p. 324.

44 O. Khazova, Russia, in this volume, pp. 291–292 (although there is no evidence that this has ever occurred).

45 M. Keyes, Australia, in this volume, pp. 90–91.

46 H. Friðriksdóttir, Iceland, in this volume, p. 268.

47 N. Cahn and J. Carbone, United States of America, in this volume, pp. 324–325.

rights then will vest in her.[48] Similarly, in *Greece*, following court authorisation of the agreement, the courts can compel the surrogate to hand over the child at birth using the Code of Civil Procedure on judicial execution. However, where the ovum of the surrogate is used, she can challenge legal motherhood within six months of birth.[49]

In *Israel*, the surrogate has slightly wider scope to challenge the legal parenthood of the commissioning parents. Unlike *South Africa* and *Greece*, this does not rely on a genetic relationship, but on a change of circumstances which justifies her change of mind. This will then go before the court for determination, which must then be satisfied that awarding parenthood to the surrogate would not harm the welfare of the child.[50]

Interestingly, *Portuguese* law contained a provision that would assign legal parenthood to the commissioning parents from birth, with an associated obligation on the surrogate to hand over the child. However, following a challenge to the Constitutional Court, this provision was struck down as unconstitutional. The court made clear that the surrogate *must* have the opportunity to change her mind post-birth, even if the surrogacy contract has been confirmed pre-birth before the National Council for Medically-Assisted Procreation.[51]

2.1.2.2.3. Behaviour and Health

The extent to which the commissioning parents can control the behaviour of the surrogate through contractual obligations is a contentious issue. In *Greece*, the surrogate must observe general standards for a healthy pregnancy, including not smoking and drinking. If she does not comply with this, and it affects the health of the child, she may be held liable both in contract and in tort, vis-à-vis the intended parties and the child born. However, contractual terms that lead to 'undue' restriction on the surrogate's freedom – for example the surrogate being subject to the constant control of the commissioning parents, or even extreme precautions she must take during pregnancy – are void.[52] On the other hand, in *Portugal* behavioural restrictions are explicitly prohibited,[53] and a *Taiwanese* draft Bill, whose future is uncertain, proposes to enshrine respect for the autonomy of the surrogate to decide health and physical condition-related matters during pregnancy.[54]

More common than these behavioural provisions, however, are those that require details of the medical procedures to be carried out. In *South Africa*, the

48 J. Sloth-Nielsen, South Africa, in this volume, pp. 191–192.
49 E. Zervogianni, Greece, in this volume, pp. 152–153.
50 R. Schuz, Israel, in this volume, p. 178.
51 R. Teixeira Pedro, Portugal, in this volume, pp. 236–237.
52 E. Zervogianni, Greece, in this volume, p. 150.
53 R. Teixeira Pedro, Portugal, in this volume, p. 241.
54 C. Ho, Taiwan, in this volume, p. 389.

agreement must set out the details of when the artificial insemination will take place,[55] while in *Israel*, details must be provided as to the medical procedures, and the period of time for which attempts to secure pregnancy will continue.[56]

Portugal has perhaps the most extensive list of medical terms and conditions that must be included in a surrogacy arrangement, including not only rights of the surrogate, but also duties. In relation to the surrogate's rights, the arrangement must acknowledge her right to psychological support before and after childbirth; the right to participate in the decisions concerning the choice of obstetrician, the type of delivery and the place where it will take place; and the right to information on clinical techniques and their potential health risks. The contract must also set out her duty to comply with medical guidelines, and undergo examinations, which safeguard the normal evolution of the pregnancy and the well-being of the child. Finally, the contract must contain provisions on what will occur in the event of malformations or any health matters occurring during pregnancy, both to the foetus and to the surrogate.[57]

2.1.2.2.4. Welfare of the Child

Interestingly, terms concerning the welfare of the child are only mandatory in one of the jurisdictions discussed. In *South Africa*, any agreement put before the court must include provisions regarding the care, contact, upbringing and general welfare of the child, including what the position will be in the event that one/both of the commissioning parents die or separate.[58] One of the *Taiwanese* draft Bills also proposed a right to contact with the child for the two years following birth, but this was framed in the context of the right of the surrogate, rather than being for the welfare of the child.[59]

This is a significant difference from those jurisdictions that tolerate surrogacy through approving the transfer of parenthood post-birth (see Section 8.1.2. below). In the 'tolerant' jurisdictions, the welfare of the child is paramount, something that is made possible by the fact that there is a living child being presented before the court whose future has to be decided. On the other hand, one of the greatest criticisms of this approach has been that there can be no control over the other aspects of the agreement post-birth, as the welfare of the child demands legal recognition of the de facto situation – that is, the parenthood of the commissioning parents.[60]

---

55 J. Sloth-Nielsen, South Africa, in this volume, p. 190.
56 R. Schuz, Israel, in this volume, pp. 170–171.
57 R. Teixeira Pedro, Portugal, in this volume, p. 242.
58 J. Sloth-Nielsen, South Africa, in this volume, p. 190.
59 C. Ho, Taiwan, in this volume, p. 389.
60 C. Fenton-Glynn, England and Wales, in this volume, pp. 120–22. See also C. Fenton-Glynn, 'The Regulation and Recognition of Surrogacy in English Law' (2015) 27(1) *Child and Family Law Quarterly* 83.

As a result, we see a tension between pre-birth authorisation – where the welfare of the child is measured *in abstracto*, through the setting of eligibility criteria for surrogates and commissioning parents, and thus gets sidelined to a certain extent – and post-birth authorisation – where we can judge the welfare of the child *in concreto*, but the paramountcy given to the child's interests cancels out any other restrictions we might wish to place on surrogacy.

2.1.2.2.5. Termination of the Agreement

In *Portugal*, *South Africa* and *Israel*, before a surrogacy contract will be confirmed, the appropriate authority must be satisfied that it includes provisions contemplating the breakdown of the relationship between the surrogate and the commissioning parents. In *South Africa*, this must take the form of provisions concerning the termination of the agreement, and the effect of this termination,[61] while in *Israel*, this involves setting out remedies for a breach of the agreement.[62] *Portugal* takes this one step further, requiring that the contract set out mechanisms for conflict resolution in the event of a dispute, as well as setting out the possibility of termination of the surrogacy contract by either party in the event of a number of failed attempts of pregnancy and the terms upon which such termination may occur.[63]

2.1.2.2.6. Termination of the Pregnancy

One issue that remains under-explored in relation to surrogacy is whether a surrogate can choose to terminate the pregnancy, or whether the commissioning parents can demand that she do so.

In *Portugal*, before the Council can approve the surrogacy contract, it must be satisfied that it contains clauses concerning the termination of the pregnancy – although it does not state what the content of these provisions must be, save that they must comply with criminal law. Thus the surrogate must be permitted to obtain an abortion where she wishes to do so – as the criminal law states she is the sole decision-maker in this respect – but the question remains whether she will be liable for contractual damages should she do so.[64] This raises a very difficult legal and ethical issue: should a woman ever be liable in contract for her decision to have, or not to have, an abortion? In most jurisdictions, we do not have an answer for this question.

Only the new *Thai* law has explicitly contemplated the scenario where the commissioning parents wish for the surrogate to have an abortion. Under the

---

61 J. Sloth-Nielsen, South Africa, in this volume, p. 190.
62 R. Schuz, Israel, in this volume, p. 170.
63 R. Teixeira Pedro, Portugal, in this volume, p. 242.
64 Ibid.

new law, termination of pregnancy is only possible with the express written consent by the commissioning couple and the surrogate. However, if the surrogate mother does not give her consent, no termination can be performed. Moreover, if the surrogate does not consent to the abortion, the contract will be null and void, yet the surrogate will not be liable for any damages for termination of the contract.[65] What the law apparently fails to consider, however, is what would happen if the surrogate wished to have an abortion, but this was resisted by the commissioning parents. Could she really be forced to continue a pregnancy she no longer wished for?

This is an area where the law needs significantly more clarity, especially in jurisdictions where the commissioning parents are assigned legal parenthood from birth, so are more likely to view the child as 'theirs'.

2.2. COMMERCIAL, COMPENSATED OR (TRULY) ALTRUISTIC SURROGACY

One of the key debates concerning the future regulation of surrogacy is whether it should be available only on an altruistic basis, or whether commercial surrogacy should be permitted.

The term 'altruistic' is often used loosely in relation to surrogacy, referring to any agreement that is not commercial, but still leaving room for certain expenses to be paid. These often include compensatory payments for lost income, etc., so are not truly altruistic in the narrow sense. Moreover, given the nature and value of some of these ostensibly merely compensatory payments, which often are lump sums rather being itemised and proven, the line between 'altruistic' and 'commercial' can be difficult to draw. This can for example be seen in *England*, where the courts have authorised payments as 'not disproportionate' to reasonable expenses – identifying the relative comparator to be the amount given to other surrogates in the same jurisdiction.[66]

For this reason, we have divided the jurisdictions into three categories: (1) commercial, indicating a free market approach; (2) compensated; (3) and 'truly' altruistic.

2.2.1. Commercial

Very few jurisdictions allow commercial surrogacy. Interestingly, some jurisdictions, like *India* and *Thailand*, which were previously two of the most popular destinations for reproductive tourism, have both moved in recent years

65 S. Hongladarom, Thailand, in this volume, p. 504.

66 *Re X and Y (Foreign Surrogacy)* [2008] EWHC 3030 (Fam).

from a free market approach towards one which is tightly regulated – not only with respect to payments, but also with respect to who can enter into surrogacy agreements within their jurisdiction.[67] The reason for these changes in regulation are significant – in both jurisdictions, this resulted from concerns regarding the exploitation of women acting as surrogates, particularly by foreigners using the jurisdiction for reproductive tourism.

Of those jurisdictions canvassed that continue to allow commercial arrangements, neither *California* nor *Russia* put any limits on the amounts that can be paid. It is estimated that in *California*, sums paid range between US$30,000–60,000,[68] while in *Russia*, this is significantly lower at US$15,000–20,000.[69]

The only commercial jurisdiction that does exercise some oversight of payments is *Israel*, where all payments must be approved by the Committee. However, the Committee will not interfere with the sums agreed upon between the parties – as can be seen by the average cost of surrogacy in Israel reaching US$66,000. Approximately US$40,000 of this goes directly to the surrogate to compensate her for her time, suffering and impaired earning capacity, but the commissioning parents must also pay for the surrogate's independent legal advice, life insurance, counselling and direct and indirect expenses incurred due to hospitalisation resulting from pregnancy. Importantly, sufficient funds for the entire agreement must be deposited in advance in a trustee account in the name of a lawyer/accountant, who will then disperse these to the surrogate.[70]

The reasons why these jurisdictions have chosen to allow commercial surrogacy vary. For example, in *Thailand*, when commercial surrogacy originally was permitted, this was a deliberate decision by the government to promote health (and particularly reproductive) tourism.[71] For other jurisdictions, however, the use of commercial surrogacy is largely linked with pro-natalist policies. In *Israel*, this goes back to the state's cultural, religious and political context. Procreation is central in Israeli society, and there has been express judicial recognition of the right to become a parent, accompanied by policies encouraging childbirth. This is coupled with the fact that surrogacy amongst close family is not possible as it raises doubts as to the status of the child in Jewish law, meaning that commissioning parents are forced to look outside the family for a surrogate. In this context, a system based on altruistic surrogacy was not considered a realistic option.[72] Similarly in *Russia*, there is a strong

---

67 P. Kotiswaran, India, in this volume, pp. 469–498; S. Hongladarom, Thailand, in this volume, pp. 504, 507.

68 N. Cahn and J. Carbone, United States of America, in this volume, p. 324.

69 O. Khazova, Russia, in this volume, p. 291.

70 R. Schuz, Israel, in this volume, pp. 171–172.

71 See, for example, T. Noree, J. Hanefeld and R. Smith, 'Medical Tourism in Thailand: A Cross-Sectional Study' (2016) 94 *Bulletin of the World Health Organization* 30.

72 R. Schuz, Israel, in this volume, pp. 168–169, 173.

emphasis on family formation, and assisted reproduction is enshrined as a legal right for adult women, should they need it to start a family. Moreover, surrogacy is not framed in the language of 'gift relationship' or 'labour of love' as it is in many Western jurisdictions, but instead is seen as a job, deserving of compensation (or more) as with any other.[73]

2.2.2. *Compensated*

Of those jurisdictions that do permit surrogacy, the compensation model is by far the most popular. As discussed above, this is often described as 'altruistic', but the term 'compensated' or 'paid' better describes the practice.

The *Greek* regulatory system provides an example of this difference. Commercial surrogacy agreements, where the surrogate is promised 'remuneration' are unlawful in *Greece*, however, the reimbursement of all costs related to achieving pregnancy, to the pregnancy itself and post-partum period are not considered as remuneration. In addition, the surrogate may be granted compensation for her lost profits due to the pregnancy – even if she is unemployed, where the compensation will be assessed on the basis of the (hypothetical) salary she would get, if she were employed in a position which corresponded with her qualifications.[74] This goes further than other jurisdictions which allow payments for loss of earnings – for example *South Africa*, some *Australian* states, and a proposed *Taiwanese* Bill – by actually providing an income where there otherwise would be none.

Even where such compensation is not expressly permitted, the courts in some jurisdictions have taken a rather inventive interpretative approach to what is a 'reasonable expense', and what is a commercial arrangement. An example of this can be seen in *England*. Although ostensibly the legislation in this jurisdiction is based on the idea of a 'gift relationship', and it is considered inconsistent with human dignity for a woman's womb to be used for financial profit, the court can authorise the payment of 'reasonable expenses' made by the commissioning parents to the surrogate. The level of expenses is judged by the court when deciding whether to make a Parental Order, transferring parenthood from the surrogate to the commissioning parents. Given that the child's welfare must be the paramount consideration in coming to its decision, there is little choice for the court to do anything but make the order, no matter what the sums paid.[75]

---

73 O. Khazova, Russia, in this volume, pp. 282, 290.

74 Although this may not exceed €10,000: see E. Zervogianni, Greece, in this volume, p. 151.

75 C. Fenton-Glynn, England and Wales, in this volume, pp. 119–122. Hong Kong also contains the same provision on 'reasonable expenses' but how this would be interpreted in practice is unclear (D. Cheung, Hong Kong, in this volume, p. 436).

Courts have shown similar inventiveness in *New Zealand*. In this jurisdiction, commissioning parents must apply for an adoption order in order to gain legal parenthood of a child born through surrogacy. Under the Adoption Act, it is not lawful to give any payment or reward in consideration of the adoption, except with the consent of the court. When faced with adoptions flowing from a surrogacy arrangement where payments are involved, courts have determined that since the payments related to the surrogacy and not to the adoption, then the legislation had not been breached. In one case, the judge classified the payments of NZ$20,000 for pain and inconvenience and NZ$5,000 for general expenses as amounting to a 'paid' surrogacy arrangement as opposed to a 'commercial' surrogacy arrangement – though it is not clear on what basis that distinction was drawn.[76]

Other jurisdictions have been more prescriptive in what types of costs and expenses are permitted, in an effort to provide greater clarity and prevent commercial agreements through the back-door.

For example, in *Australia*, the state jurisdictions list expenses that can be reimbursed.[77] Although these vary from state to state, they include costs associated with the pregnancy and the birth and care of the child, as well as costs of counselling, legal advice and applications for parentage orders; as well as of health, disability and life insurance; and a limited amount of lost earnings.[78] In *South Africa*, such a list has been developed by case law, rather than set out in the legislation itself. Permitted payments include costs related to the artificial fertilisation, pregnancy and birth; insurance for the surrogate; loss of earnings; and legal costs. While these seem very general, the courts have cautioned against simply presenting the agreement as providing a lump sum to the surrogate, rather than itemised expenses, as this could disguise the payment of compensation.[79]

In order to combat commercial payments disguised as expenses, *Portuguese* law provides that all expenses must be itemised, be duly certified in a specific document and be accepted by the Council before they can be reimbursed.[80] Likewise, both the proposed *Icelandic* and *Taiwanese* draft Bills contain a list of types of costs that could be covered, with the anticipation that there would be certain limits for such costs set by the competent authorities.[81]

76 D. Wilson, New Zealand, in this volume, p. 211.

77 Save Victoria, which refers to costs 'actually incurred … as a direct consequence of entering into the surrogacy arrangement' (see M. Keyes, Australia, in this volume, p. 91).

78 M. Keyes, Australia, in this volume, p. 91.

79 J. Sloth-Nielsen, South Africa, in this volume, p. 196.

80 R. Teixeira Pedro, Portugal, in this volume, pp. 239–240.

81 H. Friðriksdóttir, Iceland, in this volume, pp. 268–269; C. Ho, Taiwan, in this volume, pp. 389–390.

2.2.3. *Truly Altruistic*

The final jurisdiction, in a category of its own, is *India*. Under the Surrogacy (Regulation) Bill before Parliament at the time of writing, commercial surrogacy is explicitly prohibited. Commercial surrogacy is defined as giving payment in cash or kind except for the payment of medical expenses and the insurance coverage for the surrogate.[82] Of the jurisdictions canvassed, this would then become the only one that practices surrogacy on a truly altruistic basis – perhaps linked with the requirement that the surrogate be a 'close relative' of the commissioning parents, rather than the much more common use of strangers in other jurisdictions.

3. LEGAL PARENTHOOD AND INFORMATION ON ORIGINS

3.1. LEGAL PARENTHOOD AT THE TIME OF BIRTH

In the prohibitive jurisdictions of *France*, *Germany*, *Spain*, *PR China* and *Singapore*, legal parenthood at birth is assigned according to normal rules of parenthood.[83] The same applies in the tolerant jurisdictions of *Australia*, *England* and *Hong Kong*,[84] and the jurisdictions where surrogacy is controlled by the medical authorities, *South Korea* and *Japan*.[85] This results in the surrogate being the legal mother at birth, along with her husband (if she has one).

In the regulated and free market jurisdictions, however, specialised laws make provision for legal parenthood to be vested in the commissioning parents from the moment of birth. This is the case in *California* (provided the contract has been confirmed by a court),[86] the proposed *Indian* Bill (once a court has issued a certificate)[87] and the new *Thai* law.[88] A slight difference is found in *South Africa* and *Greece*: following confirmation of the agreement by the appropriate authorities, the commissioning parents will be the legal parents from birth. However, if the surrogate is genetically related to the child, she can challenge

82 P. Kotiswaran, India, in this volume, p. 485.

83 W. Pintens, France, in this volume, p. 19; A. Dutta, Germany, in this volume, pp. 38–41; E. Farnós Amorós, Spain, in this volume, pp. 62–63; L. Shi, China, in this volume, pp. 363–365; T. Kaan, Singapore, in this volume, pp. 406–411.

84 M. Keyes, Australia, in this volume, pp. 91–92; C. Fenton-Glynn, England and Wales, in this volume, p. 121; D. Cheung, Hong Kong, in this volume, p. 433.

85 O-J. Kim and B-H. Lee, South Korea, in this volume, pp. 450–451; S. Hayakawa, Japan, in this volume, pp. 441–443.

86 N. Cahn and J. Carbone, United States of America, in this volume, p. 324.

87 P. Kotiswaran, India, in this volume, pp. 486–487.

88 S. Hongladarom, Thailand, in this volume, p. 508.

this within 60 days (*South Africa*)[89] or six months (*Greece*),[90] and parental rights will revert to her.

Portuguese law had provided that the commissioning parents would be assigned legal parenthood on birth; however, this was declared unconstitutional by the Constitutional Court, which held that the surrogate *must* have the opportunity to change her mind post-birth, even if the surrogacy contract has been confirmed pre-birth before the National Council for Medically-Assisted Procreation.[91] Similarly, in *New Zealand*, despite requiring authorisation before proceeding with a surrogacy arrangement, the surrogate retains her parental rights until the commissioning parents are granted an adoption order.[92] *Iceland's* proposed Bill would also have introduced a similar system – a pre-birth authorisation, but parenthood still assigned to the surrogate at birth, who could then choose whether to give her consent to the commissioning parents becoming the legal parents.[93]

These three jurisdictions therefore present a hybrid model of surrogacy regulation. Rather than isolating the decision-making either completely pre- or post-birth, it contains seemingly attractive elements of both. By continuing to assign parenthood to the surrogate at birth, it avoids the objections of those that believe the surrogate should not be contractually obliged to hand over the child. At the same time, by requiring pre-birth authorisation, it does not have the drawbacks of trying to control eligibility and payments post-birth, when the welfare of the child precludes any taking concrete action.[94]

Two of the jurisdictions discussed in this volume take a very different approach than the rest. In *Russia*, there is no binding rule on who is the legal parent at birth – instead, this is assigned to whoever is listed on the birth certificate. This can be the surrogate, if she so wishes, or it can be the commissioning parents, with the surrogate's consent. This is organised by the parties between themselves, with no judicial or administrative intervention.[95] In *Israel*, instead of assigning parenthood at birth, a social worker is named as the child's guardian until the Parental Order is granted to the commissioning parents. The parental order must be applied for within seven days of birth, and the court must make this order unless it is satisfied, after receiving a report from a social worker, that this course of action would not be consistent with the welfare of the child.[96]

---

[89] J. Sloth-Nielsen, South Africa, in this volume, p. 191.
[90] E. Zervogianni, Greece, in this volume, p. 152.
[91] R. Teixeira Pedro, Portugal, in this volume, pp. 236–237.
[92] D. Wilson, New Zealand, in this volume, pp. 212, 217.
[93] H. Friðriksdóttir, Iceland, in this volume, p. 269.
[94] For a greater discussion of the different approaches to this area, see Section 8.2.3.
[95] Although sometimes a court order is needed if the commissioning parents are not married, although this is a grey area where the requirements remain unclear (O. Khazova, Russia, in this volume, pp. 292–294).
[96] R. Schuz, Israel, in this volume, p. 177.

3.2. PRESERVATION OF INFORMATION CONCERNING A SURROGATE

In recent years, there has been a strong emphasis in international children's rights law on the importance of access to information on origins. In relation to surrogacy, this can be two-fold: access to information on genetic origins, and access to information on the surrogate. This can be seen in the proposed *Icelandic* Bill, under which parents would be obliged to inform the child of the surrogacy arrangement before the child reaches the age of six. Furthermore, the child can access information about this arrangement, including on gamete donors, at the age of 16.[97]

In *England*, although there is no obligation to tell a child they have been born through surrogacy, the child can find out this information through official records. As the legal mother at birth, the surrogate will be listed on the original birth certificate, and the child will be issued a new, amended, version when the Parental Order is made transferring parenthood to the commissioning parents. The child can access their original birth certificate once they reach 18. Donor-conceived children can also access non-identifying information on donors at 16, and identifying information at 18.[98]

Likewise, in *Russia*, there will not be any indication on the birth certificate that the child has been born as a result of a surrogacy arrangement, but information on the surrogacy and the surrogate is kept in the registry books. Children born through surrogacy can access these records once they reach 18. However, as discussed below in Section 4.4.3. if the child is born of donated gametes, and the donor chooses to remain anonymous, the child will not be able to access this information.[99] Similarly, in *Israel*, the name of the surrogate, together with her identity number, nationality and religion are recorded in the register of Parental Orders, which the child can access once they reach 18. They will not similarly be able to access information on gamete donors – children born through donated gametes can apply to be informed whether there is a genetic relationship between themselves and a potential marriage partner, but no other identifying information can be obtained.[100]

Conversely, in *South Africa*, the child has the right to access information concerning their genetic parents when they reach 18. However, the identity of the surrogate, if she is not the genetic parent (and she usually will not be) is not disclosed.[101]

---

97 H. Friðriksdóttir, Iceland, in this volume, p. 273.

98 C. Fenton-Glynn, England and Wales, in this volume, p. 129.

99 O. Khazova, Russia, in this volume, pp. 294–295.

100 R. Schuz, Israel, in this volume, pp. 172, 176–177.

101 J. Sloth-Nielsen, South Africa, in this volume, p. 196.

In *India*, the draft Bill proposes that the appropriate authority must maintain details of surrogacy arrangements – but there is no provision for children to access this information. This may be due to the fact that because only a 'close relative' will be able to act as a surrogate under this Bill, the child will know the woman who has acted as the surrogate in any case.[102] Similarly, in *Greece*, although anonymity is not expressly guaranteed to the surrogate, there is no rule granting the child the possibility to access the relevant information, nor can the child access information on gamete donations.[103]

On the other hand, under the new *Thai* law, no information is preserved on either the surrogate, or the gamete donors. The child will therefore not have any mechanism for finding out information on their genetic and biological origins, save that which the commissioning parents are able, or willing, to provide.[104]

4. ELIGIBILITY FOR SURROGACY

4.1. ELIGIBILITY CRITERIA FOR WOMEN ACTING AS A SURROGATE

4.1.1. Genetic Relationship

In *Russia*, *Portugal*, the *Australian* jurisdictions of *Victoria* and the *Australian Capital Territory*, and under the proposed *Icelandic* Bill, surrogacy can only be gestational – that is, the genetic material of the surrogate cannot be used in the surrogacy.[105] One rationale behind this is to prevent surrogates having the 'double' parental claim of gestation and genetics – which in turn may make her more likely to want to keep the child; another presumably is to prevent situations where the surrogate is, at least from one point of view, seen as 'selling' not only her services but also her gametes, and also to prevent the circumvention of adoption laws.

In *South Africa*, having a genetic relationship will change the nature of the surrogacy arrangement, and thus the rules concerning legal parenthood. As discussed above, where the surrogate has a genetic relationship with the child, she may be able to change her mind and keep the child within the first 60 days after birth, whereas this option would not be available to her if she was 'merely' a gestational carrier.[106] This is also the case in *Greece*, although by law only

102 P. Kotiswaran, India, in this volume, p. 487.
103 E. Zervogianni, Greece, in this volume, pp. 158–159.
104 S. Hongladarom, Thailand, in this volume, pp. 507–508.
105 O. Khazova, Russia, in this volume, p. 295; R. Teixeira Pedro, Portugal, in this volume, p. 241; M. Keyes, Australia, in this volume, p. 97; H. Friðriksdóttir, Iceland, in this volume, p. 271.
106 J. Sloth-Nielsen, South Africa, in this volume, pp. 191–192.

gestational surrogacy is permitted; but where the surrogate's genetic material nevertheless has been used, she can challenge the legal parenthood of the commissioning parents within six months of birth.[107]

4.1.2. Relationship with Commissioning Parents

In most of the jurisdictions covered, there are no provisions concerning the existence, or lack thereof, of a relationship between the surrogate and the commissioning parents. The notable exceptions to this are the new *Thai* law, and the proposed *Indian* Bill. Under the *Indian* Bill, the surrogate must be a close relative of the commissioning parents,[108] whereas in *Thailand*, the surrogate must be related by blood (although not a parent or child of the commissioning parents).[109] An exception to this is only available where neither of the commissioning parents have any blood relatives. These provisions are a reaction to the previous widespread commercial surrogacy in these jurisdictions, which were subsequently shut down due to concerns regarding exploitation of the women involved. In response to this, the restriction to relatives ensures that surrogacy cannot revert to the commercial industry it once was, and is confined within the private sphere.

On the other end of the scale, under the *Icelandic* Bill, neither the surrogate nor her spouse can be siblings, or in direct lineage with the commissioning parent that supplies any gametes. This is intended to decrease the likelihood of undue pressure on the surrogate to enter into an arrangement.[110] Similarly, in *Israel* the surrogate *cannot* be a relative of either of the commissioning parents. This prohibition is due to the complications that would otherwise arise concerning the child's status under Jewish law, and was one of the factors that led to the decision that commercial surrogacy *should* be permitted in that jurisdiction. Also for reasons concerning Jewish law, *Israel* requires that the surrogate be of the same religion as the commissioning mother, unless none of the parties are Jewish and the cleric on the Committee approving the arrangement agrees.[111]

A unique provision has been introduced in *Portuguese* law, prohibiting surrogacy arrangements between commissioning parents and surrogates where there is a 'relationship of economic subordination', namely a labour/employment relationship.[112] The aim of this condition is to safeguard the autonomy of the surrogate, protecting her against economic pressure to enter into a surrogacy

---

107 E. Zervogianni, Greece, in this volume, p. 152.
108 P. Kotiswaran, India, in this volume, p. 488.
109 S. Hongladarom, Thailand, in this volume, p. 507.
110 H. Fridriksdóttir, Iceland, in this volume, pp. 271–272.
111 R. Schuz, Israel, in this volume, p. 173.
112 R. Teixeira Pedro, Portugal, in this volume, p. 241.

arrangement. Of course, the employment relationship is only one, very narrow, form of economic pressure that a surrogate may be exposed to, but it does provide protection for those in that situation.

4.1.3. *Marital Status*

Two jurisdictions covered – *Israel* and the proposed *Indian* Bill – make marital status a condition of eligibility for a surrogate.

In *Israel*, the surrogate cannot be married, although an exception can be made by the Committee if it is satisfied that the commissioning parents could not with reasonable effort locate an unmarried surrogate. Again, this relates to religious restrictions. It is not entirely clear that a child born to a married Jewish surrogate is not treated like a child born from an adulterous or incestuous relationship (*mamzer*). The majority view is that a child born as a result of IVF cannot be a *mamzer* because there was no forbidden sexual contact, but a minority opinion takes the view that the status derives from the presence of a forbidden man's gametes in the married woman's womb. As a result, to avoid any doubt, the law requires that the surrogate not be married.[113]

In *India*, on the other hand, the proposed Bill would require that the surrogate be 'ever married'. Although it is unclear what this term means, it is presumed to require the surrogate to be in an existing marriage.[114]

Even in those jurisdictions where marital status is not a part of the eligibility criteria, it can still play an important role in the choice of surrogate, and the subsequent parenthood of the child. For example, in *England*, where the surrogate is married, her husband becomes the legal father on birth (provided he has consented to the treatment), no matter the genetic relationship, and therefore must give his consent to the transfer of parenthood to the commissioning parents.[115] This is also the case in *Australia*, *Hong Kong*, the *Icelandic* Bill, *Japan*, *New Zealand* and *PR China*.

4.1.4. *Age Limits*

An age limit for the surrogate is present in many of the jurisdictions considered. This is sometimes set as a minimum – for example *Hong Kong* (21)[116] and *Australia* (25 in most states)[117] – or a maximum – for example *South Korea* (45)[118] and *Portugal* (50).[119] Other jurisdictions set both minimum and maximum ages

113 R. Schuz, Israel, in this volume, p. 173.
114 P. Kotiswaran, India, in this volume, p. 488.
115 C. Fenton-Glynn, England and Wales, in this volume, p. 122.
116 D. Cheung, Hong Kong, in this volume, p. 434.
117 M. Keyes, Australia, in this volume, p. 94.
118 O-J. Kim and B-H. Lee, South Korea, in this volume, p. 462.
119 R. Teixeira Pedro, Portugal, in this volume, p. 249.

for the surrogate – 22–38 in *Israel*,[120] 20–35 in *Russia*,[121] 25–35 under the *Indian* Bill[122] and 25–39 under the *Icelandic* Bill.[123]

The maximum ages are in place for the purpose of ensuring the health of the surrogate, and the viability of the pregnancy. For the minimum age, the purpose of restrictions is not as clear, although may be due to the desire to ensure that the surrogate has had some life experience and is of sufficient maturity to understand the gravity of what she is entering into. This, in turn, ties in with another eligibility criterion – that the surrogate has had a previous birth.

4.1.5. Family and Previous Birth

In *Thailand*, under the *Indian* Bill and the *Australian* jurisdictions of *Tasmania*, *Victoria* and *Western Australia*, the law requires that the surrogate must have had a child in order to undertake a surrogacy agreement.[124] In *Russia*, this is even framed in the present tense – the surrogate must *have* one child, and that child must be 'healthy'.[125] Likewise, in *South Africa*, the surrogate must have had at least one pregnancy and a viable delivery, as well as having a living child.[126] In *Israel*, the surrogate must have given birth at least once, but the law also sets a maximum of no more than four times.[127]

The proposed *Icelandic* Bill is even more prescriptive, requiring that the surrogate must have had at least one child following a 'normal' pregnancy and birth, and her youngest child must be at least two years old. Her last pregnancy must not have terminated unexpectedly or with a still birth, and she must not have lost a child within the past two years.[128] In *New Zealand*, on the other hand, prior births or existing children are not strict criteria for eligibility, but before the Ethics Committee allows the surrogacy arrangement to go ahead, it must take into account whether the surrogate has completed her family. This criterion presumably is in place to provide greater certainty that the surrogate will not change her mind and decide to keep the child.[129]

Two jurisdictions also place a limit on the number of surrogacy arrangements a surrogate can enter into. In *Israel*, this is not more than twice

120 R. Schuz, Israel, in this volume, p. 173.
121 O. Khazova, Russia, in this volume, p. 295.
122 P. Kotiswaran, India, in this volume, p. 488.
123 H. Friðriksdóttir, Iceland, in this volume, p. 270.
124 S. Hongladarom, Thailand, in this volume, p. 504; P. Kotiswaran, India, in this volume, p. 488; M. Keyes, Australia, in this volume, p. 95.
125 O. Khazova, Russia, in this volume, p. 295.
126 J. Sloth-Nielsen, South Africa, in this volume, p. 192.
127 R. Schuz, Israel, in this volume, p. 173.
128 H. Friðriksdóttir, Iceland, in this volume, p. 270.
129 D. Wilson, New Zealand, in this volume, p. 214.

previously[130] while in *India* under the proposed Bill, a woman can only act as a surrogate (or give gametes away) once in her lifetime.[131]

4.1.6. *Medical and Psychological Wellbeing*

A common eligibility requirement for surrogates is confirmation that she is medically fit to undertake the surrogacy. In *Greece*, the surrogate must be in a physical and psychological condition that allows her to bear a child,[132] while in *South Korea*, the surrogate must be a healthy woman, who has no physical or other obstacles to pregnancy or childbirth.[133] In *Iceland*, the draft Bill proposes that the surrogate be of sufficient mental and physical health to be able to undertake fertility treatment, pregnancy and birth with only standard risks,[134] and in *Hong Kong*, there must be 'no high medical risk'.[135] Finally, in *Thailand*, it must be confirmed that the body, mental health and environment of the surrogate is 'ready' to undertake a surrogacy, and that she does not have any hereditary or other diseases.[136]

In addition to certifying the surrogate's physical suitability, in *South Africa*, the court must be provided with a report from a clinical psychologist.[137] Further, to ensure that the surrogate is psychologically prepared, in *New Zealand* and the *Australian* states of *New South Wales* and *Western Australia*, the surrogate must have received counselling.[138]

In *Russia*, *South Africa* and the *Australian* states of *South Australia* and *Western Australia*, the requirement is rather more general, referring to a 'satisfactory state of health' (*Russia*),[139] or simply being 'suitable to act as a surrogate' (*South Africa*, *South Australia* and *Western Australia*).[140] This phrase 'suitable to act as a surrogate' has been particularly important in the *South African* context, where courts in their pre-approval process have been willing to probe in some detail the suitability of would-be surrogates. For example, in one case, the court found that a prospective surrogate was ineligible to enter into a surrogacy arrangement, due to concerns regarding her psycho-social status: the fact that she did not appear to made good decisions in her best interests

---

130 R. Schuz, Israel, in this volume, p. 173.
131 P. Kotiswaran, India, in this volume, p. 488.
132 E. Zervogianni, Greece, in this volume, p. 153.
133 O-J. Kim and B-H. Lee, South Korea, in this volume, p. 462.
134 H. Friðriksdóttir, Iceland, in this volume, p. 270.
135 D. Cheung, Hong Kong, in this volume, pp. 431, 434.
136 S. Hongladarom, Thailand, in this volume, p. 503.
137 J. Sloth-Nielsen, South Africa, in this volume, pp. 190, 193.
138 D. Wilson, New Zealand, in this volume, p. 215; M. Keyes, Australia, in this volume, p. 95.
139 O. Khazova, Russia, in this volume, p. 295.
140 J. Sloth-Nielsen, South Africa, in this volume, p. 193; M. Keyes, Australia, in this volume, p. 95.

as a teenager (including marrying at 13, dropping out of school at 16, and having two children before the age of 20), and the fact that there was nothing in the papers to indicate that she had gained the maturity to understand the implications of her decisions.[141]

This is one of the advantages of a pre-approval system, as it gives the court the ability to thoroughly and diligently scrutinise the eligibility and suitability of surrogates (and commissioning parents, on which see Section 4.3. below), without their options being narrowed – almost to the point that there are no options but to recognise the legal parenthood of the commissioning parents – by concerns about the welfare of a child who is already in existence.

4.1.7. *Residency or Domicile*

In terms of the residence of the surrogate, *Israel* requires that the surrogate be a resident, while *South Africa* requires that the surrogate be domiciled in the jurisdiction, with the clear intention that these jurisdictions do not become destinations for reproductive tourism.[142] *Greece* also previously required domicile on the part of the surrogate – again to prevent reproductive tourism – but has since relaxed these rules to allow an arrangement where either the surrogate or the commissioning mother has domicile or temporary residence in Greece. This was seen as a pragmatic change, recognising that domicile was not difficult to prove in practice, and that reproductive tourism was an inevitability given Greece's more permissive rules than any other western European jurisdictions.[143]

The proposed *Icelandic* Bill would require legal domicile and continuous lawful residence for the previous five years. This requirement is meant not only to deter reproductive tourism to *Iceland*, but also to ensure that all the parties involved are informed of social conditions and attitudes in Iceland and more likely to fully comprehend all elements of the surrogacy arrangement.[144]

4.1.8. *Other Eligibility Criteria*

In *Hong Kong*, the *Icelandic* Bill, *South Africa*, *Thailand* and *Russia*, there is a requirement that the surrogate's husband consent to her entering into the surrogacy arrangement.[145] While this may be understandable in the former

---

141 J. Sloth-Nielsen, South Africa, in this volume, p. 193.

142 J. Sloth-Nielsen, South Africa, in this volume, p. 187.

143 E. Zervogianni, Greece, in this volume, p. 154.

144 H. Friðriksdóttir, Iceland, in this volume, p. 269.

145 D. Cheung, Hong Kong, in this volume, p. 434; H. Fridriksdóttir, Iceland, in this volume, p. 270; J. Sloth-Nielsen, South Africa, in this volume, p. 187; S. Hongladarom, Thailand, in this volume, p. 504; O. Khazova, Russia, in this volume, p. 295.

two jurisdictions, where the husband would become a legal parent upon birth, in the latter jurisdictions, where the commissioning parents are deemed the legal parents, this appears rather paternalistic.

In *South Africa*, the surrogate must not be using the surrogacy as a source of income, reinforcing the requirement that the agreement is altruistic, rather than commercial.[146] Similarly, under the *Icelandic* proposed Bill, the surrogate must have good financial and social conditions.[147]

In *South Africa*, police clearance must have been obtained in relation to the surrogate. It is interesting to note here that while the surrogate – who will not get to keep the child – cannot have such a record, there is no similar limitation on the commissioning parents.[148]

4.2. CHARACTERISTICS OF SURROGATES

In very few jurisdictions is information available concerning the characteristics of women who act as surrogates. This is due to a variety of factors, including the private nature of the procedure (for not only the commissioning parents, but also the surrogate and resulting child), the fact that traditional surrogacy can be undertaken without any medical intervention, and the fact that in many jurisdictions official involvement is not required, leaving the practice largely in the shadows.

In her report on *Russia*, Olga A. Khazova noted that there is no reliable research in this area, but in the opinion of a manager of one of Saint-Petersburg's surrogacy firms, the surrogates 'are young, lower- or lower-middle-class women with no higher education. They generally do not have enough money to support their family and no education to find a good job'. It was also noted that 'they are typically single, divorced or widowed women from small towns'.[149]

In relation to *India*, Prabha Kotiswaran observed that the popular perception of women resorting to surrogacy out of poverty is not born out by the empirical evidence. This is because very poor women are not in sufficiently good health to meet clinics' requirements for healthy surrogates. Instead surrogates tend to be working-class women in their 20s and 30s, who are married, already have children, have sympathetic husbands to help with the household and have adequate resources for taking care of the surrogate's children without making demands on the surrogate when she is in the surrogates' hostel. Of course, given the recent changes to the law in this India, this profile is bound to change.[150]

---

146 J. Sloth-Nielsen, South Africa, in this volume, p. 193.
147 H. Friðriksdóttir, Iceland, in this volume, p. 269.
148 J. Sloth-Nielsen, South Africa, in this volume, p. 190.
149 O. Khazova, Russia, in this volume, p. 296.
150 P. Kotiswaran, India, in this volume, pp. 488–489.

In *Israel* and *Greece*, there have been more comprehensive studies undertaken of women acting as surrogates, facilitated by the regulatory system requiring all applications to go through the appropriate authority. In *Israel*, research on a sample of 275 surrogacy applications submitted between 1996 and 2002 found that 75 per cent of the surrogates were divorcees, with an average age of 31. Thirty per cent were born abroad (with 20 per cent from the former Soviet Union), and only seven per cent had post-high school education. Twenty-five per cent did not work, and another 33 per cent worked in menial jobs. Unsurprisingly in a jurisdiction that permits commercial surrogacy, 80 per cent stated that their motive for participating in the process was financial.[151] This research is now 17 years old, and it is not clear whether this profile has remained consistent since that time. Nevertheless, it provides an interesting insight into the socio-economic circumstances of the women acting as surrogates, and their motive for doing so.

In *Greece*, a study of 248 court decisions that granted authorisation to surrogacy in the years 2003–2016 found that the average age of surrogates was almost 35, with almost half married, and more than half having children of their own. Two-thirds were foreign nationals, mostly from other countries in Eastern Europe. Where Greek nationals were acting as surrogates, they were on average more likely to be older and married compared to foreign surrogates. A quarter of surrogates were a relative of the intended mother, in another half, she was a 'close friend' or previously employed by her (for example, as household help).[152]

It is difficult to draw any clear conclusions from such scarce information, save for the more general point that there is a vital need for more research in this area. A lot of assumptions are made concerning the profile of surrogates, and conclusions concerning surrogacy drawn from this, and it is imperative that we have comprehensive and up-to-date empirical evidence in order to legislate appropriately.

4.3. ELIGIBILITY CRITERIA FOR COMMISSIONING PARENTS

4.3.1. Marital Status

In *Hong Kong*, *Israel* and *South Korea* only an opposite-sex married couple can enter into a surrogacy arrangement.[153] In *Thailand*, there is the additional

151 R. Schuz, Israel, in this volume, p. 174.
152 E. Zervogianni, Greece, in this volume, pp. 154–155.
153 D. Cheung, Hong Kong, in this volume, p. 434; R. Schuz, Israel, in this volume, p. 174; O-J. Kim and B-H. Lee, South Korea, in this volume, p. 462.

requirement that the couple have been married for at least three years, if one of the couple is not a Thai citizen;[154] in *India* under the proposed Bill, the couple must have been married for five years.[155] By contrast, in *Greece*, *Russia* and the Australian states of *South Australia* and *Western Australia*, surrogacy is extended to unmarried opposite-sex couples also.[156]

In *New Zealand*, only couples who are married or de facto partners (i.e. qualifying cohabitants) can enter into a surrogacy arrangement together, but these can be same-sex or opposite-sex partnerships.[157] Likewise in *Iceland* under the proposed Bill, the couple – same-sex or opposite-sex – must have lived together for three years prior to the application.[158] On the other hand, in *Portugal*, both married and unmarried couples may apply, but they must either be in an opposite sex-relationship, or a same-sex relationship involving two women – two men cannot enter into a surrogacy arrangement.[159]

The most liberal in terms of the ability of couples to enter into surrogacy arrangements are *England* and *South Africa*, which allow any couple to enter into a surrogacy arrangement – married, unmarried, opposite- or same-sex.[160]

In relation to single commissioning parents, this is possible in all *Australian* states save *South Australia*, as well as in *England*, *New Zealand*, *Greece*, *South Africa*, *Russia* and under the *Icelandic* Bill.[161] However, in *Russia* and the state of *Western Australia* this is restricted to women only, and single men cannot apply, while in *New Zealand* single men can only adopt male children (unless special circumstances apply).[162]

4.3.2. Genetic Relationship

In most jurisdictions covered, there must be a genetic relationship between the commissioning parents and child. In *England*, the proposed *Icelandic* Bill,

---

154 S. Hongladarom, Thailand, in this volume, p. 503.

155 P. Kotiswaran, India, in this volume, p. 490.

156 E. Zervogianni, Greece, in this volume, p. 156; O. Khazova, Russia, in this volume, pp. 296–297; M. Keyes, Australia, in this volume, p. 96.

157 D. Wilson, New Zealand, in this volume, p. 216.

158 H. Friðriksdóttir, Iceland, in this volume, p. 270.

159 R. Teixeira Pedro, Portugal, in this volume, pp. 248–249. The differentiation between same-sex relationships involving two women, and those involving two men, raises questions regarding discrimination, and may be open to Constitutional challenge: see fn 68, ibid.

160 C. Fenton-Glynn, England and Wales, in this volume, pp. 123–124; J. Sloth-Nielsen, South Africa, in this volume, pp. 186–187.

161 M. Keyes, Australia, in this volume, p. 96; D. Wilson, New Zealand, in this volume, p. 215; E. Zervogianni, Greece, in this volume, pp. 156–157; J. Sloth-Nielsen, South Africa, in this volume, pp. 187–189; O. Khazova, Russia, in this volume, pp. 297–299; H. Friðriksdóttir, Iceland, in this volume, p. 270 (although this is only under special circumstances, and if the interests of the child are adequately secured).

162 D. Wilson, New Zealand, in this volume, pp. 215–216; O. Khazova, Russia, in this volume, pp. 298–299; M. Keyes, Australia, in this volume, p. 96.

Israel, *New Zealand*, *Portugal* and *Thailand*, a connection with only one commissioning parent is required – with *Israel* specifying that this must be the commissioning father.[163] In *Hong Kong* and *South Korea*, on the other hand, the gametes of both the commissioning mother and the commissioning father must be used in the surrogacy.[164] This limits the scope of fertility problems that can be resolved by surrogacy in these jurisdictions, as surrogacy is often sought where the commissioning mother is not only unable to carry a child, but whose gametes also are not viable.

In *California* and *Greece*, there is no need for the commissioning parents to have a genetic relationship with the child, while in *Russia*, the situation is unclear, but it is often the case in practice that there is no genetic relationship.[165] This was seen in the case of *Paradiso and Campanelli v Italy* before the European Court of Human Rights, where the 'family life' between the commissioning parents and child was not recognised, in part due to the lack of genetic link.[166]

In *South Africa*, there has been litigation concerning the requirement that both the commissioning parents be genetically connected to the child, or if that is not possible, at least one of them. A single woman, who was unable to use her own gametes, challenged the refusal to allow her to enter into a surrogacy arrangement, arguing that this violated her rights to equal treatment, and to reproductive autonomy. The Constitutional Court found that there was a rational reason behind this requirement – to ensure the child's best interests by creating a bond between the child and the commissioning parent, as well as preserving the child's right to know his or her genetic origins – and thus there was no discrimination. Controversially, it was further held that the applicant was not treated unfairly on the grounds of her infertility, as she could always enter into a relationship with a fertile person, and qualify for surrogacy with them.[167]

---

163 C. Fenton-Glynn, England and Wales, in this volume, p. 125; H. Friðriksdóttir, Iceland, in this volume, p. 271; R. Schuz, Israel, in this volume, p. 174; D. Wilson, New Zealand, in this volume, p. 215; R. Teixeira Pedro, Portugal, in this volume, pp. 249–250; S. Hongladarom, Thailand, in this volume, p. 504.

164 D. Cheung, Hong Kong, in this volume, p. 426; O-J. Kim and B-H. Lee, South Korea, in this volume, p. 462.

165 N. Cahn and J. Carbone, United States of America, in this volume, p. 326; E. Zervogianni, Greece, in this volume, p. 157; O. Khazova, Russia, in this volume, pp. 300–301.

166 *Paradiso and Campanelli v Italy*, no. 25358/12, 24.01.2017. See P. Beaumont and K. Trimmings, Surrogacy before the European Court of Human Rights, in this volume, pp. 332–354.

167 *AB and others v Minister of Social Development and Others (Centre for Child Law intervening as Amicus Curiae)* CCT 155/15; on this see J. Sloth-Nielsen, South Africa, in this volume, pp. 187–189.

4.3.3. Age Limits

A minimum age limit of 18 is set for commissioning parents in *Hong Kong*, *England* and the *Australian Capital Territory*;[168] 21 in the Australian state of *Tasmania*;[169] and 25 in *New Zealand*, *Western Australia* and *Queensland*.[170]

Other jurisdictions set an age range: for example the proposed *Icelandic* Bill requires commissioning parents to be between 25 and 45.[171] In *Portugal* and the draft *Indian* Bill, however, the age range differs depending on the gender of the commissioning parent – for commissioning mothers it is 23–50 in *India*, and 18–50 in *Portugal*, while for commissioning fathers, it is 26–55 in *India* and 18–60 in *Portugal*.[172] The reason for the different ages for men and women in these jurisdictions is not clear.

In *Greece* and *Israel*, the only restriction is on the maximum age of commissioning mothers, at 50 and 53 respectively.[173] In *Greece*, Zervogianni notes that this provision is meant to ensure the parents' capability to take good care of the child – which is likely to be the rationale behind other jurisdictions also, even if it is not explicitly stated.[174] Having said this, it is not clear why only the commissioning mother must be of an age that she can take care of the child: most likely this reflects patriarchal views concerning child-rearing.

4.3.4. Medical or Social Need

In the majority of jurisdictions discussed in this volume, there must be a medical need for the commissioning parents to enter into a surrogacy arrangement.

In *New Zealand*, surrogacy must be the best or only opportunity for the commissioning parent(s) to have a child, and reasons of personal or social convenience are explicitly ruled out.[175] In *South Africa*, the legislation refers to the inability to give birth to a child due to a permanent and irreversible condition;[176] in *Greece*, the legislation simply states that the commissioning couple cannot have a child in the 'natural' way.[177] In *Israel*, the commissioning

168 D. Cheung, Hong Kong, in this volume, p. 435; C. Fenton-Glynn, England and Wales, in this volume, p. 125; M. Keyes, Australia, in this volume, p. 95.
169 M. Keyes, Australia, in this volume, p. 95.
170 D. Wilson, New Zealand, in this volume, p. 219 – although this is lowered to 20 if the commissioning parent is a relative of the child; M. Keyes, Australia, in this volume, p. 95.
171 H. Friðriksdóttir, Iceland, in this volume, p. 271.
172 R. Teixeira Pedro, Portugal, in this volume, p. 249; P. Kotiswaran, India, in this volume, p. 490.
173 E. Zervogianni, Greece, in this volume, p. 155; R. Schuz, Israel, in this volume, p. 175.
174 E. Zervogianni, Greece, in this volume, p. 155.
175 D. Wilson, New Zealand, in this volume, p. 215.
176 J. Sloth-Nielsen, South Africa, in this volume, pp. 187, 194.
177 E. Zervogianni, Greece, in this volume, p. 155.

mother must have medical problems preventing her from bearing a child (or making it medically risky for her to do so), while under the *Icelandic* Bill, it must be impossible – for medical or biological reasons – for the commissioning mother to have a child through her own pregnancy.[178]

In *India* under the draft Bill, on the other hand, the commissioning parents must be 'infertile' – defined as an inability to conceive after five years of unprotected sex, or other proven medical condition preventing conception.[179] In *Russia* and *Hong Kong*, this is more general, referring to only a fertility problem or inability to carry a pregnancy to term.[180] In *South Korea*, the medical guidelines are much more prescriptive, setting out a list of specific medical issues that the commissioning mother must suffer from before she will be eligible to enter into a surrogacy (where she has no uterus; where there are severe risks to the mother's health during pregnancy due to major organ diseases; where there is endometrial damage due to severe endometriosis or uterine tuberculosis; or where there has been a repetitive failure in maintaining pregnancy, and thereby the possibility of pregnancy retention is very low).[181] Likewise, *Portugal* would require the absence of a uterus, injury or disease of this organ that absolutely and definitively prevents the woman's pregnancy or in clinical situations that justify it.[182]

In three Australian jurisdictions – *New South Wales*, *Queensland* and *Tasmania* – there must be a 'medical or social need' for the surrogacy arrangement. The 'medical' side of this requirement is similar to those above – requiring that the commissioning mother have a medical condition that prevents her from conceiving, or where carrying a child and/or giving birth would significantly affect her health. However, the law also explicitly provides for surrogacy arrangements where the commissioning parent will be a single man, or two men – in such case a medical condition will not have to be shown. Interestingly, these jurisdictions also make provision for a surrogacy arrangement to be permitted where the child would be affected by a genetic condition or disorder, the cause of which is attributable to the commissioning mother.[183]

In four of the jurisdictions in this volume, there is no requirement that there be any medical need for the commissioning parents to enter into a surrogacy arrangement – *England*, *Thailand*, *California* and the Australian jurisdiction

---

178 R. Schuz, Israel, in this volume, p. 174; H. Friðriksdóttir, Iceland, in this volume, p. 271.
179 P. Kotiswaran, India, in this volume, p. 490.
180 O. Khazova, Russia, in this volume, p. 296; D. Cheung, Hong Kong, in this volume, pp. 434–435.
181 O-J. Kim and B-H. Lee, South Korea, in this volume, p. 463.
182 R. Teixeira Pedro, Portugal, in this volume, pp. 234, 239.
183 M. Keyes, Australia, in this volume, p. 95.

of *Australian Capital Territory*.[184] Therefore in these jurisdictions, the commissioning parents could enter into a surrogacy arrangement for reasons of personal or social convenience. This is particularly the case in *California* where commercial surrogacy is permitted, therefore opening the door to the outsourcing of pregnancy and birth from rich women to those who are economically disadvantaged.

4.3.5. *Medical Fitness*

In addition to some jurisdictions requiring commissioning parents to show a medical need to enter into a surrogacy arrangement, some jurisdictions conversely require that they are medically fit to enter into the arrangement – and thus look after any resulting child.

In *Thailand*, it must be certified that the commissioning parents are ready in terms of their mind, bodies and environment, whereas under the *Icelandic* Bill they must show that they are in good mental and physical health.[185] In *South Africa* and the Australian state of *Western Australia*, the focus is on psychological health, requiring a confirmation of psychological suitability to enter into the surrogacy agreement prior to conception.[186]

4.3.6. *Pre-Existing Family*

In three jurisdictions covered, there are restrictions in place in relation to the number of children the commissioning parents already have. In *Israel*, the commissioning parents must not have more than two joint children, whereas under the *Icelandic* Bill, the commissioning parents must not have a child, or legal responsibility for a child, under the age of two.[187] The draft *Indian* Bill is the most restrictive in this respect: to enter into a surrogacy arrangement, commissioning parents may not have any surviving children. However, an exception is made when they have a child who is 'mentally or physically challenged' or suffers from a life-threatening disorder or fatal illness with no permanent cure.[188]

---

184 C. Fenton-Glynn, England and Wales, in this volume, p. 125; S. Hongladarom, Thailand, in this volume, p. 507; N. Cahn and J. Carbone, United States of America, in this volume, pp. 325–326; M. Keyes, Australia, in this volume, p. 95.

185 S. Hongladarom, Thailand, in this volume, p. 503; H. Friðriksdóttir, Iceland, in this volume, p. 270.

186 J. Sloth-Nielsen, South Africa, in this volume, p. 193; M. Keyes, Australia, in this volume, p. 96.

187 R. Schuz, Israel, in this volume, p. 175; H. Friðriksdóttir, Iceland, in this volume, p. 271.

188 P. Kotiswaran, India, in this volume, p. 490.

4.3.7. *Residence*

As with the eligibility of surrogates, many jurisdictions have put in place residence requirements for commissioning parents to avoid becoming a destination for reproductive tourism.

In *Israel* and the *Australian* jurisdictions commissioning parents must be residents, while in *Greece* they can be temporary residents.[189] *South Africa* and *England* are stricter with their criteria, requiring not just residence, but domicile.[190] Likewise, under the proposed *Icelandic* Bill, the commissioning parents must have been domiciled in the jurisdiction for the last five years.[191]

To enter into a surrogacy arrangement in *India* under the proposed Bill, or in *Thailand*, the commissioning parents must be citizens.[192] This is both narrower and wider than the other jurisdictions listed – it allows the (particularly Indian) diaspora to return to the jurisdiction to undertake a surrogacy, which would not be possible with residence or domicile, but simultaneously excludes foreigners, even if they have been living in the jurisdiction for some time.

4.3.8. *Criminal Record*

What is interesting is that in only one jurisdiction – the Australian state of *Victoria* – is a criminal record check conducted as part of the authorisation process for commissioning parents.[193] While in some jurisdictions this might nevertheless be covered by a more general 'suitability' or 'best interests of the child' criteria, in others, this seems not to be a consideration.

One reason for this may be that we conceptualise surrogacy as an extension of natural reproduction – since we do not stop people procreating naturally when they have a criminal record, then it would be discriminatory to do so simply because an individual (or their partner) has a fertility problem. On the other hand, since intervention – both medical and legal – is required in surrogacy, it could be argued that there is an obligation on the state to ensure that the commissioning parents will be able to provide a safe and loving home for the child. This issue came to the fore in Australia, when a paedophile specifically commissioned twin daughters for sexual abuse, or the Baby Gammy case,

---

189 R. Schuz, Israel, in this volume, p. 177; M. Keyes, Australia, in this volume, p. 96; E. Zervogianni, Greece, in this volume, pp. 154–155.

190 J. Sloth-Nielsen, South Africa, in this volume, p. 187; C. Fenton-Glynn, England and Wales, in this volume, p. 125 (for at least one of the commissioning parents).

191 H. Friðriksdóttir, Iceland, in this volume, p. 271.

192 P. Kotiswaran, India, in this volume, p. 490; S. Hongladarom, Thailand, in this volume, pp. 503, 507. The Thai law allows an exception where only one of the commissioning parents is a Thai citizen, as long as the couple have been married for three years.

193 M. Keyes, Australia, in this volume, p. 96.

where it was later revealed that the father had previous convictions for child sex offences.[194]

4.4. USE OF GAMETES

4.4.1. *Whose Gametes can be Used?*

In *Hong Kong* and *South Korea*, only gametes from the commissioning parents can be used, which obviously restricts surrogacy to only those couples where the commissioning mother has a problem carrying a pregnancy, rather than those where the cause of infertility is the egg or sperm itself.[195]

In those jurisdictions that do allow other gametes to be used, three discussed in this volume place restrictions on this. In *New Zealand*, the donor cannot be a member of the commissioning parents' family, if there is an inter-generational link between them.[196] In *Iceland*, under the proposed Bill, the gametes cannot come from siblings of the commissioning parents, or anyone in direct lineage to them. Moreover, not only is the surrogate not permitted to donate her gametes (see Section 4.1.1. above for more discussion on this in various jurisdictions), those in direct lineage to her (or her spouse/partner) are also prohibited.[197]

In *Israel*, the restrictions are more wide-ranging. Only donated eggs are permitted, not sperm; the donor must be aged 21–35, unmarried, and not related to the 'donee' – the surrogate. In addition, she must be of the same religion as the surrogate.[198]

4.4.2. *Payments for Gametes*

In two of the jurisdictions covered – *California* and *Russia* – there are no restrictions as to payments for gametes, and therefore this can be conducted on a commercial basis.[199] However, in *Australia*, *England*, *Greece*, the *Icelandic* Bill, *Israel*, *New Zealand* and *Portugal*, the gametes and embryos must be donated – although some of these jurisdictions also allow certain

194 J. Pascoe, A View from the Bench, in this volume, p. 107; S. Hongladarom, Thailand, in this volume, pp. 499–500. This issue will be discussed further in Section 8.2.4.2.
195 D. Cheung, Hong Kong, in this volume, p. 426; O-J. Kim and B-H. Lee, South Korea, in this volume, p. 462.
196 D. Wilson, New Zealand, in this volume, p. 216.
197 H. Friðriksdóttir, Iceland, in this volume, pp. 271–272.
198 R. Schuz, Israel, in this volume, pp. 176–177.
199 N. Cahn and J. Carbone, United States of America, in this volume, p. 326; O. Khazova, Russia, in this volume, p. 299.

remuneration or reimbursement.[200] For example, in *Israel*, this is set at 19,000 New Israeli Sheqel (NIS) for eggs (approximately £4,000), whereas in *Greece*, this is €2,000, and *England* £750.[201]

4.4.3. Anonymity

In *Russia*, donors can choose to be anonymous, and if they do so, children cannot gain any information on their genetic origins.[202] Similarly in *Greece*, donors are guaranteed anonymity, although the child is able to access non-identifying medical information, if this is deemed necessary for medical reasons.[203] In *Portugal*, anonymity again is guaranteed, but the court can disclose information if there are 'significant reasons' for doing so.[204]

Conversely, in *Australia*, *England* and *South Africa*, individuals born of surrogacy are able to access information about their genetic parents as of right. In *South Africa*, the child has the right to access information when they reach 18;[205] in *Australia*, identifying information can be given once the child reaches 18, or when they are sufficiently mature;[206] and in *England* a child can receive non-identifying information at 16, and identifying information at 18.[207]

In *Israel*, the focus on providing details of gamete donors is not to provide information on origins, but to prevent incestuous relationships. Israeli law set up a registry of children born through egg donations, and will inform adult applicants whether they were born as a result of such a donation, and if so, whether there is a genetic relationship between themselves and a potential marriage partner.[208]

5. TRANSFERRING PARENTHOOD

5.1. PROCESS FOR TRANSFERRING LEGAL PARENTHOOD

In *California*, *Greece* and *South Africa*, there is no need for a transfer of legal parenthood – the commissioning parents will already be the legal parents

---

200 M. Keyes, Australia, in this volume, pp. 96–97; C. Fenton-Glynn, England and Wales, in this volume, pp. 124–125; E. Zervogianni, Greece, in this volume, p. 158; R. Schuz, Israel, in this volume, p. 176; D. Wilson, New Zealand, in this volume, p. 216; R. Teixeira Pedro, Portugal, in this volume, p. 250.

201 R. Schuz, Israel, in this volume, p. 176; E. Zervogianni, Greece, in this volume, p. 158; C. Fenton-Glynn, England and Wales, in this volume, pp. 124–125.

202 O. Khazova, Russia, in this volume, pp. 299–300.

203 E. Zervogianni, Greece, in this volume, pp. 158–159.

204 R. Teixeira Pedro, Portugal, in this volume, p. 250.

205 J. Sloth-Nielsen, South Africa, in this volume, p. 196.

206 M. Keyes, Australia, in this volume, p. 98.

207 C. Fenton-Glynn, England and Wales, in this volume, p. 125.

208 R. Schuz, Israel, in this volume, p. 176.

at birth.[209] In *Portugal*, this was intended to be the case, but the Constitutional Court deemed this provision unconstitutional, ruling that the surrogate must be given a chance to change her mind and not consent to the transfer.[210] As discussed in Section 3.1. above, in *Russia*, the parties can simply decide between themselves who will be entered on the birth certificate. Thus there is no transfer of parenthood, and the parties have autonomy in this respect.[211]

In one jurisdiction, an administrative solution is proposed for the transfer of parenthood. The draft *Icelandic* Bill suggests that commissioning parents would have to apply to an administrative body within two months of the child's birth, which could then confirm their parenthood. Only if there was a dispute between the commissioning parents and surrogate would the parties have to go before the court, in which case the decision on parenthood would be made according to the child's best interests.[212]

More commonly, however, it is the court who bears sole responsibility for transferring legal parenthood – as can be seen in *Australia*, *England*, *Hong Kong*, *Israel* and under the proposed *Indian* Bill.[213] In *Israel*, this will simply be a post-birth confirmation of what the Approvals Committee has already authorised pre-birth. The commissioning parents must apply for parenthood to be recognised within seven days of birth, and the court must be satisfied that the order will be consistent with the welfare of the child. In practice, there are no known cases where the order has not been made.[214] In *India*, the proposed Bill requires a post-birth application to a magistrate by the commissioning parents and surrogate, although no further information is given on how this mechanism would work, or what conditions would have to be satisfied.[215]

In *Australia*, *England* and *Hong Kong*, commissioning parents must apply to the court for a 'parentage' (Australia) or 'parental' (England and Hong Kong) order within six months of birth, in order for parenthood to be transferred from the surrogate. In all these jurisdictions, the child must already be living with the applicants, and the surrogate (and any other legal parent) must have given their consent to the transfer. In *Australia* and *England*, when deciding whether to authorise the order, the court is guided by the paramountcy of the best interests

---

209 N. Cahn and J. Carbone, United States of America, in this volume, pp. 324, 326; E. Zervogianni, Greece, in this volume, p. 151; J. Sloth-Nielsen, South Africa, in this volume, p. 195.

210 R. Teixeira Pedro, Portugal, in this volume, pp. 236–237.

211 O. Khazova, Russia, in this volume, pp. 292–293.

212 H. Friðriksdóttir, Iceland, in this volume, pp. 272–273.

213 M. Keyes, Australia, in this volume, pp. 97–98; C. Fenton-Glynn, England and Wales, in this volume, pp. 125–127; D. Cheung, Hong Kong, in this volume, pp. 435–436; R. Schuz, Israel, in this volume, p. 177; P. Kotiswaran, India, in this volume, p. 493.

214 R. Schuz, Israel, in this volume, p. 177.

215 P. Kotiswaran, India, in this volume, p. 493.

of the child.[216] Interestingly, however, this is not required by the *Hong Kong* legislation.[217]

The difficulty – indeed one could almost say, the futility – with such a mechanism is that once the child is in existence, and has been handed over to the commissioning parents, it is rarely going to be in the child's best interests not to legally recognise that factual tie – no matter what the conduct of the commissioning parents has been.[218] Save in exceptional circumstances, we have seen that the child's welfare will generally override considerations of illegal payments, procedural irregularities, deception of authorities, or breach of eligibility requirements. Effectively the court is forced to rubber stamp behaviour that is explicitly prohibited by the legislation, in order to protect the child.

Where surrogacy is prohibited, commissioning parents have had to come up with inventive ways to achieve legal recognition of their parenthood. The most common of these is step-parent adoption – where the commissioning father will claim paternity based on his genetic relationship with the child, and the commissioning mother will then adopt the child. This can be seen in domestic cases in *France*, *Germany*, *South Korea* and *Spain*.[219] Obviously, such an ad hoc solution is only possible if the gametes of the commissioning father have been used – if not, then a 'stranger' adoption would be the only option. And this is what is used in *Japan* and *New Zealand* – adoption must be undertaken by both commissioning parents, rather than just the commissioning mother.[220] While this is a valuable mechanism for commissioning parents in jurisdictions where there is no other solution, as a mechanism for regulating surrogacy, it leaves much to be desired, as will be discussed in Section 8 below.

5.2. CAN THE SURROGATE CHANGE HER MIND?

In prohibitive jurisdictions – *France*, *Germany*, *Spain* and *Singapore* – the surrogate is indisputably the legal mother of the child, and this cannot be challenged by the commissioning parents.[221]

---

216 M. Keyes, Australia, in this volume, pp. 97–98; D. Cheung, Hong Kong, in this volume, pp. 435–436; C. Fenton-Glynn, England and Wales, in this volume, p. 125.

217 D. Cheung, Hong Kong, in this volume, pp. 435–436.

218 However, see the discussion of *Paradiso and Campanelli v Italy*, no. 25358/12, 24.01.2017 in P. Beaumont and K. Trimmings, Surrogacy before the European Court of Human Rights, in this volume, pp. 332–354.

219 W. Pintens, France, in this volume, p. 20; A. Dutta, Germany, in this volume, pp. 41–42, 44–45; O-J. Kim and B-H. Lee, South Korea, in this volume, p. 463; E. Farnós Amorós, Spain, in this volume, p. 65.

220 S. Hayakawa, Japan, in this volume, pp. 443–445; D. Wilson, New Zealand, in this volume, pp. 217–218.

221 W. Pintens, France, in this volume, p. 19; A. Dutta, Germany, in this volume, p. 39; E. Farnós Amorós, Spain, in this volume, p. 62; T. Kaan, Singapore, in this volume, pp. 406–409.

In tolerant jurisdictions such as *Australia* and *England*, the surrogate's consent is needed for the transfer of parenthood through the Parentage or Parental Order respectively. This consent cannot be dispensed with or overridden.[222] However, it is notable that in both these jurisdictions, the courts have nevertheless found ways to get around this by using private law ordering. That is, if the surrogate refuses her consent, the dispute becomes an issue of who should have 'custody' of the child – known as a 'parenting order' (*Australia*) or 'child arrangements order' (*England*) – with an order made in favour of whoever is best placed to bring up the child. In this way, although the commissioning parents will not gain legal parenthood, the surrogate still does not get to keep the child.[223] Similarly, in *PR China*, if the surrogate refuses to hand over the child, the commissioning father can apply for custody – but rather worryingly, considerations such as economic status will be brought into the determination of where the child should live.[224]

In *New Zealand*, where the transfer of parenthood is achieved through an adoption order, the surrogate's consent can be dispensed with if the court is satisfied that the parent or guardian (so in the case at hand the surrogate and her partner if she has one) has abandoned, neglected, persistently failed to maintain, or persistently ill-treated the child, or failed to exercise the normal duty and care of parenthood in respect of the child. This gives authorities slightly more scope to override the wishes of the surrogate, and remove parenthood from her against her will – although this is nevertheless a very high standard to meet.[225]

In *Greece*, *Israel* and *South Africa*, by virtue of the system of pre-birth approval, the circumstances in which the surrogate can change her mind and refuse to hand over the child are very narrow. In *Israel*, this can only occur if the court is satisfied that there has been a change in circumstances which justify her change of mind, and this will not harm the child's welfare – and in practice, no such cases have been reported.[226] In *Greece* and *South Africa*, as discussed above, the surrogate can only contest parenthood if she is genetically connected to the child – in which case she has six months or 60 days respectively to terminate the agreement, and keep the child.[227]

Interestingly, in *Russia*, a free market jurisdiction where commercial surrogacy is possible, and there is no oversight of surrogacy arrangements, the surrogate retains strong prima facie rights to parenthood. The surrogate has

---

222 M. Keyes, Australia, in this volume, p. 97; C. Fenton-Glynn, England and Wales, in this volume, pp. 125, 127.

223 M. Keyes, Australia, in this volume, p. 98; C. Fenton-Glynn, England and Wales, in this volume, pp. 128–129.

224 L. Shi, China, in this volume, p. 366.

225 D. Wilson, New Zealand, in this volume, pp. 219–220.

226 R. Schuz, Israel, in this volume, p. 177.

227 E. Zervogianni, Greece, in this volume, p. 152; J. Sloth-Nielsen, South Africa, in this volume, p. 191.

the choice as to whether to register the commissioning parents directly on the birth certificate, or whether to keep the child and register her own name. If she chooses the latter, it is not possible for the commissioning parents to contest parenthood, even if the surrogate has no genetic connection to the child.[228]

Under the proposed *Icelandic* Bill, parenthood of the commissioning parents can be confirmed, with the surrogate's consent, by administrative measures following birth. However, if the surrogate changes her mind, the case will go before the court, who will decide to whom parenthood should be awarded. However, there appears to be a preference in favour of the surrogate, with the proposal suggesting that parenthood could be transferred without the consent of the surrogate if the child is or has been in care of commissioning parents, and if the transfer would be highly in the child's favour. This moves away from a pure welfare assessment, and instead puts in place additional barriers that commissioning parents must overcome.[229]

The proposed *Taiwanese* law is remarkable for the weak position of the surrogate. While she can change her mind and renege on the agreement within the first 24 weeks of pregnancy, to do so she would have to have an abortion, rather than being able to keep the child herself. Moreover, if the commissioning couple decides that they don't want the child, the surrogate is only given 'preference' for adoption, rather than parental rights reverting to her automatically.[230]

5.3. CAN THE COMMISSIONING PARENTS CHANGE THEIR MINDS?

While most jurisdictions have considered how to deal with a situation in which the surrogate changes her mind and wishes to keep the child, few have explicitly dealt with the converse issue – where the commissioning parents decide they no longer want the child they have 'commissioned'. This seems odd, particularly given the express desire in many jurisdictions to protect the surrogate, but it seems that protection is only offered in case a child is 'wanted' by the surrogate, but not if she does *not* want to be the parent.

Two jurisdictions which have dealt with this issue are *Thailand* and the *Icelandic* Bill. Under the new *Thai* law, commissioning parents would be explicitly prohibited from changing their mind, and they will acquire legal parenthood whether they wish for this or not. This is coupled with criminal sanctions for commissioning parents refusing a baby born after surrogacy, punishable by up to five years' imprisonment. These provisions stem directly

[228] O. Khazova, Russia, in this volume, pp. 294–295, 302.
[229] H. Friðriksdóttir, Iceland, in this volume, pp. 272–273.
[230] C. Ho, Taiwan, in this volume, pp. 392–393.

from the Baby Gammy case, which was a major impetus behind the new restrictive laws in *Thailand*. In that case, it was alleged that the commissioning parents took the non-disabled twin born through a surrogacy they had arranged, but left the child with disabilities with the surrogate.[231] Likewise, the proposed *Icelandic* Bill would also make provision for parenthood to be transferred to the commissioning parents against their will, at the request of the surrogate.[232]

While in each case, the commissioning parents could simply place the child in foster care, or for adoption, such a provision does transfer the risk of having to care for an unwanted child from the surrogate to the commissioning parents.

5.4. WHAT ROLE DO CHILDREN'S RIGHTS PLAY IN DETERMINING TRANSFER?

In *Australia* and *England*, where legal parenthood is transferred by a post-birth Parentage or Parental Order, the child's best interests are the central consideration.[233] Likewise, in *New Zealand*, when making an adoption order, the court must be satisfied that the adoption will promote the best interests of the child;[234] while under the *Icelandic* Bill, if there is a dispute concerning parentage, the child's best interests will be a primary consideration.[235]

In one Australian jurisdiction – *Western Australia* – before the court can make a Parental Order, a 'plan' must be put before the court. The plan must include, at least, information regarding any time that the child is to spend, or communication that the child is to have, with the surrogate, and any information that will be conveyed to the surrogate about the child in future. Before approving the plan, the court must be satisfied that it adequately balances the rights and responsibilities of the parties; that it promotes the child's long-term welfare; and is reasonable in the circumstances.[236]

In *South Africa*, when deciding whether to allow the parties to enter into a surrogacy agreement, the court must have uppermost in its mind the best interests of the child to be born.[237] In other jurisdictions that control surrogacy arrangements pre-birth, it is the very screening process, and the eligibility

---

231 S. Hongladarom, Thailand, in this volume, pp. 499–500.
232 H. Friðriksdóttir, Iceland, in this volume, p. 273.
233 M. Keyes, Australia, in this volume, p. 99; C. Fenton-Glynn, England and Wales, in this volume, pp. 129–130.
234 D. Wilson, New Zealand, in this volume, p. 219.
235 H. Friðriksdóttir, Iceland, in this volume, p. 273.
236 M. Keyes, Australia, in this volume, p. 87. Surrogacy Act 2008 (WA) ss. 21, 22.
237 J. Sloth-Nielsen, South Africa, in this volume, pp. 194–195.

criteria set for the parties, which is intended to protect the child's future welfare, rather than an explicit consideration of the welfare of the child.

In *California*, on the other hand, the child's rights are not a consideration – either implicitly or explicitly. There are no eligibility criteria set by the relevant authorities for the commissioning parents or the surrogate (although individual agencies may set their own criteria), and parenthood is assigned according to contract, rather than an individual assessment.[238] Similarly, in *Russia*, the transfer of parenthood is organised between the parties themselves, and there is no external oversight of what would be in the child's best interests.[239]

6. AGENCIES AND CRIMINALISATION

6.1. THE ROLE OF MIDDLEMEN AND AGENCIES

The role of mediators, agencies and middlemen is particularly controversial in relation to surrogacy, tying in, as it often does, with concerns regarding commercialisation and commodification.

In *Russia*, and *South Korea*, there are no rules regarding agencies. In *South Korea*, this reflects a larger lacuna in the law regarding surrogacy in general, while in *Russia*, this is the result of the free market approach to surrogacy.[240] Unsurprisingly, in the other free market jurisdiction, *California*, agencies are also permitted, including on a commercial basis.[241]

In *Israel*, another jurisdiction where commercial surrogacy is permitted, there is also no regulation on the activities of agencies. However, any contract that is entered into with an agency must be submitted to the Approvals Committee before the surrogacy can go ahead. While in theory, the Committee has the power to reject the agreement, in practice it does not interfere with this.[242] In this same way, in *South Africa*, when an agency is involved in a surrogacy arrangement, the parties must present the agreement to the court. Unlike in Israel, however, the South African courts have taken a more active role in scrutinising the content of the agreement, and have been prepared to strike out and find unenforceable agreements with agencies.[243]

In *Portugal*, any person who derives economic benefit from the conclusion of a surrogacy contract or from the promotion thereof commits an offence,[244]

238 N. Cahn and J. Carbone, United States of America, in this volume, pp. 325, 327.
239 O. Khazova, Russia, in this volume, pp. 301–303.
240 O-J. Kim and B-H. Lee, South Korea, in this volume, pp. 463–464; O. Khazova, Russia, in this volume, p. 303.
241 N. Cahn and J. Carbone, United States of America, in this volume, p. 327.
242 R. Schuz, Israel, in this volume, p. 171.
243 J. Sloth-Nielsen, South Africa, in this volume, pp. 196–199.
244 R. Teixeira Pedro, Portugal, in this volume, p. 252.

while in the Australian states of *Australia Capital Territory*, *Queensland* and *Western Australia*, the provision of services in relation to commercial arrangements is prohibited.[245]

In a similar way, in *England* and *Hong Kong*, the negotiation of surrogacy arrangements on a commercial basis is prohibited, although in *England*, non-profit agencies can receive 'reasonable payments' for their services.[246] Under the proposed *Icelandic* Bill, all agencies would also be banned, but this would not prevent interest groups providing a platform for sharing general information and knowledge on issues relating to surrogacy.[247]

The issue of non-profit organisations is a grey area in many jurisdictions – for example, *New Zealand* prohibits receiving valuable consideration for another person's participation in a surrogacy arrangement, although whether non-profit organisations can receive remuneration for 'reasonable expenses' has yet to be tested.[248] In *India*, undertaking or providing commercial surrogacy and 'related component procedures or services' is prohibited according to the Bill. While the proposal does not discuss non-profit agencies, given the requirement that the surrogate be a 'close relative' of the commissioning parents, there would not appear to be scope – or demand – for this.[249]

In *France* and *Germany*, on the other hand, any agency or association dealing with surrogacy is prohibited – whether on a commercial, or non-profit basis.[250] Likewise in *Thailand*, where there is a specific offence of 'acting as a middleman' in a surrogacy arrangement.[251]

6.2. ADVERTISING SURROGACY

Advertising surrogacy is also prohibited in *England*, *Greece*, *Hong Kong*, the *Indian* Bill, *PR China* and all *Australian* states except *South Australia*.[252] Interestingly, although surrogacy contracts are illegal in *PR China*, surrogacy agencies still play a significant role in helping commissioning parents to find surrogates.

245 M. Keyes, Australia, in this volume, p. 100.
246 C. Fenton-Glynn, England and Wales, in this volume, pp. 130–131; D. Cheung, Hong Kong, in this volume, pp. 427, 436.
247 H. Friðriksdóttir, Iceland, in this volume, p. 274.
248 D. Wilson, New Zealand, in this volume, p. 221.
249 P. Kotiswaran, India, in this volume, p. 495.
250 W. Pintens, France, in this volume, p. 20; A. Dutta, Germany, in this volume, p. 36.
251 S. Hongladarom, Thailand, in this volume, p. 509.
252 C. Fenton-Glynn, England and Wales, in this volume, p. 131; E. Zervogianni, Greece, in this volume, p. 161; D. Cheung, Hong Kong, in this volume, p. 427; P. Kotiswaran, India, in this volume, p. 495; L. Shi, China, in this volume, pp. 366–367; M. Keyes, Australia, in this volume, pp. 99–100 (although in Western Australia, the prohibition only applies to advertisements regarding commercial surrogacy, not altruistic).

The only restriction on them is a Ministry Circular prohibiting advertisement, however, even those measures are noted to be largely ineffective.[253]

6.3. PENALTIES FOR BREACH OF SURROGACY LAWS

In all jurisdictions considered in this volume, save *California* and *Russia*, penalties are imposed for the breach of surrogacy laws. However, approaches differ as to *who* is penalised, and for *what*.

A very effective way of restricting domestic surrogacy is through imposing penalties on medical professionals. Where a doctor or clinic is liable to lose their licence to practice for breaching surrogacy laws, the likelihood of illegal arrangements is significantly narrowed. This can be seen in prohibitive jurisdictions, for example, *France*, *Germany*, *PR China*, *Singapore* and *Spain*,[254] while under the *Indian* Bill medical professionals are liable to imprisonment or financial penalties.[255] Likewise, in regulated jurisdictions such as *Greece*, *Israel* and *Portugal*, and under the new *Thai* law, providing medical services without the authorisation of the appropriate body is criminalised.[256]

On the other hand, some jurisdictions also, or alternatively, penalise commissioning parents and/or surrogates for participating in illegal surrogacy arrangements. In *Hong Kong*, the *Icelandic* Bill, *New Zealand*, *Portugal*, *Thailand*, and the proposed *Indian* Bill, the action penalised is negotiating or entering into a commercial surrogacy agreement, or accepting or paying benefits in relation to surrogacy.[257] In *Greece*, entering into a surrogacy arrangement that does not comply with all the conditions set by law is criminalised, including the surrogate and the commissioning parents; while in *Israel*, offering or accepting payment in relation to the carrying out of a surrogacy arrangement, other than authorised by the Approvals Committee, is a criminal offence.[258] In the Australian jurisdiction of *Victoria*, on the other hand, the offence is aimed specifically at the surrogate herself, who commits a criminal offence for being in receipt of a material benefit or advantage in relation to a surrogacy.[259]

---

253 L. Shi, China, in this volume, pp. 366–367.

254 W. Pintens, France, in this volume, p. 20; A. Dutta, Germany, in this volume, pp. 36–37; L. Shi, China, in this volume, pp. 367–368; T. Kaan, Singapore, in this volume, p. 404; E. Farnós Amorós, Spain, in this volume, pp. 66–67.

255 P. Kotiswaran, India, in this volume, p. 495.

256 E. Zervogianni, Greece, in this volume, p. 151; R. Schuz, Israel, in this volume, p. 179; R. Teixeira Pedro, Portugal, in this volume, p. 253; S. Hongladarom, Thailand, in this volume, p. 504.

257 D. Cheung, Hong Kong, in this volume, p. 427; H. Friðriksdóttir, Iceland, in this volume, pp. 268–273; D. Wilson, New Zealand, in this volume, p. 221; R. Teixeira Pedro, Portugal, in this volume, p. 252; S. Hongladarom, Thailand, in this volume, p. 508; P. Kotiswaran, India, in this volume, p. 495.

258 E. Zervogianni, Greece, in this volume, p. 151; R. Schuz, Israel, in this volume, p. 179.

259 M. Keyes, Australia, in this volume, p. 99.

In *PR China* and under the *Indian* Bill, commissioning parents and surrogates can be changed with the offence of 'abandoning a child', or 'selling/disowning an unwanted child'.[260] Likewise, in *France*, convincing a mother to abandon her child is criminalised, as is 'wilful substitution and simulation leading to modification of civil status'.[261]

While other jurisdictions have tried to combat the exploitation of surrogates indirectly, through criminalising commercial surrogacy, the new *Indian* Bill would introduce a specific criminal offence of exploiting the surrogate. What exactly this offence would cover is as yet unclear, but in principle, it provides a broad scope for ensuring that surrogacy arrangement has been entered into voluntarily.[262]

In contrast to these jurisdictions, *England* has deliberately excluded commissioning parents and surrogates from the scope of their criminal law prohibitions on commercial arrangements. The reason behind this is simple – the legislators wished to avoid the possibility of children being born with the 'taint of criminality', no matter how the actions of the adults involved may be viewed.[263]

Interestingly, although both *Australia* and *New Zealand* include commissioning parents within their criminal laws regarding surrogacy, in practice, these are not often pursued. In particular, courts in *New Zealand* have noted that when they are faced with the competing policy objectives of acting in the best interests of the child and of prohibiting commercial surrogacy, it is the best interests of the child which should take precedence, and not the enforcement of criminal sanctions.[264] There is also a widespread perception amongst commissioning parents in *Australia* that offences are unlikely to be prosecuted, and this appears to influence the decisions of some commissioning parents to enter into commercial surrogacy agreements abroad.[265]

6.4. EXTRA-TERRITORIAL JURISDICTION

Of the jurisdictions canvassed, only the surrogacy laws of *Hong Kong* and the Australia jurisdictions of *Queensland*, *Australian Capital Territory* and *New South Wales*, have extra-territorial effect. However, in relation to the *Australian* jurisdictions, the Australian Family Law Council noted that there is an apparent lack of interest in prosecuting people for breaches of such laws.[266]

260 L. Shi, China, in this volume, p. 367; P. Kotiswaran, India, in this volume, p. 495.
261 W. Pintens, France, in this volume, p. 20.
262 P. Kotiswaran, India, in this volume, p. 495.
263 C. Fenton-Glynn, England and Wales, in this volume, p. 131.
264 D. Wilson, New Zealand, in this volume, p. 222.
265 M. Keyes, Australia, in this volume, pp. 100–101.
266 Family Law Council, Report on Parentage and the Family Law Act (December 2013), p. 86.

In *France*, domestic laws can have extra-territorial effect, as long as the act was also illegal in the jurisdiction that it was undertaken – which does not make much sense in the case of surrogacy, where the destination jurisdictions are often chosen precisely for their very leniency.[267]

This raises the issue of circumvention tourism – commissioning couples going to other jurisdictions to deliberately circumvent their own, more restrictive, domestic laws.[268] When the commissioning parents come home with the resulting child, the domestic authorities are left with the dilemma as to whether to recognise the legal parenthood established abroad – a dilemma that has been central to the discussions of the future regulation of surrogacy.

7. INTERNATIONAL SURROGACY ARRANGEMENTS

Of the jurisdictions discussed in this volume, only in *Russia* is a birth certificate issued abroad automatically recognised, provided it was issued by a competent body and apostilled.[269] In all other jurisdictions canvassed, there is a need for some sort of procedure in the home country – either through recognition, or through the application of domestic law.

7.1. RECOGNITION OF PARENTHOOD ESTABLISHED ABROAD

In continental European jurisdictions, which operate under civil law, the authorities will first seek to determine whether the foreign birth certificate can be recognised domestically.

The decision of whether or not to recognise parenthood established abroad has been heavily influenced by the rulings of the European Court of Human Rights in *Mennesson v France*[270] and *Labassée v France*,[271] which held that where a child has a genetic connection with one of the commissioning parents, the child's right to respect for private life demands that legal parenthood must be recognised.[272] Of course, this decision only directly bound the *French* authorities, but we have seen other jurisdictions also adapting their rules to comply with the guidance set down by the court in this area.[273]

267 W. Pintens, France, in this volume, p. 21.

268 See C. Fenton-Glynn, 'Outsourcing Ethical Dilemmas: Regulating International Surrogacy Arrangements' (2016) 24(1) *Medical Law Review* 59.

269 O. Khazova, Russia, in this volume, p. 304.

270 *Mennesson v France*, no. 65192/11, 26.06.2014.

271 *Labassée v France*, no. 65941/11, 26.06.2014.

272 See W. Pintens, France, in this volume, pp. 24–26.

273 See, for example, F. Klinkhammer, Surrogate Motherhood under German National and International Private Law, in this volume, pp. 49–58.

In *France*, following *Mennesson*, the authorities must register a birth certificate issued abroad of a child who has at least one French biological parent, as long as it is genuine, and 'reflects reality'. The fact that the child has been born as a result of surrogacy is not sufficient to refuse the registration.[274] Where there is no genetic tie with the commissioning parents, however, registration will not be possible – a policy that is in line with the decision of the Grand Chamber of the European Court of Human Rights in *Paradiso and Campanelli v Italy*.[275]

This line of reasoning can also be seen in the *German* Federal Court of Justice, as described by Prof. Dr Klinkhammer in his chapter providing a judicial perspective on the regulation of surrogacy. According to the decision of the Federal Court, there must be recognition of a foreign decision on parenthood if at least one of the commissioning parents is a genetic parent. Reversing previous decisions, the court held that recognition was not against public policy, even though surrogacy is illegal within Germany, and based on the best interests of the child, the foreign law allowing the transfer of parenthood to the commissioning couple does not contravene fundamental principles of Germany law.[276]

In *Spain*, a foreign judicial decision assigning parenthood to the commissioning parents will be registered, however, a foreign administrative decision, or birth certificate, will not be. This reflects the desire to make sure that a court has considered the welfare of the child, especially in relation to the right to know one's biological origins, and that the capacity of surrogate women and the freedom and revocability of their consent are guaranteed.[277] Conversely, in *Portugal*, a foreign birth certificate can be recognised, as long as it has been registered with the competent foreign authority. However, a foreign judicial decision requires revision and confirmation prior to recognition to ensure that it is not contrary to the *ordre public*. Given that Portugal has only very recently introduced legislation regulating altruistic surrogacy, it is not clear how this will be interpreted in the future.[278]

In *Greece*, again the recognition of parenthood arising out of a surrogacy arrangement in another jurisdiction depends on the compatibility of recognition with the Greek *ordre public*. In one extreme case, a woman who commissioned two Russian surrogates to give birth using the sperm of her deceased son, and subsequently adopted the children, then sought recognition of the Russian court decision in Greece. This was denied on the basis of *ordre public* – on the grounds (*inter alia*) that the deceased son had not given his consent to the use of his

---

274 W. Pintens, France, in this volume, pp. 27–32.

275 *Paradiso and Campanelli v Italy*, no. 25358/12, 24.01.2017. See P. Beaumont and K. Trimmings, Surrogacy before the European Court of Human Rights, in this volume, pp. 332–354.

276 F. Klinkhammer, Surrogate Motherhood under German National and International Private Law, in this volume, pp. 49–58.

277 E. Farnós Amorós, Spain, in this volume, pp. 73–75.

278 R. Teixeira Pedro, Portugal, in this volume, p. 255.

sperm; the ova of the surrogates was used (traditional surrogacy), and that the commissioning mother (or grandmother) had exceeded the age limit set by law for both surrogacy and adoption. However, Zervogianni noted in her chapter that in cases where the deviations from Greek law are neither so blatant nor act cumulatively, it does not seem probable that the assignment of parenthood to the intended parents would be considered to be against the *ordre public*. In fact, she argues, recognition would actually promote the *ordre public*, a central part of which is ensuring the best interests of the child.[279]

In contrast to these jurisdictions, the *Japanese* Supreme Court has refused to recognise a foreign judgment on parenthood (issued in Nevada) on the grounds that surrogacy is contrary to the *ordre public*, in that it is incompatible with a fundamental principle of Japanese Family Law: a woman who has given birth to a child should be identified as the mother of the child. It held that

> 'a judgment rendered by a foreign court acknowledging the establishment of a natural parent-child relationship between the persons who are not eligible for such relationship under the Civil Code, is incompatible with the fundamental principle or fundamental philosophy of the rules of law in Japan … '

Despite this ruling, however, the commissioning parents were permitted to adopt the child, and thus legal parenthood was established through a different mechanism.[280]

In *South Korea* and *South Africa*, it is currently unclear how parenthood established abroad will be treated. In *South Africa*, Sloth-Nielsen suggests that if the surrogacy were commercial, the public policy exception may result in the court declining to recognise the legal tie, while again in *South Korea* it will depend on how the public policy exception is interpreted, but there is as yet no indication as to how this will be resolved.[281]

Finally, in *PR China*, Shi notes that foreign decisions will 'probably' be recognised, but that even if not, Chinese law – as the place of habitual residence of the commissioning parents – will apply. Where this occurs, the courts will find in favour of the status quo: that is, the people who have custody.[282]

7.2. APPLYING DOMESTIC LAW

In the common law jurisdictions of *Australia, England, Hong Kong, New Zealand* and *Singapore*, rather than focusing on recognition of foreign decisions, domestic

279 E. Zervogianni, Greece, in this volume, pp. 162–163.
280 S. Hayakawa, Japan, in this volume, pp. 443–445.
281 J. Sloth-Nielsen, South Africa, in this volume, pp. 199–200; O-J. Kim and B-H. Lee, South Korea, in this volume, pp. 464–465.
282 L. Shi, China, in this volume, pp. 368–370.

law will apply, and the question thus becomes whether there is a domestic mechanism able to recognise parenthood for commissioning parents.

In *England* and *Hong Kong*, this is done through a Parental Order, on the same grounds as would a surrogacy within the jurisdictions. This obviously runs into difficulties when there has been a commercial arrangement, with the courts forced to decide between upholding the prohibition against commercial surrogacy, and ensuring the best interests of the child by transferring legal parenthood to those who will be caring for him or her.[283] This has been particularly problematic in England, as was discussed by Sir Mark Hedley in his chapter in this volume on 'Legal Implications of International Surrogacy Agreements: A View from the Bench in England and Wales'.

In *New Zealand* and *Singapore*, commissioning parents will have to go through domestic adoption proceedings in order to have their parenthood recognised. This itself raises significant difficulties, especially in light of restrictions on payments and strict eligibility criteria (see Section 5.1. above).[284]

On the other hand, in *Australia*, 'Parentage Orders' that can be used to transfer legal parenthood in domestic surrogacy arrangements, cannot be used where the surrogacy has been carried out abroad. This is due to a number of different factors, including that some states require medical procedures to be carried out within the jurisdictions, while others require counselling and legal advice to be provided by local practitioners. The most influential factor, however, is that Parentage Orders can only be granted in altruistic arrangements, which excludes most international cases coming before the Australian courts, and in fact, there are no published decisions in which Parentage Orders were granted in an international arrangement. Instead, Australian commissioning couples will either apply for adoption, or private law 'parenting' orders, which grant custody and decision-making authority, without transferring legal parenthood.[285]

7.3. SPECIAL PROCEDURES FOR FOREIGN SURROGACY

In *Israel*, and under the proposed *Icelandic* Bill, special guidelines have been set up in relation to foreign surrogacy. These mechanisms do not follow domestic law, but also do not simply rely on recognition of a foreign judgment.

In *Israel*, this procedure is based on administrative guidelines, which are not publicly available, but are referred to by the courts. Under these guidelines,

---

283 C. Fenton-Glynn, England and Wales, in this volume, pp. 132–133; D. Cheung, Hong Kong, in this volume, pp. 436–437.

284 D. Wilson, New Zealand, in this volume, pp. 218–221; T. Kaan, Singapore, in this volume, pp. 411–412.

285 M. Keyes, Australia, in this volume, p. 101.

the commissioning parents must produce documents evidencing the surrogacy arrangement, its legality under foreign law, and the surrogate's consent to the child's removal to Israel (which must be given in the Israeli consulate in the country of birth). The commissioning father must also show proof that he is the biological father, and once this is proven, he will be registered as the legal parent. Interestingly, a number of cases have held that where the commissioning mother is the genetic mother, she will be treated as legal mother, and will not need to go through separate adoption. This is a unique provision, as most jurisdictions explicitly exclude the commissioning mother's genetic relationship when considering motherhood, instead relying on the biological/gestational connection to the surrogate.[286]

The *Icelandic* Bill proposes setting up a Committee specially authorised to consider parenthood established abroad under a surrogacy arrangement, and to decide whether or not to recognise this. The Committee would be instructed to deny recognition of foreign decisions if not consistent with the best interests of the child involved, or where it would be in violation of fundamental principles of law (including commercial surrogacy agreements), though it is not clear what the outcome would be if these two principles clashed – as they have been shown often to do.[287]

8. CONCLUSIONS

Given the sensitivity of the issues and the widely differing views on them, it would be presumptuous to claim to be able to draw 'final' conclusions or make general recommendations about the best way to approach surrogacy, with a view of them being implemented in various jurisdictions. There can be no doubt that all law, but perhaps the law of surrogacy in particular, remains specific to the culture, social environment and legal tradition in which it is meant to apply. In this contentious area, any concrete recommendations would be inappropriate for implementation in many legal and social environments. Moreover, our own inevitable jurisdictional biases, much as we strive to suppress them, necessarily influence how we personally perceive the best way to regulate surrogacy, both in form and in content. Especially in a volume discussing both Eastern and Western perspectives, we must be careful not to let our own background lead us to make one-size-fits-all recommendations.

But what this final section *can* do is to look at emerging trends and regulation (Section 8.1. below). In doing so, the picture that emerges is that *not* regulating surrogacy – or simply prohibiting it domestically – obviously does not deal with

[286] R. Schuz, Israel, in this volume, pp. 180–183.

[287] H. Friðriksdóttir, Iceland, in this volume, pp. 275–276.

the issues arising from surrogacy. Moreover, it ultimately leads to the exportation of many social and legal problems to other jurisdictions, often to the detriment of everyone involved, including the citizens of the non-regulating state. Sticking one's head in the sand and hoping that the phenomenon of surrogacy, and the legal problems that arise in relation to it, will go away, is not an acceptable option for any jurisdiction.[288] Therefore one definite conclusion is that some regulation is not only desirable but necessary. While of course no comprehensive framework can be suggested here, for the reasons just mentioned, this final part will look at some aspects of regulation (Section 8.2. below), highlighting in particular which legislative (or judicial) approaches have failed to generate the effects desired by the decision-makers, and what has emerged in practice. The chapter will conclude with some brief observations regarding the way forward (Section 8.3. below).

8.1. EMERGING TRENDS AND REGULATION

8.1.1. The Failure of the Prohibitive Approach

The reaction to the emerging practice of surrogacy in some of the jurisdictions canvassed (for example *France*, *Germany* and *Spain*) was unambiguous, principled and clear: that this practice should be prohibited. But while this means that no surrogacies are taking place, at least officially, in these jurisdictions, the reality is that this has simply exported the issue to other jurisdictions with a more permissive approach.[289] The desire to become a parent is greater than the barriers put in place by the legislature.

This is problematic in a number of ways. Firstly, and probably most alarmingly, if the intention was to protect women (and children) from potential exploitation and commodification, then this approach has failed as the exploitation and commodification simply takes places elsewhere as couples will go to more permissive jurisdictions for the surrogacy they desire. This is discussed in more detail in Section 8.2.1. below. When commissioning parent(s) return to the jurisdiction following international surrogacies, this prohibitive approach has had to surrender to the practical realities, and the need to safeguard the rights of the children born through international surrogacies. Thus in cases of international surrogacy, even jurisdictions with the prohibitive approach now generally recognise the parenthood of the intended parents,

---

288 For such a view see for example *Report of the Committee of Inquiry into Human Fertilisation and Embryology*, HMSO, London 1984, reprinted 1988, Cm 9314.

289 See W. Pintens, France, in this volume, pp. 17–34; A. Dutta, Germany, in this volume, pp 35–48; E. Farnós Amorós, Spain, in this volume, pp. 59–84.

at least where the gametes of one of the commissioning parents are involved.[290] As a result, international surrogacy now practically is an acceptable (but largely unregulated) way to parenthood in these jurisdictions. So while the 'prohibitive' jurisdictions may, at least to a certain extent, succeed in protecting their own citizens from exploitation, the price of this protection is paid by citizens of other jurisdictions. Therefore, these jurisdictions uphold their own moral principles but turn a blind eye to what as a result happens elsewhere; but realistically this can only be characterised as wilful blindness. Claiming the moral high ground when knowing full well that the undesired practices take place elsewhere and the 'results' are then accepted is, at best, cynical.

Secondly, this leads to a de facto discrimination on the basis of wealth, as only more affluent couples can afford to enter into an international surrogacy arrangement. Such arrangements require not only knowledge and sound legal advice (although unfortunately this is not always present), which itself comes at a price, but also involve payment of considerable expenses, including (but not restricted to) medical expenses, travel, payments to the surrogate and agents, etc. Therefore, only couples who can afford embarking on this difficult and expensive path of circumventing the domestic restrictions can avail themselves of international surrogacy. Less wealthy couples with a fertility problem will simply not have that option. Surrogacy thus becomes the privilege of the wealthy.

Finally, the restriction on surrogacy could be viewed as potentially discriminatory on the grounds of gender. In these jurisdictions, male fertility problems can be dealt with – through use of donated sperm – but female fertility problems relating to gestation cannot (and are often coupled also with a prohibition on egg and embryo donations in the same jurisdictions). While they are not directly comparable, such differential treatment must be carefully justified, and the reasons for it clearly articulated.

In any event, attempts at prohibiting surrogacy must, in the light of the realities of a global surrogacy market, be deemed a failure – at least in the way it is currently practiced. Without extraterritorial restrictions, and where parenthood is simply recognised in any case, they do not prevent surrogacy – except perhaps in excluding those who do not have the financial means – and prohibition merely ensures that surrogacies take place elsewhere.

8.1.2. The Capitulation of the Tolerant Approach

While the 'tolerant approach' – where jurisdictions do not regulate surrogacy itself, but only permit the transfer of parenthood post-birth in limited

[290] See for example for France: *Mennesson v France*, no. 65192/11, 26.06.2014; *Labassée v France*, no. 65941/11, 26.06.2014; for Germany: German Federal Court of Justice, XII ZB 463/1 (10.12.2014), BGHZ 203, 350; for Singapore: *UKM v Attorney-General* [2018] SGHCF 18.

circumstances – cannot necessarily be called a complete failure, it is safe to say that it has not been a success either. The difficulties faced by this approach result from the same circumstances that undermine the 'prohibitive approach': namely, the availability of international surrogacies. Reality simply has overtaken what may have been a well-intended approach.

England can serve as a paradigm example, being a jurisdiction which – very reluctantly – decided to allow surrogacy only in very limited circumstances, including the requirement of altruism on the part of the surrogate. One of the consequences of this has been a shortage of surrogates willing to take on this role, leading commissioning parents to seek surrogates in other jurisdictions who are able to enter an arrangement for commercial gain.[291] Moreover, the *ex post facto* examination of the surrogacy, and the transfer of parenthood only after the birth, lacks legal certainty for commissioning parents, resulting in them travelling to jurisdictions where they are assured that the child will be handed over to them. The practice of international surrogacy is so common and so accepted that it is now even included in the UK passport application as a specific category. Of course, the exact number of international surrogacy arrangements leading to children living in the jurisdiction is unknown as many may not apply for an official transfer of parenthood upon their return. However, the General Register Office stated that in 2013, 69 of 185 (so some 37 per cent) Parental Orders were made concerning children who were born outside the United Kingdom; in 2014, this figure was 107 of 258 (41 per cent), and in 2015 the number 156 of 281 (56 per cent).[292] Thus, even under the data available the number of foreign surrogacies has increased significantly, and this trend is likely to continue.

This may seem surprising, given that the vast majority of these foreign surrogacies will have been of a commercial nature: i.e. precisely what the legislation set out to avoid. But what is the court to do when asked for a Parental Order in a case where the commissioning parents obviously and deliberately decided to undertake a commercial surrogacy elsewhere? Again, as with the prohibitive approach, the interests of the child – who is an innocent party in all this – must dictate the outcome, meaning that other policy considerations give way to legal certainty regarding parenthood and identity. The dilemma has been described most aptly by Mr Justice Hedley in *Re X and Y (Foreign Surrogacy)*, the first English case dealing with a foreign commercial surrogacy:

> 'I feel bound to observe that I find this process of authorisation most uncomfortable. What the court is required to do is to balance two competing and potentially

291 See Section 8.2.2.1.

292 These figures were provided by the Registrar's Office to Dr Marilyn Crawshaw, University of York. Although it is not clear that this information is entirely accurate (see C. Fenton-Glynn, England and Wales, in this volume, pp. 117–118), it at least gives some kind of indication of the prevalence of the practice.

> irreconcilably conflicting concepts. Parliament is clearly entitled to legislate against commercial surrogacy and is clearly entitled to expect that the courts should implement that policy consideration in its decisions. Yet it is also recognised that as the full rigour of that policy consideration will bear on one wholly unequipped to comprehend it let alone deal with its consequences (ie the child concerned) that rigour must be mitigated by the application of a consideration of that child's welfare. That approach is both humane and intellectually coherent. The difficulty is that it is almost impossible to imagine a set of circumstances in which by the time the case comes to court, the welfare of any child (particularly a foreign child) would not be gravely compromised (at the very least) by a refusal to make an order.'[293]

Thus, as the same judge observed in *Re L (Commercial Surrogacy)*, 'only be in the clearest case of the abuse of public policy that the court will be able to withhold an order if otherwise welfare considerations supports its making'.[294] In other words, when presented with the 'result' of a commercial surrogacy, i.e. the child, the courts will virtually always be compelled to make the Parental Order. As a consequence, commercial surrogacy is being practised, and given sanction by the courts, both within and outside England and Wales, despite this being prohibited. The law in essence is not enforced, meaning that commercial agreements are being permitted through the back door. The 'tolerant approach' has morphed into a state where it does not, as it was set out to do, just tolerate surrogacy in certain limited cases, but in fact now tolerates a practice that was expressly prohibited by the legislature, seriously undermining the rule of law.

In tolerant jurisdictions the courts therefore have been set an unachievable task – they are expected to balance the regulation of surrogacy, while also protecting the best interests of children. Sensibly and humanely, they have decided to give preference to the latter: an approach that is also in line with the developing international jurisprudence.[295] As a result, however, the tolerant approach, which attempted to operate a partial prohibition, just like the (fully) prohibitive approach ultimately had to capitulate to the realities of the global surrogacy market.

8.1.3. *The Problems of the Free Market Approach*

Having considered that both the 'prohibitive' and the 'tolerant' approach fail to achieve their aims, this may seem to lead to the conclusion that therefore a

293 *Re X and Y (Foreign Surrogacy)* [2008] EWHC 3030 (Fam), at [24].

294 *Re L (Commercial Surrogacy)* [2010] EWHC 3146 (Fam), at [10].

295 See, for example, *Mennesson v France*, no. 65192/11, 26.06.2014; *Labassée v France*, no. 65941/11, 26.06.2014; *Paradiso and Campanelli v Italy*, no. 25358/12, 24.01.2017; German Federal Court: XII ZB 463/1 (10.12.2014), BGHZ 203, 350.

'free market' approach is what inevitably will happen. However, this approach – which would allow individuals to assign parenthood according to a private contract – also has many problems, to say the very least.

As a – perhaps rather abstract – starting point, leaving surrogacy to 'the free market' is anathema to the very purpose of family law. Family law as a distinct area of law exists precisely because the personal relations between family members, adults and children as well as the wider kin, are fundamentally different than those between strangers. There are many considerations that do not arise in similar form in the general law, particularly (but not exclusively) the need to protect weaker parties and especially the children, and that is why family law steps in.[296] Hence it would be extraordinary to simply cede a part of the law of filiation to the free market. It would be contrary to what family law stands for.

A complete absence of regulation leaves everyone vulnerable: surrogates, commissioning parents and children alike. Interestingly, the paucity of this approach has been recognised by a number of jurisdictions which were once at the forefront of the surrogacy industry. For example, *India* and *Thailand*, have taken measures to seriously curtail and regulate the practice of surrogacy in their jurisdictions.[297] One of the reasons for this was that there was effectively no oversight of surrogacy, and consequently little or no protection of surrogates and children, or indeed the commissioning parents. In this lacuna, exploitative practices had developed: profiteering by individuals and agencies, abuse up to the level of human rights violations and exploitation had become the norm. Even where that was (or is) not the case, in many instances commissioning parents from wealthy regions would make significant payments for surrogacy arrangements; for women from poorer backgrounds in less developed countries this creates substantial financial incentives and indeed pressures to agree to act as surrogates, which otherwise they would not have. In these cases, the exploitation is a financial one.

Where there is a functioning market, arguably the worst practices may be curbed, and a measure of protection indeed may be afforded, because the surrogacy agreement and its conditions can be freely negotiated. Realistically, however, in most parts of the world this 'freedom' to negotiate is limited at best, and illusionary at worst.[298] In particular, the inequality of bargaining power may result in overly restrictive contracts, which unacceptably curtail the freedom of the surrogate.

---

296 As is common in other areas of law, where there is an obvious imbalance of power which can be exploited, for example in consumer law or labour law.

297 P. Kotiswaran, India, in this volume, pp. 469–498; S Hongladarom, Thailand, in this volume, pp. 499–511.

298 An exception to this may be California, where the surrogate may in fact have *greater* bargaining power as a result of the free market (see, for example, *J v G* [2014] 1 FLR 297).

Moreover, this freedom can only be exercised by the negotiating parties and certainly not the future person or persons they are negotiating about. Neither surrogate nor commissioning parents will necessarily always act with the best interest of the child in mind. Arguably, as a bare minimum, the preservation of the best interest of the child must be central to any decision or legislation on surrogacy. One only needs to imagine the scenario of the child sex offender commissioning children, or, perhaps somewhat more realistically, the couple that was denied adoption for pertinent reasons.[299]

Irrespective of whether one agrees with surrogacy, in the absence of regulation, it is the stronger party who can enforce their preferences and in the international context this is very likely to be the wealthy commissioning parent(s). Ultimately, proper protection of all involved, but especially the surrogate and the children, can only be achieved by regulation, not the free market.

8.1.4. *Why International Instruments Cannot be the Answer to All Problems*

As this analysis demonstrates, both the prohibitive approach and the tolerant approach have been undermined by the availability of international surrogacy. This has led not only to circumvention tourism, but also to conflicts of law concerning parenthood and nationality, leaving children in a state of legal uncertainty. Given this reality, ideally there would be an international treaty or convention on these issues, which could provide legal certainty and protection for all involved. Therefore it is to be welcomed that attempts at drafting such treaties are being undertaken – for example, by the Hague Conference on Private International Law.[300] However, realistically one must concede that such initiatives are not very likely to be successful in regulating surrogacy globally, given the widely divergent approaches; absent at least a very basic international consensus no international treaty can come into existence. Moreover, as the views on surrogacy are so fundamentally different, treaties are extremely unlikely to yield results quickly enough, or indeed even within the next decades, to deal with the issues we already are facing at the moment.

There are two issues that fall to be regulated by international treaty. First, the legal and civil status of the child. Article 8 of the UN Convention on the Rights of the Child provides that every child has the right to identity and to a nationality, something which has been put in jeopardy by the operation of conflicts of law rules in tolerant and prohibitive jurisdictions. As has been discussed in Section 7. of this chapter, some jurisdictions initially refused to register parenthood arising from a foreign surrogacy, on the grounds that it would involve recognising a

---

299 Both these situations have arisen in practice – see M. Keyes, Australia, in this volume, p. 103; *Paradiso and Campanelli v Italy* no. 25358/12, 24.01.2017.

300 See <https://www.hcch.net/en/projects/legislative-projects/parentage-surrogacy> accessed 05.03.2019.

procedure explicitly prohibited by the state. However, in most cases, the best interests of the child have now been recognised as paramount, and parenthood recognised, even if surrogacy is domestically prohibited.[301]

The second issue that falls to be regulated is the potential violations of the rights of surrogates and children in the process of gestation and transfer to commissioning parents. But as the contributions in this volume show, jurisdictions remain deeply divided as to how to respond to surrogacy, both in legal, social and cultural terms. Some perceive surrogacy as a violation of the dignity of women and the commodification of children, others allow commercial surrogacy for the highest bidder. That jurisdictions holding such divergent views could agree on international regulation is highly unlikely. In addition, surrogacy challenges traditional assumptions concerning the mother-child bond, and indeed womanhood in general. The advent of surrogacy requires nothing less than reconceptualising legal parenthood, something that simply cannot – and indeed should not – be done by an international instrument. It is part of a much wider, much more fundamental, debate about parenthood and parent-child relations, and at its core is one that must be had on a national level.

So realistically, for any international treaty to have any chance of being ratified by many jurisdictions, it would probably have to be a very basic one,[302] thus presumably limited to mutual recognition of parental status across jurisdictions in cases of surrogacy. This may be acceptable to many jurisdictions irrespective of their basic views on surrogacy, given the acknowledgement of the child's interests as paramount. But what would be gained by such a treaty? For most jurisdictions that would find such a convention acceptable, it would do nothing more than codify the already existing practice.[303] But crucially, such a convention may ultimately aggravate some of the problems of and concerns raised against surrogacy, particularly the potential exploitation and commodification of women and children. Indeed, this is precisely what has occurred in several jurisdictions, as explained above (see Sections 8.1.1. and 8.1.2.): when presented with the child as a result of a surrogacy agreement, jurisdictions deal with what they can deal with, namely civil status and the best interests of the child in question, turning a blind eye to the issues of exploitation and commodification on which

---

301 See, for example, W. Pintens, France, in this volume, pp. 27–28; F. Klinkhammer, Surrogate Motherhood under German National and International Private Law, in this volume, pp. 49–58; E. Farnós Amorós, Spain, in this volume, pp. 73–75.

302 See also the discussion by the Hague Experts' Group on the Parentage/Surrogacy Project on their meeting on 25–28.09.2018, available at <https://www.hcch.net/en/projects/legislative-projects/parentage-surrogacy> accessed 05.03.2019.

303 See, for example, W. Pintens, France, in this volume, pp. 27–28; F. Klinkhammer, Surrogate Motherhood under German National and International Private Law, in this volume, pp. 49–58; C. Fenton-Glynn, England and Wales, in this volume, pp. 125–127. See also C. Fenton-Glynn, 'The Regulation and Recognition of Surrogacy in English Law' (2015) 27(1) *Child and Family Law Quarterly* 83.

they have no real influence as they happen elsewhere. Hence, as described, the exploitative practices would continue unabated, now potentially aided by the international instrument. This would be, as Eekelaar has put it in another context, regularisation, rather than regulation,[304] and in doing so, it would essentially legitimise practices that domestic authorities had rejected as contrary to (their) human rights principles. In other words: when a government enters into an international treaty saying that it will recognise the effects of a surrogacy arrangement, it sends the explicit message that it is a legitimate transaction, making it an acceptable practice. In any event, such a convention would only address the civil status of the child and fail to address other concerns, making it unlikely that such a convention would be ratified widely.[305]

Having said that, a convention going beyond that and addressing the wider issues surrounding surrogates, commissioning parents, and the best interests of the child, would be even less likely to be widely recognised. While it is possible that some common ground could be found concerning eligibility of surrogates, of commissioning parents, and medical standards, the sticking point for such a model lies with questions as to the enforceability of the surrogacy contract, the identity of the legal parent at birth, and whether the surrogate can change her mind and decide to keep the child. Given the divergence in approaches between jurisdictions on these issues, there is little that could be codified in a treaty.

If the instrument were to allow commercial surrogacy (which would indicate that there should be some form of contractual enforceability, and recognition of the commissioning parents as legal parents), this would severely limit the number of countries willing to ratify the agreement. As the jurisdictions canvassed in this volume show, while the jurisdictions in which international surrogacy takes place are predominantly those that allow commercial surrogacy, very few jurisdictions where the commissioning parents reside permit this – in fact, it is this very difference that drives the international surrogacy industry.

On the other hand, if the international treaty prohibited commercial surrogacy, allowing only reasonable expenses, it would so severely limit its scope that it would be rendered useless. Given the scarcity of altruistic surrogates in those jurisdictions that have opted for a 'tolerant approach', and the growing need for reproductive services, the same problems would occur, and couples would seek commercial arrangements – which would fall outside of the treaty.

---

304 This concept is used by Eekelaar when discussing the law's role in divorce (J. Eekelaar, *Regulating Divorce*, Clarendon Press, Oxford 1991). Whereas regulation attempts to direct society's actions, taking a more interventionist approach, regularisation is more fatalistic, accepting that the phenomena will happen regardless of what the law does, and confines the legal process to ensuring that the legal process does not add to the harm (at p. 142).

305 For a more extensive discussion of the possibilities of an international treaty, see C. Fenton-Glynn, 'Creating International Families: Private International Law and the Industry of Parenthood' in G. Douglas, M. Murch and V. Stephens (eds), *International and National Perspectives on Child and Family Law: Essays in Honour of Nigel Lowe* (Intersentia, Cambridge 2018).

This leaves the international community at an impasse. While multilateral cooperation is not only desirable but quite obviously necessary, there do not seem to be any viable approaches to a truly globally acceptable treaty or convention. Even soft instruments, like guidelines of good practice, face similar problems. In the meantime, the number of children born through international surrogacy arrangements continues to rise.

8.1.5. The Rise of the Regulatory Approach

In the light of this, the burden must lie with domestic legislatures to create stable and reliable legal frameworks that at least mitigate or minimise the risks for surrogates, children and commissioning parents.

Looking at developments in a number of jurisdictions, there is a clear trend going towards regulation and – albeit reluctant – recognition of surrogacy as a (global) fact. When new legislation is being drafted, such as in *Iceland* or *Portugal* for example, this legislation focuses on pre-birth approval/procedures, constituting what in this book is referred to as the 'regulatory' approach. This pre-birth approval gives greater legal certainty to commissioning parents, while simultaneously providing protection to surrogates against potential exploitation by allowing the authorities to have control over the conditions in which surrogacy takes place. This legislation builds on the experiences of other jurisdictions, such as *Greece*, *Israel* and *South Africa*, and has been used to regulate both altruistic and commercial arrangements.

Nevertheless, a regulatory approach does not solve all problems. First, for prohibitive jurisdictions, where opposition to surrogacy does not rest on the conditions in which it takes place, but in the very nature of the practice itself, regulation would not be consistent with these principles. This is discussed further in Section 8.2.1. below. Second, while a regulatory approach may provide greater control domestically, there will always be those that fall outside the regime – for example, same-sex couples in *Israel* – who will continue to resort to international surrogacy to achieve their desire for a family. Where this occurs, authorities are left with the same dilemma as prohibitive and tolerant jurisdictions face – whether to authorise a surrogacy arrangement that does not comply with domestic law. In this way, regulatory approaches rely on creating conditions that entice commissioning parents and surrogates to stay within the jurisdiction, which may potentially result in the reduction of protection to the lowest common denominator.

8.2. ASPECTS OF REGULATION

The comparison of the different forms of regulation (or lack thereof) shows that no solution is without its own difficulties. The aim of the comparison therefore was not to find 'the' solution, but to lay these difficulties bare, thus providing a foundation from which legislators can consider the best way forward for their jurisdiction.

Of course, the form of regulation is only one part of the equation. The decision as to which form to choose is necessarily influenced by the deeper philosophical questions concerning exploitation, commodification, and autonomy.

8.2.1. Competing Ideas of Exploitation, Commodification and Autonomy

At the heart of the debate concerning surrogacy – and whether a prohibitive, tolerant, regulated or free market approach is taken – lies the question of women's rights: is surrogacy an expression of reproductive autonomy, or does it involve the exploitation of women?

On the one hand, surrogacy could be viewed as the ultimate form of reproductive empowerment – allowing women to move beyond imprisonment by their biological capacities, and choose when and how to have children.[306] Further, it recognises that where a woman chooses to provide such services for another, she is entitled to payment for her reproductive labour in the same way as she would any other type of labour. On the other hand, it could be argued that this is false empowerment – a type of self-deception by which rather than exercising autonomy, women are in fact reinforcing oppressive gender roles, and social expectations of women.[307] As Andrea Dworkin has argued, reproductive technologies 'make the womb extractable from the women as a whole person', and the unique differences between individuals are erased.[308] Moreover, surrogacy may create hard choices for poor women – she may find it degrading to use her reproductive capacities in such a manner, but feel that it is preferable to other life options open to her.[309] This may then lead to a system characterised by power imbalance, where those who are financially able are employing poor women to bear children for them.

This chapter will not go into greater detail concerning the competing theories in this respect, as they have been extensively covered by other authors.[310]

---

306 See, for example, L.B. Andrews, 'Surrogate Motherhood: The Challenge for Feminists' in L. Gostin (ed), *Surrogate Motherhood* (Indiana University Press, Bloomington IN 1990).

307 A.L. Allen, 'Surrogacy, Slavery and the Ownership of Life' (1990) 13 *Harvard Journal of Law and Public Policy* 139; M.J. Radin, 'Market Inalienability' (1987) 100 *Harvard Law Review* 1849, 1930.

308 A. Dworkin, *Right Wing Women* (Perigee Press, New York 1983), p. 187.

309 M.J. Radin, 'Market Inalienability' (1987) 100 *Harvard Law Review* 1849, 1930.

310 See, for example, P. Laufer-Ukeles, 'Mothering for Money: Regulating Commercial Intimacy' (2013) 88 *Indiana Law Journal* 1223; K.B. Lieber, 'Selling the Womb: Can the feminist critique of surrogacy be answered?' (1992) 68(1) *Indiana Law Journal* 205; A. Van Niekerk and L. Van Zyl, 'The Ethics of Surrogacy: Women's Reproductive Labour' (1995) 21 *Journal of Medical Ethics* 345; C.L. Kerian, 'Surrogacy: A Last Resort Alternative for Infertile Women

Instead, taking as a starting point the position taken by the jurisdiction in question, it seeks to explore how this affects the possibilities for effective regulation.

8.2.1.1. Prohibitive Jurisdictions

In the prohibitive jurisdictions, such as *Germany* and *France*, all arrangements, either altruistic or commercial, are viewed as violating the dignity of women. The concern is not about the individual woman as such but about the way in which it treats female body parts as a means to an end, rather than for their essential value as part of humanity. On this view, surrogacy does violence to the way we think about the body, life, and women's reproductive capacities in commodifying them, and thus reducing them to an economic value.[311] If one accepts this philosophical position as the starting point, a regulatory approach would not be appropriate, as it would be sanctioning a process that is deemed exploitative. However, as discussed above, the prohibitive approach has been unable to prevent citizens from these jurisdictions travelling abroad to achieve their desire to create a family, meaning that authorities have had to accept the outcomes of such arrangements whether they agree with them or not.

This leaves these jurisdictions with three options. First, they can continue in their current approach, prohibiting surrogacy domestically, but tacitly permitting it when it takes place in another jurisdiction. There are advantages to this approach – it sends a clear message of what domestic law deems acceptable, while also allowing for expressions of moral pluralism. For example, Guido Pennings argues that:

> 'The final result of a policy of external tolerance is that a certain norm is applicable and applied in society as wanted by the majority while simultaneously the members of the minority can still act according to their moral view by going abroad. On deeply felt moral issues concerning life and death (such as reproduction, abortion, euthanasia etc), this policy prevents a frontal clash of opinions which may jeopardise social peace. Obtaining the desired treatment by travelling partially defuses the conflict and prevents the frustration and indignation of the minority group from accumulating.'[312]

On the other hand, such an approach undermines the integrity of domestic legislation, and allows for those with sufficient means to circumvent the law, while those who are less well-off cannot afford to do so – as discussed

or a Commodification of Women's Bodies and Children' (1997) 12 *Wisconsin Women's Law Journal* 113.

311 C. Fenton-Glynn, 'Outsourcing Ethical Dilemmas: Regulating International Surrogacy Arrangements' (2016) 24(1) *Medical Law Review* 59.

312 G. Pennings, 'Reproductive Tourism as Moral Pluralism in Motion' (2002) 28(6) *Journal of Medical Ethics* 337, 340.

in Section 8.1. It also has the effect of protecting women domestically, while allowing citizens to engage in what is viewed as exploitation in other countries, and then reap the benefits.

The second option for such jurisdictions would be to retain the prohibition on surrogacy, but to make this prohibition enforceable with extraterritorial effect. Currently, in the prohibitive jurisdictions discussed, criminal sanctions are only imposed if the arrangement takes place domestically, or if the act was also illegal in the jurisdiction in which it was undertaken – which is not usually the case with practices involved in circumvention tourism.[313] This leaves the only limitation on international agreements as the possibility of non-recognition of parental status, which has now been found to be incompatible with the rights of the child. However, if these jurisdictions really wanted to stop international surrogacy, they could impose sanctions with extraterritorial effect – either in the form of fines, or even prison sentences. If the commissioning parent(s) were aware that they faced years in prison, this could prove a significant disincentive.

Of course, there are downsides to this approach also. The *Australian* experience, discussed in Section 6.4. above, shows that despite having the relevant provisions enshrined in law, there is little appetite for imposing sanctions on commissioning parents in practice, with no reported arrests or convictions. Moreover, criminal sanctions could drive surrogacy underground, leaving *less* opportunity to regulate, and greater scope for exploitation and undesirable practices. A study by Everningham, Stafford-Bell and Hammarberg asked respondents to imagine they were considering an international commercial surrogacy arrangement, but lived in a jurisdiction that made this a criminal offence. They found that '[s]uch laws were a deterrent for only 9% of respondents (23). Of the 114 who actually lived in Australian states with criminalisation laws, 63 (55%) would enter an overseas compensated surrogacy contract, based on a low probability of prosecution, and another 26 (23%) would move to a state where overseas compensated surrogacy is not criminalized'.[314]

The third and final option would be to re-evaluate the domestic prohibition, and consider whether it is sustainable in light of the global marketplace of reproductive tourism, or indeed if it continues to reflect the views of its citizens. Does the fact that individuals and couples are travelling to other jurisdictions where the laws are more lenient in this respect indicate a change in attitude towards surrogacy? In an area where technology and medicine are rapidly advancing, it is vital that the law continues to respond to the challenges this poses.

---

313 Some tolerant jurisdictions do have extraterritorial jurisdiction – see Section 6.4. above.

314 S. Everingham, M. Stafford-Bell and K. Hammarberg, 'Australians' use of surrogacy' (2014) 201(5) *Medical Journal of Australia* 1, 3.

8.2.1.2. Tolerant Jurisdictions

Tolerant jurisdictions that allow surrogacy but only under specific circumstances, advance a different position on the nature of surrogacy. Rather than being an *intrinsic wrong*, inherent in every arrangement no matter what its content, surrogacy in these jurisdictions is viewed as *contextually wrong* – that is, only problematic if the arrangement exploits the individual woman in question. In such cases, the issue of exploitation rests on the question of moral agency, and the ability to make a free and informed choice to carry out an act that serves the ends of others. Exploitation, or lack thereof, depends on whether the arrangement was entered into voluntarily, whether the surrogate has the capacity to fully understand the risks involved, and has the ability to make an informed decision regarding these.[315]

Where the wrong is contextual, and based on decision-making autonomy, the obligation on states is thus to ensure that the optimal conditions for this are developed. As discussed above in Section 8.1.2., this cannot occur where the authorities are undertaking an *ex post facto* examination of an agreement, especially where it has taken place outside the jurisdiction. Pro-active, rather than reactive, regulation is needed to provide the necessary control over agreements, and ensure that they are adequately scrutinised. In this way, a shift to a regulatory regime may be the best approach for jurisdictions currently operating a 'tolerant' model. While there remains the risk that commissioning parents may continue to go abroad where they do not fit within the requirements of the regime, for all other arrangements, it would provide a greater level of control.

8.2.1.3. Free Market Jurisdictions

As discussed in Section 2.2.1., the reasons for adopting a free market approach vary, however the idea of reproductive autonomy has a strong influence in many jurisdictions. Under this approach, surrogacy is viewed as a legitimate job, and therefore individuals should be free to set their own terms and conditions of engagement. This can be seen in the idea of contractual freedom in *California*, as well as the attitudes of surrogates in *Russia* that they are merely providing a 'service' like any other form of employment.

This position in turn has an impact on the type of regulation that the authorities can impose – the law should not restrict the woman's autonomy, and freedom of contract, unduly, and instead let her decide what conditions best suit her. Such a model does have drawbacks, however. Most importantly, it views autonomy in a very superficial manner, looking only to understanding and

---

[315] C. Fenton-Glynn, 'Outsourcing Ethical Dilemmas: Regulating International Surrogacy Arrangements' (2016) 24(1) *Medical Law Review* 59.

agreement, without considering the contextual factors that might lead a woman to accept a certain arrangement. In doing so, it fails to have regard to the unequal playing field, so often seen in international surrogacy arrangements, where one party has significantly greater bargaining power than the other. This goes back to the discussion above concerning tolerant jurisdictions, and the need to ensure that the optimal decision-making conditions are in place. Within this oversight, what needs to be considered is the extent to which conditions should be regulated, and how strictly this should be supervised – as will be discussed in Section 8.2.4. below.

8.2.2. Commercial or Altruistic?

If states do decide to regulate surrogacy, this then raises a number of important policy questions, the first and foremost being: commercial or altruistic?

8.2.2.1. The Practical Failure of the 'Truly' Altruistic Approach

As seen in Section 2.2. above, while many jurisdictions describe their surrogacy regime as 'altruistic', this is rarely the case in practice. Despite formal restrictions of payments to expenses only, as the Brazier Report in England stated 'it is clear that in many cases a component of the amount paid to the surrogate mother is a direct payment for services rendered rather than the reimbursement of actual expenses'.[316] This was demonstrated by the recent survey by Surrogacy UK, in which 68 per cent of respondent surrogates said they received between £10,000 and £15,000 compensation, with the mean for all respondents being £10,859.[317] While this is still a long way from adopting a purely commercial approach, it demonstrates a practical reality that surrogacy arrangements rarely take place without a financial element – in the Surrogacy UK survey, in only one per cent of arrangements did no money at all change hands. The problem with this lies in the fact that payment for services of surrogates is being hidden behind the shield of undefined and unmonitored 'expenses'. This term can mask an almost limitless range of payments, undermining the altruistic intention of the regime.

On the other hand, such payments may be necessary to maintain a supply of surrogates. This was recognised by *Israel* when it was first drafting its surrogacy legislation: given that family members would not be permitted to act as surrogates, the authorities accepted that they would have to introduce a commercial regime in order to provide incentives for others to step forward.[318] However, in those

316 'Surrogacy: Review for Health Ministers of Current Arrangements for Payments and Regulation – Report of the Review Team', HMSO, London 1998, Cm 4068, p. 43.
317 Surrogacy UK, 'Surrogacy in the UK: Mythbusting and reform' (11.2015), p. 20.
318 See R. Schuz, Israel, in this volume, pp. 168–169, 173.

regimes that continue to adopt a nominally 'altruistic' domestic system many commissioning parents are turning to international surrogacy as a remedy for the lack of individuals willing to undertake a surrogacy domestically.

While the reasons for individuals and couples seeking surrogacy abroad are varied, a small survey by Surrogacy UK indicated that one of the most common reasons for choosing international surrogacy was the availability of surrogates – as well as certainty, ease of setting up arrangements, and 'ethical reasons'.[319] However, this question only received 14 responses, so only gives a bare indication of what might be occurring on a larger scale. A larger survey in *Australia*, however, found that 114 of the 259 respondents did not even consider uncompensated surrogacy domestically, with 68 per cent having no one of the right age or life stage to ask. Of those who did consider using an uncompensated surrogate, only 41 per cent were able to find a surrogate.[320] Hence legally accessible altruistic arrangements apparently are not meeting the needs of the demographics seeking surrogacy, which in turn leads to reproductive tourism. Authorities are regulating to protect women domestically from what they deem exploitative practices (e.g. commercial surrogacy), while simply exporting the problem elsewhere.

Overall, few 'altruistic' regimes live up to that name (the proposed *Indian* Bill being the notable exception), and instead most jurisdictions are moving towards a model that – in practice at least – allows for compensation, rather than expecting surrogacy to be purely a gift relationship. This has the result of creating a discord between principle and practice, where what the law says is at odds with what the law does. Moreover, it fails to come to terms with the reality of the global surrogacy market – where there are insufficient candidates willing to act as surrogates domestically, commissioning parents can, and do, simply travel abroad to other jurisdictions where there is a greater supply. As Chief Judge Pascoe wrote, 'where there is demand and a profit to be made, a market almost inevitably will open up.'[321] This is not to say that regulation should be driven by the desires of commissioning parents, nor that a free market approach should be adopted (see below). Rather authorities must be alive to the practical implications of any policy choice, and how this will affect not only their own citizens, but those in other jurisdictions also.

8.2.2.2. The Risks of the Purely Commercial Approach

While adopting an altruistic model has its downsides, so too does regulation (or lack thereof) on the other end of the spectrum – the commercial model.

---

319 Surrogacy UK, 'Surrogacy in the UK: Mythbusting and reform' (11.2015), p. 24.

320 S. Everingham, M. Stafford-Bell and K. Hammarberg, 'Australians' use of surrogacy' (2014) 201(5) *Medical Journal of Australia* 1, 2.

321 J. Pascoe, A View from the Bench, in this volume, p. 106.

Commercial surrogacy has been linked to the increased risk of exploitation of women – both inherent, and contextual. With regard to the former, commercialisation of surrogacy can be viewed as inherently exploitative as it monetises women's personal attributes, and through the pricing of their services, undermines their personhood and the way they are conceived and perceived.[322] On the other hand, it could also be seen as a contributing factor to potential exploitation, where the ability to make truly autonomous decisions may be compromised by financial considerations. A purely commercial approach also raises the issue of the commodification of children. Article 2 of the Optional Protocol on the sale of children, child prostitution and child pornography defines the sale of children as the (a) transfer of a child; (b) for remuneration or any other consideration. Unlike child trafficking, this does not require that there be any resulting exploitation of the child, and Art. 3 of the Optional Protocol mentions the sale of children in the context of the transfer of parental rights, albeit in the context of adoption. In recent years, the UN Committee on the Rights of the Child has applied this provision to commercial surrogacy arrangements. In relation to the *United States*, it connected the sale of children with situations when parentage issues are decided exclusively on a contractual basis at pre-conception or pre-birth stage.[323] In relation to *Israel*, it expressed concern that there was no appropriate procedure for screening prospective parents, which may lead to the hidden sale of children (in relation to international surrogacy arrangements).[324]

On a more philosophical level, critics such as Radin have warned against the danger of a 'capitalist baby industry': 'how could any of us ... avoid subconsciously measuring the dollar value of our children? How could our children avoid being preoccupied with measuring their own dollar value?'[325] On this view, the very fact of conceiving of a child in the context of the market is a moral wrong – children are not a 'good' that should exist in the marketplace.[326]

As stated above, this chapter will not take a position on the issue of exploitation, however, it is important to note that jurisdictions which were once central to the market in reproductive tourism – for example, *India* and *Thailand* – are now moving from a free market approach to one that is tightly regulated, driven largely by concerns surrounding the exploitation of their citizens by foreign nationals. This mirrors a pattern that was seen in relation to inter-country adoption in the 1990s – countries would become very popular due to permissive (if any) rules, only to subsequently introduce strict regulation in following years due to concerns about exploitation of women and children.

322 See M.J. Radin, 'Market Inalienability' (1987) 100 *Harvard Law Review* 1849.

323 CRC/C/OPSC/USA/CO/3-4, para. 24.

324 CRC/C/OPSC/ISR/CO/1, para. 28.

325 M.J. Radin, 'Market Inalienability' (1987) 100 *Harvard Law Review* 1849, 1926.

326 Ibid, 1927.

Unfortunately, in their place another destination would arise, only for the cycle to repeat. In many respects, international surrogacy has replaced inter-country adoption as the way to found a family – it is only to be hoped that it does not repeat its failures in this respect.

8.2.2.3. A Compensatory Model as the Realistic Way Forward?

Surrogacy is usually characterised as either altruistic – out of the goodness of the surrogate's heart – or as a free market commercial transaction, with no in between. However, the practice is quite different: there is a middle ground, in the form of compensated surrogacy. Such a model, which can be seen in *Greece* and *South Africa*, allows for some individual compensation for time and inconvenience – as well as for medical and pregnancy expenses – but this amount is monitored, and required to be within certain guidelines. This also operates as a matter of practice in tolerant jurisdictions which allow for a payment for services under the guise of 'reasonable expenses', as is discussed above in Section 8.2.2.1. This is distinguished from the commercial approach, as the payment is not reliant on market forces, but on an adjudication of what is reasonable and acceptable.

This may be a way forward for 'altruistic' jurisdictions that are struggling with recruitment of surrogates. Given that these arrangements are occurring in any case in an unregulated manner, as very few jurisdictions live up to the name of truly 'altruistic', this would provide the benefit of bringing such payments into the open, rather than being hidden for fear of illegality, or obfuscated by general references to 'expenses'.

8.2.3. The Enforceability of the Surrogacy Contract

The second question that arises in relation to the content of regulation relates to the surrogacy contract itself – whether it is enforceable, and if so, to what extent.

The greatest concern in this regard relates to the allocation of parenthood. Should surrogates have the chance to change their mind and keep the child? Or should commissioning parents be recognised as the legal parents from birth? While this is usually characterised as the 'rights' of commissioning parents versus the 'rights' of the surrogate, the reality is not that simple. It is true that this is a key concern of commissioning parents: an *Australian* study found that 75 per cent of participants indicated that concern that the surrogate might keep the child was a reason for entering into an international, rather than a domestic, arrangement.[327] However, there is evidence to suggest that many

[327] S. Everingham, M. Stafford-Bell and K. Hammarberg, 'Australians' use of surrogacy' (2014) 201(5) *Medical Journal of Australia* 1.

surrogates would also endorse this position. For example, in *England*, a survey by Surrogacy UK found that 64.9 per cent of the surrogates surveyed thought the legal parents of the child should be the commissioning parents, whether genetically related or not, and 68.5 per cent stated that the surrogate should not be able to change her mind about handing over the child.[328]

It is also important to consider the inequality of risk between the parties. For the commissioning parents, the risk is that they will not have a child at the end of the process, despite having outlaid a lot of money.[329] For the surrogate, on the other hand, if the commissioning parents walk away, not only does she have no recourse for recovering payments for the expense of the pregnancy (not to mention, she loses any financial gain she may have contracted for), but she is also left with a child that she did not plan to raise. This was seen in the case of Baby Gammy, where the mother was left with the child with disabilities while the parents took his non-disabled twin. Indeed, it was this case that prompted the *Thai* government to radically change their laws on surrogacy, and now includes a new criminal offence for commissioning parents who refuse parenthood. As Chief Judge Pascoe stated: 'the foreign location, lax laws, and/or poor law enforcement assists the industry by providing commissioning parents a back-out option if they decide not to go through with the arrangement – what can be seen as a crude "returns policy"'.[330]

One solution to this would be to adopt a free market model of regulation – simply let the commissioning parents and surrogate negotiate for the consequences that they desire. However, this is to ignore the third party that must be part of the equation: the child themselves. As discussed in Section 8.1.3., leaving parenthood to private contract goes contrary to the very purpose of family law. The parent/child relationship is not one that should be bargained for between adults, but must reflect policy considerations that promote the best interests of the child. Moreover, it has been argued by many, including the UN Special Rapporteur on the sale of children,[331] that commercial surrogacy will constitute the sale of the child if the contract is enforceable against the surrogate. According to this view, where the surrogacy contract involves the payment of money, in return for the transfer the child after birth – either explicitly through physically enforcing the transfer, or implicitly by virtue of financial penalties if this does not occur – then the child is being bought and sold. This is the case even if it is not characterised as such by the parties to the agreement – for example, the payments being listed as for the surrogate's

328 Surrogacy UK, *Surrogacy in the UK: Myth Busting and Reform* (11.2015), pp. 21–22.

329 Although some of this may be recoverable under the doctrine of unjust enrichment, or similar.

330 J. Pascoe, A View from the Bench, in this volume, p. 107.

331 United Nations Human Rights Council, Report of the Special Rapporteur on the sale and sexual exploitation of children, including child prostitution, child pornography and other child sexual abuse material (A/HRC/37/60, 15.01.2018).

'services'. While this view is not universally accepted,[332] it remains a powerful argument from an influential source, and cannot be dismissed lightly.

A middle ground has been sought in jurisdictions which allow the surrogate to enforce a contract against the commissioning parents, through the demand of payments, while not similarly allowing the commissioning parents to demand the handing over of the child against the surrogate's wishes. This mechanism protects surrogates by ensuring that they are not subject to financial risk, while still allowing them the flexibility to change their minds with regard to handing over the child and avoiding the charge of 'baby selling'. On the other hand, however, commissioning parents remain vulnerable to going through the emotional journey of the surrogacy, without any guarantee that their parenthood of the child – who they had planned for, and to whom they are mostly likely genetically connected – will be recognised. Moreover, this approach does not address the concern that the surrogate may, quite literally, be left 'holding the baby'.

A third approach that presents itself is a regulatory regime where the enforceability of the terms of the surrogacy rely not on the contract itself, but on the order of a court. This would operate the same way as a consent order – the court would scrutinise the arrangement as envisaged by the parties, ensure that its terms are acceptable (while changing those that are not), and make an order accordingly. This overcomes the concern regarding private allocation of parenthood: as soon as it moves into the hands of the court to decide whether or not to grant parenthood, then it is not the surrogate/commissioning parents themselves effecting the transfer – even if the court would usually follow the approach that the private agreement sets out. Nevertheless, it provides an important check and balance against the free market, ensuring that unsuitable terms and unfair agreements are not enforced, thus providing protection for the weaker party. Moreover, it avoids the charge of 'baby selling' – the UN Special Rapporteur has indicated that as long as a court is involved *post*-birth, and is able to allocate parenthood as it sees fit (and not simply according to what the contract determines) then there will not be a sale of the child, even if money has changed hands. Thus only where the court is *obliged* to effect the transfer, rather than making its own substantive evaluation of whether transfer is desirable, does it fall foul of the prohibition against the sale of children.

---

332 Of course, this is only one view, and is not universally accepted. McLachlan and Swales, for example, argue that payments in commercial surrogacy are for the surrogate's services in carrying and delivering the baby, not the baby itself. (H.V. McLachlan and J.K. Swales, 'Babies, Child Bearers and Commodification: Anderson, Brazier et al., and the Political Economy of Commercial Surrogate Motherhood' (2000) 8 *Health Care Analysis* 1). Another perspective is given by van Niekerk and van Zyl, who suggest that what is being bought and sold is not the child, but parental rights. (A. van Niekerk and L. van Zyl, 'Commercial Surrogacy and the Commodification of Children: An Ethical Perspective' (1995) 14 *Medicine and Law* 163).

Having said this, the intervention of the court post-birth, as well as pre-birth, may create unnecessary bureaucracy – especially at a time when the surrogate will be recovering from the birth, and the commissioning parents will be spending time with their newborn child. One solution may be to require the agreement to be approved pre-birth, which will then be binding post-birth, *unless* the surrogate chooses to revoke it within a certain period after the birth. This is the system used in *South Africa* and *Greece*, where following the confirmation of the agreement by the authorities pre-birth, the commissioning parents will become the legal parents unless the surrogate objects post-birth. Such a system avoids a second court hearing where all parties are in agreement, while still giving the surrogate post-birth control over whether parenthood is transferred.

8.2.4. *Eligibility Conditions for Surrogacy*

The conditions placed on entering into a surrogacy arrangement, and particularly the eligibility criteria for surrogates and commissioning parents, go to the heart of how we conceptualise the family, and the place of the state in the private sphere. This chapter will not attempt to set guidelines for what is most appropriate, but rather explores the parameters of the issues that must be decided upon in designing domestic regulation.

8.2.4.1. Eligibility of Surrogates

As discussed in Section 4.1. above, there are many different eligibility criteria that jurisdictions impose on surrogates: age limits; marital status; previous child birth; lack of genetic relationship with a child. However, the differences between jurisdictions appear to be practical, rather than philosophical. The criteria are all imposed with the same aim: to ensure that the surrogate is fully informed and acting autonomously, that she is in good health, and that the risk of her wishing to keep the child is minimised. The only difference lies in which criteria are imposed to achieve this.

A key divergence is that of the relationship with the commissioning parents. While some jurisdictions require such a relationship – for example, *Thailand*, and the proposed *Indian* Bill – others expressly prohibit it (the proposed *Icelandic* law).[333] Even these diametrically opposed conditions, however, have the same end goal – to ensure that the surrogate is not exploited. For *India* and *Thailand*, the aim is to prevent commercial transactions, and ensure that the surrogacy truly is based on a gift relationship. Likewise, the aim of the *Icelandic* Bill is to prevent the exploitation of women by ensuring that pressure cannot be put on family members to be surrogates.

---

[333] See Section 4.1.2.

8.2.4.2. Eligibility of Commissioning Parents

The more interesting question from a comparative perspective relates to the eligibility of commissioning parents, as this is where we can see important philosophical differences in the respective approaches.

When thinking about regulating who may or may not be eligible as commissioning parents for surrogacy, the core question is the underlying conception of surrogacy and its place in the creation of a family. If surrogacy is seen as akin to natural reproduction, then the role of the state in regulating this should be minimal. However, if surrogacy is perceived as similar to adoption, involving the transfer of parenthood, then eligibility should be equally carefully scrutinised before individuals are to become parents in this way.

There are a small number of jurisdictions that seem to lean towards the former position: for example, *Israel*, with its pro-natalist approach, or *Russia* where the creation of a family is conceptualised as a right.[334] However, it appears that more jurisdictions see surrogacy as involving the transfer of parenthood, and thus, like in cases of adoption, putting the state under a duty to ensure that the transfer is in the child's best interest. Otherwise the state may become complicit in bringing about a state of affairs that may be detrimental to the best interest of the child. Having said this, few jurisdictions put comprehensive checks on the suitability of commissioning parents,[335] as they would in cases of adoption – in most cases, checks are largely limited to ensuring that certain criteria are met, rather than more general suitability for parenthood.

The problem of course is that surrogacy (at least in most cases) has elements of both natural conception and adoption. On the one hand, the gametes of at least one of the commissioning parents are usually used and there is a genetic connection with the child.[336] On the other hand, in most jurisdictions the full effect of the commissioning parent(s) achieving the full and sole legal status of a parent depends on a judicial intervention by the state. This tension can be seen in the decisions of the European Court of Human Rights in this area. Where there is a genetic link between the child and commissioning parents, the child's right to respect for private life, and the right to identity, requires recognition of parenthood.[337] However, where there is no genetic connection, the link to natural procreation may be deemed to be lost, leaning (even) more strongly

---

334 See Section 2.2.1. *Israel* also has rules that prohibit family members becoming surrogates, but this is based on religious considerations, so is a special case.

335 Cf. D. Wilson, New Zealand, in this volume, pp. 215–216.

336 This is a requirement in all jurisdictions discussed, except for Greece, California, and possibly Russia: see N. Cahn and J. Carbone, United States of America, in this volume, p. 326; E. Zervogianni, Greece, in this volume, p. 157; O. Khazova, Russia, in this volume, pp. 300–301.

337 *Mennesson v France*, no. 65192/11, 26.06.2014.

towards a regulation by the state, or even an ineligibility for the recognition of parenthood.[338]

But if the eligibility of commissioning parents is to be regulated in some shape of form, the question is which criteria ought to be applied. Those who argue that surrogacy should be seen as akin to natural reproduction would obviously want to see minimal (if any) regulation. This then raises the spectre of 'unsuitable' parents – the paradigm case being the child-sex offender – commissioning children. The simplistic argument then is that since child sex offenders cannot be stopped from having children through natural means, why should they then be prohibited from having a child through surrogacy? However, the response to this is obvious, and applicable beyond the scenario just outlined. Natural reproduction generally is beyond regulation; it is simply unfeasible to do so. However, surrogacy requires medical intervention, and thus is not a natural liberty being curtailed, but a practice being facilitated. Hence the state has a legitimate role in deciding whether, and under what circumstances, an individual should become a parent in this way. Artificial reproduction through this particular aspect thus becomes analogous to adoption, where there is strict scrutiny of prospective parents, rather than pure natural reproduction. Thus state intervention is not only desirable but also necessary, as otherwise the state would be in breach of its international human rights obligation with regard to the child.

8.2.4.2.1. Requirement of a Genetic Link

As discussed above, significant emphasis is placed on the genetic link with at least one commissioning parent. Before exploring whether this ought to be a criterion for eligibility, it is worth pointing out that this emphasis on the genetic link appears to be somewhat one-sided and, at least in some cases, brings with it a potential discrimination on the basis of gender. This arises from the fact that although the reasons for wanting to have a child via a surrogacy agreement usually is a fertility problem related to the female partner, this problem in many cases relates to gestation only, rather than the woman's gametes. Therefore, in many surrogacies the gametes of both the female and the male partner are used. If a child then is born to an unmarried surrogate, the current law enables the man (commissioning father) to claim paternity solely because of his genetic contribution, and thus immediately acquires legal rights and duties. However, the genetic contribution of the female partner (commissioning mother) has no such consequences in most jurisdictions, as the mother is deemed to be the woman giving birth to the child, irrespective of any genetic contribution. Thus, it does not matter legally whether her gametes or donor gametes were used: the legal

[338] *Paradiso and Campanelli v Italy*, no. 25358/12, 24.01.2017.

position of the commissioning mother is the same. So despite both partners having contributed the same – the gametes – the legal consequences are different based on their gender. This can have grave consequences, for example in case of relationship breakdown before the commissioning mother acquires legal parenthood, as the man will have more legal rights in relation to the child – and indeed the status of parent – than the woman. Hence the focus of the genetic link appears somewhat male-centric, at least in these cases.

But the wider question of course is whether a genetic link should be required in the first place, or whether a couple (or indeed a single person) should be eligible as commissioning parents in the absence of such a link. Before gestational surrogacy became a possibility, in such cases (as indeed most cases of infertility of the female partner) the obvious avenue to becoming parent(s) would be, and in many cases still is, through adoption. That said, in many jurisdictions the number of children available for adoption is very low, thus leading to a move towards inter-country adoptions, which brings with it a significant number of very serious issues which cannot be addressed here.[339] Yet the creation of a child that is not genetically related to the commissioning parents, possibly in exchange for money, is a very different matter and can with some justification be seen as 'buying a baby'.[340] Given that comprehensive protective legal frameworks have been created for precisely this situation of parenthood by people not genetically related to the child, namely the legal rules on adoption, jurisdictions need to weigh very carefully whether they should allow those to be circumvented through surrogacy.[341] Moreover, availability of surrogacy in these situations may have a significant, and potentially very adverse, impact on the realities of adoption, state care and the welfare of those children. In any event, where permitting 'genetically unrelated' surrogacy is being contemplated, the arguments for aligning the eligibility requirements for parents in surrogacy and adoption become even stronger.

8.2.4.2.2. Requirement of Infertility

Another core issue that arises concerning the eligibility of commissioning parents is the requirement of infertility: should surrogacy only be available where natural reproduction is not possible? Or should it be available on a wider basis? Even the category of 'infertility' itself can be given different definitions.

339 For a comprehensive comparative analysis see C. Fenton-Glynn, *Children's Rights in Intercountry Adoption: A European Perspective* (Intersentia, Cambridge 2014).

340 On this see also the South African case of *AB and others v Minister of Social Development and Others (Centre for Child Law intervening as Amicus Curiae)* CCT 155/15, discussed by J. Sloth-Nielsen, South Africa, in this volume, pp. 187–189.

341 On this, see *Paradiso and Campanelli v Italy*, no. 25358/12, 24.01.2017. See P. Beaumont and K. Trimmings, Surrogacy before the European Court of Human Rights, in this volume, pp. 332–354.

It can be narrowly interpreted, meaning that only medical conditions will qualify, i.e. some medical 'disability' relating to fertility; or it could be given a much wider meaning, thus encompassing what may be called 'social' or 'structural' infertility – for example single males, as well as male couples, or indeed couples who are past childbearing age.[342] Whether this interpretation of infertility is acceptable in a jurisdiction of course largely depends on the broader family law context.

Whichever definition of infertility is adopted, this needs to be distinguished from situations where the couple or individual woman in question could have a child naturally, but nevertheless chooses surrogacy; in the latter group the surrogacy therefore could be said, perhaps somewhat derogatorily, to be a 'life-style' choice. Anecdotal evidence suggests that for some couples these are very real considerations, and that some women who would like to have children are preferring not to undergo pregnancy and birth themselves because of the potential physical consequences on their bodies or the impact on their work and private lives.

Undoubtedly those jurisdictions who have put infertility requirements in place will have done so mostly because of concerns relating to this latter group. When 'outsourcing' the pregnancy for reasons other than infertility becomes available and acceptable, this truly makes the 'transaction' one of commodification of the gestational process. If commercial (or even compensated) surrogacy is also available, gestation then merely becomes a service that is for hire, leaving the inconveniences of pregnancy to those who are willing to accept them in return for payment. This unquestionably brings with it not only the dangers of (financial) exploitation, but also the danger of a dystopian world where the rich for their convenience could (and probably would) pay the poor for gestational services. Arguably by detaching childbirth from the personal experience to something that can be outsourced at will, it loses its humanity.

While in principle the same can be said about surrogacy in cases of infertility, in practice, the social situation is very different. Here a person or a couple who would otherwise have a child in the natural way (and indeed would have to, if 'life-style' surrogacy was not permitted) for medical or social/structural reasons *has* to resort to surrogacy to have a child to which they genetically are related.[343] The venture therefore is driven by the very human desire to have and raise a

---

342 Arguably these persons fall into the category of 'medical' infertility, as it would be possible for them to procreate, but for the cessation of functioning of their reproductive capacities. However, they are included as a form of 'social' infertility as their reproductive capacities are not inhibited by a medical *problem*, but from the natural passing of time.

343 Whether the desire to have a genetically related child in itself is sufficient to justify resorting to surrogacy may be debatable. If not, then obviously adoption would be the way to become a parent. However, this may not always be possible, given strict eligibility requirements usually in place for adoption.

child, and not by rejecting the humanity of the gestational process and wanting to avoid the inconveniences of pregnancy or child birth.

8.3. THE REGULATION (OR NOT) OF SURROGACY: THE WAY FORWARD

The regulation of surrogacy in today's world requires a fine balancing act between principles and pragmatism. It exposes deep tensions between domestic regulation and international consequences; between individual autonomy and protection from exploitation; and between adult desires and children's rights. There is no easy answer to these questions, nor, indeed, is there only one answer. This volume has not attempted to prescribe a universal framework that would work in every jurisdiction: this would be a pointless task, doomed to failure. The value of comparative law lies not in finding the 'best' approach, but in exploring different solutions to difficult legal and moral dilemmas, to better understand our own.

Having said this, there are five key features that we have identified that must define any legal framework for surrogacy. Whatever approach is taken, these must be the central considerations for any legislators grappling with this difficult, and ever evolving, area.

1. *The Need for Change.* First and foremost, it is clear that the status quo is unsatisfactory, and there is a significant amount of work to be done in this area. Every commentator identified areas where the law in their jurisdiction was unclear, unsatisfactory, or unworkable. Many states continue to rely on laws that were enacted decades (or even centuries) ago, and have failed to respond to the emerging challenges that come with the rapid development of reproductive technology. Even those with more modern frameworks face challenges in ensuring that they continue to reflect current norms, for example concerning family forms, and that they are able to address issues arising out of international surrogacy. For this reason, every state must continuously re-evaluate their current legal framework, to ensure that it is fit for purpose.
2. *Legal Certainty.* This begs the question: what makes a law on surrogacy fit for purpose? When considering how best to respond to surrogacy, any framework that is adopted must provide legal certainty. This is an element that is missing in many current regimes, either because of a lack of legislation, or because the laws that are in place are not tailored to the practice of surrogacy. Surrogates need to know what remuneration they can receive, whether the contract is enforceable, and require the protection of clear legal rules to prevent exploitation. Commissioning parents, on the other hand, also require certainty concerning remuneration and the

enforceability of contracts, but also whether they will be able to return to their own jurisdiction with the resulting child, and whether they will be recognised as legal parents. Most importantly, however, is that the law provides certainty for the children themselves, concerning their identity, nationality, and legal parenthood.

3. *Effective Laws*. Third, and related to the need for legal certainty, is the necessity that the law be effective. This may sound self-evident – a necessary feature for *any* law – but currently many regimes operate knowing that their laws are not only unenforced, but unenforceable. This means that commissioning parents can circumvent the law, achieving their desired result by simply going ahead with a surrogacy arrangement, and trusting that this will be approved retrospectively. The consequence of this is that there is uncertainty for all parties in the process to some extent, if the law is little more than words on paper. Crucially, such a situation is unacceptable given the centrality of the rule of law in modern societies.
4. *The Rights of the Child*. Fourth, the law must be designed to promote and protect children's rights. Children are at the heart of surrogacy, but too often they are viewed as the objects resulting out of the arrangement, rather than legal subjects in their own right. Children's rights must be the paramount consideration in surrogacy: both *in abstracto*, when determining the structure of the legal framework, and *in concreto* when making decisions within that framework. While the latter has been a feature of some legal regimes – particularly the prohibitive and tolerant jurisdictions – the former is of equal importance. Rules on the enforceability of contracts, the eligibility of commissioning parents, the transfer of parenthood, and the availability of information on origins, must all be framed with the rights of the child in mind.
5. *The Global Marketplace*. Finally, any legislative framework must recognise the reality of the global surrogacy market. On the one hand, the law must be able to adequately respond to international surrogacy arrangements in a way that provides certainty, is effective, and protects the rights of children. On the other hand, states must recognise the impact that their own laws have on other jurisdictions, in the context of reproductive tourism. Legislators cannot bury their heads in the sand: surrogacy is not going to go away. It is now an established artificial reproductive technique, and in a global marketplace, there is always going to be somewhere, somehow, that it is available. The only question is how we deal with the consequences.

INDEX

ABOUT THE EDITORS

Jens M. Scherpe is Reader in Comparative Law at the University of Cambridge, a Fellow of Gonville and Caius College, Cambridge, Cheng Yu Tung Visiting Professor at the University of Hong Kong and Honorary Professor at the University of Aalborg. He also is an Honorary Fellow of St. John's College, Hong Kong and an Academic Door Tenant at Queen Elizabeth Building, London. Before coming to Cambridge, he was a Senior Research Fellow at the Max Planck Institute for Comparative and International Private Law in Hamburg, Germany. He specialises in comparative law and particularly comparative family law. Jens' publications include major comparative studies on same-sex relationships (2000), cohabitation (2005), the legal status of transgender and transsexual persons (2004 and 2015), matrimonial property and marital agreements (2012), registered partnerships (2017) and the legal status of intersex persons (2018). In 2016 he also edited a four-volume book set on European Family Law, including a monograph *The Present and Future of European Family Law*.

Claire Fenton-Glynn is a Lecturer in Law at the University of Cambridge, and Fellow at Jesus College. She specialises in human rights and the protection of children, in particular focusing on issues such as intercountry adoption, international surrogacy and cross-border child protection. At the core of her research is the interaction between international and regional human rights instruments and domestic law, and the way in which these frameworks can be used to implement children's rights. Her first book, *Children's Rights in Intercountry Adoption*, was awarded the Inner Temple Book Prize for New Authors, as well as the Faculty of Law's Yorke Prize. Claire is an Associate Member of Harcourt Chambers and an Academic Fellow of Inner Temple. She has worked with organisations such as the United Nations Office of the High Commissioner for Human Rights, the European Union, Save the Children and Avocats Sans Frontieres on issues concerning child protection, human rights and rule of law.

Terry Kaan is Associate Professor of Law at the University of Hong Kong and also Co-Director of the Centre for Medical Ethics and Law of the University of Hong Kong. He specialises in bioethics and medical law, and is especially interested in the governance of biomedical research; as well as the ethical, legal and social implications of the application of new and emerging technologies in medical practice, particularly in precision medicine and the use of whole genomic sequencing in clinical practice and in research. Terry is also interested in the privacy implications of the development of large-scale genetic and genomic databases for both clinical and biomedical research purposes, and has co-edited a book on genetic privacy.

www.ingramcontent.com/pod-product-compliance
Ingram Content Group UK Ltd.
Pitfield, Milton Keynes, MK11 3LW, UK
UKHW051917100926
8556IPUK00021B/1233

9 781780 68652